AMERICAN LITERATURE IN TRANSITION, 1930–1940

American Literature in Transition, 1930–1940 gathers together in a single volume preeminent critics and historians to offer an authoritative, analytic, and theoretically advanced account of the Depression era's key literary events. Many topics of canonical importance, such as protest literature, Hollywood fiction, the culture industry, and populism, receive fresh treatment. The book also covers emerging areas of interest, such as radio drama, bestsellers, religious fiction, internationalism, and middlebrow domestic fiction. Traditionally, scholars have treated each one of these issues in isolation. This volume situates all the significant literary developments of the 1930s within a single and capacious vision that discloses their hidden structural relations – their contradictions, similarities, and reciprocities. This is an excellent resource for undergraduate and graduate students, and for scholars interested in American literary culture of the 1930s.

ICHIRO TAKAYOSHI teaches modern American literature and social thought at Tufts University. He is the author of *American Writers and the Approach of World War II, 1935–1941: A Literary History* (Cambridge University Press, 2015) and editor of *American Literature in Transition, 1920–1930* (Cambridge University Press, 2017). He is currently at work on a literary and intellectual history of the interwar decades.

American Literature in Transition captures the dynamic energies transmitted across the 20th- and 21st-century American literary landscapes. Revisionary and authoritative, the series offers a comprehensive new overview of the established literary landmarks that constitute American literary life. Ambitious in scope and depth, and accommodating new critical perspectives and approaches, this series captures the dynamic energies and ongoing change in 20th- and 21st-century American literature. These are decades of transition, but also periods of epochal upheaval. These decades – the Jazz Age, the Great Depression, the Cold War, the sixties, 9/11 – are turning points of real significance. But in a tumultuous century, these terms can mask deeper structural changes. Each one of these books challenges in different ways the dominant approaches to a period of literature by shifting the focus from what happened to understanding how and why it happened. They elucidate the multifaceted interaction between the social and literary fields and capture that era's place in the incremental evolution of American literature up to the present moment. Taken together, this series of books constitutes a new kind of literary history in a century of intense cultural and literary creation, a century of liberation and also of immense destruction too. As a revisionary project grounded in pre-existing debates, American Literature in Transition offers an unprecedented analysis of the American literary experience.

Books in the Series

American Literature in Transition, 1910–1920 edited by MARK W. VAN WIENEN
American Literature in Transition, 1920–1930 edited by ICHIRO TAKAYOSHI
American Literature in Transition, 1930–1940 edited by ICHIRO TAKAYOSHI
American Literature in Transition, 1940–1950 edited by CHRISTOPHER VIALS
American Literature in Transition, 1950–1960 edited by STEVEN BELLETTO
American Literature in Transition, 1960–1970 edited by DAVID WYATT
American Literature in Transition, 1970–1980 edited by KIRK CURNUTT
American Literature in Transition, 1980–1990 edited by D. QUENTIN MILLER
American Literature in Transition, 1990–2000 edited by STEPHEN J. BURN
American Literature in Transition, 2000–2010 edited by RACHEL GREENWALD SMITH

AMERICAN LITERATURE IN TRANSITION, 1930–1940

EDITED BY

ICHIRO TAKAYOSHI

Tufts University

CAMBRIDGE
UNIVERSITY PRESS

CAMBRIDGE
UNIVERSITY PRESS

University Printing House, Cambridge CB2 8BS, United Kingdom

One Liberty Plaza, 20th Floor, New York, NY 10006, USA

477 Williamstown Road, Port Melbourne, VIC 3207, Australia

314–321, 3rd Floor, Plot 3, Splendor Forum, Jasola District Centre, New Delhi – 110025, India

79 Anson Road, #06–04/06, Singapore 079906

Cambridge University Press is part of the University of Cambridge.

It furthers the University's mission by disseminating knowledge in the pursuit of education, learning, and research at the highest international levels of excellence.

www.cambridge.org
Information on this title: www.cambridge.org/9781108429382
DOI: 10.1017/9781108563895

First published 2018

Printed in the United States of America by Sheridan Books, Inc.

A catalogue record for this publication is available from the British Library.

Library of Congress Cataloging-in-Publication Data
NAMES: Takayoshi, Ichiro, editor.
TITLE: American literature in transition, 1930–1940 / edited by Ichiro Takayoshi.
DESCRIPTION: Cambridge, United Kingdom ; New York, NY : Cambridge University Press, 2018. | Series: American literature in transition | Includes bibliographical references and index.
IDENTIFIERS: LCCN 2018022355 | ISBN 9781108429382 (alk. paper)
SUBJECTS: LCSH: American literature – 20th century – History and criticism. | Literature and society – United States – History – 20th century.
CLASSIFICATION: LCC PS223 .A44 2018 | DDC 810.9/0052–dc23
LC record available at https://lccn.loc.gov/2018022355

ISBN 978-1-108-42938-2 Hardback

Contents

Figures

Notes on Contributors

JEFF ALLRED is Associate Professor of English at Hunter College, City University of New York, where he has taught since 2005. He is the author of *American Modernism and Depression Documentary* (2010) and has published articles and reviews on American literature, modernism, digital pedagogy, and new media studies in *American Literature, American Literary History, Criticism, Arizona Quarterly,* and *Transformations.* He is currently working on a book project on pedagogy and literary modernism entitled *ABC of Modernism.*

AMY L. BLAIR teaches American literature at Marquette University. She is the author of *Reading Up: Middle-Class Readers and the Culture of Success in the Early Twentieth-Century United States* (2012) and coeditor with James L. Machor of the journal *Reception: Texts, Readers, Audiences, History.* Her current project investigates middlebrow reading during the 1920s and 1930s and reading advice in *Good Housekeeping* magazine.

MILTON A. COHEN, Professor of Literary Studies at the University of Texas at Dallas, has published books on cummings, Hemingway, and modernist groups, and on Stevens, Frost, cummings, Williams, and leftist critics in the 1930s. He is presently completing a study of Steinbeck, Hemingway, Richard Wright, and the left in the late 1930s, and is also editing a Norton Critical Edition of E. E. cummings.

MORRIS DICKSTEIN is Distinguished Professor Emeritus at the City University of New York Graduate Center and the author of *Dancing in the Dark: A Cultural History of the Great Depression* (2009) and *Why Not Say What Happened: A Sentimental Education* (2015).

DAVID EKBLADH is Associate Professor of History and Core Faculty in International Relations at Tufts University. His books include *Beyond 1917: The United States and the Global Legacies of the Great War* (with Thomas Zeiler and Benjamin Montoya, 2017) and *The Great American*

Mission: Modernization and the Construction of an American World Order (2010), which won the Stuart L. Bernath Prize of the Society of American Historians and the Phi Alpha Theta Best First Book Award.

JOSEPH B. ENTIN is Associate Professor of English and American Studies at Brooklyn College, City University of New York. He is the author of *Sensational Modernism: Experimental Fiction and Photography in Thirties America* (2007), and coeditor, with Franny Nudelman and Sara Blair, of *Remaking Reality: U.S. Documentary Culture after 1945* (2018), and, with Robert Rosen and Leonard Vogt, of *Controversies in the Classroom: A Radical Teacher Reader* (2008). His current research explores narratives of precarious, low-wage labor in contemporary American fiction and film.

MARK FEARNOW writes about theater history and theory. He is the author of *The American Stage and the Great Depression* (Cambridge University Press, 1997), *Clare Boothe Luce* (1995), and *Theatre and the Good* (2007). He has published many articles and chapters focusing on American drama and theater of the twentieth century. He has retired from university teaching and lives in Palm Springs, California.

DONAL HARRIS is the author of *On Company Time: American Modernism in the Big Magazines* (2016). His work has appeared in *PMLA, Modern Language Quarterly*, and *The Los Angeles Review of Books*, among other venues. He is Assistant Professor of English at the University of Memphis.

JENNIFER HAYTOCK teaches American literature at the College at Brockport, State University of New York. She is the author of *At Home, At War: Domesticity and World War I in American Literature* (2003), *Edith Wharton and the Conversations of Literary Modernism* (2008), and *The Middle Class in the Great Depression: Popular Women's Novels of the 1930s* (2013). Her essays have appeared in the *Hemingway Review, Legacy*, and *Mosaic*.

JERROLD HIRSCH, Professor Emeritus of History at Truman State University, is coeditor with Tom Terrill of *Such as Us: Southern Voices of the Thirties* (1978), a collection of previously unpublished Federal Writers' Project (FWP) life histories; author of *Portrait of America: A Cultural History of the Federal Writers' Project* (2003); and coeditor, with Larry Rogers, of *America's Folklorist: B. A. Botkin and American Culture* (2010). He has published numerous articles on the FWP, the history of

American folklore studies, oral history, and disability history in journals, chapters in edited books, and introductions to books. He is currently working on a study of the creative folklore and writing projects of the FWP and on a biography of B. A. Botkin.

MICHAEL KREYLING received his PhD from Cornell in 1975 and thereafter taught at Mississippi State University, Tulane University, and Vanderbilt, where he retired as Gertrude Conaway Vanderbilt Professor of English in 2015. His early work includes studies of the fiction of Eudora Welty, *Eudora Welty's Achievement of Order* (1980) and *Figures of the Hero in Southern Narrative* (1987). More recently he is the author of *The South That Wasn't There* (2010) and *A Late Encounter with the Civil War* (2014).

JOHN MARSH is Associate Professor of English at the Pennsylvania State University. In addition to numerous articles and reviews, he is the author or editor of *You Work Tomorrow: An Anthology of American Labor Poetry, 1929–1941* (2007); *Hog Butchers, Beggars, and Busboys: Poverty, Labor, and the Making of Modern American Poetry* (2011); *Class Dismissed: Why We Cannot Teach or Learn Our Way Out of Poverty* (2011); and most recently, *In Walt We Trust: How a Queer Socialist Poet Can Save America from Itself* (2015). He is at work on a cultural history of the 1930s called "This Dark Hour: The Emotional Life of the Great Depression."

CHRISTOPHER PHELPS is Associate Professor of American History teaching in the Department of American and Canadian Studies at the University of Nottingham. He is the author of *Young Sidney Hook: Marxist and Pragmatist* (1997; 2nd edn, 2005) and, with Howard Brick, *Radicals in America: The U.S. Left since the Second World War* (Cambridge University Press, 2015).

CHARLES J. RZEPKA is Professor of English at Boston University, where he teaches British Romanticism and detective and crime fiction. He is the author of numerous articles in both fields, as well as several books, including *Being Cool: The Work of Elmore Leonard* (2013) and *Detective Fiction* (2005). Together with Lee Horsley, he also coedited *A Companion to Crime Fiction* (2010). His latest essay, "Red and White and Pink All Over: *Vacilada*, Indian Identity, and Todd Downing's Queer Response to Modernity," on the gay, part-Choctaw detective writer of the 1930s Todd Downing, appeared in a special issue of *Texas Studies in Literature and Language* on the New Modernism in the fall of 2017.

YAEL SCHACHER has a BA in English and comparative literature from Columbia University, an MA in history, and a PhD in American studies from Harvard University. She specializes in the literature and history of immigration, on which she has taught courses at the University of Connecticut's Hartford campus for several years. In 2016 she received a Cromwell Fellowship from the American Society for Legal History to revise her dissertation, "Exceptions to Exclusion: A Prehistory of Asylum in the United States, 1880–1980," for publication. She will be working on this monograph, among other projects related to migration, displacement, and exile, as a postdoctoral fellow at the Institute for Historical Studies and The University of Texas at Austin in 2017–18. She served on the editorial board of *New Literary History of America* (2009) and was a research assistant for Harvard's digital archives on immigration to the United States.

WILLIAM SOLOMON is Professor of English at the University at Buffalo. He is the author of *Literature, Amusement and Technology in the Great Depression* (2002) and *Slapstick Modernism: Chaplin to Kerouac to Iggy Pop* (2016). He has published numerous articles on American literature and film in journals such as *American Literature, Mosaic, Texas Studies in Literature and Language*, and *Arizona Quarterly*.

JASON STEVENS has taught at Harvard University and the University of Maryland, Baltimore County, and he has been a fellow of the National Humanities Center and the University of Pittsburgh, Humanities Center. His work focuses on twentieth-century American literature and US cultural and intellectual history, with emphases on modernism, secularization theory, and Christianity. He is the author of *God-Fearing and Free: A Spiritual History of America's Cold War* (2010) and the editor of *This Life, This World: New Essays on Marilynne Robinson's Housekeeping, Gilead, and* Home (2015). His writings have also appeared in *boundary 2, American Literature, Literature/Film Quarterly*, and *The Immanent Frame*. He is completing a book project on American film noir and preparing an additional book on Robert Penn Warren and the rhetoric of prophecy in Southern letters.

ICHIRO TAKAYOSHI teaches in the Department of English at Tufts University. His books include *American Writers and the Approach of World War II* (2015) and *American Literature in Transition, 1920–1930* (2017).

ETSUKO TAKETANI is Professor of American Literature at the University of Tsukuba, Japan. She is the author of *U.S. Women Writers and the Discourses of Colonialism, 1825–1861* (2003) and *The Black Pacific Narrative: Geographic Imaginings of Race and Empire between the World Wars* (2014). Her current research examines African American literature of the air-atomic age.

NEIL VERMA is Assistant Professor in Radio/Television/Film at Northwestern University. He is the author of *Theater of the Mind: Imagination, Aesthetics, and American Radio Drama* (2012), winner of the Best First Book Award from the Society for Cinema and Media Studies. He is coeditor of *Anatomy of Sound: Norman Corwin and Media Authorship* (2016) and the winner of the Best Moving Image Book Award from the Kraszna-Krausz Foundation. Verma has published on topics ranging from film history to experimental listening and podcasting in *The Cine-Files, Critical Quarterly, The Journal of American Studies, The Journal of Sonic Studies, RadioDoc Review, Recherches sémiotiques/Semiotic Inquiry*, and *The Velvet Light Trap*. He is the co-network director for the Radio Preservation Task Force at the Library of Congress, the former special editor at the site *Sounding Out!*, and the founder of the Great Lakes Association for Sound Studies. He was a Harper-Schmidt Fellow at the University of Chicago from 2010 to 2014.

DAVID WELKY is Professor of History at the University of Central Arkansas, specializing in twentieth-century American history, the history of film, and the history of popular culture. He is the author of *Everything Was Better in America: Print Culture and the Great Depression; The Moguls and the Dictators: Hollywood and the Coming of World War II; A Wretched and Precarious Situation: In Search of the Last Arctic Frontier*, and other books.

ROBERT B. WESTBROOK is Joseph F. Cunningham Professor of History at the University of Rochester, where he has taught since 1986. He is the author of *John Dewey and American Democracy, Democratic Hope: Pragmatism and the Politics of Truth*, and *Why We Fought: Forging American Obligations in World War II*, as well as many essays and articles on American cultural and intellectual history.

DAVID M. WROBEL is a native Londoner who came to the United States for graduate school in 1985 and never left. He is the Merrick Chair in Western American History, the David L. Boren Professor, and the Faculty Director of the Western History Collections at the University of Oklahoma, where he teaches courses on the American West, American thought and culture, and John Steinbeck. His books include: *America's West: A History, 1890–1950* (2018), *Global West, American Frontier* (2013, winner of the Western Heritage Award for nonfiction), *Promised Lands* (2002), and *The End of American Exceptionalism* (1993). He is currently working on "John Steinbeck's America: A Cultural History, 1930–1968." He is a past president of the Pacific Coast branch of the American Historical Association and of Phi Alpha Theta, the National History Honor Society, and is a frequent collaborator with K–12 teachers across the country.

Chronology

1929   Books: *Sartoris* (William Faulkner), *The Sound and the Fury* (Faulkner), *A Farewell to Arms* (Ernest Hemingway), *Look Homeward, Angel* (Thomas Wolfe), *Daughter of Earth* (Agnes Smedley), *Middletown* (Robert and Helen Lynd).

April. The Gastonia Strike begins. It will be the subject of at least four proletarian novels and two plays.

May. *The Little Review* ceases publication.

July. *The Dial* ceases publication.

October. Black Thursday. The Dow Jones Industrial Average plunges 11 percent. The beginning of the Wall Street Crash.

October. Staff members of *The New Masses* found the John Reed Club.

November. The Museum of Modern Art opens.

1930   Books: *Jews without Money* (Michael Gold), *The Woman of Andros* (Thornton Wilder), *Ash Wednesday* (T. S. Eliot), *The Bridge* (Hart Crane), *The 42nd Parallel* (John Dos Passos), *I'll Take My Stand* (the Southern Agrarians), *Cimarron* (Edna Ferber), *The Maltese Falcon* (Dashiell Hammett), *As I Lay Dying* (William Faulkner), *Not without Laughter* (Langston Hughes), *Laughing Boy* (Oliver La Farge), *Dance Night* (Dawn Powell), *Exile* (Warwick Deeping), *Black Manhattan* (James Weldon Johnson), *Mixed Marriage* (Margaret Banning), *A Draft of XXX Cantos* (Ezra Pound).

February. Time Inc. launches *Fortune* magazine.

August. *Amos 'n' Andy* starts broadcasting.

October. The first "soap opera," *Painted Dreams*, debuts on Chicago radio station WGN.

October. Ethel Merman makes her Broadway debut in the Gershwin brothers' musical *Girl Crazy*. One of her most famous songs is "I Got Rhythm."

November. Sinclair Lewis wins the Nobel Prize for Literature.

Agnes Smedley crosses paths with Soviet spy Richard Sorge in Shanghai. She introduces him to Hotsumi Ozaki.

Deaths: D. H. Lawrence, Herbert Croly, Pauline Hopkins.

1931   Books: *Axel's Castle* (Edmund Wilson), *Hard Lines* (Ogden Nash), *The Good Earth* (Pearl Buck), *Sanctuary* (William Faulkner), *Black No More* (George Schuyler), *The Forge* (T. S. Stribling), *ViVa* (e. e. cummings), *A White Bird Flying* (Bess Streeter Aldrich), *American Humor* (Constance Rourke), *Shadows on the Rock* (Willa Cather).

February. A special issue of *Poetry* dedicated to Objectivism appears.

February. Dr. Seuss's first book, *The Pocket Book of Boners*, is released. The term "boner" means a silly mistake.

March. "The Star-Spangled Banner," by Francis Scott Key, is approved by the government as the national anthem.

March. Nevada legalizes gambling.

April. The trials of the Scottsboro Boys start in Alabama.

May. The Empire State Building, the world's tallest, is opened by President Hoover.

October. The Dick Tracy comic strip appears.

October. Eugene O'Neill's trilogy, *Mourning Becomes Electra*, opens on Broadway.

November. H. L. Mencken's *American Mercury* quantifies the South's backwardness in "The Worst American State: Part III."

Harold Clurman, Cheryl Crawford, and Lee Strasberg form the Group Theater. The Group launches the career of Clifford Odets.

The exodus of Broadway talent to Hollywood picks up.

Deaths: Khalil Gibran, Vachel Lindsay, Bix Beiderbecke.

1932   Books: *Death in the Afternoon* (Ernest Hemingway), *Tobacco Road* (Erskine Caldwell), *Young Lonigan* (James T. Farrell), *Guys and Dolls* (Damon Runyon), *Light in August* (William Faulkner), *1919* (John Dos Passos), *The Conjure Man Dies* (Rudolph Fisher), *Infants of the Spring* (Wallace Thurman), *The Knife of the Times* (William Carlos Williams), *Sons* (Pearl S. Buck), *The Fountain* (Charles Morgan), *Laughing in the Jungle* (Louis Adamic), *Moral Man and Immoral Society* (Reinhold Niebuhr), *Southern Road* (Sterling Brown).

March. The infant son of Charles and Anne Morrow Lindbergh is kidnapped.

April. Hart Crane kills himself, aged thirty-two.

May. William Faulkner arrives in Culver City, California. The beginning of a long captivity in Moviedom.

May. Al Capone goes to jail for tax evasion.

June. Langston Hughes arrives in Moscow as part of a group of African Americans hired to act in a Soviet film about race relations in the American South.

The stock market bottoms out. The Dow Jones Industrial Average sinks to 41.22 (down from 381.17 in September 1929). The market doesn't regain its previous peak until November 1954.

November. Franklin Delano Roosevelt defeats incumbent President Hoover.

T. S. Eliot returns to the United States to assume the Charles Eliot Norton professorship at Harvard for the 1932–33 academic year.

Whittaker Chambers goes underground as a spy for a GRU apparatus.

Deaths: Charles Chestnutt.

1933   Books: *My Life and Hard Times* (James Thurber), *The Autobiography of Alice B. Toklas* (Gertrude Stein), *God's Little Acre* (Erskine Caldwell), *Miss Lonely Hearts* (Nathanael West), *Anthony Adverse* (Hervey Allen), *Banana Bottom* (Claude McKay), *The Disinherited* (Jack Conroy), *Mis-Education of the Negro* (Carter G. Woodson), *Eimi* (e. e. cummings), *Hungry Men* (Edward Anderson), *Unfinished Cathedral* (T. S. Stribling), *Ann Vickers* (Sinclair Lewis).

January. Adolf Hitler is appointed as Chancellor of Germany. The beginning of the Third Reich.

March. FDR is inaugurated. The beginning of the New Deal.

May. Book burnings in Germany are carried out by the German Student Union, mainly works by Jewish intellectuals.

May. Disney cartoon *Three Little Pigs* is released.

October. Men's magazine *Esquire* is founded and thrives, mixing men's fashion with highbrow literature. Fitzgerald's *The Crack-Up* and Pietro di Donato's "Christ in Concrete" originally appear in this magazine.

November. A strong dust storm takes place in South Dakota. The beginning of the environmental crisis in the "Dust Bowl."

November. Billie Holiday's recording debut with Benny Goodman, produced by John Hammond. Two recordings: "Your Mother's Son-in-Law" and "Riffin' the Scotch."

December. Raymond Chandler debuts in *Black Mask*.

December. *Tobacco Road* opens on Broadway. It plays for an astonishing 3,182 performances, breaking Broadway records.

December. In *United States* v. *One Book Called Ulysses*, Judge John M. Woolsey rules James Joyce's novel is not obscene.

December. The Twenty-First Amendment is repealed. The end of Prohibition.

Unemployment peaks at 24.9 percent.

Albert Einstein takes up a position at the Institute for Advanced Study in Princeton, NJ.

Deaths: Ring Lardner.

1934   Books: *Tender Is the Night* (F. Scott Fitzgerald), *ABC of Reading* (Ezra Pound), *Eleven New Cantos: XXXI-XLI* (Pound), *Tropic of Cancer* (Henry Miller), *The Thin Man* (Dashiell Hammett), *The Postman Always Rings Twice* (James M. Cain), *A Cool Million* (Nathanael West), *Jonah's Gourd Vine* (Zora Neal Hurston), *Appointment in Samarra* (John O'Hara), *Call It Sleep* (Henry Roth), *Patterns of Culture* (Ruth Benedict), *The Young Manhood of Studs Lonigan* (James T. Farrell), *It Can Happen Here* (Sinclair Lewis), *The Last Puritan* (George Santayana), *The League of Frightened Men* (Rex Stout), *The Story of a Country Boy* (Dawn Powell), *Summer in Williamsburg* (Daniel Fuchs), *Technics and Civilization* (Lewis Mumford), *After Strange Gods* (T. S. Eliot), *The Land of Plenty* (Robert Cantwell), *Heaven Is My Destination* (Thornton Wilder), *Ladies Go Masked* (Margaret Widdemer), *Beauty's Daughter* (Kathleen Thompson Norris).

January. Following *United States* v. *One Book Called Ulysses*, Random House publishes the first authorized edition in America. It has 12,000 advance sales.

May. A *Pravda* article hints at a turn in the Communist International (Comintern) policy toward Western democracies. The end of the ultra-left "Third Period" and the beginning of the Popular Front.

July. John Dillinger is gunned down in front of the Biograph Theater in Chicago by FBI agents.

October. Gertrude Stein begins her tour of America. She will return to France in May 1935.

October. The Chinese Red Army begins the Long March.

November. Lillian Hellman's first successful play, *The Children's Hour*, premieres on Broadway.

November. Cole Porter's musical, *Anything Goes*, opens on Broadway. "You're the Top," "I Get a Kick Out of You."

December. The murder of Sergei Kirov in Leningrad. Stalin uses this as a pretext to launch the Great Purge.

The Motion Picture Association of America begins strictly enforcing the Production Code (the so-called Hays Code), which was adopted in 1930.

Deaths: Wallace Thurman, Rudolph Fisher.

1935   Books: *Tortilla Flat* (John Steinbeck), *Judgment Day* (James T. Farrell), *Green Hills of Africa* (Ernest Hemingway), *The Daring Young Man on the Flying Trapeze* (William Saroyan), *Somebody in Boots* (Nelson Algren), *Theory of Flight* (Muriel Rukeyser), *They Shoot Horses, Don't They?* (Horace McCoy), *no thanks* (e. e. cummings), *An Early Martyr* (William Carlos Williams), *Vein of Iron* (Ellen Grasgow), *Green Light* (Lloyd C. Douglas), *Selected Poems* (Marianne Moore), *The Journeyman* (Erskine Caldwell), *Of Time and the River* (Thomas Wolfe), *Permanence and Change* (Kenneth Burke).

January. Clifford Odets's *Waiting for Lefty*, a play inspired by a 1934 strike of New York City cab drivers, premieres at a benefit for *New Theater* magazine.

February. The Group Theatre produces Clifford Odets's *Awake and Sing* on Broadway.

March. Germany unilaterally declares rearmament.

April. The First Congress of the League of American writers is held. The Americanization of Communism.

April. The Resettlement Administration (RA), the brainchild of Rexford Tugwell is founded, and is reorganized as the Farm Security Administration in 1937. Its Historical Section (the Photography Section under the FSA) is headed by Roy Stryker. FDR appoints filmmaker Pare Lorentz to the RA, who makes *The Plow That Broke the Plain* and *The River*.

June. The greatest hitter in the history of baseball, Babe Ruth retires.

June. Alcoholics Anonymous is founded in Akron, Ohio.

Summer. A flurry of legislative activities occurs (the Second New Deal): the Social Security Act, the Works Progress Administration (WPA), the Wagner Act.

July. The WPA funds a number of programs that employ writers and artists, such as the Federal Writers' Project (FWP) and the Federal Theater Project.

August. Benny Goodman performs for a three-week engagement at the Palomar Ballroom in Los Angeles. The beginning of the swing era.

August. The Social Security Act is passed.

September. The Hoover Dam is dedicated.

October. Langston Hughes's play *Mulatto* opens on Broadway.

October. Italy invades Ethiopia.

October. Huey Long is assassinated.

October. The Gershwins and DuBose Heyward opera, *Porgy and Bess*, opens on Broadway. "Summertime," "I Got Plenty O' Nuttin'," "It Ain't Necessarily So."

November. Charles Coughlin founds the National Union for Social Justice.

November. F. Scott Fitzgerald moves to Hendersonville, North Carolina, stays at a cheap hotel, and writes "The Crack-Up" while eating canned food and tens of thousands of dollars in debt, with less than 40 cents in cash and a $13 deficit at his bank.

Deaths: Charlotte Perkins Gilman.

1936   Books: *Gone with the Wind* (Margaret Mitchell), *Absalom, Absalom!* (William Faulkner), *The Big Money* (John Dos Passos), *Black Thunder* (Arna Bontemps), *Double Indemnity* (James M. Cain), *We the Living* (Ayn Rand), *In Dubious Battle* (John Steinbeck), *How to Win Friends and Influence People* (Dale Carnegie), *Turn, Magic Wheel* (Dawn Powell), *Homage to Blenholt* (Daniel Fuchs), *Ideas of Order* (Wallace Stevens), *Owl's Clover* (Wallace Stevens), *The Surrounded* (Darcy McKnickle), *Nightwood* (Djuna Barnes).

April. The opening of the "voodoo" *Macbeth* at the Lafayette Theater in Harlem, directed by Orson Welles.

June. Pope Pius XI issues an encyclical to US bishops entitled "On Motion Pictures."

June–July. James Agee and Walker Evans travel from New York City to Alabama on assignment for *Fortune* magazine.

July. Ralph Ellison moves from Alabama to New York City.

July. The Spanish Civil War starts.

August. The Berlin Summer Olympics are held. Jesse Owens wins four gold medals. Hitler refuses to be photographed with him.

October. Eugene O'Neill is awarded the Nobel Prize in Literature.

Fall. John Steinbeck tours the San Joaquin Valley with Eric H. Thomsen, regional director of the federal migrant camp program, and sees the plight of migrant laborers firsthand.

November. FDR is reelected.

November. Henry Luce's Time Inc. launches *Life* magazine.

December. George S. Kaufman and Moss Hart's *You Can't Take It with You* premieres on Broadway.

December. The United Auto Workers, part of the Congress of Industrial Organizations, begins a sit-down strike at the General Motors plant in Flint, Michigan.

The fertility rate hits the bottom. 75 per 100,000 women aged 15–44 (93 in 1928).

Deaths: Harriet Monroe, Irving Thalberg.

1937   Books: *Of Mice and Men* (John Steinbeck), *The Citadel* (A. J. Cronin), *The Fifth Decad of Cantos* (Ezra Pound), *To Have and Have Not* (Ernest Hemingway), *Their Eyes Were Watching God* (Zora Neale Hurston), *The Good Society* (Walter Lippmann), *Red Star over China* (Edgar Snow), *A Long Way from Home* (Claude McKay), *Low Company* (Daniel Fuchs), *Middletown in Transition* (Robert and Hellen Lynd), *The Man with the Blue Guitar* (Wallace Stevens), *White Mule* (William Carlos Williams), *You Have Seen Their Faces* (Margaret Bourke-White and Erskine Caldwell), *Thieves Like Us* (Edward Anderson), *Northwest Passage* (Kenneth Roberts), *And China Has Hands* (H. T. Tsiang), *The Importance of Living* (Lin Yutang), *Attitudes toward History* (Kenneth Burke), *American Stuff: An Anthology of Prose and Verse by Members of the Federal Writers' Project*.

April. Archibald MacLeish's "The Fall of the City" is broadcast over the Columbia Broadcasting System as part of the Columbia Workshop radio series.

April. Guernica is bombed.

May. The Golden Gate Bridge opens.

June. The League of American Writers holds its Second Congress. The civil war in Spain is the main concern.

June. Valery Chkalov flies nonstop from Moscow, Soviet Union to Vancouver, Washington, US, via the North Pole.

June. Theodore Adorno leaves England for New York.

July. The Marco Polo Bridge Incident occurs in which Japan invades China proper.

July. F. Scott Fitzgerald reports at MGM, $22,000 in debt.

November. Musical revue *Pins and Needles* opens on Broadway. The cast are all members of the International Ladies' Garment Workers' Union. An unexpected hit, it runs for 1,108 performances.

FDR prematurely tries to balance the budget. The Roosevelt Recession ensues.

Deaths: George Gershwin, H. P. Lovecraft, Edith Wharton, Don Marquis.

1938   Books: *In Dreams Begin Responsibilities* (Delmore Schwartz), *The Coming Victory of Democracy* (Thomas Mann), *Homage to Catalonia* (George Orwell), *The Late George Apley* (John P. Marquand), *Uncle Tom's Children* (Richard Wright), *The Happy Island* (Dawn Powell), *I Should Have Stayed Home* (Horace McCoy), *Life along the Passaic* (William Carlos Williams), *All This, and Heaven Too* (Rachel Field), *My America* (Louis Adamic), *The World's Body* (John Crow Ransom), *Understanding Poetry* (Cleanth Brooks and Robert Penn Warren), *The Hill Grows Steeper* (Fannie Cook).

February. Thornton Wilder's *Our Town* opens on Broadway.

July. The Justice Department begins antitrust proceedings against Hollywood studios. The beginning of the end of the studio system.

October. The Munich Crisis.

October. Archibald MacLeish's radio drama "Air Raid" is broadcast.

October. Orson Welles's radio adaptation of *The War of the Worlds* is broadcast in The Mercury Theatre on the Air series.

October. Pearl S. Buck wins the Nobel Prize in Literature.

November. Irving Berlin's "God Bless America" is sung by Kate Smith on her radio show on Armistice Day.

Whittaker Chambers breaks with the Communist Party and goes into hiding with his family.

Deaths: James Weldon Johnson, Thomas Wolfe, Arthur Schomburg.

1939   Books: *Tropic of Capricorn* (Henry Miller), *The Grapes of Wrath* (John Steinbeck), *The Big Sleep* (Raymond Chandler), *The Day of the Locust* (Nathanael West), *Let Me Breathe Thunder* (William Attaway), *Drums at Dusk* (Arna Bontemps), *Ask the Dust* (John Fante), *Moses, Man of the Mountain* (Zora Neale Hurston), *Finnegans Wake* (James Joyce), *Pale Horse, Pale Rider* (Katherine Anne Porter), *Johnny Got His Gun* (Dalton Trumbo), *U.S. 1: Poems* (Muriel Rukeyser), *The New England Mind* (Perry Miller), *The Idea of a Christian Society* (T. S. Eliot), *Knowledge for What?* (Robert Lynd), *Factories in the Field* (Carey McWilliams), *Moment in Peking* (Lin Yutang), *Christ in Concrete* (Pietro di Donato), *An American Exodus* (Dorothy Lange and Paul Schuster Taylor), *Kitty Foyle* (Christopher Morley), *Career by Proxy* (Faith Baldwin), *The Main Stream* (Hilda Morris).

January. W. H. Auden and Christopher Isherwood emigrate together to America.

March. The *Anschluss*, the German annexation of Austria, takes place.

March. T. S. Eliot's *Family Reunion* opens at the Westminster Theatre, London.

April. Norman Corwin's radio drama "They Fly through the Air with the Greatest of Ease" is broadcast.

April. The New York World's Fair opens in Queens, NY. The Fair will draw 45 million paid visitors in the next two years.

April. Marian Anderson sings at the Lincoln Memorial.

April. Ezra Pound sails for the United States, convinced that he will stop American involvement in the approaching war.

June. The League of American Writers holds its Third Congress.

August. The Nazi–Soviet Pact is signed. The fatal blow to the Popular Front.

August. Albert Einstein meets with FDR and discusses an A-bomb possibility.

September. Germany invades Poland. The beginning of World War II in Europe.

A banner year on Broadway: *Abe Lincoln in Illinois* (Robert Sherwood), *The Philadelphia Story* (Philip Barry), *The Little*

Foxes (Lillian Hellman), *The Man Who Came to Dinner* (Kaufman and Hart), *The Time of Your Life* (William Saroyan).

A banner year in Hollywood: *The Wizard of Oz, Gone with the Wind, Stagecoach, Mr. Smith Goes to Washington, Wuthering Heights, Ninotchka.*

Simon & Schuster starts its paperback division, Pocket Books, revolutionizing the publishing industry.

Congress ends funding for the FWP.

Thomas Mann emigrates to the United States.

Deaths: Sigmund Freud, W. B. Yeats, S. S. Van Dine (Willard Huntington Wright), Havelock Ellis, Zane Grey, Heywood Broun, Sidney Howard.

1940 Books: *Native Son* (Richard Wright), *For Whom the Bell Tolls* (Ernest Hemingway), *Cantos LXII-LXXI* (Ezra Pound), *The Heart Is a Lonely Hunter* (Carson McCullers), *To the Finland Station* (Edmund Wilson), *Sapphira and the Slave* (Willa Cather), *Farewell, My Lovely* (Raymond Chandler), *How to Read a Book* (Mortimer J. Adler), *My Name Is Aram* (William Saroyan), *Angels on Toast* (Dawn Powell), *Harlem: Negro Metropolis* (Claude McKay), *50 Poems* (e. e. cummings), *In the Money* (William Carlos Williams), *From Many Lands* (Louis Adamic).

February. Woody Guthrie writes "This Land Is Your Land," the antiwar rejoinder to Irving Berlin's "God Bless America."

April. Robert Sherwood's interventionist play, *There Shall Be No Night,* opens on Broadway and wins Sherwood his third Pulitzer Prize.

August. Varian Fry arrives in Marseilles. He will smuggle out anti-Nazi intellectuals and artists, including Marc Chagall, André Breton, Max Ernst, and Hannah Arendt.

October. Louis Adamic launches the *Common Ground* magazine.

September. Congress passes the first peacetime conscription bill.

November. FDR is reelected, becoming the first man to hold the presidency for three terms.

Deaths: F. Scott Fitzgerald, Nathanael West, Marcus Garvey.

1941 Books: *Let Us Now Praise Famous Men* (James Agee, Walker Evans), *Twelve Million Black Voices* (Richard Wright), *The Last*

Tycoon (F. Scott Fitzgerald), *What Makes Sammy Run* (Budd Schulberg), *The Ground We Stand On* (John Dos Passos), *American Renaissance* (F. O. Matthiessen), *A Leaf in the Storm* (Lin Yutang), *The New Criticism* (John Crow Ransom), *Philosophy of Literary Form* (Kenneth Burke).

January. FDR gives his "Four Freedoms" speech.

January. From Rome, Ezra Pound starts broadcasting a seemingly incoherent medley of economic analysis, political commentary, and literary divagations.

February. Henry Luce declares that his country owns the twentieth century. "The American Century" appears in *Life*.

June. Germany invades the Soviet Union in Operation Barbarossa.

September. Melvin Tolson's "Dark Symphony" appears in *Atlantic Monthly*.

September. Walter Benjamin kills himself in Portbou, Spain. He was on his way to the United States, reading Herman Melville to brush up on his English.

December. The Japanese attack Pearl Harbor. The United States enters World War II.

Introduction

Ichiro Takayoshi

"In a real dark night of the soul it is always three o'clock in the morning, day after day," wrote F. Scott Fitzgerald in his country's darkest hour.[1] It was February 1936. At that juncture, in the last year of Franklin Roosevelt's first term, the clock must have looked eternally stuck at three in the morning to countless Americans, especially those of Fitzgerald's generation. Around midnight, the most expensive orgy of all generations – the high jinks and careless laughs and reckless speculations, both emotional and financial, of the 1920s – had reached its vertiginously lofty acme. Then, crash! It was the sound of the postwar boom falling apart. Immediately, all the panicked guests fled the party. That was a while ago, and now the time is three in the morning, sharp. Hugging their naked souls, they are alone in the dark. The first light, the glimmer of economic recovery and political stability, will be several dark and solitary hours in coming. Will it really come, ever? They are not so sure any more. Down and out but still wide awake, they find themselves suspended in an unaccustomed zone of transition. It's neither night nor day. A buzz from too much champagne is giving way to the onset of a hangover, the piercing headache. They have tumbled down to the bottom of the worst depression in the nation's history, the worst depression of their lives, but they want to believe that the dawn is just around the corner.

I commissioned the following chapters specially for this book with a view to capturing the decade with all of its transitional contradictions, all of its darkest nights and its bravest days. The "test of a first-rate intelligence is the ability to hold two opposed ideas in the mind at the same time, and still retain the ability to function." This is another famous maxim taken from Fitzgerald's essay "The Crack-Up." I thought this test was pertinent to this volume. To be first-rate, it must hold a multitude of oppositions and contradictions. To be first-rate, this book must offer a coherent account of an incoherency: how the nation despaired and hoped all at once at three in the morning. This book's syncretic contents and its elastic framework are the devices I consciously chose to achieve this goal.

It presents no surprise that nocturnal themes dominate many of the subsequent chapters. "Hunger makes thief of any man." "As God is my witness, I'll never be hungry again." "To hell with the truth! As the history of the world proves, the truth has no bearing on anything." "With *usura* hath no man a painted paradise on his church wall." "Christ is a nigger, beaten and black." "Why do you hate the South?" "Knights had no meaning in this game. It wasn't a game for knights." "God Bless America," sung not in a jingoistic growl but in a scared croak.[2] Hunger, confusion, hate, isolation, cynicism, and fear motivated these memorable locutions. The general emotional tone of this volume is grave.

And yet the ensemble that my contributors play in concert is never monotonous. You will find in the following chapters literary expressions of sunny sentiments, sung, declaimed, or muttered in an unterrified cadence. "Good-morning, Revolution." "Everything that is is holy." "After all, tomorrow is another day." "For whom the bell tolls." "This land is your land." "Night and day, you are the one." "Love is lak de sea." "There ain't no sin and there ain't no virtue. There's just stuff people do." "Toto, I've got a feeling we're not in Kansas anymore." And Tonto's endearing "Ke-mo sah-bee."[3] These utterances, as intimately enmeshed with our idea of the 1930s as their despairing opposites, came from another place in American culture, a seemingly impregnable bastion of hope, camaraderie, elegance, and wonderment that survived the most trying of circumstances. Throughout, my goal has been to let this book register the crush of all these contradictory melodies and sentiments that found expression in the era's literature.

To design a volume of essays that meets Fitzgerald's first requirement – holding a multitude of opposed ideas – was, then, my first goal. The second consisted in giving a book of such internal tension "the ability to function." This is where the concept of "transition," central not only to this volume but to the Cambridge series as a whole, came in handy. As you can see, the table of contents relies on a rather conventional way of organizing multifarious topics. It divides the materials into "Themes," "Formats," and "Institutions," and under these headings, diverse chapters address themselves to diverse but clearly defined problems. Such a system makes these problems assignable to specific contributors equipped with specific expertise, showcases the rich variety of the contents, and easily accommodates additions and substitutions. Underneath this conventional surface, however, lies another, simpler, and more organic principle – a dialogue between problems of literary representation that arose out of the social conditions of the time and those that might have been made acute by historical circumstances of the 1930s but were not created by the major political, social, and technological developments of that era.

Since even in the most turbulent of epochs there seldom emerges a wholly original literary problem, an argument could be made that many of the topics examined by the contributors in what follows were actually preexisting creative issues endemic to the act of representation as such. In other words, contemporary writers discovered new solutions to old problems. Take for example the radical writers' relationship with the Communist Party of the United States of America (CPUSA), the subject of Chapter 21. Even this topic, as uniquely characteristic of the historical situation in the 1930s as any other, can be argued to be an iteration of an enduring literary theme. Didn't Henry James, a half century before, already dissect the morality of political violence and the perils of the individual's total assimilation into a radical and quasi-religious organization in *The Princess Casamassima* (1886)? Didn't William Shakespeare explore the same dangerous territory of subversive conspiracy in *Julius Caesar* (1599)? Although it may not be always easy sharply to distinguish problems of literary representation unique to the 1930s from those that are not so, I remain convinced that this distinction can be seen as seminal for a larger insight that is at the heart of this volume. The insight consists in this: the best way to model a literary history is by treating it as a bundle of themes, formats, and institutions always *in transition* at divergent paces. If you apply this model to the distinction between literary problems that are context-bound and literary problems that are relatively autonomous, then you will be able to see this distinction not as a given line but as a changeable value that reflects a particular quantity of turbulence generated at a particular moment of transition. On this account, literary problems popularly associated with the 1930s, such seemingly *sui generis* events as the political radicalization of literary culture, government funding of arts, and the rise of documentary journalism, are revealed as especially stormy manifestations of traditional literary concerns at a time of transition. Likewise, literary pursuits that kept the pressures of the immediate context at arm's length, such as the novelistic exploration of women's changing roles in the family and at work, can be understood as relatively quiescent phases of long-standing concerns enduring through the 1930s. Needless to say, these two kinds of literary problems stand at the extremes of an elastic spectrum that can accommodate a number of intermediate cases. For example, the problem of national identity and literature's responsibility for evolving a series of its definitions, the subjects of Chapters 9, 10, and 11, were intermediate issues that were neither completely context-bound nor autonomous.

My aim in the remainder of this introduction is to unpack the contents housed discretely in "Chapters" and "Parts" and reassemble them in accordance with the logic of variable transition. An image of a sparser but deeper structure emerges from this re-assemblage, and affords a glimpse into the blueprint of this volume that underlies its table of contents.

***

Let's begin with the literary themes whose transitional processes were particularly turbulent in the decade, those problems to which the historical moment appeared to writers to demand immediate and radical solutions. One of the most memorable of these, the one probably most intimately associated with the 1930s in our collective memory, is what Joseph Entin calls in Chapter 3 the "precarity" of the working class. Americans had always been working people. On farms, in towns, and increasingly since the Civil War on factory floors, an overwhelming majority of the nation toiled daily to produce and subsist. Precisely because of its accustomed presence at the center of American life, however, labor was never truly among the topics fit for literary endeavors until its precarious character was exposed to the working men and women and to the "intellectual workers" of the 1930s. A proximate cause that forced the nation to reflect on the life of the "proletariat" (originally a Roman term meaning "those who produce the offspring," applied in the Roman Republic to citizens possessing only children and no property, revived by Marx in the nineteenth century and imported into the American lexicon around the turn of the century) was mass unemployment. When jobs evaporated overnight in staggering numbers and when much national anxiety was attached to the problem of relief and job creation, writers and readers became curious about what these jobs – cannery work, fruit packing, welding, mining, tobacco farming, logging, and so on – actually entailed. It was the frightful dearth of jobs that, defamiliarizing them, made them a worthy object of aesthetic interest and social passion for writers and artists. Forensic and worshipful descriptions of the logistics of cotton farming in James Agee and Walker Evans's *Let Us Now Praise Famous Men* (1941), a Zola-esque delineation of Virginia miners in Muriel Rukeyser's *U.S.1* (1938), or at once allegorical and action-packed descriptions of bricklayers in Pietro di Donato's *Christ in Concrete* (1939) spoke to this emergent interest in the physics of laboring.

The national office of the Federal Writers' Project (FWP) caught onto this trend very late in the decade, but when it did, as Jerrold Hirsch discusses in Chapter 18, it brought its full institutional resources to bear on their new project, titled *Men at Work*, which documented a diversity of jobs done by ordinary workers.[4]

These writers recorded labor itself in vivid detail. Harold Rosenberg, editor of *Men at Work*, even stipulated that writers contributing to the anthology see the jobs firsthand or preferably perform these jobs themselves. Meanwhile, other writers, the majority of those responding to the precarious life of the working class, chose to focus on the class's experiences outside of work. Such a choice was logical for a number of reasons. To begin with, an overwhelming majority of writers were after all college-educated intellectuals with little or no experience of backbreaking manual labor. Di Donato, who left school at the seventh grade to work as a construction worker, was a rare exception; James Agee, a graduate of Phillips Exeter and Harvard, was the norm. Another reason for the relative absence of actual labor in 1930s literature was the fact that what heightened the sense of working-class insecurity was the threat or the reality of joblessness. Structurally, the proletariat's vulnerable position as a class without property that only produced offspring was bound up less with hazardous working conditions than with the ever-imminent possibility of unemployment. At the lowest circle of the hell that was Depression-era America, writers found not men at work but men who were either out of work or facing the imminent risk of falling out of work. The most famous Depression-era fictional characters, the Joads of John Steinbeck's *The Grapes of Wrath* (1939), travel in their jalopy 1,500 miles from Oklahoma to California, in search of work and cause anxious rejection in the communities through which they pass.

The ambit of the writers' interest in the working class extended beyond the economic challenge of breadwinning; their attitude took an anthropological turn. Alive to this development, Agee wrote in 1935 to Father Flye, his high school mentor in Tennessee, "that in most present writing that is any good there is a strong consciousness of 'anthropological' correctness, i.e. the writer takes great care, in writing of millhands, that they speak an exact Pittsburgh instead of Gary dialect."[5] Although works of fiction about the working class introduced a variety of ethnic groups, regions, and occupations to the readers, many of them couldn't have been written in the first place if their authors hadn't been driven by a certain shared vision about the life-world of workers. Stylistically, authors like Mike Gold, Henry Roth, James T. Farrell, Carlos Bulosan, Dalton

Trumbo, and Richard Wright experimented with miscellaneous techniques. Yet, notwithstanding the resulting diversity in terms of aesthetic effect, these authors all wrote on the assumption that the working class had developed a unique way of life. This new "way of life" has been interpreted from differing points of view since its discovery in the 1930s. You could, for example, place it in the liberal narrative of progress. Then, you would be able to see how the working-class status came to be recognized as a cultural identity in the 1930s thanks to the rise of unions and their contributions to popular culture.[6] Or, alternatively, you could adopt a Marxist viewpoint. Then, you might realize that the idea that to labor in America is to practice a way of life patterned by unique rituals and symbols could gain acceptance precisely because the working class was losing its edge, its intractable outsider-ness. Dissolving the "contradiction" between labor and capital that radicals pointed to as the engine behind history's inexorable progression toward social revolution, the new working-class culture saved capitalism from itself.

Whatever your evaluation of the social implications of the discovery of the working-class culture, what you find in these books exploring the proletarian way of life is an attention fastened on the minutiae of individual daily existence. These books collected particular scenes and confused but honest emotions that were meaningful enough to sustain the interest of the main story, meaningful enough to dispense with a didactic author editorializing about their political usefulness. Certainly, this does not mean that the authors did not handle these concrete and particular materials with an eye toward exposing their injustice. Speeches connecting working-class life as it actually was to a theoretically spectated destination in history often obtruded themselves at the very end of these usually autobiographical stories. But as far as the all-informing literary sensibility was concerned, these authors of working-class fiction were more naïvely experiential than theoretically rigorous. Gold, Roth, Farrell, Bulosan, and Trumbo were committed socialists and several of them were card-carrying members of the CPUSA at some point during the 1930s. The irony is rich. Whatever dire prophesies they made about the inevitability of a working-class uprising, whatever yearnings for a classless society they gave voice to through their political actions, the stories they actually told painted a surprisingly claustrophobic picture of working life.[7] Like it or not, and they often seem quite attached to it, the workers in these stories appear to be trapped in a culture that does what all cultures do so well – prevent its members from historicizing their conditions.

If class interest could be rewritten as cultural experience, it is not so surprising that many 1930s writers, readers, and publishers reduced, *ad absurdum*, the problem of class to the problem of style. The 1930s were "an age of the present tense, the stevedore style," Dawn Powell writes in *Turn, Magic Wheel* (1936), a scream of a satire on literary celebrities and the Manhattan publishing industry. The "stevedore style" is on display in a piece of pulp fiction that draws the attention of young, ineffectually ambitious editor Johnson, always on the lookout for new talents in order to one-up his competitors:

> The freight slows up just outside the yards. As she jerks around the bend by the tower Spud gives Butch a kinda push and out they rolls outa the side door onto the gravel. Wot the hell, sez Butch, take it easy, take it easy. Ya wanna kill us?

"To achieve this virile, crude effect," Powell's bemused voice glosses, "authors were tearing up second, third, and tenth revised drafts to publish their simple unaffected notes, plain, untouched, with all the warts and freckles of infancy. The older writers who had taken twenty years to learn their craft were in a bewildering predicament, learning, alas, too late, that Pater, Proust, and Flaubert had betrayed them, they would have learned better modern prose by economizing on Western Union messages."[8] In fairness to all the literary performers of proletarian virility, let me repeat that Powell's pastiche is an absurd reduction. But, besides being funny, her ridiculous reduction inadvertently serves to make the political point: by figuring the worker as a speaker with a distinctive voice, instead of a rational actor with an economic interest, the author risks translating economic disagreement into terms of expressive difference.

In 1930s culture, the interest in the marginalized class was connected with the interest in marginalized geographical regions, as Chapters 4, 6, and 7 explain. If the class protagonists of the literary culture of the previous decade were elites, that is to say, the at least imaginatively free souls whose resources of consciousness were more than equal to the troubling consequences of war, urbanization, and commercialism, the class protagonists of the 1930s were decidedly the plebeians whose consciousness struggled to digest the world around them. In parallel with this shift, the regional focus of literary culture also moved from New York City, the playground of sophisticates and snobs, to the rest of the nation. Under conditions of economic depression, populism and regionalism were on the rise in tandem. Because during the Jazz Age he had wagered, with more romantic abandon than anyone else, all of his phenomenal ability to feel on the

promise of the city, F. Scott Fitzgerald was ready to dramatize the
Depression-era rediscovery of the hinterland, the vast country that was
not New York, with more piquancy than anyone else. In July 1932,
Fitzgerald revisited his Babylon – Manhattan – for the last time. What
struck him was how the economic crisis actually normalized American life.
Customs agents were curiously polite. His barber was back at work in his
shop. The head waiters at his old haunts again bowed people to their tables.
And from

> the ruins, lonely and inexplicable as the sphinx, rose the Empire State
> Building and, just as it had been a tradition of mine to climb to the Plaza
> Roof to take leave of the beautiful city, extending as far as eyes could reach,
> so now I went to the roof of the last and most magnificent of towers. Then
> I understood – everything was explained: I had discovered the crowning
> error of the city, its Pandora's box. Full of vaunting pride the New Yorker
> had climbed here and seen with dismay what he had never suspected, that
> the city was not the endless succession of canyons that he had supposed but
> that *it had limits* – from the tallest structure he saw for the first time that it
> faded out into the country on all sides, into an expanse of green and blue
> that alone was limitless. And with the awful realization that New York was
> a city after all and not a universe, the whole shining edifice that he had
> reared in his imagination came crashing to the ground.[9]

Then as nowadays, typical writers were cosmopolitan *flâneurs*, and so it was
not as though the Great Depression precipitated among writers a mass
hegira to small towns and the countryside. But as a place to live and work,
cities in general became impractical for writers, many of whom took to the
road for significant portions of the decade. Probably the most dramatic
case in point was Langston Hughes. Leaving a cabinet of his files, suitcases,
and a few books in his friends' homes in Carmel, CA and New Jersey, he
crisscrossed the nation in his new Model A Ford sedan for much of the
decade, relying on the proceedings from his public readings for his livelihood. Moral and creative reasons also compelled writers to hit the road,
because the most urgent topic of the era, legions of forgotten men and
women, resided in rural America. Their travels down many unfamiliar
ways and byways of their own country resulted in a host of road narratives
and on-the-ground accounts of the plights of ordinary people. Field reports
filed by journalists on Federal Emergency Relief Administration (FERA)
assignments, including Martha Gellhorn, belong to this genre. These
officially sponsored writings were joined by a wealth of reportage produced
by progressive writers at once driven by anger at the inequitable social
system and tempted by the chance to gather new materials for their artistic

endeavors. Works belonging to this genre include Edmund Wilson's *The American Jitters* (1932), Sherwood Anderson's *Puzzled America* (1935), James Rorty's *Where Life Is Better* (1936), and Nathan Asch's *The Road: In Search of America* (1937). Another group of authors, who, often literally, had lived as hobos themselves, overlaid their works of fiction with the conventions of travel narrative. Edward Anderson's *Hungry Men* (1933) follows a hobo-musician, narrated in the third person, in a desolate dead-pan voice. Tom Kroner's only novel, *Waiting for Nothing* (1935), also relates the life of a hobo, in a similarly dry and hard-boiled prose. African American writer William Attaway's first novel, *Let Me Breathe Thunder* (1939), the story of two white hobos with a Mexican boy they take under their wing on a whim, promotes vagabondage as a counter-value to the bourgeois obsession with productivity and domesticity. Carlos Bulosan's *America Is in the Heart* (1946) paints a determinedly upbeat picture of the precarious and violent world of Asian migrant workers who follow the crops along the West Coast. John Steinbeck's two most popular works, *Of Mice and Men* (1937) and *The Grapes of Wrath* (1939), also drew on the format of the road narrative.

As New York City was marginalized, the events of the 1930s thrust two regions on the nation's margin, California and the South, to the center of attention. The prominence of the West Coast in Depression literature owes much to the entrenched tradition of labor radicalism there (though the political class leaned strongly Republican), to Upton Sinclair's End Poverty in California (EPIC) campaign in 1934, and to Steinbeck's commercial and critical success. David Wrobel covers these issues and much more in Chapter 7. Chapter 6 is about the South. As Michael Kreyling convincingly shows, the South was the nation's Other: the depository of all the anachronisms that Americans had sloughed off as they modernized and liberalized themselves. The *American Mercury* survey Kreyling discusses paints a familiar picture of a region woefully deficient in all the requisite attainments of modern civilization: wealth, education, public health, and public order. As much a fact as a fascinating myth, such a picture influenced literary representations of the poor whites there in works such as William Faulkner's *As I Lay Dying* (1930), Erskine Caldwell's *Tobacco Road* (1932; turned into a Broadway hit in short order and adapted to screen by John Ford in 1941), and James Agee and Walker Evans's *Let Us Now Praise Famous Men* (1941). The images of the South created by these works evoke conflicting emotions that range from disgust to empathy and reverence, as John Marsh explains in Chapter 4, but all these divergent emotional reactions somehow end up confirming the South's irredeemable backwardness. The economic, political, and social setbacks combined to expose whatever advances the South had made toward reconstruction and regeneration up to that point as an inept sham. Even the incidence of lynching increased after a steady decline. If anything, the South now seemed more barbarous than it did when the Menckenian condescension peaked during the Scopes trial in the previous decade.

Was the Great Depression, then, an unrelieved nightmare for the South? Not necessarily, at least in the realm of cultural politics, for the decade-long pause in modernization complicated the meaning of the South's foreignness. The collapse of the economy called into question progress, modernity, and liberalism: in short, everything that had given the North license to think of itself as the nation's destiny. Restated from the Dixie side, the 1930s represented a brief interlude in history, a moment of confusion when there was a chance, however illusory, to appeal history's final verdict on its eternal guilt. Perhaps it should not surprise anyone that, in reaction to capitalism's failure to self-adjust, white and Jewish writers romanticized the Southern way of life. The Heyward/Gershwin opera *Porgy and Bess* (1934) portrayed Catfish Row as the kind of warm and organic neighborhood no longer to be found in the harsh industrialized North, a romantic characterization that the pimp from Harlem, Sportin' Life, who is upgraded to a major character in the opera, sharpens through his Northern sophistication and slickness.[10] Margaret Mitchell's *Gone with the Wind* came out in 1934 to become the bestseller of the decade. David O. Selznick's film version premiered in Atlanta five years later, to win ten Oscars and to become the highest-grossing film of the century. In their depictions of war and slavery, both versions were friendly to the Lost Cause, but this alone cannot explain its phenomenal popularity north of the Mason-Dixon line. David Welky persuasively argues in Chapter 12 that what actually added to its resonance was Scarlett O'Hara's life trajectory that culminates in her rejection of the ethic of capitalism, symbolized by Richmond, and her return to Tara, which stands for the promise of escape from modernity.

African-American writers never mistook the crisis in industrial capitalism for a vindication of the Lost Cause. Some of the most sensational events that galvanized black communities across the country took place in the South, such as the trial of nine black boys falsely accused of the rape of a white woman in Alabama and the trial of Angelo Herndon, a black labor organizer arrested and convicted for insurrection in Atlanta. Clear-eyed, black writers found the popularity of a book like *Gone with the Wind* nothing but ominous. At the NAACP, Walter White even got into an extensive correspondence with Selznick, urging him to hire experts to advise on historical details. Thanks to the campaign by the press and Hattie McDaniel's demand (McDaniel went on to win the Oscar for Best Supporting Actress), "nigger," which pockmarks countless dialogues and internal monologues in the original book, was entirely dropped from the film version.[11]

All the same, the unforgiving living conditions in Northern cities, combined with nostalgia for childhood, also led some African-American writers to construct an intimate and organic picture of black lives in the South. In Richard Wright's *Uncle Tom's Children* (1938), the South comes across as no different than Hitler's police state. Instead of the Gestapo, white vigilantes hunt, torture, and burn the blacks there. His autobiographical novel, *Black Boy* (1945), also dwells on Wright's miserable childhood in the South. But the aesthetic framework in which he places the South is rather conventional. What Wright manages, inadvertently or not, to etch in the reader's memory is a way of life receptive to the power of nature, the power that assumes a magical glow in the alienated consciousness of the anomic Negro in the North. In the hands of a much more romantic writer like Zora Neale Hurston, whose "facile sensuality" Wright attacked in his review of *Their Eyes Were Watching God* (1937), the black communities in the South slip out of history altogether.[12] Using her preternatural gift of magical realism, Hurston would turn the earthy South into Africa, nature, a myth:

> So they danced. They called for the instrument that they had brought to America in their skins – the drum – and they played upon it. With their hands they played upon the little dance drums of Africa. The drums of kidskin. With their feet they stomped it, and the voice of Kata-Kumba, the great drum, lifted itself within them and they heard it. The great drum that is made by priests and sits in majesty in the juju house. The drum with the man skin that is dressed with human blood, that is beaten with a human shin-bone and speaks to gods as a man and to men as a God. Then they beat upon the drum and danced.[13]

The Southern revival I have been trying to sketch raises an unanswerable but interesting question: was it necessary that the 1930s coincided with William Faulkner's most productive years? With the exception of *The Sound and the Fury*, which was published a few weeks before Black Thursday, all of the books that critics consider his highest achievements were written between the Crash and Pearl Harbor: *As I Lay Lying* (1930), *Light in August* (1932), *Absalom, Absalom!* (1936), *The Hamlet* (1940), and much of *Go Down, Moses* (1942). Additionally, he wrote and published two lesser novels and two collections of stories. And let us not forget that he maintained this level of productivity while commuting back and forth between Hollywood and Oxford, Mississippi for most of the decade.

Such an unusually high degree of productivity must be powered by a complex vision holding opposed ideas: hope and disillusion. The unique way in which the meaning of the South transitioned through the 1930s provided Faulkner with exactly this kind of tragic vision. During Faulkner's *anni mirabiles*, a series of challenges to democratic capitalism created an appearance that liberalism had been dealt a potentially fatal setback. This perception spread not just domestically but, as Ekbladh and Takayoshi and Taketani show in Chapters 11 and 5, internationally. The crisis of confidence in liberalism opened up some space for creative thinking in the mind of writers and in American culture at large, the space in which the future of America, as avatar of liberalism, was made open to debate. Which is to say: the meaning of American history, especially the meaning of the defeat of the nation's most intimate enemy, the South, standing athwart its path to freedom and justice, was made, for a moment, subject to reinterpretation. The Southern agrarians, led by John Crowe Ransom, Donald Davidson, Allen Tate, and Robert Penn Warren, eagerly utilized this newfound room for opportunistic maneuvering. Their revisionist attempt resulted in the publication of *I'll Take My Stand* in 1931. Faulkner similarly recognized an opening. But unlike the apologists of the Old South, Faulkner apparently concluded that, even when reevaluated in light of the most favorable circumstances, the Southern past was still beyond redemption. His attempt at reevaluation was not half-hearted. It is not as though the North emerged more and more victoriously irreproachable in proportion as the South's guilt appeared inarguable in Faulkner's 1930s fiction. For Faulkner, being on the right side of history supplies no evidence that the North has greater moral insight. Rather the North as portrayed indirectly in his Depression-era fiction lacks historical consciousness, and Faulkner does not shrink from intimating that this lack is the source of the North's political power, its economic dynamism, and its moral innocence that is as rapacious as it is ill-deserved. In "The Bear," Southern speculators and politicians may be the direct cause of the paving of the Delta jungle, but the obsession with development and capital that makes this obsession actionable are unequivocally of a Northern origin. After the Crash, the crisis of capitalism initially tempted Faulkner, as it tempted countless other Southerners, to reassess the Southern past in political – strategic – terms. If the North got history wrong, their wishful thinking ran, maybe the South unintentionally got something right about history. But soon Faulkner rejected this view, not because after comparing the relative merits of the North and the South he reconfirmed the South's relative blameworthiness but because he accepted that the South's eternal damnation resulted not from a political miscalculation or a wrong economic policy but from its crimes against the absolutes – "the old verities and truths of the heart."[14] It is hard to see how Faulkner could have plumbed his tragic vision to such a depth, had the Depression not tempted him with the illusory promise of the South's exoneration.

Besides the incentive to reinterpret traditional themes, the economic crisis also gave the literary world new employers. Since the nineteenth century, journalism had served as the most reliably available employer, on whom writers could count for steady income and the occasional vent for their creative energy. Their relationship did not radically change during the 1930s. Chapter 20 offers a case study of this continued trend, with special attention to Henry Luce's multimedia empire, Time Inc. Unsurprisingly, the Depression skewed the labor market for intellectual workers in favor of employers, and the quality of writers available for hire was at a historic high. This was a golden opportunity for creative publishers, and Luce exploited it more deliberately than any of his competitors. As Donal Harris explains, Luce bet that his era's general anxiety over information overload would translate into a demand for a new type of print journalism. The fear, according to many alarmed social scientists, was that there was simply too much printed information, all cheap and accessible, and that this not only created confusion among consumers but also destabilized a democracy that was premised on well-informed rational citizens. Who else would be better trained for the new task, the new business of gathering, digesting, condensing, and repackaging this plethora of information, than the unemployed symbol manipulators of the literary world? Some, like Archibald MacLeish, thrived working in a buttoned-up corporate environment; others, like James Agee and Dwight MacDonald, chafed under by no means onerous requirements, such as deskwork, regular attendance at meetings, and editorial rules meant to create unique house styles for Luce's flagship publications, *Fortune*, *Time*, and *Life*. For a brief moment, however, individual talents and anonymous organizational structures came together to amalgamate bureaucratic machinery and personal ambition into stylish and often penetrating pieces of reportage and commentary, which catapulted Luce's magazines to the forefront of journalistic innovation.

Other emerging sectors also beckoned writers with the promise of money, security, and the chance to experiment with new media. As print culture was reaching the saturation point, other producers of contents, most importantly radio and Hollywood, rose to challenge the former's market share and prestige. The cinema had just started talking when the market crash inaugurated the Depression decade. Despite the initial downturn in their business in the immediate aftermath of the crash (a few studios underwent bankruptcy or merger), by the early 1940s, Hollywood studios and the distributors and theater chains that owned these studios emerged as the nation's most powerful purveyor of mass entertainment. Meanwhile, radio was also taking more and more leisure hours from its competitors, making inroads into millions of households with cheaper radio sets and enticing programing. The copy needs of these two industries were phenomenal. In Chapter 13, Neil Verma drives this point home vividly: "At the height of the radio age, according to Erik Barnouw, American stations broadcast some 20 million words each day; to put that figure in today's perspective, every 145 days or so the industry aired as many words as there are in the entire English-language Wikipedia." We lack statistics for the movies, but one imagines that all those studios had to produce words on an industrial scale. The copy needs naturally translated into the demand for talents fast with words, and the best were found among poets, playwrights, and novelists. The list of the talents who wrote for the radio at some point or other during the decade is long and illustrious: Archibald MacLeish, Orson Welles, Stephen Vincent Benét, Alfred Kreymborg, Langston Hughes, W. H. Auden, Alfred Kazin, Maxwell Anderson, William Saroyan, Robert Sherwood, Marc Connelly, and Edna St. Vincent Millay. The list of authors who moved to Southern California is long enough to defeat even the most cursory of attempts in this space, but William Solomon offers an astute analysis of these Hollywood writers' experiences and their fictionalized accounts in Chapter 19.

Two more institutions extended temporary haven to unemployed writers: the federal government and the CPUSA. The list of authors who took refuge in various programs sponsored by the Works Progress Administration is at least as long as that of writers in Hollywood. One of these programs, the FWP, alone employed more than 6,000 writers and editors. Among them were some of the most talented African-American authors of their generations, Claude McKay, Zora Neale Hurston, Sterling Brown, Richard Wright, and Ralph Ellison, a development whose circumstances are carefully elucidated by Etsuko Taketani in Chapter 5. The FWP, like its sister programs in art, music, theater, and historical research, was conceived of as a relief program. Its goal was economic: to absorb idle labor that the free market could not put to productive use while alleviating the misery caused by mass unemployment. However, these programs were directed by progressive political appointees (FWP director Henry Alsberg was a liberal journalist), and their ranks and files were filled with artists and writers, all known for their sympathy for the New Deal or causes farther to its left. Despite conscious efforts to keep to politically anodyne subjects and projects, then, it was inevitable that these federally funded programs came to be informed by a vision, a "cultural strategy," a certain mentality back of the New Deal that celebrated the nation's diversity. This is the main topic of Chapter 18, contributed by Jerrold Hirsch.

Unlike Hollywood, radio networks, and the federal programs, the CPUSA's main appeal to penurious writers was political instead of financial. Working as activists, organizers, and in rare cases as spies (Whittaker Chambers), Communist writers were remunerated by the Party for their labor, but most card-carrying members were not salaried employees. They relied on some other source of income, which under 1930s conditions usually meant the government, Hollywood, popular journalism, or radio. What drove these writers into the Party's embrace was a mixture of motives: despair over the free market, admiration for Soviet Russia as an economic utopia and a staunch opponent of authoritarian antidemocratic regimes like Germany, and as Christopher Phelps reminds us in Chapter 21, a "philosophical existentialism *avant la lettre*, in which Communist commitment is cast as a desperate way of imbuing life with purpose."

Writers' sojourns in these institutions resulted in distinct literary products that were indelibly stamped with the conditions of the time. Writers' experimentation with radio led to the new form of radio drama in which radio's medium-specific properties were discovered. Writers' work for Time Inc. accidentally gave birth to the postwar subgenre of anti-Time crime procedurals. Writers in Hollywood wrote Hollywood novels. Writers in the federal programs bequeathed to later generations documentary records of the nation's folkways, such as the American Guide Series and interviews of ex-slaves. And in the case of Communist writers, their involvement in the Party resulted in countless proletarian novels, stories, poems, songs, and, during the postwar years, in a bevy of Dostoevskian autobiographies in which ex-Communists recounted the dangers and allures of a life totally possessed by politics.

***

The literary questions discussed thus far were all closely bound up with the most immediate circumstances of the Depression decade. While most of them were not unique to the 1930s, these questions resonated strongly with the temporarily heightened concerns of the era. And as a result, in the process of transitioning through the decade, they wound up ingesting various contingent elements specific to their social surroundings, so much so that these questions are today regarded in some quarters as exotic flora and fauna indigenous to this peculiar time.

How writers handled these questions tells only half the story, however. The other half concerns questions that often fail to be associated in our collective memory with the decade under the shadow of severe economic depression and approaching world war, those literary questions that transitioned through the 1930s without having their internal structures modified too drastically thanks to their muted resonance with the era's most divisive issues. One such question is the focus of Chapter 1, where Amy Blair investigates middle-class readers' attitudes toward literature. As it turns out, the economic upheavals and political turmoil did not fundamentally change their reading habits: this demographic kept reading the so-called middlebrow books it had been known for reading since the 1910s. If anything, they read even *more* fiction of this sort during this time of hardship and stress. Blair, though, unearths a subtle change: the main criterion for choosing books shifted from their educational value to their "fit" with the readers' tastes, preferences, and personality types. Here you see a germ of market segmentation, a trend that is commonly associated with the rise of postmodern consumer culture in the late twentieth century.

In Chapter 2, Jennifer Haytock takes you to the deepest stratum of the literary culture: middle-class women readers. If those distinctively 1930s literary questions discussed in the chapters dealing with sociological topics and techno-commercial innovations were the white and frothy waves of a choppy ocean, then the world reflected in the best-selling books by Margaret Banning, Edna Ferber, Faith Baldwin, Fannie Hurst, Margaret Widdemer, Kathleen Norris, Margaret Ayer Barnes, and Fannie Cook was the deep sea. You could barely hear the economic commotion and the approach of war churning the ocean's surface. In contrast to economic disasters, political fights, and ethical dilemmas that often assumed world-historical proportions in the topical writings of engaged, and mostly male, writers, a host of problems that beset the average female writer and the average female reader were small, quotidian, pervasive, and, in a way, more intractable, because they arose from women's unending efforts to readjust to the shifting meanings of courtship, sex, marriage, and motherhood as the ideology of free love, a new cultural emphasis on self-expression, the availability of contraception and divorce, and the opening up of the labor market to women complicated their lives.[15]

Few things change as glacially as family structure and gender roles, except the country's overall religious sensibilities, and that is the main object of analysis in Chapter 8. Addressing an astonishingly wide array of authors, Jason Stevens surveys the decade-long, low-grade but unrelenting conflict between the forces of secularization and Christianity. Christian leaders recognized the Depression as a man-made disaster. This was tantamount to admitting that dogmas and pieties would not suffice as an efficacious response to the crisis. Writers who still insisted on the value of religion in the face of the man-made crisis, therefore, had to be particularly creative – a creativity that led some to rediscover America's puritan beginnings, some to aestheticize Christianity, some to appropriate with modernist twists evangelical styles and scriptural allegories for leftist purposes, and still others to model the individual's role in the community after enduring religious teachings.

Suspended between these dramas unfolding in slow motion in the deep sea and the volatile currents on the surface were the twinned issues of national unity and pluralism, explored in Chapter 9 by Yael Schacher and Chapter 10 by Robert Westbrook, respectively. Schacher reconstructs the thinking of many prominent advocates of diversity, including FWP directors Morton Royse, Benjamin Botkin, and Henry Alsberg, as well as a number of minority authors such as Herant Armen, William Saroyan, D'Arcy McKnickle, and H. T. Tsiang. Westbrook's main interest is in social and cultural theorists who appreciated the importance of agreement on national identity but at the same time wrestled with its impossibility: Alfred Kazin, Ruth Bennedict, Constance Rourke, and Robert Lynd, among others.

It is worth remembering that "multiculturalism" was a coinage of the 1930s. In 1941, Edward Haskell published his first and only novel, *Lance: A Novel about Multicultural Men*. According to the *Oxford English Dictionary*, the term "multicultural" was introduced by this bizarre novel about a new breed of men, "multinational men." Enriched by variegated life experiences, multiculturals switched among multiple perspectives with ease. In Haskell's optimistic vision, these people of fluid identities heralded a world in eternal peace where ancient tribal antagonisms would give way to cross-cultural understanding.[16] It was not entirely a coincidence that the term "multicultural" was coined on the eve of World War II. As the United States scrabbled its way through the years shadowed by economic slump, political unrest, and the increasing threat from dictatorships, it did so as the

world's most diverse modern nation-state. Of its total population of
120 million, about 30 million consisted of American-born children of
immigrant parents of various nationalities: German, Italian, Polish, Czech,
Slovak, Serbian, Croatian, Slovenian, Bulgarian, Jewish, Russian, Ukrainian,
Lithuanian, Finnish, Hungarian, Norwegian, Swedish, Danish, Dutch,
French, Flemish, Spanish, Portuguese, Romanian, Armenian, Syrian, Lett,
Albanian, Greek – the list can go on. An additional 10 million were first-
generation immigrants, many of whom had not yet gained citizenship by the
1929 Wall Street crash. And these were just Americans of what the census
called "the old white stock." In thinking about the ethnic and racial strife
during the Depression decade, we need to account for 12 million Americans
of African descent. At least, then, more than 40 percent of Americans did not
fit the white Anglo-Saxon Protestant (WASP) norm. In itself, this demographic conjuncture was destabilizing enough. Two additional developments unique to the 1930s exacerbated it and turned it into a social
problem that clamored for cultural and political solutions. First, the 1930s
coincided with the volatile period when the bulk of second-generation
immigrants began assimilating. The fact that these "new Americans" had
been born in the United States worked to their advantage. Unlike those of
their parents, their endeavors to Americanize themselves were not hindered
by deep attachments to their old countries. And yet they were not entirely
accepted by the mainstream either. This state of belonging to neither the
new world nor the old, as Slovene-American journalist Louis Adamic
warned, psychologically unbalanced tens of millions of second-generation
immigrants. Writers, especially those of minority backgrounds, grew increasingly conscious of the need to make a new language of justification available
to these struggling new Americans so that they could make sense of their
unique place in society (it was during the 1930s that "minority," formerly
applied to religious groups, came to designate racial and ethnic
status). Second, as if to buck the pan-Western trend toward anti-racism
and anticolonialism that accelerated in the previous decade, the retrograde
political philosophy that justified aggression and violence on racist grounds
spread in Europe throughout the 1930s. This created a palpable need among
intellectual circles for a new counter-vocabulary to celebrate America's
cultural and racial diversity, a way of, as Adamic put it, "accepting and
welcoming and *exploiting* diversity, variety, and differences," which should
inoculate the psychologically unstable second-generation Americans against
the call of ethnocentrism emanating from their old countries.[17]

   This celebration of diversity contended against the centripetal force of
cultural nationalism. F. O. Matthiessen, whose *American Renaissance*

(1941) solidified the legitimacy of American literature as a worthy academic discipline, opened that classic with a Whitman-inspired creedal statement: the scholar's "works must ... prove that it has drawn him toward his people, not away from them. That his scholarship has been applied for the good and the enlightenment of all the people, not for the pampering of a class. His works must prove that he is a citizen, not a lackey, a true exponent of democracy, not a tool of the most insidious form of anarchy. In a democracy there can be but one fundamental test of citizenship, namely: Are you using such gifts as you possess for or against the people?"[18] Nationalism, the fantasy of communion expressed in "We, the People," had always constituted a vital part of literary culture since the colonies began actively agitating for independence. In varying degrees, then, the question of national character always had a place in literary conversations of this young republic. Yet this obvious continuity should not blind one to a farrago of new cultural purposes that Americanism served in the 1930s. As if to compensate for liberal democracy's failure to deliver on its extravagant promises, patriotic phrases like "American dream" and "the American way of life" entered the popular lexicon in the 1930s. The republic was riven by class antagonisms, and class was by definition transnational. The Depression-era writers' almost incantatory invocation of the uniqueness and resilience of "the people" was aimed at diffusing these economic contradictions in the solvent of a supposedly unified national culture. The rhetoric was popular across the political spectrum. The utility of this language for those hoping to minimize reform was obvious, but with the formation of the Popular Front in the middle years of the decade, leftists and liberals also availed themselves of it. It is perhaps impossible to find clearer evidence of the versatility of this rhetoric than the fact that in the 1940 presidential election John La Touche's "Ballad for Americans" was chanted in both the Republican National Convention and that of the CPUSA. Westbrook analyzes how the defensive investment in the potent symbolism of Americana and the many intellectual exertions to forge an imaginary national unity came in conflict with a normative and empirical view of American culture as pluralistic. The era's most enduring cultural achievements, such as Walker Evans's photos and Faulkner's fiction, he suggests, resulted from the artists' self-conscious assimilation of this tension into the aesthetic and moral fabric of their works.

Three literary genres traveled through the 1930s and en route were modified considerably but not entirely by the strains of the time. Chapter 17, Mark Fearnow's survey of American theater, recounts the rise of realism as the dominant style, a pivotal development that resulted in a number of classic realist plays by Lillian Hellman, Clifford Odets, Sherwood Anderson, Kaufman/Hart, and Philip Barry. The figure that dwarfed all these popular playwrights was Eugene O'Neill. As much as William Faulkner did to American prose fiction, O'Neill's major works during this period, *Mourning Becomes Electra* (1931), *The Iceman Cometh* (written in 1939), *Long Day's Journey into Night* (written in 1941), and *A Moon for the Misbegotten* (written in 1941) elevated the status of American drama as a serious art to an unprecedented height. Chapter 14 relates a similar process that crime fiction underwent. Over the course of the decade, authors writing under British influences, such as John Dickson Carr, S. S. Van Dine, Rex Stout, and Ellery Queen, ceded ground to writers like Dashiell Hammett, Raymond Chandler, Frederic Nebel, and Raoul Whitfield, who "gave murder back to the kind of people that commit it for reasons, not just to provide a corpse; and with the means at hand, not with hand-wrought dueling pistols, curare, and tropical fish."[19] With this new approach, a hard-boiled prose emphasizing action, objectivity, and dark humor was born, and quickly came of age, staking a claim to the status of a serious art in its own right. Charles Rzepka reconstructs this process of genre elevation, while at the same time attending to the widespread cynicism toward the corruption of public institutions that fueled the genre's popularity, the invention of nonwhite detectives by Earl Derr Biggers (Charlie Chan), John P. Marquand (Mr. Moto), and Rudolph Fisher (Perry Dart, John Archer), and the rise of *noir* fiction, which paved the way for the *noir* aesthetic of the early Cold War years. The title of one representative of the latter genre, Horace McCoy's *They Shoot Horses, Don't They?* (1935), epitomized its pervading mood. The myth of the "American Dream," a phrase popularized by James Truslow Adams's *Epic of America* (1931), survived the nation's worst crisis since the Civil War. The ordinary Americans continued to throw themselves into the frenzy of the "race of life" with even greater desperation than ever. As in the horse race, the odds of winning were astronomically long. As in the horse race, men and women, delicate creatures, suffered injuries along the way. Unlike those brisk and beautiful racehorses that had the fortune of getting euthanized right away, however, Americans of the Depression era had to crawl their way to an undignified death while enduring slowly spreading infections and piercing pains.

Modernist writers, now all in middle age, splintered in all directions under the external and internal pressures to subordinate self-expression to a variety of competing collective causes. A small minority of libertarians radicalized their individualism in reaction to what they saw as a global trend to "totalize" populations into collectivities made up of robotic subjects. e. e. cummings is one notable case in point discussed in Chapter 16, contributed by Milton Cohen. Another was Henry Miller, who wrote around 1938:

> I put no trust in the men who explain life to us in terms of history, economics, art, etc. They are the fellows who bugger us up, juggling their abstract ideas. I think it is a piece of the most cruel deception to urge men to place their hopes of justice in some external order, some form of government, some social order, some system of ideal rights ... I don't need an explanation of our capitalistic society. Fuck your capitalistic society! Fuck your Communistic society and your Fascist society and all your other societies! Society is made up of individuals. It is the individual who interests me – not the society.[20]

The opinion expressed here is out of key with his time, at once recalling the attitude of transcendentalists like Emerson and foreshadowing the post-1960s neoliberal obsession with the self, individuality, and identity. Miller was one of the few late bloomers belonging to the generation of the 1890s. After spending the boom years of the 1920s writing copiously and futilely stories in imitation of one literary hero after another, he finally hit his stride in the 1930s. At the age of forty-three, he published his debut novel *Tropic of Cancer* (1934) to critical acclaim among a motley group of connoisseurs and cognoscenti that included Ezra Pound and George Orwell. That novel, set in 1930s Paris, was soon followed by *Black Spring* (1936), a collection of short stories about his upbringing as a German-American boy, and *Tropic of Capricorn* (1939), a reminiscing book about his life in Brooklyn in the 1920s. Miller was arguably America's closest counterpart to D. H. Lawrence. His views on the self and culture were implacably anti-Freudian. He saw, as Freud did, life as an endless war between the pleasure principle and the reality principle, as a combat between the internal world of freedom and external constraints. But unlike Freud and like Lawrence, he saw the internal world's adjustment to the external world not as a civilizing process conducive to the health of the self and society but as an avoidable tragedy. The vast world outside the small but free self, to his way of thinking, was not some efficiently patterned order trying to discipline the chaotic psyche of the individual so that the latter can function and be productive. On the contrary, it was the external world that was chaotic. On this logic, then, by conforming to the demands and conventions of society, the self made itself more chaotic and confused, in addition to robbing itself of confidence in its integrity. The countermeasure that such a theory prescribed is easy to imagine: a life-long denial of adjustment as a source of value. "Equilibrium is no longer the goal – the scales must be destroyed," so Miller's autobiographical protagonist orates on the final page of *Tropic of Capricorn*.[21] With the scales destroyed, you have a free fall. Society is obliterated from your consciousness, as your subjectivity recoils into itself until it shrinks to the smallest size possible – a fetus in the womb. This is why regression and self-infantilization are the key themes in all of Miller's writings. Once you learn to listen to Miller's logorrhea as you would listen to a fetus that can brag with a Shakespearian vocabulary about the instant *in utero* gratification of all of its most authentic – because the most basic – desires, everything will begin making sense to you.

Apart from Marianne Moore and Robert Frost, however, most modernists willy-nilly braved the 1930s outside the womb. Cohen's chapter chronicles how politics of the time colored the lives and works of John Dos Passos, Ernest Hemingway, William Carlos Williams, Wallace Stevens, William Faulkner, T. S. Eliot, and Ezra Pound. Hues of their politics – whether red, brown, or black – were rather variegated, their calculations and priorities that led to these tinctures even more so. The only pattern that emerges here is that very few modernists, even those who maligned the relevance of social theories to literature and life, managed to elude entirely what Wallace Stevens called ambivalently "the pressures of the contemporaneous."[22] Literary modernism too, then, changed its course significantly during the 1930s under the impact of depression and war. It negotiated its way through a complicated transition, as Jeff Allred elucidates in Chapter 15, to be succeeded by late modernism, modernism's offspring that specialized in representing things beyond representation: fissures, dislocations, and irruptive forces unleashed by the maturation of capitalism and the consolidation of mass society.

In this regard, modernism in the 1930s, along with the development of crime fiction and the maturation of realism in theater, nominates itself as the paradigm case of transition, the mean of all the cases studied in the following chapters. The complex of modernist attitudes – self-consciously worked out during the fin-de-siècle, energized by the utopian politics of the 1910s, and popularized in the climate of 1920s prosperity, disaffection, and snobbery – readjusted itself under the pressures of the unusually disrupting impingements of 1930s politics in order to survive, albeit in a modified form, into the postwar decades. To one side of this moderate case of transition, you see more dramatic cases of transition such as proletarian literature, working-class realism, works of compassionate disaster tourism, the Southern revival, the experimental radio drama, and Hollywood novels. These were relatively context-bound, ultimately ephemeral avatars of preexisting literary concerns under the strain of unusually intense social, political, and technological changes. To the opposite side, you will find stable cases of transition such as the domestic novel of courtship, marriage, and parenting, middlebrow fiction, and literary explorations of national identity and the nation's religious traditions. The contemporaneous turmoil threatened to extinguish the problems of representation and communication that these entrenched genres of writing had traditionally sought to solve, but they managed to transition through the era without their deep, enduring internal structures radically rewritten.

Notes

Thanks to Ann Douglas, Michael Kreyling, and Christopher Phelps for the care they took in commenting on earlier versions of this introduction.

1. F. Scott Fitzgerald, "The Crack-Up," *The Crack-Up* (New York: New Directions, 2009), 69.
2. My allusions are to Pearl Buck, *The Good Earth*, Margaret Mitchell, *Gone with the Wind*, Eugene O'Neill, *The Iceman Cometh*, Ezra Pound, *The Cantos*, Langston Hughes, "Christ in Alabama," William Faulkner, *Absalom, Absalom!*, and Raymond Chandler, *The Big Sleep*. Irving Berlin's "God Bless America," the version that survives to this day, debuted in 1938 as an antiwar song.
3. My allusions are to Langston Hughes, "Good-morning Revolution," James Agee and Walker Evans, *Let Us Now Praise Famous Men*, Margaret Mitchell, *Gone with the Wind*, Ernest Hemingway, *For Whom the Bell Tolls*, Woodie Guthrie, "This Land Is Your Land," Cole Porter, "Night and Day," Zora Neale Hurston, *Their Eyes Were Watching God*, John Steinbeck, *The Grapes of Wrath*, *The Wizard of Oz* (motion picture), and *The Lone Ranger* (radio drama).
4. The project was completed, but a Congress hostile to the New Deal shut down the FWP before it made its way into print. Its manuscript was recently discovered in the Library of Congress. See Matthew Basso, ed., *Men at Work: Rediscovering Depression-Era Stories from the Federal Writers' Project* (Salt Lake City: University of Utah Press, 2012).
5. James Agee, *Letters of James Agee to Father Flye* (New York: George Braziller, 1962), 75.
6. The most influential study that pursues this angle is Michael Denning, *The Cultural Front: The Laboring of American Culture in the Twentieth Century* (London: Verso, 1998).
7. See Ann Douglas's reading of Farrell's *Studs Lonigan*, "Studs Lonigan and the Failure of History in Mass Society: A Study in Claustrophobia," *American Quarterly* 29 (Winter 1977): 487–505.

8. Dawn Powell, *Dawn Powell, Novels 1930–1942* (New York: Library of America, 2001), 454.

9. F. Scott Fitzgerald, "My Lost City," *The Crack-Up* (New York: New Directions, 2009), 32.

10. See Morris Dickstein, *Dancing in the Dark* (New York: W. W. Norton, 2009), chapter 13.

11. Kenneth Robert Janken, *White: The Biography of Walter White, Mr. NAACP* (New York: The New Press, 2003), 266–68.

12. Richard Wright, "Between Laughter and Tears," *New Masses* (October 5, 1937), 22.

13. Zora Neale Hurston, *Jonah's Gourd Vine* (New York: Harper, 1990), 29–30.

14. William Faulkner, "Address upon Receiving the Nobel Prize for Literature," *Essays, Speeches and Public Letters*, ed. James B. Meriwether (New York: Modern Library, 2004), 120.

15. Needless to say, there are exceptions to this admittedly crude generalization. Male authors who explored domestic concerns are too numerous to be listed in this space. See Gordon Hutner, *What America Read: Taste, Class, and the Novel* (Chapel Hill: University of North Carolina Press, 2009), chapter 2. Female authors whose works explored political and economic issues include Meridel Le Sueur, Agnes Smedley, Josephine Herbst, Muriel Rukeyser, Tillie Olsen, Elizabeth Leonard, Grace Lumpkin, and many others.

16. Werner Sollors, "The Word 'Multicultural,'" in *A New Literary History of America* (Cambridge, MA: Harvard University Press, 2012).

17. *Common Ground* (Autumn 1940), 66.

18. F. O. Matthiessen, *American Renaissance: Art and Expression in the Age of Emerson and Whitman* (New York: Oxford University Press, 1968), xv.

19. Raymond Chandler, "The Simple Art of Murder," in *Raymond Chandler: Later Novels and Other Writings* (New York: Library of America, 1995), 989.

20. Henry Miller, "An Open Letter to Surrealists Everywhere," *The Cosmological Eye* (New York: New Directions, 1939), 162.

21. Henry Miller, *Tropic of Capricorn* (New York: Grove Press, 1961), 348.

22. Wallace Stevens, "The Irrational Element in Poetry," *Collected Poetry and Prose* (New York: Library of America, 1997), 789.

PART I

Themes

CHAPTER I

The Middle Class

Amy L. Blair

The May 1933 issue of the popular homemaking magazine *Good Housekeeping* opened with an unusual full-page, signed editorial provocatively titled "The Wages of Labor." In this piece, the editors of the magazine, whose hallmark was a devotion to consumer advocacy through testing of all advertised products, turned their critical gaze not on the behavior of the producers of household appliances, cosmetics, clothing, and prepared foods but on their middle-class readership as consumers of such products. The editorial leveled a charge at the consumers of America to eschew cheaply produced goods in favor of items manufactured by laborers who would receive a fair wage for their work:

> We are not criticizing those who are buying the best they can afford. Millions are out of work. But millions more are working, and a vast multitude of them have been driving the wage scale downward, and making it harder for business to get on its feet again, by buying low-quality products or deliberately waiting until merchants have been forced to sacrifice their legitimate profits and, to forestall a complete loss, sell their goods for whatever they will bring.[1]

The *Good Housekeeping* reader was presumably among those who, with her pocketbook, would be able to make this patriotic contribution to economic recovery. As a member of the vast middle, she was able to "assure the worker of his wage – and his buying power – by spending wisely now."[2] The *Good Housekeeping* reader, by virtue of her ability to purchase, had an obligation to the national economy to stop economizing. This editorial, published at the pivot point of the Great Depression,[3] is emblematic of the ideological construction of the middle class in the 1930s as a group that needed literally to buy into the economic and social reforms of the New Deal.

While many inhabitants of the United States were destitute during the Depression era, many more were making ends meet, even if feeling a bit

27

more pinched than before. This group has been variously termed the
"middle class," because of its relative financial stability, because of its
alignment with business ownership and white-collar positions, or because
of aesthetic inclinations that scholars have come to term "middlebrow."
It is crucial to recognize the cultural underpinnings of middle-class identity
during the transitional moment of the 1930s; middlebrow aesthetics in
particular demonstrate acutely the degree to which class, as Wai Chee
Dimock and Michael Gilmore put it in their introduction to *Rethinking
Class*, "can be understood as a mediate relation between the economic and
the noneconomic, as a mode of structuration, a set of constitutive relays
linking economic identities with social identities."[4] Social identifications
could not fluctuate as rapidly as personal finances, and thus it becomes
apparent during the 1930s that "middle class" was more of an ideological
position than a financial one, "middle-classness" being expressed through
and defined in relation to middlebrow cultural modes. Historian Burton
Bledstein writes that the question "what did people mean when they
represented themselves as middle class?" is one of the most important in
American history; that he does so in the language of representation underscores the degree to which class is a set of social constructions that are
linked to economic conditions, but are not dependent on them.[5]

   On their return to Muncie, Indiana, in 1935, Robert S. Lynd and Helen
Merrill Lynd found the local newspapers and businessmen expounding the
notion that "depressions are merely 'psychological'": "This whole depression business is largely mental . . . If tomorrow morning everybody should
wake up with a resolve to unwind the red yarn that is wound about his old
leather purse, and then would carry his resolve into effect, by August first,
at the latest, the whole country could join in singing, 'Happy Days are
Here Again.'"[6] Business owners – as opposed to the working people of
Muncie – escaped from the Depression largely unscathed; to them, the
Lynds observed, "'good times' mean 'profits'; to the latter, 'a steady job.'"[7]
While articles such as these could clearly be read as symptoms of the civic
booster's stubborn reluctance to admit the underlying structural weaknesses of unregulated capitalism, we might also grant that prosperity was
both culturally relative and a function of individual psychology. Indeed, in
the 1930s, middle-classness was less a function of finances and more, as
Jennifer Parchesky argues, an identity interpolated by middlebrow cultural
products that "position[ed] their audiences in particular relationships to
the cultural formations they represented; that is, they shaped the way their
audiences perceived and interpreted their experiences of everyday life."[8]
Robert Seguin describes the middle class as "not so much . . . [a] thing or

idea, but more as a social-semantic structure capable of a range of invest-ments, and supporting a range of practices and beliefs."[9] As Jaime Harker puts it, "the very notion of 'middle America' was a creation of middlebrow culture during the interwar period."[10] My fellow contributor to this volume, Jennifer Haytock, contends that "buying a book is a social and economic act, as is reading it; and within the pages of that book, 'class actions' are represented and imaginatively experienced."[11] In the process of selecting and choosing to read a novel, or choosing to stop reading the novel, or choosing to carry around a novel without reading it, readers enact and shore up any number of identifications, class among them. It is then less a Marxian version of "class" than this performance of class – or of "middleness" – that we must try to excavate in a study of the "middle class" of American literature and American readership in the 1930s.

"Middlebrow" has become the shorthand for the tastes of nonprofes-sional, nonradical readers from the 1920s onward, but the recent uptick in critical attention to the middlebrow has not resolved the question of whether the middlebrow is an aesthetic category or a mode of reception, or some combination of the two. Joan Shelley Rubin's discipline-defining *The Making of Middlebrow Culture* described the various means by which culture, once decoupled from wealth, became a commodity in the twen-tieth century, particularly after World War I. "Middlebrow" cultural striving was facilitated in the 1930s by an attitude that culture might be acquired – that, for example, "one might become refined by reading *about* books rather than by reading the books themselves."[12] "Midcult" fell somewhere between "high culture" and "low culture," but without the authenticity of either and threatening to undermine both. Janice Radway's *A Feeling for Books* took a closer focus on a particular institution of middlebrow culture – the Book-of-the-Month-Club – in order to high-light the ways in which gatekeeping institutions produced a "transformed self, whose particular mode of realization was entirely integral to the functioning of the larger system within which she or he was incorporated."[13] Gordon Hutner, in his *What America Read*, rejects the term "middlebrow" as "promot[ing] criticism as an Arnoldian quest for connoisseurship" and thereby facilitating continued critical disparagement of "middle-class realist" texts; preferring to discuss a "majoritarian tradi-tion of middle-class realism – especially regionalism, historical fiction, family photos, and novels of middle-class manners" in the 1930s – Hutner draws from best-seller lists to create his alternative portrait of the reading of middle-class midcentury readers.[14]

Lisa Botshon and Meredith Goldsmith, introducing their collection *Middlebrow Moderns*, intervene in the debates by describing the middlebrow as "a richly textured area of cultural production" that is naturally interdisciplinary.[15] They and their contributors work to reclaim the middlebrow from the margins to which it was relegated by scholars and critics who denigrated it as lacking both cachet and edginess. In a monograph that builds on her essay in Boston and Goldsmith's volume, Jaime Harker argues that many popular women authors in the 1930s consciously chose to write texts targeted toward readers who embraced middlebrow aesthetics in the hopes of attracting a wider audience for their various social agendas (with mixed results, she concedes). Admittedly "constructing a category of authorship that the authors in question likely would have disavowed," Harker contends that "[m]iddlebrow authors assume a sympathetic communion between reader and writer; the text offers vicarious experience, understanding, and wisdom. This primary emphasis drove many professional and aesthetic decisions of middlebrow writers, from choice of publisher to choice of genre and form, and it led some middlebrow writers to disavow, deliberately, the cultural capital of 'serious' authorship."[16] In sum, the middlebrow became a literary and aesthetic mode in the 1930s in response to an extant middle-class reading formation.

What, in the meantime, has happened to the notion that middlebrow culture looks anxiously to highbrow notions of cultural capital for validation? To begin to answer this question, I would like to return to the pages of *Good Housekeeping* magazine and the recommendations offered by Emily Newell Blair therein. *Good Housekeeping* was one of the "big five" mass-market magazines in the opening decades of the twentieth century. Like *Ladies' Home Journal* and *Woman's Home Companion*, *Good Housekeeping* focused on advice to women in the administration of their homes and families. In 1900, the magazine set up an "Experiment Station" to test products and housekeeping practices; in 1909 it became the Good Housekeeping Institute, set up on a laboratory basis and eventually employing independently renowned specialists such as the former chief chemist of the US Department of Agriculture Dr. Harvey W. Wiley.[17] The Good Housekeeping Seal was introduced in 1909 as a sign that certain products had been "tested and approved" by the Institute. In addition to the Seal, the magazine promised in every issue that "[e]very article advertised in *Good Housekeeping* carries with it a money-back guaranty whether the article is susceptible of some laboratory test or not."[18] Every product and process mentioned in the magazine, then, was covered by the imprimatur of expert evaluation. When Rexford Tugwell became the assistant secretary of agriculture in 1933 and began a heated campaign against what he saw as abuses in advertising, he set his sights directly on the Good Housekeeping Seal. This would result in two years of hearings, between 1939 and 1941, that ended in a Federal Trade Commission (FTC) order that the magazine cease and desist using language about "testing" in its promotion of the Seal. Throughout the 1930s, though, the magazine persisted in using the language of "testing," and waged a campaign against the FTC in its pages and in numerous side publications.[19] The magazine's circulation grew dramatically during the same period, reaching 2.5 million by 1943,[20] while the Seal became an icon of the authority and power of the middle-class consumer.

Blair became the book columnist for *Good Housekeeping* in 1926 and remained at the post through August 1934, during the period when the Seal and the guaranty were most powerful. During her tenure at the magazine, Blair published nearly 100 columns and discussed more than 1,000 book titles. Unlike the columns written by Hamilton Wright Mabie in *Ladies' Home Journal* at the beginning of the century, Blair's *Good Housekeeping* columns rarely mentioned a book more than once; Blair's mandate was more about contemporaneity than acculturation.[21] While Blair very rarely mentioned books that we now think of as the "canonical," high-modernist texts of the period, she also steered a very different course through literature then that traced by those who we have come to think of as the middlebrow cultural arbiters of her day, such as the literary lights of the Book-of-the-Month club, Harry Scherman and Henry Seidel Canby. *Contra* Rubin and Radway, I read Blair's recommendations in *Good Housekeeping* as a move that rejects, or at the very least contests, the notions of proper reading and acculturation (even proper middlebrow acculturation) that drove the Book-of-the-Month Club and the publication of best-seller lists – and certainly worked against prescriptive entities like the still-popular Five Foot Shelf of Books and the more flexible, but still prescriptive, Modern Library.

Blair saw her job in *Good Housekeeping* not as that of gatekeeper but, in keeping with the rest of the magazine's content, as that of consumer advocate – her readers needed someone to help them find the kinds of books they wanted to read, and her job was not to dictate to them, but to screen literature like the Institute screened other consumer products and processes. Her advice, while given in the relatively impersonal setting of the magazine column, was actually tailored to personality types; her job was not to dictate proper reading to her audience but to match readers with the kinds of books that they would like but might not be able to find on their own.[22] This stance does not shift from Blair's first column in 1926 to her last in 1934, in which she goes back into the archives for books that should not be "overlooked by the very readers who would most enjoy them."[23] These are not books that have won awards, though Blair claims that she was inspired to write this column by the conferral of the Pulitzer Prize on a dark horse novel, *Lamb in His Bosom*, by Caroline Miller. "Why, I asked myself, should only prize novels be recalled to the attention of readers? Why not also a few others which should not be missed?" And so Blair offers *Mandoa-Mandoa*, by Winifred Holtby, for "any one seeking to revalue his own concepts of civilization." On the other hand, "[i]f it is smiles you wish, then another spring book should be read, *The Flowering Thorn* by Margery Sharp. It is that rare thing, a light novel altogether wholesome, which appeals to your intelligence rather than your emotions and has, besides, importance."[24] Blair took care, even in the mid-1920s, to validate her readers' desires for leisure, refusing to insist that reading should always be instructive or intellectual. In fact, the habitual and intelligent reader is the one who is most likely to need such escape.

> Most omnivorous readers experience at times a desire to indulge in a story that makes no demand on their intelligence but carries them along in a conventional plot, with conventional characters, through conventional emotions, without at the same time being so crude that they are forced to question its verisimilitude or English. It is like one's pleasure in meeting a "yellow dog from home," or eating greens in the spring, or hanging up one's stocking at Christmas. Freud doubtless can tell us just what emotions it sets loose – at any rate, we do it.[25]

Difficult times called for more self-medicating through literature. In *Middletown in Transition*, the Lynds observe that the Depression actually stimulated the reading of fiction in Muncie, Indiana; an illuminating chart of the public library's circulation figures shows that, at least in the 1930s, "Middletown reads more books in bad times and fewer in good times. Circulation failed even to keep up with population growth in the busy years from 1925 through 1929, increasing by only 15 per cent during these four years while the population was growing by 25 per cent."[26] By contrast, "by 1933 every cardholder was reading, on an average, 20 books a year, as against 11 in 1929."[27] The Lynds point out that even in prosperous times,

> Middletown is not a book buying city, though in this respect it is probably not different from other similar midland cities of its size. Book reading in Middletown means therefore, overwhelmingly, the reading of public-library books. There is not even a strong book-rental service in the city and this type

of service again is performed by the "new book" rental library in the public library.[28]

Best-seller lists, then, would not necessarily register the type of reading being done in such places.

If we take *Good Housekeeping*'s readership as a snapshot of the diverse "middle class" of the interwar period, we can see through Blair's recommendations that their reading was similarly multifarious, with tastes running the gamut from authors whose works have remained a part of our notion of the 1930s – Zora Neale Hurston, Somerset Maughan, and Virginia Woolf – to authors we no longer easily recognize – Blaise Cendrars, Rosamond Lehman, and Percy Waxman. In the context of Blair's columns, then, we can think of the middlebrow as less a genre of literature than a mode of readership, a way of approaching literature so that it is applicable to everyday life and in order to reinforce the middle-class identifications of her readers. Or, as Blair terms it in her May 1933 column titled, poignantly, "Books as Trouble Antidotes," literature was an anodyne, either an aid or an antidote to quotidian concerns. Observing that "it is the patient one prescribes for, not the trouble,"[29] Blair suggests a number of different novels, some that offer vicarious escape to different geographies or to historical settings, and others that simply offer "a sense of proportion," but in all cases she recommends the reading of fiction:

> I would prescribe fiction – but fiction of a special kind. Not "Ann Vickers," with its arraignment of a criminal system under the guise of a novel, and its distorted characters; nor even Fannie Hurst's "Imitation of Life," sound and sane though it may be as a study of the self-made woman pushed into success through economic need and paying the price for her success without whining. Rather I would select a novel about simple people going their daily round and meeting their daily problems with a nobility which makes one proud to be human, with no realization themselves that they are noble, and no insistence on the author's part that they are.[30]

The celebration of the "nobility" of "simple people going their daily round" is a hallmark of the 1930s valorization of a middle-class identity, as against that of the worker (workers needed to be aided by, and existed to serve, the middle-class consumer, per the *Good Housekeeping* editorial cited earlier) or the wealthy elites. Where Gordon Hutner sees *Ann Vickers* as a salient example of "what America read," Blair's explicit recommendation against it suggests that, while it may have been purchased, and may even have been discussed, *Ann Vickers* could not be properly thought of as a text that met the needs of the middle-class audience. Hutner notes that Lewis's novel was both the "fifth leading seller among novels" in 1933 and "critically respected in some quarters too," reading the book as a hallmark of "the era's reexamining of the relation between the public and private spheres" in the wake of the Crash, which "led novelists to wonder what effects its disillusioning aftermath would have on how Americans conducted intimate life, a concern ultimately dominating middle-class writing for the rest of the decade."[31] Blair's synopsis, brief as it is, points only to the novel's prison reform plot – there is no suggestion here that the novel is at all engaged with the prevalent domestic strain of middle-class literature in the 1930s. *Imitation of Life*, likewise, is too much melodrama to fit the needs of Blair's middlebrow reader. Both texts have been thought of as exemplars of the middlebrow, for many of the same reasons that Blair says readers should turn to fiction, but twenty-first-century tastes seem to be determining this classification. Rather than these texts, Blair recommends two books that she says are "as free from mawkish sentiment as from maudlin cynicism" (the former presumably the fault of Hurst, the latter the fault of Lewis). These books will help "restor[e] the reader's sense of proportion," and "give a new connotation to that threadbare adjective, 'wholesome.' Perhaps they are the vanguard of a new type which, though it can treat the simple annals of the poor realistically, reveals also the dignity and beauty that lies in meeting bravely the conditions of life, whatever the estate to which one is called."[32] *Jenny Wren* by E. H. Young and *Enchanted Winter* by Martin Hare do not portray exceptional lives that end dramatically like those of Ann Vickers or the Pullmans; they are more kosher examples of interwar "domestic modernism" than either Lewis's or Hurst's novels.[33]

It might make sense at this point to pose the question: what was *not* middlebrow? Despite attempts by modernist authors, "Smart Set" critics, and university professors, among others, to define some literature as anathema, and completely external to the lives and needs of those who constituted the "vast middle" of American society, it does seem as if nearly anything could potentially be middlebrow if approached through a middlebrow interpretive lens. Two examples from the pages of Blair's *Good Housekeeping* columns can serve as examples of both the possibilities and the limitations of this flexibility: Virginia Woolf's *The Waves* and Zora Neale Hurston's *Jonah's Gourd Vine*.

Since the middlebrow, unlike the early-century mode of "reading up" that I have described elsewhere, was relatively unconcerned with living up to a cultural arbiter's notion of proper reading, there was less anxiety in Blair's columns about attempting to read the books "we are supposed to read" in the prescribed fashion of people who were "in the know." Still,

Blair's charge, as outlined in her inaugural column, extended to the task of telling her readers "the books we'll like, the books we ought to read, and what we ought to know about the new books."[34] In that spirit, Blair would recommend one of the most experimental of Virginia Woolf's books, *The Waves*, in her March 1932 column. Telling her audience that "March is the Time to Read the Best Books of the Season," in part because there are few social events during Lent, Blair takes this opportunity to name the books

> that can not be ignored . . . Either they have been acclaimed as especially fine of their kind, or we have heard Something about them that makes a special appeal to us. Not to read them would be to forgo a great pleasure or deny ourselves some knowledge we should gain. In other words, they are books we simply can not afford to miss.[35]

The Waves, she admits, is one of those books, largely because Woolf is a "writer who must command the attention of those who take literature seriously," despite the fact that "[t]here are not lacking critics to complain that [her methods or her material] limits her claim to greatness. Her innovations as to form, they contend, make her too difficult to understand. The things she chooses to write about are merely separate things, poignant enough in themselves, but revealing no new version of the universe."[36] But it turns out that it is the critical debate that actually recommends Woolf as someone who should be read. "When there is such a difference of opinion as this about an author's work, what reader interested in the development of literature can afford to miss her latest book? . . . Indeed, he will need to read it if he is to know what it is all about, for it is impossible for any outline to give an adequate idea of the book."[37] Blair's subsequent attempt to offer a general summary of *The Waves* leaves no question about the text's experimental form. Her audience will know that they are in for an uphill climb, that they will need to stop and reread and reread in order to make sense of Woolf's text.

Blair goes so far as to quote the final lines of the novel to demonstrate their opacity to interpretation. She performs a series of alternate readings of the lines, and of Woolf's use of the wave imagery, to demonstrate the text's complexity to her readers:

> What does Mrs. Woolf mean by placing these descriptions of the sea before the soliloquies of these characters, each soliloquy concerned with some experience vital to the speaker? Does she mean to suggest the futility or the pathos of the human insistence on the experience of the moment – when it is seen against the ceaseless ebb and flow of events; or does she intend to

remind us that years in a human life are but as an hour of the ocean's restless life? In her exclusion of background, domestic experiences, all the paraphernalia of daily life, is she trying to show us, as one critic suggests, just what is left to human life without them; or, by concentrating on the feelings of her characters, is she attempting to value life in terms of pure emotion? Is she, by omitting all social experience, and dealing wholly with individual experience, trying to picture the inner spirit which is independent of time and place; or is she only showing us what men would really tell about themselves and the world if they could express exactly what they felt?[38]

Blair refers to critical debates over the text's meanings, even as she offers a multiplicity of interpretations to her *Good Housekeeping* audience; we could on the one hand see these as discussion questions, suitable for importation into book group discussions of the novel (Blair addresses book clubs specifically in many of her columns, and she opens the series with a discussion of her own Joplin, Missouri, book group). But Blair goes on to reassure her reader that "[t]hese questions will be answered differently by different readers." Woolf's book "will not prove interesting to every reader," but "those who like to solve puzzles for themselves" will enjoy the challenge of tackling Blair's questions, and they need not answer them in the same way. Just as there are readers who enjoy different types of books, not all of the readers who enjoy the same type of books will interpret those books the same way. Blair's job is to describe the book well enough for her readers to identify it as their type of book; the reader's job is to make an accurate assessment of their tastes to choose wisely from among the books Blair describes. This tacking back and forth between readerly desires is typical of Blair's columns – she summarizes books so as to fit them to readers, and even goes as far on occasion as to warn her readers not to complain if they read against type and end up dissatisfied with their books. After a lengthy summary description of one novel, about which Blair was admittedly ambivalent but that did have several redeeming qualities (Rosamond Lehmann's *Dusty Answer*), Blair cautions her readers:

> Now, having heard what the story is about and what it means, the question is up to the reader, "Is it your book?" Do you want to know what Judith wanted from the world and see her disillusionment? Do you enjoy the companionship of young and innocent and slightly stupid girls? Will the pleasure of viewing her child world through rose-colored glasses make up to you for the pain of seeing her break them and throw them away? Will you endure the murkiness produced by these implications for the sake of the beauty unobscured? If you can not answer these questions in the affirmative, then the book is not for you. If you can, it will probably give you, as it did to the critics, extraordinary pleasure. But I beg of you, do not answer these

questions "No," then read it and complain because you do. Or worse, never answer these questions at all, read it, and feel that a "bad book" was imposed on you.[39]

If a double edge can be discerned in this summary of *Dusty Answer*, we can trace it to the situation that occasions Blair's decision to discuss the novel: it was, apparently, a book that had "taken the book reviewers by storm."[40] Reading between the lines, one might guess that Blair felt some pressure to address the book in her column; her apparent chafing at the strong critical consensus for the book comes through when she notes that it gave the critics "extraordinary pleasure." Blair, like her readers, wanted to have the freedom to "Choose for yourself" – this being the title of the self-same January 1928 column – and she does have opinions, which she does not always withhold from her audience. In the case of *The Waves*, Blair seems a fan: "for those who would enjoy it to miss it would be a calamity," she avows; but, lest her readers think that they are somehow lacking if they do not find themselves drawn to *The Waves*, Blair closes with one of her typical caveats: "it has not been my intention to suggest that every one of these books should be read by every reader, but only that each is so excellent of its kind that it would be a pity for any reader who enjoys the type to which it belongs to let the season pass without having had it."[41] While a reader might reasonably feel some degree of compulsion to read this modernist novel, Blair can plausibly deny her role in that compulsion.

Blair's recommendation of *Jonah's Gourd Vine* is an example both of the expansion of the middlebrow mode of reading and the ways in which a middle-class identification could be exclusionary. In her final column for *Good Housekeeping*, Blair lists Hurston's novel as one of the "Distinctive Books of 1933–1934," telling her readers that "[i]t is a novel about Negroes by a Negro, which reveals them as members of their own race with its own characteristics, and members of the human family with the characteristics common to it. This is a social document which one who wishes to be 'up' on fiction or sociology will find valuable."[42] This moment recalls Mary Church Terrell's complaint, cited by Jamie Harker, that she could not be published in an "average magazine" (read: one with a primarily white audience) because "[n]obody wants to know a colored woman's opinions about her own status or that of her group. When she dares express it, no matter how mild or tactful it may be, it is called 'Propaganda,' or is labeled 'controversial.'"[43] Terrell was writing about the publishing environment of the late 1880s; by 1934, the presumption seems to have shifted. Now, the work of a black writer about black subjects is presumed to be sociology, and the black subjects represented therein have become metonymy for the race. This qualified embrace of Hurston's work is arguably more thoroughly othering than the simple exclusion encountered by Terrell or, in Harker's example, the black middlebrow writer Jesse Fauset. Hurston's work, particularly when couched in these terms, could rest easy with an audience that "tended to see the African-American community as uniform: primitive, sensual, funny, musical, rhythmic, and simple."[44] Fauset's name is never mentioned in Blair's columns, despite Blair's agenda of resuscitating works that have slipped past the best-seller lists. On the other hand, Blair is a repeat advocate of DuBose Hayward's *Porgy*, which is set, like Hurston's novel, in the Deep South and centers on a romance plot. Blair recommends Porgy in similar terms to those she uses to recommend *Jonah's Gourd Vine*; it is a book that one must read if one wants to keep up with the literary times: "Since so many people say it is *the* book of the year, the girls should have an opportunity to read that. College-bred girls, teachers like mine, who are essentially interested in the trend of literature, hate to get out of it as you hate to get away from a daily newspaper. You feel something must be happening."[45] Blair's standard operating procedure of book summary fails her when it comes to *Porgy*, however; she insists that it must be read to be understood, that "it would be sacrilege as well as idiocy for me to paraphrase, because it is the way Hayward tells the story that makes you accept Porgy as a great tragic character and so all that happens to him as of significance."[46] In other words, you need the Gullah dialect, you need the sultry Charlestonian atmospherics, you need all of the literary technique that will enable a sociological or aesthetic distance from the subject.

One might notice that many of the novels I have discussed here are not properly considered "American fiction." Blair's recommendations, like the best-seller lists and the Modern Library contents, were international in flavor. One of her most-recommended authors is Norwegian Nobel Laureate Sigrid Undset. Blair discusses her 1933 novel *The Wild Orchid* just before tackling *The Waves*. Blair seems to be addressing a reader who might object to the foreignness of the novel at some length:

> It is a Norwegian novel. On every page, in nearly every line, we are made aware of it. The names of the people, places, and things, the scenes, the

setting, belong to that country and no other. The people, too, belong to it.
We could never mistake them for Irishmen or Americans. Specifically, what
we are shown is a cross-section of Norwegian society as it breaks with its past
and imbibes new doctrines. In spite of the distinctly Norwegian setting we
realize, as we read, how like it all is to our society in pre-war days. In ours,
too, you remember, were to be found rebels like Paul, radicals like his
mother; the same concentration on wealth and material goods, the same
progressivism in social welfare, the same idolatry of personal liberty, the
same smugness and sense of security, the same conventionality and respectability. Thus what Mme. Undset has given us is not alone a cross-section of
Norwegian pre-war society, but of pre-war society. Strip it of the Norwegian
background and there is a complete study of the society of a period.[47]

Just as her discussion of *Jonah's Gourd Vine* reinforces the whiteness (and
non-Southern-ness?) of her audience, Blair's discussion of Undset shores
up the national identifications of the middle-class, middlebrow audience.
The Norwegian story is stripped of its national specificity and becomes
a portrait of "society" – an historically specific portrait, to be sure, but
applicable across borders in ways that the Hurston and Hayward texts are
not transferrable across racial designations. The middlebrow reading
mode, in which all readers chose texts because of their utility for themselves, could and did accommodate a range of international literatures in
translation as either universal visions of humanity or as anthropology or
travelogues.

   Blair's columns for *Good Housekeeping* ended in 1934, just as the
national recovery from the Depression began to occasion a decline in
middle-class reading. The Lynds noted that 1933 was the high-water mark
for library use in Middletown; by 1935, the circulation numbers had
decreased by 20 percent, though they were still above 1929 levels.[48]
Blair was not on staff at *Good Housekeeping* to respond to – or to ignore –
the profound popularity of *Gone with the Wind*, though her silence on
Anthony Adverse, the runaway bestseller of 1933–34, suggests that she
might have declined to comment on Mitchell's novel too. If we consider
Blair's columns, appearing as they did in the largest circulating mass-
market magazines at the beginning of the 1930s, as a reflection of and
a significant contributor to middle-class and middlebrow reading culture,
we can broaden even further the scope of both. Her "test kitchen"
mentality, and her address to middling (and middle-aspiring) readers
from all geographic areas of the country, re-centers reading in the 1930s as
a leisure practice that enabled international identifications at the same
time as it worked to shore up racial differences within the United States
itself.

Notes

1. William Frederick Bigelow, "The Wages of Labor," *Good Housekeeping* (May 1933), 4.
2. Ibid.
3. Franklin Delano Roosevelt was inaugurated in March 1933; by May 1933, New Deal reforms such as the Emergency Banking Act and the establishment of the Civilian Conservation Corps were already in place. May would see the creation of the Federal Emergency Relief Administration and the Tennessee Valley Authority, as well as the passage of the National Industrial Recovery Act.
4. Wai Chee Dimock and Michael Gilmore, "Introduction," in *Rethinking Class: Literary Studies and Social Formations* (New York: Columbia University Press, 1994), 3.
5. Burton J. Bledstein, "Introduction," in *The Middling Sorts: Explorations in the History of the American Working Class* (New York: Routledge, 2001), 3.
6. Robert S. Lynd and Helen Merrell Lynd, *Middletown in Transition* (New York: Harcourt Brace Jovanovich, 1937), 17.
7. Ibid., 16.
8. Jennifer Parchesky, "Melodramas of Everyday Life: 1920s Popular Fictions and the Making of Middle America," unpublished dissertation, Duke University, 5.
9. Robert Seguin, *Around Quitting Time: Work and Middle-Class Fantasy in American Fiction* (Durham, NC: Duke University Press, 2001), 3–4.
10. Jaime Harker, *America the Middlebrow: Women's Novels, Progressivism, and Middlebrow Authorship between the Wars* (Amherst: University of Massachusetts Press, 2007), 20.
11. Jennifer Haytock, *The Middle Class in the Great Depression: Popular Woman's Novels of the 1930s* (New York: Palgrave Macmillan, 2013), 8.
12. Joan Shelley Rubin, *The Making of Middlebrow Culture* (Chapel Hill: University of North Carolina Press, 1992), 288.
13. Janice Radway, *A Feeling for Books: The Book-of-the-Month-Club, Literary Taste, and Middle-Class Desire* (Chapel Hill: University of North Carolina Press, 1997), 197.
14. Gordon Hutner, *What America Read: Taste, Class, and the Novel, 1920–1960* (Chapel Hill: University of North Carolina Press, 2009), 9–10, 119.
15. Lisa Boston and Meredith Goldsmith, "Introduction," in *Middlebrow Moderns: Popular American Woman Writers of the 1920s* (Boston: Northeastern University Press, 2003), 4.
16. Harker, America the Middlebrow, 13–14.
17. For the full story of the *Good Housekeeping* Institute, see "Who, What, Why, and Wonderful: The Good Housekeeping Institute," *Good Housekeeping* (May 1960), 116–24.
18. "Index to Good Housekeeping Advertisements," *Good Housekeeping* (February 1926), 6.

19. This history is discussed at some length in Frank Luther Mott, *A History of American Magazines 1741–1930*, vol. V (Cambridge, MA: Harvard University Press, 1930), 138–42.

20. Ibid.

21. For a discussion of Mabie's columns in *Ladies' Home Journal*, please see my *Reading Up: Middle-Class Readers and the Culture of Success in the Early Twentieth-Century United States* (Philadelphia, PA: Temple University Press, 2012).

22. I also discuss this dynamic in "Tasting and Testing Books: Good Housekeeping's Literary Canon for the 1920s and 1930s," *REAL: Yearbook of Research in English and American Literature* 31 (2015), 167–83.

23. Emily Newell Blair, "Emily Newell Blair Discusses Some Distinctive Books of 1933–1934," *Good Housekeeping* (August 1934, 96).

24. Ibid., 179.

25. Emily Newell Blair, "Tasting and Testing Books," *Good Housekeeping* (May 1926), 260.

26. Lynd and Lynd, *Middletown in Transition*, 252.

27. Ibid.

28. Ibid.

29. Emily Newell Blair, "Emily Newell Blair Names Some Books as Trouble Antidotes," *Good Housekeeping* (May 1933), 96.

30. Ibid., 90.

31. Hutner, *What America Read*, 135.

32. Blair, "Antidotes," 90.

33. Jenny Wrenn is treated at length as "domestic modernism" in Chiara Briganti and Kathy Mezei, *Domestic Modernism, the Interwar Novel, and E. H. Young* (Burlington, VT: Ashgate Publishing, 2006).

34. Emily Newell Blair, "Tasting and Testing Books: A New Service for the Readers of Good Housekeeping," *Good Housekeeping* (February 1926), 45.

35. Emily Newell Blair, "March is the Time to Read the Best Books of the Season, Says Emily Newell Blair," *Good Housekeeping* (March 1932), 192.

36. Ibid., 195.

37. Ibid.

38. Ibid.

39. Emily Newell Blair, "Choose for Yourself," *Good Housekeeping* (January 1928), 138.

40. Ibid., 51.

41. Blair, "March," 196.

42. Blair, "Emily Newell Blair Discusses Some Distinctive Books of 1933–1934," 181.

43. Harker, *America the Middlebrow*, 61.

44. Ibid., 65.

45. Blair, "Tasting and Testing Books," 259.

46. Ibid.

47. Blair, "March," 194.

48. Lynd and Lynd, *Middletown in Transition*, 253.

CHAPTER 2

Romance, Marriage, and Family

Jennifer Haytock

In 1934, best-selling novelist Margaret Culkin Banning published *Letters to Susan*, ostensibly a collection of missives that she sent to her daughter at college. In a preface, Banning outlines the aspirations that she has for her daughter and, by implication, all young white middle-class women: she should be able to "pass examinations in Chemistry, French, Latin and Mathematics"; earn a living; be polite to everyone; manage money; learn a sport; "read intelligently," including works by Dickinson, Hemingway, Woolf, Kay Boyle, and Faulkner; shop and order food; select her clothes and keep them clean; avoid alcohol "without being priggish"; manage young men's desires; keep the house in order; be kind to family members; "drive a car without accidents, wash it, change a tire if necessary"; and "keep some of her day for herself."[1] While Banning recognizes the wide scope of her expectations as well as the apparent contradictions within them, she justifies her list as necessary for a young woman of the age: "Her equipment must be diversified because I do not know what her future will be. Her future set-up is not as clear as that of a young man, because a woman's destiny today is being altered by her changing relationships to the world."[2] While Banning's delineation of female behavior is decidedly conservative, her list and rationale offer a useful starting point for considering fiction by and for women in the 1930s. We may think discussions of women's "having it all" began with the women's liberation movement of the 1970s; in fact, early twentieth-century changes in attitudes about women's sexuality and companionate marriage as well as the financial struggles of the 1930s opened this conversation significantly earlier. Realist fiction by and about women in this decade reflects and engages with a variety of changing expectations and opportunities for women, influenced by the deepening connection between sex and marriage and the role of work in developing and expressing a woman's individuality and her place in the family.

With the rise of literary modernism by the 1920s and the spread of proletarian literature in the following decade, critical judgment has dismissed realist and popular literature as outdated and irrelevant. Yet even as consumer spending decreased, people still bought these novels. The Book-of-the-Month Club, established in 1926, provided readers with access to the most recent books and a critical apparatus that pronounced those texts to meet a particular standard. As Joan Shelley Rubin demonstrates in her foundational study *The Making of Middlebrow Culture*, in the early part of the twentieth century a reading public hungered for fiction that would expand their horizons and identify them as members of an educated middle class. At the same time, fiction that might not make the Book-of-the-Month Club's reading list, sometimes called "light fiction," circulated both in magazines, including pulp publications, and in book form. Plots about women – particularly those of courtship, romance, and family – remained central to 1930s fiction. This chapter looks at the realist fiction that Gordon Hutner has recently drawn attention to in *What America Read: Taste, Class, and the Novel, 1920–1960* as well as the light fiction that sold extremely well: both sets of literature were in demand because both circulated contemporary ideas about women's lives and opportunities.[3]

Concerns about novels for women, particularly those with courtship and marriage plots, date back to the origins of the form. In 1785, Clara Reeve captured the public debate about novels and romances, including the apprehensions of those worried about the spread of fiction: "the press groaned under the weight of novels, which sprung up like mushrooms every year," and poor imitations of worthy novels became a "public evil."[4] Later, Nathaniel Hawthorne infamously railed against the "damned mob of scribbling women" who he believed to be preventing his popular success. These concerns about women's writing and novels in particular twine around several threads: the belief that women were intellectually incapable of understanding what they read and thus they could be led astray, and an anxiety about the economic power of women writers in the marketplace. In 1936, the attack on "feminine fiction" was spearheaded by Katharine Fullerton Gerould, who pronounced it to be "escape literature ... that states no vital problem for the mind to solve, that lays on us no duty of moral selection; fiction that is less vicarious experience than vicarious dreaming" and that essentially teaches women to be consumers.[5] Banning, one of Gerould's targets, responded with "The Problem of Popularity," in which she rejects Gerould's argument on the grounds that "life is usually not one vital problem but a succession of small problems, most of them recurrent, many of them incapable of solution."[6] Indeed,

Banning's 1933 novel *Path of True Love* exemplifies such a plot: opening just after the wedding of a young couple, the novel explores the challenges of fidelity and sacrifice and the need for the wife to find an interest apart from wife- and motherhood, and while it ends with the wife's illusions about love tarnished, she's better prepared to face the future. For many women (and men too) in the 1930s, as well as before and after, finding the right partner and constructing a daily life that provides individual satisfaction constitute "vital problems."

Most of the best-selling authors of fiction about women discussed here were established in the marketplace well before the 1930s. Banning, Edna Ferber, Faith Baldwin, Fannie Hurst, Margaret Widdemer, and Kathleen Norris had been publishing for at least a decade if not two prior to the Depression. Margaret Ayer Barnes is one of the few who built a successful career as a popular novelist after the Crash, while Fannie Cook produced her first novel late in the decade and went on to publish several more in the 1940s. Notably, these women all came from the middle or upper class and were white, and their characters tend to mirror them and their presumed readers. While many black writers chose to employ innovative literary forms, Jessie Fauset published realist fiction about middle-class African Americans, although her readership was considerably more circumscribed than some of her white peers. Popular representations tended to inscribe white, middle-class, heterosexual women as normal, and these novels' plots focus on problems that beset this particular subset of the population.

Negotiating Sex and Love

In many women's novels of the 1930s, female characters continue to navigate the changing attitudes toward sex, marriage, love, and divorce that germinated in the early part of the twentieth century. As historian Christina Simmons explains in her study *Making Marriage Modern*, changes in behavior, law, and technologies altered mainstream beliefs about marriage.[7] The Bohemian free love movement of the 1910s led to more open regard for female pleasure in sexual encounters, in or out of marriage (in fact, this shift began even earlier, with the free-thinker and sex radical reform movement in the nineteenth century). Advances in contraceptive technologies and birth control campaigns helped more couples consider childbearing as optional, separating the role of sex from that of reproduction and facilitating the view that sex was an expression of love for its own sake. The increased availability of divorce meant that couples were no longer obligated to stay in a relationship that one or both of them found unsatisfactory. By the 1930s, even though the economic crash strained marriages, decreased the number of couples who could afford to divorce, and caused many individuals to postpone marriage and childbearing, the ideal of marriage had developed into a relationship that emphasized a personal connection between two individuals rather than a union that focused on economic stability and childrearing. The practice of dating, in which young couples paired off and enjoyed public entertainments rather than kept company in the young woman's family home, had become the primary model of courtship, made possible by consumer culture, including the cheap production of automobiles and the rise of public amusements. When a couple married, they were more likely to do so because they found something in the other that they liked. Judith Cole in Banning's *Path of True Love* declares to her husband, "I married you. I didn't hire a man to work for me,"[8] suggesting a desire for the modern marriage founded on individual freedom and companionship rather than an economic contract.

As part of the modern marriage model, the emotional intimacy of sexual relations, rather than their reproductive function, was considered essential to a healthy union. As Ira Wile and Mary Day Winn explain in *Marriage in the Modern Manner* (1929), "[s]ex communion . . . makes sex pleasure not an end itself but a means to a greater enrichment of life for both partners, a drawing together into closer spiritual relations."[9] This belief, coupled with inquiries into the state of marriage by scientists and social scientists, created a public demand for more information about sex. In the early 1930s, revisions to the Comstock laws, which prohibited dissemination of "obscene" material through the US mail system, meant that information became more available, including such scientific studies as Robert Latou Dickinson and Lura Beam's *A Thousand Marriages: A Medical Study of Sex* (1931) and Rachelle S. Yarros's *Modern Woman and Sex: A Feminist Physician Speaks* (1933).[10] The decade saw a rapid growth of relatively explicit sex manuals, including Theodore Van de Velde's *Ideal Marriage: Its Physiognomy and Technique* (1930), M. J. Exner's *The Sexual Side of Marriage* (1932), and Millard S. Everett's *The Hygiene of Marriage* (1932). These advice books emphasized female pleasure, the use of birth control, and the connection between a satisfactory sex life and healthy marriage.

In courtship plots of the 1930s, female characters tend to seek not a marriage that will support them economically or offer safety, but rather one that will provide companionship and fulfill their sexual desires.

In Baldwin's *That Man Is Mine* (1937) and *Career by Proxy* (1939), the female protagonist dismisses the male suitor who has been by her side since childhood because she recognizes him as a friend and not a sexual partner. That the women acknowledge this problem while the men do not suggests that Baldwin's heroines appreciate the importance of physical desire for their own happiness. Women as well as men were expected to know about sex, so when, in Baldwin's *Skyscraper* (1931), Lynn Harding moves from her women's club to an apartment shared with a roommate, she understands the dangers of what could happen when she entertains a man alone in that space. She's not an innocent victim or puppet of convention; she takes active steps to prevent being placed in a situation in which her desires, not simply her suitor's, may compromise her decision not to have sex before marriage.

Literature suggests that openness about female sexuality could be a double-edged sword in the 1930s, as characters often must interpret their desires independently from a religious or social order. Many novels about courtship and marriage in this decade explored what the equation between sex and love meant. Should one marry the person one finds sexually attractive? Should one divorce if sexual desire occurs outside the marriage? In Katharine Brush's *Red-Headed Woman* (1931), for example, a married male character discovers that he feels attracted to his secretary, so both he and his wife conclude that he's in love with the other woman, resulting in a divorce and incompatible second marriage that leaves everyone miserable. A similar situation arises in Margaret Ayer Barnes's Pulitzer Prize–winning *Years of Grace* (1930) when the main character's daughter Cicely leaves her husband for a more passionate relationship, only to decide in the 1938 sequel *Wisdom's Gate* that she will commit to an unfaithful husband rather than secure a second divorce. Barnes's Sally McLeod, in *Within This Present* (1933), finds it easier to accept the thought that her husband may have been in love with another woman than to forgive his alleged sexual infidelity. In all of these novels, characters contend with an ideology of love, sex, and marriage that picked up steam in the previous two decades and that sometimes left them unsure of the meaning of their emotions and desires.

Often in these novels, the resolution to the conflict between sexual desire and relational stability is a return to more conservative values. In Margaret Widdemer's *Eve's Orchard* (1935), indiscriminate flirtatious behavior by both men and women so obscures actual desire and affection that friends don't realize the central couple is engaged, and when the male character decides to use a well-positioned female friend to advance his career, his behavior leads to at least the appearance of infidelity. Ultimately, Eve Mannersfield renounces modern city life in favor of the rural existence led by her ancestors and the more transparent behaviors that come with it. In Widdemer's *Ladies Go Masked* (1934), a novel loosely organized through the stories of the women in a large family, Dorothea and Tom agree that if their marriage isn't happy, they'll simply separate, "the sort of thing every decent man and woman would do," yet when "the ardent certainties of their marriage in the Scott Fitzgerald era" – that is, "the insistence on mutual fairness, justice and mutual freedom"[11] – are tested by a long visit from Dorothea's school friend, Dorothea sends her friend packing, much to her husband's relief.

These authors' views of marriage – and of what women should do when faced with an unfaithful husband – were by no means uniform. Kathleen Norris's *Beauty's Daughter* (1934) and Widdemer's *This Isn't the End* (1936) begin with similar plots: both novels focus on women whose husbands commit adultery, and each wife determines to wait out the affair, treating it as her husband's passing whim. While Norris's heroine is rewarded with the return of her husband, Widdemer's Penelope realizes, once her husband asks for her back, that his indifference to their daughter's well-being has opened her eyes to his selfishness. Unlike her namesake, she happily marries someone else. The values of marriage and motherhood are upheld, although Penelope needs divorce to save her from a lifelong commitment to the wrong man.

While lesbians occupied public space more than they had previously, they tended not to appear, and often not positively, in mainstream fiction. Some novels allude to lesbians, such as the unmarried women in Barnes's *Years of Grace* and *Within This Present*. In *The Hill Grows Steeper* (1938), Fannie Cook explicitly includes a lesbian character, a female friend from whom the main character distances herself and who ends up with a career but apparently no personal life. Still, more rounded depictions of lesbians began to circulate: Gale Wilhelm, for example, published two lesbian novels during the decade, *We Too Are Drifting* (1935) and *Torchlight to Valhalla* (1938). While popular literature continued to insist on heterosexual plots, by the end of the decade lesbian stories blossomed in the pulp fiction market.[12]

Managing Work and Romance

In Baldwin's *Career by Proxy*, Joan Armstrong errs in her romantic life by falling in love with her boss, which she attributes to the "adventure" of

work: "Being with him, seeing him, I can't dissociate him from the freedom, the excitement, the gratification I've had from the experience" of
holding a job, she reflects.[13] Although a romantic misadventure was precisely what Americans feared several decades earlier when women began
moving to the cities to work and live on their own, Joan's mistake stems
not from an inherently dangerous workplace for women but rather from
the personal satisfaction she finds in being useful and earning money.
In *Tales of the Working Girl: Wage-Earning Women in American Literature,
1890–1925*, Laura Hapke notes that since women's wide-scale introduction
to the labor market around 1890, plots about working women were laced
with the danger of their sexual vulnerability in the workplace. In her
Afterword to the Feminist Press's 2003 reissue of Baldwin's *Skyscraper*,
Hapke points out that by the 1920s, "the female clerical worker was no
longer the imperiled virgin or single-minded temptress, but 'an honest,
resourceful, hard working-fun-loving, good girl.'"[14] Indeed, *Skyscraper*'s
Lynn Harding manages to enjoy her work and marry her man.

While white middle-class women had worked outside the home prior to
this decade, many writers continued to address the significance of women's
work and its relation to the roles of wife and mother, particularly given the
insistent problem of money during the Great Depression. During this
period, economic realities seemed to lend weight to the argument that
women should leave jobs to men who needed to support their families.
As Elaine S. Abelson shows, such arguments and public policies ignored
the realities that many families needed two incomes and that women were
sometimes the sole wage earner in the family.[15] These public arguments
also failed to recognize the sense of fulfillment that many women found in
work. Fiction of the 1930s often reflected middle-class women's negotia-
tion of their need and sometimes desire to work with individual and
collective pressure to stay in, or return to, the home.[16]

The stress point in much of this fiction is the intersection of work and
marriage: many female characters in these novels hold jobs, by necessity or
choice, before marriage, and stories often turn on when or whether they
will quit for the sake of the couple's domestic life. Courtship plots often
invoke the male character's inability to provide financially as an obstacle to
marriage, and conflicts over the woman's desire to keep working further
fuel tensions. In Baldwin's version of these plots, the couple generally
decides to marry on both incomes, with varying degrees of speculative
happiness in the marriage. In *Skyscraper*, the couple postpones marriage
several times because of quarrels and financial setbacks, and only when
Tom accepts that he'll have a working wife is the plot resolved; they need

the money she'll earn, and, further, he realizes that her work brings her personal satisfaction, as his does him. They also must outwait company policy to fire married women. *Men Are Such Fools!* (1936) ends with the unlikeable, manipulative Lina saving her marriage by accepting a position working for her husband, even as both husband and wife secretly scheme to control the other through office machinations. In *That Man Is Mine*, the couple goes into business together. In all these novels, Baldwin portrays women as achieving fulfillment through work, and resolution of the plot leaves the woman in the workforce but the couple not ready to address the question of childrearing.

While childless marriages conveniently if temporarily resolve the tensions of courtship plots, other novels more closely examine many couples' decision to delay childbearing for economic reasons. In Fauset's *Comedy, American Style* (1933), Phebe Cary, who enters what Simmons' calls a "partnership marriage," a model she sees as particular to African Americans,[17] continues her dressmaking business after marriage and brings her husband's family into her home when they lose their money in the Depression. While Phebe enjoys her profession, she also sometimes feels overwhelmed by the day's work, particularly when she comes home to a tired husband and quarreling family. Tempted almost to infidelity, she remembers her love for her husband and remains faithful, yet the ending is not wholly satisfying. The couple wants children but sees no way to support them given the economic realities of their situation. In 1933, the situation looked insolvable.

Several 1930s novels about working women end with unsettling decisions by those characters to give up their thriving careers in capitulation to the demands of domestic life. At the end of Baldwin's *Self-Made Woman* (1932), Cathleen McElroy, a successful real estate agent, chooses her marriage over her business at her husband Bill's insistence. Here, the emancipation of women's sexual desire works against Cathleen: she makes her decision not out of conservative values but rather because her physical attraction to her husband makes her vulnerable. Bill's emotional dominance over Cathleen, Cathleen's dislike of the social world he wants her to facilitate for him, and Cathleen's genuine interest and satisfaction in work leave the ending disturbing. Harriet Andrews, in Cook's *The Hill Grows Steeper*, resists traditional expectations for women by building a career, enjoying an out-of-wedlock affair, and having a baby before marrying its father – only to end up feeling that she can't successfully fill the roles of worker, wife, and mother at the same time. She chooses to give up her job, yet it's not a happy victory for domesticity: she feels that the dress she wears to attend her first dinner as her husband's wife is her "shroud."[18] Both of these novels conclude with the main character giving up work reluctantly, and these endings suggest that traditional expectations of women in the home retain their power despite the individual freedom these characters would prefer.

This imaginative inability to portray women thriving as wives and workers permeates the fiction of the decade. Fannie Hurst's novels *Back Street* (1931) and *Imitation of Life* (1933) present a striking pair of critiques of both romance and work for women or, rather, the devastation that can ensue when women fail to balance them. In *Back Street*, Ray Schmidt gives up her successful career to be the mistress of a married man. She retreats into an apartment, hardly ever leaving in case he calls, and winds up destitute when he dies without making provision for her. Through Ray's complete devotion to love apart from contractual marriage, Hurst condemns the idealization of love and warns of the dangers for women who cannot support themselves financially. *Imitation of Life* examines the inverse situation: Bea Pullman, a young widow with a daughter to support, reluctantly becomes hugely successful in business. Obsessed with making enough money to provide a secure home, Bea never actually spends time with her daughter nor finds a romantic partner. Taken together, Hurst's novels of the early 1930s argue for a necessary balance between women's work and domestic lives while they illuminate the drives and ideologies that limit that possibility.

The Middle-Class Family

Given the long-standing interest of the novel in the middle class and the financial uncertainties of the Depression, class identity remains a fixture in 1930s women's novels. Not surprisingly, many popular novels by and about women portray characters working toward a middle-class income, although, unlike in proletarian fiction, the threat of poverty usually remains vague or obscured. Baldwin's plots, for example, are full of couples who have to wait to marry until they earn enough to support themselves, and while obstacles in the novels frequently revolve around insufficient income, the real hardships of poverty never loom large. These characters have certain expectations for married life that are distinctly middle class: enough space, often a maid or cleaning woman, particular clothes, and eventually a house in the suburbs. These plots follow the recognizable trajectory of the American Dream. In contrast, Josephine Lawrence's *If I Have Four Apples* (1935) explores the structural obstacles in American society that block the climb to the middle class: each member of the family of five has his or her own vision for betterment, but the erosion of their income during the Depression makes their hold on middle-class identity increasingly tenuous. All of the characters end up sacrificing some part of their beliefs in themselves and their options by the end of the novel as they come to recognize the American Dream as a myth.

Much women's fiction of the decade tends to drive toward middle-class status; as one might expect, many of these plots follow characters who try to move "up," with different degrees of success. Occasionally, however, authors portray characters who intentionally move "down" toward middle-class normalcy. Baldwin's *Career by Proxy* follows a wealthy female character whose parents refuse to allow her to work not out of snobbery but rather out of a sense of obligation to leave wage-earning opportunities for women who need them. Joan only gets a job when her less fortunate friend becomes seriously ill. Joan's desire to work rather than live a frivolous life leads ultimately to her marriage to a highly committed doctor, a relationship that will provide the basics but no frills. This fiction offers readers the opportunity to identify with working women and their romances while the characters avoid the material anxieties of most readers' actual experiences: Joan can afford to take a cab home if she works late, and she has a maid to cook her dinner.

Women's fiction of the 1930s, while very invested in middle-class identity, often erases differences in class behavior to which a writer like Edith Wharton was highly attuned and made visible in her novels, such as *The Custom of the Country* (1913). That Udine Spragg must learn about dinner party behaviors and note-writing practices from magazines and newspapers signifies her outsiderness to the class she wishes to join. In contrast, in some popular 1930s fiction, class differences become simplified to financial ones. In Baldwin's *That Man Is Mine*, for example, although the main female character comes from a higher class background than her male love interest, the difference between them is portrayed solely as one of money. Since the couple's friends are Greenwich Village Bohemians and so many people have lost money in the Depression, his lack of morning coat to wear to a wedding fails to matter. What's at stake in the novel is not the bridging of classes – although that happens – but rather the need for the main characters to recognize their love for each other, despite competing romantic interests and a general confusion over what love actually is. Hilda Morris's *The Main Stream* (1939) also obscures class differences by normalizing middle-class behavior. The novel follows three siblings as they move away from the family farm into different destinies and social positions: one a factory worker, one married to a business tycoon, and the third, Flora, a teacher. Flora, the central figure and observer, suggests that "[c]lass in America has nothing to do with birth"; she also argues that the middle class "isn't a class . . . it's just people,"[19] thus making any middle-class markers invisible.

While many of the main characters of popular fiction appear in the city with few or no family relations, the decade saw the publication of a number of novels that present a vast family history, including Barnes's *Years of Grace* and *Within This Present*. *Years of Grace* charts differences in behavior and values from one generation, beginning around 1890, to the next, with the main character wondering at her children's choices, particularly those of her daughters. With conscious attention to national history, *Within This Present* tracks the central family's fortunes from financial success to a rocky period after the Crash. Fauset's *Comedy, American Style* traces three generations with particular attention to racial identity and the possibilities of passing, while her *Chinaberry Tree* (1931), though covering a shorter span of time, dwells on the family history through Laurentine Strange's resentment of her "tainted" blood and the past relationships shaped by desire and race that nearly lead to the incestuous marriage of Melissa Paul and Malory Forten. In other words, the decade saw the production of novels invested in the histories of middle- and upper-class families and in intergenerational conflicts and relationships, often shaped by social change.

In many novels about white middle-class families, children appear at well-spaced intervals that suggest the couple's informed use of contraception, sometimes linked to the values of eugenics. Controlling the number and timing of children was considered a responsibility of educated couples even while native-born whites were expected to reproduce to balance out the impact of large immigrant families. In *Beauty's Daughter*, the young wife has five children in very short order, leading a friend to remark that having so many children is "dreadful," "too much," and "distinctly *different*,"[20] reinforcing the belief in one or two children as "normal." Banning's *Mixed Marriage* (1930) explores a union between a devout Catholic who cannot use contraception and her Protestant husband, who simultaneously respects her faith and wants to protect her from too many pregnancies. However, both husband and wife feel sexual passion and want to act on it, so not until the wife accepts that she's willing to have "a dozen children with my head up" does the marriage achieve a secure footing.[21] With the increasing availability of birth control, limiting the number of children in a marriage was considered a sign of education and respect for women's independence, both markers of class status.

Novels representing motherhood contended with various contemporary ideologies, most significantly popularized Freudian psychology and eugenics. In Anne Parrish's *Mr. Despondency's Daughter* (1938), the self-centered mother damages everyone around her. Her sexual frigidity seems to cause her husband to commit suicide, and her need for attention drives away one son and apparently turns the other one gay, as encoded in his affection for clothes, flowers, and art. Although she recognizes her own destructive behaviors, she can't control them, so she secludes herself from her family in order to protect them. In *The Hill Grows Steeper*, the doctor's diagnosis of Harriet's son as "neurotic" serves as the tipping point that convinces her to give up her work.[22] In *This Isn't the End*, Penelope must recognize her primary responsibility as mother to her daughter, not as wife to her husband, as part of her own maturation. Olivia Cary's poor mothering in *Comedy, American Style* stems from her desire to be white and to have her children pass into whiteness; her rejection of her dark-skinned son leads to his suicide and ultimately to her exile from her family.

Fluid class boundaries – both upward and downward – and public recognition of female autonomy and sexual desire support plots in which female characters create their own families through nonbiological and extramarital means. In Edna Ferber's *American Beauty* (1931), Temmie Oakes, descendent of once-prominent original New England settlers, creates a family of "freaks," including her giant aunt Bella, her dwarf uncle Jot, her spinster aunt Judith, and her immigrant husband, as well as biological and adopted children.[23] In *Eve's Orchard*, Eve Mannersfield builds a family with her "uncle" Henry, a suitor of Eve's dead aunt, and the neglected child of friends, eventually marrying her steady neighbor George rather than the selfish Denny, who destroys his relationship with Eve by refusing to accept the child. *The Hill Grows Steeper*'s Harriet Andrews, finding herself unmarried and pregnant with a job on the line, rejects abortion because "having a baby was an integral part of being Harriet Andrews!"[24] In these novels, personal desire trumps biology and custom in the forming of a family.

Conclusion

In Banning's *Path of True Love*, after learning that her husband loves another woman but chooses to remain in their marriage, Judith Cole realizes that "I can't expect a marriage to do all the work of my life for me, can I?"[25] She must, she discovers, cultivate other interests, even if the work to which she devotes herself is tending to children and domestic life rather than employment outside the home. Even the "light fiction" of the decade seldom ended with a "happily ever after," as these novels attended to the complexities of modern life for women. Through these unsettled endings, writers recognized that their fiction does a particular kind of work: it sketches in social values and economic realities, suggests ways readers can imagine their lives, and illuminates the ambiguities and contradictory expectations for women in the decade.

During the 1930s, fiction for and by white middle-class women focused not just on financial hardship: novels continued to reflect and investigate how women experienced the world. Their lives were shaped by changes in access to birth control, which in turn altered how marriage was conceived. When reproduction became optional, fiction grappled with the new possibilities for women's existence and relationships, including new questions about love and commitment to which there were more open answers. Fiction mapped new paths as well as illuminated how traditional arrangements maintained their hold. Concerns surrounding work continued to loom large in women's lives and in their fiction, and it often served as a fulcrum on which tensions of marriage and family balanced. Even as women's situations and prospects changed with the social and economic tides, writers found that the realistic form served a useful purpose: it allowed them to imagine and portray the material and social realities that shaped women's emotional lives and aspirations.

Notes

1. Margaret Culkin Banning, *Letters to Susan* (New York: Harper & Brothers, 1934), 4–6.
2. Ibid., 7–8.
3. This chapter focuses on fiction by women, although such a decision may be considered arbitrary. Sinclair Lewis's *Ann Vickers* (1933) and Christopher Morley's *Kitty Foyle* (1939) follow female protagonists through their experiences with work and romance, including out-of-wedlock sexual affairs and abortions.
4. Clara Reeve, *The Progress of Romance*, vol. II (Dublin, 1785), 7.
5. Katharine Fullerton Girould, "Feminine Fiction," *Saturday Review of Literature* (April 11, 1936), 3–4, 15.
6. Margaret Culkin Banning, "The Problem of Popularity," *Saturday Review of Literature* (May 2, 1936), 3–4, 16–17. See also Gordon Hutner, *What America Read: Taste, Class, and the Novel, 1920–1960* (Chapel Hill: University of North

Carolina Press, 2009), 137–41, for a full account of the debate between Girould and Banning and the response from editor Henry Canby.

7. Christina Simmons, *Making Marriage Modern: Women's Sexuality from the Progressive Era to World War II* (New York: Oxford University Press, 2009).

8. Margaret Culkin Banning, *Path of True Love* (New York: Harper & Brothers, 1933), 124.

9. Ira Wile and Mary Day Winn, *Marriage in the Modern Manner* (New York: Century Company, 1929), 53.

10. See Simmons, *Making Marriage Modern*, 183–86.

11. Margaret Widdemer, *Ladies Go Masked* (New York: Farrar & Rhinehart, 1934), 32.

12. See Paula Rabinowitz, *American Pulp: How Paperbacks Brought Modernism to Main Street* (Princeton, NJ: Princeton University Press, 2014), chapter 7.

13. Faith Baldwin, *Career by Proxy* (New York: Farrar & Rinehart, 1939), 216.

14. Laura Hapke, "Afterword," *Skyscraper* (New York: Feminist Press, 2003), 251.

15. Elaine S. Abelson, "The Times That Tried Only Men's Souls: Women, Work, and Public Policy in the Great Depression," in *Women on Their Own: Interdisciplinary Perspectives on Being Single*, ed. Rudolph M. Bell and Virginia Yans (New Brunswick, NJ: Rutgers University Press, 2008), 219–38, 221.

16. Poor women had to work, though fiction shows that they might experience backlash from men for doing so. In Meridel Le Sueur's *The Girl*, for example, the main character waitresses and prostitutes herself to provide money for herself and her male partner, only to have him beat her and try to force her to have an abortion as he compensates for his economic helplessness.

17. Simmons, *Making Marriage Modern*, 150–64.

18. Fannie Cook, *The Hill Grows Steeper* (New York: G. P. Putnam's Sons, 1938), 276.

19. Hilda Morris, *The Main Stream* (New York: G. P. Putnam's Sons, 1939), 299.

20. Kathleen Thompson Norris, *Beauty's Daughter* (Garden City, NY: Doubleday Doran, 1934), 174.

21. Margaret Banning, *Mixed Marriage* (New York: Harper & Brothers, 1930), 310.

22. Cook, *Hill Grows Steeper*, 271.

23. See Susan Edmunds, *Grotesque Relations: Modernist Domestic Fiction and the U. S. Welfare State* (New York: Oxford University Press, 2008) for a further discussion of the meaning of "freaks" in the context of the 1930s in *American Beauty*.

24. Cook, *Hill Grows Steeper*, 208.

25. Banning, *Path of True Love*, 222.

CHAPTER 3

The Working Class
Joseph B. Entin

The 1930s was a period of both crisis and opportunity for working people in the United States. Soaring unemployment and environmental catastrophes, such as the Dust Bowl, left millions of Americans out of work, drifting into an uncertain future. The economic collapse underscored the contingency of labor under capitalism, in which unemployment precedes employment, and insecurity, rather than stability, is the norm. At the same time, the 1930s also witnessed the expansion of Fordism, as assembly-line production and mass consumerism became increasingly hegemonic in American economic life. Faced with hard times on one hand, and intensified labor discipline on the other, many working people organized and fought for change through labor unions, unemployment councils, and mutual assistance networks of all kinds. Indeed, the decade marked a watershed in working-class resistance and unrest. Millions of workers struck – in textile factories and coal mines, in a wave of sit-down strikes across the retail, auto, and steel industries, and in cities like San Francisco and Minneapolis, which were immobilized by general strikes in 1934. After the passage of the National Labor Relations Act in 1935, the Congress of Industrial Organizations (CIO) was formed and grew rapidly, inaugurating what historian Michael Denning has called the "Age of the CIO," a prolonged period of union power and working-class influence in US culture.

This chapter examines novels of working-class crisis and struggle produced during the long Depression decade. In what follows, I suggest these novels constitute a literature of precarity, in several senses.[1] First, these texts place great stress on the violence of capitalist production and the vulnerability of working people to injury and harm. These dynamics are often condensed in striking, at times grotesque, rhetorics of distortion, excess, or disfiguration, as writers attempt to put into literary form the decade's propulsive dialectics of disaster and possibility, abjection and agency, emergency and emergence. Further, while these texts feature many kinds of work – from factory and mine labor, to farm work, housework, and prostitution – they also devote substantial attention to the absence of and exclusion from work, and to displacement, dispossession, and destitution. In charting the movement of laboring people between work and non-work, employment and unemployment, these texts underscore the porousness and fluidity, rather than coherence and stability, of the working class as a category of belonging. These novels highlight the fundamentally contradictory position of working people under capitalism, as the source of productive power and surplus labor value, but also as a population that capital aims to render expendable, itself surplus. Finally, these novels underline the precarious and contradictory location of working-class literature itself, poised between the concerns, voices, and perspectives of the working people it depicts and the predominately middle-class readers to whom it is addressed. Rather than a discrete or singular genre, working-class fiction from the Depression displays a remarkably heteroglossic range of voices, languages, and styles, as writers blend and extend the innovations of early twentieth-century realists, naturalists, and modernists to address the material hardships and dynamic modernity of an era in which revolution seemed possible, and yet from which a fortified monopoly capitalism emerged. In the end, I contend, due to its emphasis on the unpredictability of working-class life and labor, the pervasiveness of capitalist logics in social and personal experience, and the volatility of economic existence, writing from the 1930s feels remarkably contemporary to our own moment of economic recession, extreme inequality, and contingent work.

***

Fiction of the 1930s about working-class life and labor cannot be limited to proletarian literature, but much of the period's most potent writing about work, class struggle, and economic suffering was penned under the banner of proletarianism. For decades, mainstream literary critics, influenced by Cold War anticommunism, tended to disparage, even dismiss, proletarian literature as a didactic, rigidly formulaic subgenre advanced and actively policed by the cultural apparatus of the Communist Party of the United States of America (CPUSA). The CPUSA was indeed central to the left literary landscape, but revisionist historians have demonstrated that rather than "the literature of a party disguised as the literature of a class," as Phillip Rahv famously charged, proletarian literature in fact constituted a fluid and capacious cultural formation that supported and trained writers from varied class positions, regions, genders, and ethnic and racial backgrounds, who collectively produced a heterogeneous body of literary work.[2]

In fact, from its very inception in the American context, proletarian literature was a contested term, the subject of a lively, often contentious, conversation, hosted in an array of venues, from meetings of the John Reed Clubs that sprang up around the country after 1932, to publications such as the *Daily Worker*, *The New Masses*, *Anvil*, *Left Front*, *Partisan Review*, and many others, in which no single set of interpretive ideas or formal criteria dominated. Even the era's allegedly most doctrinaire critic, Mike Gold, insisted: "There is nothing finished or dogmatic in proletarian thought . . . Proletarian literature is taking many forms. There is not a standard model which all writers must imitate, or even a standard set of thoughts."[3]

One can grasp the scope of ideas articulated in the name of proletarian literature by glancing at the proceedings of the 1935 American Writers Congress, published as the CPUSA was shifting from a militant early-1930s stance to the more alliance-focused strategies of the Popular Front. In his talk to the Congress, novelist John Conroy, author of *The Disinherited* (1933), advanced the ideal of the worker-writer who aims "to attempt an interpretation of those aspects of American life important to the masses," and to "communicate this material as simply and clearly as we are able to the largest body of readers we can command."[4] By contrast, John Dos Passos compared the radical writer's position to a professional technician, whose chief aim is to apply "discovery, originality, and invention" to their craft.[5] In turn, critic Edwin Seaver, attempting to "eliminate a whole cadre of dogmas whose effect is to clog the creative process," insisted that proletarian literature cannot be identified by the author's class origin, or even the class portrayed, but rather by a writer's "political orientation."[6] Kenneth Burke went so far as to suggest that writers should exchange a focus on "the worker," which Burke felt had limited political appeal, to the more inclusive symbol of "the people," which, he argued, "contains connotations both of oppression and of unity."[7] The varied perspectives expressed at the Congress underscore that, rather than a unified school governed by predetermined aesthetic dictates, proletarian literature represented an experimental, speculative endeavor that took a diverse range of forms.

One of the earliest Depression-era novels by a working-class writer active in the proletarian movement was *Jews without Money*, Mike Gold's fictionalized autobiography about growing up on the Lower East Side. Published in February 1930, just months after the 1929 crash, the novel went through eleven printings by October. Looking back to Abraham Cahan's *Yekl* (1896) and Anzia Yezierska's *Bread Givers* (1925), as well as James Joyce's *Portrait of the Artist as a Young Man* (1916), Gold's novel opened the door for a host of 1930s novels that, like his, narrate stories of working-class hardship as tales of ethnic childhood and youth: John Farrell's *Young Lonigan* (1932), Henry Roth's *Call It Sleep* (1935), John Fante's *Wait Until Spring, Bandini* (1938), Nelson Algren's *Never Come Morning* (1942), Tillie Olsen's *Yonnondio* (1974), and others.

Although Gold was well known for his efforts, as literary editor of *The New Masses*, to articulate a coherent theory of proletarian writing, his own novel is noteworthy for its fractured, unruly textuality. *Jews without Money* is less a linear narrative of working-class *bildung* than an episodic series of vignettes about life in the tenements, as seen through the eyes of the narrator, Mikey, and his "gang of little Yids."[8] In fact, Melvin Levy, in a review of the novel in the *New Republic*, claimed that Gold's novel failed as a work of proletarian literature. "The characters are not proletarians," Levy complained, "they are merely poor people." Further, "labor organization and strikes are not mentioned ... nor [is] the Triangle Fire."[9] Gold responded that he did "not believe any good writing can come out of the mechanical application of the spirit of proletarian literature," but Levy's comments gesture to some of the social and literary contradictions at the heart of the book.[10]

For instance, while *Jews* is a novel about working people, it foregrounds the absence of work and the anxious, often desperate, struggle of Gold's family, and other immigrant slum residents, against privation. Further, while the text does, contrary to Levy's claim, recount a shirtwaist strike, in which young Mikey's Aunt Lena participates, it also underscores the lack of radicalism among workers. "I spit on a union!," declares Mikey's father, Herman. "What nonsense! In America each man should make his own fortune."[11] Yet Herman Gold, the voice of economic self-sufficiency, in fact spends much of the novel incapacitated and unable to earn a living due to the lead poisoning he acquires as a house painter and an injury he suffers falling from a scaffold. As a result, his family hovers on the cusp of destitution. Coming to the United States, he insists soberly to his son, "was the greatest mistake in my life."[12] Gold's novel, so focused on the material hardships of ghetto life and the precariousness of his family's well-being, thus inverts the conventional narrative of immigrant assimilation and upward mobility, turning the classic story of ascent into a descent.

The text's contradictions are condensed in the black humor and graphic hyperbole that Gold employs to puncture genteel literary expectations. In his description of sleeping on the roof to beat the mid-summer heat, Gold writes: "Like rats scrambling on deck from the hold of a burning ship ... we poured on the roof at night to sleep."[13] The sleepers are "heaped like

corpses," "mounds of pale stricken flesh, tossing against an unreal city" –
vamping T. S. Eliot in this last phrase to delineate the desperation of the
city's impoverished populations.[14] Written to challenge a potentially picturesque or pathetic treatment of the poor, *Jews* is a novel of rats, flies, flying
garbage,[15] heads severed by horse carts,[16] bedbugs,[17] and alley cats – "not the
smug purring pets of the rich, but outcasts, criminals and fiends . . . hideous
with scars and wounds . . . smeared with unimaginable sores and filth."[18]
Gold's assault on bourgeois literary tastes is allegorized when the tenement
children chase a "big sightseeing bus" out of the neighborhood, pelting
"rocks, garbage, dead cats and stale vegetables at the frightened
sightseers . . . What right had these stuckup foreigners to come and look at
us?"[19] Here, we can sense Gold's awareness of the contradictory position of
working-class writing: unlike the young ghetto dwellers, who simply want to
chase the bus away, Gold himself is suspended *between* the slum and outsiders, writing for the very literary sightseers whose motives and capacity to
understand he finds suspect.

The gritty, grotesque elements of the novel are in turn contradicted by
the sentimental and melodramatic threads, such as the saintly portrait of
Gold's mother and the depiction of his younger sister's death beneath the
wheels of a street wagon. More broadly, the novel is a cacophonous literary
fabric, a site of "crazy mingling"[20] like the tenement itself, in which a wide
range of references and languages, high and low, converge: from
Shakespeare to dime novels, James Joyce to Buffalo Bill, Walt Whitman
to folk tales, all peppered with Yiddishisms. The novel's polyglot textuality
is echoed in the various hybrid, boundary-crossing figures that populate
the novel, such as the talking bear in the story that Herman Gold spins for
Mike and his sister; Harry the Pimp, a criminal who gives young Mikey his
first book to read;[21] and Mikey himself, the school drop-out who "hated
books,"[22] yet becomes a tenement memoirist.

The kind of industrial accident that Herman Gold experiences in *Jews
without Money* is elevated to a primary motif in *Christ in Concrete* (1939),
Pietro di Donato's harrowing novel about the precarious position of
immigrant construction workers in capitalist New York. Based on a short
story published to great acclaim in *Esquire* in 1937, *Christ in Concrete* was
chosen over *The Grapes of Wrath* as a Book-of-the-Month Club main
selection in 1939. Di Donato's novel narrates the story of a young Italian-
American, Paul, whose immigrant father, Geremio, is killed when
a building he is working on collapses on Good Friday when Paul is twelve
years old. The oldest of six children, Paul takes up bricklaying to support
his family; in the course of the novel, Paul's uncle loses a leg during

a construction accident and Paul's godfather plummets off a scaffold to his death.

Similar to *Jews, Christ in Concrete* is a disjointed novel comprised of multiple, often conflicting, voices, styles, and ideological registers. Perhaps the most pervasive aspect of the novel's formal hybridity is its fusion of Italian and English, visible in di Donato's habit of translating the characters' speech into English, but retaining the metaphors and rhythms of their native Italian. More broadly, di Donato deploys the modernist tactics of linguistic estrangement to render the almost unbearable pressures of physical labor in a capitalist system poised between collapse and structural reorganization. A resolutely political modernism that grounds avant-garde techniques in material incongruities and conflicts, di Donato's novel captures the perverse and perilous quality of social existence for immigrant workers in a country that, as one character puts it, "has contradicted itself," in which "to rebel is to lose all of the very little. To be obedient is to choke."[23]

The contradictions the novel traces are illustrated most powerfully in the innovative renderings of the labor process – the "terror of production," as the novel describes it – and of the working and wounded bodies of the laborers themselves, which serve both as analogues of the novel's chaotic form and as spectacular figures of social protest.[24] For Paul and the other construction workers, labor represents a figure of immense power and persuasion, "Job," which di Donato describes in a language that blends excitement and danger, coordination and confusion, in "an inferno of sense-pounding cacophony":

> Compression engines snort viciously – sledge heads punch sinking spikes – steel drills bite shattering jazz in stony-stone excitedly jarring clinging hands – dust swirling – bells clanging insistent aggravated warning – severe iron cranes swivel swing dead heavy rock high – clattering dump – vibrating concussion swiftly absorbed – echo reverberating – scoops bulling horns in rock pile chug-shish-chug-chug aloft – hiss roar dynamite's boomdoom loosening petrified bowels – one hundred hands fighting rock – fifty spines derricking swiveling – fifty faces in set mask chopping stone into bread – fifty hearts interpreting labor hurling oneself down and in at earth planting pod-footed Job.[25]

Adopting Cubist and Futurist techniques to render the enthralling dynamism and the ominous fury of large-scale construction work, di Donato fashions a labor modernism that overwhelms standard syntax. Like Job itself, di Donato's prose is a "balanced delirium," combining naturalism's emphasis on gritty details with a Joycean-like stream-of-consciousness.[26]

Labor in *Christ in Concrete* is an enduring state of struggle depicted in deeply dichotomous terms. On one hand, working bodies are ironically dismantled as the very structures they build take shape. As he works, Paul's "back . . . broke and seemed to come apart. The bending point severed and became a gap connected with trickling, shocking electrical flashes."[27] Yet Job not only splits and severs, it paradoxically sustains and empowers the bricklayers: "Brick and mortar was to become for Paul as stuff he could eat, and the constant motion from brick pile and tub to wall was to become a motion that fed upon itself."[28] Labor is the process of world building, of transforming hope and desire into concrete reality; it is thus both the brutalizing extraction of human energy – the "soul's sentence to stone"[29] – and a potentially revolutionary realization of spiritual and physical energy: "Paul was now bricklayer worker . . . welded to the hands whose vibrations could shatter the earth."[30] The rhetoric here is deeply gendered: the power Paul and other laborers sense as they raise towering buildings is decidedly phallic. Yet the at-times overblown quality of the masculinist rhetoric, which reinforces the compensatory images of brawny male workers that cut across 1930s art and literature, is tempered by the novel's stress on the susceptibility of workers to injury and harm, especially in several searing scenes of industrial accidents.

The most graphic of these scenes is the death of Paul's father, Geremio, when the partially constructed building he is working on collapses, crushing several workers beneath steel beams and smothering them in wet concrete. As the building gives way, the "floor vomited" as "frozen men went flying explosively" – "Walls, floors, beams became whirling, solid, splintering waves crashing with detonations that ground man and material in bonds of death."[31] In a dream-like sequence, the familiar forms of the material world are transformed into a shattered array of component parts. Geremio's own "bones cracked mutely and his sanity went sailing distorted in the limbo of the subconscious."[32] While *Christ in Concrete* narrates Paul's growth, it is punctuated by these and other brutally rendered moments of danger, injury, and loss, which underscore the radical precariousness of immigrant, working-class life. In the end, the volatile, sensationalized depictions of work and the harm working bodies suffer can be read as responses to the challenges of address that di Donato, like Gold and other working-class writers, faces: to write in a way that draws attention to, and tries to breach, the social and aesthetic distance that often prevents middle-class readers from grappling with working-class exploitation.

If *Christ in Concrete* offers an arresting portrayal of men's manual labor, Meridel Le Sueur's *The Girl* centers on women's labor as waitresses, sex workers, and mothers. Le Sueur's novel narrates the story of an unnamed barmaid in St. Paul, Minnesota, who falls in love, suffers the death of her lover in an ill-fated bank robbery, and finally gives birth to a baby girl. The narrative foregrounds the collective power of women's productive and reproductive capacities, but also the vulnerability of women to violence perpetrated by men and the patriarchal state during an era of extreme economic instability.

In *The Girl*, the process of coming to class consciousness is simultaneously the realization of the Girl's unity with other women and her identity as a mother.[33] The Girl affirms her identity as a worker – "*I have worked all my life*"[34] – while she is confined to a state-run maternity home, where she learns about the organizing of the Workers' Alliance. After she escapes the home, she joins a group of women living collectively in an abandoned warehouse; she gives birth to her daughter there just as "all the street girls and the sewing women"[35] return from a demonstration calling for milk and iron pills to sustain the Girl during her pregnancy. Subverting traditional divisions between public and private, the novel makes reproductive labor the grounds for collective political action, maternity the avenue through which women enter history.

Le Sueur's narrative is propelled by an experimental, highly sensuous, and unstable language of desire, which is coded as both empowering and unsettling. In the first chapter, when the Girl sees her lover, Butch, she is at once excited and frightened: "I felt hot and strange and the sweat ran down my armpits clean down my side . . . Then something kind of exploded in my eyes and I saw him come in," she explains. "I was scared [and] shaking in all my bones."[36] Sex with Butch produces a similar sense of rupture – of physical and affective precariousness – that in turn catalyzes a new understanding of the world: "Something had entered me, broken me open, in some kind of terrible hunger," she says.[37] "I would always now know the naked skin of man and woman, their hearts and hungers . . . I wouldn't see us flat anymore but great burning balls of fire turning into each other, piercing, breaking, howling, singing, melting together and tearing apart."[38]

The novel's volatile discourse of desire is not only sexual, but more broadly metaphorical, and frequently channeled through an expansive rhetoric of hunger. When Butch asks the Girl what she wants, she replies: "I want everything. Sure, I got hungers. I want earth . . . I want meat, bread, children. I am starving."[39] This language of hunger – of both starving and wanting, lack and longing, precarity and persistence – pervades the novel, registering not only the literal hungers of the Depression era's undernourished poor, but also deeper existential, physical, and political yearnings for contact, love, fulfillment, and togetherness. "I was full but I was hungry," the Girl notes, suggesting that even on a full stomach, she longs for things to be otherwise.[40] "I'm hungry," she reiterates after reuniting with the other women. "Nobody can shut me up, I'm not going to be good, be happy, make plans, act like nothing has happened."[41] Here, the language of hunger signifies a refusal to accept the subordinate roles men have tried to give her, the commands to comply and be quiet.

The novel's discourse of precarity is not only economic, but also sexual. The stories about sexual relationships the Girl hears from her female coworkers, and her own experiences with men, both underscore women's vulnerability and lay the groundwork for gender and class solidarity. Clara, a barmaid who also works as a prostitute, shares her stories about being beaten by clients; Belle tells the Girl about her thirteen abortions, and admits that her husband, Hoinck, abuses her; the Girl herself is harassed and eventually raped by a local gangster, Ganz. After the rape, the Girl thinks: "Now I knew it . . . Down below you know everything and there are some things you can never tell, never speak of, but they are inside you like yeast."[42] Here, the book reflects on the challenges of representing knowledge of and through the body. On one hand, one's visceral experiences are "inside you like yeast." Yet those things cannot always be communicated. Or, as Amelia, the lead female activist in the novel, says, "[t]here are things the poor suffer that they can't even bear to mouth to each other."[43] After burying Butch's body, the Girl experiences a new sense of self, linked to the body, and a new awareness of collective possibility. "Now I know the whole city," she says to Belle and Amelia, "and the way it is and the way those in it can be together. This you can't know or be at home with until you have lived it. No one can tell you. Now I am at home with my own body and the bodies of others and I will do whatever there is to do."[44] The novel's lyrical language of hunger and desire represents an effort to address this dilemma, which is at the heart of 1930s labor literature: how to render the materiality of working-class experience, the knowledge generated "down below" that "no one can tell you," in literary form. It is, *The Girl* and other novels suggest, a project at once imperative and impossible.

The questions at the heart of *The Girl* about language's capacity, or incapacity, to limn the body, desire, and destitution during precarious times are also crucial to William Faulkner's *As I Lay Dying*, which the celebrated Southern writer wrote in a six-week burst immediately following the 1929 stock market crash. Structured by fifty-nine discrete

monologues, delivered by nine characters, the novel narrates the impoverished Bundren family's nine-day odyssey to bury Addie, wife to Anse and
mother to Cash, Darl, Jewel, Dewey Dell, and Vardaman. Held delicately
together by the interplay of the characters' voices, rendered in stream-of-
consciousness prose and unframed by an omniscient narrator, *As I lay
Dying* is not only one of Faulkner's most formally daring novels, but one of
his most socially and politically responsive texts as well.

In many ways, the Bundrens' journey to inter Addie constitutes, in
Darl's words, a "monstrous burlesque."[45] The image of the indigent family,
towing a rotting corpse for days in the hot sun, followed by a passel of
buzzards, is pitiful to the point of being absurd. Several episodes, such as
the casting of Cash's injured leg in wet cement and Vardaman drilling
holes through the coffin lid into Addie's face, generate a macabre comedy
out of the family's pathetic situation, making them seem like hapless
stereotypes of rural white trash. However, the text's monologues undermine a reductive image of the poor farmers as simple-minded, inarticulate
folk. Words and images of unusual beauty appear not only in sections
narrated by Darl, the character many critics identify as a proto-modernist
figure of the artist, but also by other family members, such as Vardaman's
bizarre and bracing imagistic formulation "my mother is a fish,"[46] and the
lyrical sensualism of Dewey Dell's encounter with a cow she milks:
"The cow breathes upon my hips and back, her breath warm, sweet,
stertorous, moaning ... I feel like a wet seed wild in the hot blind
earth."[47] Dewey Dell's rapturous, poetic account belies her public inarti-
culateness, reminding readers that her seeming lack of sophistication is
countered by a rich, complex sense of self and beauty.

In the lone chapter narrated by Addie, the novel also provides a potent
mediation on the paradoxical power and poverty of language, and by
extension, literature itself. Words, Addie states, "don't ever fit even what
they are trying to say at."[48] The word "love," she contends, is "like the
others: just a shape to fill a lack."[49] Addie explains that words are ultimately
incommensurate with experience, insufficient containers for her own pain
and desire. The novel seems to be suggesting that understanding her
experience entails questioning the very terms and conventions – linguistic,
social, and ideological – through which we are accustomed to compre-
hending the world and people before us. Here, social critique is linked to
aesthetic instability and innovation, as modernism is deployed to express
the precarity of both language and social existence for people like the
Bundrens, who persist in the face of extreme material hardship and emotional loss.

If *As I lay Dying* is the decade's most aesthetically experimental novel about hard-pressed working people on the move, the most high-profile 1930s narrative of itinerant labor was John Steinbeck's Pulitzer Prize-winning epic of precarious life, *The Grapes of Wrath* (1939). *Grapes* recounts the story of an impoverished family of Oklahoma sharecroppers, the Joads, who are driven from their land with thousands of other migrants by drought, corporate bank schemes, and the mechanization of the agricultural industry, and head to California's Central Valley looking for work.

Formally, Steinbeck's novel blends multiple literary threads, including a social realist narrative of dispossession, poverty, and struggle; a sentimental narrative about the redemptive power of mothers and families; an experimental rendition of migrant conditions, universally conceived; and a prophetic allegory of human development and progress. The book was inspired by several sources, from early American captivity narratives, to *Huckleberry Finn*'s vernacular picaresque, to the stark migrant photos of Dorothea Lange and the sequential filmmaking of Pare Lorenz, as well as folk music, Darwinian theory, and the King James Bible.[50] Noted Steinbeck scholar Robert DeMott describes the novel as "a relational field"[51] that "contains multitudes."[52]

In an effort to convey, and at some level contradict, the acute instability and uncertainty of the Joads' migrant existence, the novel oscillates between a robust, at times radical, critique of capitalist development, and a more conservative sentimental and racial populism. On one hand, the novel offers a forceful denunciation of what Marx called primitive accumulation, as well as the environmentally destructive nature of capitalist expansion, which displace whole populations of working people from the land and create conditions of pervasive material and affective instability. The story of the Joads' precarity – their expulsion from Oklahoma and their uneven struggle to find work on the move in California – is essentially a story of corporate accumulation by dispossession,[53] in which vast tracts of land are appropriated by a small group of owners who protect their property with both state-sanctioned and extra-state violence: "The land fell into fewer and fewer hands [and] the number of dispossessed increased ... The great owners formed associations for protection and they met to discuss ways to intimidate, to kill, to gas."[54] Yet, the novel suggests, as mass displacement and misery increase, so do the chances of mass revolt: "Three hundred thousand [migrants], hungry and miserable; if they ever know themselves, the land will be theirs and all the gas, the rifles in the world won't stop them."[55] Passages like these, alongside others that illustrate Marx's reserve army of labor theory and condemn the profit motive that encourages farmers to destroy crops while thousands starve, explain why the Associated Farmers of California mounted a campaign to impugn the book, and why radical critic Granville Hicks, reviewing the novel in *The New Masses*, asserted that Steinbeck's "insight into capitalism illuminates every chapter of the book." "No writer of our time," Hicks continued, "has a more acute sense of economic forces, and of the way they operate against the interests of the masses of the people."[56]

On the other hand, however, the novel's critique of capitalism and narrative of precarious migration rub up against a deeply embedded discourse of organic vitalism. The book repeatedly reframes economic and social questions as matters of "faith" and "soul," "people" and "species" – large, transhistorical concepts that effectively lift the Joads and their struggles out of their immediate political context and into the realm of nature and myth. "Why, we're the people," Ma Joad tells Tom, "we go on."[57] As Tom glances at her, he sees a "curious look in her eyes, eyes like the timeless eyes of a statue."[58] In this "timeless" image of Ma Joad as a static work of art, we can see how *Grapes* aspires to elevate the Joads to the plane of allegory, above and beyond history. Elsewhere, the novel suggests the Joads merge into an organic migrant collective that moves by instinct, "obey[ing] impulses which registered only faintly in their thinking minds."[59] The migrants, we are told, "had no argument, no system, nothing but their numbers and their needs."[60] Here, the Joads and their peers seem to move according to basic physiological demands. They lack analysis, and any sense of themselves as an exploited class, relying instead on animal impulses. "[L]ike ants," the narrator explains, the people "searched for food, work."[61]

The novel's language of natural impulse and organic connection stresses the value of "wholeness" and unity: "all we got is the family unbroken," says Ma.[62] A counterweight to the discourse of loss and uncertainty, this language of wholeness is ultimately linked to a politics of racial purity. Eliding the ethnically mixed composition of California's agricultural workforce, as documented in Dorothea Lange's photographs and Cary McWilliams's *Factories in the Field*, published the same year as *Grapes*, Steinbeck's novel foregrounds the "simple agrarian folk,"[63] figured as the embodiment of an essentialized – and white – American spirit. The text almost entirely obscures the Mexican, Japanese, Filipino, and Chinese workers who worked the fields of California in the early 1930s, and undertook a series of powerful strikes in 1933 and 1934 that ironically served as one inspiration for Steinbeck's writing in the first place.

These struggles by ethnic and immigrant farmworkers occupy the fore-ground of Carlos Bulosan's semi-fictionalized autobiography, *America Is in the Heart*, published in 1946, but set largely in Depression-era California. *America* tells the story of Allos, a migrant Filipino fieldworker who becomes an activist and writer. Yet the book not only recounts the narrator's education and development; it also offers a piercing portrait of ethnic labor precarity, of "despair and rootlessness,"[64] centered on the dispossession of working people, the violence of capitalist production, and the viciously discriminatory treatment of Filipinos and other immigrants and minority populations in the Western United States.

The tensions between materiality and transcendence, exploitation and aspiration, collapse and collective possibility that organize so much work-ing-class writing from the 1930s are central to *America Is in the Heart*. On one level, Allos's story is a tale of intellectual awakening and the emergence of class and ethnic solidarity. Yet every positive opportunity is intertwined with violence and upheaval. After Allos's mother informs him that he can start attending school rather than continuing to sell salted fish, his sister Irene dies suddenly and mysteriously, blood pouring from her mouth and ears, "like an animal that has been strangled with a rope."[65] His arrival in the United States, punctuated by "a sudden surge of joy" and an optimistic sense that "I must find a home in this new land,"[66] is followed immediately by the realization that he and his companions have had their savings stolen, forcing them into indentured labor in the fishing canneries. Later, just as his writing starts to make him feel "like a new man" who can "fight the world with my mind, not merely with my hands," he realizes, "I was sick [with tuberculosis]: the years of hunger had found me at last."[67] The oscillation between hope and despair, positive possibility and violent betrayal, shapes the narrative throughout, as abstract ideals and aspirations are continually undercut by the harsh social and economic realities con-fronting impoverished, racially marked immigrant laborers. *America* thus narrates not just the instability of migrant life in Depression-era California, but the particular precariousness experienced by the novel's Filipino char-acters under a system of neocolonial, racial capitalism that renders them especially vulnerable to exploitation.

The acutely insecure position occupied by Allos and his peers is echoed and reinforced by the text's formal structure, which is highly episodic and fragmented. When *America Is in the Heart* appeared, it was acclaimed as a testimony of immigrant assimilation and achievement. Yet the novel's jagged plot line, which depicts Allos shuttling quickly between a bewildering array of farms and hardscrabble cities in search of work, and its stress on pain and hunger, defy the forms of narrative closure and continuity that give coherence to traditional immigration stories.[68] It is, rather, a novel of loose ends, relationships cut short, and abrupt transitions, relayed in a detached, proto-hard-boiled style. Although framed as a *bildungsroman*, then, and underpinned by Bulosan's socialist hopes for progressive collective action, the novel's focus remains largely on loss and displacement – on the precariousness of existence for minority migrant workers on the West Coast. As emblems of hardship, images of violence and injury inflicted on the bodies of working and poor people litter the book: limbs severed in canneries, a foot torn off by the wheels of a freight train, a young woman raped in a boxcar, men shot in dance halls, a labor organizer "found dead in a ditch."[69]

Allos is a figure of the artist, and consequently a figure of mediation, poised between working-class subjects and middle-class readers. For Bulosan, writing is a contradictory project of limning absences, finding substance in lack and negativity, "giv[ing] significance to all that was starved and thwarted in my life."[70] This is one reason *America* takes on such an unmistakably noirish tone: it is an effort to render the dark shadow beneath the shiny American dream, the horrific misdeeds committed in the name of profit, the sense of illegitimacy and desperation foisted onto poor immigrants who realize "that in many ways it was a crime to be a Filipino in California."[71] For Filipino workers, shunted to the margins of American prosperity, discriminated against by legal and extralegal means, the United States becomes "a world of corruption"[72] best rendered in the perverse chiaroscuro of noir.

In its final two sections, Allos becomes a writer and decides to devote his life to social justice. He begins work on the socialist magazine *The New Tide*, joins the Committee for the Protection of Filipino Rights, and collaborates with organizers who are unionizing farm workers. The experience of collective action gives Allos a "new heroism: a feeling of growing with huge life."[73] Yet the harrowing violence and existential insecurity linger, as several union organizers and activists are lynched, shot, intimidated, and beaten. The novel ends on a note of resounding uncertainty. Aware that an "other world – new, bright, promising – " is being born, Allos nonetheless insists that he and his brothers "belonged to the old world of confusion" and "would be unable to meet the [new era's] demands."[74] The novel's final pages depict Allos on a bus from California to Oregon, waving good-bye to a group of Filipino pea pickers. He asserts that "no man . . . could destroy my faith in America again."[75] Yet this scene of solitary flight into an uncertain future represents an eerie repetition of other moments of departure that structure the novel, and seems to emphasize less the start of something new than the persistence of what has come before: dark, despair-filled episodes of hunger, poverty, precarity, and stunted, if valiant, resistance.

Bulosan's stress on the violent terror of US racial antagonisms, and the particularly hazardous conditions of life for racialized workers in modern American capitalism, finds resonance in the work of Richard Wright, whose autobiography *Black Boy* (1945) served as one of the models for *America Is In the Heart*. Wright came of age as a writer in the Chicago John Reed Clubs and worked as a reporter for the CPUSA's *Daily Worker*, and his writing demonstrates a keen grasp of the interlocking power of oppressive social systems to create insidious forms of racial and economic insecurity. Wright is best known for his hard-hitting 1940 novel, *Native Son*, about Bigger Thomas, a young black chauffer who accidentally kills the daughter of the Chicago real estate magnate for whom he works. Blending a naturalist emphasis on environmental determinism, a pulpy murder plot, and modernist experiments in point of view, *Native Son* was written to disable the kind of sentimental reception that Wright felt had greeted his 1938 story collection, *Uncle Tom's Children*; Wright aimed for *Native Son* to be "so hard and deep that [readers] would have to face it without the consolation of tears."[76]

In its focus on the conditions of Bigger's life on Chicago's South Side, and his murder trial and execution verdict, *Native Son* traces the ways in which capital, the mass media, and the state combine to form what the novel calls "a vast but delicate machine"[77] that enforces black destitution, galvanizes racist opinion, and normalizes premature black death. Precarity here is not only economic, but also, and more fundamentally, a matter of life and death, as Bigger's literal death is preceded and made possible by his social death.[78] As Bigger realizes while contemplating the "anti-Negro epithets" used to depict him in the press, "[t]o those who wanted to kill him he was not human."[79] In the courtroom presentation during the murder trial, the prosecutor adopts and inflates the newspapers' sensationalized depictions of Bigger, referring to him as a "black mad dog,"[80] a "rapacious beast,"[81] a "maddened ape," and an "infernal monster."[82] Whites, Bigger understands, "regarded him as a figment of that black world which they feared and were anxious to keep under control."[83]

Caught within the mechanisms of white supremacy and capitalist exploitation, Bigger occupies a fundamentally paradoxical and deeply precarious position: he is at once perpetrator and victim, subject and object, character and symbol, both "an American, because he was a native son," but also "not allowed to live as an American," as Wright put it in his essay "How 'Bigger'

Was Born."[84] Bigger is thus "hovering unwanted between two worlds – between powerful America and his own stunted place in life," and Wright "took it upon [himself] the task of trying to make the reader feel this No Man's Land."[85] "No Man's Land" is Wright's name for the overdetermined yet indeterminate and highly insecure space that Bigger, as a young, black, working-class man, inhabits. It denotes the "shadowy region" that Bigger enters when he feels most racially marked by "the badge of shame which he knew was attached to black skin."[86] But it is also Wright's term to describe the novel's mode of address to white, middle-class readers – his effort to construct a point of view that captures Bigger's interior thoughts, yet also allows readers to understand the larger social forces beyond Bigger's field of vision that shape his existence. In its efforts to render for readers the harrowing vulnerability of Bigger's position in US racial capitalism, *Native Son* takes its place alongside so many novels about working-class life in 1930s America, which aimed to represent, in both content and form, the economic, social, and emotional precarity that pervaded this era of economic crisis for laboring and other dispossessed peoples.

Notes

1. While much recent critical discourse has asserted that precarity is a contemporary condition, and that the "precariat" may even be a new class, specific to the freelance, contingent, and immaterial labor regimes that mark post-Fordist production, labor literature from the 1930s suggests that economic and social precariousness has a long historical trajectory and that the economic and social uncertainty so palpable in the current economic recession is less a late-breaking exception than a long-standing capitalist norm. The literature of precarity is substantial, and growing; for starters, see Brett Neilson and Ned Rossiter, "Precarity as a Political Concept, or, Fordism as Exception," *Theory, Culture & Society* 25(7–8) (December 2008): 51–72; Dimitris Papadopoulos and Vassilis Tsianos, "Precarity: A Savage Journey to the Heart of Embodied Capitalism," *Transversal* (October 2006). Web. February 10, 2016. http://eipcp.net/transversal/1106/tsianospapadopoulos/en; Guy Standing, *The Precariat: The New Dangerous Class* (London: Bloomsbury, 2011).
2. See James D. Bloom, *Left Letters: The Culture Wars of Mike Gold and Joseph Freeman* (New York: Columbia University Press, 1992); Michael Denning, *The Cultural Front: The Laboring of American Culture in the Twentieth Century* (New York: Verso, 1996); Barbara Foley, *Radical Representations: Politics and Form in U.S. Proletarian Fiction, 1929–1941* (Durham, NC: Duke University Press, 1993); Lawrence Hanley, "'Smashing Cantatas' and 'Looking Class Pitchers': The Impossible Location of Proletarian Literature," in *The Novel*

and the American Left: Critical Essays on Depression-Era Fiction, ed. Janet Casey (Iowa City: University of Iowa Press, 2004), 132–50; Paul Lauter, "American Proletarianism," in *The Columbia History of the American Novel*, ed. Emory Elliot (New York: Columbia University Press, 1991), 331–56; James Murphy, *The Proletarian Moment: The Controversy over Leftism in Literature* (Urbana: University of Illinois Press, 1991); Paula Rabinowitz, *Labor and Desire: Women's Revolutionary Fiction in Depression America* (Chapel Hill: University of North Carolina Press, 1991).

3. Michael Gold, "A Proletarian Novel?" *The New Republic* (June 4, 1930), 74.
4. Jack Conroy, *The Disinherited* (Columbia: University of Missouri Press, [1933]1991), 86. Also see his "The Worker as Writer," in *American Writers' Congress*, ed. Henry Hart (New York: International Publishers, 1935).
5. John Dos Passos, "The Writer as Technician," in *American Writers' Congress*, ed. Henry Hart (New York: International Publishers, 1935), 78–82.
6. Edwin Seaver, "The Proletarian Novel," in *American Writers' Congress*, ed. Henry Hart (New York: International Publishers, 1935), 98–102, 100, 101.
7. Kenneth Burke, "Revolutionary Symbolism in America," in *American Writers' Congress*, ed. Henry Hart (New York: International Publishers, 1935), 87–93, 93.
8. Michael Gold, *Jews without Money* (New York: Public Affairs, [1930] 2009), 16.
9. Melvin P. Levy, "Mike Gold," *New Republic* (March 26, 1930), 161.
10. Gold, "A Proletarian Novel?"
11. Gold, *Jews without Money*, 235.
12. Ibid., 101.
13. Ibid., 126.
14. Ibid., 126.
15. Ibid., 57.
16. Ibid., 49.
17. Ibid., 71.
18. Ibid., 63.
19. Ibid., 55.
20. Ibid., 174.
21. Ibid., 29.
22. Ibid., 305.
23. Pietro di Donato, *Christ in Concrete* (New York: Signet, [1939]1993), 211, 13.
24. Ibid., 13.
25. Ibid., 36.
26. Ibid., 180.
27. Ibid., 143.
28. Ibid., 142.
29. Ibid., 143.
30. Ibid., 143.
31. Ibid., 14.
32. Ibid., 16.

33. See Rabinowitz, *Labor and Desire*.

34. Meridel Le Sueur, *The Girl* (Boston, MA: West End Press, [1939/1978] 1990), 118.

35. Ibid., 129.

36. Ibid., 4.

37. Ibid., 45.

38. Ibid., 46.

39. Ibid., 43.

40. Ibid., 99.

41. Ibid., 101.

42. Ibid., 64.

43. Ibid., 110.

44. Ibid., 102.

45. William Faulkner, *As I Lay Dying* (New York: Vintage International, [1930] 1990), 78.

46. Ibid., 84.

47. Ibid., 64.

48. Ibid., 171.

49. Ibid., 172.

50. Robert DeMott, "Introduction," in *The Grapes of Wrath*. John Steinbeck (New York: Penguin Classics, [1939]2006), ix–xlv.

51. Ibid., xvi.

52. Ibid., xiv.

53. See David Harvey, "Accumulation by Dispossession," in *The New Imperialism* (New York: Oxford University Press, 2003), 137–82.

54. John Steinbeck, *The Grapes of Wrath* (New York: Penguin Classics, [1939] 2006), 238.

55. Ibid., 238.

56. Granville Hicks, "Steinbeck's Powerful New Novel," *New Masses* (May 2, 1939), 22–24.

57. Steinbeck, *Grapes of Wrath*, 250.

58. Ibid., 281.

59. Ibid., 99.

60. Ibid., 283.

61. Ibid., 284.

62. Ibid., 169.

63. Ibid., 282.

64. Carlos Bulosan, *America Is in the Heart* (Seattle: University of Washington Press, [1946]1973), 29.

65. Ibid., 42.

66. Ibid., 99.

67. Ibid., 224–25.

68. See Lisa Lowe, *Immigrant Acts: On Asian American Cultural Politics* (Durham, NC: Duke University Press, 1996).

69. Bulosan, *America Is in the Heart*, 144.

70. Ibid., 62.

71. Ibid., 111.

72. Ibid., 136.

73. Ibid., 196.

74. Ibid., 324.

75. Ibid., 326.

76. Richard Wright, "How Bigger Was Born," in *Native Son and "How Bigger Was Born"* (New York: HarperCollins, [1940]1993), 503–40, 531.

77. Richard Wright, *Native Son*, in *Native Son and "How Bigger Was Born"* (New York: HarperCollins, [1940]1993), 429.

78. See Abdul JanMohamed, *The Death-Bound-Subject: Richard Wright's Archaeology of Death* (Durham, NC: Duke University Press, 2005).

79. Wright, *Native Son*, 328.

80. Ibid., 477.

81. Ibid., 478.

82. Ibid., 480.

83. Ibid., 318.

84. Wright, "How 'Bigger' Was Born," 527.

85. Ibid., 527.

86. Wright, *Native Son*, 76.

CHAPTER 4

Sympathy and Poverty

John Marsh

On November 16, 1936, just two weeks after winning reelection, and perhaps feeling the pressure of an ongoing strike among tenant farmers in the South and egregious attacks on their civil liberties, President Franklin Delano Roosevelt convened a committee on what he called "farm tenancy." It was not just, as Roosevelt noted in his letter of instruction to Secretary of Agriculture Henry A. Wallace, that "the rapid increase of tenant farmers over the last half century" had violated, as Roosevelt put it, "the American ideal of owner-operated farms."[1] It was also that the increase in tenant farmers brought with it "soil depletion and declining living standards," which, Roosevelt warned, somewhat vaguely, "presents a challenge to national action."[2] Despite this initial vagueness, the document that the committee produced – *Farm Tenancy* – is one of the more useful summaries of what its authors (and Roosevelt) called "farm insecurity," which those not in thrall to New Deal jargon would simply call rural poverty.

By farm tenancy, Roosevelt and others meant those – tenants and sharecroppers – who lived and worked on a farm but did not own it. Instead, they contracted with a landlord who did. Although the distinctions could blur and differ from place to place, tenants usually paid rent on the land in advance and had most if not all of the tools and livestock needed to raise a crop. At the end of the season, they kept what they could get for the crops they had raised, less of course the rent they had paid on the land at the start of the season. Like tenants, sharecroppers did not own land, but as a rule they had neither the cash to pay rent nor the tools or livestock to raise a crop. Instead, at the beginning of the season, the owner of the land or a nearby merchant would loan them – at exorbitant interest rates – everything they needed to raise a crop, not just tools, livestock, seed, and fertilizer but food to live on as well. At the end of the season, by way of rent, sharecroppers would turn over a portion, usually half, of the crops they had raised to the landowner. In addition, they would surrender still more of the crop they had raised to the owner or merchant to repay the initial loan (plus interest) of everything (tools, livestock, seed, fertilizer, food) they had used to raise the crop. Although few envied the lot of tenants, next to share-croppers they at least had a chance. If tenants had a good harvest, they could turn a profit. Sharecroppers, by contrast, no matter how good the harvest, did well to end the season simply out of debt to their landlord or furnishing merchant.

Whether tenants or sharecroppers, the number of farmers who did not own their land was on the rise. In the late nineteenth century, the authors of the report calculated, one out of every four farmers was a tenant. By 1935, two out of every five were.[3] In total, nearly 3 million farmers did not own the land they farmed, with 40,000 added to their number every year.[4] Except for migratory laborers, those who worked for brief periods harvest-ing crops before moving on to the next harvest or the next crop, and who could be found everywhere but especially in the western states, the authors of *Farm Tenancy* acknowledged that farm tenancy and the resulting insecurity – read poverty – mostly occurred in the South, where two out of every three tenant farmers in the country lived.[5] Moreover, although the Midwest and West had their share of tenants, only in the South did the percentage of farmers who did not own their land exceed those who did. Of the 3.422 million farmers in the South, more than 1.831 million of them were tenants.[6] In the Cotton Belt states of Georgia, Tennessee, Alabama, Arkansas, and Mississippi, the rate of tenancy exceeded 60 percent and, in Mississippi, rose as high as 70 percent.[7]

The problem was not just that tenancy had increased and continued to increase, but the appalling poverty and problems – disease, illiteracy – that accompanied it. In a section entitled "The Erosion of Our Society," the authors of *Farm Tenancy* got as close to outright damnation as they would in the otherwise rhetorically muted document. "The extreme poverty of one-fifth to one-fourth of the farm population," the authors wrote, "reflects itself in a standard of living below any level of decency." They continued:

> Large families of tenants or croppers, or hired farm laborers, are living in houses of two or three rooms. The buildings are frequently of poor con-struction, out of alinement [*sic*], weather-beaten, and unsightly. The doors and windows are rarely screened. Often the roofs are leaky. The surroundings of such houses are bleak and unattractive. Many have no outside toilet, or, if one is available, it is highly unsanitary.
>
> Many of these families are chronically undernourished. They are readily subject to diseases. Pellagra, malaria, and the hookworm and other parasites

exact heavy tolls in life and energy. Suitable provision for maintaining health and treating disease among these families is lacking or inadequate in many localities.

   Clothing is often scarcely sufficient to afford protection to the body, much less to help maintain self-respect.[8]

Just to be clear, when the authors of the report note that many families have no outside toilet, they do not mean that families do not have indoor plumbing, but that they do not have an outhouse. They use the bushes.

   Unlike the problem of unemployment, which would decrease as economic prosperity returned, farm tenancy and its accompanying poverty, while made worse by the Depression, had also predated it and, in all likelihood, would outlast it. In other words, when it came to farm insecurity, especially in the South, something must be done, something beyond the ordinary New Deal measures to restore the national economy to prosperity *and* beyond earlier New Deal efforts, like the Agricultural Adjustment Act of 1933, to raise crop prices by limiting supply, which harmed as much as it helped farmers who did not own land. In essence, the authors of *Farm Tenancy* reasoned that if the problem was farmers who did not own land, the solution lay in helping farmers acquire land, which the federal government would accomplish through a series of reforms: low-interest loans to those capable of owning a farm now; aid to tenants who, with guidance and education from federal extension agents, could after a year or several years responsibly own a farm; and the resettlement of tenants currently on depleted land to more promising homesteads, where they too might eventually own a farm. Whereas now few landlords owned a majority of the land on which a majority of farmers scratched out an insufficient living, eventually, or so the authors of *Farm Tenancy* hoped, a majority of farmers would own their own farms, on which they would raise crops to eat and cash crops to sell. In short, the Jeffersonian ideal of prosperous, independent yeoman farmers would return.

   In order to lend urgency to the cause of farm tenancy, the authors turned to a rhetorical strategy – documentary photography – that in the coming years would assume more and more of a place in efforts to influence American attitudes toward poverty. That is, the authors of the report sought to put a face to the problem of rural poverty. After the section reprinting Official Documents, they included eight black-and-white photographs depicting the areas and people discussed in the report. One photograph, titled "The Home and Family of a Cropper in the Cotton Belt," shows three shoeless children, one smiling winsomely, standing in front of two grown women. One of the women has her eyes closed, and the other stares forcefully into the camera. All stand before a rotting cabin, though this one has screens on the window.

In all likelihood, this and the other photographs came from the files of the Historical Section of the Resettlement Administration, a New Deal agency that had already begun, in limited form, to undertake the reforms recommended by *Farm Tenancy*. In the Resettlement Administration, soon renamed the Farm Security Administration, the head of the Information Division, Roy Stryker, employed a handful of photographers – initially, Dorothea Lange, Walter Rothstein, Carl Mydans, Walker Evans, and Ben Shahn – to produce, in Stryker's words, "a pictorial documentation of our rural areas and rural problems."[9] As Cara Finnegan has argued, the photographs, distributed to newspapers and magazines, would win public and congressional support for New Deal programs in general and the sort of reforms proposed by the authors of *Farm Tenancy* in particular.[10]

The photographs taken by those employed by the Farm Security Administration embody the emotional contract that sought to shape American attitudes toward poverty during the Great Depression. Through words and, increasingly, through photographs, Americans could witness an injustice – rural poverty – that would otherwise have remained hidden from them. Informed of such injustices, they would sympathize with those subject to them and support the efforts of those institutions – in the case of rural poverty, the federal government or the Southern Tenant Farmers' Union – that sought to do something about them. In short, exposure – somewhat literally in the case of photographs – would equal sympathy would equal reform.

That formula lies behind much of the literature of social justice written during the 1930s, all the more so literature about sharecropping. The latter includes Sterling Brown's poem "Sharecroppers" and the stories collected in Richard Wright's *Uncle Tom's Children*, but especially those works that mixed text and photograph, like *Farm Tenancy* and, from the same period, Richard Wright's *Twelve Million Black Voices* and Erskine Caldwell and Margaret Bourke-White's 1937 collaboration *You Have Seen Their Faces*. Yet that formula, which predated the Great Depression but gained new urgency during it, has made works that treated rural poverty but broke with its emotional contract seem downright strange, if not, politically speaking, perverse. In this chapter, I follow writers – Erskine Caldwell, William Faulkner, and James Agee – who, while occasionally inviting Americans to feel the conventional emotions about poverty, also offered readers other, radically different ways to feel about the poor during the

Great Depression. I do so in order to complicate our understanding of the emotional life of the Great Depression, which, in retrospect, too often clusters around a few canonical emotions like despair (on the part of those brought low by the Depression) or sympathy (for those in despair). Of course, those emotions did appear during the decade, even predominate, but to understand the decade more fully, it helps to understand the range of emotions that characterized it. That said, I also follow these writers in their pursuit of alternative emotions because these other ways of feeling about poverty that they offer – hopelessness, fear, and awe – may have something useful to teach us about poverty, including whether the predictable emotions are the best ones to summon when we seek to do something about it.

I

When it comes to strange, possibly perverse novels about sharecropping, few can match Erskine Caldwell's 1932 novel *Tobacco Road*, one of the least sympathetic and therefore most disturbing books of the Great Depression. *Tobacco Road* concerns a family of Georgia tenant farmers, the Lesters, who no longer even count as tenant farmers since, for the past seven years, the man who owns their land, Captain John, has refused to loan them what they need to raise a crop. "There was," the narrator tells us, "no longer any profit in raising cotton."[11] Unable to borrow money elsewhere, or mercilessly taken advantage of by loan companies when he does, the patriarch of the family, Jeeter Lester, slowly starves, as does the rest of his family: Ada, his wife; Ellie May, his daughter; Dude, his son; and Mother Lester, the grandmother. Reluctant to give up on farming, his only passion, Jeeter refuses to move his family to the nearby cotton mills where they might, at least, find work and enough to eat. Instead, the Lesters scratch out a desperate life on depleted, hopeless land. The novel ends with Jeeter and Ada burned alive while they sleep in their house, consumed by the fire Jeeter sets to scorch his land in the vain hopes of raising a crop that season.

That synopsis makes *Tobacco Road* sound like a tragedy when, in fact, it reads more like a farce, albeit a deeply unsettling farce. In its review, the *New York Times* referred to the "grotesque humor" of the novel, though contemporary readers will likely find it infinitely more grotesque than humorous.[12] Indeed, the novel is hard to read. Not because it is difficult, in the modernist sense, but because Caldwell repeatedly shows human beings at their very worst. Jeeter marries off his twelve-year-old daughter,

Pearl, to a neighbor, Lov Bensey, who abuses her when she refuses to speak
or sleep with him. Although at various times Jeeter has enough money, he
never pays for the surgery that would fix the harelip that disfigures his older
daughter, Ellie May, which leaves her unmarriageable and sexually frustrated. Throughout the novel, the entire Lester family treats Mother
Lester, the grandmother, as an intolerable burden. She is shoved out of
the kitchen when the family sits down to eat what food there is, and worse
awaits. The teenage son, Dude, marries an older friend of the family, Sister
Bessie, a self-styled preacher who lacks a nose. Looking at her, the reader is
told, repeatedly, is "like looking down the end of a double-barreled
shotgun."[13] Dude marries Bessie because she promises to buy him a new
car, which they ruin within days, but not before they crash it into a wagon
driven by a "nigger," whom they leave helplessly dying by the side of the
road. "Niggers will get killed. Looks like there ain't no way to stop it,"
Jeeter observes with mild resignation.[14] The first set piece in the novel ends
when Lov, come to complain to Jeeter about Pearl and carrying a bag of
turnips, is seduced in the open by Ellie May, then set upon by the rest of
the family while Jeeter makes away with his bag of turnips. It only gets
worse from there. The novel reads like Green Acres as scripted by
Harmony Korine.

The climax of the novel – or the nadir, really – comes when Bessie
refuses to let Jeeter ride in her car because the load of wood he persuades
her to let him haul into town to sell puts holes in the back seat. Offended,
Jeeter tells Bessie to get off his land, where she and Dude had moved
because the roof of the house where Bessie lives had rotted away.
Infuriated, Bessie starts scratching Jeeter's face with her fingernails, where-
upon Ada rushes to her husband's defense. Bessie and Dude then jump in
the car to escape and accidentally back over Mother Lester, then run over
her again on their way out. The chapter quickly ends with no further
mention of Mother Lester. The next chapter, however, begins with Ada
and Jeeter callously peering down at her.

> [She] still lay there, her face mashed on the hard white sand. From the
> corner of the house, Ellie May looked at what had happened.
> "Is she dead yet?" Ada asked, looking at Jeeter. "She don't make no sound
> and she don't move. I don't reckon she could stay alive with her face all
> mashed like that."
> Jeeter did not answer her. He was too busy thinking of his hatred for
> Bessie to bother with anything else. He took another look at the grand-
> mother and walked across the yard and around to the back of the house. Ada

went to the porch and stood there looking back at Mother Lester several minutes, then she walked inside and shut the door.[15]

Only later in the chapter, after Lov has come to protest to Jeeter about Pearl running away, and Jeeter offers him Ellie May in her place, does Jeeter finally tend to Mother Lester.

> "Looks like she's dead," [Lov] said. "Is she dead, Jeeter?"
> Jeeter looked down and moved one of her arms with his foot.
> "She ain't stiff yet, but I don't reckon she'll live. You help me tote her out in the field and I'll dig a ditch to put her in."[16]

Notice that Jeeter does not dig a grave for Mother Lester, who may not even have died yet, but a ditch. Throughout the makeshift funeral, Jeeter continues to dicker with Luv about Ellie May, disposing of daughters as readily as he does mothers.

As these and other scenes suggest, Caldwell has thoroughly broken the emotional contract that usually rules how readers regard the pain of others. We get a brief glimpse into what Mother Lester feels as she lies on the ground, her body and face crushed, and therefore sympathize with her suffering. But any sympathy for her is overwhelmed by our horror at the Lester family. The entire family looks at Mother Lester's crushed body with indifference. Worse, those who appear so callous toward the pain of others – the Lesters – are starving, suffering tenant farmers for whom, in the 1930s, we would have been expected to feel the most sympathy. Yet with the possible exception of when Bessie and Dude go to town to buy a car and are ridiculed and taken advantage of by salesmen, at no point do we feel sympathy for the Lesters. They do not seem aware of their own suffering, and when they do – their hunger, for example – their suffering turns them so mean that it actively repels sympathy. In her classic account of the Southern poor white in fiction, Sylvia Jenkins Cook writes of the Lesters: "Caldwell creates in them people who are so intellectually debased and emotionally brutalized that we scarcely recognize them as being of our own species."[17] In short, the emotion Caldwell evokes in readers is not anger, sympathy, or even pity, but despair, hopelessness, or perhaps disgust.

Why would Caldwell do this? Why make his characters, whose counterparts in reality suffered horribly, look irredeemably repulsive? Although he sympathized with the plight of farm tenants, Caldwell did not – as his fellow documenter of the Southern poor white James Agee would shortly be accused – believe that "a sure and simple virtue" grows out of "hard, unlovely poverty."[18] Rather, Caldwell appears to have believed very much the opposite. Poverty does not ennoble people but degrades them, a belief that seems at least as plausible – and politically relevant – as its opposite. True, Caldwell may have exaggerated the extent to which poverty degrades. The Lesters have no redeeming features whatsoever. But that exaggeration seems no more harmful than the exaggerated portrait of total innocence and undeserved suffering that characterized many sympathetic accounts of the poor during the Great Depression.

If one wanted to rescue Caldwell still further, one could argue that he expects readers to transfer the horror they feel for the Lesters to the system that has made them so. In *You Have Seen Their Faces*, published in 1937, just five years after *Tobacco Road*, Caldwell charges "farm tenancy, and particularly sharecropping" with making the white tenant farmer "wasteful and careless," "bestial," "cruel and inhuman."[19] "The institution of share-cropping does things to men as well as to land," Caldwell concludes. "Plantation and tenant-farm owners alike are to be held responsible, and in the end to be called upon to answer for the degeneration of man as well as for the rape of the soil in the South."[20] Admittedly, asking readers to shift their horror from the Lesters in particular to the institution of share-cropping in general may ask more from them than they can give, especially since most readers will simply want to put the novel away and wipe its characters out of their mind as quickly as possible. But one cannot do that easily. Like scenes from certain horror movies, one cannot unwatch or, in this case, unread the Lesters. They remain to haunt. Still, if one wants to speak in terms of politics, that haunting may accomplish as much good – as much urgency toward reform – as a more conventional approach built around sympathy for innocent victimhood.

II

As many critics have observed, William Faulkner could do "grotesque humor" of the *Tobacco Road* sort as well as anyone. Recall that Anse in *As I Lay Dying*, published in 1930, believes that "if he ever sweats, he will die" or, in that same novel, the medically dubious decision to set Cash's broken leg in cement.[21]

As critics have also pointed out, though, Faulkner could generate incredible sympathy for his characters too. Indeed, few moments in American literature move me quite as much as when Dewey Dell, impregnated by a farm laborer, Lafe, finally arrives in Jefferson and is taken advantage of by a drug store clerk, MacGowan, who fools her into having sex with him by promising that doing so – in addition to some bogus medicine he offers her – will rid her of her pregnancy.

To be sure, Dewey Dell is not the victim of a ruthless landlord, as in most sharecropper dramas from the 1930s, and the Bundrens may not even technically qualify as tenants. Still, her ignorance – of human anatomy, of basic science, and of human nature – and profound vulnerability, which at least in part result from her poverty, leave her deeply exposed to the rest of the world. Even so, even after MacGowan rapes her and gives her the sham medicine, she maintains some dignity. "It ain't going to work," she says immediately afterward, in the chapter narrated by her younger brother, Vardaman. "That son of a bitch."[22]

As Jenkins Cook notes, and the example of Dewey Dell confirms, Faulkner accomplishes something in *As I Lay Dying* that few had before him: he humanizes the poor. "Poverty is at every point a compelling and obvious factor in the Bundrens' lives," Jenkins Cook observes, "but Faulkner does not permit it to interfere in any direct way with the kinds of moral decisions the various members of the family make; idleness, suffering, and victimization typify but do not explain or dismiss them."[23] The problem with humanizing the poor, however, especially when you could do it as well as Faulkner could, lay in Faulkner's growing antipathy to the New Deal. No one knows when exactly Faulkner began to resent efforts on the part of the federal government to aid poor farmers, but it had certainly fully formed by 1941, when he published the anti–New Deal short story "The Tall Men" in the *Saturday Evening Post*.[24] In all likelihood, his antipathy developed much earlier. In any case, as the 1930s progressed, and the plight of the sharecropper gathered national attention, by humanizing the rural poor, by showing them to be independent of yet still victims of their poverty, and thereby generating sympathy on their behalf, Faulkner risked licensing the sort of federal antipoverty programs he deeply resented.

That risk provides the context for one of Faulkner's most accomplished short stories, "Barn Burning," published in *Harper's* in 1939. Although set in the last decade of the nineteenth century, the story reads like a parable of 1930s debates about the justice or injustice of sharecropping. Faulkner tells the story through the eyes of Colonel Sartoris ("Sarty") Snopes, the ten-year-old son of Abner Snopes, a former Civil War soldier and horse trader turned sharecropper. As the story opens, Abner Snopes stands trial for burning the barn of his landlord, which he has in fact done. Hoping to prove that Snopes did it, but otherwise lacking proof, the landlord calls Sarty to testify. For reasons that Faulkner does not make clear, Sarty is not

questioned, but the possibility sets the central theme of the story into
motion. Sarty is pulled between loyalty to his family and loyalty to flawed
but nevertheless compelling ideals like law, fairness, or, perhaps slightly less
inspiring, property.

In a crucial scene after the trial, as the Snopes leave one farm for another,
Abner confronts his son:

> "You were fixing to tell them. You would have told him." He didn't answer.
> His father struck him with the flat of his hand on the side of the head, hard
> but without heat, exactly as he had struck the two mules at the store, exactly
> as he would strike either of them with any stick in order to kill a horse fly, his
> voice still without heat or anger: "You're getting to be a man. You got to
> learn. You got to learn to stick to your own blood or you ain't going to have
> any blood to stick to you. Do you think either of them, any man there this
> morning would? Don't you know all they wanted was a chance to get at me
> because they knew I had them beat? Eh?" Later, twenty years later, he was to
> tell himself, "If I had said they wanted only truth, justice, he would have hit
> me again." But now he said nothing. He was not crying. He just stood there.
> "Answer me," his father said.
> "Yes," he whispered. His father turned.[25]

On the one hand, as when earlier at the trial Sarty refers to the landlord and
the justice of the peace not just as his father's enemy but as his enemy too,
Sarty identifies with his father. (All the more so when he attacks a boy
outside the store who calls his father a "Barn Burner!") On the other hand,
Sarty can also sympathize with the landlord whom Abner has wronged by
destroying his property, and the justice of the peace – aptly named – who
seeks to restore the justice and peace that his father has disturbed. Indeed,
when the story propels forward twenty years, and the narrator relates what
Sarty "was to tell himself," the divide between father and son – and
between family and, say, the law – suddenly widens. Yet his father recognizes no such thing as the law or truth or justice; or, rather, his father
believes that these abstractions merely paper over other truths and injustices, including but not limited to his own exploitation as a sharecropper.
In his slightly paranoid way, Abner believes that those in power – the
landlord, the justice of the peace who tries him – only want "a chance to get
at me." Abner divides the world into us and them, and when his son
abandons him, or would have abandoned him, he feels, perhaps rightly,
betrayed.

When Sarty invokes ideals like truth and justice, he may prejudice
readers against his father. Yet Faulkner goes to some lengths to portray
Abner as a heroic – or, at least, an intimidating – figure. The first words out

of his mouth are a curse. Found innocent by the justice of the peace but told to leave the area nonetheless, Abner responds, "his voice cold, harsh, level, without emphasis: 'I aim to. I don't figure to stay in a country among people who . . . ' he said something unprintable and vile, addressed to no one."[26] Later, Sarty refers to the "wolflike independence and even courage" of his father, and the narrator often describes how Abner looks, with his "harsh, level stare beneath the shaggy, graying, irascible brows."[27] Even his attitude toward fire – "as the one weapon for the preservation of integrity" – is, in a way, equally venerable.[28] Who can argue with integrity?

Abner's ferocious insistence on his integrity continues after he and his family arrive at their new homestead, where he laconically announces, "I reckon I'll have a word with the man that aims to begin to-morrow owning me body and soul for the next eight months."[29] We know from Thomas Sutpen in *Absalom, Absalom!* that poor whites should enter mansions in the back – and how doing so may inspire a lifetime of resentment and ambition on their part – but Abner, insisting on his equality, enters the mansion of his landlord through the front. Worse, or better, depending on your perspective, he has deliberately stepped in horseshit on the way and proceeds to grind his filthy boot into an immaculate white rug in the entryway. In doing so, he tries to break the spell of admiration that young Sarty has for the mansion and its opulence: "'Pretty and white, ain't it?,' he said. 'That's sweat. Nigger sweat. Maybe it ain't white enough yet to suit him. Maybe he wants to mix some white sweat with it.'"[30] As statements of racial solidarity go, this one leaves a lot to desire. Nevertheless, coming from a former Confederate soldier – albeit one less than fully committed to the cause – this observation reads like a surprisingly acute perception into the racial and economic dynamics of the accumulation of wealth in the South before and after the Civil War.

Primed to resent landlords and sympathize with sharecroppers, as most readers would have been in 1939, at this point in the story Faulkner instead invites us to admire Abner, especially since we never learn the details of why he set fire to the first barn. Perhaps, as the story suggests, he believes it really is to preserve his integrity. In any event, while some may sympathize with Abner – he has traded the independence of horse-trading for the demeaning dependence of sharecropping – he does not make it easy to sympathize with him, for at no point does he exude despair, the emotion sharecroppers supposedly feel at all turns. Rather, Abner illustrates the emotions other than despair that, in Faulkner's rendering, sharecropping and poverty also inspire, namely, pride and rage. Far from pitying Abner, then, readers may respect him. After the soiled rug has been dropped at his cabin for him to clean, Sarty observes his father "at the door, framed against that shabbiness, as he had been against that other bland perfection, impervious to either."[31] The "bland perfection" here is the mansion, and the point seems to be that Abner, like Dewey Dell, does not let his poverty or lack of social status define him. He is his own man. The difference, in keeping with Faulkner's reluctance to generate too much sympathy for him, is that, unlike with Dewey Dell, at no point do we pity Abner, though we may well fear him.

For all but a few readers, however, our admiration for Abner soon enough dissipates when we see how little it takes to stoke his rage. Ordered to clean the white rug he has soiled, Abner instead takes a sharp rock to it, leaving it with "long, water-cloudy scoriations resembling the sporadic course of a lilliputian mowing machine."[32] Fined $100 by his landlord, Abner sues him and gets the fine reduced. Even so, back at home, he orders Sarty to get a can of oil. He intends to burn another barn.

To continue to admire Abner after this decision, one must believe, with Proudhon, that property is theft, and that when Abner burns barns he does not do so out of a "ravening and jealous rage," as the narrator observes at one point, but out of purer political motives. Some – notably critic Ted Atkinson – can sustain that belief, but more readers will see Abner as Faulkner invites them to see him: as someone disfigured by his pride and rage, someone whose violence is unwarranted and therefore unpardonable.[33]

Just as our admiration for Abner diminishes, however, our admiration for Sarty develops. Sarty recognizes his father for what he is – or for what Faulkner represents him to be: an unhinged, egoistic threat to his family and the social order. Before Abner can burn another barn, Sarty breaks free and warns their landlord. Running from the mansion, Sarty is overtaken by the landlord on horseback and, in the distance, hears three shots, which, in all likelihood, mean his father, caught setting fire to the barn, has been killed. Here Faulkner might tempt readers to sympathize with and even pity Sarty, forced, by an unjust system of sharecropping, to choose between loyalty to a father damaged by that system and an irresistible set of socially sanctioned ideals like truth, justice, and peace. Yet as soon as we start to sympathize with Sarty, he too, like his father, turns into his own man, and we start to admire rather than pity him. Fleeing the country, setting out on his own, the last lines of the story – "He did not look back" – similarly cast him as a man beyond his years.[34] Although Sarty may feel some guilt about betraying his father, Faulkner knows – and invites readers to believe – that he has made the mature, ethical decision. His father was not a brave cavalryman in the Civil War, as Sarty tells himself at the end of the story. He had no loyalties to anyone but himself. Sarty has done the right thing. Once again, Faulkner has humanized the poor, shown them as resentful or pulled between competing and mutually exclusive loyalties, though unlike in *As I Lay Dying*, he does so in a way that does not invite sympathy or, worse, reform.

III

In the middle years of the 1930s, *Fortune* magazine had a mostly frivolous "Life and Circumstances" series devoted to documenting the ordinary lives of ordinary Americans. In the summer of 1936, the poet and staff writer for the magazine, James Agee, accepted an assignment to produce an entry in the series on cotton tenant farmers. He and Walker Evans, a photographer on loan from the Resettlement Administration, traveled to rural Alabama, found a suitably representative family – and two nearby ones – and spent four weeks living with them. Afterward, Agee wrote an unwieldy article – the recently rediscovered "Cotton Tenants: Three Families" – which the editors of *Fortune* asked him to revise and, when he refused, eventually returned to him to do with as he pleased.[35] In the year that followed, Agee turned a long but manageable article distinguished by its touches of poetic language and moral outrage into a 400-page meditation on the political, philosophical, and cosmological significance of three families of tenant farmers. Drafting off the success of Erskine Caldwell and Margaret Bourke-White's *You Have Seen Their Faces*, Agee and Evans eventually found a publisher for the book. Despite positive reviews – including one from Lionel Trilling calling it "the most realistic and most important moral effort of our generation" – it sold poorly and quickly went out of print.[36]

As Trilling recognized, the book was nominally about the lives of three Alabama tenant families. But its moral importance arose from another question: "How may we – 'we' being the relatively fortunate middle class that reads books and experiences emotions – how may we feel about the – and the word itself proclaims the difficulty – underprivileged?"[37] In the course of the book, Agee tries out a number of possible answers to that question, rejecting none, really, except the one we might expect. From the start of the book, and renewed throughout, Agee attacks not just those who would sympathize with his cotton tenant families but with the concept of sympathy itself. Indeed, the word appears on the – admittedly lengthy – list of suspect "anglosaxon monosyllables" that Agee prints at the end of the book.[38] Of all writers during the 1930s, Agee makes the strongest and most self-conscious brief against sympathy.

That is not to say, of course, that Agee does not sympathize with his subjects or, through his sympathy, occasionally lead readers to a similar emotion. Early in the book, for example, Agee describes the plight of Emma, daughter of one of the tenant farmers and sister of another, as she reluctantly prepares to leave her family to join a husband who treats her badly and whom she does not love. (Agee's speech to her, which begins "nobody has a right to be unhappy, or to live in a way that makes them unhappy," is one of the most moving episodes in the book.)[39] Moreover, in the second and third parts of that section, Agee speaks in the voice of Annie Mae, the wife in the tenant family whom he knows and likes the best, whose refrain – "How was it we were caught?" – suggests the depths of her despair and hopelessness.[40] In addition, Agee tenderly describes the literally crippling work the families perform, and the humiliations the children absorb at school because of their poverty, and these too break your heart.

Yet before, during, and after nearly every incident or description in the book that might invite sympathy, Agee warns against it. He sets the keynote in the Preamble, when he offers this ironic précis of the book and its audience:

> [T]his is a book about "sharecroppers," and is written for all those who have a soft place in their hearts for the laughter and tears inherent in poverty viewed at a distance, and especially those who can afford the retail price; in the hope that the reader will be edified, and may feel kindly disposed toward any well-thought-out liberal effort to rectify the unpleasant situation down South, and will somewhat better and more guiltily appreciate the next good meal he eats; and in the hope, too, that he will recommend this little book to really sympathetic friends, in order that our publishers may at least cover their investment and that just the merest perhaps) some kindly thought may be turned our way, and a little of your money fall to poor little us.[41]

The passage suggests a number of reasons why Agee has come to distrust sympathy as much as he does. To start, he fears that sympathy may oversimplify why people feel sorry for others. That is, sympathy may arise as much out of self-interest as it does out of genuine interest in the well-being of others. Obviously, this fear accounts for his own, recurring concern that he might in any way profit from – whether in terms of money or reputation – his "parading the nakedness, disadvantage, and humiliation of these lives before another group of human beings."[42] But Agee also fears that not just writers but readers might profit from the parade too.

By reading of human suffering, they get to feel like the sort of person who sympathizes with others, who seeks to be "edified," and who as a result appreciates what they have. That is not to say one should not do or feel these things, only that they complicate what many would prefer to think of as a simple, purely altruistic emotion, and Agee has set himself the task of complicating all such simplicities.

In addition, Agee worries about the political implications of sympathy. A carelessly written book may lead people to "feel kindly disposed toward any well-thought-out liberal effort to rectify the unpleasant situation down South." That may not sound sinister, but what if the situation down South resists or exceeds those liberal efforts? In that case, sympathy, by offering easy answers, may do more harm than good. In a long passage discussing tenant houses, Agee writes:

> The tenant house as a shell is, then, a thing to itself, created by the tenant system, but having much in common with southern company houses in general. But beyond that, to talk as if tenantry as such were responsible, as is often done or seldom guarded against, is dishonest or ridiculous, or in any case deceptive and dangerous. It is dangerous because by wrong assignment of causes it persuades that the "cure" is possible through means which in fact would have little effect save to delude the saviors into the comfortable idea that nothing more needed doing, or even looking-to. It is deceptive because ... these homes have more than less in common with the homes of the whole poorest class of *owning* cotton farmers.[43]

The "economic source," he adds, "is nothing so limited as the tenant system but is the whole world-system of which tenantry is one modification; and there are in the people themselves, and in the land and climate, other sources quite as powerful but less easy to define, far less to go about curing; and they are, to suggest them too bluntly, psychological, semantic, traditional, perhaps glandular."[44] In other words, as part of the whole world-system, tenantry may change, but the abuses it gives rise to will not change save the changing of the whole world-system. To be sure, well-thought-out liberal efforts of the sort suggested by the authors of *Farm Tenancy* – having the government furnish sharecroppers at no interest or helping tenants acquire land – will help at the margins, but they will not fundamentally alter the conditions that inspired our sympathy in the first place. (Unless, that is, out of our desire to be done with the "unpleasant situation down South," we deceive ourselves that, as Agee puts it, "nothing more needed doing.") In other words, if you think tenantry is the problem, Agee suggests, look at the lives of those who own their own farms rather than rent them, or those who live in company housing in the nearby mill towns, and say whether you would trade places with them. The problem, that is, goes beyond sharecroppers. Even if it did not, sympathy tends to narrow our view of cause and effect.

Finally, in addition to simplifying motives and solutions, Agee fears sympathy may simplify poverty or, at least, those who live in it. In the first passage quoted earlier, Agee puts "sharecroppers" in quotation marks not just because by the time he writes the Preamble they have become a familiar cause, but because thanks to *You Have Seen Their Faces* and other works, the mere mention of sharecroppers sets off a whole preexisting, prepackaged discourse of the poor best captured in the phrase "the laughter and tears inherent in poverty." As Agee shows, his families do occasionally laugh and cry, but from his view nothing inheres about poverty, no essence precedes its individual existences. Only poverty "viewed at a distance," which viewing it through the lens of sympathy may encourage, allows one to believe that there is much that is permanent, essential, or even characteristic about it.

Elsewhere, Agee refers to sympathy as one of the "various possible reflexes" that readers may have for and while reading the book, and once sympathy becomes a reflex, it ceases to respond adequately to its object, other human beings. In the Notes and Appendices section of the book, for example, Agee reprints a fluff article about Margaret Bourke-White that appeared in the *New York Post* following the publication of *You Have Seen Their Faces*. Discussing Erskine Caldwell's new play, *Journeyman*, which takes place in a church for poor whites in the South, Bourke-White observes:

> The Negro churches are not, somehow, so shocking, because you think of Negroes as being actors and emotional, but with the white people the whole business is so sordid and desperate and out of place. It isn't as though the church played any role, as we know religion. It's just a place where people go to shout and scream and roll on the floor. They are so beaten down and their lives are so drab and barren and lonely that they have nothing. This terrible thing Sunday is their only release.[45]

Many people who write about *Let Us Now Praise Famous Men* follow Agee in making Caldwell and, especially, Bourke-White, into villains, and I do not want to pile on, especially since, as I said earlier, their approach has merit. Still, Bourke-White, who had a chance to view poverty not just at a distance but up close – or through a camera lens, anyway – should know better than that the poor "have nothing." No one doubts Bourke-White's sympathy for sharecroppers, or her desire to do something for them, but her sympathy for them – as may sympathy in general – reduces them to their suffering and leads her to believe nonsense such as the poor "are so beaten down and their lives are so drab and barren and lonely that they have nothing." A decent, perhaps less sympathetic artist would look harder for what they do have.

By contrast, Agee devotes the better part of his book to expanding on those who suffer from poverty, not in observing what they do not have but dilating on what they do. Agee emphasizes over and over again not what makes the members of his tenant families representative – of whites or blacks or of their class – but what makes them specific. Early in the book, he speaks of their "irreparable, unrepeatable exis-tences," meaning both that they will not get to repeat their lives but also that no other human being will repeat them.[46] They are unique. Not "one of these persons is ever quite to be duplicated," Agee writes later in the book, "nor replaced, nor has it ever quite had precedent."[47] "Each of you," he addresses the members of the tenant families directly, "is a creature which has never in all time existed before and which shall never in all time exist again and which is not quite like any other."[48] Moreover, to withhold those "specifications," Agee believes, "I could but betray you still worse."[49]

This emphasis on human specificity leads to the emotion Agee offers readers in place of the now discredited sympathy. To rephrase Trilling, how should we feel about the underprivileged? Not love, exactly, as William Stott, in his influential study of documentary expression in the 1930s describes it, though Agee does insist how much he loves the tenant families and how much he desires their love in turn. Rather, I think Agee wants us to feel awe and, at times, sorrow for his tenant families. Awe that all the forces of the universe have conspired to make this world, and these unprecedented people in it, and sorrow at all that the world subjects them to, the shaping and damaging – what Agee calls the "world's bombard-ment" – some of which can be rectified, but most of which cannot.[50] Hence the phrase that Agee offers early on to describe the true subject of his book: "an independent inquiry into certain normal predicaments of human divinity."[51] We are to feel awe in the face of human divinity, but also sorrow at the predicaments that habitually afflict it. Rarely, if ever, though, are we to feel sympathy, which, unlike sorrow, implies a possible end to those predicaments.

IV

In July 1937, just months after Roosevelt forwarded *Farm Tenancy* to Congress, that body passed the Bankhead Jones Farm Tenant Act, which among other provisions would assist tenant farmers in purchasing family-sized farms. Earlier versions of the bill called for $1 billion in funding, but the final version set aside just tens of millions of dollars annually, which greatly limited its influence. No matter. In 1946, Congress killed the program altogether. All told, the agency made 44,300 loans, far fewer than its original supporters or the authors of *Farm Tenancy* had hoped.[52]

Despite its limited success, the problem that Bankhead Jones and its early supporters sought to address – farm tenancy – all but disappeared over the next decade, not because of mass ownership of farms, as Roosevelt and the authors of *Farm Tenancy* had hoped, but because of agricultural mechanization. By the late 1920s and early 1930s, John Deere and International Harvester had perfected the general-purpose tractor, which made it far easier for farmers to till soil and plant crops on a much larger scale. Still, someone needed to harvest the crop – that is, pick the cotton – so the influence of tractors remained less than it would otherwise. All that changed in 1944, though, with the appearance of the International Harvester cotton picker, which, together with tractors, made tenant farmers completely redundant.[53] Indeed, the cotton picker made family-sized farms, whether tenant or owner operated, all but redundant too. From that point forward, scale and efficiency mattered, as they never had before.

By 1944, the *annus mirabilis* of the cotton picker, many tenant farmers – and the sons of tenant farmers – had been drafted into the Second World War, while others had migrated to the cities for jobs in factories that turned out material for the war. Few returned to sharecropping after the war, and even those who did would not last long. Of course, they would face other challenges, and many remained in poverty. (Here Agee was right: the problem was not just sharecropping.) Still, by the 1950s, the days of tenant farming had largely passed, which few, not even Agee, had anticipated, and fewer still mourned.

The eclipse of tenant farming makes the literature of sharecropping more of an artifact of history than it otherwise would be. Nevertheless, that literature offers readers the opportunity to consider the by no means simple or easy relationship among literature, sympathy, and poverty. In truth, and despite the criticisms that Caldwell, Faulkner, and Agee indirectly or directly level at it, when it comes to poverty, we probably need more and not less sympathy, as much as that sounds like a liberal truism. Moreover, some of the strategies these writers adopt when they challenge sympathy – especially Agee's focus on human specificity and how it qualifies individuals for far better treatment than they receive – may actually aid in generating that sympathy.

Even so, like these writers, I have my doubts about the role that literature can or should play in generating sympathy, especially since sympathy and its foundation in empathy remain so tied to affect and the immediate, which often disappears when we put the book down or allow our attention to wander, as Agee well knew. Even if you have more optimism about the relationship between literature and sympathy, though, or between sympathy and poverty in general, these writers revealed the liabilities of sympathy, where it – and those who cultivate it, whether in themselves or others – may go wrong, or, at the least, how the emotion is far more complex and difficult than the conventional wisdom would suggest. Of course, the best literature, like *Let Us Now Praise Famous Men*, has it both ways: generating sympathy for those who suffered, and keeping us honest about the very real limits of that emotion.

Notes

1. United States, *Farm Tenancy: Report of the President's Committee* (Washington, DC: Government Printing Office, 1937), 25.
2. Ibid., 25.
3. Ibid., iv.
4. Ibid., iv.
5. Ibid., 35.
6. Ibid., 35.
7. Ibid., 89.
8. Ibid., 7.
9. Quoted in Blanche M. G. Linden, "Photography," in *Encyclopedia of the Great Depression*, vol. 2 (New York: Thomson Gale, 2004), 756.
10. See Cara Finnegan, *Picturing Poverty: Print Culture and FSA Photographs* (Washington, DC: Smithsonian Institution Scholarly Press, 2003).
11. Erskine Caldwell, *Tobacco Road* (New York: Grosset and Dunlap, 1932), 82.
12. "'Tobacco Road' and Other Recent Works of Fiction." *New York Times*, Feb. 21, 1932.
13. Caldwell, *Tobacco Road*, 58.
14. Ibid., 159.
15. Ibid., 215.
16. Ibid., 225.
17. Sylvia Jenkins Cook, *From Tobacco Road to Route 66: The Southern Poor White in Fiction* (Chapel Hill: University of North Carolina Press, 1976), 67.

18. See Lionel Trilling, "Greatness with One Fault in It," *Kenyon Review* 4.1 (1941), 102.
19. Margaret Bourke-White and Erskine Caldwell, *You Have Seen Their Faces* (new edn) (Athens: University of Georgia Press, 1995), 19.
20. Trilling, "Greatness," 20.
21. William Faulkner, *As I Lay Dying* (new edn) (New York: Vintage, 1991), 17.
22. Ibid., 251.
23. Jenkins Cook, *From Tobacco Road*, 42.
24. William Faulkner, "The Tall Man," *Saturday Evening Post*, May 31, 1941, 14–19.
25. William Faulkner, "Barn Burning," *Selected Short Stories* (New York: Modern Library, 2012), 8–9.
26. Ibid., 5.
27. Ibid., 7, 9.
28. Ibid., 8.
29. Ibid., 9.
30. Ibid., 13.
31. Ibid., 13.
32. Ibid., 14.
33. See Ted Atkinson, *Faulkner and the Great Depression:* Aesthetics, Ideology, and Cultural Politics (Athens: University of Georgia Press, 2006).
34. Faulkner, "Barn Burning," 26.
35. James Agee and Walker Evans, *Cotton Tenants: Three Families* (New York: Melville House, 2014).
36. Trilling, "Greatness," 102.
37. Ibid., 99.
38. Agee and Evans, *Famous Men*, 404.
39. Ibid., 59.
40. Ibid., 80.
41. Ibid., 11–12.
42. Ibid., 5.
43. Ibid., 182.
44. Ibid., 182.
45. Ibid., 400.
46. Ibid., 7.
47. Ibid., 51.
48. Ibid., 88.
49. Ibid., 89.
50. Ibid., 256.
51. Ibid., x.
52. Paul E. Mertz, "Bankhead Jones Farm Tenant Act of 1937," in *Encyclopedia of the Great Depression*, vol. 1. (New York: Thomson Gale, 2004), 87–88.
53. Neil Fligstein, *Going North: Migration of Blacks and Whites from the South 1900–1950* (New York: Academic Press, 1981), 147–49.

CHAPTER 5

Black Culture at Home and Abroad

Etsuko Taketani

In his prize-winning book *Black Manhattan* (1930), James Weldon Johnson illustrated the story of Harlem with black-and-white maps that depict its expanding "boundaries." Johnson's maps of the "black metropolis in the heart of the great Western white metropolis" are not merely an example of this illustration, a visual representation of the Harlem real estate market from 1925 to 1930; they render the idea of a nation within a nation , or a "black nation" within a "white nation," with finite, if not solid, boundaries.[1] By the same indication, George S. Schuyler's immensely popular work of pulp fiction, *Black Empire* (1936–38), the story of Harlem physician Henry Belsidus, who plotted a black revolution inside and outside the nation's borders, would have been impossible without cartography. In this story, Belsidus renders the spectacle of "an international race war," deploying "maps" – in regions ranging from the United States, Liberia, and Africa to the entire world – that enable his "Black Internationale" organization to execute an arsenal of strategies to destroy European colonialism and establish a Black Empire.[2] In each case, the use of maps, whether as a paratext (Johnson) or a narrative prop (Schuyler), is bound up with the ways in which African Americans interpret spaces, both domestic and global, as a whole text to redefine their place within those spaces.

In many ways, 1930s African American culture is a story of geographic imaginings in transition – a transition that the Great Depression, as a *national* and *global* phenomenon, effected. In the United States, a decade-long financial crisis, marked at its beginning by the Wall Street Crash, and President Franklin Roosevelt's New Deal domestic programs in response to it, affected numerous aspects of African Americans' relation to the nation.[3] African American writers who emerged both as subjects and as authors of a geographic knowledge of the nation is of particular interest for the purposes of this chapter. In the 1920s, African American arts and letters had a symbolic focal point, as suggested by the geographical metaphor

"Harlem Renaissance." However, African American writers of the New Deal era, hired as "federal" authors across the nation, inscribed blackness on America's lily-white image of itself beyond Harlem. The catalyzing force was the prominent role that the federal government came to assume as a cultural producer through four arts projects under the Works Progress Administration (WPA), in particular the Federal Writers' Project (FWP), whose core undertaking was the American Guide Series.[4] The guides officially sanctioned tourism as the nation's industry and as "a ritual of citizenship,"[5] but one significant consequence for black America was that African American writers, for the first time in their history, made inroads into the production of the geographic knowledge of the nation, which was often a function of state power as it defined what counted as legitimate knowledge and who could produce such knowledge. Among African Americans hired as federal writers, both on public relief rolls and otherwise, were Sterling A. Brown in Washington, DC; Claude McKay, Ralph Ellison, Dorothy West, and Richard Bruce Nugent in New York; Zora Neale Hurston in Florida; Arna Bontemps in Illinois; Chester Himes in Ohio; and Richard Wright, who worked at different times in Illinois and New York, where "the intellectual and artistic lines between the Communist Party and the Federal Writers' Project were blurred."[6]

The FWP (1935–43) demonstrated the New Deal's liberal interest in mapping and narrating the diversity of the nation and its citizenry and landscape. The American Guide Series, a comprehensive set of travel guides to the forty-eight states, the District of Columbia, Alaska, and New York City, was a showcase of the FWP's orchestrated attempt to capture American culture and the voices of various ethnic groups and to "position America as a modern folk nation."[7] Sterling Brown accepted the appointment as national editor of the Negro Affairs division of the FWP, and himself contributed an essay, "The Negro in Washington," to *Washington: City and Capital* (1937), in which he told the story of black Washingtonians and their "profound influence" on the destiny of the nation's capital, which had been created between the two slave-holding states of Maryland and Virginia. While "Benjamin Banneker, a Negro mathematician ... appointed by George Washington to serve on Major L'Enfant's commission for the surveying and laying out of the city" is symbolic of African American participation in the establishment of the nation's capital, the paradox of "the profession of democracy and the practice of slavery" left its marks on the Washington cityscape. In the nineteenth century, "William Wells Brown, in *Clotel*, the first novel by a Negro," captured this paradox by having the title character "jump into the Potomac to escape slave catchers." Sterling Brown's essay closes with a claim to contemporary African American status and belonging as "a citizen," not "a ward."[8]

In New York City, Richard Bruce Nugent, one of the more openly gay members of the Harlem Renaissance, wrote biographical vignettes of black personalities for the FWP. "Gloria Swanson" (a Mr. Winston) is about a celebrated "chocolate-brown" drag queen. "A perennial winner at the 'drags' in Chicago," he came to Harlem "at a time when 'male' and 'female' impersonation was at a peak as night club entertainment" and "became and remained queen of them all" until the intervention of "Mayor La Guardia's police."[9] Jamaican-born author Claude McKay found rich material through the FWP Harlem project, drawing on which he wrote *Harlem: Negro Metropolis* (1940). Portraying the social geography of Harlem, "the Negro capital of the world," McKay depicted Father Divine and cultists, Madame C. J. Walker (who "revolutionized Negro Beauty Culture") and businessmen, numbers (a gambling game) as "the most flourishing clandestine industry," and Marcus Garvey and politicians, while condemning the Communists for overrunning Harlem and the New York Writers' Project. The Communists, he quips, "injected the poison of Segregation" with an allegation that "the Negro writers were segregated on the project" though "some of us preferred [special research work], because the facts we unearthed were of intrinsic value to those of us who were writing about Negro life in our off-project time."[10] McKay lost his job at the FWP in 1939 "after a new rule barred aliens from such employment" – a dismissal that he ascribed to "Communist animosity."[11]

With the John Reed Club – a leftist cultural organization founded after the stock market crash, whose Chicago chapter Richard Wright had joined – disbanded by the Communist Party in 1935, the FWP proved pivotal in launching Wright's fledgling writing career. Wright got a job with the Illinois Writers' Project, where he was promoted to a supervisor position, and subsequently transferred, as he had hoped, to the New York Writers' Project. Although he recalls it as the time when "I tried to earn my bread by writing guidebooks,"[12] the FWP afforded him the opportunity to write his own work. Wright's autobiographical sketch "The Ethics of Living Jim Crow" was published in *American Stuff: An Anthology of Prose and Verse by Members of the Federal Writers' Project* (1937), a collection of the best off-project-hours works whose social realism depicted "the American scene to the life."[13] Likewise, Wright's first published book, *Uncle Tom's Children* (1938), a collection of short novellas, "came through the WPA publishing machine"[14] ("Fire and Cloud," one of the stories, won first prize in *Story* magazine's contest, which was open to all writers associated with the FWP, and the entire collection was published by Harper and Brothers). After his transfer to the creative work program, which was "effectively a fellowship," of the New York Writers' Project, Wright began serious work on what would become *Native Son* (1940), the first novel by an African American writer to become a Book-of-the-Month Club selection.[15] As Henry G. Alsberg – national director of the FWP – phrased it, Wright was "the most promising new writer that the Federal Writers' Project has turned up."[16]

On the route linking African American folklore to the American landscape in the American Guide Series, there was no better guide than Zora Neale Hurston in the Florida FWP. She collected folklore, added her vignettes of African American lore to "the tours section of the Florida guidebook," and contributed extensively to a proposed volume, *The Florida Negro.*[17] *Florida: A Guide to the Southernmost State* (1939), embellished with a highway tour map on the front endpaper, describes US 90 as an east–west route passing through important landmarks including "[Negroes'] mythical cities and countries" – Diddy-Wah-Diddy, Beluthahatchie, Heaven, and West Hell – whose folkloric descriptions came out of Hurston's pen.[18] The tour of US 17, a north–south route, takes a side trip "right from Maitland on a paved road to EATONVILLE," which is "the birthplace and home of Zora Neale Hurston (1903–), and the locale of her novel, *Their Eyes Were Watching God* (1937)." Hurston flavors "Eatonville in her eyes" with an African American folktale about "Eatonville's most celebrated resident, the world's largest alligator" in Lake Belle:

> This legendary alligator, it is said, is no other than a slave who escaped from a Georgia plantation and joined the Indians during the Seminole War. When the Indians retreated, he did not follow but instead made "big medicine" on the lake shore, for he had been a celebrated conjuring man in Africa. He transformed himself into an alligator, the god of his tribe, and slipped into the water. Now and then he resumes human form, so people say, and roams the country about Eatonville. At such times all the alligators in the surrounding lakes bellow loudly all night long. "The big one has gone back home," whisper the villagers.[19]

This alligator/conjuring man is a recurring figure in Hurston's work, appearing as "Old Man Massey" or "Uncle Monday."

Slave Narratives: A Folk History of Slavery in the United States from Interviews with Former Slaves, consisting of more than 2,000 interviews, is an ambitious supplementary project that the FWP developed. It was derived from an initiative taken by the Florida Writers' Project, where African American field workers conducted interviews with surviving ex-slaves.[20] When the slave narrative collection formally began, Sterling Brown sent to sixteen states a dispatch of instructions on the transcriptions of "dialect" in interviews, in which he suggested that the example of "Zora Neale Hurston in stories of Florida Negroes," an author who makes "truth to idiom be paramount" rather than phonetic spelling, should be followed "in order to make this volume of slave narratives more appealing and less difficult for the average reader."[21] In her essay "Art and Such," written for the art and literature chapter of *The Florida Negro*, Hurston herself boasted of her innovation in dialect writing in African American fiction: namely, "the telling of the story in the idiom – not the dialect – of the Negro." "The Negro's poetical flow of language, his thinking in images and figures," Hurston claims, "was [thus] called to the attention of the outside world."[22]

The Illinois Writers' Project is undoubtedly best known for having been a hotbed for budding African American writers. "No other writers' project in the country produced comparable Negro talent during the depression," recalls Arna Bontemps, who worked as a supervisor of the Illinois Writers' Project. From Richard Wright and Margaret Walker to Katherine Dunham (who was also a choreographer and dancer), they all "tested" their talents "on WPA." Federal funding of the arts took the place of white patrons such as Charlotte Osgood Mason and Carl Van Vechten, under whose patronage the Harlem Renaissance had flourished. The effect was a change in African American literary geography, in which Chicago, Bontemps declares, was "definitely the center of the second phase of Negro literary awakening" – a period that has come to be known as "the Chicago Renaissance."[23] An undertaking under Bontemps's editorial supervision, the projected volume *The Negro in Illinois* opens with Chicago's first "white" settler, Jean Baptiste Point Du Sable, who "the Indians used to say . . . was a Negro." It delineates black Chicago's cultural renaissance and its roots – "Iola" (Ida B. Wells), theater, jazz, and religious groups such as the Nation of Islam – while depicting the Great Depression period "Slave Market" (a labor exchange between black women domestics standing on the street and local white housewives, "bidding for their services much as southern blacks had been appraised on the block before emancipation").[24] Bontemps also edited *Cavalcade of the American Negro*, a booklet for Chicago's 1940 American Negro Exposition celebrating the Diamond Jubilee of Emancipation. The Exposition, "meant to constitute the first Black-organized World's Fair," drew contributions from various fields (music, literature, newspapers, art, sports, and others) and included an exhibit from the Republic of Liberia, Africa.[25] The opening pages of *Cavalcade of the American Negro* present a black past that is at the same time a future projection, entitled "Toward Freedom," telling how "Negro servants, traders, and explorers" – among them Alonzo Pietro, who captained Columbus's ship *Niña* – first came to America, antedating African slaves in chains.[26] Bontemps worked alongside white proletarian writer Jack Conroy and formed a close friendship that would lead to their literary collaboration on books, including the best-selling children's book, *The Fast Sooner Hound* (1942), with Virginia Lee Burton's pictures. Adapted from Conroy's industrial folktale for the Illinois Writers' Project, "The Boomer Fireman's Fast Sooner Hound," this is the story of a dog that outruns a train, about which Conroy had heard in the "Wabash Railway shops" in Moberly, Missouri, and it has become a children's classic.[27]

The Federal Theatre Project (FTP, 1935–39), another of the New Deal arts programs under the WPA, stamped its influence on geographic imaginings in African American stage productions that became rich with transnational and racial crossovers, departing from nineteenth-century America's cross-racial minstrel tradition. It established sixteen racially marked "Negro units" in FTP theaters across the four geographic divisions of the East, the South, the Midwest, and the West. The April 1936 opening of the New York City Negro unit's *Macbeth*, known as the "voodoo" *Macbeth*, at the Lafayette Theatre in Harlem, was a watershed moment. Directed by Orson Welles, the Harlem stage production of Shakespeare transposed the temporospatial setting of *Macbeth* from feudal Scotland to the nineteenth-century Caribbean island of Haiti and cast Macbeth's witches as voodoo priestesses. This black Atlantic rendition of *Macbeth* also altered the soundscape of Shakespeare's classic play. Including a troupe of African drummers and dancers led by Asadata Dafora, a native of Sierra Leone who had created *Kykunkor, or the Witch Woman* (1934) based on "authentic" African dance rhythms, the Harlem unit's *Macbeth* crafted an Afro-Caribbean sound.

No discussion of the black Federal Theatre would be complete without mentioning the Chicago Negro unit, directed by African American playwright Shirley Graham (Du Bois). She mounted her opera *Tom-Tom: An Epic of Music and the Negro* (1932) with an all-black cast and at the Chicago Negro unit she helped adapt Gilbert and Sullivan's operetta *The Mikado*. This production "blackened" the Savoy tradition, in which British actors played Oriental comic-opera roles. The production was ultimately reconceived as what came to be known as *The Swing Mikado*

Figure 5.1 The Chicago Negro unit's *The Swing Mikado* (1938).

(1938), under Harry Minturn, white director of the Chicago FTP. *The Swing Mikado* at the Great Northern Theatre moved the setting of the operetta from the genteel town of Titipu in medieval Japan to a coral island in the South Seas reminiscent of US insular territories such as the Philippines, Guam, Samoa, and Hawai'i, representing what might be termed the "black Pacific" (Figure 5.1).[28] The idea of putting "swing" at the core originated from the Negro unit's improvisations. *The Swing Mikado*'s modern soundscape – spicy rhythms and a contagious jitterbug dance – against the backdrop of a primitive coral island took audiences by storm in the Windy City. After its successful Chicago run, the FTP brought the production to Broadway in March 1939, with a gala opening at the New Yorker, attended by the first lady, Eleanor Roosevelt, and WPA directors, former and incumbent. Preeminent African American aesthetician Alain Locke remarked on the cultural significance of *The Swing Mikado* that "because of its exotic character, it was perhaps pardonable for Broadway to have overlooked the suggestive novelties of *Kykunkor*, the African dance-ballet, but not to have seen in the *Swing Mikado* the new horizons of Negro musical comedy was, it seems to me, unpardonable."[29]

The black Federal Theatre's streamlined *Mikado* fueled a boom of *Mikado* productions. *The Hot Mikado* (1939), a commercial version of *The Swing Mikado* by Broadway producer Michael Todd, starred tap

dancer extraordinaire Bill "Bojangles" Robinson in the role of the emperor
of Japan. Having featured in the Shirley Temple films *The Little Colonel*
and *The Littlest Rebel*, in which he played Southern servant roles and
danced with the white child star, Robinson was America's favorite enter-
tainer at the time. In *The Hot Mikado*, Robinson appeared in full regalia –
a diamond-encircled derby hat, gold uniform, and sparkling shoelaces –
amid brigades of jitterbugging girls and boys. He tap danced and sang his
version of the *Mikado* song "My Object All Sublime," making topical
allusions to such aspects of contemporary black society as Father Divine,
Joe Louis, and numbers games in Harlem (of which he was an honorary
mayor) and presented the image of "a gold-embossed Mayor of some
Japanese Harlem," or the "Harlemperor of Japan," in the words of white
reviewers.[30] The audience at the premiere of *The Hot Mikado* at the
Broadhurst Theatre in New York included J. Edgar Hoover, who traveled
from Washington for the occasion. The black–Japanese nexus – stylized
and repackaged for Broadway consumption – was a production that even
the chief of the FBI could enjoy (though wartime FBI special agents would
surveil it after Pearl Harbor).[31]

***

The story of black culture and the Great Depression is not just about
government patronage of the arts in the New Deal. It is inextricably linked
to the development of fascism and militarism in Europe and Asia, yet
another response to the Great Depression, leading to local wars whose
global implications were captured by African American arts and letters.
African Americans, in their efforts to comprehend those implications, also
reconfigured their relation to global space. Fascist Italy's invasion of
Ethiopia in 1935 was a primal moment, which set black spatial reconfigura-
tion in motion, galvanizing pan-African racial solidarity and anti-imperial
activism across the Atlantic while complicating the idea of "empire" for
African Americans. In campaigning against empire (Mussolini's neo-
Roman Empire in the fascist worldview), the African American public
supported a black empire and its ruler, Ethiopian emperor Haile Selassie I,
whose dynastic genealogy stretches back to Menelik I, son of King
Solomon and the Queen of Sheba. Langston Hughes, a poet identified
with the communist left, made a pan-racial appeal in his poem "Call of
Ethiopia" (1935), calling upon "all Africa" to "arise" for freedom "in answer
to the call of Sheba's race."[32] In November 1936, when it was no longer
possible to save Ethiopia from Mussolini's modern war machine,
Schuyler – a conservative journalist and the author of *Black No More*

(1931), a satiric science fiction novel – began his two-part serial *Black Empire*, which played on the fantasies of international race war, in the *Pittsburgh Courier*. He created a charismatic black leader, Dr. Belsidus, and his "Black Internationale" organization, which commanded superior and futuristic technologies. The narrative of the first serial climaxes with Ethiopia's liberation from the Italian occupation force, and the second with the complete destruction of the Italian air base in Libya, the last stronghold of Mussolini's vanishing empire in Africa. While abolishing the polity of a republic – the Republic of Liberia – for the black race, Belsidus does not reinstate black rule in Africa with Selassie restored to the throne. *Black Empire* instead closes with a future projection of a new black empire, a "Black Internationale" imperium whose "outlying districts" encompass America, Malaysia, and India.[33]

Ethiopia would continue to serve as a critical lens after the Second Italo–Ethiopian War (1935–36), which afforded African American writers and artists a view of local conflicts in Europe and Asia. During the Spanish Civil War (1936–39), which came on the heels of the Ethiopian crisis, about ninety African Americans joined the Abraham Lincoln Brigade, a contingent of American volunteers that fought in support of the Spanish Republic against General Francisco Franco. Oscar Henry Hunter, one of those "black Lincolns" and a Communist Party member from Chicago, wrote a short story entitled "700 Calendar Days" in which an African American volunteer from Georgia, dying of tuberculosis, remembers that "I wanted to go to Ethiopia and fight Mussolini. Couldn't get there ... I got to Spain. This ain't Ethiopia, but it'll do."[34] Through the prism of Langston Hughes, who crossed the sea to Spain as a correspondent covering the Spanish Civil War for the *Baltimore Afro-American*, the Spanish theater presented a more complex spectacle. It was not only because he met "more white American writers than at any other period in [his] life" in Spain away from home, including Ernest Hemingway, "a big likable fellow whom the men in the Brigades adored," but also because of the "Moors" in Franco's Army of Africa.[35] That dark-skinned combatants were fighting on both sides unsettled the meaning of the Spanish Civil War as a substitute for fighting in Ethiopia. Hughes writes in a dispatch (October 30, 1937) from Spain: "I knew that Spain once belonged to the Moors, a colored people ranging from light dark to dark white. Now the Moors have come again to Spain with the fascist armies as cannon fodder for Franco. But, on the loyalist side there are many colored people of various nationalities in the International Brigades. I want to write about both Moors and colored people."[36] In a speech delivered in Paris immediately before he entered Spain, Hughes had observed that the wars in Ethiopia and Spain, coupled together, showed how "race means nothing when it can be turned to Fascist use." "The same Fascists who forced Italian peasants to fight in Africa," he remarked, "now force African Moors to fight in Europe." Onto this world map of fascism, Hughes added "the Military Party in Japan," a colored people dominating another in Korea and Manchuria at gunpoint.[37] He wrote a poem entitled "Roar China!" (1937) in *The Volunteer for Liberty*, organ of the International Brigades, in response to the Sino–Japanese War (1937–45). Opening with a direct imperative, "Roar, China! / Roar, old lion of the East!," the poem called for resistance to Japanese and Western imperialists.[38]

Paul Robeson, who earned international acclaim for his starring roles in Eugene O'Neill's *The Emperor Jones* as Brutus Jones, who rose from being a Pullman porter to the emperor of a Caribbean island, and in Shakespeare's *Othello* as the Moor of Venice, went to Spain in 1938 with his wife, Eslanda Goode Robeson. Having met volunteers from the Lincoln Battalion, both white and black, who came to "fight and die that another 'government of the people, by the people and for the people shall not perish from the earth,'" Robeson reminisces in his autobiography *Here I Stand* (1958) that the Spanish Civil War was "a major turning point in my life."[39] Steadfast in defending democracy, the singer and activist declared his support for Chinese aspirations for self-determination against Japanese aggression in the Sino–Japanese War, as well. He performed the song "Chee Lai!" (Arise!) – the future national anthem of the People's Republic of China (1949–) – in English and Chinese, calling upon the Chinese masses "who refuse to be bond slaves" to "stand up and fight for liberty and true democracy."[40]

A card-carrying member of the Communist Party, Richard Wright served as Harlem Bureau editor of the *Daily Worker*, organ of the Party, and in this capacity reported on boycotts, pickets, and rallies against Japan, Italy, and Germany in 1937.[41] However, the potential appeal that fascism and militarism could have held for African Americans in dire poverty, who experienced the Great Depression differently from whites, was not lost on him. Wright's *Native Son* (1940) tells the story of Bigger Thomas, a working-class black youth living in Chicago's South Side ghetto, providing an insight into his psychic interior. In Wright's depiction, Bigger "liked to hear of how Japan was conquering China; of how Hitler was running the Jews to the ground; of how Mussolini was invading Spain" – a black geo-psychic map on which Ethiopia is significantly displaced or "substituted" by Spain.[42] Lest Wright's readers miss the dangerous allure of fascism and militarism, which dovetailed with pan-racial appeal as a shaping influence in the world of Bigger (whom Wright calls "a meaningful and prophetic symbol"), the author discusses in his essay "How 'Bigger' Was Born" (1940): "As I grew older, I became familiar with the Bigger Thomas conditioning and its numerous shadings no matter where I saw it in Negro life . . . I've even heard Negroes, in moments of anger and bitterness, praise what Japan is doing in China, not because they believed in oppression (being objects of oppression themselves), but because they would suddenly sense how empty their lives were when looking at the dark faces of Japanese generals in the rotogravure supplements of the Sunday newspapers. They would dream of what it would be like to live in a country where they could forget their color and play a responsible role in the vital processes of the nation's life."[43] The rise of fascism and militarism, and wars in Africa, Europe, and Asia as a corollary, expanded the international horizons of African Americans, redefining their place within a global space (beyond national space) at a time when US foreign policy had become increasingly reflective of isolationism due to the Depression.

Some African American writers were globetrotters and traveled widely around the world. Running through channels not explicitly routed through Europe, black internationalism moved beyond what Paul Gilroy has termed the "black Atlantic."[44] In the fall of 1929, James Weldon Johnson, on leave of absence from the National Association for the Advancement of Colored People (NAACP), where he served as executive secretary, sailed across the Pacific Ocean from Seattle to Japan as an American delegate to the third biennial conference of the Institute of Pacific Relations (IPR) (1925–61). Founded in Honolulu in the US territory of Hawai'i, the IPR was a nongovernmental organization that advocated the concept of a Pacific Community, challenging the Atlantic-centric perspective on the world. Reflecting this, Johnson's autobiography, *Along This Way* (1933), traces the crisscrossing routes that he navigated for (black) internationalism, reaching beyond US borders, the Caribbean, Latin America, and Europe, to embrace the Pacific in the penultimate chapter. In the process, the autobiography links two distinct memories of Pacific Rim nations – namely, the US Marine occupation of Nicaragua in which Johnson "ha[d] a hand" as a consul in 1912 and the Japanese military occupation of Manchuria in 1931 – that came to resonate in the (black) Pacific. As he reminisces, Johnson's participation in the implementation of Big Stick diplomacy in Latin America, under the Roosevelt Corollary to the Monroe Doctrine as US international policy in the region, was cited as "a precedent" that the Japanese Empire appropriated and emulated in Northeast Asia to justify both its occupation of Manchuria in China to create the puppet state of Manchukuo and its attempt to integrate, or rather to invent, the area.[45] *Along This Way* addresses the complex field of forces that went into the making of the regional order in the Pacific that trapped Johnson, even as they circumscribed the black internationalism to which they gave shape.[46]

Langston Hughes crossed the Atlantic to the Soviet Union in 1932, with a group of twenty-two African Americans, including Dorothy West and Louise Thompson Patterson, to make *Black and White*, an ill-fated motion picture about US race relations. Hughes stayed for twelve months in the Soviet Union, where he wrote and published several revolutionary poems, such as "Good Morning Revolution" and "Goodbye Christ," and toured extensively in Soviet Central Asia. However, Hughes's journey to the Soviet Union did not end in the ambit of the black Atlantic; he traveled further east, to China and Japan, returning to the United States via the Pacific. Hughes's wide travels in Moscow, Shanghai – where he met Madame Sun Yat-sen and Lu Xun – and Tokyo, transpired under the gaze of state security forces: the US State Department, the Shanghai Municipal Police (SMP) (the Special Branch of the SMP operated, in effect, as a Far Eastern arm of MI6, the British Secret Intelligence Service), and the Tokyo police, which all opened files on Hughes in 1932–33. As he recounts in his memoir *I Wonder as I Wander* (1956), having freshly arrived from the Soviet Union, the poet found himself a focus of the anticommunist paranoia of the Japanese authorities, which resulted in his expulsion from the country on suspicion of being a Soviet spy. He makes the following observation about this humiliating experience: "I, a colored man, had lately been all around the world, but *only* in Japan, a colored country, had I been subjected to police interrogation and told to go home and not return again. The word 'Fascist' was just coming into general usage then. When I got to Honolulu, I said in a newspaper interview that in my opinion Japan was a Fascist country." However, the narration of this final scene in Honolulu, US territory in the Pacific, in *I Wonder as I Wander* registers the presence of an "F.B.I. man" spying on him. Introduced by a newsman, Hughes "shook hands" with the FBI man and the man subsequently "stood around while [he] repeated for Honolulu newsmen the details of [his] Tokyo police experience." Why the FBI agent turned up "to *meet*" him is not explained.[47] Yet given that *I Wonder as I Wander* was published in the 1950s, when Hughes was suffering through another ordeal resulting from anticommunist fervor, this time at the hands of Joseph McCarthy in the United States and of General Douglas MacArthur, the supreme commander of the Allied powers in American-occupied postwar Japan, the appearance of the FBI agent may be understood to signal to the reader that the intelligence dragnet to track the mobility of the black radical literary traveler and to silence dissenters had spread beyond the black Atlantic.[48]

The globe-girdling journey that W. E. B. Du Bois embarked on in 1936 included five months in Nazi Germany, sponsored by the Oberlaender Trust, and a Eurasian continental rail tour across the Soviet Union to China and Japan. While his 1928 novel *Dark Princess* is a prime example of "Afro-Orientalism,"[49] the actual journey at once expanded and complicated the Asian arc of his internationalism. Du Bois landed in Manchuria as the first African American reporter to cover Manchukuo (1932–45), a Japanese puppet state on the Pacific Rim that had appeared in atlases only four years prior. The travel narrative tracing Pacific itineraries – recorded in dispatches that he sent to the *Pittsburgh Courier* and a chapter entitled "I Gird the Globe" in his unpublished, book-length manuscript "Russia and America" – makes a strong case for the socio-economic experiment in Manchuria of departing from capitalist development, imagining that "Japanese colonialism" in Manchuria furnished the promise of Asian "socialism."[50] There was ambivalence at the heart of Du Bois's sympathies for Japan that coexisted with those for Soviet Russia and China in pre–World War II Asia, but the (sometimes unnervingly) pro-Japanese messages that he issued in his newspaper columns gave rise in 1939 to unsubstantiated rumors in the US Congress that Du Bois was a paid propagandist for the Japanese imperial government.[51]

Richard Wright applied to cover the Sino–Japanese War as a foreign correspondent for the Associated Negro Press (ANP) in 1941. The author of *Native Son* wanted "to see how men and women of color are living in other parts of the world."[52] He also sought this assignment out of envy of white American writers – amongst them Ernest Hemingway, who had recently left for Chungking, the wartime capital of China's Nationalist government, as a correspondent for the New York leftist newspaper *PM*, along with his wife, Martha Gellhorn, a war correspondent for *Collier's* magazine. "Many white writers learn, study, and broaden themselves by doing jobs of this sort, while most of our Negro writers cling close to the fireside," Wright wrote in a letter to Claude Barnett, director of the ANP, alluding to intractable inequalities in modern mobility.[53] Nowhere is this frustration better expressed than in an episode of Bigger Thomas's denied dream of becoming an aviator in *Native Son* (Bigger is instead given the job of chauffeur for a wealthy white family through a relief agency).[54] However,

Wright's application to the State Department for a passport to travel to China and the Soviet Union as a reporter for the ANP was denied. The Department "did not intend to issue a passport to a black foreign correspondent critical of the American government."[55]

The right to international travel was not always guaranteed to African American authors and artists. Their relationship to the passport, a device to verify citizenship and control the movement of citizens abroad, was politically strained. (This situation would culminate in the State Department's revocation of the passports of Paul Robeson and Du Bois in the 1950s because of their political opinions). For writers of the black left, mobility and vulnerability to statelessness went hand in hand. The liberal landscape that was engendered by the state power through the New Deal cultural programs during the Great Depression decade was haunted by racism and the repression of that racism. In the end, government-funded arts projects – taking the place of white patrons in the Harlem Renaissance – acknowledged the value of African Americans as citizens and allowed African American federal writers to inscribe blackness (and even the political color red) in America's lily-white capitalist democratic image of itself, insofar as they did not challenge or undermine it.

Notes

1. James Weldon Johnson, *Black Manhattan* (New York: Da Capo Press, 1991), 4, 146.
2. George S. Schuyler, *Black Empire*, ed. Robert A. Hill and R. Kent Rasmussen (Boston, MA: Northeastern University Press, 1991), 51.
3. For instance, during the crisis in which racial inequality was ever more egregiously manifested in unemployment and poverty, Roosevelt's programs for direct relief, economic recovery, and financial reform produced a major realignment of African American voters in relation to the federal government, who switched their political allegiance from the Republican Party (the party of Abraham Lincoln) to the Democratic Party. Under the leadership of African American educator Mary McLeod Bethune, the unofficial "Black Cabinet" was formed within the Roosevelt administration to advise the president on racial matters (Harvard Sitkoff, *A New Deal for Blacks: The Emergence of Civil Rights as a National Issue: The Depression Decade* [thirtieth anniversary edn] [New York: Oxford University Press, 2009], 58–76).
4. The best and most comprehensive treatment of this subject is found in Wendy Griswold, *American Guides: The Federal Writers' Project and the Casting of American Culture* (Chicago: University of Chicago Press, 2016).
5. Marguerite S. Shaffer, *See America First: Tourism and National Identity, 1880–1940* (Washington, DC: Smithsonian Institution Press, 2001), 203.

6. Lawrence P. Jackson, *The Indignant Generation: A Narrative History of African American Writers and Critics, 1934–1960* (Princeton, NJ: Princeton University Press, 2011), 62.

7. Shaffer, *See America First*, 203.

8. [Sterling A. Brown], "The Negro in Washington," in *Washington: City and Capital* (Washington, DC: Government Printing Office, [1937]), 68, 70, 89.

9. Thomas H. Wirth, ed., *Gay Rebel of the Harlem Renaissance: Selections from the Work of Richard Bruce Nugent* (Durham, NC: Duke University Press, 2002), 221–23.

10. Claude McKay, *Harlem: Negro Metropolis* (New York: Harcourt Brace Jovanovich, 1968), 16, 98, 101, 240.

11. Tyrone Tillery, *Claude McKay: A Black Poet's Struggle for Identity* (Amherst: University of Massachusetts Press, 1992), 162.

12. Richard Wright, *American Hunger* (New York: Harper and Row, 1977), 127.

13. Henry G. Alsberg, foreword to *American Stuff: An Anthology of Prose and Verse by Members of the Federal Writers' Project* (New York: Da Capo Press, 1976), viii.

14. Jackson, *The Indignant Generation*, 109.

15. Hazel Rowley, *Richard Wright: The Life and Times* (New York: Henry Holt, 2001), 150.

16. Quoted in ibid., 157.

17. Pamela Bordelon, "Zora Neale Hurston: A Biographical Essay," in *Go Gator and Muddy the Water: Writings by Zora Neale Hurston from the Federal Writers' Project*, ed. Pamela Bordelon (New York: W. W. Norton, 1999), 25.

18. Federal Writers' Project, *Florida: A Guide to the Southernmost State* (New York: Oxford University Press, 1939), 431–32.

19. Ibid., 361–62.

20. Norman R. Yetman, "The Background of the Slave Narrative Collection," *American Quarterly* 19.3 (Autumn 1967), 549.

21. [Sterling A. Brown], "Notes by an Editor on Dialect Usage in Accounts by Interviews with Ex-Slaves," in *From Sundown to Sunup: The Making of the Black Community*, ed. George P. Rawick (Westport, CT: Greenwood, 1972), 176.

22. Zora Neale Hurston, "Art and Such," in Bordelon, *Go Gator and Muddy the Water*, 144.

23. Arna Bontemps, "Famous WPA Authors," *Negro Digest* 8.8 (June 1950), 44, 46.

24. Brian Dolinar, ed., *The Negro in Illinois: The WPA Papers* (Urbana: University of Illinois Press, 2013), 2, 144.

25. Adam Green, *Selling the Race: Culture, Community, and Black Chicago, 1940–1955* (Chicago: University of Chicago Press, 2007), 20.

26. *Cavalcade of the American Negro* (Chicago: Diamond Jubilee Exposition Authority, 1940), 11.

27. Jack Conroy, "Memories of Arna Bontemps: Friend and Collaborator," *American Libraries* 5.11 (December 1974), 602.

28. Stephanie Leigh Batiste, *Darkening Mirrors: Imperial Representation in Depression-Era African American Performance* (Durham, NC: Duke University Press, 2011), 151–53.

29. Alain Locke, "Broadway and the Negro Drama," *Theatre Arts* 25.10 (October 1941), 748.

30. Burns Mantle, "'The Hot Mikado' Burns Up All the Colored Show Records," *Daily News* (New York), March 24, 1939, reel 15, Collection of Newspaper Clippings of Dramatic Criticisms, Billy Rose Theatre Collection, New York Public Library for the Performing Arts, New York; "New Play in Manhattan," *Time*, April 3, 1939, 23.

31. See, for instance, "Japanese Influence and Activity among the American Negroes," in *The FBI's RACON: Racial Conditions in the United States during World War II*, ed. Robert A. Hill (Boston, MA: Northeastern University Press, 1995), 507–49.

32. Langston Hughes, "Call of Ethiopia," in *The Collected Poems of Langston Hughes*, ed. Arnold Rampersad (New York: Vintage, 1994), 184.

33. Schuyler, *Black Empire*, 256.

34. O. H. Hunter, "700 Calendar Days," in *The Heart of Spain: Anthology of Fiction, Non-Fiction, and Poetry*, ed. Alvah Bessie (New York: Veterans of the Abraham Lincoln Brigade, 1952), 299.

35. Langston Hughes, *I Wonder as I Wander: An Autobiographical Journey* (New York: Hill and Wang, 1993), 362–63.

36. Langston Hughes, "Hughes Finds Moors Being Used as Pawns by Fascists in Spain," *Afro-American*, October 30, 1937, in *The Collected Works of Langston Hughes, Volume 9, Essays on Art, Race, Politics, and World Affairs*, ed. Christopher C. De Santis (Columbia: University of Missouri Press, 2002), 161.

37. Langston Hughes, "Too Much of Race," in *Good Morning Revolution: Uncollected Social Protest Writings by Langston Hughes*, ed. Faith Berry (Westport, CT: Lawrence Hill, 1973), 97–98.

38. Langston Hughes, "Roar China!," in *The Collected Poems of Langston Hughes*, 198.

39. Paul Robeson, *Here I Stand* (Boston, MA: Beacon Press, 1988), 53.

40. *Chee Lai! (Arise!): Songs of New China* (New York: Keynote Recordings, 1941), 5.

41. See *Byline, Richard Wright: Articles from the "Daily Worker" and "New Masses,"* ed. Earle V. Bryant (Columbia: University of Missouri Press, 2015), 95–122.

42. Richard Wright, *Native Son* (New York: HarperPerennial, 1998), 115; Ichiro Takayoshi, *American Writers and the Approach of World War II, 1935–1941: A Literary History* (New York: Cambridge University Press, 2015), 46.

43. Richard Wright, "How 'Bigger' Was Born," in *Native Son*, 439–41.

44. Paul Gilroy, *The Black Atlantic: Modernity and Double Consciousness* (Cambridge, MA: Harvard University Press, 1993).

45. James Weldon Johnson, *Along This Way: The Autobiography of James Weldon Johnson* (New York: Da Capo Press, 2000), 286.

46. Etsuko Taketani, *The Black Pacific Narrative: Geographic Imaginings of Race and Empire between the World Wars* (Hanover, NH: Dartmouth College Press, 2014), chap. 1.

47. Hughes, *I Wonder as I Wander*, 277, 278–79.

48. Taketani, *The Black Pacific Narrative*, chap. 4.

49. Bill V. Mullen, *Afro-Orientalism* (Minneapolis: University of Minnesota Press, 2004), chap. 1.

50. W. E. B. Du Bois, "Forum of Fact and Opinion," *Pittsburgh Courier*, February 13, 1937, 7, 15; W. E. B. Du Bois, *Newspaper Columns by W. E. B. Du Bois*, ed. Herbert Aptheker (White Plains, NY: Kraus-Thomson Organization, 1986), 1:167–68; W. E. B. Du Bois, "Russia and America: An Interpretation," draft manuscript, 132, reel 85, Papers of W. E. B. Du Bois (microfilm), University of Massachusetts, Amherst, MA; Taketani, *The Black Pacific Narrative*, chap. 5.

51. Waldo McNutt to W. E. B. Du Bois, February 13, 1939; Du Bois to McNutt, February 25, 1939, in *The Correspondence of W. E. B. Du Bois*, ed. Herbert Aptheker (Amherst: University of Massachusetts Press, 1973–78), 2: 184–85.

52. Richard Wright to Claude A. Barnett, March 4, 1941, box 93, folder 1187, Richard Wright Papers, Yale Collection of American Literature, Beinecke Rare Book and Manuscript Library, Yale University, New Haven, CT.

53. Quoted in Rowley, *Richard Wright*, 235.

54. Wright, *Native Son*, 16–17, 353.

55. Rowley, *Richard Wright*, 251.

CHAPTER 6

The Southern Heritage

Michael Kreyling

"The Southern Heritage" of the 1930s presents a paradox. On the one hand, it supplied raw material for the most vulgar appetites (for erotic titillation, for "disaster tourism," for plantation escapism, for racial stereotype) while on the other it provided American literature with connections to modern European and continental literary criticism. Not to overlook Mt. Everest – Mississippi gave us William Faulkner, our greatest modern novelist.

The paradox of the 1930s began in 1917. Or 1920. H. L. Mencken originally published his notorious demolition of highbrow culture south of Mason–Dixon, "The Sahara of the Bozart," as a newspaper column in the *New York Evening Mail* in 1917. It was published anew in his *Prejudices: Second Series* in 1920, enlarged and more venomous.[1] Depending on when you – the Southerner Mencken roasted – read the piece, would depend the date of your resolve to prove the Yankee cultural occupier dead wrong.

Mencken's indictment of Southern culture is Shermanic: scorched earth. The epigraph he chose, a maladroit couplet by South Carolinian J. Gordon Coogler (1865–1901), has achieved minor sideways fame as the motto of a poetaster:

> Alas, for the South! Her books have grown fewer –
> She never was much given to literature.

Mencken's opening paragraph continues the bashing:

> In the lamented J. Gordon Coogler, author of these elegiac lines, there was the insight of the true poet. He was the last bard of Dixie, in the legitimate line. Down there a poet is now almost as rare as an oboe-player, a dry-point etcher or a metaphysician. It is, indeed, amazing to contemplate so vast a vacuity. One thinks of the interstellar spaces, of the colossal reaches of the now mythical ether. Nearly the whole of Europe could be lost in that stupendous region of fat farms, shoddy cities and paralyzed cerebrums. (971)

In Mencken's gleeful scorn, the South lacks artistic potency, not to mention taste. There might be a few genteel writers in and around Richmond (Ellen Glasgow, James Branch Cabell) who guard the remnants of a once-proud Virginian culture, but they are drowning in a rising tide of small-town mediocrity, Protestant fundamentalism, and inferior education. "Virginia is the best of the South today," in Mencken's estimation, "and Georgia is perhaps the worst. The one is simply senile; the other is crass, gross, vulgar, and obnoxious" (973).[2] As a "republic of letters," the South is a failed state. When Mencken traveled to Dayton, Tennessee in 1925, to report on the trial of John Scopes, who had been brought to the bar for teaching evolution, he found precisely the botched culture he expected to find. He would not be the last to explore "down there," in America's subconscious, its repressed Other.[3]

If you were a college student, in the South, in the 1920s, seriously intent on making a mark in literature, you were probably white, male, and eager to show Mencken that he was wrong. Not because he had overlooked legions of poets and fiction writers; listing them would only bolster his indictment because there would be too many Cooglers. But because you had already recognized indigenous mediocrity and fled from it to cultural values more permanent than the progressive, American agenda Mencken personified. You had embraced transatlantic literary modernism.

Perhaps the most notable group of such individuals coalesced at Vanderbilt University in the 1920s. They called themselves "Fugitives" (because they had agreed to flee from the regional chauvinism all around them) when they began to meet, discuss, and write their own poetry. They produced a "little magazine" called *The Fugitive* from 1922 until 1925, by which time most of them had graduated. The senior players were John Crowe Ransom and Donald Davidson. Both were professors, and both bore the luster of having participated in the Great War – they had spent time in the "waste land" that functioned as the historical correlative of the ruined civilization T. S. Eliot evoked in his modernist masterpiece. Ransom and Davidson were joined in meetings of the Fugitives by undergraduates Allen Tate and Robert Penn Warren. (Cleanth Brooks, B. A. 1928, was just a little too late to bask in the Fugitive radiance.) Tate considered Eliot's poetry and critical temperament to be the only way out of a stultifying and moribund Southern (and Victorian) artistic sensibility, and urged his comrades to follow him. Not all were equally persuaded, but the heat generated by their debates brought *The Fugitive* into being in 1922 and kept it going for three years.

The Fugitive and its principal contributors might have gone the way of other "little magazines" that sprouted in the "sahara of the bozart" in the 1920s: *The Reviewer* in Richmond, Virginia (1921–25), and *The Double-Dealer* in New Orleans (1921–26), for example. But many of the participants in *The Fugitive* reunited later in the decade for a symposium they titled *I'll Take My Stand: The South and the Agrarian Tradition* (ITMS) (1930).[4] The symposium's impulse was to adapt and extend the poetics of *The Fugitive* into a Southern politics: conservative, wary of progressive social policy, anti-industrial, and anti-urban. Feeling that the South was being browbeaten into modernity against its traditions, the movers of the volume (Ransom, Davidson, Tate) concluded that the South needed watchmen to warn the region of invading change. The twelve essays in the manifesto (covering economics, Civil War history, religion, racial mores, education, and other topics) are previewed in Ransom's unsigned "Introduction." He proffers a serious, traditional, and seasoned culture that Mencken had, apparently, missed ten years earlier. As outlined by Ransom, the Agrarian South was realistic rather than romantic and individualistic, rural without being countrified, landed (or agrarian) rather than industrial, provincial rather than urban. It was in fact European rather than American, a "community" held together by "heart" and "genius" (ITMS xlviii), not "some fabulous creature called society" (ITMS xlvi) engineered by a "government" in thrall to industrial capital (ITMS xli).

Some of Ransom's complaints echo familiarly in the twenty-first century, the era of STEM dominance. National resources, he warned, are flowing to the applied sciences: "The capitalization of the applied sciences has now become extravagant and uncritical; it has enslaved our human energies to a degree now clearly felt to be burdensome" (ITMS xxxix). Ransom's allusion to slavery, however, is part of the reactionary rhetoric and ideological work of *I'll Take My Stand*; these essays are largely intended to confound historical memory and replace it with a myth. The objective of the rhetoric is to maintain that slavery does not accurately name the condition of Africans in the antebellum South, nor is guilt for that institution part of the "burden" of the modern Southerner. If there are burdens, they have been created by the modern infatuation with "the applied sciences."[5] Ransom extends his conservative revision of history in his signed essay "Reconstructed but Unregenerate." There he argues that traditional Southern society was not so much an aristocracy (as depicted in *Gone with the Wind* [1936] most notably) but rather a squirearchy –more modest in its social gradations and therefore more stable, less competitive, less tied to international commodity markets: "Their [squirearchy's social] relations were personal and friendly. It was a kindly society, yet a realistic one; for it was a failure if it could not be said that people were for the most part in their right places. Slavery was a feature monstrous enough in theory, but, more often than not, humane in practice; and it is impossible to believe that its abolition alone could have effected any great revolution in society" (ITMS 14). "Impossible" for whom?

The sole notable engagement with Southern race relations in *I'll Take My Stand* is Robert Penn Warren's "The Briar Patch." In this essay Warren sidles up to Booker T. Washington's theory of separate spheres for white and black, with the black sphere remanded to vocational training rather than professional education: "There are strong theoretical arguments in favor of higher education for the negro, but those arguments are badly damaged if at the same time a separate negro community or group is not built up which is capable of absorbing and profiting from those members who have received this higher education" (ITMS 251). W. E. B. Du Bois is not mentioned by name in "The Briar Patch."[6] Warren later, in *Who Speaks for the Negro?* (1965), disavowed this position.

Insofar as the South was a field for literature, the consensus among the Agrarian fellowship established a conservative bulwark against innovation. The literary work produced under this consensus would be formal rather than experimental, always mindful, as was T. S. Eliot, of the necessary relationship between tradition and the individual talent. Except for Warren, whose poetry over the course of his career developed a distinctive free verse, the other poets of the group (Tate, Ransom, Davidson) clung to canonical forms. Tate wrote in *terza rima*, and his most famous poem, "Ode to the Confederate Dead" (1928), utilizes the conventions of both ode and elegy. Ransom's poems are intricately metered, carefully interlocking structures of erudite vocabulary and metaphor; they resemble completed, highly complex crosswords. Davidson's signature poem, "Lee in the Mountains" (1938), hews to the guidelines of the traditional ballad.

The Agrarian South is, fundamentally, a region imagined rather than empirically observed, a set of "deep structures" of belief intuitively sensed by insiders but beyond the ken of outsiders. Its "way of life" – including of course its racial behaviors – is organically generated by these deep structures and therefore resistant to progressive tinkering. Ransom tacitly included these mores in his encomium to the South: "For it is the character of a seasoned provincial life that it is realistic, successfully adapted to its environment, and that as a consequence it is stable, or hereditable" (ITMS 5). That is, the South is an identity grasped intuitively, not a set of empirical data to be counted and measured (and, it follows, socially engineered or legally changed). Here Mencken reenters the frame.

In three consecutive issues of *The American Mercury* (A-M) (September, October, and November) in 1931 (as *I'll Take My Stand* was still in its first flush), Charles Angoff and H. L. Mencken, managing editor and editor, respectively, produced aggregated data purporting to locate "The Worst American State." Using the 1930 census, Angoff and Mencken put an empirical floor under many of the negative regional stereotypes Mencken alone had trumpeted in "The Sahara of the Bozart." In Part III of the series, they collated data into five lists ranking the forty-eight states and the District of Columbia according to four general attainments of modern civilization: wealth, education, public health, public order. "These tables," the authors claim, "selected for their apparent fairness, seem to show clearly that the New England States lead the country on all counts, with the Pacific and Middle Western States following, and that the Cotton States are at the bottom" (A-M 355).[7]

To be sure, the Angoff-Mencken interpretation of statistics is skewed and unprofessional – neither was a demographer. They purport, for example, to see correlations between states in which Baptists predominate in religion and states high in numbers of homicides and lynchings (A-M 360). They extend the lynching implications from religion to states highest in support for Prohibition. There too, "of the States which vote dryest [*sic*] five [Alabama, Mississippi, Tennessee, Arkansas, Georgia] are also champion lynching States" (A-M 364), The overall Angoff-Mencken conclusion is, by their own admission, predictable. "Most Americans," they pronounce, "asked to name the most generally civilized American State, would probably name Massachusetts at once, and nine out of ten would probably nominate Mississippi as the most backward" (A-M 371).[8] Not surprisingly, that is the outcome of their "data" as well. And Mississippi's ills are metonymic to the South as a region: "The Cotton Belt . . . is the least advanced part of the United States, and of all the Cotton States Mississippi is the most unfortunate . . . In the midst of its hordes of barbaric peasants there is some native stock of excellent blood. But the young men of this stock, finding few opportunities at home, have to go elsewhere" (A-M 371). "Elsewhere" being, of course, Massachusetts.[9]

Angoff and Mencken discover a South dominated by two races, white and Negro, by evangelical Protestant religion, and by public support for Prohibition. In what constitutes a modern civilization, the South is deficient. The region lacks daily newspapers and the hotel lobbies and restaurants (presumably) in which white men could read them (A-M 366).

Southern states spend markedly less than the rest of the nation on "education, hospitals, roads, etc." (A-M 366), and therefore fall short in public
wit, health, and mobility. At the outset of the 1930s, then, as economic
stagnation was strengthening its grip on the nation, one region was by all
metrics, valid or not, so much worse than the rest of the country that it, the
South, qualified as a civilization of a different order altogether – if indeed it
was a civilization at all. So much less American in quantifiable terms than
the rest of the country, it was rather a segment of (what would come to be
called) "the third world" internal to a nation struggling to sort out
a modern, first world industrial economy and its entailed culture.
The Angoff-Mencken statistics also identify the South as the region with
the highest average temperature and the highest annual rainfall: an
American, onshore tropics (A-M 370).

In the 1930s, the South was the arena where the champions and opponents of the modern, industrial state fought their battles. It was either an
idealized island of stability in the spreading wreckage of Depression-era
America (Agrarian conservatives), or "hordes of barbaric peasants" comically (at best) or viciously (at worst) bungling the basic elements of human
civilization.

"Barbaric peasants" proved popular and profitable in the 1930s. Erskine
Caldwell's *Tobacco Road* (TR) (1932) is perhaps the most prominent
example of the peasant South: human beings living beneath the minimum
level of civilization. The novel was a best seller at publication and
a Broadway adaptation ran for eight years in New York (1933–41). John
Ford's film version (1941), consciously bowdlerizing the stage version,
treats the impoverished lives of the Southern sharecroppers as farce. Ford
had presented the lives of the Joads, in his classic film version (1940) of
John Steinbeck's *The Grapes of Wrath* (1939), as tragic, but his suffering
Crackers were not vouchsafed the stature of his Okies.

Caldwell's *Tobacco Road* dwells in excess. The action focuses on
a seasonal cycle in the lives of one Georgia sharecropping family, the
Lesters. The patriarch, Jeeter Lester, is an agrarian grotesque. He still
feels the primal urges of the soil even though economic pressures to
move to the cotton mills of Augusta represent the inevitable conquest of
industry:

> I think more of the land [he muses] than I do about staying in a durn cotton
> mill. You can't smell no sedge fire up there, and when it comes time to break
> the land for planting, you feel sick inside but you don't know what's ailing
> you. People has told me about that spring sickness in the mills, I don't know
> how many times. But when a man stays on the land, he don't get to feeling

like that this time of year, because he is right here to smell the smoke of burning broom-sedge and to feel the wind fresh off the plowed fields going down inside his body.[10]

There is a grotesque irony in Caldwell's narrative, however; it is a field-clearing sedge fire burning out of control that, in the end, consumes the Lester shack and erases the family from the land altogether.

Caldwell's novel, unlike the subsequent stage and film adaptations, juxtaposes Jeeter's doomed nostalgia for agrarian harmony in the land with modern innovations in agronomy. The Lesters, like Steinbeck's Joads, have been swept up in national (if not global) tides of finance and commodity production of which they feel (rather than understand) only the results. The original owner of the plantation the Lesters now work on shares that (Captain John)

> abandoned the farm and moved to Augusta. Rather than attempt to show his tenants how to conform to the newer and more economical methods of modern agriculture, which he thought would have been an impossible task from the start, he sold the stock and implements and moved away. An intelligent employment of his land, stocks, and implements would have enabled Jeeter, and scores of others who had become dependent upon Captain John, to raise crops for food, and crops to be sold at a profit. Co-operative and corporate farming would have saved them all. (TR 60)

Few in Caldwell's immense audience were aware of his progressivist message. They were instead titillated by the code-stretching sensuality of Jeeter's daughters: the twelve-year-old blonde nymph Pearl, married to a neighboring man but eluding his attempts to consummate the nuptials, and her older sister, eighteen-year-old Ellie May, willing to do almost anything for food but shuffled to the bottom of the erotic economy because of a harelip that "spread open across her upper teeth, making her mouth appear as if she had no upper lip at all"(TR 22).[11] The audience, following Mencken's paradigm, was instead fascinated by the presence within the United States of an enclave of white primitives resistant to the momentum of modernity that would lift the nation out of economic ruin in the decade of the New Deal.

This "fascination" – scopophilia, the near-erotic pleasure of looking at the primitives of the South – reaches its epitome in *Let Us Now Praise Famous Men* (1941), the record (in prose by James Agee and black-and-white photographs by Walker Evans) of the pair's sojourn among several white sharecropping families in rural Alabama in the summer of 1936. They had been sent (Agee was freelance, Evans on loan from the Farm Security

Administration) by Henry Luce's *Fortune* magazine to document the lives of white "cotton tenants" in the South under New Deal programs – the techniques of "modern agriculture" that might have rescued Caldwell's Jeeter Lester. But what had been planned as a magazine article grew into a 400-page book (it was not published until 1941), and Agee's choice of an epigraph from *The Communist Manifesto* could not have fit in well with the pro-capitalist philosophy of *Fortune*.[12]

Let Us Now Praise Famous Men is significant to the literature of the South in the 1930s in several ways. As a hybrid work of prose and photographs, it is an important indicator of the process by which the nation pictorialized its "view" of the region. South Carolina writer Julia Peterkin and photographer Doris Ulmann had collaborated on a similar hybrid book about the Lowcountry, *Roll Jordan, Roll* in 1933. In 1941, Richard Wright wrote the text and Edwin Rosskam edited the photographs for *12 Million Black Voices: A Folk History of the Negro in the United States*.[13] Rosskam's photographic archive was the Farm Security Administration, New Deal employer of many of the era's distinguished documentary photographers. The Agee–Evans collaboration is, however, arguably the most important of these hybrid books. In it we find the iconic portraits of Floyd and Lucille Burroughs, the porch portrait of Bud Fields and his family, the riveting images of the tenant cabins and the arresting minimalism of their interiors. Evans's images have become staples of modernist art; in fact, his still life of Floyd Burroughs's empty brogans has become an American counterpart to Van Gogh's *A Pair of Shoes* (1886).[14]

Agee strove to make his prose capture the same pristine objectivity he envied in Evans's photographs. "If I could do it," he writes in his overture, "I'd do no writing at all here. It would be photographs; the rest would be fragments of cloth, bits of cotton, lumps of earth, records of speech, pieces of wood and iron, phials of odors, plates of food and excrement" (FM 10). But there was a double edge to the modernist distance from the object of the artist's consciousness. As much as Agee strove to present the Southern poor in their own aura, as if without words, there were words nonetheless.

Agee's writing connects with Caldwell's within the inescapable cultural logic of scopophilia, the gaze. If Caldwell saw the Lester women, Pearl and Ellie May, as objects of erotic titillation, Agee saw the women he encountered as if they were primitive or classical sculpture. In one of his first encounters, he approaches a group on the porch of their shack:

> The young man's eyes had the opal lightings of dark oil and, though he was watching me in a way that relaxed me to cold weakness of ignobility, they fed too strongly inward to draw to a focus: whereas those of the young woman had each the splendor of a monstrance and were brass. Her body also was brass or bitter gold, strong to stridency beneath the unbleached clayed cotton dress, and her arms and bare legs were sharp with metal down. (FM 30)

Agee makes the tenant farmer South a modernist acropolis; despite his urgent efforts to sear the economic hardship of these humans into his readers' complacent, bourgeois minds, we see them as almost totally mute statuary of a distant time before we lived in metropolises, drove in cars, captured images with a photographic apparatus. Caldwell's South is "other" in the style of a P. T. Barnum gallery of freaks and curiosities; Agee's South is "other" the way Cycladic sculpture or Egyptian hieroglyphs suggest a locked-away form of human consciousness we in the modern present can in no way fathom, but for which we feel a distant nostalgia.

Agee's attempts to fathom the South, to shape into words what he thinks human consciousness must sound like within the minds of his Southern subjects, are significant moves in the modernist aesthetic, dating at least to Pablo Picasso's experiments with Cubism in the first decades of the twentieth century. Here is a moment when Agee seems to dissolve the hard edges of the real into "other" forms:

> The light in this room is of a lamp. Its flame in the glass is of the dry, silent and famished delicateness of the latest lateness of the night, and of such ultimate, such holiness and silence and peace that all on earth and within extremest remembrance seems suspended upon it in perfection as upon reflective water: and I feel that if I can by utter quietness succeed in not disturbing this silence, in not so much as touching this plain of water, I can tell you anything within the realm of God, whatsoever it may be, that I wish to tell you, and that what so ever it may be, you will not be able to help but understand it. (FM 46)

If the language of Angoff and Mencken, for the South, is a language of signifiers connecting laterally to still other signifiers – numbers of churched Baptists to number of lynchings to the name of a state in the Union – then the language of Agee is the language of nearly pure signifieds. As if the South, lagging the modern industrial state in the materialist things of civilization, had grasped the "ultimate," "extremest" essence of being, of being written.

William Faulkner defines the decade in many ways; defining the modernist aesthetic is just one. Here is mad Darl Bundren, the clairvoyant eye of *As I Lay Dying* (AILD) (1931), prefiguring Agee:

> When I was a boy I first learned how much better water tastes when it has set a while in a cedar bucket. Warmish-cool, with a faint taste like the hot July wind in cedar trees smells. It has to set at least six hours, and be drunk from a gourd. Water should never be drunk from metal.
>
> And at night it is better still. I used to lie on the pallet in the hall, waiting until I could hear them all asleep, so I could get up and go back to the bucket. It would be black, the shelf black, the still surface of the water a round orifice in nothingness, where before I stirred it awake with the dipper I could see maybe a star or two in the bucket, and maybe in the dipper a star or two before I drank. (AILD 8)[15]

With so few things to focus the eye upon in the primitive, impoverished South, there was, it seems, that much more clarity. Darl's cedar bucket, gourd, and dipper charge forward with undeniable thingness, like the mundane yet luminous objects in Walker Evans's still life images of share-cropper interiors, or Agee's "fragments of cloth, bits of cotton, lumps of earth." Darl, epitome of the modernist artist, becomes the "orifice in nothingness" he strives to represent, as Agee is consumed in the lamplight he contemplates hypnotically. The dipper Darl drinks from becomes the Dipper that swallows him. Appropriately, he is carted off to an asylum, laughing uncontrollably, in the final pages of the novel.

William Faulkner looms over Southern writing of the 1930s with such totality that it is difficult to remember that (a) there were many other writers besides him who worked in the decade, and (b) by 1940, all of Faulkner's books were out of print. It was Malcolm Cowley, reassembling Faulkner's work into *The Portable Faulkner* (1946), who brought him back to critical attention and wove his work into the realistic narrative of American literature more generally. "The job [*The Portable Faulkner*] is splendid," Faulkner wrote to Cowley upon seeing the finished volume. "Damn you to hell anyway. But even if I had beat you to the idea, mine wouldn't have been this good. By God, I didn't know myself what I had tried to do, and how much I had succeeded."[16]

Over the span of the 1930s Faulkner wrote several of the most important novels in US literature, and at least one of the most notorious. The modernist masterwork *The Sound and the Fury* (1929) was followed by *As I Lay Dying* (1930), *Sanctuary* (1931), *Light in August* (1932), *Pylon* (1935), *Absalom, Absalom!* (1936), *The Wild Palms* (1939), *The Hamlet* (1940), and – stretching the decade just slightly because we must not omit "The Bear" – *Go Down, Moses* (1942).

In two of these novels, *The Sound and the Fury* and *Absalom, Absalom!*, Faulkner examines the image of the South, the automatic recognition of a cultural identity and the imperative to defend it in spite of the under-minings of historical fact. The protagonist in both novels, Quentin Compson, is the symbol for the white Southern male doomed to defend an indefensible identity. His torment in both novels and his suicide in *The Sound and the Fury* are directly if not solely attributable to his failure to make abstractions (the past, family name, honor, virginity) stable mean-ings in a modern world dismissive of all abstraction. In *Absalom, Absalom!* Quentin comes face to face, in the climactic scene, with his alter ego: a white Southern man, Henry Sutpen, who at Quentin's age in the 1850s and 1860s had been similarly baffled by the absence of fixed meanings in honor, blood, sexuality, race, incest, virginity, and more. What these two novels accomplish together is the thorough insertion of the South and its brutal past into the poetics of modernist narration and the politics of regional memory. Engaging the former, Faulkner pushes the limits of writing's power to represent the real. Like Agee, Faulkner strives to eliminate mediations between words and world, but unlike Agee, he cannot find an instrument (like the camera) for accomplishing the task. Faulkner's novels then become ongoing, self-examining exercises in trying to separate the teller from the tale.

At the same time Faulkner was undertaking his deep examination of the ideas of Southern history and culture, he exploited the popular image of the region as an aborted civilization: the version summed up in Mencken's phrase "hordes of barbaric peasants" and in Caldwell's tribes of primitive sharecroppers. *Sanctuary* is saturated with this South: nymphomania, binge drinking, rape with a corncob, murder. Indeed, the most domestic space in the novel is a Memphis brothel. Henry Seidel Canby, reviewing the novel in the *Saturday Review of Literature*, voiced genteel and main-stream revulsion from "Mr. Faulkner's Mississippi," the enabling site of "his [Faulkner's] characterizations – Popeye, the filthy politician, the boot-legger's woman, the nit-wit. Nor can any sane reader doubt that some-where along the path he is following lies the end of all sanity in fiction. Here in this sadistic story is decadence in every sense that criticism has ever given the word ... The emotions are sharpened to a febrile obsession with cruelty, lust, and pain which exaggerates a potentiality of human nature at the expense of human truth."[17] At one end of the 1930s spectrum, the South as "Mr. Faulkner's Mississippi" could be seen (and rejected) as an American Bedlam or unconscious where appetites kept carefully in check in polite civilization break the surface in characters, places, and situations studiously censored by the watchmen of public morality. At the other end of the spectrum, Faulkner had also mobilized the South as a site of modernist exploration where the very mechanisms of understanding could be questioned: language, writing, history, time.

None of which, however, impinged in any way on the popularity, in the decade and since, of Margaret Mitchell's *Gone with the Wind* (1936) and David O. Selznick's film version (1939). In Mitchell's South, Mammy, Pork, Prissy, and Big Sam are never more contented than when they serve white O'Haras and Wilkeses and Butlers. Mammy's prejudice for white skin is just as unquestioning as any of her various masters'. Yankees are predatory, marauding rapists who deserve to be shot. Reconstruction was a merciless and unlawful appropriation of white Southern property and political sway; in this belief Mitchell was one with Thomas Dixon, the author of *The Clansman* (1905), the film version of which, D. W. Griffith's *Birth of a Nation* (1915), is a direct ancestor to Selznick's film.

Still, there are segments of *Gone with the Wind* (print and film) that connect less directly to its dissemination of racist stereotype and false history. The second half of both novel and film, covering the career of Scarlett (now Butler) in Reconstruction Atlanta, functions as a motivational narrative for an America, in the late 1930s, still waiting for New Deal policies to bear fruit and not yet swept up in the war economy of the 1940s. It is as if Scarlett had heard and taken to heart the official New Deal message. On August 5, 1938, Harry L. Hopkins, administrator of the Works Progress Administration in Franklin Delano Roosevelt's second administration, delivered a radio address from Memphis in which he laid out the New Deal plan for national economic recovery, with the South as a special beneficiary. That Hopkins had traveled to Memphis for this broadcast was not an accident; President Roosevelt had previously proclaimed the South as "America's Economic Problem Number 1." Without ever mentioning myriad denials of legal rights to African Americas under brutal Jim Crow racial segregation, Hopkins prescribed a tonic of diversified industrial economy, more public schools, better public health, and liberation from the monoculture of cotton. Demonstrating particular tone deafness to a particular Southern cultural icon, Hopkins implied that a tractor might be a better farm implement than a mule.[18] Mules were still, in Scarlett's time, the preferred means of hauling and plowing and grinding and lifting – when she could not rent black convicts more cheaply.

African-American writers were not entirely stifled in the decade. Richard Wright (1908–60) was a prominent voice. His collection of short stories, *Uncle Tom's Children*, first published in 1938 and reissued with an additional story, "Bright and Morning Star," and with his autobiographical account of growing up in Mississippi, "The Ethics of Living Jim Crow" positioned as the introduction (1940), directly rebuts the white myth of a civilized Southern way of life. Not organic stability rooted in an agrarian order, but savage, paternalistic violence is the controlling instinct of the white population. This is the theme explored in "Big Boy Leaves Home," a story of black innocence, white sexual hysteria, lynching, and flight North. The self-serving and comfortable "Mammy" stereotype of *Gone with the Wind* is rewritten in "Bright and Morning Star" as an armed, dangerous, and willing martyr prepared to die exercising retributive justice on the white men who have killed her beloved son.

Wright's novel *Native Son* (1940) conveniently closes the decade. The life and death by execution of Bigger Thomas – the continuation of the Big Boy who leaves Mississippi for the North in "Big Boy Leaves Home" – roughly sums up one powerful iteration of black, male experience in 1930s America. Life in a Chicago ghetto sparks desires that the actual limits on black life can never fulfill. Wright converts all of Bigger's stifled desires into one desire: sexual. Bigger commits one murder – of a black woman whom he sees as a barrier to his ultimate freedom – for which he is not pursued. And a second panicked, diminished-capacity homicide of a white woman for which he is, theatrically, tried and convicted. One white Mississippi writer who, better than most of his race, place, and time, realized what Wright sought to express, wrote to Wright a few years later after reading his autobiographical *Black Boy* (1945). William Faulkner praised the later book, but remembered the earlier one in a conflicted way: "I have just read *Black Boy*. It needed to be said, and you said it well. Though I am afraid (I am speaking now from the point of view of one who believes that the man who wrote *Native Son* is potentially an artist) it will accomplish little of what it should accomplish, since only they will be moved and grieved by it who already know and grieve over this situation."[19]

There are few American myths as durable as this one: the intractable otherness of the South, rooted in what is either a dismal failure or a principled refusal to become a modern democracy, to succeed (or acquiesce) in becoming like the rest of America. As the 1930s inevitably became the 1940s, a world war brought the South more directly into the social, cultural, and economic currents of that modern nation. Still, to stretch Faulkner's meaning, many in the South were not "moved" into the present.

If the South had been, in the 1930s, exclusively a "national problem," it became, in the 1940s, international. Gunnar Myrdal (and his collaborators) identified this as the paradoxical theme of his massive study *An American Dilemma: The Negro Problem and American Democracy* (AD), researched in the 1930s and published in 1942.[20] The South was crucial to the "Dilemma" Myrdal studied because the South was the part of "America" resistant to racial change as America fought a totalitarian state in Europe. "We shall find," Myrdal writes hopefully in his introduction, "that even a poor and uneducated white person in some isolated and backward rural region in the Deep South, who is violently prejudiced against the Negro and intent upon depriving him of civic rights and human independence, has also a whole compartment in his valuation sphere housing the entire American Creed of liberty, equality, justice, and fair opportunity for everybody" (AD lxxii). In his uplifting conclusion to *An American Dilemma*, Myrdal foresaw a redeemed South in a progressive nation:

> The South has been, and is, changing rapidly, and Southern liberalism has been coming to be a force though it was practically nowhere in political power and today [1930s] is fearfully timid on the Negro issue. Even the ordinary conservative white Southerner has a deeply split personality. In the short run this can be suppressed, and the tension can lead to violent reactions. But in the long run it means that the conservative white Southerner himself can be won over to equalitarian reforms in line with the American Creed. (AD 1015)

It must be said, in conclusion, that the "long run" has proven to be much longer than Myrdal was willing to admit. In the "Author's Preface to the Twentieth Anniversary Edition" of *An American Dilemma*, Myrdal confirms his unwillingness to revisit the project (AD xxiv), leaving reassessment to his collaborator on the original work, Arnold Rose. To Rose was left the sobering task of assessing progress in race relations in the two decades since original publication. The usual suspects, apparently, are still in play in the aftermath of *Brown* v. *Board of Education* and Little Rock. While white liberals "know and grieve" rather than act, passionate intensity is the mode of resistance for "those, mainly in the lower classes, who get psychological satisfaction out of a sense of racial superiority" (AD xxxvii). Mencken's "hordes of barbaric peasants," and the fearful subconscious they represent, still lurk in those "lower classes."

Notes

1. See Richard Beale Davis, C. Hugh Holman, and Louis D. Rubin Jr., eds. *Southern Writing 1585–1920* (New York: The Odyssey Press, 1970), 970–79. Rubin selected Mencken's essay for inclusion and wrote the introductory note.

Immediately following the conclusion of "The Sahara of the Bozart" is "Postscript: The Southern Literary Renascence" (980–87), implying a strong causal connection.

2. And Georgia had, Mencken reminds his readers, recently lynched Leo Frank.

3. Chuck Thompson, *Better Off without 'Em: A Northern Manifesto for Southern Secession* (New York: Simon & Schuster, 2012); V. S.Naipaul, *A Turn in the South* (New York: Alfred A. Knopf, 1989); Peter Appelbome, *Dixie Rising: How the South Is Shaping American Values, Politics, and Culture* (New York: Times Books, 1996); Tony Horwitz, *Confederates in the Attic: Dispatches from America's Unfinished Civil War* (New York: Pantheon, 1998); Paul Theroux, *Deep South*. Photos by Steve McCurry (New York: Houghton Mifflin Harcourt, 2015). And others.

4. Twelve Southerners, *I'll Take My Stand: The South and the Agrarian Tradition* (1930; rpt. Baton Rouge: Louisiana State University Press, 1977).

5. The discourse of "burden" will be familiar to readers of Robert Penn Warren's novel *All the King's Men* (1946), whose narrator, Jim Burden, works both in the present for demagogic governor Willie Stark and in the past on the journals of an ancestor eaten away with guilt over slavery. Historian C. Vann Woodward picks up the discourse with *The Burden of Southern History* (1960).

6. See my " Robert Penn Warren: The Real Southerner and the 'Hypothetical Negro,'" in *The South That Wasn't There: Postsouthern History and Memory* (Baton Rouge: Louisiana State University Press, 2010), 49–75.

7. Charles Angoff and H. L. Mencken, "The Worst American State: Part III," *The American Mercury*, 24.95 (November 1931), 355–71.

8. At least Mencken was willing to change his mind on one thing: the worst Southern state in "The Sahara of the Bozart" was Georgia; in 1931, it was Mississippi. Not much has changed in eight decades: The Economic Innovation Group, a more contemporary version of Angoff and Mencken, has found, after crunching its own supply of census data, that among the now fifty states, Mississippi has the largest component of its population living in "economic distress": 40 percent. In general, "the South is home to more than half of the 50.4 million Americans living in distressed zipcodes." See Nelson D. Schwartz, "Poorest Areas Have Missed Out on Boons of Recovery," *New York Times*, February 24, 2016. www.nytimes.com/2016/02/25/business/economy/poorest-areas-have-missed-out-on-boons-of-recovery-study-finds.html?_r=0

9. William Faulkner's young Southern man of "excellent blood," Quentin Compson, had made the move (*The Sound and the Fury* [1929]) – and drowned himself in the Charles River.

10. Erskine Caldwell, *Tobacco Road* (1932; rpt. New York: New American Library, 1959), 25.

11. Pearl is part of the iconography of Southern literature. As archetype, she appears in the character of Dewey Dell in William Faulkner's *As I Lay Dying* (1931) and later in Tennessee Williams's screenplay for *Baby Doll* (1956), directed by Elia Kazan. Ellie May, relieved of her harelip, appears archetypally

as well in almost every Southern farmer's daughter, and by name in the very popular television series *The Beverly Hillbillies* (1962–71) played by Donna Douglas.

12. "Workers of the world, unite and fight. You have nothing to lose but your chains, and a world to win." In a footnote, Agee cryptically added: "These words are quoted here to mislead those who will be misled by them." He intended the quotation as one theme in a double-themed "sonata form." The other epigraph is taken from *King Lear*, Act III, scene iv: "Poor naked wretches . . . ." James Agee and Walker Evans, *Let Us Now Praise Famous Men* (1941; rpt. Boston: Houghton Mifflin, 2001), n.p.

13. Julia Mood Peterkin and Doris Ulmann, *Roll Jordan, Roll* (New York: Bobbs-Merrill, 1933); Richard Wright, *12 Million Black Voices* (New York: Viking Press, 1941).

14. See Fredric Jameson, *Postmodernism; or, The Cultural Logic of Late Capitalism* (Durham, NC: Duke University Press, 1991), 6–15.

15. William Faulkner, *As I Lay Dying*, ed. Michael Gorra (1930; rpt. New York: W. W. Norton, 2010).

16. William Faulkner to Malcolm Cowley, April 23, 1946. In Joseph Blotner, ed., *Selected Letters of William Faulkner* (New York: Random House, 1977), 233.

17. Henry Seidel Canby, "The School of Cruelty," *Saturday Review of Literature* (March 21, 1931), 673–74, 674.

18. http://newdeal.feri.org/works/wpa06.htm

19. William Faulkner to Richard Wright, September 11, 1945. Blotner, *Selected Letters of William Faulkner*, 201.

20. Gunnar Myrdal, *An American Dilemma: The Negro Problem and American Democracy, Twentieth Anniversary Edition* (New York: Harper & Row, 1962).

CHAPTER 7

The Literature of Social Protest in California

David Wrobel

I'm trying to write history while it is happening and I don't want to be wrong.

John Steinbeck (1938)

California: A Guide to the Golden State (1939), compiled by the California division of the Federal Writers' Project under the auspices of the New Deal's Works Progress Administration (WPA), did not shy away from the pressing social and economic issues facing the Golden State. Part of the New Deal's monumental state guides series (one of the nation's great cultural treasures), the California guide included coverage of Upton Sinclair's remarkable 1934 gubernatorial campaign built around his End Poverty in California (EPIC) program, and of Sinclair's literary contributions to the Golden State.[1] Most famous for his Progressive Era muckraking classic *The Jungle* (1906), Sinclair moved to California in 1916 and wrote a series of exposés, of the coal, oil, and automobile industries, organized religion, Hollywood, the press, and the University of California. Most importantly, he crafted a sixty-three-page work of "futurist fiction" titled *I, Governor of California and How I Ended Poverty: A True Story of the Future*, published in October 1933. In *I, Governor*, Sinclair predicted his gubernatorial victory and outlined the EPIC program he planned to institute once in office. The small book became a big seller, facilitated no doubt by its price – twenty cents a copy.[2] EPIC, which centered on the idea of production for use instead of production for profit, was influenced by the cooperatives that had sprung up in Los Angeles, Seattle, and Denver. The plan involved opening up shuttered factories and fallow farmland across California to provide labor for the state's unemployed, who would in turn be compensated in scrip notes that could be used to purchase food, clothing, furniture, and other goods within the production-for-use system.[3]

The California guidebook also chronicled the heavy reliance of the state's agricultural sector on cheap migrant labor from China, Japan, South Asia, Mexico, and the Philippines, and the recent journey of several hundred thousand migrants driven out of the Southern Plains by the terrible dust storms and drought. "An effective approach to the migrant problem is now being made, for the first time in California history, by the Federal Government," the guide declared, and proceeded to detail the efforts of the Farm Security Administration in setting up sanitary camps, providing emergency food supplies, and organizing medical services for migrant families. The guide highlighted the horrendous conditions those migrants faced in California, quoting the National Labor Relations Board's 1934 description of "filth, squalor, and entire absence of sanitation, and a crowding of human beings into totally inadequate tents or crude structures built of boards, weeds, and anything that was found at hand to give a pitiful semblance of a home at its worst." The contributing authors then proceeded to describe the failure of workmen's compensation laws to protect those laborers, the California agribusiness sector's practice of ignoring minimum wage laws for women and minors, the denial of medical aid to desperately ill people, the corrupt practices of labor contractors, and the role of violent vigilantism, sponsored by those same corporate agricultural interests, in breaking up strikes.[4] In short, the *WPA Guide to California* provided a crystal clear delineation of its authors' and the federal government's support for migrant workers and their families (and for labor in general). In this regard, the California guide was among the most progressive and social justice-oriented of all the WPA state guides and clearly benefited in this regard from its staff of young activist writers such as poet Kenneth Rexroth, novelist Tillie Olson, and labor advocate (and future author of mysteries and science fiction) Miriam Allen de Ford.[5]

The guide's section on the state's literary heritage paid special attention, as one would expect, to luminaries such as Mark Twain, Bret Harte, Robert Louis Stevenson, and to late nineteenth- and early twentieth-century social activist writers Frank Norris and Jack London. The volume also emphasized the contemporary literary scene, particularly the work of Sinclair, as well as California native John Steinbeck, highlighting his critically acclaimed strike novel *In Dubious Battle* (1936), and his popular novella *Of Mice and Men* (1937) about the struggles of migrant workers George and Lennie.[6] Published in May 1939, the guide had gone to press too soon to include mention of Steinbeck's 1939 novel *The Grapes of Wrath* (which appeared in April), and predated journalist and social activist Carey McWilliams's influential study *Factories in the Field*, published in July of the same year. Without overtly saying as much, the guide's authors had underscored the connections between literature and social protest in the state.[7] Sinclair put his literary talents to work in the cause of his own gubernatorial campaign. Steinbeck, as he worked on *The Grapes of Wrath*, remarked in a letter to a friend, "I'm trying to write history while it is happening and I don't want to be wrong." McWilliams's exposé of California's corporate agriculture served as a sort of nonfiction historical and sociological companion to Steinbeck's epic novel. This chapter charts the efforts of these authors to chronicle and transform social conditions through their writing, and in doing so suggests that the literature of social protest characterized California writing during the Depression decade.[8]

The Depression hit California hard. Between 1929 and 1932, the value of the state's agricultural output dropped by half from $750 million to $372 million. Republican Governors James Rolph (1931–34), who died in office in 1934, and his successor, Frank Merriam (1934–39) proved largely unreceptive to New Deal initiatives to bring relief and recovery to the state.[9] California's resistance to the New Deal was in keeping with its recent history of brutal opposition to labor; the New Deal, in contrast, was supportive of labor's right to unionize and bargain collectively. The agricultural sector was particularly volatile. Dominated by corporate interests long before the Depression decade, California farming was characterized by large farms worked by temporary laborers, rather than small owner-operated homesteads. Daily wages for California field workers averaged $2.55 a day in 1930, but by 1933 had dropped to $1.40, or fifteen to sixteen cents an hour. No fewer than thirty-seven strikes took place across the state in 1933. In the fall of that year, 12,000 cotton pickers in the lower San Joaquin Valley (mostly Mexicans and Filipinos, but also some African Americans and white Southern Plains migrants), organized by the Cannery and Agricultural Workers Industrial Union (CAWIU), went on strike. The action met with a violent response from local authorities; several strikers and sympathizers were gunned down. Sherriff's deputies even prevented the union from delivering food supplies to the striking workers and their families. The New Deal's National Industrial Recovery Act (NIRA) provided no significant protections for agricultural workers. Nonetheless, the National Recovery Administration (NRA) did intervene to help broach a compromise, which provided for a small pay increase for the workers, but no formal recognition for the CAWIU. The federal government was clearly leaning toward labor, but not yet fully committed to the cause.[10] However, in the spring of 1934, a rigidly anti-labor organization, the Associated Farmers of California, formed to shore up profit margins for the state's corporate agricultural interests by systematically repressing labor activism and oppressing migrant workers.

Then in San Francisco in the summer of 1934, militant Australian labor leader Harry Bridges, empowered by the NIRA, led a walkout of longshoremen that turned horribly violent on July 5, "Bloody Thursday," when thousands of strikers faced 800 uniformed and armed police employing tear gas and fire hoses. Two workers were killed and more than seventy were injured. Workers across the city supported the longshoremen and a general strike followed; San Francisco was paralyzed. Governor Merriam declared martial law and the National Guard was called in; for two weeks the city seemed to be on the brink of even more violent clashes before the strikers submitted to arbitration. The resulting agreement actually met many of labor's demands. Nonetheless, the backdrop of organized resistance to labor and, in the state legislature and the governor's office to New Deal programs, ensured a climate of "New Deal, No Deal" in California.[11]

It was in this dangerous atmosphere of labor activism and violent repression of those efforts during the mid- to late 1930s that Sinclair, Steinbeck, and others helped make California an example of what literature could do to transform society. It was not just the written word that proved a tool for social protest. King Vidor's critically acclaimed film, *Our Daily Bread*, which lauded the virtues and benefits of life on an American collective farm, was released in October 1934, during the height of the California gubernatorial campaign.[12] And the New Deal's Resettlement Administration (founded in 1935 and expanded into the Farm Security Administration in 1937) included a photography division that employed Dorothea Lange, Russell Lee, and other socially conscious artists who captured the trials and tribulations of migrant workers and their families in an effort to generate public support for the New Deal's assistance programs. Lange, of course, provided the single most powerful and influential photographic image of the thirties, her "Migrant Mother" (1936) portrait of Oklahoma native Florence Owens Thompson and her children in a migrant camp in Nipomo, in California's Central Valley. Lange, with her husband, labor economist Paul Schuster Taylor, also published a powerful photo essay, *An American Exodus: A Record of Human Erosion in the 1930s*, later in the same year (1939) that *Factories in the Field* and *The Grapes of Wrath* appeared. Their book charted the migration to California and declared that the frontier of Western promise was gone, and the "opportunity to obtain intermittent employment in a disorganized labor market – no experience required – is our new frontier, our new West." Yet Lange and Taylor also found a glimmer of hope in their subjects: "When they arrive in the fertile valleys of the West, the migrants are ragged, half-starved, needy … but with a surprising morale in the midst of misery, and a will to work."[13] By the late thirties, Lange and Taylor, Vidor, and other committed chroniclers of human suffering had drawn the attention of the nation and its government to the Southern Plains' migration to the Golden State, and their works were vital accompaniments to the efforts of Sinclair, McWilliams, and Steinbeck to help to effect social change.

Sinclair's whole career had been devoted to social justice issues, so for him the 1930s were no great departure, but rather the natural continuation of his work at the intersections of literature and muckraking journalism dating back to *The Jungle*. But in 1933, Sinclair took the genre of literature as social protest to a new place. *I, Governor of California* predicted the future and laid out the plan (nothing new there – utopian fiction had been doing as much for half a century, from William Dean Howells and Edward Bellamy forward), but then the author actually acted out the narrative and ran for office. "First, I portray events," he wrote, "and then I put down my pen and try to make them happen." Moreover, he added, "so far as I know, this is the first time a historian has set out to make his history true." Adding to the drama of the moment, Sinclair declared that "forty nations as well as forty centuries," and "forty-seven other States in the Union" were watching to see California's peaceful democratic salvation. Providing further evidence of his remarkable self-confidence, or plain hubris, Sinclair went on in the very pages of his book to predict its future sales – more than a quarter million by September 1934.[14]

Sinclair's bold EPIC plan was lauded by those on the left for its attentiveness to the needs of the unemployed and underemployed and the hungry and the destitute, and lambasted by conservatives for being socialistic. Sinclair summed up the "The Twelve Principles of EPIC" in *I, Governor*, and the document was reprinted in newspapers across the country:

1. *God created the natural wealth of the earth for the use of all men, not a few.*
2. *God created men to seek their own welfare, not that of masters.*
3. *Private ownership of tools, a basis of freedom when tools are simple, becomes a basis of enslavement when tools are complex.*
4. *Autocracy in industry cannot exist alongside democracy in government.*
5. *When some men live without working, other men are working without living.*

6. *The existence of luxury in the presence of poverty and destitution is contrary to good morals and sound public policy.*

7. *The present depression is one of abundance, not scarcity.*

8. *The cause of the trouble is that a small class has the wealth, while the rest have the debts.*

9. *It is contrary to common sense that men should starve because they have raised too much food.*

10. *The destruction of food or other wealth, or the limitation of production, is economic insanity.*

11. *The remedy is to give the workers access to the means of production, and let them produce for themselves, not for others.*

12. *This change can be brought about by action by a majority of the people, and that is the American way.*[15]

To put these principles into action, finance the production-for-use system, and thereby prevent California's "drifting towards Fascism," Sinclair outlined a progressive tax system that included the eradication of the state sales tax and its replacement by a tax on stock transfers, a graduated state income tax on annual earnings of more than $5,000 a year, including a 30 percent tax on incomes over $50,000o, and a very high inheritance tax rate of 50 percent on the wealthy. Revenues generated would provide $50-a-month pensions for all the state's citizens over sixty, $50 a month to those with disabilities, and the same amount to widowed women with dependent children.[16] The plan proved attractive, not because California was filled with doctrinaire socialists and communists seeking a thoroughgoing redistribution of wealth in the state, but because many residents were tired of corporate domination and monopoly and fully aware of, or themselves caught up in, the awful economic conditions. By August there were more than 1,000 EPIC Clubs operating in the state. Sinclair's efforts resulted in the registration of 350,000 new Democratic Party members, and for the first time, Democrats outnumbered Republicans in California. At the end of the month, Sinclair won the Democratic primary with a 436,000-vote majority.

Sinclair met with Franklin D. Roosevelt in early September, but failed to get the president's endorsement for the fall election. FDR feared that Sinclair's radicalism would damage the Democratic Party and the New Deal nationally, particularly his own efforts to develop a social security program. Whether the president's overt support would have swung the election away from Republican incumbent governor Merriam and toward Sinclair is debatable. The longshoremen's strike and the resulting general strike in San Francisco that summer made the public nervous about labor radicalism and undercut Sinclair's support. The Republicans launched a comprehensive campaign against Sinclair, supported by big business, agribusiness (*I, Governor* was highly critical of the mistreatment of workers by the large farming interests), organized religion, the press (particularly newspaper giants William Randolph Hearst and Harry Chandler), most of the Hollywood film industry, and the University of California; those organizations relished the opportunity to pay Sinclair back for his scathing portrayals of them in his novels in the twenties and early thirties. Sinclair was roundly condemned as a dangerous radical out to bankrupt the Golden State. Studio chiefs in Hollywood actually blocked the release of *Our Daily Bread* in the state, fearing that the film's powerfully uplifting portrayal of cooperatives would boost Sinclair's chances. The carefully coordinated red baiting campaign against Sinclair in the *L.A. Times* and other newspapers and in newsreels created by Louis B. Mayer and MGM Studios proved highly effective. Fabricated newsreels were shot depicting tramps and vagrants pouring into the state to take advantage of the welfare and work programs that Sinclair promised.[17]

The much-needed endorsement from FDR never came, and right before the election the California Democratic Party stuck a deal with Merriam to throw its support to him in return for his announcement upon reelection of support for New Deal programs in the state. Merriam won quite comfortably in November 1934 with close to 49 percent of the vote to Sinclair's less than 38 percent. Raymond Haight, a third-party candidate for the Commonwealth/Progressive Party ticket, offered a moderate alternative to Sinclair and got 13 percent of the vote. Haight's and Sinclair's vote totals together actually exceeded Merriam's, and Sinclair had done better than any other Democratic gubernatorial candidate in the state's history. Twenty-six EPIC candidates, including future governor Culbert Olson, were voted into the state legislature despite Sinclair's defeat. The EPIC campaign, while a failure in the short term, had contributed to the forces pushing FDR to the left and would impact California and the nation in the long term.[18]

Never one to pass up an opportunity to put pen to paper, three days after the election Sinclair began writing a new book, which appeared before the year was out. Sinclair described *I, Candidate for Governor: And How I Got Licked*, as "a revelation of what money can do in American politics."[19] Almost four times the length of the ostensible self-fulfilling prophecy pamphlet *I, Governor*, the post-election protestation *I, Candidate for Governor*, generated only modest sales and was not republished for sixty years. Reflecting in the book on one of the particularly notable missteps of his campaign – his premature claim that FDR was about to endorse his "production for use" program in a pending speech – Sinclair lamented that "[t]he future, if it remembers me at all, may forgive blunders caused by a too impetuous desire to stop the starving of men and women, and especially of little children, in a world that has learned to produce more than it can consume." Sinclair at least took some comfort in the election of Olson as state senator for Los Angeles County, along with other EPIC candidates, and he declared that "[t]he political life of this state is going to be different from now on; the reactionaries will not take everything for granted."[20] On this point Sinclair's predictive powers turned out to be quite prophetic indeed.

By January 1935, the nation had suffered through five long years of economic depression. FDR's New Deal programs, enacted during the First Hundred Days (the congressional session from March to June 17, 1933), had alleviated the suffering of millions. But critics on the left, such as Louisiana Senator Huey Long, were attacking the president for not doing enough to help those Americans suffering the most. For example, the New Deal's initial response to the nation's terrible agricultural crisis was to raise commodity prices by encouraging farmers to scale back production, thus reducing supply. Those efforts included the destruction of crops that were already in the ground and payment of cash subsidies to farmers to take land out of production. Some large landowners found it financially advantageous to evict tenant farmers and leaseholders from the land in return for these subsidies. This was an unintended consequence of federal policy, but to radical critics of the New Deal it was evidence that FDR's administration cared primarily about saving capitalism rather than helping the nation's poorest citizens. In *I, Candidate for Governor*, Sinclair insisted that FDR "has to choose between EPIC and Hoover."[21] Meanwhile, critics on the right, including ex-President Herbert Hoover, accused FDR of instituting state socialism, or even worse, communism.

During that month, January 1935, John Steinbeck wrote to a friend about a "brutal" book manuscript he was completing. He had started down the path that would lead to *The Grapes of Wrath*, one that could be traveled only through personal experience with his subjects. In 1934, he had interviewed Cicil McKiddy and Carl Williams, the key organizers of the 1933 San Joaquin Valley cotton pickers' strike. In addition to drawing inspiration from that strike, *In Dubious Battle* made direct reference to the San Francisco longshoremen's strike and "Bloody Thursday." John Steinbeck had begun to write history while it was happening.[22]

The novel opens with Jim Nolan walking into a local Communist Party headquarters in San Jose; his father (a labor organizer) has been dead for three years and his mother just a month in the grave. Jim announces, "I feel dead. Everything in the past is gone" (537). At that point, his life begins again. Jim meets Mac, his mentor-to-be, and starts his apprenticeship in strike organizing. He and Mac travel to a California apple orchard where conditions for the migrant laborers and their families are deteriorating and Mac immediately works to earn the trust of the strikers, even going so far as to help deliver a baby, despite his complete lack of medical training. Mac is fully committed to the principle that the Communist Party's revolutionary ends justify any means (no matter how violent or unethical) employed in the struggle. In the wake of the successful birth, Mac callously remarks to Jim, "We've got to use whatever material comes to us. That was a lucky break. We simply had to take it. 'Course it was nice to help the girl, but hell, even if it killed her – we've got to use anything" (576). Mac uses people again and again in pursuit of the cause and Jim, far from being repelled by Mac's approach, becomes the perfect apprentice. Then, as the strike moves toward its inevitably unsuccessful conclusion, after a series of graphically violent confrontations, Mac holds up Jim's dead body to the crowd of striking workers, under the light of a lantern, with the face completely blown off by gunfire, and proclaims, "Comrades! He didn't want nothing for himself – " (793).

Not surprisingly, communists found little to aid their cause in Steinbeck's novel, and the book incensed California's agribusiness interests. Steinbeck depicted the desperate conditions faced by the workers, and the violently oppressive actions of the organized large growers. But in showing so clearly the matching inhumanity of a methodically applied radical ideology, wherein the ends always justify the means, he had created a work devoid of heroes. He had charted the anatomy of a strike, with horrendous acts of violence on both sides. But he had also begun to develop a foundational theme of *The Grapes of Wrath*: the need "for an end to man's inhumanity to man."[23]

October 1936. The nation was a month removed from the assassination of Louisiana senator and potential presidential candidate Huey Long (not everyone was enamored with his "Share the Wealth" program, designed to make "Everyone a King"), and a month away from the election that would see FDR and the Democratic Party win the most comprehensive victory in modern American history. The Second New Deal programs saw a hardening of FDR's criticism of big business and a growing attention to the needs of those Americans at the bottom of the socioeconomic structure, and were enormously popular with the majority of Americans. Reform was in the ascendancy, in no small part because photographers, writers, and intellectuals were highlighting the plight of the downtrodden and dispossessed, just as had been the case during the first period of modern American reform, the early twentieth-century Progressive era, when Sinclair wrote *The Jungle*.

Steinbeck's "The Harvest Gypsies," a series of seven articles, appeared in the *San Francisco News* between October 5 and 12, 1936.[24] Tom Collins, manager of the federal Resettlement Administration's Arvin Sanitary Camp for migratory laborers in Kern County, California (more familiarly known as the Weedpatch Camp), helped educate Steinbeck about the migrants' culture and the conditions they faced. A character based on Collins appears in *The Grapes of Wrath*, and the novel was dedicated to both Collins and to Steinbeck's wife, Carol ("To Carol who willed it. To Tom who lived it" – not Tom Joad, Tom Collins). Steinbeck observed Collins at work, establishing structures for the migrants to govern themselves and thereby restore some pride and dignity, and Steinbeck read the detailed reports on conditions that Collins filed. Steinbeck also toured the San Joaquin Valley in the fall of 1936 with Eric H. Thomsen, regional director of the federal migrant camp program and a former preacher, in order to better understand the landscape of migratory labor. He spent time with migrant families (mainly from Oklahoma) between 1936 and 1938, learning about their labor conditions, values, diets, and speech patterns, and sometimes using his own funds to help support them.[25]

Steinbeck was clearly disturbed and angered by these experiences. The second of the *San Francisco News* articles chronicled the fortunes of three migrant families in a typical California squatters' camp, each in a different stage of decline and despair. It is one of the most moving and disturbing journalistic accounts of American poverty in the thirties. The first family (husband, wife, and three children), formerly proprietors of fifty acres, with a bank balance of a thousand dollars to their name, had now been reduced to building a ten-by-ten-foot house with corrugated paper. But the first rain would turn the house into a "brown, pulpy mush," and combined with the lack of good nutrition would subject the whole family to pneumonia (996). Steinbeck wrote, "there is still pride in this family," and appropriate sanitary practices are still followed since the father is "a newcomer and his spirit and decency and his sense of his own dignity have not been quite wiped out" (996–97).

The second family (husband, wife, and four children), former grocery store proprietors, now live in a tattered, rotting tent; their sanitary standards are lower than the first family's, their diet less varied, and their number already reduced by one as a result – their four-year-old boy has just died of malnutrition. "This is the middle class of the squatters' camp," Steinbeck explained," but "[i]n a few months this family will slip down into the lower class. Dignity is all gone, and spirit has turned to sullen anger before it dies" (998). The third family (husband, wife, and three children) have tried to build a home from willow branches and weeds, paper, tin, and old carpet strips. They sleep on an old piece of carpet on the floor, folding it up over them. "The three year old child has a gunny sack tied about his middle for clothing. He has the swollen belly caused by malnutrition ... He will die in a very short time. The older children may survive. Four nights ago the mother had a baby in the tent, on the dirty carpet. It was born dead, which was just as well because she could not have fed it at the breast; her own diet will not produce milk ... This woman's eyes have the glazed, far away look of a sleep walker's eyes ... [The husband] has lost even the desire to talk" (998–99).

Steinbeck described what happens to women and men as their "children have sickened and died, after the loss of dignity and spirit have cut [them] down to a kind of sub-humanity," insisting that "malnutrition is not infectious, nor is dysentery, which is almost the rule among the children" (999–1000). He emphasized that these are curable and correctible conditions and the fact of their persistence was not attributable to the failings of the parents, or to their cultural background, but to the meanness and inhumanity of California's organized agricultural interests. Steinbeck next outlined the role of federal camps at Arvin and Marysville in "restor[ing] the dignity and decency that had been kicked out of the migrants by their intolerable mode of life" (1006). Steinbeck described these camps as thoroughly positive "experiments in natural and democratic self-government" that "reduce the degenerating effect of the migrants' life" as effectively as California agribusinesses' oppressive labor system promoted those effects (1007–08).

In addition to calling for an expansion of the Resettlement Administration's sanitary camp system for migrant workers, Steinbeck went much further in the last of his *News* articles, advocating that state and federal land be set aside to provide subsistence farms for migrant laborers. They would be able to either lease the land at affordable rental rates, or purchase it with long-term mortgages, and thus be able to grow their own food to supplement their wages as crop pickers, and escape the worst excesses of the current labor system. The women and children would be able to tend the subsistence farms, and once again enjoy the fruits of education and geographic rootedness – a sense of place – while only the employable men traveled to meet the seasonal demands of California agribusiness. Steinbeck angrily noted that the cost to the government of providing small plots of land, small houses, and schools for migrant families "would not be that much greater than the amount which is now spent for tear gas, machine guns and ammunition, and deputy sheriffs" (1020). Steinbeck insisted that only the support of the federal government in guaranteeing the rights of farm workers to organize and in prosecuting acts of "vigilante terrorism" sponsored by California agribusiness could guarantee the peaceful future of the state. He called for the direct intervention of the US Attorney General, declaring, "if the terrorism and reduction of human rights, the floggings, murder by deputies, kidnapings [sic] and refusal of trial by jury are necessary to our economic security," then "California democracy is rapidly dwindling away." Steinbeck further added that "Fascistic methods are more numerous, more powerfully applied and more openly practiced [in California] than in any other place in the United States" (1022).

Not surprisingly, around this time, Steinbeck's friends began to worry about his safety and such concerns only increased after his novella *Of Mice and Men* appeared in March 1937, and was adapted successfully for the stage later that year; the play was performed more than 200 times on Broadway to great critical and public acclaim. The popular movie adaptation, starring Lon Chaney Jr. as Lennie and Burgess Meredith as George, was released in December 1939. While not directly concerned with labor troubles or the suffering of migrant families, *Of Mice and Men* was set in the same region as *In Dubious Battle* and "The Harvest Gypsies," on a ranch near Salinas, and centered on George and Lennie's unattainable dream of owning a few acres and living "off the fatta the lan,'" and seemed to underscore that the dream of landownership in California was now unattainable. George's mercy killing of Lennie symbolizes the death of that dream. That theme was explored again in "The Leader of the People," the last installment in Steinbeck's *The Red Pony* story cycle, which appeared in his 1938 collection *The Long Valley*. Lange and Taylor conveyed the same message in *An American Exodus*.[26]

The death of the California dream was at the heart of the big novel that Steinbeck was planning. Originally conceived under the title "The Oklahomans," which was to have been about the indomitable spirit of California's newest migrants, the novel eventually evolved into something much more expansive. Events on the ground shifted Steinbeck's direction. He would write to his friend and agent Elizabeth Otis in early February 1938 about the conditions in Visalia and Nipomo, California:

> I must go over into the interior valleys. There are about five thousand families starving to death over there, not just hungry but actually starving. The government is trying to feed them and get medical attention to them with the fascist group of utilities and banks and huge growers sabotaging the thing ... In one tent there are twenty people quarantined for smallpox and two of the women are to have babies in this tent this week ... I must get down there and see it and see if I can't do something to help knock these murderers on their heads (LL, 158)[27]

Steinbeck then implored Otis to keep the matter under wraps, "because when I have finished my job the jolly old associated farmers will be after my scalp again" (LL, 158).

A few weeks later Steinbeck was in Visalia to witness the conditions firsthand and try and help the thousands of migrant families stranded by the floods. He wrote to Otis again in early March about what he experienced:

> A short trip into the fields where the water is a foot deep in the tents and the children are up on the beds and there is no food and no fire, and the county has taken off all the nurses because "the problem is so great that we can't do anything about it." So they do nothing ... It is the most heartbreaking thing in the world ... I break myself every time I go out because the argument that one person's effort can't really do anything doesn't seem to apply when you come on a bunch of starving children and you have a little money ... I want to put a tag of shame on the greedy bastards who are responsible for this. (LL, 161–62)

Steinbeck was saddened and enraged by the nightmarish conditions in Visalia. He published a piece titled "Starvation under the Orange Trees" in the *Monterey Trader* in April, and the Simon J. Lubin Society of California published an expanded version of "The Harvest Gypsies" articles (accompanied by photographs, mostly by Dorothea Lange) in pamphlet form, under the new title *Their Blood Is Strong*, for twenty-five cents a copy to raise money for migrant families; the popular work quickly went through four printings.[28] Steinbeck's next attempt at the novel was titled "L'Affaire Lettuceberg," a scathing work focused on the systematic mistreatment of the migrants by the municipal leaders of Salinas and by citizen vigilantes, not on the migrants' suffering. By May 1938, Steinbeck had completed about 60,000 words of the manuscript and planned on 10,000 more to complete it, but he recognized that "L'Affaire" was "a vicious book, a mean book," one that failed to capture the full drama, significance, and tragedy of the story he wanted to tell. Covici announced the publication of the book, but Steinbeck wrote to Otis and Covici informing them that he would not be delivering the work: "My whole work drive has been aimed at making people understand each other and then I deliberately write this book the aim of which is to cause hatred through partial understanding." He destroyed the manuscript. Writing "L'Affaire," though, had been a cathartic exercise, and *The Grapes of Wrath* would not have become the epic work it did without the detours of "The Oklahomans" and "L'Affaire."[29]

In late May 1938, Steinbeck began writing *The Grapes of Wrath*. Exactly five months later, on October 26, after a monumental hundred days of creativity, he wrote in his journal: "Finished this day – and I hope to God it's good." Carol came up with the title (in early September), drawing from "The Battle Hymn of the Republic," which John Steinbeck insisted appear on the inside front and back covers of the novel – both the music and all the verses. He wrote to Covici on New Year's Day, 1939:

> The fascist crowd will try to sabotage this book because it is revolutionary. They will try to give it the communist angle. However, the Battle Hymn is American and intensely so. Further, every American child learns it and then forgets the words. So if both words and music are there the book is keyed into the American scene from the beginning. (LL, 174)

Steinbeck was right: the book would meet with vigorous opposition upon its publication, but what he had created was simply too powerful and relevant to suppress. He had, indeed, created a novel that was at once both revolutionary and intensely American, and had somehow balanced the most extreme tragedy with a measure of hopefulness. This remarkable equilibrium is evident in the book's controversial final scene. Speaking of Rose of Sharon's act of human kindness in another letter to Covici, Steinbeck refused to change the ending, dismissing all concerns about its appropriateness:

> I am sorry but I cannot change that ending ... if there is a symbol, it is a survival symbol not a love symbol, it must be an accident, it must be a stranger, and it must be quick ... The fact that the Joads don't know him, don't care about him, have no ties to him – that is the emphasis. The giving of the breast has no more sentiment than the giving of a piece of bread ... I am not writing a satisfactory story. I've done my damnedest to rip a reader's nerves to rags. I don't want him to be satisfied. (LL, 178–79)

In addition to its powerful closing scene, the enduring power of *The Grapes of Wrath* also comes in part from its "Old and New Testament themes, parallels, analogies, allusions, and inversions" – the Exodus theme; Rose of Sharon's stillborn child placed in an old apple crate and floated down the river like Moses in the basket; and Jim Casey – initials "JC" – who goes "into the wilderness, like Jesus, to try to find out somepin," is killed and is born again in the newfound, other-centered consciousness of Tom Joad.[30] Moreover, the novel is also a great Western epic, and an anti-Western of sorts: it is not romantic or triumphal, not a heroic saga of settlement. At its core, and much like Lange and Taylor's *An American Exodus*, it is a book about the West, from the dried-out and dust-blown Southern Plains and consequent displacement of sharecroppers, tenants, and small landowners, to the failure of California's fertile valleys to live up to their great promise (334). And, very much related to the theme of the death of the dream of a promised land, *The Grapes of Wrath* is also a novel about the failure of the residents of one American region to welcome the migrants from another.

When the Joads reach California (without Grandma and Grandpa, who have died on the journey), we know the dream is fragile from the casual comment of one service-station attendant to another: "Them goddamn Okies got no sense and no feeling. They ain't human. A human being wouldn't live like they do. A human being couldn't stand to be so dirty and miserable. They ain't a hell of a lot better than gorilla's" (445). Steinbeck was demonstrating how the Joads and other newcomers to the Golden State were being dehumanized because of their regional background and how that process helped to justify inhumane acts against them. "These goddamned Okies are dirty and ignorant," we learn. "They're degenerate, sexual maniacs. These goddamned Okies are thieves. They'll steal anything. They've got no sense of property rights" (510). Steinbeck was highlighting the disturbing way that some people developed their own attachment to a place by deriding newer arrivals to that same place.

In illuminating this "regionalism through reaction," Steinbeck showed the true nature of his literary efforts on behalf of social justice. *The Grapes of Wrath* is not a proletarian novel, or even a particularly political one. It is a novel about what human beings are capable of doing to each other, and for each other, and one that urges "an end to man's inhumanity to man." This is the great power of the final scene, where Rose of Sharon, after delivering her stillborn child, offers her milk-laden breast to a dying man, a total stranger, to sustain his life. These are the awful depths to which California's migrants have been sunk, and the stirring heights to which they have risen. This is the scene Steinbeck steadfastly refused to delete, and one that Hollywood could not depict, choosing instead to end the movie on another powerful, but far less controversial note of noble and enduring struggle as Ma Joad reminds Pa "we're the people that live." As the novel and the film come to their respective endings, the Joads are able to maintain their dignity. "The Harvest Gypsies" articles chronicled dignity's decline among the residents of the camps and displayed Steinbeck's palpable anger; *The Grapes of Wrath* celebrated dignity's survival and illustrated his determination to find some measure of hope amidst the desperation wrought by drought and displacement and then by California's corporate agricultural interests.

In March 1939, Steinbeck heard a rumor that the FBI was investigating him and he became seriously concerned that the Associated Farmers were planning violence. Around that time "he was warned to not stay alone in hotel rooms, in case a rape or assault charge might be set up against him."[31] Then, after the novel was published in April 1939, his literary representation of a contemporary problem literally created history as controversy raged over whether he had told the truth about the migrants and about California agribusiness. The following April, Eleanor Roosevelt visited a migrant workers' camp and testified before Congress on the migrants' plight (the first First Lady to offer congressional testimony), and wrote, much to Steinbeck's relief, that "I never believed that *The Grapes of Wrath* was exaggerated."[32]

Nonetheless, enemies of the book and later of the film engaged in actions that amounted to life imitating art imitating life, as they sought to repress a literary depiction of their own repression of migrant workers and their families. By February 1940, ten months after its publication, *The Grapes of Wrath* was already in its eleventh edition and had sold more than 430,000 copies. The novel's very success nurtured a more determined response; it was banned or burned in several places, including Kern County, California. California agribusiness organized a protest against the book at San Francisco's Palace Hotel. The Associated Farmers in California spread the rumor that Steinbeck was a Jew, acting for Zionist-communist interests to undermine the US economy. The rumor that hurt Steinbeck the most, though, was one spread by California newspapers claiming "the Okies hated him and had threatened to kill him for telling lies about them." Tom Collins told Steinbeck that the Okies at the Weedpatch Camp were deeply angered by this smear campaign against him.[33]

By trying to write history while it was happening Steinbeck had struck a major chord in California, in Oklahoma, and in the national consciousness, but the pressures of success and fear for his personal safety were taking a toll. In October 1939, Steinbeck wrote to Elizabeth Otis, "[t]he last year has been a nightmare all in all," and added, "[o]ne nice thing to think of is the speed of obscurity. In a month [*Grapes*] will be off the [bestseller] list and in six months I'll be forgotten" (LL, 189). He was resoundingly wrong on both counts. John Ford's film version of *The Grapes of Wrath* was released in late January 1940. The movie benefited significantly from Tom Collins's work as technical advisor, and much of the filming took place at the Weedpatch government camp. Steinbeck described the film as "a harsher thing than the book."[34] It was a massive box office success and garnered academy awards for director John Ford and Jane Darwell, who played the indomitable Ma Joad. In April 1940, Steinbeck received the Pulitzer Prize for the novel.

Upton Sinclair, because of his EPIC campaign, dominated the California consciousness in the mid-1930s in a way that few writers can ever hope to do. Steinbeck was considerably more private and less politically active than Sinclair. Yet, nonetheless, Steinbeck's writings in the late 1930s (the period referred to as "the years of greatness" by Steinbeck scholars) captured the social inequities and injustices of the Golden State more profoundly than any other writer and placed them before the American public so poignantly that we remember the Joads, just as we remember the Oklahoman Florence Owens Thomson, as the most representative faces of the nation as it endured hard times.[35] We remember the Joads so well in no small part because of the brilliant casting in Ford's adaptation of the novel, which relied heavily on the photographs of migrant workers and their families taken by Horace Bristol while traveling with Steinbeck to camps in the Central Valley in late 1937 and early 1938 while on assignment for *Life Magazine*. Those photographs of the movie Joads and the "real" Joads appeared side by side in the magazine in January 1940 under the title "Speaking of Pictures ... these by *Life* prove facts in 'Grapes of Wrath,'" and provided further validation for Steinbeck's novel. Also, in April 1940, the same month that Eleanor Roosevelt testified before Congress, Oklahoma singer–songwriter Woody Guthrie was in New Jersey recording his famous *Dust Bowl Ballads* album, which included "Tom Joad," a six-minute summation of Steinbeck's novel, and a suite of other songs charting the displacement, migration, and struggle of Oklahoma's refugees. Released in July 1940, *Dust Bowl Ballads* was Guthrie's most successful recording and provided one more layer of support for the veracity of Steinbeck's depictions of the migrants' plight.

Carey McWilliams's *Factories in the Field* also proved pivotal to the migrants' cause, serving as a sort of nonfiction companion to *The Grapes of Wrath*. Published just a few months after Steinbeck's novel, McWilliams's book elicited a comparably vehement response from California agribusiness interests: he was denounced as "Agricultural Pest No. 1, worse than pear blight or boll weevil."[36] Nonetheless, for all their critics, Steinbeck's and McWilliams's books generated public support for bringing Robert La Follette's Senate Committee on Education and Labor to California to investigate the "violations of the rights of labor" that both had described. Moreover, McWilliams, by then, was serving as the state commissioner of immigration and housing under the new Democratic governor Culbert Olson, who had ridden the EPIC tide into office five years earlier, and assumed the governorship in January 1939 (partly through the support of Southern Plains migrants).[37] McWilliams helped prepare Governor Olson's testimony before the La Follette Committee, which included hallmark McWilliams phrases such as "large-scale industrialized corporate farms," designed to explode romantic notions of California growers as salt-of-the-earth yeoman farmers. The committee hearings were conducted in December 1939 and January 1940.[38] The report established that agricultural workers were suffering a "shocking degree of human misery" and that the Associated Farmers had engaged in "the most flagrant and violent infringement of civil liberties."[39] La Follette's report would not be released until October 1942, but the hearings were enough to ensure that the federal government provided more aid to the migrant families and more protection for workers, all of which was made easier by Olson's supportive presence in the governor's office.

Like Steinbeck, McWilliams was drawn to social justice advocacy by events on the ground. A native Coloradan, McWilliams had moved to California as a teenager in 1922 after his family's ranch failed.[40] By 1934, the young lawyer was representing labor unions throughout California, including those representing Mexican-origin workers, and he was campaigning for Upton Sinclair and the EPIC plan. In May 1935, he toured the Sacramento Valley with journalist Herbert Klein to investigate labor conditions for field workers and the two published a series of powerful articles in the *Pacific Spectator* in 1936 under the title "Factories in the Fields."[41] The articles served as a sort of prelude to McWilliams's 1939 book, much like Steinbeck's "The Harvest Gypsies" series did for *The Grapes of Wrath*. Also in 1936, McWilliams defended Hollywood studio hands, and in 1937 represented Filipino domestic workers and women walnut workers of Mexican and Eastern European backgrounds, as well as Chinese, East Indian, and Japanese workers.[42] In the summer of 1938, the Committee to Aid Agricultural Organization was established and Steinbeck was named its state chairman (a largely honorific title), and the organization's name was strategically changed to the Steinbeck

Committee to Aid Agricultural Organization. McWilliams, who despite their shared efforts on behalf of migrant labor had not met Steinbeck, was placed in charge of the southern division of the state committee.[43] These wide-ranging experiences in labor advocacy would shape *Factories in the Field* and the many social justice-driven books that followed from McWilliams's impassioned pen during the late 1930s and the 1940s.

In *Factories in the Field* McWilliams titled one of his chapters "The Rise of Farm Fascism" and included a section on "Gunkist oranges," leaving no confusion concerning his perspective on the large growers and their repression of migrant workers. In "The Harvest Gypsies" Steinbeck had spoken too of the "fascistic methods" of California agribusiness and the money that was being spent on guns and ammunition to repress migrant workers that could have been directed to the provision of humane conditions. Steinbeck deeply appreciated McWilliams's study since it provided clear evidence of the conditions he described in *The Grapes of Wrath*, and he wrote a blurb for McWilliams's publisher to use.[44] But McWilliams departed from Steinbeck in several areas. For example, he provided considerably fuller coverage of the exploitation of Chinese, Japanese, Filipino, and Mexican field workers and their families prior to the arrival of white migrant workers. Still, like Steinbeck, McWilliams insisted that the landscape of labor exploitation had changed with the arrival of this new flood of refugees from the Southern Plains: "[t]hese despised Okies and Texicans were not another alien minority group (although they were treated as such)," and with their arrival, McWilliams wrote, "a day or reckoning approaches for the California farm industrialists."[45] However, the reckoning that McWilliams envisioned involved the development of working-class consciousness among this new white underclass and, ultimately, "the substitution of collective agriculture for the present monopolistically owned and controlled system." Steinbeck certainly did not go so far as to propose collectivization and had proposed in "The Harvest Gypsies" that the government purchase small plots of land for migrant families to provide them once more with a measure of independence, self-sufficiency, and rootedness.[46]

Still, the more immediate reckoning that both *Factories in the Field* and *The Grapes of Wrath* worked most tangibly toward was the matter of whether the La Follette Committee would come down on the side of the migrants or California's corporate agricultural sector. Steinbeck's heart-rending portrayal of the Joads' suffering and McWilliams's careful detailing of the migrants' living and working conditions and his caustic cataloging of the violently repressive practices of the Associated Farmers in crushing labor activity – "the organization ... has many points of similarity with organizations of a like character in Nazi Germany," he wrote – together won the day.[47] The evidence that both writers amassed on the migrants' behalf, and against the Associated Farmers and the corporate agricultural sector more broadly, serves as one of our clearest examples of the capacity of writers for effecting social change in the United States.

The WPA Guide to California, in its coverage of California migrant labor, echoed Steinbeck's and McWilliams's empathy, and their condemnatory tone toward California agribusiness. Like Steinbeck, the guide's authors advocated government intervention on the migrant workers' behalf and praised the sanitary camps that had been established across the state by the Farm Security Administration. The guide concluded that the state's future would be marked by "an intensive struggle to solve the social and economic problems which are the inevitable heritage of California's four centuries of development."[48] Emphasizing the complicated and often lamentable history of California race relations and the contemporary mistreatment of migrant worker families, the California guide was a far cry from the simple boosterism of previous guides to the state, and it remains one of the most compelling of all the WPA guides. Indeed, this federally sponsored project was, at its heart, as much an example of California social protest literature as it was a celebration of the cultural heritage of the state.

While FDR's administration had by no means been in perfect alignment with Sinclair (out of concern that his radical programs could undermine the New Deal coalition), the EPIC campaign had succeeded in tilting California to the left, at least for a few years. It was in those years, in the late 1930s and early 1940s, that Steinbeck's and McWilliams's writings in support of migrant workers and their families – the novelist's efforts "to write history while it is happening," and the journalist's mission to chart the historical roots of California's mistreatment of field workers – were very much in keeping with the goals of the New Deal Farm Security Administration, whose photographers produced images designed to generate public support for federal aid programs. The federally funded California state guide was marked by the same tilt toward social justice. Those works, *I, Governor of California*, *The WPA Guide to California*, *Factories in the Field*, and *The Grapes of Wrath*, together changed lives in California and across the country and remind us of why the intersections of history and literature matter.

Whether the literary enterprise somehow becomes adulterated at those moments when it intersects with social causes is a matter for the literary critics to consider. Sinclair, one suspects, would have been little bothered by such concerns over artistic integrity since he always placed his art in the service of social protest; indeed, Sinclair's writing was first and foremost a vehicle for social change. McWilliams was a journalist and prolific author of books (he published ten between 1939 and 1949, mostly detailing the lamentable legacies of racism in California) who consciously plied his trade in the service of social activism. He was a superb prose stylist, but had no literary pretensions. Steinbeck has certainly been the subject of such musings about the writer's social responsibilities and literary merits. In October 1962, Steinbeck learned that he was the recipient of the Nobel Prize in Literature. That December, right before the ceremony, *New York Times* literary critic Arthur Mizener published his dismissive piece "Does a Moral Vision of the Thirties Deserve a Nobel Prize?" Steinbeck, it is worth noting, had been quite productive in the years after *The Grapes of Wrath*, writing classics such as *Cannery Row* (1945) and *East of Eden* (1952), but he was devastated by the criticism he received from Mizener and others and never wrote another novel. Nonetheless, in his memorable Nobel acceptance speech Steinbeck declared that:

> The ancient commission of the writer has not changed. He is charged with exposing our many grievous faults and failures, with dredging up to the light our dark and dangerous dreams for the purpose of improvement.
>
> Furthermore, the writer is delegated to declare and to celebrate man's proven capacity for greatness of heart and spirit – for gallantry in defeat, for courage, compassion and love. In the endless war against weakness and despair, these are the bright rally flags of hope and emulation.[49]

Steinbeck certainly upheld that "ancient commission" in *The Grapes of Wrath*, and in his other writings during the late 1930s, and in doing so played a vital role in improving social conditions in California, and more than three quarters of a century later those works are still widely read. Steinbeck, McWilliams, Sinclair, and the contributors to the WPA state guide were among the California writers who performed this service or writing history while it happened, and they did so at a cultural moment when, thankfully, the stars seemed to align in support of literature as social protest.

Notes

1. *The WPA Guide to California*, compiled and written by the Federal Writers' Project of the Works Progress Administration (New York: Pantheon Books, 1984; originally published under the title *California: A Guide to the Golden*

State, New York: Hastings House, 1939), page numbers from reprint, 63–64 for EPIC, and 148–49 for Sinclair's literary contributions.

2. Upton Sinclair, *I, Governor of California and How I Ended Poverty: A True Story of the Future* (New York: Farrar and Rinehart, 1933, and Los Angeles: End Poverty League, 1933).

3. Kevin Starr, *Endangered Dreams: The Great Depression in California* (New York: Oxford University Press, 1996), 120–55, "futurist fiction" quotation on p. 122.

4. *The WPA Guide to California*, 69 and 106–07.

5. Gwendolyn Wright's "Introduction" to the reprint edition of *The WPA Guide to California*, xv–xxiv, provides further discussion of the contributing authors; see especially xvii.

6. Ibid., 141–50.

7. Susan Shillinglaw examines the theme of social protest as a central tenet of California literature in "The Protest Fiction of Frank Norris, Upton Sinclair, Jack London, and John Steinbeck," in Blake Allmendinger, ed., *A History of California Literature* (New York: Cambridge University Press, 2015), 157–70; Jan Goggans, "Dreams, Denial, and Depression-Era Fictions," in Allendinger, *History of California Literature*, 171–81; and Editors' "Introduction" to "Part Four: Dreams and Awakenings, 1915–1945," in *The Literature of California: Writings from the Golden State: Volume I: Native Beginnings to 1945*, ed. Jack Hicks, James D. Houston, Maxine Hong Kingston, and Al Young (Berkeley: University of California Press, 2000), 393–406.

8. John Steinbeck to Elizabeth Otis, ca. March/April 1938, in John Steinbeck, *A Life in Letters*, ed. Elaine Steinbeck and Robert Wallsten (New York: Viking Penguin Inc., 1975; quotations from Penguin reprint edition, 1989), 162.

9. For more on California's political resistance to the New Deal, see Richard Lowitt's chapter, "California Is Different," in his The New Deal and the West (Norman: University of Oklahoma Press, 1992), 172–88; and Rick Wartman, "New Deal, No Deal: The 1930s," in William Deverell and David Igler, eds., *A Companion to California History* (Malden, MA: Wiley-Blackwell, 2008), 292–306.

10. Lori A. Flores, *Grounds for Dreaming: Mexican Americans, Mexican Immigrants, and the California Farmworker Movement* (New Haven, CT: Yale University Press, 2016), 32.

11. Wartman, "New Deal, No Deal," especially 296–99.

12. John H. M. Laslett, *Sunshine Was Never Enough: Los Angeles Workers, 1880–2010* (Berkeley: University of California Press, 2012), 118–23.

13. Dorothea Lange and Paul Schuster Taylor, *An American Exodus: A Record of Human Erosion in the 1930s* (New York: Reynal and Hitchcock, 1939; republished for the Oakland Museum by Yale University Press, 1969, page references from reprint), 110 and 113.

14. Sinclair, *I, Governor of California*, 9.

15. Ibid., 10.

16. Ibid., 63 and 22–23.
17. Starr, *Endangered Dreams*, 120–55, especially 142–50; T. H. Watkins, *The Great Depression: America in the 1930s* (Boston, MA: Little Brown and Company, 1993), 238–39; and David Kennedy, *Freedom from Fear: The American People in Depression and War, 1929–1945* (New York: Oxford University Press, 1999), 225–27.
18. Laslett, *Sunshine Was Never Enough*, 122; Watkins, *The Great Depression*, 239; and Starr, *Endangered Dreams*, 154.
19. Upton Sinclair, *I, Candidate for Governor: And How I Got Licked* (New York: Farrar and Rinehart, 1934), 3. The work was republished, with an introduction by James N. Gregory (Berkeley: University of California Press, 1994); quotations are from the original.
20. Ibid., 183 and 203.
21. Ibid., 184.
22. For a fuller discussion of Steinbeck's work in relation to the social context of the late 1930s, see David Wrobel, "Regionalism and Social Protest during John Steinbeck's 'Years of Greatness,' 1936–1939," in Michael C. Steiner, ed., *Regionalists on the Left: Radical Voices from the American West* (Norman: University of Oklahoma Press, 2013), 327–51; and Morris Dickstein's section "Steinbeck Country," in his *Dancing in the Dark: A Cultural History of the Great Depression* (New York: W. W. Norton, 2009), 70–80. For more on the background to *In Dubious Battle*, see Warren French's "Introduction" to the Penguin Classics edition of the novel (New York: Penguin, 1992 and 2006). All quotations from the novel are from John Steinbeck, *Novels and Short Stories, 1932–1937* (New York: Library of America, 1994).
23. See Warren French, "Introduction" to his *John Steinbeck* (New York: Twayne, 1961), xxvii. French's study was one of the very first critical works on Steinbeck and remains one of the best.
24. Quotations from "The Harvest Gypsies" are from John Steinbeck, *The Grapes of Wrath and Other Writings, 1936–1941*, ed. Robert DeMott and Elaine A. Steinbeck (New York: Library of America, 1996).
25. James N. Gregory's *American Exodus: The Dust Bowl Migration and Okie Culture in California* (New York: Oxford University Press, 1989) remains the most important work on the migrants.
26. For an early exploration of this theme, see Warren French, "Death of the Dream" (unpublished seminar paper for Walter Prescott Webb, University of Texas, Austin, ca. 1953; copy in author's possession).
27. Quotations from Steinbeck's correspondence are drawn from Elaine Steinbeck and Robert Wallsten, eds., *Steinbeck: A Life in Letters* (New York: Viking, 1975; Penguin 1976, reissued 1989) (hereinafter LL).
28. James R. Swensen, "Focusing on the Migrant: The Contextualization of Dorothea Lange's Photographs of the John Steinbeck Committee," in Cyrus Ernesto Zirakzadeh and Soimon Stow, eds., *A Political Companion to*

John Steinbeck (Lexington: University Press of Kentucky, 2013), 199–226, especially 196–97.

29. Robert DeMott, "'This Book Is My Life': Creating The Grapes of Wrath," in *Steinbeck's Typewriter: Essays on His Art* (Bloomington, IN: iUniverse, 2012), 146–205, especially 168–69.

30. Ibid., 173.

31. Jackson Benson, *John Steinbeck, Writer: A Biography* (New York: Penguin, 1990; originally published as *The True Adventures of John Steinbeck: Writer*, New York: Viking: 1984; quotations from the 1990 edition), 402.

32. "The Roosevelts and John Steinbeck: 75th Anniversary of *The Grapes of Wrath*," at: www.roosevelthouse.hunter.cuny.edu/roosevelts-john-steinbeck-75th-anniversary-grapes-wrath/ (accessed October 19, 2016).

33. Benson, *John Steinbeck*, 421. Also see Rick Wartzman, *Obscene in the Extreme: The Burning and Banning of John Steinbeck's The Grapes of Wrath* (New York: Public Affairs, 2008).

34. Wartzman, *Obscene in the Extreme*, 411.

35. See Tetsumaro Hayashi, ed., *John Steinbeck: The Years of Greatness, 1936–1939* (Tuscaloosa: University of Alabama Press, 1993).

36. Carey McWilliams, *The Education of Carey McWilliams* (New York: Simon & Schuster, 1979), 77, quoted in Michael C. Steiner, "Carey McWilliams, California, and the Education of a Radical Regionalist," in Steiner, *Regionalists on the Left*, 353–76, quotation on 358.

37. Olson performed particularly well in the election in those areas of the state where Southern Plains migrants resided, including the southern San Joaquin Valley; see Gregory, *American Exodus*, 97.

38. Douglas C. Sackman, "Foreword" to Carey McWilliams, *Factories in the Field: The Story of Migratory Farm Labor in California* (Berkeley: University of California Press, 1999; originally published in Boston by Little, Brown, 1939), ix–xviii, quotation on xiii of reprint edition.

39. Ibid., 422.

40. Robert L. Dorman, *Hell of a Vision: Regionalism and the Modern American West* (Tucson: University of Arizona Press, 2012), 86–87.

41. Richard Steven Street, *Everyone Had Cameras: Photography and Farmworkers in California, 1850–2000* (Minneapolis: University of Minnesota Press, 2008), 299.

42. For more on McWilliams's social justice work leading up to the writing of *Factories in the Field*, see Steiner, "Carey McWilliams," 366–72.

43. Swensen, "Focusing on the Migrant," 192–93.

44. Benson, *John Steinbeck*, 421–22.

45. McWilliams, *Factories in the Field*, 306.

46. Ibid., 324. McWilliams's emphasis on developing working-class consciousness and the conflicting individualist orientation of Southern Plains migrants is discussed by Charles J. Shindo in *Dust Bowl Migrants in the American Imagination* (Lawrence: University Press of Kansas, 1997), 19–22.

47. McWilliams, *Factories in the Field*, 231.
48. *The WPA Guide to California*, 65 and 69.
49. The "Nobel Prize Acceptance Speech" appears in John Steinbeck, *America and Americans and Selected Non-Fiction*, ed. Susan Shillinglaw and Jackson J. Benson (New York: Penguin, 2002), 172–74, quotation from 173.

CHAPTER 8

Reckoning with Christianity

Jason Stevens

A 1935 editorial in *The Christian Century* concluded that the Great Depression was perhaps "the first time men have not blamed God for hard times."[1] Christian leaders' recognition that the Depression was a man-made crisis occasioned vocational reflection: what was the proper relation between Christ and culture, the Kingdom of God and American society? The decade's literature also weighed the fund of Christian experience against this-worldly challenges. As a response to the rise of secularism and non-belief, T. S. Eliot's 1927 conversion to Anglo-Catholicism was exceptional, and to "Eliotic leftists," a scandal, yet his writings on the subject – particularly "Religion and Literature" (1935) – staked out conceptual territory that many of his peers shared even when they disliked his prescriptions.[2] The West had become only nominally Christian; too many of its religious institutions, especially its Protestant ones, were captive to bourgeois and nationalistic ("pagan") values. The responsibility of art, however, was not to become dogmatic. Religion and literature were basically autonomous of each other, related, in Eliot's ideal society, through an integrated cultural sensibility that shaped aesthetic perception unconsciously. American authors drawn to the Marxist and Popular Front ambits of thought in the thirties had a pluralistic vision that led literature far away from Christian orthodoxy and traditionalism, but they recognized, at times rued, the imaginative power that historic faith exerted and saw it, as Eliot did, permeating culture and ideology. Precisely because they discerned how even tottering pieties, when refreshed through irony and defamiliarization, could motivate and inspire, writers on the left often adapted the language, myth, and song of Christianity to assail humanly created injustice. Authors who did not participate in the "cultural front," like Marianne Moore, Thornton Wilder, and Zora Neale Hurston, discovered Christian sources of community and individualism in the usable past.[3]

   Examining a range of fiction, poetry, and nonfiction across the political
spectrum of the thirties, this chapter considers how the period's literature
addressed US Christian thought and culture in connection to several key
themes. The first of these is the Depression itself. For some authors, the
social catastrophe occasioned reflections on American identity that led
back to Puritanism as ailment or corrective. Many others combined
modernist experiments with a literature of protest and social fact designed
to speak for "the common man" and the multiethnic (Jewish and Catholic)
proletariat. African American writers in the proletarian movement joined
its political critiques of Christianity with the Harlem Renaissance's deep
renovation of black evangelical traditions. Regionalism was also a crucial
theme of the thirties, as local authors highlighted the religious features
particular to the "ill-clothed, ill-housed, ill-nourished" South.[4] Finally, the
advance toward World War II tested the conscience of many writers.
The drumbeats instigated, on the one hand, *Johnny Got His Gun*,
a major pacifist work revising the Passion, and, on the other,
W. H. Auden's poetry and nonfiction addressing the tragic choices forced
by sin.
   Marianne Moore's "The Octopus"(1924) had rejected *The Wasteland*'s
despair for a tempered affirmation of American democracy. During the
Depression, Moore was politically conservative, though she did not react to
Marxist prognoses with outsized optimism for the nation-state. She forged
a "counter-heroics" designed to resist US nationalist mythologies, which
shaded into fascist ideologies of "authentic identity."[5] Moore's skeptical
attitude toward nationalism is partially creditable to her study of Puritan
texts. Raised Presbyterian in a family of ministers, Moore became more
religious during World War II, but her "interest in seventeenth century
poetry and the Protestant sermon, fostered in early youth," already marked
her work in the thirties.[6] In this period, she also discovered theologian and
activist Reinhold Niebuhr, who lectured at her own church (Lafayette
Avenue Presbyterian, Brooklyn) in 1938.[7] Stressing the Calvinist side of
American Protestantism, Niebuhr taught that self-doubt was a salutary
regulative principle, for it acted as a check to sinful pride that defies
mystery. The Puritan literary tradition and its accent on human finitude,
strongly echoed in Niebuhr's work, finds a correlate in Moore's modernist
experiments with form. Hers is a "poetics of profound self-suspicion" that
assumes its subjectivity is hybrid and particular, and offers no escape from
this fortunate impurity into moral certitude.[8] She avoids a fixed lyric
persona, preferring to distribute the speaking voice across a collage of
quotations, which could include bits of sermonic citations and biblical

commentaries. Her symmetrical stanzas of syllabic verse evoke fixed limits, while her wordplay invites readers to discover latent associations not only between words, but also between the things that her poems describe. Nature, for Moore as for Edward Taylor and Jonathan Edwards, was a source of analogies that rewarded receptive observation with singularity of expression. Her religiously inflected modernism made her an intuitive critic of "national egoism," which confers on the patriot an illusion of destiny and unrestrained power based on rootedness in home and kinship.[9] In several of her Depression-era poems, Moore swerves from American mythologies connecting freedom, acquisition, and colonial expansion to "nationalistic identification."[10] Her triptych – "The Steeple-Jack," "Hero," "The Jerboa" (1932) – her animal poem, "The Pangolin" (1936), and her Jamestown-set "Virginia Brittania"(1935) admire figures in their environments whose ways of being exemplify Moore's own artistry and temperament, but she does not authorize their behavior by deference to place or affiliation. They remain individuals carefully perceived, unhallowed by any rhetoric of connatural ties.

In his Depression-set best seller, *Heaven Is My Destination* (1934), Thornton Wilder gently satirized American self-reliance and its perfectionist Protestant traces. While Marianne Moore was a believing Presbyterian, Thornton Wilder had to wean himself from his Congregationalist father Amos's faith to become a writer. Calvinism left a residuum in his literary career, but his second and third novels, *The Bridges of San Luis Rey* (1927) and *The Woman of Andros* (1930), have a humanist cast and universalize Christian virtues as potentials of the mortal heart. Hope and love, rather than reason or will, are the provident forces in Wilder's universe, and the hero of *Heaven Is My Destination* is a determined optimist whose buoyance floats on his resolve and whose charity is a matter of principle. Traveling textbook salesman George Brush, devoted to his own improvement and society's, is "a Baptist 'Don Quixote.'"[11] The allusion to "Don Quixote" points to Brush's innocence, which never graduates to madness, but makes his quest for perpetual reform comically earnest. "Baptist" not only describes Brush's background, but points to a characteristically American adaptation of Calvinism that imprints his personality and makes him innocent of the crevasse between his ideals and the people who would live under them. As in *Pilgrim's Progress*, to which the novel's style, incident, and very title allude, the protagonist's picaresque adventures are also a moral education, but, in contrast to Bunyan's Christian, Wilder's hero may miss the instruction.[12] A living manual of advice literature, George draws his personal philosophy from eclectic sources, including Gandhi, Tolstoy, and Epictetus. All of this accumulated wisdom is put to the service of a drive to sanctify the whole of his life and transmit the power he gains from self-discipline to others. When disillusionment overtakes him, George falls into a slough of despond that is disturbing. The implied author's laughter at brittle principle is displaced by George's mordant laughter at a world that now appears absurd to him. He is rescued from nihilism by a posthumous gift from Father Pasziewski, a Polish priest who had never met George yet kept him in his prayers. The priest's gesture, made from kindness and esteem, should chasten George's self-reliance and remind him that people need *caritas*, and not only uplift, to nurture them in benevolence and sustain them through despair. The novel's ending suggests instead that George recovers his former innocence. He launches from his sickbed and, in a list of episodes that rhymes with the book's opening chapters, repeats his adventures. The novel's epigraph, from *The Woman of Andros*, states that "[o]f all the forms of genius, goodness has the longest awkward age," and as George's mission resumes, it seems that he will have to mature a good deal more before he is fit to enter the Celestial City.

While Moore and Wilder dealt with America's Puritan legacy, the proletarian literary movement decentered Protestantism. Appearing less than four months into the Depression, Mike Gold's *Jews without Money* (1930) established "a new genre of city novel." Michael Denning has coined the term *ghetto pastoral* to refer to these fictions of "growing up in the ethnic working-class neighborhoods" of New York and Chicago, which were written by "plebeian men and women" who came of age there. Succinctly put, they were "tales of how *our* half lives."[13] Adopting a proletarian outlook that transcends the subjectivities of their protagonists, the narratives critically examine the symbolic structures – rituals and emblems – of ethnic communities. WASP society is remote, culturally if not geographically. Ghetto pastorals pay far more attention to Jewish–Catholic relations, to class and ethnic tensions within Catholicism and Judaism, and to the dueling meanings of Messianism across Jewish, Gentile, and Marxist eschatologies.

Jews without Money is a fictionalized memoir set in Manhattan's Lower East Side and narrated autobiographically in the first person. Then editor in chief of the *New Masses*, Gold tells a coming-of-age story that leads to political conversion. On the way to this transformation, young Gold wrestles with prophecies of deliverance. He first encounters Christianity through mutual insults and profanations ("Christ-Killer!" versus "goy!") that render it an ominous abstraction. The messiah of the Gentiles,

Momma explains, is false, the god of liars and thieves.[14] Yet, for the adult Gold, the messiah of the Jews is also specious, and the narrator's deflating commentaries on Chasidism anticipate young Gold's religious disenchantment. The ghetto educates the child (who ages from five to fifteen) in the problem of injustice, which neither Christianity nor Judaism can satisfactorily answer. His childhood self tries to resolve the question by parsing the roles of the Jewish messiah, stressing his part as a warrior who avenges the poor, but the afflictions that tenement Jews endure from both Gentiles and their pious rich brethren continue to weaken the boy's sense of a Hebrew covenant with God. In response to teenaged Gold's prayer for the world's redemption, the narrator curtails the rest of the character's youth and closes on a night when a slightly older Gold is proselytized by a street-corner communist. The character's consciousness has now caught up with its narrator's, and the novel ends: "O workers' Revolution ... you are the true Messiah" (309). The secular critique of soulless conditions absorbs religion's protest against suffering.

Henry Roth's ghetto pastoral *Call It Sleep* (1934), set in Brownsville and the Lower East Side before World War I, gives intimate access to a Galician Jewish family as perceived by its only child, David Schearl. Diverging from *Jews without Money*, Roth's modernist focalization and parody mediate a conceptual point of view that treats Christianity and Judaism as incomplete, rather than false ideological, forms of consciousness. In Gold's novel, the child's theodicy is the father of the adult's radicalism, which kills the Jewish faith while glowering at the Christian. In Roth's, the child turns from one faith to the other while the author's Joycean practice, unbolting the symbols of each religion from worn theological grooves, clears a fissure for apophatic revelation.

Call It Sleep climaxes with Lower East Side denizens gathered around an unconscious David, electrocuted while trying to purify himself by touching the light flashing between trolley tracks. Prior to his near death, David has been drawing closer to Christian mysteries in a spirit of fear and curiosity. An opportunistic Polish Catholic boy, Leo, has befriended him, and David has traded entry to his female cousins for Leo's rosary, seemingly a magical talisman. Discovering David's sacrilege and familial betrayal, his father has driven the boy from the home and denounced him as a *goy*. Some critics have seen *Call It Sleep* as a Jewish novel of Christian supersession.[15] Yet Roth's allusions to the Crucifixion and Easter Sunday are not deferential. Throughout Book IV, Chapter XXI, as David lies unconsciousness, the narration's free association – across the snatches of reported dialogue from multiple, synchronous conversations – strikes surprising, irreverent, and discordant linkages. The literal referent of "Three Kings," a character's hand at poker, profanes the authorial allusion to the Nativity's wise men. The mention of "Red Cock" calls to mind Christ's betrayal, but also an erect phallus. There is a further embedded allusion to Emma Lazarus's subversive poem, "The Crowing of the Red Cock" (1900), in which Gentiles desert their Christ by persecuting his "folk," the Jews.[16]

The puns and double-voiced discourse unsettle a reading that would weld the child's near-death experience to a Christological schema, as Chapter XXI builds instead to an afflatus within David's stream of consciousness. In the moment before David awakens, he hears "Zwank! Zwank!" followed by a description of mental phenomenon in the narrator's lexical register: "Nothingness beatified reached out its hands." The Yiddish *zwank* (meaning "tongs" or "pincers") has appeared in the text twice before, once as Genya Schearl, holding kitchen tongs, describes how little the human brain can widen to comprehend Eternity, and again as the rabbi at *Cheder*, translating Isaiah 6:6, describes a seraphim picking up a fiery coal to purge the prophet's tongue (69, 227). Embraced by a timeless and unnamed Word, David seems to have reached a mystical intuition that the language of religion and holy knowledge can only obscure. This mystical contact may comfort David and free him to speak, untimorously, in the profane tongues of man, but it fulfills no prophecy and provides for no supersession, whether of Judaism by Christianity or religious messianism by communism. In the passage, "a red-faced" radical proclaiming the day of the proletariat from a nearby street corner becomes but one fragmentary voice among others (415, 417). Though he was a communist when writing *Call It Sleep*, and remained one until the late 1960s, Roth's conclusion to his first novel supplants disenchantment and political conversion for negative theology.

At age twenty-five and as a communist, Pietro di Donato wrote a short story, "Christ in Christ" (published in *Esquire*, 1937) that recounted the on-the-job death of an Italian-American bricklayer based on his father, who perished in a construction accident on Good Friday. Di Donato expanded the story into *Christ in Concrete* (1939), a novel-length ghetto pastoral that, after its second chapter, shifts the narrative focus to the surviving family, particularly twelve-year-old Paul. After his father, Geremio, is killed, Paul is forced to take up bricklaying in order to support his pregnant mother, Annunziata, and six siblings. While Annunziata ("Annunciation") finds solace in the Catholic Church, Paul matures through his workplace relationships with older Italian laborers and his friendship with a fourteen-year-old secular Russian Jew, Louis Molov. Paul's relationship with Louis, who is intellectual and literate, introduces him to Bolshevism and to the possibility of secularism. The novel ends with Paul repudiating the Church, but making no positive statement of political faith.

Di Donato famously mixes allegory with realism. While his allegorical technique has occasionally been faulted, di Donato does not deploy it to impose an ideological totality.[17] Rather, the cosmic image and ritual structure of allegory – iconographic names, repetition of action, and ruling demonic powers – attack capitalism's drive to automatize the immigrant laborer's life.[18] The recurrent allegorical symbol of "Job" ("the great God Job"), for example, personifies the condition of alienated labor and the institutional power of the ruling class: "Job tore down upon them madly," "Job had arrested each" (8, 14, 137, 142, 221). The narrator's allegorical discourse also enters characters' consciousness through dream visions and interior monologues. In these wishful, prayerful passages, Christ emerges in Annunziata's and Paul's thoughts not only as the High Priest and Church of the Catholic liturgy but also as the representative son whose body is daily sacrificed to Job to make bread for the family. The risk of di Donato's allegorical technique is that its emblems and cyclical action, instead of super-scribing societal structures that reduce workers to abstract individuals, will have an "anesthetizing" effect on the reader.[19] However, *Christ in Concrete*'s Italian-American English (slang, dialect, and literal translation) and sensual realism enfleshes its characters and gives them expressive tongues.[20] Thomas Ferraro has noted the novel's unembarrassed emphasis on "sensory perception rather than psychological portrayal," as the laborers bond with each through shared "physicality": the trials of bodies strained by toil and the elements, the rituals of bodies resting, healing, and, occasionally, indulging (55, 59). This "material sacramentalism," which vies with the Church's signs of grace, is "semi-blasphemous" and becomes explicitly so when the workers stage a carnival-like mock crucifixion of one of their own (55). Though only Paul renounces Catholicism, none of the bricklayers is so pious that he is willing to forego the opportunity for pleasure, even gluttony and fornication, when means of life and happiness are already being extracted from his body for wages. In such passages, di Donato locates the possibility of hope and clarifies the anti-affirmative function of his allegory. Its proletarianization of Christ anticipates an agential renunciation of the worker's sacrificial role, for only then will hope take form in history.[21] Hence, in the finale, Paul must refuse his father's fate as one of the "Christ in Concrete," a fate decreed by "Job," uncontested by the Church, and sanctified by his mother's passive faith.

"Who nails us to the cross?" Paul asks incredulously (226). There is no mistaking the novel's answer.

Trotskyist James T. Farrell's Studs Lonigan trilogy (published 1932–35) expands the ghetto pastoral over a character's lifetime.[22] The narrative time frame of the three novels spans the post–World War I era to the onset of the Great Depression, as its protagonist William "Studs" Lonigan ages from teenager to thirty-year-old cipher. In its slow tracing of an Irish Catholic male's debauched and brutish life, Farrell imagined the fate that might have enveloped him had he not escaped Chicago's South Fifties. The first and most poignant of the novels, *Young Lonigan*, opens with fourteen-year-old Studs posing in front of a mirror on the occasion of his graduation from parochial elementary school. In view of the final novel of the trilogy, *Judgment Day* (1935), this early image of Studs "on the verge of fifteen, and wearing his first long trousers," looking bullish for his reflection and ejaculating, "[w]ell, I'm kissing the old dump good-bye tonight," is sadly ironic, for though he may leave parochial school, he will never grow beyond the social matrices that have formed him in Farrell's naturalistic scheme.[23] Every personal battle he wins in his roughhouse gang, every triumph in the eyes of his peers, only mires him in his environment. The narrator introduces the character by his street moniker rather than his baptismal name, for it marks his aspiration to be feared as a local tough who has proven his mettle in territorial contexts. Both "Catholicism" and "Irishness" are masks of difference that Studs and his companions project and perform in their daily boundary-drawing with boys from other ethnic and religious purlieus: "sheenies," "kikes," "jigs," and "smokes."[24] Theologically, the Church has little purchase on Studs's mental life apart from the vague, occasionally shuddering, sense that he "must be a bastard."[25] Lucifer, whom Father Gilhooley describes as poaching boys' souls, is but one more enemy for Studs to imagine emulating and crushing as he reacts belligerently to structural injustices that he cannot, and will never, understand. At the close of *Judgment Day*, as a socialist demonstration marches nearby, Studs lies in a terminal coma receiving last rites, having kept fealty with Irish Catholic nationalism and its increasingly fascistic tendencies.

Outside the genre of the ghetto pastoral, the proletarian literary movement on the African American left strengthened a secular impulse that had coursed through the Harlem Renaissance. While some connected their work to the politics of Franklin Roosevelt's New Deal and others to socialism (Du Bois), a number of the most prominent black writers (Richard Wright, Langston Hughes, Arna Bontemps, Ralph Ellison, and

Paul Robeson) were affiliated with the American Communist Party or were fellow travelers. Responding to Christianity, African American literary Marxists balanced their complaints against the Harlem Renaissance's acknowledgment that black evangelical ministers and churches had been sources of leadership and vernacular artistry. Langston Hughes and Richard Wright sharply denounced Christian hypocrisy and violence while rechanneling the prophetic and communal spirit in black religious history.

With the controversy that ensued over his poem "Goodbye Christ" (1932), Langston Hughes discovered how the Depression's contentious climate of opinion could wedge apart what he blended: a radical critique of Christian culture combined with sympathy for the Christ-like in spirit. Written while Hughes was on a trip to the USSR, the poem was published without his permission in the German COMINTERN journal, *Negro Worker*, and then reprinted in the *Baltimore Afro-American*, where it drew strong objections. In contrast to his anti-lynching poem, "Christ in Alabama" (*Contempo*, December 1, 1931), "Goodbye Christ" was addressed to both black and white churches and mentions by name Harlem's Saint Becton as well as Los Angeles's Aimee Semple McPherson. Assailed and debated in editorials by black and white authors across the country, "Goodbye Christ" would dog Hughes into the Cold War as a statement of Marxist atheism.[26] African American reverend and activist Benjamin Mays, in a classic 1938 study, characterized the poem as the most communistic of its era: "Christ is not only of no use in perfecting social change, but He is a decided handicap. He gets in the way of things."[27] Hughes, who was unhappy to have the poem in the public domain, offered qualifications. "Goodbye Christ," he stated in 1941, was a satire on all profiteers from religion that was written in the genre of a dramatic monologue, and its communist persona was not representative of the author's ideology.[28] The second point is only partially true. While Hughes was never an official party member, he supported affiliate organizations, published frequently in *New Masses*, and closed his one-act play, *Scottsboro Limited* (1931), with the raising of the red flag and the singing of the Internationale. However, his denial of the communist persona was partly a response to imputations of antireligious atheism that followed him after "Goodbye Christ" was published. Hughes had become a free thinker, but he did not feel that Christian ideals were valueless. The poem's anger is summoned by hypocrisy; the speaker says farewell to the Christ of Christendom, which had placed its most sacred figure "in the service of ecclesial and State power" and in the service of mammon.[29]

Against the blasts for militant atheism, the most trenchant defense that Hughes could have offered was his semi-autobiographical novel, *Not without Laughter* (1930), winner of the Harmon Award administered by the Federal Council of Churches. Protagonist Sandy Rogers's evangelical grandmother, a member of the First Ethiopian Baptist Church, joins Sister Johnson in lamenting how parishes "now'days. . ... don't care nothin' 'bout po' Jesus. . ... Money! That's all 'tis! An' white folkeses' religion – Lawd help!"[30] The critique of "Goodbye Christ" had already been spoken in this earlier text, and by black Christian characters. Moreover, the novel's ending conveys that as a fledging artist Sandy distills from his grandmother's faith a vocational purpose: to be "a dancer of the spirit"(211). Pausing outside "a little Southern church on a side street," he hears in the song (Charles Albert Tindley's "We'll Understand It Better By and By") "a stream of living faith" that will flow into his own poetry (218).

The attribution of committed atheist more aptly fits Richard Wright, who resented his rearing in the household of strict Seventh Day Adventists and a Methodist mother. The "Southern Night" section of his autobiography *Black Boy* (1945) begins symbolically with four-year-old Richard setting fire to his devout grandmother's house, much as the autobiographical narrator has burned his ties to the religious culture of his familial past. *Black Boy* is narrated in a tone that matches the anger of young, embattled Richard, for whom Granny's and mother's religion impedes his self-making and belongs to "the culture from which I sprang . . . the terror from which I fled."[31] Wright never participated in any church after leaving the rural South, and he assumed that African American Christianity would decline as blacks migrated to Northern cities and became modernized.[32] He also called Christianity "counter-revolutionary" in print, though his fiction gives a more complex sounding of the matter than this statement.[33] His first published book, *Uncle Tom's Children* (1938, expanded 1940), written while he was a Communist Party of the United States of America (CPUSA) member, is based on "oral histories of African-American Southern radicals and replete with songs and religious references."[34] In the final stories in the collection, "Fire in the Cloud" (1938) and "Bright and Morning Star" (1938) the Christian beliefs of the characters (respectively, a reverend and a layperson) are not simply represented as reactionary or atavistic. Instead, using the technique of limited omniscience that he had mastered from Henry James, Wright explores the characters' transitions from evangelical faith to movement consciousness.

In "Bright and Morning Star," the more compelling of the two stories, Aunt Sue is a scrubwoman living in Memphis, where she and her son are members of the local Communist Party. The title, a hymnal allusion to Jesus, spotlights the psychology of faith, "a bright star" transferred in Sue's life from a kerygmatic framework to a political cause in which she has discovered interracial solidarity and friendship. This "new faith" radiates with a subjective intensity that she likens to grace (225). Over the course of one night, Sue's conviction dims when a white "Judas," Booker, cozens her into divulging the secret location of the next Party meeting.[35] Feeling abandoned, she calls out "Jesus, hep me," her old faith resurfacing "from a vacant place" (244). Though she discounts this cry as a moment of weakness, Sue's subsequent choice owes to her religious sensibility, as "her whole being leaps with will," overriding doubt, in response to out-rushing of love for her white comrade Reva, whose pure devotion to the movement she determines to protect (253). In a finale befitting the story's thriller pacing, Sue intercepts and shoots Booker before he shares his information. As she and her son Johnny Boy, already the sheriff's prisoner, are slain in retaliation, the narrator uplifts Sue into martyrdom: "Focused and pointed she was, buried in the depths of her star, swallowed in its peace and strength; and not feeling her flesh grow cold, cold as the rain that fell from the invisible sky upon the doomed living and the dead that never dies"(263). As elsewhere in the story, Wright's language, in keeping with the post-Christian mentality of his protagonist, is at once desacralizing and sacred; to achieve the task of history, Sue dies into the permanence of the revolutionary spirit.

Though the proletarian literary movement had long aftershocks, its heyday was the early thirties, which saw the John Reed Club open chapters in major cities across the country. The Popular Front shifted focus away from proletarian radicalism and developed rhetoric for unifying the industrial working-class, white-collar workers, small farmers, and displaced labor as "the people" or "the common man."[36] John Steinbeck's *The Grapes of Wrath* (1939), an instant best seller and the most influential of Popular Front narratives, salvages from the disintegration of the fictional Joad family an image of the people groping toward a spiritual epiphany.[37] The Joads are biblical Protestants, and their fellow migrants appear to come from Holiness or fundamentalist molds. Straddling this belief culture and a religionless one to come is Jim Casy, an ex-preacher who has abandoned his flock because he could not stop sinning and has ceased to even believe in sin. In one respect, Casy's lapses satirize Protestantism and tap into the vein of Southwestern humor. With some justness, Colleen McDannell has faulted these burlesque elements for obscuring the serious evangelicalism of migrants leaving the Dust Bowl: "They might have left

their places of worship behind them [but] ... [f]ew gave up gave up on
Christianity, as had Jim Casy ... [M]ost migrant preachers set up prayer
circles and devised plans for building churches" (33). To focus on the
novel's irreverence and what it omits, however, is to miss the other side
of Casy's witness. He articulates the text's Whitmanesque spirituality:
liberal, post-Christian, and immanent. Casy moves from doubt to an
expanded sense of his boundaries: "Sometimes I'd pray like I always
done. On'y I couldn' figure out what I was prayin' to or for ... I got
thinkin' how we was holy when we was one thing, and' mankin' was holy
when it was one thing. An' it on'y got unholy when mis'able little fella got
the bit in his teeth an' run off his own way, kickin' and draggin' and
fightin'."[38] Hard-bitten Tom Joad internalizes Casy's heart: "[H]e foun' he
jus' got a little piece of a great big soul ... Funny how I remember. Didn't
even think I was listenin'. But I know now a fella ain't no good alone."[39]

The narrator educes the collectivist ethical implications of its characters'
intuitions: "The quality of owning freezes you forever in 'I,' and cuts you
off forever from the 'we.'"[40] Mystical socialists like Horace Traubel,
founder of the Walt Whitman Fellowship, had long interpreted *Leaves of
Grass* as a new gospel proclaiming love of man and providing an anti-
authoritarian alternative to revolutionary Marxism.[41] Steinbeck was
a naturalist rather than a mystic, and Casy's spirituality does not sail
above the novel's oft-noted biological metaphors. Rather, Whitman's
motifs are employed to grow altruistic consciousness for the survival of
communities. The idea that souls belong to an interdependent whole
challenges the normativity of individual interest and the pursuit of personal freedom through wealth. It also undermines the priorities behind the
communist strategy skeptically examined in Steinbeck's *In Dubious Battle*
(1936). That novel's union organizers, such as Mac McLeod, depend on the
striking workers to function like "group-men," kneaded into utilizable
mass agents by the Party's cadres.[42] While the flawed organizers in this
former text place the Party's teleology above the local needs of the workers,
Casy's homilies universalize the Joads' immediate pain, loss, desire, and
yearning into an identification with struggling humanity. Unfortunately,
The Grapes of Wrath's immanent and unifying spirituality is at odds with
Steinbeck's ethnic bias and "negative portrayal of the urban and industrial
poor." The novel's iconography, which contracts the one big soul to plain
white Protestant agrarians, contrasts decisively with the more pluralistic
image of America promoted by the Popular Front.[43]

Begun as a series of articles on migrant workers written for the *San
Francisco News*, *The Grapes of Wrath* is indicative of the thirties writer's

endeavor to combine social fact and advocacy. Under the aegis of the Works Program Administration and the Farm Security Administration, writers and photographers combed rural America in the thirties to document the common man, often captured in religious worship or surrounded by religious images. There was a propagandistic purpose to some of these representations: even amidst dire circumstances, Americans were not turning to "godless communism or socialism," but holding fast to "enduring faith."[44] In other cases, the depiction of rural faith served a secularization thesis anticipating the end of hard religion, or it occasioned a modernist formalism elevating the "folk" sacred into a timeless and impersonal style.[45] None of these motives adequately accounts for the voice of James Agee's *Let Us Now Praise Famous Men* (1941). Idiosyncratically for the documentary genre, it is a devotional and confessional text. Erskine Caldwell's *You Have Seen Their Faces* (1937), to which *Let Us Now Praise Famous Men* is often compared, gives more explicit attention to the spiritual practices of the poor and, in contrast to Walker Evans's photographs for Agee's text, includes Margaret Bourke-White's many shots of worshippers. However, it is not the piety of the poor that awakens Agee, but an inner luminous quality. Morris Dickstein has described how Agee, a lapsed Anglo-Catholic, invests his tenant families with religious "awe." Beyond his attempts to understand the sharecroppers, he seeks redemption from their trust and his truthful recording.[46] Avowedly burdened by the contrast between his status and the destitution of his subjects, Agee avoids aestheticizing the families in a fashion tasteful to middle-class benevolence. Without concealing his disgust, he meticulously describes the absence of privacy, the odor of moldy oil cloth, the dullness of "sour and greasy wood," "the peculiar taste and stench" of cheap silverware, the filthy "iron blackness" of every wall, a "steady shame and insult of discomforts, insecurities, and inferiorities."[47] More than scrupulous accuracy drives these moments. Agee draws near the abject in self-humbling, and such passages as the night he spends on a bedbug-infested pallet rolling and scratching evoke the mortification of the flesh (374). To see families like Gudger's honestly, he would empty himself, and knowing this is impossible for art, he meditates on the limits of prose to penetrate their lives.[48] Reviewing *Let Us Now Praise Famous Men* one year after its publication, Lionel Trilling faulted Agee for sentimental error. He had ennobled his farmers for enduring poverty. Walker Evans's recollections suggest that the quality in Agee's perception that discomfited Trilling might be traced to a root other than a reflexive need to find virtue in suffering. Agee's belief in the "sacred" and "possibly immortal" human

soul, perhaps, required him to remove the buffer of tasteful representation and still try to restore to his subjects the *Imago Dei.*[49]

The Depression had transformed the South from America's "shoved
around" "country cousin" into the nation's underdog: knocked on its back,
trying to find its morale and persevere despite joblessness, poverty, and
scarcity.[50] The South as working-class dark horse competed with the still
powerful Menckenite legend of the atavistic South, its backwardness
reinforced by puritanical fundamentalism. For writers in the thirties, the
economic crisis had underscored the region's incomplete modernization
and the consequences of maintaining Southern habits. They did not arrive,
however, at a uniform valuation that Christianity was on the side of
traditionalism or that Christianity should not act as a brake to change.
Their judgments differed, partly because of the examples of Southern
religion they chose to highlight, and also because they varied in their
moral estimates of progress and in the lessons they drew from the
Southern past.

T. S. Stribling (b. Tennessee) from youth thought himself an infidel and
travestied "a kind-hearted Christian lady" in one of his earliest stories.[51] He
turned his critical realism to the theme of secularization in *The Unfinished
Cathedral* (1934), the third title in his popular trilogy spanning three
generations from the Civil War to the 1920s.[52] Set in the twenties, the
novel examines contemporary transition through the clash between reg-
nant, middle-class and insurgent, plebian forms of the South's evangelical
Protestantism. In this conflict, Stribling uniquely focuses on Southern
Rotarians from the narrative perspective of a minister inside their ranks.
Jerry Caitlin, newly appointed for his public relations and fund-raising
skills, has joined the personnel of the theologically modernist Pine Street
Methodist Church. The unfinished building of the novel's title is Pine
Street's under construction mega-church, "All Souls Cathedral," designed
to be a monument to the economic "progress" fueled by booming real
estate values. Caitlin is a cagy, prosperous liberal Protestant: *Elmer Gantry*'s
Frank Shallard, but with the political acumen to package his religious
doubts as a means of attracting secular society to Christianity. His contender in the novel is a simple evangel, Willie Rutledge, the founder of the
Drownders, a spirit-filled sect that practices full immersion baptism,
embraces voluntary poverty, and collect no tithes. Once the sect takes
over a Methodist church and spreads to Baptist and Presbyterian assem-
blies, Caitlin is given the mission of neutralizing them. As always, he
succeeds, though he is ambivalent over his triumph. The Drownders, he
knows, revive the impulses of primitive Christianity that were present in

the early Methodist-Holiness movement. Converting laborers that Pine Street cannot, the Drownders offer succor to those who have departed an economic system that filled the thought of every morrow with uncertainty. Quietly, Caitlin is saddened that he has fallen so far from the minister he had once desired to be, "moving among the poor and the humble ... praying for and healing the afflicted" (45). Stribling's implied author sympathizes with the Drownders, but, like Caitlin, he sees them as too pietistic to stop the Rotarians from carrying the South into a future where everything, including religion, is a function of industry and commerce. Only the fallout from greed and financial over-speculation, combined with stirrings of racial protest and class revolt, bode any serious challenge.

In *The Unfinished Cathedral*, Stribling wryly depicts the modern evangelical church's adaptation to the structure of business enterprise. Erskine Caldwell (b. Georgia), like Flannery O'Connor in the fifties, focuses on the faith of those left behind: the evangelical Protestantism of poor whites and small farmers in decline. The Lesters, for example, in his first and best-known novel, *Tobacco Road* (1932), are Protestant sharecroppers in rural Georgia who cobble together lay theology, folk belief, and revival teaching. The son of progressive minister Reverend Ira Sylvester Caldwell, of the Associate Reformed Presbyterian Church, Caldwell kept his father's social consciousness but jettisoned his faith, becoming an agnostic and a supporter of the Communist Party ticket in 1932. In his nonfiction, he baldly criticized Christianity, whether it was the modernist Caitlin variety or "Holy Rollers," for impeding social reform. His best-selling fiction, at its most simplistic, treats Southern evangelicalism as a farce and an absurdity for pretending to curb the poor's maundering desires. Material environment diminishes his characters' agency, but does not anesthetize them biologically. *Tobacco Road*'s antinomian preacher Sister Bessie is a hypocrite who both shames and rationalizes improvident desires. Though she prays for Jeeter Lester to lose his devilish fleshly urges, she forms the two-member "Holy" sect chiefly to satisfy her lusts for Jeeter's teenaged son. Sister Bessie is strictly the butt of satire, but Protestants like patriarch Ty Ty Walden in *God's Little Acre* (1933) and the protean revivalist Semon Dye in *The Journeyman* (1935) voice Caldwell's own naturalism. Both believe that the animal in man is God's image; preachers forbid, and they make biology evil. At his most sympathetic, in the narration of Jeeter Lester's thoughts, Caldwell allows the character's lay theology to register moral shock at his squalor and at the apparent reversal of the biblical God's care for the poor. Jeeter Lester struggles to understand, without understanding, why he has nothing and never will. He

accuses God of being unfair since the rich reap rewards while the sharecroppers grow hungry and diseased. Jeeter is able to affirm God's original
goodness, if not quite His justness, because He gave the farmer Creation to
till and a body to reproduce. Jeeter therefore distinguishes his present
condition from a displaced state of nature in which existing and laboring
as divinely intended would be intrinsically satisfying. It is the textile mills,
employing men forced from the land to make goods not their own, who
have marred God's first design. When Caldwell does not simply settle for
burlesque or bromide, he is able to imagine that his characters' Protestant
discourse is their way of quarreling with fate. It may not pierce through to
the political economy of their situations, but it can call progress to account,
ask God's purposes, question whether clergy know God, and affirm the
satisfactions of creaturely existence. This speculative depiction of belief is
more provocative than trite statements in his nonfiction of the period that
religion "serve[s] as a release and an escape."[53]

William Faulkner (b. Mississippi) saw Christianity as a heritage that
haunts the modern Southern mind and sometimes consoles it. Baptized
Methodist, and as an adult attending the Episcopal Church in Oxford,
Mississippi, he took a capacious view of the region's diverse religiosity.
Titles in his Yoknapatawpha saga, *The Sound and the Fury* (1929), *As I Lay
Dying* (1930), *Light in August* (1932), and *Absalom, Absalom!* (1936), together
provide a cross-section of Southern Christianity: black Holiness churches,
folk belief, Baptist Calvinism, and the region's civil religion.[54] While the
practices of Faulkner's African Americans and peasantry condition them to
compassion, stoicism, and humor, Calvinism and the civil religion create
grotesques. Calvinists loathe human depravity, but doom others to servi-
tude and mortification so that they may purchase redemption for the elect.
The civil religion, which displaces Christology to a national body, mili-
tantly defines the South as a separate civilization covenanted with God and
sanctified by the blood of Confederate martyrs. In *Light in August*, the two
religious ideologies lethally reinforce each other and keep the South
enthralled to the racist past. Fugitive Joe Christmas, who believes himself
to be mulatto, has internalized a predestinarian logic that justified slave-
holding and persists in the Jim Crow era: black blood dooms one to sin
expungable only by the whim of the white man's god. The civil religion is
embodied by maniacal Doc Hines, who pursues Joe from childhood; Percy
Grimm, who slays and castrates him; and defrocked Reverend Hightower,
who prefers a dream world, wrapped around the legend of his Confederate
grandfather's death. When Joe's life pierces Hightower's Civil War fantasy,
it moves the former minister to pity. Against the clear night sky, Hightower

has a vision, a circle of faces merging Joe and his bigoted killer, that briefly leaves the catastrophe of racial violence for the promise of forgiveness and the recognition of universal suffering.

The aftermath of Joe and Hightower's encounter moves the novel beyond the conventions of anti-lynching fiction, a radical genre in the thirties. For some, *Light in August*'s turn toward Christian reconciliation is evidence of Faulkner's rejection of the literary left. In a classic study of the Depression era, cultural historian Richard Pells points also to *Absalom, Absalom!*, an indictment of "Faustian" modern man, as evidence that Faulkner's ethic was "profoundly conservative" compared to his contemporaries.[55] This is a simplistic characterization from the evidence. A moderate Democrat, Faulkner did support some Popular Front causes, and he was particularly fervent about antifascism.[56] *Absalom, Absalom!* exhibits a tragic view of history, at least partially rooted in a Judeo-Christian pessimism about human nature and temporality, that runs counter to utopian and revolutionary politics. However, *Absalom, Absalom!* is also about the perversion of the covenantal relationship between God and His people by a character, Thomas Sutpen, whom Faulkner considered a regionally grown fascist personality. Sutpen is both an embodiment of the will-to-power, intended to have contemporary overtones, and a sublime example of sinful hubris, defying "creaturely" evanescence and incurring a curse upon future generations.[57] To cleave the two meanings or negate one with the other ignores how religious discourses had more than one ideological vector in this period. In Faulkner's fiction, sin-consciousness can lead, horrifically, to the rationalization of oppression or to humility, forgiveness, and the refusal of complicity in social evil. These attitudes were not inimical to "liberal" or "Popular Front" ethics, and not exclusive to "conservative" ethics.

Zora Neale Hurston's regional rediscovery took her afield of her Southern contemporaries. Her personal background in Eatonville, Florida's Macedonian Missionary Baptist assembly and her extensive anthropological fieldwork on black congregations, posthumously collected in *The Sanctified Church* (1981), had persuaded her that religion could function effectively as a cultural system and provide for creative encounters between self and social forms. She strongly supported African American churches because their ritual art and liturgical performances could anchor individuality in local communities. Black congregations, she had documented, also hybridized with Caribbean and West African religions. In her fiction, Hurston constructed a theological romance between these traditions and Christianity. Escaping their Southern Baptist homes, John

Buddy in *Jonah's Gourd Vine* (1934) and Janie Crawford in *Their Eyes Were Watching God* (1937) come into contact with nature divinities, respectively the African-Vodun deity Dumballah Ouedo and the Haitian-Vodun storm god Shango. At the climax of *Jonah's Gourd Vine*, John Buddy (now the Rev. John Pearson) gives a sermon fusing the gospel and Vodun and thus underscoring their spiritual "complementarity."[58] Many Southern authors, white and black, had depicted African American services, notably Faulkner in Part IV of *The Sound and the Fury*, but only Hurston presented an oratory demonstrating that "Congo gods" have acquired "Christian names."[59] Uniquely for the thirties' endeavor to capture folk experience and Southern life in transition, Hurston showed the syncretic nature of black Christianity while trusting that it could adapt to a changing world.

By 1939, the war in Europe and the question of American intervention had divided the anti-Stalinist left and put Christian pacifists on the defensive. Dalton Trumbo's National Book Award–winning *Johnny Get Your Gun* (1939) adapted the Christological motifs of antiwar literature to make a proletarian case for nonintervention. In keeping with the Soviet Union's neutrality at the time, Trumbo (who would officially join the CPUSA in 1943) takes the stance that the war is a battle between imperialist nations and not a crusade to stop fascism. During World War I, twenty-year-old draftee Joe Bonham, from Colorado, survives a bomb blast that leaves him sightless, deaf, mute, and limbless. Interior narration (alternating second and third person) represents Joe's subjective experience of his new universe, suspended in a permanent twilight where dream and wakefulness become nearly indistinguishable and time has no mark. Since the character is a Catholic by training, his memories and fantasies about the Son of Mary furnish the premise for Trumbo to revisit "the Crucified Christ" of World War I memoirs. As in these antiwar texts, Christ is a universal infantryman, but Trumbo ironically alters the memoirs' tripartite "romantic structure": "training, 'combat,' recovery. Or, innocence, death, rebirth." The third phase, usually at a pastoral remove, sees the former soldier apotheosized into "a literary rememberer" who makes the madness of war cohere through "emotional motifs."[60] For Joe Bonham, there is no pastoral compass. His scene of recollection is living death, in which consciousness remains intact but incommunicable. Joe undergoes two self-designated "resurrections" from his eternal night. In the first, he establishes a nonverbal means of communicating with other humans. This victory over death is shortly stolen from him when he learns that the military has denied his request to be made a living exhibit of the horrors of war. The dead never get to confirm whether the cost of war justifies it; church and state always testify for them, eulogizing their bloodshed and making a patriotic symbol of the cross. Like the worker's Christ of di Donato, Trumbo's must *renounce* his sacrificial role.[61] In the novel's closing, Joe's spirit dilates to become one with all sons drafted into service, regardless of nationality. He is resurrected once more, this time as a secularized eschatological symbol: revolutionary, immanent, having no stench of glory (204–08, 238–42, 227). As "the new Christ," he will not participate in his own crucifixion.

While Trumbo remolded the Passion to discourage intervention, W. H. Auden was coming round to Reinhold Niebuhr's anti-pacifism and anticommunism. Auden's journey back to Christian belief, following his socialist phase, is a paradigmatic instance of the pilgrimage that many intellectuals took in the forties. Shortly after emigrating to the United States, Auden began attending St. Mark's Episcopal Church in New York, and he reaffirmed his faith in 1940. The book of poetry *The Double Man* (written 1939, published 1940) marked his return. Its epilogue explicitly names Jesus for the first time in his poetry, while its many allusions (Dante, Pascal, Kierkegaard, and Tillich) trace the reading that led him back to Christianity. The title "refers to man's dual nature, that he is neither pure spirit nor pure flesh," and much of Auden's subsequent work would be preoccupied with "human self-division" and misleading secular quests to transcend the problem or deny it.[62] Marxism, he endeavored to show, suppresses the element of faith in its vaunted rationality. In the dialogue with the Devil that comprises part of *The Double Man*, Auden likens Marx's theory of history to Millennialism, and, in his essay "Purely Subjective" (1943), he derisively calls Marx's and Hegel's "Dialectic" the "new God" of the "pure epistemological I."[63] Lacking a philosophical cognate for the doctrine of original sin, Marxism made humankind forget that reason is always confounded with ego. The Pulitzer Prize–winning *The Age of Anxiety* (1947, begun in 1944), addressed the experience of World War II, but ended up giving a name to the early Cold War. Taking as its theme mankind's creaturely fallenness and desire for restoration,[64] the poem's mingling of religious and psychoanalytic self-searching made it a cultural touchstone at a time when intellectuals and artists were faulting the prior decade's left for lacking inwardness. The "age of anxiety" was also, as Harold Rosenberg dubbed it, "the Confession Era," as ex-radicals renounced political innocence and defined their former Marxist commitments as false secular faiths that resembled Christian heresies or parodies of prophetic revelation. Instructed by Reinhold

Niebuhr, who would become America's premiere establishment theologian in the fifties, liberals and conservatives alike concluded that despite the Party's official atheism, communism was a political religion, or a God that failed.[65]

While the former left told a narrative of violated innocence, McCarthyism purveyed a cruder, ideologically instrumentalized story of Marxist guile advancing treason through atheism. The repressive effect on art and thought in the Cold War is evident in the controversy that pursued Langston Hughes over "Good-Bye Christ." Hughes was called before the Permanent Subcommittee on Investigations in 1953. During the interrogation, Republican senator Everett McKinley Dirksen of Illinois read aloud from "Goodbye Christ" and followed up with questions "to determine if the poem represented Hughes's atheism, and therefore, his belief in Communism."[66] At the public hearing chaired by Joseph McCarthy, Hughes protected his career and his reputation by not only denying that he had ever been an atheist or a communist, but also denouncing the poem and muting its intent. The questions the subcommittee asked of Hughes vulgarly posed an either-or that left no conceptual space for the poem's dialectic. "Goodbye Christ" was never just a statement of unbelief, and Hughes, like a number of his contemporaries in the thirties, was not simplistically anti-Christian. Beyond disillusionment, writers on the left diversely appropriated Christianity, refusing to wait upon messianic time though secularizing messianic hope, denying redemptive character to labor's suffering yet redeeming suffering in behalf of labor, and challenging churches' bigotry and social captivity while judging them by the gospel's ideals. As Cold War America recoiled from "the Red Decade," these literary examples persisted in cultural memory, their heterodoxy reclaimed in Norman Mailer's theodicies, James Baldwin's prophetic witness, Philip Bonosky's liberation theology, Jack Kerouac's hobo saint, and Harriet Arnow's migrant Gerda, seeking in postwar Detroit the face of another Jesus.[67]

Notes

1. *The Christian Century* 52 (September 18, 1935), 1168–70. Qtd. in Martin E. Marty, *Modern American Religion V. 2: The Noise of Conflict, 1919–1941* (Chicago: University of Chicago, 1993), p. 253.
2. Harvey Teres, "Remaking Marxist Criticism: Partisan Review's Eliotic Leftism. 1934–1936," *American Literature* 64 (1992), pp. 127–53.

3. Michael Denning, *The Cultural Front: The Laboring of American Culture in the Twentieth Century* (New York: Verso, 1997). Denning's term *the cultural front* refers to the cultural formations of the Popular Front era, which were imprinted by Marxist, socialist, and "laborist" aesthetics.
4. Phrasing from FDR's second inaugural address (January 20, 1937).
5. Charles Berger, "The 'Non-Native' Moore: Hybridity and Heroism in the Thirties," in *Critics and Poets on Marianne Moore: "A Right Good Salvo of Barks,"* ed. Linda Leavell, Cristianne Miller, and Robin Schulze (Lewisburg, PA: Bucknell University Press, 2005), pp. 150–64. Qt. pp. 159, 156.
6. Patricia C. Willis, "Marianne Moore and the Seventeenth Century," in Leavell, Miller, and Schulze, *Critics and Poets on Marianne Moore*, pp. 40–55. Qt. p. 53.
7. Linda Leavell, *Holding on Upside Down: The Life and Work of Marianne Moore* (New York: Farrar Straus & Giroux, 2013), p. 324.
8. Judith Merrin, "Sites of Struggle: Marianne Moore and American Calvinism," in *The Calvinist Roots of the Modern Era*, ed. Carol J. Singley (Hanover, NH: University Press of New England, 1997), pp. 91–106. Qt. p. 98.
9. Niebuhr, *Moral Man and Immoral Society* (New York: Charles Scribner's Sons, 1932), p. 91.
10. Berger, "The 'Non-Native' Moore," p. 153.
11. The phrase "Baptist 'Don Quixote'" is from Wilder's papers, as quoted in the Afterword to the McClatchy edition of *Heaven Is My Destination*, p. 188.
12. Lincoln Konkle, *Thornton Wilder and the Puritan Narrative Tradition* (Columbia: University of Missouri Press, 2006).
13. Denning, *The Cultural Front*, p. 230.
14. Mike Gold, *Jews without Money* (Philadelphia, PA: Public Affairs, 2009), p. 189.
15. Leslie Fiedler, "The Christian-ness of the Jewish American Writer," in *Fiedler on the Roof: Essays on Literature and Jewish Identity* (Boston, MA: David R. Godine, 1991), pp. 59–71; Hana Wirth-Nesher, "Afterword: Between Mother Tongue and Native Language in Call It Sleep," in Roth, *Call It Sleep* (New York: Noonday, 1995), pp. 443–62.
16. Wirth-Nesher notes that the phallic image and allusion to Lazarus's poem are "satiric," but argues that Roth requires the Christ symbol to demonstrate his, and David's, transcendence of Jewish particularity; p. 459.
17. See Allen Tate's dismissive remark that Marxists had become the twentieth century's allegorists in "Three Types of Poetry" (1934), in *Essays of Four Decades*, rev. edn. (Chicago: Swallow Press, 1968), pp. 187–88.
18. Angus Fletcher, *Allegory: The Theory of a Symbolic Mode* (Princeton, NJ: Princeton University Press, 2012), pp. 24–68.
19. Fletcher, *Allegory*, p. 369.
20. Thomas J. Ferraro, *Feeling Italian: The Art of Ethnicity in America* (New York: New York University Press, 2005), pp. 51–71.
21. Fletcher, *Allegory*, p. 343.

22. Alan Wald covers Farrell's Trotskyist years in Alan M. Wald, *The New York Intellectuals: The Rise and Decline of the Anti-Stalinist Left from the 1930s to the 1980s* (Chapel Hill: University of North Carolina Press, 1987), pp. 82–85.

23. James T. Farrell, *Young Lonigan* (New York: Penguin Classics, 2003), p. 5.

24. Paul Giles, *American Catholic Arts and Fictions: Culture, Ideology, Aesthetics* (Cambridge: Cambridge University Press, 1992), pp. 153–67.

25. Farrell, *Young Lonigan*, p. 64.

26. On the poem's publication history and reception, see Arnold Rampersad, *The Life of Langston Hughes, Volume 1: 1902–1941* (New York: Oxford University Press, 2002), pp. 252–53, 393–94; Wallace Best, "Concerning 'Goodbye Christ': Langston Hughes, Political Poetry, and African American Religion," *Religion and Politics* (November 26, 2013). http://religio nandpolitics.org/print/?pid=6813 (accessed March 3, 2016).

27. Benjamin E. Mays, *The Negro's God: As Reflected in His Literature* (Eugene, OR: Wipf and Stock, 2010), p. 239. First published Chapman and Grimes, 1938.

28. Hughes, "Concerning 'Good-bye Christ'"(1941), discussed in Rampersad, *Life of Langston Hughes*, p. 393, Best, "Concerning 'Goodbye Christ,'" p. 4.

29. Best, "Concerning 'Goodbye Christ,'" p. 3.

30. Langston Hughes, *Not without Laughter* (Mineola, NY: Dover, 2008), p. 49.

31. Wright, *Black Boy* (New York: Harper Perennial, 2007), p. 257.

32. Colleen McDannell, *Picturing Faith: Photography and the Great Depression* (New Haven, CT: Yale University Press, 2004), pp. 200, 219.

33. Wright called Christianity counterrevolutionary in " Blueprint for Negro Writing" (1937), in David Levering Lewis, ed., *The Portable Harlem Renaissance Reader* (New York: Viking, 1995), p. 197. First published in the Marxist magazine *The New Challenge*. Wright joined the CPUSA through Chicago's John Reed Club.

34. Alan Wald, *Writing from the Left: New Essays on Radical Culture and Politics* (New York: Verso, 1994), p. 174. Stories in his first published book, *Uncle Tom's Children* (1938, expanded 1940), were originally published separately. "Fire in the Cloud" was first published in *Story* (1938), and "Bright and Morning Star" was first published in the *New Masses* (1938).

35. Wright, *Uncle Tom's Children* (New York: Harper Perennial, 2004), pp. 226, 228.

36. Denning, *The Cultural Front*, p. 24.

37. On *The Grapes of Wrath* as a key Popular Front text, see Morris Dickstein, *Dancing in the Dark: A Cultural History of the Great Depression* (New York: W. W. Norton, 2009), pp. 124–43; Denning, *The Cultural Front*, pp. 266–67.

38. John Steinbeck, *The Grapes of Wrath*, (New York: Penguin Books, 1992 [1939]), 84.

39. Steinbeck, *The Grapes of Wrath*, 440.

40. Steinbeck, *The Grapes of Wrath*, 159.

41. Michael Robertson, *Worshipping Walt: The Whitman Disciples* (Princeton, NJ: Princeton University Press, 2009). Esp. chapters 1, 3, and 6.
42. Steinbeck, *In Dubious Battle* (New York: Penguin, 2006), p. 113. On Steinbeck's deep ambivalence about communism, see Dickstein, *Dancing in the Dark*, 84–91.
43. Cyrus Ernesto Zirakzadeh, "Revolutionary Conservative, Conservative Revolutionary? John Steinbeck and The Grapes of Wrath," in *A Political Companion to John Steinbeck*, ed. Cyrus Ernesto Zirakzadeh and Simon Stow (Lexington: University Press of Kentucky, 2013), p. 51. On the affinities between the novel's iconography of "the people" and racial populism, see Denning, *The Cultural Front*, 266–67.
44. McDannell, *Picturing Faith*, p. 50.
45. For instances of the secularization thesis, see McDannell, pp. 86–87, 198–221. On modernism, see in particular McDannell's discussion of Walker Evans, pp. 53–78.
46. Dickstein, *Dancing in the Dark*, p. 109.
47. *Let Us Now Praise Famous Men* (Boston, MA: Houghton Mifflin, 2001), pp. 159–160, 173, 184.
48. Dickstein, *Dancing in the Dark*, p. 107.
49. Lionel Trilling, "Greatness with One Fault in It," *The Kenyon Review* 4.1 (1942), pp. 99–102. Qt. p. 102; Walker Evans, "Preface"(1960), in *Let Us Now Praise Famous Men* (Boston, MA: Houghton Mifflin, 2001), p. vii.
50. Preface (1937) to Erskine Caldwell and Margaret Bourke-White, *You Have Seen Their Faces* (Athens: University of Georgia Press, 1995). Originally published 1937.
51. Kenneth W. Vickers, *T. S. Stribling: A Life of the Tennessee Novelist* (Knoxville: University of Tennessee Press, 2003), p. 25.
52. T. S. Stribling, *The Unfinished Cathedral* (Tuscaloosa: University of Alabama Press, 1986). The trilogy began with *The Forge* (1931) and *The Store* (1933), each focusing on the fictional Vaiden family and set in and around Florence, Alabama.
53. *You Have Seen Their Faces*, p. 39.
54. Charles Reagan Wilson, "Faulkner and Southern Religious Culture," in *Faulkner & Religion*, ed. Doreen Fowler and Ann J. Abadie (Jackson: University Press of Mississippi, 1991), pp. 21–43.
55. Richard Pells, *Radical Visions and American Dreams: Culture and Social Thought in the Depression Years* (Urbana-Champaign: University of Illinois Press, 1998), pp. 242–46.
56. On Faulkner's political affiliation and sympathies, see Ted Atkinson, *Faulkner and the Great Depression: Aesthetics, Ideology, and Cultural Politics* (Athens: University of Georgia Press, 2005).
57. Robert Alter, *Pen of Iron: American Prose and the King James Bible* (Princeton, NJ: Princeton University Press, 2010), pp. 78–113. Qtd. p. 89.

58. Nancy Ann Watanabe, "Zora Neale Hurston's Vodun-Christianity Juxtaposition: Theological Pluralism in Their Eyes Were Watching God," in *Zora Neale Hurston, Haiti, and* Their Eyes Were Watching God, ed. La Vinia Delois Jennings (Evanston, IL: Northwestern University Press, 2013), pp. 237–55. Hurston's father, a minister in the Macedonian Missionary Baptist church of Eatonville, FL, was the basis for John Buddy/John Pearson in *Jonah's Gourd Vine*. On the ritual interaction between individual and community in Hurston's *The Sanctified Church* and her first two novels, see M. Cooper Harriss, "The Preacher in the Text: Zora Neale Hurston and the Homiletics of Literature," *Religion and Culture Web Forum* (February 2008). https://divinity.uchicago.edu/religion-and-culture-web-forum-archive-20092008 (accessed June 8, 2018).

59. *Jonah's Gourd Vine* (New York: Harper Collins, 2008), p. 89.

60. On Trumbo's political leanings, see Daniel Aron, *Writers on the Left: Episodes in American Literary Communism* (New York: Columbia University Press, 1992), pp. 385–86. On romance and Christology in World War I memoirs, see Paul Fussell, *The Great War and Modern Memory* (New York: Oxford University Press, 2013), pp. 127–29, 134, 139–42.

61. *Johnny Got His Gun* (New York: Citadel Press, 2007), p. 241.

62. Arthur Kirsch, *Auden and Christianity* (New Haven, CT: Yale University Press, 2005), pp. 33, 32.

63. Edward Mendelson, *Later Auden* (New York: Farrar, Straus & Giroux, 1999), p. 112.

64. The poem is subtitled "a baroque eclogue." Auden closely associated the pastoral genre with the Christian myth of prelapsarian innocence; in *The Age of Anxiety*, the dream of returning to the Garden (Arcadia) cannot be teleogized as a utopian goal.

65. On the Confession Era, see Harold Rosenberg, "Couch Liberalism and the Guilty Past," in *The Tradition of the New* (New York: Da Capo, 1960), pp. 221–40; Michael Kimmage, *The Conservative Turn: Lionel Trilling, Whittaker Chambers, and the Lessons of Anti-Communism* (Cambridge, MA: Harvard University Press, 2009), pp. 142–47, 222–25; Jason Stevens, *God-Fearing and Free: A Spiritual History of America's Cold War* (Cambridge, MA: Harvard University Press, 2010), pp. 87–111.

66. Best, "Concerning 'Goodbye Christ,'" p. 5.

67. Allusion to Philip Bonovksy's novel *Burning Valley* (1953). "[A] laughing Christ uncrowned with thorns and with the scars of the nail holes in his hands all healed away; a Christ who had loved people, who had loved to mingle with them and laugh," Harriet Arnow, *The Dollmaker* [First published 1954] (New York: Scribner, 2009), p. 67.

CHAPTER 9

Diversity and American Letters

Yael Schacher

Was Depression-era pluralism dependent upon the belief that, as a vigorous proponent of the "nation of nations" idea insisted in 1931, "immigration is now ended"?[1] Some recent historians and literary critics have implied that exclusion was a prerequisite for the multiculturalism of the 1930s. As Wendy Wall writes, "casting American variety in ethnocultural terms proved politically easier than it had been in the past, in part because of the clapdown on immigration to the U.S. in the 1920s. The restrictive legislation of that decade effectively took immigration off the table as a subject of national debate and hastened the acculturation of ethnic communities. In doing so, it made declarations of cultural diversity less threatening."[2] A related position is that the multiculturalism of the 1930s and 1940s was distinctively whitening. As Matthew Frye Jacobson puts it, the restrictionist 1924 immigration law "laid the way for a redrawing of racial lines" and marked "the beginning of the ascent of monolithic whiteness." African Americans, Native Americans, and Asian Americans were outside the pale. By the 1930s and 1940s, the children of European immigrants were perceived as culturally, not racially, distinct; the term *Caucasian* would surface in novels by Irish-American James Farrell and Jewish American Laura Hobson.[3] Ethnic literature of the Depression era, scholars note, focused on acculturation and the second generation and presented the process of immigrating and mono-ethnic enclaves as of the past – "ghetto pastorals" in Michael Denning's words.[4] Another important but incomplete shift was toward a relationally constructed understanding of race and ethnicity.

If assimilation of European ethnics was a preoccupation of writers in the 1930s, a minor strain of literature grappled directly with the implications of restrictionist immigration policies. This literature deserves attention because immigrant rights, like civil rights, gained some cultural traction in the New Deal era, though policy changes were a long way off. Some writers in the 1930s realized that portraying America as a nation of past immigrants was not a sufficient response to policies of exclusion and deportation in the present. One such writer insisted in 1935 that there was a "hidden history" – one marked by exploitation and violence – behind the romantic myth of migration to the Golden Land.[5] As recent scholars have noted, there were also writers of the decade who refused to think of immigration from Europe in isolation. For them, it was related to other forms of migration (of African Americans from South to North, of Mexicans back and forth across the border, for example) and to racial violence (against Native Americans and Asians, for example). This more radical pluralism was linked to transnational solidarity and interracial cooperation on the American left, particularly antifascist and anti-imperialist movements. More than in the previous decade, writers depicted interactions between individuals from different backgrounds.[6]

Many scholars have pointed to the significance of the Federal Writers' Project (of the Work Progress Administration) and other folklore and oral history–gathering projects for the development of 1930s cultural pluralism. This chapter addresses not only the ways these projects influenced "the invention of ethnicity" but also the ways they tenuously addressed racism and restrictionism. It similarly analyzes literary contributions to the early issues of the first American magazine explicitly devoted to diversity, *Common Ground*. It also discusses the ways that ethnic writers participated in the search for a distinctly diverse or radical "usable" American past. Sometimes they did this through interpretive imitations of canonical American writers. Finally, this chapter discusses fiction that contended directly with the literary output of nativists and with poetry that challenged exclusionary immigration policies.

The relationship of the folklore and oral history projects of the Federal Writers' Project (FWP) to the depiction of cultural diversity in literature is complicated. Morton Royse and Benjamin Botkin, academic overseers of the FWP's late 1930s ethnic studies and folklore projects, respectively, wanted amateur interviewers familiar with local immigrant and African American communities to collect "human documents" that would convey "the contemporary scene with all its variety and richness." Royse's goal was then to put together a series of books, entitled "Composite America," that emphasized cultural diversity and were written in "creative" literary form.[7] The bogey for Henry Alsberg, head of the entire FWP, was "secondhand" and "statistical" data. An unanticipated problem was that some of the data were secondhand and literary. An anonymous project worker in Connecticut submitted a portion of Mary Antin's autobiographical novel as the life history of a Jewish immigrant in New Haven.[8] Though Zora

Neale Hurston presented "Love ain't nothing but the easy-going heart disease" as primitive local folklore in her writing for the FWP Florida guide, Hurston's Florida subjects may have been riffing off of Langston Hughes's bluesy poem "Gypsy Man" (which ends with a stanza about "Love, Oh love is/Such a strange disease), a poem Hurston shared to kick off storytelling contests.[9] In a way, sophisticated, adaptive story-collecting and storytelling like this was the best proof of what Royse and Botkin set out to find: "the dynamics of cultural diversity" and participatory creative expression by African Americans and immigrants who were in the process of making American culture (rather than antiquarian tracing lore back to past homogeneous origins). Botkin also thought that folklore involved a process of "interchange between cultural groups" and of "creative listening." "Wherever we set up living lore units – in New York, in Chicago, in New England," Botkin wrote, "it was imaginative and speech values of 'own stories' that interested and impressed the workers most."[10] Botkin was interested in how the subjective or intimate, the symbolic or abstract, and the external environment or daily experience were integrated and conveyed through speech. This, and Botkin's approach to New York City work and street songs, resonate with the proletarian aesthetics of Michael Gold and the modernist aesthetics of Henry Roth.[11]

Langston Hughes and Mary Antin – whose writing surfaced in the FWP interviews – were writers particularly sensitive to racism and immigration restrictionism; overall, the former received more recognition in the FWP's guidebooks, despite resistance from some state editors. Academic and poet Sterling Brown, who was the director of Negro affairs for the FWP, reviewed copy in the state guides for stereotypes and paternalism and insisted, albeit with mixed success, that racial violence and inequality – like the ferocity of the East St. Louis, Illinois race riot of 1917 or the discrepancy between white and black public education in South Carolina and Mississippi – not be "glossed over" or whitewashed. For the DC guidebook, Brown himself wrote the chapter "The Negro in Washington," providing a history of the city's role in the interstate slave trade and emphasizing, along with African American achievements, contemporary discrimination and segregation.[12] Richard Wright wrote the Harlem section of the Project's guide to New York City; it is mostly descriptive, rather than analytical, but it does point to the neighborhood's poverty, overcrowdedness, high rents, shoddy housing, tension over employment at white-owned businesses, "racial discrimination and lack of opportunity to learn skilled trades," and inadequate health care.[13] Wright's autobiographical litany of cruelties, "The Ethics of Living Jim

Crow," was published in the FWP's 1937 anthology *American Stuff,* and Wright's "Fire and Cloud" – which details the brutal, but ultimately unsuccessful, attempt to suppress a communist-backed relief protest in a Southern city – won a story contest for FWP workers in 1938. The story begins with the protagonist, an African American preacher, half laughing and half shuddering as the bitter words of a folk saying "rolled without movement from his lips": "A naughts a naught/ N fives a figger/ All fer the white man/ N none fer the nigger." (A variant on this saying was reprinted in another FWP *American Stuff* literary collection in 1938.[14]) The story ends with the preacher confidently marching with an interracial crowd and singing the spiritual, "So the sign of the fire by night/ N the sign of the cloud by day/ A-hoverin oer/ Jus befo/ As we journey on our way," then "exultingly" adding the phrase "Freedom belongs to the strong," thereby shifting the emphasis of the song from the power of God to the power of the people.

Nativism and exclusionism did not figure as prominently as anti-black racism in FWP publications. Some of the most interesting writing expressly dealing with immigration policy that came out of the FWP was revised or never published because it touched on politically sensitive issues at a time when Alsberg and the Project were under scrutiny by the red-baiting and nativist Congressman Dies of the House Un-American Affairs (HUAC) Committee. Dies claimed any reference to historical or contemporary economic strife and racial injustice effectively "promoted class or racial hatred" and "stimulated racial intolerance." Another controversial topic was the Spanish Civil War. At the time of the congressional hearings, Italian American writer Mari Tomasi, who was collecting "living lore" from Vermont granite workers (that she would eventually incorporate into her novel *Like Lesser Gods*), did an interesting interview at Barre's Spanish Club, which supported the Loyalists. Tomasi recorded John (formerly Juan) Bavine:

> I have a wife an' three children in Spain. My wife she took the children there just before the war to see their grandmother ... After the war is start' they are not allow' to come home ... Always it has been in my heart to become the American citizen. Always I say, tomorrow I will take out the papers. But always there is something else to do, an' so I wait. But now – I have take them out – quick ... It makes me sick an' afraid to have them over there. My wife, she writes, an' I write to her; but what good is that? The letters, they have been open'. She cannot say what is in her heart, she cannot tell the truth about what is go' on. An' my letters to her, they are open', too.

Bavine was making direct reference to the difficulty Spanish refugees had coming to the United States; as a noncitizen, Bavine could not bring his family to America outside the quota and, even after naturalizing, the process could be difficult. Though this story (and the entire "Men against Granite" collection it was part of) did not make it into print at the time, the interview was edited for publication to read, "But now I have them [citizenship papers], I will send for the family," thereby deemphasizing the harshness of US immigration policy.[15] Volumes that made it into print received intense scrutiny: Royse was very disappointed that Alsberg kept deleting passages from a manuscript on Albanians in Massachusetts out of concern about stirring up trouble between the US State Department and the Albanian government.[16]

Royse believed there was an aesthetic corollary to this kind of political timidity. Of Harlan Hatcher, director of the Ohio project, who complained about Royse's approach, Royse wrote to Alsberg: "The main reason Hatcher is dubious of the work is that Hatcher is a teacher of English, schooled in the [Booth] Tarkington manner, somewhat timid of the world we live in. I've read two of his books, and think them nice, even praiseworthy, but certainly not a [James] Farrell etc., let alone the more plunging writers. I know you like his local guidebooks and agree that they are well written, but I can't reconcile myself to the thought that we must limit ourselves to such stuff."[17] Royse associated the Tarkington school with a style and approach to American culture opposed to diversity. Tarkington's most famous protégé at the time, *Saturday Evening Post* journalist, best-selling historical fiction writer, and outspoken nativist Kenneth Roberts, epitomized this. Having spent much of the 1920s calling for further immigration restriction, Roberts spent the 1930s writing "lost cause" books about the era of the American Revolution that betrayed a reactionary's worry about the claimants of the legacy of democracy. *Arundel* (1930) told the story of Benedict Arnold's 1775 expedition through the Maine and Canadian wilderness accompanied by some of Roberts's own ancestors; a sequel, *Rabble in Arms* (1933), told of the retreat and battles of the American army through 1777. These books captured a sense of grievance and appealed to those opposed to the New Deal: Benedict Arnold was, for Roberts, a heroic victim, a man who got a "raw deal."[18] Roberts's *Northwest Passage* – the biggest fiction seller of 1937 – was about Robert Rogers, a commander of Colonial soldiers during the French and Indian War who was known for his attack on the Abenaki at St. Francis, for securing support from the British to find an overland route to the Pacific and the Orient (the Northwest Passage), and then for treacherous squandering and desertion. Roberts depicts Rogers as a tragic hero: a fearless Indian fighter foiled by bureaucratic red tape, jealous rivals, a shrewish wife, and his own human weaknesses. Roberts's novels were just a few of an "unprecedented" number of popular historical romances that "smoothed over the anxiety of diminishment" felt by white, middle-class readers of the era. These readers "developed a special appetite for challenges that elicited their forebears' fortitude, believing that somehow reliving those adversities might spark their hereditary strength now . . . If the Writers' Project mapped the forty-eight states culturally and thereby made familiar the rich, contradictory panoply of life in the United States, historical novels aimed to recast and reclaim the consoling American history from which the Depression had alienated the citizenry."[19] As literature critic and professor Howard Mumford Jones noted, "the gulf between the Boston Brahmins and the Boston Irish, old Detroiters and . . . thousands of automobile workers, the first families of Cleveland and the Poles, the Armenians, the Czechs, the Ruthenians . . . is not . . . going to be bridged by a bright recital of the French and Indian Wars" by "'Old Americans' (hateful phrase!) who tend to take the point of view that American history is their private possession because they were here first."[20]

Nativist sentiment and the harsh immigration laws and policies of the 1930s complicated representations of diversity even for its champions. In late 1932, President Herbert Hoover instructed State Department officials to dramatically restrict visa issuance under an expansive definition of those ineligible to immigrate because they were "likely to become a public charge." Hoover's secretary of labor, William Doak, was nicknamed "Deportation Doak" by opponents for his notorious roundups of radicals. President Franklin Delano Roosevelt's administrators expressed more sympathy for immigrants, but the visa regulations remained intact, and deportation efforts continued against radicals, those who overstayed their visits or entered without proper documents, and the unemployed and those on relief; Filipinos and Mexicans and Mexican Americans were especially targeted for "repatriation" between 1931 and 1936. FDR spoke of immigration as admirable but of the past; increasingly history textbooks stressed the same message.[21] Edward Corsi, who immigrated to the United States from Italy as a young boy and served as the commissioner of Ellis Island in the early 1930s, titled his memoir *In the Shadow of Liberty*. "I'll probably have to send more out than I let in," he correctly predicted upon assuming the office. "Economic conditions have now driven us to close the gate and lock it against all the world . . . Deportation was the big business at Ellis Island."[22] In his compilation of personal essays *My America*, popular

Slovenian American writer Louis Adamic includes a letter he wrote in 1934 but never sent to the editor of the *Saturday Evening Post* in response to a nativist editorial and a "growing movement to send or drive as many of the immigrants as possible 'back where they came from.'" Adamic's letter emphasized the "contribution to America's present-day greatness" of millions of Slavic immigrants and their American-born children. The stance he took, was, admittedly "defensive." Adamic recognized that contributionism had a nostalgic, compensatory feel. (It also implied that ethnicity was formed a priori; it did not convey a sense that ethnicity was constructed in relationship to others.) The letter, Adamic writes, "was part of my groping toward an approach to the immigrant question, and, I felt, all wrong."[23] Adamic grappled with the question, not quite knowing how best to address it for the next several years.[24] Adamic's friend Carey McWilliams, who was the opposite of defensive in his withering criticisms of the treatment of Mexicans and Filipinos, was much more attuned to the ways different nationality groups were interacting and fighting for their rights in California.[25] (McWilliams was also very much aware that publishers were not interested in books about Mexican immigrants, who were perceived as "not an integral part of the American scene" until late into the next decade.[26]) McWilliams claimed prejudice and discrimination was not a natural outgrowth of mores or a by-product of racial or cultural differences as such, but rather stemmed from conflict or competition and was induced or sanctioned by legislation and policies.

Armenian American writer Herant Armen published several stories in the mid-1930s that address the impact of immigration policies on an ethnic community and convey both the defensive contributionism of Adamic and the trenchant criticism of McWilliams. Armen's protagonists are immigrants who came to the United States in the early years of the twentieth century with the intention of later returning to their families or bringing them over to the United States. By the 1930s, they are bitter and disillusioned: most of their relatives perished in the Armenian Genocide and restrictive American immigration laws made it difficult to bring over survivors. In one story, after years of waiting, a son arrives in the United States, but he is missing a telltale birthmark. He confesses that, after the true son died in the Syrian desert, he was so desperate to emigrate that he falsely claimed the son's visa. At the end of the story, the father, Sarkis Nourian, opts not to reveal the fraud for two reasons. First, he acknowledged a commonality of suffering he shared with the boy, a tragic sense Armen refers to as "Armenian destiny." Nourian was also concerned about his image in the eyes of his non-Armenian friends, in the eyes of all the local officials, tradesmen, and customers with whom he had talked of his son for years, among whom he was known as the man whose "amazing faith recovered the lost son."[27] This concern with respectability may also explain why so few ethnic writers wrote about the effects of restrictionist immigration laws. In another story, immigration seems so remote that Armen depicts it with dark humor. The story is about a joke played on a middle-aged Armenian man named Avakian by his Armenian friends in Brighton, MA. The friends show Avakian a picture of one of their supposed relatives, a refugee waiting for a visa, they claim, and suggest he marry her and bring her to the United States. Enchanted by the picture and by the thought of this noble and chivalrous rescue (a "sacred duty" to his people), Avakian agrees, and his friends take him to the movies to celebrate. There he sees his picture bride on the screen; Avakian's friends had given him a picture of Greta Garbo. "The joke ... proved to possess an enduring quality ... It taught [Avakian] to attend moving pictures ... While on the other hand, the joke augmented a great deal the fame of the Swedish lady, the noted actress," among Armenians in Brighton, who thereafter referred to her as one of their own.[28] That Greta Garbo was considered Armenian because of an inside ethnic joke highlights the adaptability and dynamism of ethnic culture and the way that, in this story, movies helped Armenians share in a collective experience as immigrants.[29] In both stories, Armen depicts acculturation as a kind of melding of contributions: before the son arrives, Nourian dreams of him being a "lion" like fire-haired King Vahakn from the pre-Christian Armenian origin myth and like popular American boxer Jack Dempsey.[30] Armen's later writing focused more exclusively on Armenian history and mythology; he believed in looking to the Armenian cultural past for renewal at a time when new immigration was limited.

Though Armen and the better-known writer William Saroyan published stories in the same Armenian-American weekly, the English language *Hairenik*, the tone of the two writers could not be more different. Armen modeled his tales on those of Nathaniel Hawthorne; they are full of brooding, secrets, symbols, guilt, and ancestral baggage. Saroyan, on the other hand, wrote in a capacious, effusive, celebratory style reminiscent of Walt Whitman. For example, the *Hairenik* of March 22 and 29, 1934 featured "Yea and Amen," a short story by Saroyan ostensibly about Armenian-American children taking apart a clock and rescuing a hen, but actually an affirmation of the holiness of the human spirit and its connectedness to everything. Saroyan writes that: "We had the presence of vast and unseen things, oceanic ... rivers of soul, canyons of mind, tall ageless trees, the universe of remembrance, God within us, and the wailing of babes ... the surge of history, turning in us ... To be related to all things ... to be related to the coming and going of men, to the appearance and disappearance of the faces and forms in all the regions of the earth, to be a part of every act of man, the good and the evil, all things performed, all thoughts and hopes and griefs." This story by Saroyan, like so much of Whitman's writing, is full of catalogs, focused on the self, and moves both inward and outward; it is about how, one critic notes, "we are all tied together by the bonds of common humanity – within each human breast beats the same cosmic energy."[31] In another piece in *Hairenik* later in 1934, Saroyan wrote, "[t]he continuity of mortal thought occurs in the men who walk alone, who journey over a lonely, and sometimes bitter, path. My sympathies are with such men ... I find community prayer silly and blasphemous. I find political oratory false and cheap. I find social events wasteful and disgusting ... I am interested in the magnificence of my race which blossoms only in the heart and mind of the man who finds himself." Saroyan further clarified his position a few weeks later: "One man is unlike another in many things and all men are alike in basic things, the universal. Of the same family. To be conscious is all that is necessary. And energetic. Not asleep. Not timid, ashamed, small." In short, Saroyan claimed he was "opposed to groups, interested in the individual."[32] In contrast, Armen's stories, as we have seen, are preoccupied with the relationship between the two.

Armen's interest in ethnic identity and the impact of law and policy on it resembles the perspective of Native American writer D'Arcy McKnickle (of Métis and Irish descent and enrolled in the Flathead tribe of northwestern Montana), whose 1936 novel *The Surrounded* depicts an attempt to reconcile traditional Salish customs and modern life that is foiled by the racism of American Indian policy. McKnickle originally wrote the novel in the mode of James Weldon Johnson's *Autobiography of an Ex-Colored Man*; it was a story about the son of a Spanish father and a Salish mother who goes off to Paris to study music, falls in love with a white American woman, and then, upon return to the United States, becomes a successful farmer and abandons his tribal heritage. When McKnickle redrafted the novel in 1933–34, he jettisoned the assimilationist emphasis and the happy ending; the protagonist returns to the reservation and interacts with tribal elders and the younger generation, only to be arrested by an Indian agent for the killing of a game warden and sheriff.[33]

The fiction of Armen and of McKnickle, who worked for the FWP for a few months in 1935 before joining the Bureau of Indian Affairs, resonates with the FWP's emphasis on the significance of cultural pluralism but refusal to see it as a panacea for social and political problems. One early ethnic project the FWP undertook was a study of Armenians in Massachusetts that focused on assimilation and contributions to American life by individual Armenian Americans. Once Morton Royce took over, however, he changed the focus of the project, as we have seen. His book on Albanians departed from assimilationism to focus on forms of diasporic nationalism and political and religious divides within the Albanian community. It also did not shy away from discussing nativism and poverty.[34] In *The Surrounded*, one scene depicts tribal elders telling several Salish folk stories at a traditional feast. In his portrayal of ceremonies involving a whip and a dance, McKnickle emphasizes both the efficacy of tribal traditions and their change over time. Later, in a scene depicting an encounter between the protagonist and an old deaf woman, McKnickle portrays the hunger, poverty, and "desolation" of Native Americans in Montana.[35] While the FWP Montana guidebook focused on pre-reservation tribal practices, later oral history projects in the state included interviews detailing contemporary Native American participation in Montana's economy as well as old and new folk stories of Montana's many tribes. Just as in the ethnic studies, fieldworkers for FWP "Indian studies" sometimes incorporated "previously printed materials" if relevant to contemporary political concerns over tribal recognition and land claims, for example.[36] Ultimately, however, as Armen's stories and McKnickle's novel show, the recognition of cultural diversity in the 1930s did not imply expanded legal and political rights. Later in the decade, while working for the BIA to promote tribal self-government in line with the Indian Reorganization Act, McKnickle became increasingly aware of how mixed ancestries and the resistance of whites to land claims meant that Métis along the northern border in Montana remained destitute and stateless – "part Cree, part Chippewa, part European, neither Canadian nor United States citizens . . . living on the ragged edge of survival, with no land and no treaty recognition."[37] McKnickle devoted his career to finding constructive policy solutions predicated on humane respect for tribal cultures and needs.

Louis Adamic generally thought of the "over 300,000 Indians, who are mostly on reservations," as a "problem somewhat special and apart" from that of "forming a culture" of the various "white elements" present in America. (Adamic also deemed the "13,000,000 Negroes . . . a rather special and uniquely acute problem . . . destined to be . . . the most severe test . . . of our pretentions to democracy.")[38] Characteristically for the decade, Adamic turned to questionnaires and interviews, trying to gather stories from people of diverse backgrounds. Adamic's "special question-naire on the Negro" was very different from the questions he directed at "immigrants and their American born descendants."[39] Adamic did not actively oppose most immigration restriction; he felt that America needed "to give herself a chance, to take time to merge and integrate her popula-tion, study herself and determine what she really is, and gain some control over her cultural destiny." (This echoed a contemporary sentiment expressed by President Roosevelt that the children of immigrants "more and more realize their common destiny in America.") Occasionally, Adamic did note that "immigrant problems" were not limited to those of the second and third generations. For example, in 1936, Adamic wrote a piece in the *Nation* protesting the impending deportation of anti-Nazis who had overstayed temporarily allotted times in the United States. (One came to the United States as a sailor and the other as a visitor.) Though the immigration law "says, 'Deport them!'" Adamic protested, "if I know anything about America, the tradition of this country is, 'Let them stay!'"[40]

By this time, the American Civil Liberties Union (ACLU) and the American Committee for the Protection of the Foreign Born (ACPFB), the latter of with which Adamic was affiliated, were making the case that it was not enough to integrate those already in the United States and to celebrate America's cultural diversity; refugees needed asylum. The pamphlets issued by these organizations argued, like Adamic, that immigration policies should harken back to America's origins as an "asy-lum for mankind" and welcomer of exiles, a tradition that had been "negatived" in recent decades. Despite exclusionary immigration policies, an ACLU pamphlet pointed out, "hundreds of alien political refugees have managed to get in, legally and illegally. Some have come on visitor's permits or business and have stayed … Hundreds have come over the Canadian and Mexican borders … These refugees are of all sorts – anti-Fascists, Russian Czarists and other anti-Soviets, Communists of many lands under dictators, anarchists from anywhere, Chinese, Korean and other colonials escaping the tyranny of imperialism, middle class repub-licans exiled from the dictatorships that today afflict half of Europe and of South America."[41] Many of these refugees were threatened with deporta-tion. For them, "Ellis Island is in the shadow of the Swastika," the ACPFB wrote, playing off the title of Edward Corsi's memoir.

An ACPFB pamphlet from the spring of 1937 – just when *Harper's* magazine ran an "American Way" essay contest that asked contestants to separate the essential from the outdated national ideals – pointed out that

Thomas Jefferson and Abraham Lincoln "tried to make this country a safe refuge from Old World Tyrannies" and considered "the principle of asylum a cornerstone of democratic institutions." "If Thomas Jefferson and Abraham Lincoln were to come to America today as immigrants, they would be excluded for the speeches they made and the opinions they held," the ACPFB noted. The ACPFB extended its criticism beyond refugees and asylum to immigration and deportation policy more generally, which it claimed was divisive and violated "human rights." The recruitment, mal-treatment, and deportation of Mexican workers in the Southwest, the ACPFB asserted, "well illustrates the fact that immigration policy in America has been dictated throughout by the needs of the capitalist system for workers." Finally, the ACPFB challenged the fundamental assumption that, as Roosevelt put it on the campaign trail in 1932, "Our industrial plant is built ... Our last frontier has long since been reached ... There is no safety valve in the form of a Western prairie ... We are not able to invite the immigration from Europe to share our endless plenty." The ACPFB was adamant not only that "immigrants from every land made America the richest country in the world," but that "it has the natural resources and the industrial development capable of providing an abundant life for several times its present population."[42] This reopening of the frontier was part of a broader movement by writers of the decade to ground support for the rights of migrants in a revisionist account of American history. McWilliams claimed contemporary "farm fascism" in California was rooted in violence and discrimination against immigrant agricultural workers (many of them Chinese and Japanese) going back to the nine-teenth century. Muriel Rukeyser included her protest poem "The Book of the Dead" – which documents the maltreatment of hundreds of miners, many of them Southern black migrants, hired to construct the Hawks Nest Tunnel in West Virginia – in a volume she titled *US 1* (1938) in a deliberate radicalizing of the FWP's highway guidebook of that name. Guiding the reader though West Virginia at the beginning of the poem, the speaker especially notes the site of the execution of radical abolitionist John Brown; at the end of the poem, the speaker again invokes the spirit of John Brown, this time to demand justice for the migrant workers.

By the end of the decade, concern for the civil rights of migrants and the need for a less punitive and restrictive immigration policy were latent themes of numerous pieces published in *Common Ground*, a journal Adamic edited with the declared goal of "tell[ing] the story of the coming and meeting on this continent of peoples belonging to above 60 different national, racial, and religious backgrounds."[43] The opening issue, of autumn 1940, featured a poem by John Ciardi – "Letter to Mother" – about the inadequacy a child of immigrants feels in his encounter with America as compared with that of his parents; another essay in the issue suggests that up-and-coming young ethnic writers look to Saroyan for inspiration. But the issue also moved beyond concerns with feelings of inferiority among the second generation. It included an article on the Smith Act, which mandated the registration of all noncitizens and expanded those subject to deportation; the Act was an indication of wariness toward the foreign-born and marked the transfer of the Immigration Service to the Justice Department, where it became primarily an enforcement agency. The spring 1941 issue of *Common Ground* featured a story, "Red Necktie" by Joe Sinclair, about a recently arrived elderly Jewish refugee who was having difficulty adjusting and making ends meet in an economically depressed Cleveland. The next issue featured another story about newly introduced legislation that would bar refugees and provide for the indefinite detention of deportable aliens.

One young writer found himself in just that position at the time. H. T. Tsiang had come to the United States on a temporary visa and enrolled as a graduate student at Stanford in 1926. (Under the exclusion laws then in force, Chinese people who could not claim derivative citizenship could not enter the United States unless they were coming temporarily as merchants, teachers, or students.) Tsiang worked briefly at the Kuomintang (KMT) daily *Young China* and then, frustrated by its conservativism, left to edit an independent weekly periodical, *Chinese Guide in America*, led rallies against Chiang Kai-shek's persecution of party radicals, and handed out leaflets critical of the KMT. Tsiang was hassled by the immigration service, which wanted to deport Tsiang for political reasons, but went after him for technical ones of not maintaining his student status. A federal court rejected this accusation in 1928.[44] Tsiang moved to New York, where he enrolled at Columbia University in the summer of 1928, at New York University in 1930, and at the New School in 1932. Tsiang also got involved with the literary left, publishing protest poems in the *New Masses* and *Daily Worker*, and self-publishing his first novel, *China Red*, in 1931. The novel is epistolary, but it only includes the letters written to a Chinese student in America (a fictionalized version of Tsiang) from his girlfriend in China, not the letters from him to her – formally capturing Tsiang's shadowy presence in the United States. As Tsiang prefaced his 1935 (also self-published) masterpiece *The Hanging on Union Square*, "What is unsaid/ Says,/And says more/Than what is said/Says I." The fictional student is eventually deported to China and executed by the KMT; Tsiang includes a graphic illustration of what looks like dripping blood or spilled ink. If this ending was Tsiang's attempt to make a tragedy of the farce that was his 1928 deportation proceeding, the following decade he had more good material to draw upon. In 1937, the immigration service again sought out Tsiang for his failure to attend school and demanded that he "communicate monthly" with the INS office. Tsiang didn't write "and when confronted with the fact of his failure, he stated that it was up to the school to write, whereas he was not in attendance at any school."[45] Tsiang's attitude toward the immigration authorities reflected his attitude toward the American literary world: he was an outsider who thumbed his nose at authority and convention.[46]

But Tsiang did write many letters – to acquaintances, politicians, writers, and lawyers – when he spent several months at Ellis Island between the fall of 1939 and the spring of 1941. Detained in September 1939 for not maintaining his student status, Tsiang claimed that condemnation of Japanese aggression in his recent novel *And China Has Hands* (1937) would put him in danger if he was returned to occupied China. A lawyer for the ACPFB argued that Tsiang had not resumed his studies for health reasons and got him released from Ellis Island and a six-month stay. Though Tsiang began attending the New School again on a scholarship in the fall of 1940, he was detained at Ellis Island for deportation in November. The ACPFB lawyer asked the immigration service to reconsider the case, but the service, which by now had moved from the Labor to the Justice Department, would not budge. When the ACPFB's appeals were also denied by the federal courts, Tsiang's deportation was delayed by the introduction of a private bill on his behalf by Congresswoman Jeanette Rankin. When a reporter from *P.M.* visited him at Ellis Island in the summer of 1941, Tsiang gave him a poem: "Three meals a day and a bed at night/ . . . But the locked door, guard and matron,/ Yes, my boy, you are in prison/ . . . How long are you going to stay?/ Some tell you this, some tell you that,/ Wait, wait, and your hair turns grey./ . . . I smoke, I read and I write./ My first vacation in ten years, a delight."[47] Tsiang's letters from this period are mostly appeals for help, though even these contain barbs of protest. (This strategy is similar to one Tsiang perfected as a self-publishing author: he used letters of rejection or criticisms of his books as blurbs to promote them.[48]) Tsiang wrote one of these letters to New York congressman Vito Marcantonio and sent along a seventy-three-page manuscript of poems entitled "Deportation" that he composed while at Ellis Island.[49]

The manuscript is divided into two sections, "Isle of Tears" and "Kingdom of Pear," the first which refers to Ellis Island, and the second which refers to heaven or youth (a pear is a symbol of immortality, since pear trees live a long time; in Chinese culture, pears are also associated with purity, generosity, justice, benevolent administration, prosperity, and good fortune, all of which play into Tsiang's poems).[50] But Tsiang emphasizes the connection between the two sites (Isle and Kingdom) as much as the contrast, and both seem to stand for America. Tsiang explains the significance of the two parts in the "introduction" that precedes them:

> Through the aid of friends
> And mercy of the King,
> Jailed in Winter
> I was freed in Spring.
>
> Old man, Time
> Are you fair?
> Forever, you put me out of
> The Kingdom of Pear.

The Isle of Tears section contains a group of "social significance" poems describing cruelty and tragedy at Ellis Island (including the gruesome suicide of an excluded German Jew and the "brutal" treatment of a Chinese woman by immigration officials), and two poems that refer derisively to the Statue of Liberty. But it also includes a group of juvenile poems and other lyrical and colloquial poems conveying a mix of sorrow and joy, hope and despair. The Kingdom of Pear section is invested with a sense of both love and loss. It is a Chinese taboo to divide a pear among friends as the word *fen li* (sharing a pear) is pronounced the same way as separation. Tsiang translates this idea into English in the opening poem of the Kingdom of Pear section:

> Many many thanks for your pear. But look here:
>   Pear, the word, is spelled a bit like tear.
>
> Your Walter is wild – as a wild cat.
>   Your Pauline is a pretty apple – so good to look at.
>
> And your Alice is music, is a song:
>   She makes me write all day long.
>
> Many thanks for your pear. But listen here:
>   Is it a pear? Is it a tear?

The poems in this section describe the speaker's observations of and encounters with Walter, Pauline, and Alice for two weeks while at Ellis Island. The style is a cross between Gertrude Stein's *Three Lives* and Langston Hughes's Semple stories. Though one poem reminds us, "A jail is jail, it can't be heaven," when spending time with the three youngsters, the speaker is prolific: "I catch the ghost; I put it in black and white." The speaker/writer also reenacts a Chinese folktale about a pear seed. In the folktale, a poor man jailed for stealing a pear out of hunger eats the fruit but saves the seed and then claims it would yield pears of gold to a person who never cheated or lied. Saying that it was no use to him as a common thief, the poor convict offers the seed to the emperor, high officials, wardens, and guards, but no one accepts it because none has a clear conscience; in the process, they come to see the injustice of imprisoning the poor man and set him free.[51] In Tsiang's version, the jailed speaker considers whether to eat or save a pear "for some other day/when Isle of Tears will be as dry as a dried fruit,/ Let this pear smile, laugh, and then salute." But the speaker gets mad and eats the pear, only to feel "sorry for the past" and to resolve to salvage its core. Later, when he is transferred to a new cell, forgets the core, and wants to retrieve it, he tells the guard and the "guard tells the guard-king," but all they do is "sneer." This seems to hint at the speaker's desire to hold on to a positive image of America and its promise of freedom, only to have it denied. Later, Alice and Pauline give him a pear for sticking to his convictions as a writer and refusing to conform. The last lines are: "Who said 'Pear is a tear!' I say no–/ What a nice vacation, Ha, ha, ha!/I'm one book richer, Rah, rah, rah!" These last lines make sense in the context of a note Tsiang appended to *The Hanging on Union Square*, explaining that he wrote his novels in a few weeks but then spent years raising money to print and distribute them, and the observation of an immigration inspector that Tsiang was "underweight and undernourished in November 1938, having spent his money to publish books."[52] For Tsiang, Ellis Island was both a jail and a vacation. But, once freed, he was still not really let in to America. One poem from the first section captures a sense of what Tsiang could not have:

Something

Back again, looking for something –
  Looking for winter? Looking for spring?
Hat lost, shoes missing, – no harm done –
  Forget the old, buy a newer one.

If, that missed something is really something –
  By all means, find it, either in winter or spring!

Since I have missed that – my something –
  I mind not winter, mind not spring.

Tsiang's poems attest to both the power and the limits of 1930s pluralism. The poems Tsiang wrote while detained on Ellis Island combine dialogue and folklore and seem stylistically influenced by modernist writers. Tsiang more than anyone would have appreciated the irony that the same could be said about the works of better-known minority and ethnic writers such as Ralph Ellison or Nelson Algren who got their start as workers for the FWP.[53] What McWilliams wrote of Adamic in 1935 better applied to Tsiang at the end of the decade: "his voice is prompted by an awareness of the discrepancy between the advertised virtues of American life and . . . the realities he encounters."[54]

Notes

1. Louis Adamic, *Laughing in the Jungle* (New York: Harper & Brothers, 1932), ix.
2. Wendy Wall, *Inventing the American Way: The Politics of Consensus from the New Deal to the Civil Rights Movement* (New York: Oxford University Press, 2008), 65.
3. Matthew Frye Jacobson, *Whiteness of a Different Color: European Immigrants and the Alchemy of Race* (Cambridge, MA: Harvard University Press, 1998), 92–93.
4. Michael Denning, *The Cultural Front: The Laboring of American Culture in the Twentieth Century* (New York: Verso, 1997).
5. Carey McWilliams, *Factories in the Field: The Story of Migratory Farm Labor in California* (Boston, MA: Little, Brown and Company, 1939).
6. Benjamin Balthasar, *Anti-Imperialist Modernism: Race and Transnational Radical Culture from the Great Depression to the Cold War* (Ann Arbor: University of Michigan Press, 2016); Erin Royston Battat, *Ain't Got No Home: America's Great Migrations and the Making of an Interracial Left* (Chapel Hill: University of North Carolina Press, 2014).
7. Quoted in Jerre Mangione, *The Dream and the Deal: The Federal Writers' Project, 1935–1943* (Syracuse, NY: Syracuse University Press, 1996), 278, 281.
8. Laura Banks, "Immigrant Voices from the Federal Writers Project: The Connecticut Ethnic Survey, 1937–1940," in *The Mythmaking Frame of Mind: Social Imagination & American Culture*, ed. James Gilbert, Amy Gilman, Donald Scott, and Joan Scott (Belmont, CA: Wadsworth, Inc., 1993), 280.
9. David Kadlec, "Zora Neale Hurston and the Federal Folk," *Modernism/Modernity* 7.3, September 2000, 481–82.
10. B. A. Botkin, "We Called It 'Living Lore,'" 0, 14.3., Fall 1958.
11. B. A. Botkin, "The Folk and the Individual: Their Creative Reciprocity," *English Journal* (college edition) 27 (Feb. 1938), 121–35; " WPA and Folklore Research: 'Bread and Song,'" *Southern Folklore Quarterly* 3

(March 1939): 7–14. On Michael Gold's *Jews without Money*, see Denning, *The Cultural Front*, ch. 6. On Roth's aesthetics in *Call It Sleep*, see Werner Sollors, *Ethnic Modernism* (Cambridge, MA: Harvard University Press, 2008), ch. 12.

12. Brown quoted in Lauren Rebecca Sklaroff, *Black Culture and the New Deal: The Quest for Civil Rights in the Roosevelt Era* (Chapel Hill: University of North Carolina Press, 2009), 98, 101.

13. FWP of the WPA, *New York City Guide* (New York: Random House, 1939), 267.

14. See "Phrases of the People," Recorded by Harris Dickson, Vicksburg, Missouri, *American Stuff: By Workers of Federal Writers' Project*, special issue of *Direction*, Feb. 1938, 126.

15. Compare [*Memorandum to Dr. Botkin*]. Vermont, 1940. Manuscript/Mixed Material. Retrieved from the Library of Congress, www.loc.gov/item/wpal h002707 to Tomasi, Mary, et al. [*Barre's El Club Espanol*]. Vermont. Manuscript/Mixed Material. Retrieved from the Library of Congress, www .loc.gov/item/wpalh002706.The latter (edited) version of the interview was finally published in Mari Tomasi and Roaldus Richmond, *Men against Granite*, ed. Alfred Rosa and Mark Wanner (Shelburne, VT: New England Press, Inc., 2004).

16. *Dream and the Deal*, 284.

17. *Dream and the Deal*, 281.

18. Kenneth Roberts's diary quoted in Jack Bales, *Kenneth Roberts* (New York: Twayne Publishers, 1993), 56.

19. Gordon Hunter, *What America Read: Taste, Class, and the Novel 1920–1960* (Chapel Hill: University of North Carolina Press, 2009), 163–67.

20. Howard Mumford Jones, "Patriotism – But How?" *Atlantic Monthly*, 162.5 (November 1938), 592.

21. In 1936, the *America and the New Frontier* textbook noted that: "The immigrant has played an important part in the making of America in the past, but that phase of our history has probably ended" (quoted in Robert Fleegler, *Ellis Island Nation: Immigration Policy and American Identity in the Twentieth Century* [Philadelphia: University of Pennsylvania Press, 2013], 49).

22. Edward Corsi, *In the Shadow of Liberty: A Chronicle of Ellis Island* (New York: Macmillan Company, 1935), 35, 46, 95.

23. Louis Adamic, "A Letter I Did Not Mail," in *My America, 1928–1938* (New York: Harper & Brothers, 1938), 191–94.

24. Adamic, *My America*, 208. In the same collection of essays, Adamic describes how he approached the Federal Emergency Relief Administration with a proposal for an "Encyclopedia of the Population of the United States, from the Indians down to the latest immigrant group," on the premise "that Ellis Island is now in reverse and mass immigration is ended, and this is the time to determine, in as great detail as possible, of what sort of human stuff America is made; what her potentialities are; which group has

contributed what to this civilization." For a good contextualization of Adamic's dedication to contributionism, see Fleegler, *Ellis Island Nation*, chs. 2 and 3.

25. Carey McWilliams, "Getting Rid of the Mexican," *American Mercury*, March 1933, 322–24; Carey McWilliams, "Exit the Filipino," *Nation*, September 4, 1935, 265. On October 3, 1937, McWilliams wrote to Adamic about a speech he gave in Los Angeles to 1,500 women walnut pickers about their right to organize. His speech was translated into several languages for an audience of Russians, Armenians, Slavs, Mexicans, and others. "You should have been there if only to have gotten the feel of the meeting, its tension and excitement," McWilliams wrote. "And you would have been fascinated to watch some of the women get to their feet and attempt to explain how they felt about their work." (Quoted in Carey McWilliams, *The Education of Carey McWilliams* [New York: Simon & Schuster, 1978], 84).

26. Carey McWilliams, "Once a Well-Kept Secret," *Pacific Historical Review*, 42.3 (1973), 311. See also Carey McWilliams, "The Forgotten Mexican," *Common Ground*, Spring 1943, 65–78.

27. Herant Armen, "The Son," *Hairenik Weekly*, September 3, 1936, 4.

28. Herant Armen, "Ohan's Sister," *Hairenik Weekly*, October 30, 1936, 8.

29. The story supports the argument, made first by Lizabeth Cohen, about the give-and-take between ethnic and popular culture and the ability of ethnic cultures to integrate mass cultural elements rather than to be always opposed to and overwhelmed by them. (Lizabeth Cohen, *Making a New: Industrial Workers in Chicago, 1919–1939* [New York: Cambridge University Press], 1990).

30. The birth of Vahakn is depicted thus in a fifth-century history of Armenia by Moses of Khorene: "Heaven and earth were in travail/ And the crimson waters were in travail./ And in the water, the crimson reed/ Was also in travail./ From the mouth of the reed issued smoke,/ From the mouth of the reed issued flame./ And out of the flame sprang the young child./ His hair was of fire, a beard had he of flame,/ And his eyes were suns." (See *Armenian Legends and Poems*, ed. Zabelle Boyajian [New York: E. P. Dutton, 1916].)

31. Dickran Kouymjian, "Whitman and Saroyan: Singing the Song of America," in *Critical Essays on William Saroyan*, ed. Harry Keyishian (New York: G. K. Hall & Company, 1995), 77.

32. William Saroyan, "My Armenia," *Hairenik Weekly*, November 16 and December 21, 1934.

33. Darcy McKnickle, *The Surrounded* (New York: Dodd, Mead, 1936; Albuquerque: University of New Mexico Press, 1978). For details on the original manuscript, called "The Hungry Generations," see Dorothy Parker, *Singing an Indian Song: A Biography of D'Arcy McNickle* (Lincoln: University of Nebraska Press, 1992) ch. 2.

34. For an insightful comparison of *The Armenians in Massachusetts* (1937) and *The Albanian Struggle in the Old World and New* (1939), see Christine Bold,

Writers, Plumbers, and Anarchists: The WPA Writers' Project in Massachusetts (Amherst: University of Massachusetts Press, 2006), ch. 3.

35. McKnickle, *The Surrounded*, 234.

36. Mindy Morgan, "Constructions and Contestations of the Authoritative Voice: Native American Communities and the Federal Writers' Project, 1935–1941," *American Indian Quarterly* 29.1, 2 (Winter, Spring 2005), 69–71. Also, as with the ethnic studies, much collected material for the Indian studies was never published.

37. Parker, *Singing an Indian Song*, 71.

38. Adamic, "Plymouth Rock and Ellis Island" (reprint of a lecture delivered before numerous audiences in late 1939–early 1940), *From Many Lands* (New York: Harper & Brothers, 1940), 293.

39. Adamic, "The Broadside" and "Special Questionnaire on the Negro," in *From Many Lands*, 304–06, 309–10.

40. Louis Adamic, "Shall We Send Them Back to Hitler?" *Nation*, March 25, 1936, 378.

41. "The Right of Asylum: The end of the old American tradition of a land of asylum for political refugees, the plight of thousands of political refugees, Amend the immigration laws to legalize their stay!" (pamphlet), American Civil Liberties Union, March 1937, Reel 157, ACLU Records, Roger Baldwin Years, Public Policy Papers, Department of Rare Books and Special Collections, Princeton University Library.

42. A Memorandum: Right of Asylum (April 26, 1937), Box 9, Folder 1 (1935–38), American Committee for Protection of Foreign Born Records, University of Michigan Library (Special Collections Library), Joseph A. Labadie Collection; Dwight Morgan, *The Foreign Born in the United States* (New York: American Committee for the Protection of the Foreign Born, 1936), 14, 52, 72, 33, 79. For details on the *Harper's* contest, see Wall, *Inventing the American Way*, 15–17. "I have noted," Howard Mumford Jones wrote in the same essay in which he rebuked nativists for their representations of the American past, "a wonderful interest in the Bill of Rights among communists in danger of arrest and deportation … There is scarcely a pressure group in the country that cannot cite Jefferson or Lincoln." For the Roosevelt quote, see Roger Daniels, *Guarding the Golding Door: American Immigration Policy and American Immigrants since 1882* (New York: Hill & Wang, 2004), 66.

43. "Editorial Aside," *Common Ground*, Autumn 1940, 2.

44. The original warrant of deportation, issued May 5, 1927, accused Tsiang of failing to maintain the status of a student and for being "an alien who writes, publishes … or who knowingly circulates, distributes, prints, publishes … material advising … the overthrow by force or violence of the Government of the United States or of all forms of law." Even when the government officially dropped the latter as a ground of deportation, it connected Tsiang's political activity with the former ground of deportation. Tsiang was ordered deported on December 17, 1927, because he "remained in the United States for the purpose of aiding radical and Bolshevistic-inclined factions in this country,

rather than attend school" (Defendant's Pretrial Memorandum, *Tsiang Hsi Tseng* v. *Albert Del Guercio*, Civil No. 19291, Records of the US District Court for the Central District of California in Los Angeles, RG 21, NARA Riverside).

45. Quoted in Defendant's Reply Brief, *Tsiang Hsi Tseng* v. *Albert Del Guercio*, Civil No. 19291, Records of the US District Court for the Central District of California in Los Angeles, RG 21, NARA Riverside.
46. For an excellent discussion of Tsiang's outsider status, see Hua Hsu, *A Floating Chinaman: Fantasy and Failure across the Pacific* (Cambridge, MA: Harvard University Press, 2016), 11, 155.
47. This poem was published in *P.M.* on August 8, 1941. The clipping, along with information about ACPFB's defense and Rankin's bill, is in Tsiang's ACPFB case file, Box 49, ACPFB, Records, Labadie.
48. See the rejection blurbs from publishers at the beginning of *The Hanging on Union Square* (1935). At the end of this book, Tsiang also published "Comments on China Red," many of which are only partly favorable.
49. Tsiang to Marcantonio, June 12, 1941, Box 46, Folder: American Committee for the Protection of the Foreign Born, Vito Marcantonio papers, MssCol 1871, Manuscripts and Archives Division, The New York Public Library.
50. The manuscript of poems is enclosed in ibid. All poems cited in what follows come from this manuscript.
51. Robert Wyndham, "The Marvelous Pear Seed," in *Tales People Tell in China* (New York: Julian Messner, 1971).
52. Quoted in Defendant's Reply Brief, *Tsiang Hsi Tseng* v. *Albert Del Guercio*, Civil No. 19291, Records of the US District Court for the Central District of California in Los Angeles, RG 21, NARA Riverside.
53. For specific examples of how Algren and Ellison integrated their FWP interviews into *Never Come Morning* and *Invisible Man*, respectively, see Carla Cappetti, *Writing Chicago: Modernism, Ethnography, and the Novel* (New York: Columbia University Press, 1993), 164–67.
54. Carey McWillliams, *Louis Adamic and Shadow America* (Los Angeles, CA: Arthur Whipple, 1935), 25, 75–76.

CHAPTER 10

This Land Is Your Land

Robert B. Westbrook

> This is an immense country made up of overpopulated islands
> sprinkled among the prairies, the forests, and the deserts. Among
> these islets of skyscrapers there is hardly any common life.
> The newspapers of Minneapolis are not read in Cincinnati.
> The great man of Tulsa is unknown in Dallas. The Negro of
> Georgia, the Swede of Minnesota, the Mexican of San Antonio, and
> the German of Chicago, Marquand's patricians, and Steinbeck's
> tramps are all citizens of the United States, but there is slight resem-
> blance among them.
>   –André Maurois, *Etats-Unis 39: Journal d'un voyage en Amérique* (1939)

In 1938, critic Alfred Kazin, the young son of Eastern European Jewish
immigrants, began countless hours of research in the reading room of the
New York Public Library, looking for the "moral history" of modern
America in its prose literature. The fruits of his long labors, *On Native
Grounds*, was published to wide acclaim in 1942. Kazin was keenly aware
that he was not alone in his quest "to chart America and to possess it," and
he concluded his book with a chapter – "America! America!" – that
reflected on the remarkable outpouring of self-reflection and stock-
taking that had marked American culture during the years of the Great
Depression and to which he had himself now added a full measure.[1]

"Underlying the imaginative life in America all through the years of
panic, depression, and the emergence of international civil war," Kazin
observed, "was an enormous body of writing devoted to the American
scene that is one of the most remarkable phenomena of the era of crisis . . .
It is a vast body of writing that is perhaps the fullest expression of the
American consciousness after 1930, and one that illuminates the whole
nature of prose literature in those years as nothing else can." This "new
nationalism" manifested "a moving and always astonishing hunger for self-
knowledge" that enlisted a wide and diverse range of writers and other
artists.[2]

Determined efforts at "aroused self-comprehension" and "national self-scrutiny" by American intellectuals were not, by any means, unprecedented by 1929.³ They had a pedigree at least as venerable as Emerson's "American Scholar" (1837). And too often, of course, affirmative American nationalism had about it an air of smug self-satisfaction and chauvinist bravado, marked by invocations of millennial destiny and a redeeming mission toward less blessed peoples. But this was less often the case in the thirties. Cast as it was in the midst of economic collapse at home and calamity abroad, American cultural nationalism in the years between 1929 and 1941, for all its appreciation of the riches of American folkways and lapses into sentimentality, bespoke less confidence than anxiety, less certainty than perplexity, less consensus than dispute, less comforting answers than unsettling questions. Cultural nationalism during the Depression was contested terrain; it never congealed into a hegemonic form. Americans are most interesting when they are least sure of themselves, and seldom have they been less sure of themselves when it came to themselves than in the 1930s.

***

If a nation is an "imagined community," the American nation was more thoroughly imagined than most.⁴ A leader among the "creole" nations of the Western Hemisphere founded in the late eighteenth and early nineteenth centuries following anticolonial revolts against dynastic regimes, the United States found itself a largely British ethnic country with every reason to rest its national identity on something other than an ethnic foundation. Hence, the ground of American national identity was ostensibly ideological, not ethnic. For its citizens, as Philip Gleason says, "a sense of distinctive peoplehood could be founded only on ideas . . . because the great majority of Americans shared language, literature, religion, and other cultural traditions with the nation against which they had successfully rebelled and from which they were most determined to establish their spiritual as well as political independence."⁵ Americans defined themselves initially not by way of a shared heritage or inheritance, but by way of a shared creed, one that put liberty, equality, and constitutional principle at its center. *Novus ordo seclorum* – a radically new order of the ages.

Some theorists of nationalism have termed the ideological core of American nationalism an exemplary instance of "civic nationalism," a purely political conception, absent any cultural component. They confine "cultural nationalism" to nationalisms in which peoplehood is defined by shared ethnic descent. On this account, the United States is altogether free of cultural nationalism, at least in principle – which is often taken to be a good thing since such theorists attribute everything nasty about nationalism to ethnic nationalism and hold up civic nationalism as an attractive alternative. As a number of critics have pointed out, this is nonsense. "All nationalisms are cultural nationalisms of one kind or another," one such critic has said. "There is no purely political conception of the nation, liberal or otherwise."[6]

In the United States, cultural naturalism has, to be sure, been intimately tied to the ideological principles of freedom and equality that frame national identity. Although the 1930s might be the first point at which cultural nationalists put it precisely this way, since the late eighteenth century, Americans have generally agreed that the abstract principles that define American identity, if they are to be realized, will require a cultural foundation. The principles must be undergirded by norms, practices, institutions, symbols, and myths – in short, a culture – consistent with them. The principles of freedom, equality, constitutional government, and democracy are essentially contested, and hence so too are its cultural underpinnings – by its very nature American nationalism refuses closure. Much of American cultural history, not least that of the 1930s, can profitably be read as a debate, often a fierce and sometimes even a violent debate, not only over the proper understanding of freedom, equality, and democracy but also over the sort of American culture necessary to foster the concrete expression of one or another interpretation of these abstractions. Thomas Jefferson worried over the adverse consequences of urbanization; we worry over the impact of the Internet. Abraham Lincoln worried over slavery; we worry over slavery's persistent racial legacy. We have always, most of us, worried over the proper education of our children. American cultural identity has always been under construction and dispute.

Given the stakes involved, the temptation of American nationalists has persistently been to try to put an end to dispute by imposing their conception of a national culture on others. The result was often the exclusion of many Americans from citizenship or full citizenship, a practice that was at odds with the apparent inclusiveness of the prescriptive, wholly ideological understanding of American peoplehood, and the adoption of ascriptive principles of exclusion as discriminatory as those of ethnic nationalisms. Indeed, for much of American history, a not-so-covert discriminatory ethnic nationalism (white, Protestant, male, Anglo-Saxon) has held sway in the United States under the banner of a universalist civic nationalism. A key to its hegemony was the manner in which the "classical model" of American citizenship, which prevailed until after World War II, allowed for sharply discriminatory treatment of all sorts between citizens and aliens and provided even citizens with but a very thin list of rights, which left the federal and state governments free to discriminate in the distribution of other rights such as suffrage and jury service.[7] Not surprisingly, this limited understanding of freedom and equality was underpinned by a cultural nationalism no less limited.

The rights of many citizens were expanded over the course of the nineteenth and twentieth centuries (by among other developments, the Fifteenth [black male suffrage] and Nineteenth [women's suffrage] Amendments to the Constitution), and since World War II, the classical model has been displaced by a more expansive and more universalistic "modern model" that has closed the gap between the rights of aliens and citizens and promised (if not assured) citizens a more extensive charter of rights. Not least among these are rights to unimpeded suffrage and to equal opportunities in employment and housing.[8] So universalistic has this model become in its eclipse of discriminations between aliens and citizens that it has engendered discontent among those unwilling wholly to relinquish a more particularistic American identity who complain that we may be on the way to "a vision of citizenship so abstract, untethered, and universalistic that it provides no convincing reasons why Americans should be any more loyal to the party of the America than to, say, the party of the United Nations."[9]

The interest of the thirties lies in its positioning between these two American citizenship regimes. Most cultural nationalists (though not all) in the thirties aimed self-consciously to avoid covert, discriminatory ethnic nationalism, and yet they nonetheless struggled in a quest for national unity in the face of the crises of depression and war to bring the construction of a particularistic and concrete American identity persuasively to a close, to limn conclusively "the American Way of Life" (a term coined at the time). They sought, in inward-looking fashion, to connect the abstract principles of freedom and equality to a more inclusive and yet still distinctively American democratic culture. A forceful reassertion of the hubristic claim by American nationalists to represent the universal ideals of all humanity would await World War II and the Cold War.[10]

Yet the cultural nationalists of the thirties failed to end the construction of and contest over American national identity. Indeed, they heightened the dispute, and the disagreements among them and with their critics may suggest the inherent futility of the striving for its resolution.

***

I said that the thirties was the first time that a significant number of Americans spoke literally, as I have, of a "cultural" foundation for American identity. That is because it was not until this period that the anthropological concept of culture that this formulation reflects came into its own. Its impact on American cultural nationalism was profound.

The ubiquity of the anthropological "culture concept" in American thought in the thirties was most memorably formulated by historian Warren Susman. In crafting "a vision of the Thirties," he said that:

> No fact is more significant than the general and even popular "discovery" of the concept of culture. Obviously, the idea of culture was anything but new in the 1930s, but there is a special sense in which the idea became widespread in the period. What had been discovered was "the inescapable interrelated-ness of . . . things" so that culture could no longer be considered what Matthew Arnold and the intellectuals of previous generations had often meant – the knowledge of the highest achievements of men of intellect and art through history – but rather reference to "all the things that a group of people inhabiting a common geographical area do, the ways they do things and the ways they think and feel about things, their material tools and their values and symbols."[11]

The point is not merely that the period marked what Kazin termed "a moving and always astonishing hunger for self-knowledge" but that this hunger was channeled through the concept of culture in an effort to know America whole.

Franz Boas and his students – including Alfred Kroeber, Paul Radin, Robert Lowie, Ruth Benedict, and Margaret Mead (once-removed) – put the culture concept on the map of American intellectual life in the twenties, displacing the racialist and evolutionary schemes that had there-tofore underpinned American anthropology and a de facto Anglo-Saxon national identity. No one had a wider or deeper impact on American cultural nationalism in the thirties than Benedict. Her book *Patterns of Culture* (1934) was a best-seller, finding its way eventually into the hands of hundreds of thousands of readers. By the end of the thirties, prominent intellectuals such as John Dewey and Robert Lynd were hailing the culture concept as the key conceptual foundation for the social sciences and an essential part of the toolkit of American self-understanding.[12] As Mead later said, "[t]hat today the modern world is on such easy terms with the concept of culture, that the words 'in our culture' slip from the lips of educated men and women almost as effortlessly as do the phrases that refer to period and to place, is in very great part due to this book."[13]

As her title suggests, Benedict emphasized that cultures are best conceived holistically, ideally as integrated wholes, expressive of particular purposes. They "are more than the sum of their traits" and all cultures were "more or less successful attainments of integrated behavior." She acknowledged that not all cultures achieved holistic integration, but she implied that, as a consequence, they were cultures in crisis or cultures much less impressive in their achievements than the others that had fashioned themselves into a coherent work of art.[14]

Benedict warned that her injunction to find the "pattern" in a culture was, at least as far as the capacities of anthropological research stood at the time, difficult to follow in the case of modern, complex societies. She cautioned against "treating modern stratified society as if it had the essential homogeneity of a folk culture." To be sure, "cultural configurations are as compelling and as significant in the highest and most complex societies of which we have knowledge. But the material is too intricate and too close to our eyes for us to cope with it successfully." She recommended a "detour" to the investigation of less complex societies and a sharpening of tools before venturing into any effort to make sense of the culture of a society as vast and variegated as that of the United States.[15]

But the United States was a society in distress, and many American writers, artists, and intellectuals were ill disposed to make such a detour before arriving at a diagnosis. So they plunged into the difficult task of discerning the distinctive pattern of the American way of life.[16]

***

The quest for America by cultural nationalists in the thirties was dominated by two forms: documentary and history. Neither proved successful in persuasively discerning the sort of integrated patterns in American life, present or past, that Benedict's concept of culture idealized.

Documentary expression exploded in the thirties and took a variety of modes: popularized case studies by social workers, pioneered by Clinch Calkins's *Some Folks Won't Work* (1930), social scientific investigations such as Robert and Helen Lynd's *Middletown in Transition* (1937), John Dollard's *Caste and Class in a Southern Town* (1937), Wight Bakke's *Citizens without Work* (1940), Mirra Komarovsky's *The Unemployed Man and His Family* (1940), Allison Davis's *Deep South* (1941), and the first volume of Lloyd Warner's "Yankee City" studies (1941); and travelogues and reportage by prominent writers including Louis Adamic, Sherwood Anderson, Nathan Asch, Erskine Caldwell, Theodore Dreiser, James Rorty, Gilbert Seldes, and Edmund Wilson.[17]

The camera, James Agee said, was "next to unassisted and weaponless consciousness, the central instrument of our time," and the camera held sway over thirties documentary. Still photography was preeminent, particularly after Henry Luce's *Life* magazine began publication in 1936. But documentary film – movies such as Pare Lorentz's *Plow That Broke the Plains* (1936) and *The River* (1938) – also made its mark on the visual imagination of the decade. Of particular significance were a series of documentary books combining text and photographs, the most notable of which were Erskine Caldwell and Margaret Bourke-White's *You Have Seen Their Faces* (1937), Archibald MacLeish's *Land of the Free* (1938), Dorothea Lange and Paul Taylor's *American Exodus* (1939), and Agee and Walker Evans's *Let Us Now Praise Famous Men* (1941).[18]

In another distinctive feature of cultural nationalism in the thirties, a number of social documentarians went looking for America under the auspices of the national state. Lorena Hickok hit the road for New Deal relief administrators and filed confidential reports with Harry Hopkins documenting the plight of citizens in thirty-two states. Most of the decade's noteworthy photographers worked at some point for the Farm Security Administration's Photography Unit run by Roy Stryker. And the arts projects of the New Deal's Works Progress Administration – the Federal Art Project (FAP), the Federal Music Project, the Federal Theatre Project (FTP), and the Federal Writers' Project (FWP) – and other less ambitious cultural programs of the federal government all mobilized, to one degree or another, behind the documentary cause. These included oral histories, some of them published in *These Are Our Lives* (1939), edited by W. T. Couch of the FWP; the FWP investigation of American foodways, "America Eats"; the "Living Newspaper" performances of the FTP, and most impressively the state-by-state (and more) American Guides Series of the FWP, regarded nearly universally as "the WPA's finest monument" to the documentary impulse.[19] "When the New Deal came to power," William Stott observes, "it institutionalized documentary."[20]

The thirties decade was also besotted with American history. "We need to know what kind of firm ground other men, belonging to generations before us, have found to stand on," John Dos Passos said. "Driven by a pressing need to find answers to the riddles of today," he and many others

Figure 10.1 John Steuart Curry, "Tragic Prelude" (1939).

looked to the past for clues.[21] The decade witnessed the opening of the National Archives, the initiation of the Historical Records Survey and the Historic American Buildings Survey, and the completion of Colonial Williamsburg. Professional historians were no less enamored of the culture concept than anyone else, and the thirties were the seedbed of the decided turn of the discipline to social and cultural history in the decades to follow. In 1928, Arthur M. Schlesinger took editorial command of a series of volumes in *A History of American Life* (1928–44) that put social history at the forefront ("pots and pans history," some disparagingly termed it), of which Schlesinger's own *Rise of the City* (1933) was the most impressive contribution.[22] Caroline Ware vigorously promoted the cause of "the cultural approach of history," and presided over a series of landmark sessions at the meeting of the American Historical Association in 1939 at which an ambitious agenda for anthropologically savvy history was laid out.[23]

Historical fiction poured off the presses, some of it memorable (Dos Passos's *USA* trilogy [1930–36], William Faulkner's *Absalom, Absalom!* [1936], J. P. Marquand's *The Late George Apley* [1937]), and much of it not.[24] "American Scene" painters weighed in with gigantic murals such as Thomas Hart Benton's social histories of Indiana (1933) and Missouri (1936) and John Steuart Curry's dramatic vision of John Brown – complete with one of Curry's signature tornados (1939) (Figure 10.1). The decade was no less fruitful for American biography. Most of the volumes in the *Dictionary of American Biography* were published in this period, as were substantial biographies of Benjamin Franklin (Carl Van Doren), Abraham

Lincoln (Carl Sandburg), Robert E. Lee (Douglas Southall Freeman), William Tecumseh Sherman (Lloyd Lewis), Andrew Jackson (Marquis James), Sam Houston (James), Thomas Jefferson (Claude Bowers), Grover Cleveland (Allan Nevins), John C. Fremont (Nevins), and John T. Rockefeller (Nevins).

No figure loomed larger in the American historical imagination in the thirties than Lincoln. He was the subject not only of Sandburg's massive six-volume biography, completed in 1939, but of three major movies: *Abraham Lincoln* (1930), *Young Man Lincoln* (1939), and *Abe Lincoln in Illinois* (1940), based on Robert Sherwood's Pulitzer Prize–winning play of 1938. Lincoln's significance lay not only in the widely drawn parallels between the crisis of the Civil War and those of the Depression and a looming world war, but in the mythical image of him as the American leader who had managed to draw multiple strands of American identity together into a coherent self. Sandburg, the poet of *The People, Yes* (1936), led the worshippers. In Lincoln, he said, "America had at last a President who was All-American. He embodied his country ... The inventive Yankee, the Western frontiersman and pioneer, the Kentuckian of laughter and dreams, had found blend in one man who was the national head." Lincoln carried the whole of the country "in his breast." Intoning the sort of Whitmanian litany that would mark so much cultural nationalism in the thirties, Sandburg sang: "Cape Cod, the Shenandoah, the Mississippi, the Gulf, the Rocky Mountains, the Sacramento, the Great Plains, the Great Lakes, their dialects and shibboleths. He must be instinct with the regions of corn, textile mills. Cotton, tobacco, gold, coal, zinc, iron. He would be written as a Father of his people."[25] If true, of course, this left the civil war that followed hard upon Lincoln's election difficult to explain, but be that as it may, this was a Lincoln for the thirties and for readers anxious about the strength of the lineaments of national unity. As Kazin said, "Lincoln now became the measure of that whole American civilization that would find apotheosis in him," a nation imagined as "a stupendous aggregate of all those American traits," embodied in this martyred hero of the common man.[26]

The federal arts projects also contributed mightily to the recovery and interpretation of the American past. The state guides combined a great deal of history with a documentary tour of contemporary points of interest for inquisitive tourists and natives alike. The FWP also sponsored the important Ex-Slave Project, which recorded interviews with former slaves. The FAP produced the Index of American Design, a pictorial survey of American crafts and decorative arts from the colonial period to 1900. And several of the projects combined efforts under the direction of FWP folklore editor Benjamin Botkin to collect American folklore, including folk songs.

***

The upshot of the monumental documentary effort of the thirties was not a compelling vision of America whole – even Lincoln could not contain its multitudes – but, as Kazin said, "a storehouse of vivid single impressions." The mysteries of American identity were not solved but catalogued. At best, documentary revealed an aggregated culture, not a patterned one. Often moving but decidedly fragmentary, the decade's documentary expression left the matter of national identity largely unsettled. Indeed, the more richly documented the country's diverse elements became, the less certain it was that they did in fact cohere. James Rorty spoke for many when he returned from his travels "moved to confess that he did not know what America was." He suspected that "no one knows."[27]

Historians were no more successful in putting the pieces of the American puzzle together, Sandburg's Lincoln to the contrary notwithstanding. No cultural historian worked harder to do so than Constance Rourke. As her biographer Joan Shelley Rubin has demonstrated, one can instructively construe her career as dedicated to contesting the claim of an earlier generation of cultural nationalists led by Van Wyck Brooks that America lacked the cultural subsoil necessary to nourish great art.[28] Although Brooks spoke in the late teens of the need for a "usable past" if Americans were to produce a distinguished and distinctive national art, he simultaneously cast doubt on the prospect that there was much of any use to be found in a cultural history long dominated by the Puritan, the pioneer, and the philistine businessman. Rourke set out to prove him wrong.[29]

A friend to Ruth Benedict and widely read in anthropological literature, Rourke can be profitably be seen as taking up the interpretive challenge that Benedict's anthropology afforded American cultural nationalists.[30] She grasped unerringly how essential it was for American nationalism to bind together abstract principle and concrete culture:

> Can the American past offer what men live by, in the way of ideals, ambitions, methods, ways of living – a foundation for the present? We need the sense of foundations in the midst of the Tempest, obviously not by way of past glory, not as a vague "heritage," but as clarifying the Democratic way of life and furthering knowledge of the methods of

democracy. Democracy, whose principles are simple, has been infinitely complex in its workings, and these reach far beyond the economic and political sphere . . . If a democracy is a way of life as well as a political system, then this culture will offer basic clues as to its character and future.[31]

Echoing here John Dewey's oft-quoted insistence that democracy was, in the first instance, a moral principle for human community and not only a political ideal, Rourke set out to discern its rootedness in the American past.

Yet if Rourke exposed to view unexampled riches in American folk culture, she failed to find the singular, unifying, integrating pattern she so desired. At least she was honest enough to admit it. In her masterwork, *American Humor: A Study of the National Character* (1931), she took the lead in uncovering, as Kazin and Robert Cantwell said of the WPA Guides, "an America that nothing in the academic histories had ever prepared one for, and very little in imaginative writing." She led the way in opening to view "the humorous, the creepy, the eccentric side of American character: the secret rooms and strange furtive religions; the forgotten enthusiasms and heresies and cults; the relics of fashion and tumbling mansions that had always been someone's folly." Hers, in short, was what Greil Marcus would later term "old weird America."[32]

Rourke keyed her study of American humor on what she argued were its three pivotal figures: the Yankee, the backwoodsman, and the blackface minstrel. Each of these figures brought distinctive features to the making of the American. Each wandered the land (willingly or unwillingly), and each broke bonds – with the English motherland, with Eastern civilization, with white mastery (in, she said, "a cryptic and submerged" fashion). The laughter to which each contributed mightily "created ease, and even more, a sense of unity, among a people who were not yet a nation and who were seldom joined in stable communities." Eventually, Rourke said, "the comic trio tended to merge into a single generic figure," and out of this figure a pattern would emerge for American culture.[33] A pattern, she argued, that one could discern in the work of figures as diverse as Lincoln, Melville, Poe, Twain, Hawthorne, Dickinson, Brigham Young, and even Henry James.

But the pattern that Rourke wove with one hand she unraveled with the other. In the end she concluded that if the aim of American humor was "that of creating fresh bonds, a new unity, the semblance of a society and the rounded completion of an American type," its work remained undone: "the American character is still split into many characters."[34] As Marcus acutely observes, "All through *American Humor*, at the ends of paragraphs, in the midst of sentences about something else, she voiced her doubts as to whether the country existed at all. As she brought American culture to life she stressed the holes in its story, the story less as chronicle than erasure, culture as a wilderness of unknowing."[35]

Rourke insisted nonetheless that "at least a large and shadowy outline has been drawn," but she struggled vainly to bring that shadow to light. At times, as Brooks said, she seemed in the grip of an almost mystical belief that "if she could assemble materials enough, the tradition would declare itself through them."[36] This, he was polite enough not to say, was not how it works.

***

Rourke's quest for a unifying, integrating American tradition bespeaks the deeply conservative, or at least therapeutic, character of much of cultural nationalism in the thirties. She underplayed class and racial conflict in favor of accentuating what she believed was a common heritage that crossed such lines of division and held the potential for culture-wide unity. In this, she was typical of many cultural nationalists in the decade. Challenging a widespread conception of the thirties as a "red decade," Warren Susman rightly urged its historians many years ago to appreciate the manner in which "the idea of an American Way could reinforce conformity." The culture concept, with its holism and insistence on underlying patterns shaped by shared purpose, pointed to thinking "far more conservative than radical."[37]

Nationalism, as such, puts a premium on those forces that bind people together, not those that push them apart. It is meant often to heal, internally if not without. Understanding this well, historian Jean-Christophe Agnew has nicely applied the Philoctetes myth to thirties talk of culture. Suffering in exile from Greece on a remote island as a consequence of a horrible, reeking wound on his foot, Philoctetes is reunited with his countrymen because they have need of the bow and arrows he inherited from Hercules if they are to win the Trojan War. In the Depression, Agnew suggests, "the capitalist crisis of the thirties was the suppurating wound ... that paradoxically empowered the magical bow of culture." The culture concept became "a figure of thought capable of imaginatively repatriating a generation of Americans that had been emotionally and physically dislocated by years of depression and war" (Figures 10.2– 10.3).[38]

Yet the culture concept was not without radical possibilities, which some were eager to explore in the thirties. For example, sociologist Robert Lynd,

Figure 10.2 The Wound. Walker Evans, "Joe's Auto Graveyard, Pennsylvania, 1936."

Figure 10.3 The Bow. Walker Evans, "Alabama Tenant Farmer Family Singing Hymns, 1936."

a man of the left who took a back seat to none in hailing the rewards of the culture concept for the social sciences, offered a stinging indictment of the manner in which capitalism had shaped "the pattern of American culture," producing:

> A pattern of opportunity and of frustration, of strength and of careless disregard for patent weaknesses; a pattern . . . of rootless people wandering from farm to city in quest of gain; with youth favored but frustrated, and sex roles in conflict; believing in a future which for most of them will never happen; searching for "the way," which recurrently turns out to be an unmarked fork in the road; and relying on the outworn dogmas of "rational human choice" and the automaticity of "whatsoever things are good and true" to bring them to the Promised Land. It is in the main a pattern of lack of pattern, marked by the disorder and the substitution of doing for feeling that characterizes a frontier boom town.[39]

The point of uncovering this cultural pattern for Lynd and many others on the left in the thirties was not to celebrate it, nor to bathe in its healing powers, but to remake it dramatically. American culture was not the bow to rescue the society from capitalist collapse but the pus of that suppurating wound. "Private capitalism," Lynn asserted, "does not now operate, and probably cannot be made to operate, to assure the amount of general welfare to which the present stage of our technological skills and intelligence entitle us; and other ways of managing our economy need therefore to be explored." Hence, Lynd declared, social scientists should take on a deeply adversarial role.[40] The vision of American culture that Lynd advanced was not less partial than any other, but if one discounts his uncritical enthusiasm for technocratic social engineering, it was widely shared among writers, artists, and intellectuals in what Michael Denning has termed a social-democratic "cultural front."[41]

If the culture concept was malleable, the language of "Americanism" was multivocal. As Gary Gerstle says, Americanism was an arena of contest in the thirties. "For every individual looking to Americanism for comfort and security," he notes, "we can counterpose another who found in American history rhetoric and inspiration for political revolt." Cultural nationalism was the *lingua franca* of American politics, shared often by bitter opponents, an almost obligatory framing for anyone hoping to gain a hearing for their interests.[42]

One prominent example will have to do. As legend would have it, Woody Guthrie found himself in February 1940 freezing beside the road in Pennsylvania as he hitchhiked to New York. Fearful for his life, he generated some heat with his antipathy to a song he kept hearing on jukeboxes as he made his way north from Texas: Irving Berlin's "God Bless America," sung by Kate Smith in her signature martial fashion. There and then he began to compose a response, hammering out the opening lines of a new song: "This land is your land, this land is my land/From California to the New York Island." Shortly thereafter, he completed a first draft of "This Land Was Made for You and Me" – scratching out another title: "God Blessed America." Two verses stood out in decided contrast to Berlin's song, rendering Guthrie's song a competing national anthem: "Was a big high wall there that tried to stop me/A sign was painted said: Private Property/But on the back side it didn't say nothing/God blessed America for me" and "One bright sunny morning in the shadow of the steeple/By the Relief Office I saw my people/As they stood hungry/I stood there wondering if God blessed America for me."[43]

Guthrie was but one of many figures contributing to what Michael Denning has called a counterhegemonic "laboring of American culture" in "the age of the CIO" by the left-wing Popular Front. Americanism was essential to Popular Front ideology, but it was there designed not to foster unity and consensus but to evoke the divide between traditional American ideals and contemporary American practice. It was a disappointed patriotic call to resistance and revolt.[44]

As the examples of Berlin and Guthrie suggest, some cultural nationalists embraced mass culture, the markets of the "culture industries," as an arena in which to pursue the meaning of America. Yet others were slow to regard it with anything other than contempt, a realm bereft of culture, even in the anthropological sense. Curiously, for those supposedly interested in unifying, centripetal cultural forms, their complaint was that mass culture was "homogenizing." They ruefully accepted Sinclair Lewis's observation in his preface to *Main Street* (1920) that the Main Street of his fictional Gopher Prairie, Minnesota "is the continuation of Main Street everywhere. The story would be the same in Ohio or Montana, in Kansas or Kentucky or Illinois, and not very differently would it be told Up York State or in the Carolina hills." (Figure 10.4)[45]

Rather than explore the shared world of meaning evident in these homogeneous Main Streets, many cultural nationalists sought out, sometimes desperately, only the back alleys into which the tentacles of mass culture had yet to reach. If, as historian Lawrence Levine contended, mass culture is "the folklore of industrial society," then some in search of the American folk in the thirties overlooked a rich archive essential to their investigations.[46] For example, the national editors of the FWP "America Eats" project were so determined to exclude from American foodways the

Figure 10.4 Walker Evans, "Main Street, Saratoga Springs, New York, 1931."

mass-produced food that began to find its way onto more and more American tables beginning in the late nineteenth century such as canned foods, breakfast cereals, baby food, prepared meat, and mass-produced vegetables that they drew a line at the Civil War for demarcating "American" food. As a result, their version of "America Eats" (never published) was more accurately "America Ate," and was a decidedly inaccurate portrait of the contemporary American diet. Moreover, although many local FWP reporters took full note of the impact of ethnic foods and hybrid menus on American food cooking and eating, the arbitrary insistence of their superiors on "traditional" foods alone drew a decidedly WASPish perimeter around the nation's evolving cuisine.[47] Many in the Popular Front, like Guthrie, worked in the culture industries and while no less disturbed than others by its formidable presence and the threat of homogeneity it posed, they saw it as well as a site on which a struggle for American identity could and should be waged.

Kazin misled when he characterized the cultural nationalism of the thirties in *On Native Grounds* as simply "a swelling chorus of national affirmation and praise."[48] This certainly did not describe the usable past offered in the other masterpiece of American literary history published in the period, F. O. Matthiessen's *American Renaissance* (1941). Matthiessen, for all his loving, close readings of the masterpieces of Emerson, Thoreau, Hawthorne, Melville, and Whitman, was also attuned to the culture concept. Indeed, for him, close reading was an indispensable clue to cultural context. "An artist's use of language," he wrote, "is the most sensitive index to cultural history, since a man can articulate only what he is, and what he has been made by the society of which he is a willing or an unwilling part."[49]

In good cultural nationalist fashion, Matthiessen saw the writers of the antebellum American Renaissance as engaged in the project of thickening up the cultural substrate of the American Revolution's ideals. "They felt that it was incumbent upon their generation to give fulfillment to the potentialities freed by the Revolution, to provide a culture commensurate with America's political opportunity." Yet Matthiessen, a Christian socialist, was most moving when he spoke of the sober doubts of some of his subjects, especially Melville.

> Contemplating the actual, Melville saw the gap between our professions and our practice, as in the great wrong of slavery; in the difficulty of establishing adequate human contacts in our violently expanding life. When writing *Israel Potter*, he observed in Paul Jones a fascinating but terrible symbol for the American character: "Intrepid, unprincipled, reckless, predatory, with boundless ambition, civilized in externals but a savage at heart, America is, or may yet be, the Paul Jones of nations."[50]

And perhaps in a rebuke to Rourke, Matthiessen offered a less affirming view of American folklore. The tale of John Henry was the story "primarily of the tragedy of the black man subjected to the power of the white," and Paul Bunyan signified the "gutting of the forests." In the spirit of the cultural front, he concluded that "the recent attempts to retell their legends show by their factitiousness that the folk art of an industrialized society,

Figure 10.5 Walker Evans, "Houses and Billboards in Atlanta, 1936."

like that of Chaplin or Disney, must spring from new sources and new techniques of its own." (Figure 10.5)[51]

***

A seemingly irreducible diversity of American cultures thus challenged cultural nationalists in the thirties. As readers of the American Guides could readily discern, the country had more than enough *pluribus*, too little *unum* – centrifugal forces overwhelming any centripetal counter. Some turned to "cultural pluralism" for a resolution. Diversity, they argued, was not a threat to American national identity but essential to it.

On the face of it, this turn was a desperate maneuver, a way to make the best of a bad situation for nationalists. Nationalism is a jealous mistress; it does not rest easy with more than one national culture within its borders. Dynastic empires might have been able to manage this trick (sometimes), but it posed far greater difficulties for nation-states, particularly one wedded to freedom and equality. But this trick is precisely what Horace Kallen, who coined the term "cultural pluralism" in the early twenties, envisioned.[52] The context for this effort by this philosopher and Silesian Jewish immigrant to the United States was his fierce discontent with "the melting pot" as a metaphor for the integration of immigrants, particularly those from eastern and southern Europe, into American life. As Philip Gleason has demonstrated, the "melting pot" was a muddled concept that had taken on a variety of meanings by World War I. Yet at that time, the preeminent meaning, one that would guide the restrictive immigration legislation of the early twenties, was that of "Anglo conformity," that is, of the "melting" process as one of burning off of the "foreign dross and "impurities" of immigrant ethnicity and pouring newcomers into a preestablished mold of Anglo-Saxon culture.[53]

In response to this conception of the melting pot, Kallen called for a radically anti-assimilationist conception of American culture as a culture of forever distinct and circumscribed ethnic cultures and of the United States as "a nation of nations."[54] About as centrifugal a conception of American nationalism as one could imagine, Kallen's cultural pluralism contended that the glue holding the country's forever separate peoples together would be little more than shared political and economic institutions and ideology, which he distinguished sharply from cultural bonds. His, in short, was about as thin a conception of American nationalism as "civic nationalism" as anyone has proposed, one that overlooked (or more likely, implicitly assumed) the cultural character of the "overlapping consensus" binding ethnic groups together as fellow citizens.[55]

Kallen said next to nothing precise about the interaction of ethnic groups in the United States. Instead, he offered a metaphor to compete with and, he hoped, eventually displace the melting pot: the orchestra. America would be "a multiplicity in a unity, and orchestration of mankind" in which each ethnic group would play its own distinctive and unchanging instrument. The American symphony would be unscored, and its orchestra would be without a conductor. "A musical symphony," Kallen said, "is written before it is played; in the symphony of civilization the playing is in the writing, so that there is nothing so fixed and inevitable about its progressions as in music, so that within the limits set by nature and luck they may vary at will, and the range and variety of the harmonies may become wider and richer and more beautiful – or the reverse."[56]

This metaphor, the jazz symphony one might say, was attractive in many respects – certainly more attractive to many immigrants than Anglo conformity – but it was filled with ambiguities, most of them growing out of Kallen's insistence, grounded in the "racialist" assumptions he shared with his opponents, that ethnic cultures were and always would be immutable and separate. This separatism rendered the prospects of harmony highly unlikely, as Gleason says, and though Kallen allowed for dissonance and even discord, he "simply postulated the elimination of the hatred and conflict that had historically marked the coexistence of different nationalities in Europe. He said nothing about how this happy circumstance was to be attained."[57] Moreover, his ethnic instruments played their part in the symphony but they were unchanged by it. And it was unclear why they would want to play in the orchestra if all their cultural needs were met in their enclave. If the music of the orchestra was not a distinctive, hybrid American culture improvisationally composed together by the separate ethnic instruments, what was the point of the band ever tuning up?

As Gleason shows, Kallen's radically anti-assimilationist, separatist conception of American culture found few followers (and Kallen himself would abandon it). By the thirties, "cultural pluralism" had taken on fresh meanings and become nearly as confused a concept as the melting pot. Nonetheless, it had clearly incorporated a much stronger assimilationist cast, which it retained until the late 1960s and the emergence of "multiculturalism," which reversed this centripetal dynamic by again lending cultural pluralism a more centrifugal meaning, if not, for the most part, as centrifugal a meaning as Kallen's conception. In the Depression and World War II, cultural pluralism added to the American creed a tolerance for, perhaps even a respect for, diversity, but not for divisiveness. It regarded immigrants as immigrants not as national minorities, and insisted that immigration implied a willingness to "Americanize," that is, to embrace the principles of freedom, equality, and democracy and the public culture they required. Ethnicity, insofar as it persisted, was to be confined to the private sphere.[58] The most significant voice for cultural pluralism in this period was Louis Adamic, a Slovenian American who urged immigrant ethnics to drop the hyphen from their self-understanding yet retain a respect and affinity for their ancestral culture while contributing to a necessarily shared American culture. He advanced this view not only through a host of books published in the period but also as a leader of the Foreign Language Information Center and its successor organization, the Common Council for American Unity. During World War II, he edited the Council's journal (the tellingly titled), *Common Ground.*[59]

The most disruptive voices opposing cultural nationalism in the thirties were not ethnic but regional, those of the white South.[60] Such Southerners, of course, had a strong claim to the status of a national minority. They had once tried, in bloody fashion, to secure their own national state. The Civil War put an end to that possibility, but many Southerners in the thirties saw themselves as an aggrieved and colonized

218   ROBERT B. WESTBROOK

people, with an unassimilable culture of their own – "reconstructed but unregenerate," as John Crowe Ransom put it. The most vigorous proponents among intellectuals of Southern difference were the so-called Nashville Agrarians, who published their manifesto, *I'll Take My Stand*, in 1930. The South, by their lights, stood for "a Southern way of life against what may be called the American or prevailing way." As they saw it, Southern culture was agrarian, anti-industrial, anti-materialistic, and dead set against "progress" as Northerners understood it. "The South took life easy," Ransom said, "which is itself a tolerably comprehensive art." The Agrarians said as little as they had to about slavery and racial oppression, and what they did say played into the "plantation myth" of genteel, easygoing, civilized planters surrounded by well-cared-for and contented black slaves. "Slavery was a feature monstrous enough in theory," Ransom admitted, "but, more often than not, humane in practice."[61] This myth found its way into the best-selling novel Margaret Mitchell's *Gone with the Wind* (1936) and the blockbuster movie that followed in 1939.

But even those Southerners who regarded the plantation myth as so much horseshit insisted on construing the region's culture as an outlier. W. J. Cash, misanthropic Carolina journalist and debunker of the aristocratic pretensions of the planter class, eviscerated the Agrarians' South in his *Mind of the South* (1941), a brilliant demolition of their longing for a mythic preindustrial South of easygoing gentility. He portrayed a region instead committed to "The Savage Ideal," in which no one was more thoroughly savaged by white Southerners than black Southerners. "I myself have known university-bred men who confessed proudly to having helped roast a Negro," he remarked. Nonetheless, Cash still insisted that "the South is another land, sharply differentiated from the rest of the American nation, and exhibiting within itself a remarkable homogeneity."[62]

For the national leaders of the Federal Writers' Project – Henry Alsberg, Benjamin Botkin, Sterling Brown, and Morton Royse[63] – Southerners, including those employed in the state units of the project, were a thorn in the side. As Jerrold Hirsch has shown, these important figures among cultural nationalists of the thirties tried, despite the apparent paradoxes, to combine a romantic nationalism with cultural pluralism. They met particularly strong resistance from Southerners every step of the way, but they managed to grope their way to most promising conceptual territory.[64]

The key to their innovative notion of cultural pluralism was to argue that American culture was dynamic, a culture never finished but always in formation, and then to conceive of the disparate ethnic and regional cultures within the nation's borders not as "contributors" to an already formed national culture, but as "collaborators" or, even better, "participants" in the ongoing, often dissonant construction of that shared way of life. Theirs was most assuredly an assimilationist vision, but it was assimilation *with*, not assimilation *to*, American culture. Diversity would persist – indeed it was essential to American cultural development – but the expectation was that diversity would serve a hybrid national culture, a common life amid diversity, that would well serve a society with democratic aspirations.[65]

Proud of the remarkable state guides, but disappointed in the manner in which the straitjacket of the form and the resistance of local units to their vision, the FWP leaders planned an ambitious set of projects in folk history and ethnic studies to carry it forward. But though some promising material was published, their plans were thwarted. They, like the other arts projects, ran afoul of Texan Martin Dies and the newly formed House Un-American Activities Committee, a bastion of rearguard Anglo conformity and defiant white supremacy, which led the eventually successful charge to close them down.[66]

***

To my mind, the finest work of American documentary photography of the thirties is Walker Evans's *American Photographs* (1938). And the finest work of American historical fiction of the thirties (or arguably ever) is William Faulkner's *Absalom, Absalom!* (1936). Neither contributed much of anything to the cultural nationalist cause. Neither gives much comfort to those who might think that the shortcomings of that cause lay not in its guiding ambition to find or make American whole but merely in its faltering pursuit of it.

Evans was not a typical FSA photographer. His tenure at the agency was brief and turbulent. *American Photographs*, drawn from a career-making exhibition at the Museum of Modern Art in 1938, included many of his FSA photographs, and reviewers were too quick to see it as another artifact of the wider documentary impulse of the decade. But Evans stood apart from this impulse in important ways. As Alan Trachtenberg says, his book "negates the methods and styles of journalism, and of the stereotyped FSA. In *Let Us Now Praise Famous Men*, [James] Agee's insistent denial that his prose fits any of the standard categories of 'social protest' or 'reportage' also concurs with Evans' intention in that book, as well as in *American Photographs*."[67]

Evans was as deeply invested as anyone else at the time in the search for an American cultural identity, hence the title of his book. It is a book in which he showed, as Lincoln Kirstein put it in his fine afterword, "the visible effects, direct and indirect, of the industrial revolution in America, the replacement by the machine in all its complexities of the work and art once done by individual hands and hearts, the exploitation of men by machinery and machinery by men. He records alike the vulgarization which inevitably results from the widespread multiplication of goods and services, and the naïve creative spirit, imperishable and inherent in ordinary men" (Figure 10.6).[68] Even so, it was not a tendentious book, but rather, as Evans himself said, "reflective" and "in a certain way, disinterested." Bereft of text and captions (apart from a listing of the photographs at the end of each of two parts), offering no explanation for a sequencing of images that nonetheless clearly meant something, it left that meaning to the reader to discern. As Trachtenberg observes, "the very openness of *American Photographs* implies a skepticism toward closed forms and fixed meanings. The book invites its readers to discover meanings for themselves, to puzzle over the arrangement of pictures and figure out how and why they appear as they do." And it is hard, often frustrating work. Consequently, Trachtenberg concludes, "the book proposes no immanent whole named America, as Evans's friend Hart Crane attempted in *The Bridge*, but a continuous meditation upon the problem of coherence." America, Evans suggests, lies in the endless endeavor to wrench a coherent pattern from disparity – "not in a finished thesis but a continuous process, less an idea than a method," one of painstaking, detached, inconclusive, and unsparing seeing.[69]

Faulkner's South was much closer to that of Cash than to that of the Agrarians. As Peter Conn points out, "Faulkner's gallery of idiots, con men, rapists, suicides, arsonists, and twisted souls, etched the lineaments of Southern identity in the acid of deviance, incest, violence, and death."[70] This most certainly includes *Absalom, Absalom!* But the significance of the novel for the story about American cultural nationalism I have been telling here amounts to more than this. For it comprises not only a tale of the savage South at work in the nineteenth century, but a meditation on the extraordinary difficulty of forging that tale in any singular fashion.

The novel offers up a mystery: why did Thomas Sutpen, the brutal, driven builder of a plantation empire on the southwestern frontier in Mississippi, refuse to grant the hand of his daughter Judith to the apparently honorable Charles Bon, the close friend of his son Henry – a refusal that leads Henry eventually to murder Bon? The mystery is never

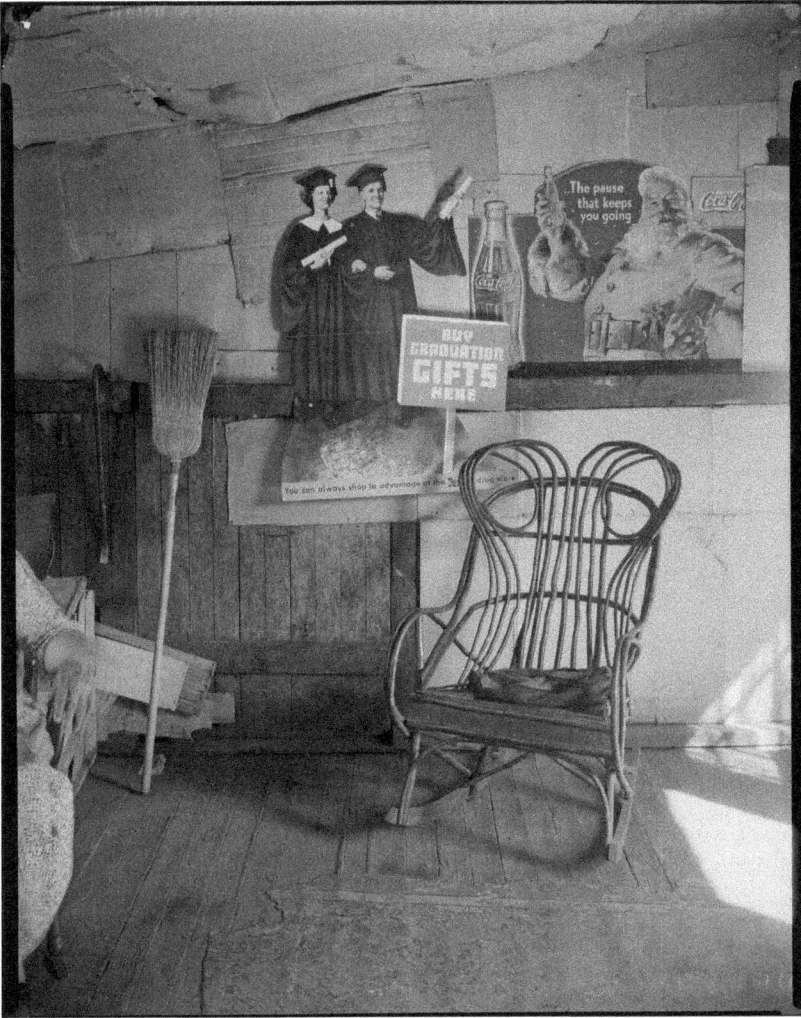

Figure 10.6 Walker Evans, "Interior Detail, West Virginia Coal Miner's House, 1935."

definitively solved. Instead, we are offered the reflections and speculations on the matter by a series of narrators: Rosa Coldfield, Sutpen's sister-in-law, Sutpen's friend Confederate General Compson and his son, and finally Compson's grandson Quentin, who puzzles over the mystery with his roommate Shreve in their Harvard dorm room in 1910. The accounts vary significantly, and, as Faulkner intended, the reader never quite pins down what truly happened.

The novel suggests that turning to the past to sort out the incoherence of the present is unlikely to yield a satisfying result for those in quest of singular patterns and uncontested traditions. Lynd had assigned historians the pivotal task of "joining parts into wholes" in the "unifying of the entire field of human behavior."[71] Faulkner implied that they were probably going to fail at this assignment no less painfully than Quentin Compson, though, unlike him, most of them would regard suicide as an unduly despairing response to this fate. Confident though historians may be that the traces of the past bump up against the stories of America they devise with enough determination to limit the range of possible narratives, they can be far less confident that the limit can be drawn at all tightly.

Perhaps we should include figures such as Evans and Faulkner prominently within the fold of the American search for self-knowledge in the thirties, not in spite of but *because of* their skepticism about its prospects for any clear resolution. Then the legacy of American cultural nationalism of the period might be said to lie not only in its considerable achievements, in its mining of the country's diverse cultural traditions and resources, but also in its failure to corral this diversity into any coherent American way, dream, or identity. Being an American might, that is, be understood in light of this failure not as integration into a stable, coherent, well-established cultural pattern but rather as participation in an ongoing, never-ending construction and reconstruction of a people: less a culturally pluralistic symphony than a culturally pluralistic argument, one often dissonant and only as civil as circumstances allow. Americans can, to be sure, be properly construed as a people committed as one to freedom, equality, and democracy, if one also allows that they are a people never settled on what these elusive abstractions can and should mean or what sort of culture they require to give them life – a nation whose citizens find their thickest adhesions elsewhere in other roles, and hang together as citizens only in constant debate and as loosely as they can safely manage.

Notes

1. Alfred Kazin, *On Native Grounds* (New York: Harcourt, Brace, and World, 1942), x, 486.
2. Kazin, *On Native Grounds*, 485. Though he was among the first, Kazin was certainly not the last observer to put cultural nationalism at the heart of an understanding of American cultural expression in the 1930s. See, for example,

Charles C. Alexander, *Nationalism in American Thought, 1930–1945* (Chicago: Rand McNally, 1969); Charles C. Alexander, *Here the Country Lies: Nationalism and the Arts in Twentieth-Century America* (Bloomington: Indiana University Press, 1980), 152–241; and Richard H. Pells, *Radical Visions and American Dreams: Culture and Social Thought in the Depression Years*, 1st edn. (New York: Harper & Row, 1973).

3. Kazin, *On Native Grounds*, 486.
4. Benedict Anderson, *Imagined Communities: Reflections on the Origin and Spread of Nationalism*, 2nd edn. (London: Verso, 2006), 6.
5. Philip Gleason, "American Identity and Americanization," in *Harvard Encyclopedia of American Ethnic Groups*, ed. Stephen Thernstrom (Cambridge, MA: Harvard University Press, 1980), 31 (Gleason is summarizing the argument of a pioneering student of nationalism, Hans Kohn, in *American Nationalism* [1957]); Anderson, *Imagined Communities*, 47–65.
6. Kai Nielsen, "Cultural Nationalism, Neither Ethnic nor Civic," in *Theorizing Nationalism*, ed. Ronald Beiner (Albany: State University of New York Press, 1999), 127. As Nielsen further says: "Defenders of the claim that civic nationalism is the only acceptable nationalism try to deny that civic nationalism is also a cultural nationalism by claiming that a civic nationalism is a purely political conception reflecting not some distinct culture but only a common commitment, across cultures, to the political principles of democracy and freedom. But this is false. Indeed, worse than being merely false, it is a piece of deceptive ideology and may even be incoherent. To be a member of any nation at all, even in the most laissez-faire liberal society, is to be accepted as being a part of a distinctive organizational culture in terms of which even this liberal individualistic nation is defined and which sets the parameters of national identity in the nation in question. It has, that is, a cultural component as much is the most traditional of ethnic nationalism's" (124). See also the essays by Bernard Yack and Will Kymlicka in the same volume. A particular target of the animus of these critics is Michael Ignatieff, *Blood and Belonging: Journeys into the New Nationalism* (New York: Farrar, Straus and Giroux, 1993).
7. This story is fully told up to 1912 in Rogers M. Smith, *Civic Ideals: Conflicting Visions of Citizenship in U.S. History* (New Haven, CT: Yale University Press, 1997). See also Alexander Keyssar, *The Right to Vote: The Contested History of Democracy in the United States*, rev. edn. (New York: Basic Books, 2009).
8. These rights remain, to be sure, subject to fresh thinning. Felons remain disenfranchised, which has decidedly discriminatory effects along racial lines, and new strategies for limiting the black vote, such as voter ID laws, have been deployed by conservative state legislators. Witness as well the recent controversy over the decision of the Supreme Court to relax key enforcement provisions in the Voting Rights Act of 1965.
9. Jeffrey Rosen, "America in Thick and Thin," *New Republic* (January 5 and 12, 1998), 34. See also Michael Lind, *The Next American Nation: The New Nationalism and the Fourth American Revolution* (New York: Free Press, 1995), 259–98.

10. One may take Henry Luce's proclamation of the "American Century" in February 1941 as the exemplary document in the rearticulation of the nation's universal mission. On its development during the fierce debate over American intervention in World War II, see Ichiro Takayoshi, *American Writers and the Approach of World War II, 1935–1941* (New York: Cambridge University Press, 2015). On its Cold War crystallization, see John Fousek, *To Lead the Free World: American Nationalism and the Cultural Roots of the Cold War* (Chapel Hill: University of North Carolina Press, 2000).

11. Warren Susman, *Culture as History: The Transformation of American Society in the Twentieth Century* (New York: Pantheon, 1984), 153. The quotations in Susman's observation are from Robert Lynd, *Knowledge for What?* (Princeton, NJ: Princeton University Press, 1939), 16, 19.

12. John Dewey, *Freedom and Culture* (New York: Capricorn Books, 1963 [1939]), 24–49; Lynd, *Knowledge for What*, 11–113.

13. Margaret Mead, "Preface" to Ruth Benedict, *Patterns of Culture*, 2nd edn. (Boston, MA: Houghton Mifflin, 1959), vii.

14. Benedict, *Patterns*, 47, 48.

15. Benedict, *Patterns*, 55, 56–57.

16. A task pioneered by Robert and Helen Lynd in the mid-twenties in *Middletown* (1929), which made explicit use of anthropological categories. The Lynds weighed in again in the thirties with *Middletown in Transition* (1937). Benedict and other "culture and personality" anthropologists themselves threw caution to the winds during World War II on behalf of the American war effort. Benedict took on Japan in *The Chrysanthemum and the Sword* (1946), while Margaret Mead took a weak stab at America in *And Keep Your Powder Dry* (1943).

17. William Stott, *Documentary Expression and Thirties America* (New York: Oxford University Press, 1973) remains the authoritative account of this phenomenon. See especially Part Two on documentary nonfiction.

18. James Agee and Walker Evans, *Let Us Now Praise Famous Men,* in *Agee, Let Us Now Praise Famous Me, A Death in the Family, and Shorter Fiction* (New York: Library of America, 2005), 26. Stott echoes Kazin in arguing that *Let Us Now Praise Famous Men*, the least commercially successful of these documentary books, was not a typical example of the genre but an effort to subvert its "facile mechanics and passivity": Kazin, *On Native Grounds*, 495, n. 1; Stott, *Documentary Expression*, Part Three. The book, Stott says, "is a classic of documentary and the 1930s because it culminates the central rhetoric of the time, and explodes it, surpasses it, shows it up" (x). See especially Agee's savaging of Bourke-White, 382–85.

19. Stott, *Documentary Expression*, 111.

20. Stott, *Documentary Expression*, 92.

21. John Dos Passos, *The Ground We Stand On* (New York: Harcourt Brace, 1941), 3.

22. See also Schlesinger's important presidential address to the American Historical Association, "What Then Is the American, This New Man?" *American Historical Review* 48 (1943), 225–44.

23. Carolyn Ware, ed., *The Cultural Approach to History* (New York: Columbia University Press, 1940).

24. Peter Conn, *The American 1930s: A Literary History* (New York: Cambridge University Press, 2009) discusses a host of these novels, including *The Store* (1932), *Anthony Adverse* (1933), *Lamb in His Bosom* (1934), *Now as November* (1935), *George Washington's Dilemma* (1938), *Gone with the Wind* (1936), *Guns along the Mohawk* (1936), *Northwest Passage* (1937), *Star of the West* (1935), and *The Yearling* (1938). It should be said that the American appetite for historical fiction was not confined to that treating the American past, which suggests that the concerns of cultural nationalism do not alone explain it. Later Malcolm Cowley suggested that "not a few of the historical romancers who flourished in these years revealed a social purpose in their writing: at a time of crisis they were turning toward the past, not simply because it was picturesque but also to find heroes whose example would assure us about the future." Cowley as quoted in Alfred Haworth Jones, "The Search for a Usable American Past in the New Deal Era," *American Quarterly* 23 (1971), 719.

25. Sandburg, *The War Years* (1939), as quoted in Conn, *American 1930s*, 112.

26. Kazin, *On Native Grounds*, 508.

27. Kazin, *On Native Grounds*, 497, 499.

28. Joan Shelley Rubin, *Constance Rourke and American Culture* (Chapel Hill: University of North Carolina Press, 1980), 45–61.

29. Van Wyck Brooks, "On Creating a Usable Past," *The Dial* (April 11, 1918): 337–41. See as well the even more influential "America's Coming of Age" (1915) in Brooks, *Three Essays on America* (New York: Dutton, 1934), 13–112. Brooks, it should be said, had by the thirties come around to Rourke's way of thinking, and the literary histories he published in that decade could be said to have found altogether too much in the American cultural past to admire lovingly. As Kazin said, Brooks thought he had discovered in antebellum New England what D. H. Lawrence termed "a living, organic, believing community." Here "he had found it, like buried treasure, under the ground men walked in America, found it in their own past – a standard, an image of belief and security" (Kazin, *On Native Grounds*, 515). In his preface to Rourke's posthumously published *Roots of American Culture* (New York: Harcourt, 1942), Brooks saluted her role in revealing "the rich stores of tradition that lie behind us, the many streams of native character and feeling from which the Americans of the future will be able to draw" (xii).

30. Rubin, *Rourke*, 69.

31. Rourke, unpublished ms., as quoted in Rubin, *Rourke*, 190–91.

32. Kazin, *On Native Grounds*, 502; Robert Cantwell, "America and the Writers Project," *New Republic* (April 26, 1939), 323–24; Greil Marcus, *Invisible Republic: Bob Dylan's Basement Tapes* (New York: Henry Holt, 1997), 89.

As Rubin shows, Rourke had her limits when it came to the weird, particularly weird violence and sex. Rubin, *Rourke*, 141–54. Rubin suggests that a "desire for broad diffusion of a common – and acceptable – heritage was Rourke's most compelling reason for mitigating the rougher aspects of frontier life" (154).

33. Constance Rourke, *American Humor: A Study of the National Character* (1931) (New York: New York Review Books, 2004), 86.

34. Rourke, *American Humor*, 232. A few years after the publication of *American Humor*, Rourke emphasized the persistence of sectionalism as "part of the stubborn variety that seems to linger with us in spite of standardization." Rourke, "The Significance of Sections," *New Republic* (September 20, 1933), 148–51. I am grateful to Joan Rubin for this reference.

35. Marcus, "Introduction" to Rourke, *American Humor*, xxii.

36. Van Wyck Brooks, "Preface" to Rourke, *Roots of American Culture*, viii. For another example of this sort of hope, see Rourke's essay on the Index of American Design project, for which she served as national editor. "If this work is carried to full completion, the questions 'What is American design?' or 'Have we an American design?' may answer themselves, possibly with some surprises, certainly with a wealth of fresh materials." Rourke, "What Is American Design," in *Art for the Millions: Essays from the 1930s by Artists and Administrators of the WPA Federal Art Project,* ed. Francis V. O'Connor (New York: New York Graphic Society, 1973), 167.

37. Susman, *Culture as History*, 164. In the case of the "American Way of Life," one may quite confidently assert its conservatism since it was a phrase coined and circulated by advertising agents of the nation's large corporations hostile to New Deal reform and determined to put households well supplied with their commodities at the heart of popular understanding of American identity. See Charles F. McGovern, *Sold American: Consumption and Citizenship, 1890–1945* (Chapel Hill: University of North Carolina Press, 2006), 261–300.

38. Jean-Christophe Agnew, "Capitalism, Culture, and Catastrophe," in *The Cultural Turn in U.S. History*, ed. James W. Cook, Lawrence B. Glickman, and Michael O'Malley (Chicago: University of Chicago Press, 2008), 384. Agnew is here ringing changes on Edmund Wilson's quite different use of the Philoctetes myth in his *Wound and the Bow* (1941).

39. Lynd, *Knowledge for What*, 105.

40. Lynd, *Knowledge for What*, 220, 203.

41. Michael Denning, *The Cultural Front: The Laboring of American Culture in the Twentieth Century* (New York: Verso, 1996).

42. Gary Gerstle, *Working-Class Americanism: The Politics of Labor in a Textile City, 1914–1960* (New York: Cambridge University Press, 1989), 8.

43. Guthrie soon thereafter replaced the last line of the verses with "This land was made for you and me." Caught up himself in the spirit of national unity during World War II, he stripped these two verses from the song when he recorded it. In 1970, Pete Seeger restored them to what is now the standard version (sung, for example, by Bruce Springsteen). John Shaw, *This Land*

That I Love: Irving Berlin, Woody Guthrie, and the Story of Two American Anthems (New York: Public Affairs, 2013), 153 (photograph of manuscript of original draft), 211–18. See also Sheryl Kaskowitz, *God Bless America: The Surprising History of an Iconic Song* (New York: Oxford University Press, 2013), 12–67.

44. Denning, *Cultural Front*, 129. Denning's book is a robust and often successful effort to rescue Popular Front culture from its reputation as simply a crude and aesthetically lame instrument of the Communist Party, a reputation fostered by its critics in the anti-Stalinist left in the thirties (think *Partisan Review*) and characteristic of much of subsequent historiography.

45. Sinclair Lewis, *Main Street in Lewis, Main Street and Babbitt* (New York: Library of America, 1992), 3.

46. Lawrence Levine, *The Unpredictable Past: Explorations in American Cultural History* (New York: Oxford University Press, 1993), 291.

47. See Camille Bégin, *Taste of the Nation: The New Deal Search for America's Food* (Urbana: University of Illinois Press, 2016).

48. Kazin, *On Native Grounds*, 502–03.

49. F. O. Matthiessen, *American Renaissance: Art and Expression in the Age of Emerson and Whitman* (New York: Oxford University Press, 1941), xv.

50. Matthiessen, *American Renaissance*, 444. Matthiessen also captured the downbeat side of Whitman, a hero of nearly all American cultural naturalists, quoting him to the effect that "if the United States, like the countries of the Old World, are also to grow vast crops of poor, desperate, dissatisfied, nomadic, miserably-waged populations, such as we see looming upon us of late years – steadily, even if slowly eating into them like a cancer of lungs or stomach – then our republican experiment, notwithstanding all its surface-successes, is at heart an unhealthy failure" (589).

51. Matthiessen, *American Renaissance*, 641.

52. Horace Kallen, *Culture and Democracy in the United States: Studies in the Group Psychology of the American Peoples* (New York: Boni and Liveright, 1924), 11. Among the essays in this book is Kallen's best-known articulation of his cultural pluralism in 1915 before he coined the term, "Democracy *versus* the Melting Pot."

53. Philip Gleason, *Speaking of Diversity: Language and Ethnicity in Twentieth-Century America* (Baltimore, MD: Johns Hopkins University Press, 1992), 3–46.

54. This phrase, "a nation of nations," subsequently used by many others encapsulates the confusion introduced into debates over American cultural diversity by a failure to distinguish carefully between national minorities and immigrants. As Will Kymlicka says, "[i]mmigrants choose to leave their original culture and homeland and move to a new country. They know that this uprooting will only be successful if they adapt to their new country, including learning its language and customs." National minorities are ethnic groups incorporated into the nation-state of another ethnic group or groups by conquest, colonization, or voluntary federation. They are minorities that

aspire to their own state or, at least, a full measure of political autonomy. National minorities – Native Americans, native Hawaiians, Puerto Ricans, do inhabit the United States, and they should be distinguished from immigrants. African-Americans descended from involuntary immigrants are an important middle case. "African-American nationalism" is conceptually coherent as, say, Italian-American nationalism is not. Will Kymlicka, "Misunderstanding Nationalism," in Beiner, *Theorizing Nationalism*, 131.

55. "Overlapping consensus" is political philosopher John Rawls's phrase, one that was essential to his important contribution to cultural pluralist theory in his *Political Liberalism* (1993).

56. Kallen, *Culture and Democracy*, 124–25.

57. Gleason, "American Identity and Americanization," 45.

58. Gleason, *Speaking of Diversity*, 47–90.

59. Adamic's books included *Laughing in the Jungle* (1932), *Native's Return* (1934), *My America* (1938), *From Many Lands* (1940), *Two-Way Passage* (1941), *What's Your Name* (1942), *My Native Land* 1943), and *A Nation of Nations* (1945). See also Carey McWilliams, *Louis Adamic and Shadow-America* (Los Angeles, CA: Arthur Whipple, 1935) and Dan Shiffman, *Rooting Multiculturalism: The Work of Louis Adamic* (Madison, NJ: Fairleigh Dickenson University Press, 2003).

60. Or, one might perhaps more wisely say, a voice often racial in the guise of the regional, since white supremacy was one of the pivotal convictions essential to white Southern identity.

61. Twelve Southerners, *I'll Take My Stand: The South and the Agrarian Tradition* (Baton Rouge: Louisiana State University Press, 1977), xxxvii, 12, 14.

62. W. J. Cash, *The Mind of the South* (New York: Vintage, 1991), 303, xlvii.

63. Not incidentally, three Jewish-Americans and an African-American.

64. Jerrold Hirsch, *Portrait of America: A Cultural History of the Federal Writers' Project* (Chapel Hill: University of North Carolina Press, 2003), 4, 179–94.

65. Hirsch, *Portrait of America*, 22–23, 30, 38, 114.

66. Hirsch, *Portrait of America*, 197–212. As this episode suggests, American ethnic nationalism, though firmly challenged, was far from defeated in the thirties. Its persistence was perhaps most fatefully evident in the failure of efforts to expand immigration quotas in order to provide refuge for the Jewish victims of Nazi tyranny.

67. Alan Trachtenberg, *Reading American Photographs: Images as History, Matthew Brady to Walker Evans* (New York: Hill and Wang, 1989), 257. My analysis here closely follows Trachtenberg's acute reading of Evans's book.

68. Lincoln Kirstein, "Photographs of America: Walker Evans," in Evans, *American Photographs* (New York: Museum of Modern Art, 1938), 196.

69. Trachtenberg, *Reading American Photographs*, 256, 258, 284.

70. Conn, *American 1930s*, 155.

71. Lynd, *Knowledge for What*, 13.

CHAPTER II

Look at the World!

David Ekbladh, Ichiro Takayoshi

Introduction

For much of the 1930s, Malcolm Cowley worked as chief book reviewer of the liberal weekly *The New Republic*. Books of all descriptions daily crossed his desk. Cowley himself reviewed many scores of them while letting young penurious writers loafing around his office review many more for a small payment. At the close of the decade, this man, who was as attuned to the cultural and political pulse of the intellectual class as anyone in his time, looked back on the notable literary and intellectual events of the past ten years and identified three trends that lent the decade a distinct color. The first trend was the most obvious, that is, the decade-long economic depression and all sorts of economic and political strife it triggered. Considered to this day the era's defining feature, this topic is explored from a number of angles in the present volume. The second was the acceleration of monopolistic tendencies in political economy. Throughout the 1930s, the corporation, the government, and the union all grew in size and influence, calling into question the myth of America as the country of fiercely independent-minded citizens. The third trend was the least visible to Cowley's contemporaries and it was to remain so to later generations: the spread of a new globalism among the nation's educated class, which reflected "the new position of the United States in world affairs." Like the two other trends, this one too shaped the ideas, sentiments, and points of view found in the most influential books of the time, Cowley thought. The Depression years, when Americans rediscovered the natural resources and rich folkways of their vast country, was also an era when finally "Americans have begun to write with their eyes on the world overseas."[1] Still left out of most accounts of the decade's intellectual ferment, this new development is the main topic of the present chapter.

The new globalism arose at the confluence of many factors. To examine it means above all to recognize the 1930s as a unique period that saw all these historical factors come together. At the center of this confluence was an array of technological breakthroughs. In 1927, America's most famous pilot, Charles Lindbergh, flew across the Atlantic from New York to Paris nonstop. In 1937, the Soviet Union's most famous pilot, Valery Chkalov, brought Europe even closer to America. He and his copilots flew nonstop, from Moscow to Vancouver, Washington, over the North Pole. The world was rapidly shrinking south of the border as well. In 1927, Pan American Airways obtained from the US Post Office the first mail contract to fly between Key West and Havana. By the time Roosevelt was elected to the White House in 1933, Pan American operated a fleet of hydroplanes that regularly shuttled the mail, cargos, and passengers among major hubs in the Caribbean and South America.[2] The advent of the age of air travel inevitably transformed Americans' relation to events unfolding oceans away. Not only did world events come to Americans from afar, from unexpected directions, they also now reached America at a speed undreamed of during the era of the ocean liner and the train.

The world also drew closer to America through the air in another way: radio. Small, locally run radio stations had spread across the nation in the previous decade, and with the arrival of the Depression, these stations came under the control of a handful of oligopolistic corporations based in New York. Over the course of the 1930s, as these "networks" developed a variety of appealing programs, radio sets became more and more affordable and, despite the prolonged economic downturn, their sales grew exponentially. Meanwhile, the invention of short wave transmission in the 1920s (the first signals crossed the Atlantic in 1926) made it possible for the networks to cover foreign news live. By the middle of the 1930s, out of a combination of these industry developments emerged a new global radio journalism, which fanned and satisfied the increasing public interest in political and military convulsions in Europe. With the ambiance of immediacy and simultaneous connection that the voice of a foreign correspondent could create, the radio permeated tens of millions of living rooms. The sound and the feel of disturbances in remote lands were now woven into the daily lives of most Americans.[3]

These disturbances were mostly of a geopolitical kind. As the Depression enveloped the world, the international system began its violent descent into normless chaos. Japan established a puppet regime in Manchuria in 1931 and started invading China proper in 1937. In Germany, the National Socialists came to power in 1933. Through a series of unilateral actions, Hitler and his satraps made clear to the world their intention to reorganize Central and Eastern Europe under the aegis of the Third Empire. Another latecomer colonial power, Mussolini's Italy also embarked on empire building across the Mediterranean and invaded Ethiopia in 1935. Germany and Italy were the vital supporters of Franco's rebel armies in the civil war that broke out in Spain the next year. All this turmoil came to a head in Europe when Hitler's army crossed the Polish border in 1939. These events came to pass exactly as the new technologies of communication and transportation like radio and airplane were changing the way Americans understood their country's connection with the world outside. Was the United States vulnerable to events in far lands? Was the United States responsible for humanitarian crises oceans away? The major geopolitical events of the 1930s were so cataclysmic that they anyway would have forced Americans to ask these questions to themselves. But with the new technologies engendering the sense that the world was fast shrinking, these questions hit America with an urgency that wouldn't have been possible under different circumstances. By the time the Japanese attack on Hawaii dragged the United States into the new world war, a new globalism, a new willingness to rethink America's role in the small, hostile world, was driving the nation's dominant narratives and reshaping its core institutions.

The Sinew of the New Globalism

Many linked the emergence of a world hostile to core US beliefs to the catastrophic effects of the Depression. Increasingly, many liberals came to see that the decaying world order demanded changes in the US posture toward it. And when these liberals began formulating new ideas and views, they benefited from the activism of a collection of institutions that harnessed new technologies to reshape how Americans imagined the world. As much as there was the new technology of the radio to hear how close a shrinking world had become, a rank of institutions were invested in getting Americans to understand how much the world had changed.

They had emerged in response to the lessons of the Great War. Many participants came back from the battlefields of the conflict and the Versailles conference seeing a need for better resources to support US engagement with the world. A set of institutions emerged quickly in the years that followed, names that still ring with influence today. Esteemed bodies in the twenty-first century such as the Council on Foreign Relations (CFR) and the Foreign Policy Association (FPA) were in the blush of youth during the period. They represented a new concept, advocacy groups aimed at promoting greater understanding of world affairs across the American public. Along with them came the newly conceptualized field of "international relations" that cobbled together existing academic disciplines to explain world affairs. All of these were just getting their footing when the Depression splashed over the world.

They were decisively in the liberal mainstream and close, if not tightly bound, to elites and established institutions. Indeed, neither the CFR nor the FPA could have functioned without the largess of hulking foundations like the Rockefeller Foundation and the Carnegie Corporation of New York – themselves just a few decades old.

But they comprised a new nexus of activity in a period of crisis. They actively responded to the increasing instability of the 1930s by drawing in fresh ideas and shaping opinion in service of liberal viewpoints. The FPA, in particular, was active in not only disseminating new ideas but also in attempting to franchise parts of the public in a discussion of those ideas. In 1935, with the aid of the Rockefeller Foundation, it embarked on something seen as experimental: a broad national program of popular education. It had a number of nodes but central to it was drawing on the Foundation's existing research department to create a "headline series" of books that made analysis of current events more accessible and affordable. Within a few years, hundreds of thousands of copies of works with titles like *Shadow over Europe, Dictatorship*, and *America Contradicts Herself* were in print. These short works were more than an attempt to shape academic debates or elite discourse. They appealed to harried middlebrow readers who were struggling to grab some context on the rush of events. The books quickly found a market with educators in adult education programs but crucially also with colleges and high schools.

Many civic organizations, from peace groups to the League of Women Voters and a variety of local Parent Teacher Associations quickly found the books useful as they aimed to foster discussions on current events. To this end, such organizations could avail themselves of the FPA's "Club Service Bureau" that not only provided books but put together packets on particular issues and even assisted organizational leaders in creating agendas, crafting reading lists, finding speakers, and preparing their speeches on particular topics. Face-to-face discussion of world affairs and the US place within them was shaped by the interventions of the FPA. The organization also made sure that voices on the airwaves of the new national radio networks were from its stable as well.[4]

Yet the activists' embrace of new technologies cut both ways. The forces aiding global interconnection were assumed to be Janus faced. Just as radio could be used to convince the American public to see how deeply they were immersed in an interconnected world, those same airwaves could be turned against them. The hangover from the First World War had left a strong impression of how states could juggle the truth for their own ends. The term "propaganda" was tossed into public discussion by a public relations man, Edward Bernays, at the end of the 1920s but quickly became attached to efforts, particularly nefarious ones, aimed at manipulating the public.[5] Part of the reason it gained such currency was the appreciation of the qualitatively and quantitatively different ways mass societies could be influenced. In new technologies like radio, individuals and regimes with dangerous ideas had a tool for their own propaganda that had no respect for national boundaries.

It is no surprise that foundational research on the impact of mass media on society was conducted in the 1930s. That so much is known about Orson Wells's famous 1938 Halloween broadcast of the "War of the Worlds" is that many were already turned on to the question of radio's corrupting impacts on a credulous public. That and the Rockefeller Foundation had funded a research institute, well stocked with social scientists, at Princeton University in 1937 to research just that question. They were the same researchers who produced the studies on which much of the historical memory of the event has rested.

What they discovered was that many of the public agitated by Wells's broadcast actually thought the United States was under attack, not by invaders from Mars but by earthly enemies. Many thought the announcers had been duped and assumed the "Martians" were Germans or Japanese using new technologies to directly strike the United States – something no longer improbable in an age of long-range aircraft and weapons of mass destruction (it can be forgotten in an era of nuclear weapons how anxious many were in the years before World War II about the possible use of chemical weapons). The new experience of hearing radio broadcasts directly from Europe and Asia had accentuated the feeling on which the researchers based their analysis. They assumed that the public, having lived in a world in a state of perpetual economic, social, and political instability over the preceding decade, was that much more primed to overreact.[6] The speed with which these concepts moved into wider discussion and perception shows that such views were not academic or simply confined to the province of a cadre of specialists.

If any place could make a claim to being a hub of the sprawling US media landscape of the 1930s, it was Henry Luce's Time-Life empire. The magazines *Time*, *Life*, and *Fortune* alone were influential tribunes of

American opinion. The decade saw the rise of a new radio satrapy, *The March of Time*, whose broadcasts started in 1932. By 1935 *The March of Time* had colonized the newsreels. These multimedia ventures deepened Time Inc.'s already extensive reach into the culture.[7] More important, Luce's empire building in new media betrays how quickly these forces had taken a commanding commercial, cultural, and political position.

Luce's more conservative voice held remarkable sway in many circles. His 1941 article "The American Century" is often seen as the clarion call marking a start of global commitment. However, well before that, his subordinates were already mapping out the US place on a shifting globe. *Fortune*, the lavishly illustrated monthly aimed at the business community, was one locus of activity. This was due, in no small measure, to the importation of Raymond Leslie Buell, previously a pioneering scholar in the evolving field of "international relations" and former head of the FPA. Buell, himself right of center, was nevertheless an internationalist. He had traveled widely and written on a wide variety of topics. His views were mainstream, including his tendency to view humanity through a racial lens. At the same time, Buell was deeply skeptical of the statist turn many governments, including his own, took in response to the Depression. Initial interest in Franklin Roosevelt gave way to worries that the New Deal would empower government at the expense of the individual and other areas of society. This was not knee-jerk reaction to a wave of domestic reform (although Buell was miffed by something the New Deal assisted: unionization of FPA staff while he was chief there) but a deep concern about global trends. The rise of "totalitarian" regimes and their addiction to state power worried liberals across the center of the political spectrum. Buell was hardly alone in worrying that such governments, born of the crisis, would use the upheaval of the period to shape the world in their image. Even if the United States avoided the bane of overweening state power, it would eventually find its own domestic life distorted by the pressures of a globe that did not conform to its tolerances.

More than words, the graphic monthly could make the problems of the period literally visible to a slice of the public. The same *Fortune* that Buell edited boasted the talents of an innovative cartographer, Richard Edes Harrison. Harrison rode the crest of a creative wave that remapped his field and with it some public perceptions of the world around them. Harrison had a knack for making the new technologies as well as the forces at work in the new world of the 1930s come alive within the two-dimensional confines of a magazine.[8] He did not merely visualize where and what was happening but grafted a sense of why and how this new world fit together.

In Figure 11.1, for example, he managed to convey the power of radio waves, showing something that many others had appreciated over the course of the decade, that the borders of the United States were now permeable in ways they had not been before.

Time-Life is one just segment of American life in the era, but it reflected the power of a complex of institutions to inject new views into American life. Globalism of the sort they pitched was neither self-evident nor natural; it had to be cultivated. Collectively, these and other bodies extended a vision of the United States as irrevocably part of an interconnected world that was threatened by the geopolitical instability brought by economic crisis and the political transformation that followed in its wake. They appreciated that new sinew was binding the world together in new ways. Even as they grasped these new muscles to articulate and defend their own visions they understood that others might bend the same tissue to different ends.

Writers and Artists under the Shadow of the World Crisis

Alongside these new institutional promoters of liberal internationalism and the multimedia corporations like Time Inc., writers and artists also facilitated the turn of public attention from domestic problems to events beyond national borders. It is well known that the 1930s were an unusually politicized era for the creative classes. The economic crisis was so deep and prolonged that writers and artists, usually known for their individualism and aesthetic preoccupations, began exploring a range of social issues affecting their nation soon after the Wall Street crash of 1929. Around the middle of the decade, however, the character of their politicization began shifting. For one thing, after hitting the bottom in 1933, the economy began a slow and painful but nonetheless steady recovery. For another, the Washington-Versaille system came under increasingly open attack by Germany, Italy, and Japan in Europe, Africa, and Asia. The political passion of writers and artists did not diminish in the latter half of the Depression decade, but the sort of issues they addressed in their works had more and more to do with violent events oceans away and less and less with the economic hardship of fellow Americans.

Experts at liberal internationalist institutions tried to explain to the public and policymakers how prosperity and stability at home were contingent on a world system based on liberal norms. Their efforts were often concerned with technical questions of world trade, military strategy, and mass communications. By contrast, the deepening interest of writers and

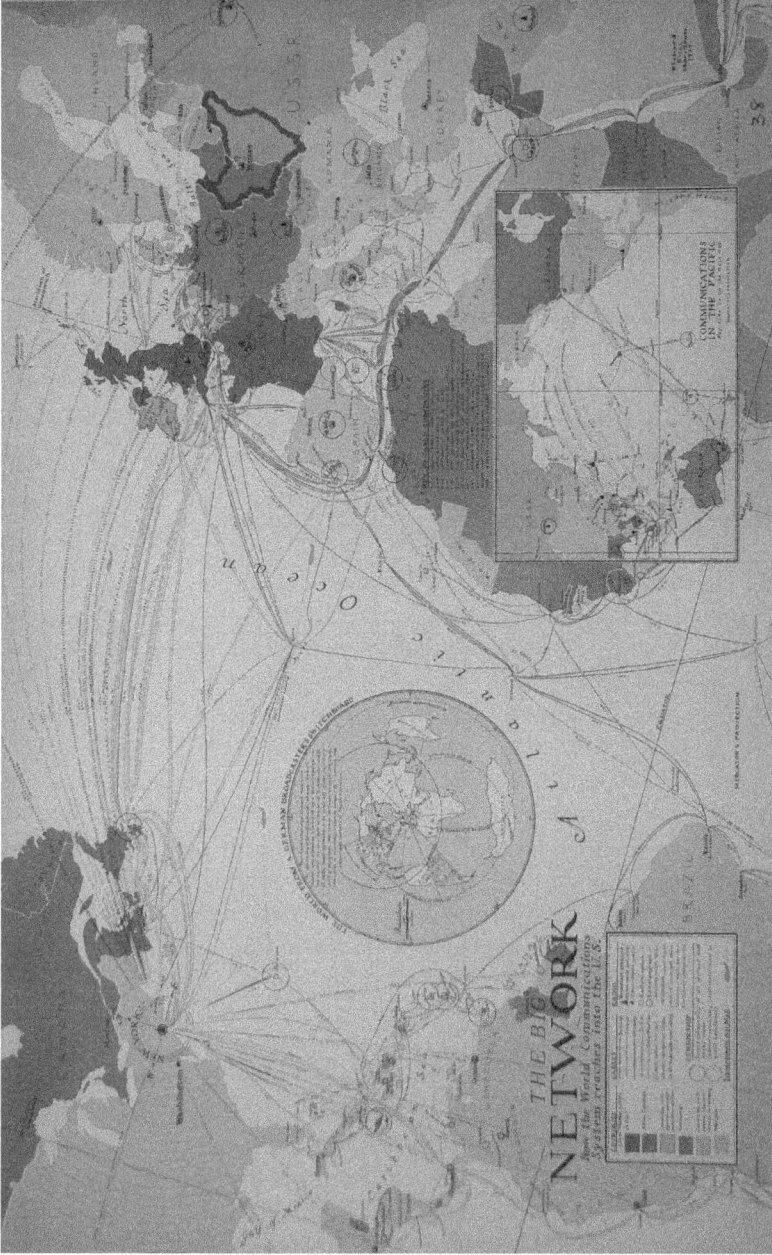

Figure 11.1 Richard Edes Harrison, "The Big Network: How the World Communications System Reaches into the U.S." (1939).

artists in world affairs was much more visceral. They specialized, after all, in the affairs of human hearts. Of all the emotional issues raised by the world crisis, they were particularly moved by two themes: heroism and civilian suffering in countries facing military aggression by undemocratic, illiberal powers and the fate of the American way of life in a world increasingly dominated by hostile ideologies. Another point of contrast between these freelancers and the globalists embedded in institutions and corporations concerned their respective attitudes toward propaganda. The latter group thought that mass susceptibility to verbal and visual manipulation was one of the most troubling weaknesses of a democratic society fighting for survival in the normless world, but nonetheless, they were willing to make a virtue of this weakness and propagandize openly for their globalist agendas. Writers and artists, on the other hand, were more ambivalent. Most of them experienced the First World War in their formative years. Almost all of them bought into Woodrow Wilson's one-world rhetoric. So the last war's illiberal consequences (the Red Scare, the Versailles Treaties) were all the more galling. Two decades later, now in their middle age, these same writers faced a twofold task of convincing themselves of the need to open up the American mind, again, to the rest of the world while taking up the weapon that once wounded them – propaganda.

As already noted, along the road to World War II, the United States passed by a number of crises: the Italo–Ethiopian War, the Spanish Civil War, the Japanese invasion of China, the Munich Crisis, and the outbreak of the European war in 1939. Each of these crises could have dragged the United States into a messy conflict against the aggressor nation, but the government and public opinion remained neutral. Writers and artists, however, reacted differently. They rushed to the rampart.

The war in Ethiopia galvanized black writers and intellectuals, while the white mainstream remained largely indifferent. African American writers did not consider the Italian invasion an attack on US interests or on a quickly crumbling liberal world order. On the contrary, they reacted as though their racial homeland was under attack by the liberal world order, whose seamy underside was imperialism and colonialism. Such a response is easy to understand, if one recalls the exploitative conditions under which the overwhelming majority of black "citizens" lived at that time. In Jim Crow America, 12 million descendants of slaves were deprived of democratic rights and responsibilities that were given automatically to white citizens. To them, the fascist soldiers besieging the last sovereign state in Africa looked like the white racists at home rather than some enemies of democracy, which was a mere abstraction as far as black people were

238   DAVID EKBLADH, ICHIRO TAKAYOSHI

concerned. To them, also, "the liberal world order" or "world peace" were just euphemisms for an agreement among white European powers, an honor among thieves, to facilitate each other in their domination of their dark-skinned subjects. Black writers and journalists, including George Schuyler, W. E. B. Du Bois, Langston Hughes, and Ralph Bunche, and young political activists like A. Philip Randolph shed few tears over these thieves finally having a falling out. The United States as well as its allies in Europe ignored Ethiopia's plea for intervention, and the war swiftly ended in Italian victory. But the war exposed how awkward it was for the United States to condemn "totalitarian" nations when their military might was directed against non-European countries. The world system that the United States claimed the "totalitarian" nations threatened clearly sanctioned colonialism and imperialism. And the Italo–Ethiopian War made it much harder for the United States to argue that it was in its national interest to preserve such a patently unjust world order. Toward the end of the decade, in the face of the escalating aggressiveness of the Axis powers, some black thinkers, notably Bunche, came to a more realistic view that the existing "liberal" world order, corrupt though it was, was still worth saving. But publicly, black writers and intellectuals did not let up their attack on liberal democracy's complicity in colonialism, so as to push their government to acknowledge publicly that preservation of colonialism would not be among its war aims in the next world war.[9] And by officially taking a stance against colonialism, the United States further undermined its commitment to the Jim Crow system at home, for the latter could be said to be a form of domestic colonialism. In short, it is to the black writers' agitation over the Italian conquest of Ethiopia that we can trace the origin of twinned movements that blacks would care most about in the 1940s and 1950s: the civil rights movement at home and decolonization abroad.

Even before the Ethiopian conflict concluded, a next war came to Spain. The Spanish Civil War occasioned a wide range of efforts – much wider than the war in Africa did – by writers and artists to alert their readers to the ominous signs of instability abroad.[10] Polls then taken show that the public was generally supportive of the Spanish Republic, but very few thought that the civil war in one of the least developed nations in Europe had any direct bearings on their country's survival. This was, however, not the case with writers and artists. To the politically engaged writers and artists, the Spanish Civil War was a proxy war: the Spanish republicans, with substantial support from the Soviet Union, were fighting America's enemies, Italy and Germany. A large contingent of authors, including Dorothy Parker, Lillian Hellman, John Doss Passos, Martha Gellhorn, and Upton

Sinclair, traveled to Spain to write about the war from the Republican point of view. Langston Hughes covered the war for the Baltimore *Afro-American*. Ernest Hemingway visited there three times during the conflict. His novel, *For Whom the Bell Tolls* (1941), an adventure tale about a heroic American guerrilla fighter, became a bestseller. Not content with cheerleading with words, some writers were eager to jump in the trenches. Among these writer-soldiers were Milton Wolff, Alvah Bessie, William Herrick, and Edwin Rolfe. Never before or since did the creative and intellectual classes side so unanimously and so viscerally with one party to a civil conflict in a foreign country, not even during the civil war in Vietnam. In part, the universal popularity of the Republican cause and the deeply felt hostility to Franco's rebel army among these authors were a testament to the effectiveness of the Soviet-led public diplomacy campaign, the Popular Front. By the middle of the decade, the Soviets had come to regard expansionist policies of Japan and Germany as the gravest threat to its existence. To draw Western nations like France, England, and the United States into an antifascist collective security scheme, the Communists and their allies in the West devised an argument: that these authoritarian nations were building up their militaries not only to destroy Russia but also to conquer the entire world. On this account, the civil war in Spain was a dress rehearsal for the coming battle between the fascist powers and the democratic nations (the Soviets tried hard to convince everyone that theirs was a democratic regime). As in Ethiopia, the world declined to intervene, and the Spanish Republic soon fell to General Franco's army. But writers' and artists' agitation on its behalf was not in vain. Their dramatic coverage of the heroism of antifascist soldiers and the suffering of civilians (the infamous bombing of Guernica took place in 1937) helped dispose the public decisively against the Axis powers while at the same time priming it for a potential alliance with the Communists in the coming world war.

Germany, Italy, or Japan instigates a new crisis in some corner of the world. Writers and artists scramble to ring the tocsin, often with some help from the various new institutions and multimedia corporations discussed earlier. This pattern repeated itself, until the next world war actually came to America in 1941 and finally forced the new globalism on the public, whether it liked it or not. Along the way, a great number of authors and artists, working with various expressive media, made sizeable contributions to the nation's conversion from isolationism to internationalism. Today, the astonishing variety and volume of these contributions are still only insufficiently appreciated. But the fullest understanding of some of the era's most important cultural events depends on doing just that. It was, for example, no coincidence that, when poet, former editor at Luce's *Fortune*, and later Librarian of Congress and a speechwriter for Roosevelt, Archibald MacLeish attempted to develop radio into a serious artistic medium with his two innovative radio dramas, *Fall of the City* (1937) and *Air Raid* (1938), he chose as their main theme an unnamed militaristic nation's invasion of a peace-loving but woefully unprepared country. The fact that MacLeish deployed a battery of new aesthetic techniques (as analyzed in Chapter 13) in his attempt to rouse the public and force it to look at the world measures the pervasiveness of such a concern in the most innovative and influential segments of the creative classes.[11] Moreover, this episode suggests that the artists' waxing interest in the world crisis was the most essential catalyst when radio finally came of age as a unique aesthetic medium.

Another good example of the cross-fueling between the artist's creativity and his interest in the US role in the world is found in Robert Sherwood, arguably the most talented playwright of the decade.[12] He won three Pulitzers in the 1930s: for *Idiot's Delight* (1936), *Abe Lincoln in Illinois* (1938), and *There Shall Be No Night* (1940). The first was written when Sherwood was a hard-bitten pacifist. It accurately prophesied the coming of a new Europe-wide war while cynically mocking the futility of political activism and idealism. The second was a period play staged in the aftermath of the Munich Crisis, which compelled Sherwood to convert to the new globalism. The play baldly drew an analogy between the coming world war and the American Civil War.[13] The third was written in response to the Soviet invasion of Finland. Featuring an American radio correspondent in Helsinki, the play argued for the inevitability of US intervention on behalf of European democracies. It is a clear indication of increasing public interest in events beyond borders that the busiest man on Broadway in the 1930s spent the decade being consumed by international themes. The fact that the Pulitzer committee, a reliable arbiter of middlebrow tastes and values, chose his three war plays in the five-year span implies that his political education, staring as a pacifist and converting to an expansive understanding of the US role in the world, mirrored exactly the political education of the nation as a whole. And most remarkably, Sherwood's career demonstrates the power of the new globalism to inspire artists and writers to the loftiest heights of creativity. Fittingly, Sherwood would receive his last and fourth Pulitzer in 1949 for his biography of Franklin Roosevelt and Harry Hopkins, two architects of the postwar global order.[14]

The press, radio, cartography, think tanks, and even Broadway contributed to the rise and spread of the new globalism. What about movies? After all, the 1930s were the golden age of Hollywood. Behind the absence of cinema from our story is a tangle of commercial and institutional conditions. Then as now, the studios did their business globally. They heavily invested in European studios and distributers; they held substantial stakes in their operations. They also regarded movies as export commodities. The ticket sales overseas accounted for large portions of their revenues. What all this meant to the moguls and caliphs of movieland was that movies dealing with controversial topics, such as the rise of authoritarianism across the globe, would hurt their bottom lines. Another complicating factor was the informal production code under which the industry put itself throughout the 1930s in order to avoid official censorship. Enforcers of this code were mainly concerned with stories and images injurious to public morals (sex, profanities, drugs, crimes), but they were at the same time sensitive to any offensive depictions of foreign nations. Under these circumstances, an adaptation of, say, Sherwood's *There Shall Be No Night*, which paints an almost diabolical picture of Germany and the USSR, would have been out of the question.

There were, all the same, some exceptions, all of which came out of Warner Bros., run by the vocally anti-Nazi Jewish brothers.[15] The most commercially successful in this genre was the blockbuster pro-intervention movie, *Sergeant York* (1941). Nominated for nine Oscars (Gary Cooper went on to win Best Actor), the movie was ostensibly about the battlefield exploits of its eponymous hero in the Great War. In this regard, it was designed as a run-of-the-mill shoot-'em-up war movie very much popular among the Depression-era theatregoers. However, the main drama of the movie was actually in York's vacillation between isolationism and the new globalism. The first half of the narrative pivots on York's religious and political transformation from a born-again hillbilly to a full-blooded patriot, a conversion experience that the studio carefully adapted to parallel the similar conversion that the spectators were undergoing in the late 1930s. The movie's emotional center, the conversion scene, depicts York sitting on the topmost crag of a mountain. Alvin York is searching his soul, torn between religious convictions against killing and love of country. Dressed in the olive drab uniform of the American doughboy, York sits alone, and in his hands he holds a leather-backed Bible and a history of the United States. York's gaze appears to turn inward, as if he is listening hard to some faint inner voices, which begin to reverberate louder and louder into the scene. The audience, along with York, overhears two distinct voices: one repeating "Obey your God" and the other "Obey your country." The close-up shot shows the face of York, distraught with these warring commands that alternate each other as they reach a maddening crescendo: "god, country, God, Country, GOD, COUNTRY ... " Then, a providential morning breeze ruffles the pages of the Bible, and his eyes drop to the page that shows Jesus's message: "Give to Caesar the things that are Caesar's, and to God the things that are God's" (Matt. 22:21). Slowly, the tortured look of indecision in York's face changes to one of firm resolve.

The theme of political conversion was topical, and it touched a raw nerve across the nation. Millions of Americans watched this movie, making it the highest grossing movie of the year. A series of carefully orchestrated publicity events in Washington, DC drew political, diplomatic, and military dignitaries, including President Roosevelt, to a special screening of the movie. An ecstatic Norman Vincent Peale gushed to Jack Warner: *Sergeant York* "will render service to our country in this crisis for it gives a sensible solution to a problem facing many young men – that is the problem of war. In fact, this picture may actually help to save this country. It will show to them that there is something worth giving everything for, namely, liberty and freedom."[16] Although the studio executives and writers prioritized box-office results over propagandizing, they exploited the topical potential of the material to the full. The "picture is crying out to be made right now," one writer wrote in an internal memo, because York represented "the prototype of the Average American," a "'Mr. Deeds Goes to War', a universal type of American boy." York "is still the ideal of American types," and "the lesson learned by York in the last war should be clear to us who are viewing the second world war."[17]

If the feature films were beginning to wrestle with the world, so were the shorts and newsreels. While Luce's favor toward Chiang Kai-shek's (or Jiang Jeshi) China against the predations of Japan was well established by the end of the 1930s, various figures at Time-Life, including Buell and Luce, were increasingly concerned by the specter of a totalitarian Germany. *The March of Time* made these plain with the pointed short documentary *Inside Nazi Germany* (1938). Through the urgent narration of Westbrook Van Voorhis and dramatic imagery the film showed Germany to be the embodiment of the dangers of the period. State power, loosed on a population, had produced a fearfully regimented society bent on expansion. This was all facilitated by the regime's all-encompassing and adroit use of propaganda (itself a popular topic and touchstone in numerous *March of Time* newsreels of the period) that seeped into every part of life. The image of the new Germany that resulted was an anti-liberal nightmare, a dangerous enemy on the leading edge of the global rise of fascism that by its nature threatened world peace and stability. Part of that threat was the fact that its ideas were spreading to the United States. In the film, the German American Bund was held up as a vessel of transmission of these alien ideas. In a key scene, the Bund's attempt to purchase land in Connecticut for its own questionable uses is stymied by a classic set piece of American democracy: dissenting views offered by seemingly average Americans at an archetypal New England town meeting. The comparison of this idealized form of participatory democracy with the regimentation and subordination to state power was understated but obvious.

Ironically, some of the evocative scenes of *Inside Nazi Germany* were filmed in Hoboken, New Jersey with anti-Nazi volunteers.[18] They were filling gaps in the visual record of course, but these only remind that no matter how accurate the documentary was about conditions in Germany, it was a construction, and, with its emphasis on the difference between statist Germany and the democratic (emphasis on the small "d") United States, it was also its own form of propaganda. Whether it was on movie screens, the airwaves, the printed page or elsewhere, various globalist forces injected their own propaganda into society so as to direct the American mind to the problems abroad.

Conclusion

The pluralistic and interconnected United States did not suddenly discover the world in the 1930s. Seeing itself as part of the world was nothing new to what some have called the "Global Republic." But all the same, the prolonged crisis that cut across so many sectors of domestic and international life rearranged conceptions and perceptions in the American mind, a rearrangement that led to a coherent globalist posture by the end of the decade. Because we are today so accustomed to this new globalism, it is important to remember that it was revealed only in increments, and seemingly irrevocable revelations were often followed by setbacks. That is to say, the road to the new consensus view of the United States as the active and assertive leader of the emerging world order was tortuous, full of twists and turns. No participant had an exact blueprint and managed to convince the nation to realize it. That was in the main a tribute to a national characteristic Americans learned to be proud of in the 1930s, namely, the nation's pluralism. The debates occurred across the diverse scholars, writers, and opinion leaders often clumsily referred to as the "epistemic community" of the United States, and this community was never monolithic. A diverse elite and even more diverse public saw their relationship with the world differently and this stoked both anxieties and responses that were qualitatively different from what had come before.

The need to confront a world disjointed by both the Depression and ideological movements spurred various groups to action. They pushed new readings of the world situation into public life with the array of technologies that had only recently appeared. At the same time, these new forms raised the questions about how US society could be influenced by outside ideas and propaganda. It forced those with their own views of how the United States should adapt to and contend with global problems to facilitate public understanding of these issues with what could rightly be called propaganda of their own.

Notes

1. Malcolm Cowley, "A Farewell to the 1930s," *The New Republic*, November 8, 1939, 42, 43.
2. D. W. Meinig, *The Shaping of America, volume 4, Global America, 1915–2000* (New Haven, CT: Yale University Press, 2004), 325–28.
3. Erik Barnouw, *A Tower in Babel: A History of Broad Casting in the United States*, vol. 1 (New York: Oxford University Press, 1966); David Holbrook Culbert, *News for Everyman: Radio and Foreign Affairs in Thirties America* (Westport, CT: Greenwood Press, 1976), 76. For the birth of radio foreign news, see also Gerd Horten, *Radio Goes to War: The Cultural Politics of Propaganda during World War II* (Berkeley: University of California Press, 2003); David Goodman, *Radio's Civic Ambition: American Broadcasting and Democracy in the 1930s* (New York: Oxford University Press, 2011); *Radio's America: The Great Depression and the Rise of Modern Mass Culture* (Chicago: University of Chicago Press, 2007).
4. "Report to the Rockefeller Foundation on the Program of Popular Education of the Foreign Policy Association for the Year 1938," RG 1.1, Box 336, Rockefeller Foundation Archives, Rockefeller Archive Center, North Tarrytown, New York.
5. Edward L. Bernays, *Propaganda* (New York: H Liveright, 1928).
6. Hadley Cantril, H. G. Wells, Howard Koch, Hazel Gaudet, and Herta Herzog, *The Invasion from Mars: A Study in the Psychology of Panic* (Princeton, NJ: Princeton University Press, 1940).
7. Alan Brinkley, *The Publisher: Henry Luce and His American Century* (New York: Alfred A. Knopf, 2010), 180–84.
8. Susan Schulten, *The Geographical Imagination in America, 1880–1950* (Chicago: University of Chicago Press, 2001).
9. Harvard Sitkoff, *A New Deal for Blacks: The Emergence of Civil Rights as a National Issue: The Depression Decade* (New York: Oxford University Press, 2009), 202.

10. The best treatment of this episode is Allen Guttmann, *The Wound in the Heart: America and the Spanish Civil War* (New York: Free Press, 1962).

11. See Chapter 13 in the present volume.

12. See Chapter 17 in the present volume.

13. See Ichiro Takayoshi, *American Writers and the Approach of World War II: A Literary History* (New York: Cambridge University Press, 2015), chapter 4.

14. See Sherwood, *Roosevelt and Hopkins: An Intimate History* (New York: Harper, 1950).

15. On the anti-Nazi campaign by the Warner brothers, see Michael E. Birdwell, *Celluloid Soldiers: The Warner Bros. Campaign against Nazism* (New York: New York University Press, 2000). For a broader treatment, see David Welky, *The Moguls and the Dictators: Hollywood and the Coming of World War II* (Baltimore, MD: Johns Hopkins University Press, 2008).

16. Letter, Norman Vincent Peale, July 2, 1941, to Jack Warner, "Sergeant York" Story-Memos & Correspondence, 1/4. Folder #1712. The Warner Bros. Archives. University of Southern California.

17. Interoffice memo, from Bob Buckner to Hall Wallis, June 4, 1940; interoffice memo, from Warren Duff to Hall Wallis, June 4, 1940. Warner Bros. Archives. University of Southern California.

18. Neil Genzlinger, "Time Marches … Backward!" *New York Times*, September 2, 2010.

PART II

Formats

CHAPTER 12

Bestsellers

David Welky

"Only the cynic and the heedless can disregard popular literature," historian Frank Luther Mott once wrote.[1] Judging by Mott's standards, most historians – with a handful of notable exceptions – are either cynical or heedless, or perhaps both.[2] A kind of circular thinking discourages academic forays into the world of bestsellers. Popular literature isn't a serious art worthy of study because it is popular, the argument goes. If it were truly art, it wouldn't be popular. Such intellectual elitism reflects a persistent bias toward the new, the strange, and the unusual, and away from the mundane, the everyday, and the common. Rather than illuminate the world of ordinary Americans, historians elevate the enduring cultural monuments of an age – the literary masterpieces – no matter how little impact they had on the society that produced them.

Decades of slanted scholarship have skewed our understandings of the print culture of the Great Depression. Most students of this period focus on either "good" fiction, meaning books that are recognized as classics, or on "proletarian literature," a genre of radical fiction that celebrated downtrodden workers' struggles against an oppressive, capitalist status quo. Both fields can yield intellectual treasures. There is no inherent reason for ignoring such landmark novels as William Faulkner's *Absalom! Absalom!* (1936) or John Dos Passos's *U. S. A.* trilogy (1930–36), or a gripping piece of proletarian fiction like Robert Cantwell's *Land of Plenty* (1934). Yet it is important to remember that, as author Louis Adamic observed in 1934, "only a few real proletarians" have "read or heard of one or more of the several recent proletarian novels." Historians seeking to grasp the culture of the Depression decade must study the books that *everyone* was reading, not just the literary elite. This demands a serious treatment of bestsellers, even such forgotten hits as Bess Streeter Aldrich's *A White Bird Flying* (1931), Caroline Miller's *Lamb in His Bosom* (1934), and A. J. Cronin's *The Citadel* (1937).[3]

Intellectuals' disregard for bestselling novels pervaded the 1930s just as much as it does our own time. One Depression-era critic warned readers to avoid "the deserts of the printed word," meaning popular novels, in favor of "the fruitful plains and valleys of literature." Traditionalists within the publishing industry feared that the rush to find the next bestseller was transforming a distinguished profession into "a business similar to that of selling washing-machines or motor cars." Bestsellers, according to this argument, squeezed serious literature out of the market and dumbed down society to the point that slack-jawed readers snapped up any book "that is sufficiently and sufficiently startlingly advertised in the papers." Overhyped bestsellers sapped the dignity from a noble art at the very moment when the worldwide economic meltdown imperiled the dignity of millions of desperate people. "Books are not vaudeville shows," an anonymous correspondent complained to *Publishers' Weekly*.[4]

Highbrow literature – the kind of works these doubters craved – offered important critiques of contemporary society. They often reflected cutting-edge philosophical, economic, and sociopolitical trends. But they are not the focus here. Instead, my goal is to create a sort of composite Depression-era bestseller by highlighting some themes that pervaded the most popular novels of the 1930s.[5]

Bestselling novels make excellent subjects because, as Peter Swirski has argued, "popular literature expresses and reflects the aesthetic and social values of its readers." The vast majority of books draw their readership from a small segment of society. They appeal to a certain age group or gender, or to people with a particular background or set of interests (elderly women rarely read books whose protagonists are young boys, and few lovers of spy novels read many romance novels). In contrast, bestsellers transcend the usual boundaries of readership, drawing their audiences from a range of demographic subdivisions. Elizabeth Long claims that they act as "a social rather than a literary phenomenon," because they suggest broad areas of agreement within a diverse mass audience.[6]

Trying to determine exactly who read bestsellers is a futile venture. Not even publishers really knew who their customers were. But a few general observations are possible. "We find that books … are not enjoyed by the majority of people," Indiana State Teachers College researcher C. T. Malan reported in 1937. "Most homes have scarcely any books at all." Although Depression-era Americans were readers, relatively few of them were *book* readers. *Publishers' Weekly* was probably right when it said that "in general … books are read by the middle classes – students, teachers, housewives in modest circumstances, professional people, white-collar workers." Copies of new fiction typically sold for about three dollars apiece, nearly a full day's wages for industrial workers and far beyond the reach of the unemployed millions. Moreover, with only about 5,000 bookstores servicing a nation of 130 million people, and only about 500 of those stocking significant quantities of new fiction, large swaths of small-town and rural America had limited contact with the latest titles. Further, industry estimates suggested that 45 million Americans, most of them in rural areas, had no access to libraries.[7]

Skeptics groused that readers desired one-dimensional tales "where the mighty fall and the lowly are lifted up; where all the women crackle with sex-appeal, and all the men manage to combine the attractions of the cave-dweller with those of the perfect English gentleman." Depression-era bestsellers actually offered their predominantly urban, middle-class audiences an intriguing mix of themes. Pre-Depression bestsellers, including Zane Grey's *The Call of the Canyon* (1924), Gene Stratton-Porter's *The Keeper of the Bees* (1925), and Harold Bell Wright's *The Mine with the Iron Door* (1923), exuded optimism and affirmed the doctrine of success through hard work, clean living, and fair play. In contrast, their 1930s counterparts exhibited three main traits. On the whole, they adopted a somber tone that shaded into a grim pessimism appropriate for an era when optimism seemed misguided. These novels also featured brutal struggles for survival against forces beyond ordinary people's control – the same kinds of unknowable forces that produced the Depression. Finally, authors won over audiences with characters who rejected the modern world in favor of exotic locations, or who embarked on personal journeys of the mind that isolated them from outside troubles.[8]

This chapter describes general trends within Depression-era bestsellers rather forcing every popular title into a grand literary design. "Who can apply a formula to public taste with any degree of success," editor and columnist Herschel Brickell asked in 1932, "or who, having such a formula, can find a book to fit it?" Individual titles exist outside of the trends listed here. Those exceptions are welcome anomalies that provide reassurance that writing a bestseller is about more than connecting dots.[9]

Bestsellers balanced hope with hopelessness, success with failure, and realism with escapism, often within the same set of covers. Such competing impulses might appear contradictory, but no society can ever articulate an entirely consistent cultural universe, particularly in a nation as large and diverse as the United States. The Depression-era Americans who turned both "Brother, Can You Spare a Dime" and "Happy Days Are Here Again" into hits were perfectly capable of reconciling opposing perspectives into a single worldview that merged a bleak awareness of hard times with a persistent faith that the individual might find better days in some better place.

***

"What if anything does literature show to be the prevailing time current of the thirties?" Book-of-the-Month Club judge Henry Seidel Canby asked in 1937. "I believe it to be fear ... This fear," he continued, "ranges from skeptical inquiry into the possible disintegration of culture as we have known it to the deep pessimism of convinced alarm." Rather than offer cheerful assurances that everything was going to be alright, popular Depression-era novelists painted vivid problems while sketching only vague solutions. Their work conveyed a gloomy perspective that both reflected and reinforced their middle-class readership's fears for themselves and their country. It was a literature of rejection that criticized materialism, authority, and modern life. It accentuated the negative and exuded pessimism about the future.[10]

The windswept central plains of Steinbeck's bestselling *The Grapes of Wrath* (1939) provide the most obvious example of this bleak outlook. Ellen Glasgow's *Vein of Iron* (1935) offers a lesser-known counterpart. Glasgow follows Ada Fincastle and her husband, Ralph, from their halcyon years in a sleepy town in Virginia's James River Valley to their turbulent life in the hustling fictional city of Queensborough. The Fincastles enjoy a relatively comfortable existence until the 1929 Stock Market Crash eviscerates the local economy. They lose their jobs, then lose their life's savings when the Queensborough Central and Savings Bank shuts down. "I'm thirty-eight," Ada laments, "and I feel as if I were fifty." Soup kitchens pop up around town. Homeless people wander the streets. Ada's neighbors commit suicide. "Wherever you looked, there was something waiting to destroy happiness," she says.[11]

Depression-era bestsellers showed that hard times could appear anywhere, at any time. Pearl Buck's *The Good Earth*, the bestselling novel of both 1931 and 1932, transplants American-style poverty to early twentieth-century China, where Wang Lung and his wife, O-Lan, fight to keep themselves and their four children alive during a famine. Exiled from their farm by drought, they scratch out a living in a soulless city. Wang Lung exhausts himself working long days as a rickshaw driver yet earns so little that he survives on rice gruel ladled out at public kitchens. O-Lan begs for coppers on the street. The children steal food.

Widespread poverty, mass starvation, social disorder – the problems of both the literary world and the real world seemed too big to conquer. It is notable that the Great Depression never produced anything like Edward

Bellamy's 1888 blockbuster utopian novel *Looking Backward*. Appearing at another time of economic upheaval, *Looking Backward* enticed followers with an upbeat vision of a future when Americans have replaced cutthroat capitalism with a humane brand of socialism. No 1930s bestsellers articulated a similarly comprehensive prescription for America's problems. Instead, they flailed at an array of targets, including materialism, the wealthy, and the powerful.

American antiauthoritarianism stretches back to Thomas Jefferson, the Boston Tea Party, and the Pilgrims, but it assumed particular relevance during the Great Depression. The pre-Depression decade of the 1920s was one of those rare moments when Americans viewed materialism and big business as signs of all that was right with their country. Former-adman-turned-author Bruce Barton even repackaged Jesus Christ into a pre-corporate, evangelical businessman in the surprise hit *The Man Nobody Knows* (1925). With businessmen taking credit for that decade's economic boom, and President Calvin Coolidge assuring voters that "the chief business of the American people is business," it is no wonder that many Americans assumed their interests and corporate interests were one and the same.

That changed with the Crash and the subsequent economic meltdown. Businessmen suddenly became the villains. Hollywood condemned them in such films as *The Match King* (1932) and *Stagecoach* (1939). The US Senate exposed them as greedy frauds during the 1932 Pecora Committee hearings. In reviling wealth and power, then, successful Depression-era novelists rejected the recent past in favor of a nihilistic-leaning worldview in which no one could be trusted, and in which striving for wealth was both pointless and destructive. Readers could therefore reassure themselves that their own monetary uncertainties did not result from personal failure. If anything, economic woes symbolized their refusal to participate in a corrupt system.

One of the most vivid literary denunciations of materialism came in the final scene of Bess Streeter Aldrich's *A White Bird Flying* (1931), a novel about a pure-hearted, small-town Nebraska girl named Laura Deal. Laura's eccentric aunt and uncle offer her a vast fortune if she agrees to move to New York and become their caretaker. She accepts their offer, then reverses herself, staying in Nebraska so she can get married. The snub outrages her relatives, who bequeath her a single silver dollar when they pass away several years later (and this with the Deal family farm on the verge of bankruptcy).

Laura, by then a mother of four, feels no disappointment. "Money does something to people," she says. "It weakens something inside them." She leads her children into a field with the dollar in her pocket. Hurling the coin with all her strength, she tells the kids to show her the most valuable thing they can find. One points at a cottonwood tree, another at a meadowlark, and a third at their infant sibling. "You were *all* right," Laura announces as they walk home, literally penniless. "Though the sun shone on [the coin] and the rain fell," Aldrich closes, "nothing ever came from it – *not a green thing nor a singing thing nor a human soul.*"[12]

This anti-materialistic spirit also manifested itself in a literary hatred of the rich. The well-to-do have made convenient villains throughout the history of American culture, but the context of the Depression gave these depictions a particularly sharp edge during the 1930s. Even the few sympathetic treatments of wealthy characters in that decade's bestsellers include disclaimers explaining why it is acceptable for readers to like them. For example, the Duc de Praslin from Rachel Field's *All This, and Heaven Too* (1938) merits a positive portrayal because, as Field explains, even though he comes from one of France's oldest noble families, he has no personal fortune. He would rather spend time with his children than count money, which makes him feel "flat." The family's wealth actually comes from his "deranged" wife, the paranoid and spiteful Duchesse.[13]

Sons (1932), Pearl Buck's bestselling sequel to *The Good Earth*, also used the wealthy as foils. The book follows Wang Lung's children through – no surprise here – a time of economic deprivation and social upheaval. The youngest, Wang the Tiger, fights in the civil wars wracking China. The middle child, Wang the Merchant, becomes a businessman, and the eldest, Wang the Landlord, a powerful landowner. Wang the Landlord is a "great fat weak man" who exploits his peasants and revels in lazy indolence. Wang the Merchant, a cold and crafty schemer, helps him pry pennies from his tenants. The two oldest Wangs even exploit a famine by re-selling grain to the farmers who raised it, at exorbitant markups. In contrast, Wang the Tiger becomes a military hero who pays his gallant troops with silver taken from undeserving tycoons.[14]

Hervey Allen's *Anthony Adverse* (1933) brought its title character into contact with several despicable rich people. *Adverse* was one of the decade's biggest books, whether measured by sales (which topped half a million hardback copies, making it the bestselling novel of both 1933 and 1934) or size (movie mogul Jack Warner once remarked, "Read it? I can't even lift it"). Anthony, a nineteenth-century orphan who spends 1,200 pages in a worldwide search for stability and personal enlightenment, learns that the affluent class follows "the fixed star of self-interest" and lacks "any social conscience whatever." Napoleonic Europe is ruled by "international pluto-crats" who manipulate stock markets in the ruthless pursuit of profits. "The chief curses to the bodies and spirits of men," Anthony concludes, come from "too great abundance."[15]

Bestselling authors compounded the literary spirit of rejection by present-ing cities, the focal points of modern America and home of the hated moguls, as corrupt, immoral places. It is in the city that *The Good Earth*'s Wang Lung, emotionally broken by grinding poverty, succumbs to a life of gambling and whoring. In *Exile* (1930), English-born Barbara Brown denounces her native London as "incredibly ugly." Boston-bred Oliver Alden, the protagonist in George Santayana's *The Last Puritan* (1936), exchanges the dehumanization inherent to the city for the "wider, more unkempt" world of the sea.[16]

Such anti-urbanism comprises one part of the bestseller's general denuncia-tion of modernity. That these novels deplored the city is especially notable considering that most of their readers were themselves urbanites. This anti-modern ethos fits into a broader Depression-era fascination with a glamorized version of rural life that took shape in the New Deal's Civilian Conservation Corps, which put unemployed young men from the cities to work in the countryside, and the Resettlement Administration, which established green-belt communities outside of disintegrating cities. Anti-modern novels also coincided with a renewed interest in rural folk music, and with the cornpone Andy Hardy movies, which cast young Mickey Rooney as the embodiment of old-fashioned, small-town values. In propagating a literature of rejection, then, bestselling novels invigorated a broader cultural backlash against the perceived sleaze, decay, and ruthlessness of contemporary America.

***

"She telescopes all that we have watched and thought about and feared as the social fabric of our age has crumbled before our eyes," *New York Times Book Review* columnist J. Donald Adams wrote after reading Ellen Glasgow's *Vein of Iron*, "and her only answer to our perplexities is for-titude." Indeed, the magnitude of the Depression closed off most narrative paths for novelists seeking a way out of the grim literary conditions they had created. Considering the dismal climate outside the bookstore, literary assertions of miraculous turnarounds or cloyingly happy endings would ring false for audiences attuned to realism.[17]

Americans had long imbibed from a stream of "luck-and-pluck" writings that promised success and security for anyone who worked hard and maintained their integrity. Benjamin Franklin's *Autobiography* (1791) established the genre by showing how a determined young rake who arrived in Philadelphia with a dollar in his pocket transformed himself into a respectable man through individual effort and clean living. A century later, Horatio Alger's famous series of young adult novels, exemplified by 1868's *Ragged Dick*, updated Franklin's formula for the industrial age.

Bestselling Depression-era novelists upended this tradition, to an extent. It is striking how often hard work proves futile in their works. Characters in bestselling Depression-era novels usually rose or fell not according to anything they did, but rather because of impersonal forces beyond their control. The overall effect is one of drift, of characters who can only hope that the fates will turn benevolent. This sense of helplessness meshed well with literary presentations of impersonal cities as the grim locus of modern life and a remote, moneyed elite as the dominant mover of society. As reviewer Dorothy Van Doren said of *Shadows on the Rock*, Willa Cather's 1931 smash about colonial-era Quebec, literary characters who try "to shape their destinies in the end are shaped by them."[18]

This sense of helplessness matched reality beyond the printed page. Despite President Franklin Roosevelt's assurances that his administration's "bold, persistent experimentation" would lift the nation out of crisis, no one could really explain why the economy had crashed, or why jobs and wages were being cut, or why enormous dust storms suddenly started tearing through the Great Plains. And no one knew when the horrors would end. With so many unanswerable questions, people felt blown about on the fickle winds of fate, or, as author Rachel Field noted when her female lead, Henriette Desportes, got swept up by scandal in *All This, and Heaven Too* (1938), "caught fast in an intricate web not of [their] own making."[19]

Consider, for example, *The Grapes of Wrath*. No one could accuse the Joad family of slacking off, yet their backbreaking efforts get them nowhere. There is always something larger, something almost intangible, working against them. John Steinbeck's symbolic celebrations of man's indomitable will to survive, whether in the famous "turtle-crossing-the-road" metaphor, or in the final scene, in which Rosasharn offers a starving man her milk-laden breast, can't conceal the blunt fact that the book ends with the Joad family disintegrating and unsure of where their next meal is coming from. The struggle will continue, but the starving man will die. The Joads will not find the promised land in California. They have plenty of pluck, but no luck, and hard work isn't enough anymore.

Fate, or dumb luck, occasionally worked to one's benefit. *The Good Earth*'s Wang Lung finds gold and jewels in an abandoned house.

Dr. Andrew Manson of *The Citadel* goes to medical school because of a scholarship benefiting students with "the baptismal name of Andrew." Fate delivers the peripatetic Anthony Adverse several lucky breaks, including an accidental apprenticeship to a merchant who turns out to be his grandfather and his rediscovery of friends and benefactors in unexpected places around the world. Even so, a humble Anthony realizes that he cannot "expect to direct, control, or even understand" his own life.[20]

More often, impersonal forces do serious harm, enhancing the sense that we all live at the whim of powers beyond our command. "The bank is something more than men," an agent explains to baffled farmers on the verge of foreclosure in *The Grapes of Wrath*. "It's the monster. Men made it, but they can't control it."[21]

Perhaps the darkest take on the arbitrary nature of existence is George Santayana's unlikely bestseller *The Last Puritan* (1936). Its protagonist, Oliver Alden, the scion of a wealthy New England family, never recovers from an early dose of hardline Calvinism that teaches him that there is "no reasonableness in rebelling" against fate. Training himself to do what is expected of him, he plays football, goes to college, and settles into a career not because he wants to, but rather because it is his duty. According to Oliver, the world is "a blind current that sweeps us on" without telling us "for how long or to what issue." He knew he was not living the life he wanted, but saw no way of escaping the accident of his birth and the impersonal forces guiding him. Ultimately, those forces carry him to the battlefields of World War I, where he meets his death in a senseless car wreck a few days after the Armistice.[22]

Nature, the epitome of irrepressible forces, played an interesting role in these novels. During the early 1930s, the weather is, if not exactly benevolent ("heaven has ordained that this year we shall starve," the peasants of 1932's *The Good Earth* lament after locusts devour their crops), at least reasonably friendly. Some early 1930s novels include loving descriptions of landscapes and scenery, whether it be the rugged splendor of territorial Oklahoma in *Cimarron* (the top seller of 1930), the lush Italian coast in *Exile*, or the awe-inspiring beauty of Shut-In Valley (overlooked by God's Mountain) in *Vein of Iron*.[23]

Authors reimagined nature as a cruel force by the late 1930s, making it one of the few elements of Depression literature that markedly evolved over the decade. This transition made sense considering what was happening in the real world. Middle America became a giant Dust Bowl. In 1937, an flood of unprecedented magnitude ravaged the Ohio and Mississippi

Valleys. With the Depression persisting without respite, nature became just one more sinister influence.

The Grapes of Wrath provides the most obvious example of this new emphasis on nature's malign whims. Hardworking though they may be, the Joad family is devastated when a drought transforms their fertile land into a "thin hard crust" capable of supporting only "weed colonies."[24]

Marjorie Kinnan Rawlings's *The Yearling* (1938) struck a similar chord. The story follows the Baxters, a family of hardworking farmers living in the backwoods of Florida. It centers on a boy named Jody who bonds with a deer he calls Flag. The Baxters do everything right only to have their crops ruined by bad weather. Determined to succeed, they plant a new crop. Flag eats it. As if that weren't enough, a cagey bear named Old Slewfoot devours the Baxters' cattle. Jody replants again, and again Flag eats all the corn. At his mother's behest, Jody shoots Flag to save his family and himself. Despite their sacrifice and toil, the Baxters are no better off than they were a year earlier. They will never escape their miserable plot of scrub-country land.

Much of the first half of *Northwest Passage* (1937) a story of the eighteenth-century French and Indian War, tracks a group of colonial rangers slogging through the "barren and miserable" wilderness after a successful raid on St. Francis, a French-occupied Canadian village. Nature exists to punish the brave soldiers. It provided them with little game or fresh water. It pummels them with frigid gales and driving rains. The brutal environment reduces the men to "draggled, hairy, feeble raccoons," more animal than human. Such is the fate of those who struggle against the elements.

***

Another defining theme of Depression-era bestsellers is that they often provided escapism wrapped in the grab of realism. Readers gravitated toward books that explained their present situation while at the same time distracting them from that situation. It is "a novel of escape, a book that carries us into a temporary world," reviewer Malcolm Cowley said of Charles Morgan's *The Fountain* (1932), a bestseller about a British POW who seeks a quiet life as a writer during World War I. And yet, added Percy Hutchinson in his *New York Times Book Review* feature on the book, Morgan "is not out of touch with the realities of daily living." "Escapism" is as good a word for this phenomenon as any, so long as we remember that people escape *from* somewhere *to* somewhere else. During hard times, readers escaped from the Depression into exotic eras or locations such as China (*The Good Earth* and *Sons*), ancient Greece (*The Woman of Andros*), and rural Maine (*Lamb in His Bosom*), or into narratives where characters isolated themselves from external events in order to search for inner peace and self-satisfaction during troubled times.[25]

Characters in bestselling novels generally experienced cataclysmic events from a physical or psychological distance, thereby separating themselves from the disruptions of the outside world. *All This, and Heaven Too* dismisses the American Civil War in fewer than ten pages, *Lamb in His Bosom* in six. *The Fountain*'s Lewis Alison actually enjoys his captivity because the "slow, empty routine" of prison life allows him time to pursue his literary goals. In *Sons*, an innkeeper, the type of person who should be up on current events, does not know that the emperor's throne is vacant, or that armies are fighting to determine who will occupy it.[26]

Feelings of detachment were common. "I am like a piano," Henriette Desportes says in *All This, and Heaven Too*. "A piano in a closed house. There it stands, capable of music, but doomed to silence because no one touches the keys." Similarly, Laura Deal (*A White Bird Flying*) is "withdrawn from the world. She lived with people, but was not one of them." In *The Woman of Andros*, the philosophical Chrysis feels the pain of her "remote" existence.[27]

Appearing as they did during the mildly social-democratic New Deal, one might expect these isolated characters to immerse themselves within larger causes or communities. That this occurred only rarely reinforced the bestseller's pervasive escapism from society and modern life. *Grapes of Wrath* is an exception, as becomes clear when Jim Casy explains that "a fella ain't got a soul of his own, but on'y a piece of a big one." Another, lesser-known example is Lloyd Douglas's *Green Light* (1934). Through the character of George Harcourt, the Episcopal dean of Trinity Cathedral and a stand-in for Douglas, himself a minister, the book urges readers to recognize themselves as "component parts of *an era* ..., all trudging along, elbow to elbow, in an endless, tightly integrated procession, in which [their] most important interests are held in common."[28]

Yet these calls for community feel incomplete and a bit haphazard. Steinbeck never shows his proposed community of the downtrodden in effect, nor does he provide clear examples of collective action producing meaningful social change. Douglas's communitarian ethos revolves entirely around the charismatic Dean Harcourt, who, like Franklin Roosevelt, was paralyzed from the waist down after being stricken with polio as an adult. "Emergencies have always been necessary to men's evolution," Harcourt assures his flock. If they stand tall in the face of their troubles, destiny will eventually flash a "GREEN LIGHT" so that progress may continue. As inspirational as it is vague and contradictory,

Douglas's novel promotes a gently communitarian message even as it concludes that each individual possesses the capacity to find a path toward happiness and contentment.[29]

More than anything else, it is this search for solid roots, for stability, for a home – however each author defined those things – that motivated the bestsellers of the 1930s. Certainty, permanence, and basic intellectual or physical comfort became a literary Holy Trinity during the Depression. In an era of social, cultural, political, and economic upheaval, this was the most escapist fantasy of all – that individuals can find a safe, secure space where they can isolate themselves from the problems of the world.

Lloyd Douglas promoted this goal, as did John Steinbeck, whose Joad family wants nothing more than a small house with a picket fence in California. Lewis Alison looks for inner security in *The Fountain*. So does Henriette Desportes in *All This, and Heaven Too*. The rangers of *Northwest Passage* spend most of the book battling obstacles to get home. Wang Lung would have understood their quest. "Land is one's flesh and blood," he declares in *The Good Earth*. It represents something solid and eternal. Even after he lucks into a fortune, his farm is the only place where he can find true contentment and happiness. It is home.[30]

In the words of Anthony Adverse, escaping a poisoned society and finding individual security requires subordinating "the physical world and the body . . . to the higher values discernable to the heart, the intellect, and the spirit of man." After spending 1,200 pages making and losing fortunes everywhere from Napoleonic France to colonial New Mexico, and at various times embracing capitalism, asceticism, mysticism, Catholicism, and rationalism, Anthony finds peace in the remote village of La Luz ("The Light"), where he rejects materialism, ministers to the poor, and frees himself from striving for social gain or worrying about the future. Like Wang Lung, his search is over, and he is home.[31]

Although their subjects range over centuries and continents, the best-sellers of the 1930s share several thematic elements. They explore the gritty realities of societies on the edge of collapse, reject wealth and power, and avoid offering systemic solutions to crushing problems. They suggest small-scale, personal paths to individual happiness while simultaneously expressing doubts that that brighter future will ever materialize. Rather than remake the world, the best we can hope for is to escape desperate situations by paring back our goals and pursing the modest goal of self-enlightenment. In a time that practically begged for dramatic shifts in direction, middle-class readers found comfort in novels that delivered order out of chaos by reasserting traditional American values such as antiauthoritarianism and individualism.

***

There is an 800-pound, Confederate-gray gorilla stomping around our library of Depression-era bestsellers. Released in the summer of 1936, Margaret Mitchell's *Gone with the Wind* tore across the United States like no novel before it. It sold a million copies by Christmas, more than tripling the total that *Anthony Adverse* racked up in its first six months. It was the bestselling novel of both 1936 and 1937, becoming a cultural touchstone that everyone seemed to have read at least once. Critics loved it. In her *Washington Post* review, Pulitzer Prize winner Julia Peterkin called it "the best novel that has ever come out of the South." It was, according to Mitchell, "a freak, a runaway, a natural, one of those things that isn't supposed to happen but does ever so often." "The bench and the bar like it," she added. "The medical profession must like it … The psychiatrists especially like it, but don't ask me why. And now," she continued, "the most confusing thing of all. File clerks, elevator operators, sales girls in department stores, telephone operators, stenographers, garage mechanics, clerks in Helpsy-Selfy stores, school teachers – oh, Heavens, I could go on and on! – like it." If Mitchell's assessment is correct, her novel's reach extended well beyond the typical, middle-class market for bestselling novels.[32]

Margaret Mitchell never planned on producing a Depression-era classic. The former newspaper features writer began drafting what became *Gone with the Wind* three years before the Crash, in 1926. Mitchell wrote mostly out of boredom after a chronic ankle injury left her bedridden and restless. She abandoned the project in 1929. The rough manuscript gathered dust until 1935, when a traveling executive from Macmillan purchased it after hearing from a mutual friend that Peggy Mitchell had something in her apartment worth reading.

So, Mitchell wasn't following some formula from a handbook entitled "How to Write a Bestseller in the 1930s." And yet, as Edward Weeks wrote in the *New York Times Book Review*, Mitchell's sprawling saga of four Southerners living through the antebellum, Civil War, and Reconstruction eras "reached us precisely at the moment when we were ready for it." Weeks explained, "there are times when ideas begin to gather in the air like thunder clouds. These ideas form a kind of atmospheric pressure which presses down upon the skulls of sensitive novelists."[33]

Weeks's clarification left much unclear. With eighty years between us and him, however, his meaning clicks into sharper focus. *Gone with the*

Wind confirms the loose thematic framework established earlier. It was the quintessential Depression-era novel. Like other 1930s bestsellers, it depicted characters suffering through hard times, denounced the pursuit of wealth and power, and offered a particular type of chronological and ideological escapism. It was "a freak" only in the sense that its author did not anticipate its unprecedented success. It was not just a bestseller, it was *the* bestseller, the novel that epitomized the literary themes swirling through contemporary bookstores.

Like many successful novels from the period, *Gone with the Wind* rejected literary frills and purple prose in favor of the blunt, documentary impulse Depression-era audiences expected. "It is a simple book, bereft of obscurity, lacking the inductive vagueness of the stream-of-consciousness school, yet frankly realistic," one observer wrote. Mitchell filled her world with tragically flawed characters who could have populated a Lost Generation novel. Scarlett O'Hara is vain, petty, and greedy. Rhett Butler is as stubborn as he is witty. Melanie Hamilton is physically frail. Ashley Wilkes, her eventual husband, cannot cope with modern sensibilities. They are psychologically complex people who balance their good and bad facets as best they can. All of them engage in moments of painful introspection, and all of them agonize over their position in a society undergoing rapid changes.[34]

The world "blew up under the unsuspecting feet of our grandparents," Mitchell observed of the Civil War generation. She imposed that same sense of dislocation on her characters, restating the now-familiar argument that impersonal factors drive people's lives. One critic noted that *Gone with the Wind* demonstrated that man "is operated on by forces over which he has no control, and . . . he must accept them as his experience and continue to exist with and despite them." Scarlett is oblivious to the titanic forces shaping the prewar South. She cannot guide the political debates swirling overhead any more than she can the massive armies that destroy the only way of life she has ever known.[35]

Once the war obliterates the antebellum order, Scarlett, like Wang Lung, Anthony Adverse, and Tom Joad, must improvise her way through an unfamiliar era "wherein every standard, every value had changed." Her first husband (Charles Hamilton) is dead, her family is in psychological shambles, and Tara is a ruined heap. Thus begins her long struggle for survival and enlightenment, a journey familiar to many figures in Depression-era popular literature.[36]

She migrates to the booming city of Atlanta in search of a fresh start. Like most Depression-era representations of cities, Mitchell's Atlanta is a grim warren populated with slick-talkers and con men. Her narrative color scheme shifts from the blood red soil of Tara to a filthy brown reminiscent of the dirty treatment the city dishes out to its inhabitants.

Scarlett possesses an immense capacity for hard work, yet hard work brings neither security nor satisfaction. She opens a lumberyard only to submit to her conviction that "money is the most important thing in the world." She undercuts her competitors, misrepresents the quality of her products, and exploits convict laborers in the name of profit. Her quest for wealth and power makes her a social pariah without providing the stability she craves. "No miser ever counted his gold oftener than she," Mitchell warned, "and no miser ever had greater fear of losing it."[37]

Besides its presentation of hard times; its depiction of people trapped by forces beyond their control; and its suspicion of cities, wealth, and power, *Gone with the Wind* parallels other contemporary bestsellers in its multi-faceted approach to escapism. Like many of its peers – to the extent that this blockbuster of all blockbusters had any peers – it is set in a distant era, allowing Depression-era Americans to escape from the dismal world around them. Placing familiar economic and social problems within an alien context universalized mankind's troubles, demonstrating that readers' difficulties were part of the general human condition. We've survived times like this before, *Wind* told its readers. We will survive again.

But *Wind*, like other 1930s bestsellers, also gave "escape" a more personal, individual meaning. True escape required that characters withdraw from grasping materialism and embark on a private search for inner fulfillment.

Scarlett, like so many of her literary peers, walks this very road to enlightenment. Her epiphany comes in Atlanta, when Rhett, the love of her life, abandons both her and her garish abomination of a mansion. I am through with "imitation gentry and shoddy manners and cheap emotions," he shouts.[38]

Scarlett is devastated. Everything she has achieved is suddenly rendered meaningless. At this nadir, she finally realizes what Mitchell has hinted at for 1,000 pages: She "belonged to the red acres" of Tara. Scarlett's colorful name alone should have told her that (Rhett/red no doubt belongs on those same crimson acres, not in grubby Atlanta). She needs the stability of the old family estate – the *terra firma* of Tara. She spent years chasing illusions, convinced that men, or money, or power, or fancy gowns would fulfill her. What she really needed was something simpler, yet more elusive: a home that provided a solid foundation in a volatile environment.[39]

Her discovery establishes a goal any reader can attain no matter their economic, family, or social status. Happiness can appear even during moments of crisis and confusion. Stability can exist even in the most disruptive times. *Gone with the Wind* does not exactly have a happy ending, but it does have an optimistic one that suggests that Scarlett's struggles will eventually produce a better life for herself.

Taken collectively, this was the promise of Depression-era bestsellers. Fiercely negative, they nevertheless delivered a positive message. Their protagonists showed a way forward even as they wallowed in struggle. Comfortingly escapist yet brutally realist, they provided a model for navigating the troubled waters of 1930s America.

Notes

1. Frank Luther Mott, *Golden Multitudes: The Story of Best Sellers in the United States* (New York and London: R. R. Bowker, 1947), 5.
2. See, for example, Amy Blair, *Reading Up: Middle-Class Readers and the Culture of Success in the Early Twentieth-Century United States* (Philadelphia: Temple University Press, 2001); Peter Conn, *The American 1930s: A Literary History* (Cambridge: Cambridge University Press, 2009); Jaime Harker, *America the Middlebrow: Women's Novels, Progressivism, and the Middlebrow Authorship between the Wars* (Amherst, MA: University of Massachusetts Press, 2008); Jennifer Haytock, *The Middle Class in the Great Depression: Popular Women's Novels of the 1930s* (New York: Palgrave Macmillan, 2013); Gordon Hutner, *What America Read: Taste, Class, and the Novel, 1920–1960* (Chapel Hill: University of North Carolina Press, 2009); Lawrence W. Levine, *Highbrow/Lowbrow: The Emergence of Cultural Hierarchy in America* (Cambridge, MA: Harvard University Press, 1988); Janice A. Radway, *A Feeling for Books: The Book-of-the-Month Club, Literary Taste, and Middle-Class Desire* (Chapel Hill: University of North Carolina Press, 2000); Joan Shelley Rubin, *The Making of Middlebrow Culture* (Chapel Hill: University of North Carolina Press, 1992); Peter Swirski, *From Lowbrow to Nobrow* (Montreal: McGill-Queen's University Press, 2005); David Welky, *Everything Was Better in America: Print Culture in the Great Depression* (Urbana: University of Illinois Press, 2008).
3. Louis Adamic, "What the Proletariat Reads," *Saturday Review of Literature*, December 1, 1934.
4. Thomas H. English and Willard B. Pope, *What to Read* (New York: F. S. Crofts, 1929), 5; Frieda Kirchway, "Books of the Month," *Nation* 128 (April 17, 1929), 474; Ford Madox Ford, "The Sad State of Publishing," *Forum* 98 (August 1937), 85; "A Few Sour Notes on the Book Business," *Publishers' Weekly* (August 17, 1935), 428.
5. Each of the titles used in this study occupied one of the top three spots in *Publishers' Weekly*'s year-end bestsellers list for fiction between 1930 and 1939, as

reported in Alice Payne Hackett, *Fifty Years of Best Sellers, 1895–1945* (New York: R. R. Bowker, 1945).

6. Swirski, *From Lowbrow to Nobrow,* 6; Elizabeth Long, *The American Dream and the Popular Novel* (London: Routledge Kegan & Paul, 1985), 4.
7. C. T. Malan, "What Should People Read in Democratic Government?" *School and Society* 46 (December 18, 1937), 806; Anonymous, "A Few Sour Notes on the Book Business," *Publishers' Weekly* (August 17, 1935), 425; Selma Robinson, "Book Clubs" *Century* 120 (Spring 1930), 297; H. A. Overstreet, "Americans Need Books – and Books Need Americans," *American Scholar* 8 (Summer 1939), 372.
8. Elizabeth Drew, *The Enjoyment of Literature* (New York: W. W. Norton, 1935), x.
9. Herschel Brickell, "The Literary Landscape," *North American Review* 233 (March 1932), 280.
10. *Saturday Review of Literature,* May 22, 1937, quoted in Halford E. Luccock, *American Mirror: Social, Ethical and Religious Aspects of American Literature, 1930–1940* (New York: MacMillan, 1940), 46.
11. Ellen Glasgow, *Vein of Iron* (1935; reprint, New York: Charles Scribner's Sons, 1938), 307, 305.
12. Bess Streeter Aldrich, *A White Bird Flying* (New York: D. Appleton, 1931), 329, 336. Emphasis in original.
13. Rachel Field, *All This, and Heaven Too* (New York: MacMillan, 1938), 195, 230.
14. Pearl S. Buck, *Sons* (New York: John Day), 218.
15. Cass Warner Spelling and Cork Millner, *Hollywood Be Thy Name: The Warner Brothers Story* (Rocklin, CA: Prima, 1994), 224; Hervey Allen, *Anthony Adverse* (New York: Farrar and Rinehart, 1933), 705, 866, 1217.
16. Warwick Deeping, *Exile* (New York: Alfred A. Knopf, 1930), 171; George Santayana, *The Last Puritan: A Memoir in the Form of a Novel* (New York: Charles Scribner's Sons, 1936), 174.
17. *New York Times Book Review,* September 1, 1935.
18. Dorothy Van Doren, "A Study in Comeliness," *Nation* 133 (August 12, 1931), 160.
19. Field, *All This, and Heaven Too,* 215.
20. A. J. Cronin, *The Citadel* (Boston, MA: Little, Brown, 1937), 15.
21. John Steinbeck, *The Grapes of Wrath* (New York: Viking, 1939), 45.
22. Santayana, *The Last Puritan,* 96, 236, 534, 584.
23. Pearl Buck, *The Good Earth* (New York: John Day, 1931), 243.
24. Kenneth Roberts, *Northwest Passage* (Garden City, NY: Doubleday, Doran, 1937), 247, 255; Steinbeck, *The Grapes of Wrath,* 1.
25. Malcolm Cowley, "The Enchanted Castle," *New Republic* 71 (July 27, 1932), 293; *New York Times Book Review,* June 5, 1932.
26. Charles Morgan, *The Fountain* (New York: Alfred A. Knopf, 1932), 10.
27. Field, *All This, and Heaven Too,* 54; Aldrich, *A White Bird Flying,* 6; Thornton Wilder, *The Woman of Andros* (New York: Albert & Charles Boni, 1930), 42.

28. Steinbeck, *The Grapes of Wrath*, 463; Lloyd Douglas, *Green Light* (New York: Grosset & Dunlap, 1934), 55.

29. Douglas, *Green Light*, 182, 183.

30. Buck, *The Good Earth*, 35.

31. Allen, *Anthony Adverse*, 1216.

32. Margaret Mitchell to Herschel Brickell, January 17, 1937, October 9, 1936, in Richard Harwell, ed., *Margaret Mitchell's* Gone with the Wind *Letters, 1936–1949* (New York: Macmillan, 1976), 109, 74; *Washington Post*, July 12, 1936.

33. Edward Weeks, "What Makes a Book a Best Seller," *New York Times Book Review*, December 1936.

34. Belle Rosenbaum, "Why Do They Read It?" *Scribner's* 102 (August 1937), 69.

35. Margaret Mitchell to Mordecai M. Thurman, February 6, 1937, in Harwell, *Margaret Mitchell's* Gone with the Wind *Letters*, 115; Rosenbaum, "Why Do They Read It?," 24.

36. Mitchell, *Gone with the Wind*, 434.

37. Ibid., 629, 667.

38. Ibid., 1035.

39. Ibid., 420.

CHAPTER 13

Radio Drama

Neil Verma

Radio in Reverse

"The situation of radio is the situation of poetry backwards. If poetry is an art without an audience, radio is an audience without an art."[1] Thus wrote Pulitzer Prize winner Archibald MacLeish (just appointed the ninth librarian of Congress by President Roosevelt) in a 1939 letter to the literary journal *Furioso* at Yale, his alma mater. It is one in a string of memorable statements that the poet made about radio as a platform for verse drama during the Depression, and while working in the leadership of several information and State Department offices during World War II and its aftermath. In the year or two before the names of Orson Welles and Norman Corwin gained national prominence as radio's most celebrated auteurs, MacLeish was perhaps the best-known public figure to emerge as spokesperson for the dramatic side of the medium. That role began in April 1937, when MacLeish previewed his upcoming blank verse radio play "The Fall of the City" on CBS's *Columbia Workshop* with an article in the *New York Times*, in which he lambasted Broadway for curtailing opportunities for modern poets to bring verse to the legitimate stage, following the recent closure of the Works Progress Administration (WPA) theater. Radio was the answer, he reckoned: "The studios, unlike the theatrical producers, are not apt to think of themselves as performing deeds of esthetic charity whenever they produce serious works of art," wrote MacLeish. "Their own need of good work is too publicly notorious."[2]

In this chapter, I'd like to explore "serious works" of radio art as embodied by MacLeish, by the group of dramatists surrounding him, and by the works they produced, in what is perhaps the most common form of narrative fiction in 1930s culture in the United States: radio. Long neglected in historical criticism, the outpouring of narrative radio that characterized the 1930s and 1940s – anthology dramas, adaptations,

thrillers, soap operas, news dramatizations, historical dramas – has recently
begun to attract scholarly interest, in part thanks to a renaissance in radio
history led by Michele Hilmes, Kate Lacey, Jason Loviglio, and others.[3]
The rise of the Mp3 file format also played a pivotal role. In one swoop,
compressed audio files made a vast amount of archived material exchange-
able, bringing the dimly recalled radio age into sonic focus for many
scholars in fields ranging from modernism to pop culture and fan studies.
Developments in audio archiving (notably the Library of Congress's Radio
Preservation Task Force) stand to expand this area, unlocking tens of
thousands of hours of broadcast transcription discs and tapes from local
and regional sources. Most importantly, listening itself occupies the center
of research for perhaps the first time (for a long time radio histories were
full of citations of printed reports, not broadcasts), and as a result radio
studies has at last become as richly "textual" as are critical traditions
associated with other expressive forms, precipitating a wholesale rethinking
of the texture of 1930s life centered on its audio storytelling habits.

With hundreds of thousands of dramas in the archives and tens of
thousands available online, any account of this culture is bound to be
partial, so I have opted to limit the ambit of this chapter. In what follows,
I focus on the "situation of radio drama" as MacLeish put it, in the years of
his two statements cited earlier – 1937–39 – a critical moment of expansion
just before the war overtook the national conversation. On the national
networks, there were some thirty radio drama shows on evening air in 1934,
but that number doubled by 1942, and we are lucky to have a number of
public statements made by key innovators during these years to help us to
understand the ideas that guided this growth.[4] The sections that follow put
the work of these years in historical context as a discursive moment by
looking at writing about radio, and finally as a sonic moment we can get
a sense of by listening. As we will see (and hear), in these years of great
expectations, it was the belief in an immanent *literary* radio that helped
a radiophonic art emerge from earlier work that tried to imitate theater and
other forms. The moment of literary aspiration catalyzed a number of
coalescing forces, prompting the radio drama field to enter a golden age
without quite knowing it, a development that often took place (appropriately enough) within narratives that involve anticipation as a dramatic
architecture.

What I'm trying to get at is the fact that although many in MacLeish's
milieu felt that a truly literary dramatic radio was never achieved in these
years, something important still did emerge: a kind of artfulness that was
something other than literary, but that likely could not have been formed

without the framework of literary art as a preliminary objective. For some, that result was not enough. Reflecting later in life, MacLeish said that radio made no progress after the middle 1930s, remarking that it got off to a good start but "a bad finish."[5] His objections were rooted in the commercialization of the medium so evident in the postwar period, but even in non-commercial contexts there was a similar feeling – in 1948, the BBC's Drama Department chief, Val Gielgud, lamented that after decades of experimentation, "we have failed to discover more than a minimum of first rate work."[6] Such pessimistic statements should not be taken at face value. In reality, as I show in what follows, vivid radio drama was under way before MacLeish got involved, and it would continue to evolve to the present, just not according to an aesthetic he might have preferred. In light of that, the 1937–39 moment is best seen not as a revolution, but as a period in which the genre self-consciously acquired two important things. First, radio drama began to accrue a surrounding rhetoric of anticipation, one that it never really shed – the rhetoric surrounding today's rise in "audio drama" sounds just like the effervescent prewar moment, the fantasy of a form about to be invented. "Radio literature" is one of those genres perpetually on the cusp of coming into being, and it was 1930s culture that first emphasized this. Second, although radio drama did not *become* serious literary work in a sustained way in the late 1930s, in the moment in which it was "about to become serious as a form of literature," it started, oddly, to become serious radio instead. MacLeish's moment, therefore, is one in which one utopian idea for the art of radio – radio literature – helped precipitate a second, allowing for the art of radio's sonic devices to set its own standards apart from those MacLeish might have deemed serious or "artful." To put it another way, it was through the mediation of an aesthetic of literary art that radio became a nonliterary art and thereby acquired recognizable medium specificity for the first time.

Catalyzing Radio "Culture"

What made radio network studios "notoriously" in need of good writing in the late 1930s? As several scholars have shown, there is great workmanship and historical resonance to Irna Phillips's "washboard weeper" serials such as *The Guiding Light* and *Young Dr. Malone*, Arch Oboler's late-night horror on *Lights Out!* and even the *Lux Radio Theater*'s glitzy film adaptations, the sort of drama that was already on the air everywhere in 1937. But it did not seem so to many at the time, including MacLeish, who heard little more than dreck coming out of these advertiser-supported programs, and who realized that there was an opportunity out there for modern writers because the networks had a "public service" mandate built in to their license to use the radio spectrum under federal law after legislation in 1927 and 1934. Radio drama focused on literary adaptation and technique could, and frequently did, fulfill that remit.

There were also business reasons to move in that direction. While local stations and regional networks focused on innovative talk and music formats in their own markets, networks created drama content as part of a campaign to offer free "sustaining" programs in between sponsored "commercial" content, providing affiliates with an unbroken stream of offerings, while also rolling out new material in order to build an audience that could attract a sponsor, a model pioneered by CBS and soon adopted by the two NBC networks.[7] A prominent example is Orson Welles's *Mercury Theater on the Air*, which started out as a summer sustaining program distributed for free, featuring adaptations of familiar novels and with a "name" from the American stage at the helm, before it was picked up by Campbell's Soup.[8] And it was the lure of the mass audience generated by that model – more than 80 percent of American homes had a radio by 1940, and audience sizes went from 1 million to the tens of millions – that made the task of bringing poetic writing to the airwaves appealing, particularly for MacLeish, who was perhaps the writer of his generation who most coveted a voice in public affairs.[9] Denigrate *Lux Radio* all you want, it still aired on eighty-four stations that year, with any single broadcast sure to reach more people than the longest Broadway run by a factor of ten, and instantly.

Of course, by the time MacLeish made his 1937 proposal to bring "serious work" to the field, the genre was already fifteen years old. According to tradition, "dramatic" programming originated in 1922, a year that saw WGY Schenectady and the Marconi station in the United Kingdom (independently of one another) adapt plays such as Eugene Walter's "The Wolf" and Edmund Rostand's "Cyrano de Bergerac."[10] The newly chartered BBC soon began experimenting with dramatic forms, airing readings from Shakespeare in 1923, then commissioning Richard Hughes's "A Comedy of Danger," the first British play written specifically for radio, in January 1924. The growth and proliferation of American radio drama over the 1920s is difficult to describe because little evidence remains of the earliest local theater shows, historical programs, and writing contests of which scholars (notably Shawn VanCour) have found traces.[11] And the category of drama is difficult to cordon off from other categories, particularly during this period of experimentation; the lines between "story," "theater," and "drama" are blurred by amateur hours, broadcasts of operas, scenes from local plays, and children's "storytime" shows with hosts (often "uncle" figures) reading aloud. Meanwhile, because they are (at minimum) dramas acted out for audiences, the phenomenal personality variety shows that arose in the 1930s such as *The Eddie Cantor Show*, *The Jack Benny Show*, and *Fibber McGee and Molly* are surely "plays" according to any strict definition of the word. And what about superhero shows and westerns from *Tom Mix* to *The Shadow*? A generation would pass before market fragmentation would make shows like these easy to wall off from mainstream dramatic programming to the extent that they merited consideration using separate criteria.

As all of those shows flourished in the 1930s, the roots of radio drama formats that would flower into their best-known form were also beginning to grow. From Chicago, New York, and other markets appeared serials that Michele Hilmes has called "dialogue sketches" (*Clara, Lu and Em, Amos & Andy, The Rise of the Goldbergs, One Man's Family*) soon to evolve into soap operas and pre-sitcom "husband and wife" shows, while playhouses, news programs, and crime shows from *Great Plays* and *Cavalcade of America* to *The March of Time* filled the airwaves from both coasts, often in hybrids that would in time become thrillers and melodramas (*Calling All Cars* is an example of all three).[12] It was a protean period. Plays could be anywhere from five minutes long to an hour, standing alone or stretching years or decades into serialization. In 1935, Montgomery Ward hired eighty actors to act out Bible stories, WENR Chicago had a fifteen-minute show called *The Vindicators* about a team fighting unjust prosecutions, while *Calling All Cars* aired a half-hour dramatization of a prison break at San Quentin as it was still unresolved. Just five years, later all three of these ideas (religious drama, fifteen-minute formats, news dramatizations) would be standardized.[13]

Dramas could also be "written" in a variety of ways in the 1930s. As Elena Razlogova has shown, many of radio's "sonic comic strips" required listener collaboration, with popular story arcs on programs such as *The Story of Mary Marlin* being rewritten along lines suggested by listener mail.[14] Writing also took place on industrial scales. One 1937 article profiled a brokerage firm that employed 112 writers to write some 2,000 drama scripts they leased for six-month increments to stations at $3 per half-hour episode.[15] The copy needs of American radio were incredible. At the height of the radio age, according to Erik Barnouw, American stations broadcast some 20 million words each day; to put that figure in today's perspective, every 145 days or so the industry aired as many words as there are in the entire English-language Wikipedia.[16]

At the edges of these programs in the years leading up to "The Fall of the City" there was also increasing experimentation with dramas pitched toward a literate public, in part thanks to ambitious program directors, and in part due to forces internal to the industry.[17] Famous names began to be associated with radio drama, slowly. In a typical week, WEAF New York, flagship of the NBC Red network, might air a romantic serial called *Peggy's Doctor*, a spy program *Stories of the Black Chamber*, but also *Great Plays*, an anthology with work by Marlowe, Shakespeare, Gilbert and Sullivan, and Corneille, as well as a skit about a celebrated cultural figure, like Clifford Odets's dramatization of the life of Sarah Bernhardt on the *Fleishmann's Yeast Hour*. There were several attempts to start up dramatic guilds on both NBC and CBS, as well as to incorporate groups like the Theater Union, which presented what were called "sociological plays" on WEVD New York, and the Actor's Repertory Company, which occasionally performed on *The Columbia Workshop*, the program that best emblematizes the "experimental" period of radio drama, and that hosted MacLeish's "The Fall of the City" in 1937. Founded by Irving Reis in 1936, the *Workshop* attracted thousands of unsolicited manuscripts each year and would have an enduring legacy of cultivating talent from John Cage to Norman Corwin, inventing techniques, and airing work from classics to surrealism, from documentary to poetry, from science fiction to science history. "Without the *Workshop*," observed the *Theatre Arts Monthly*, "the MacLeish play, in all probability, would never have been broadcast because there was no place for it."[18]

That's an exaggeration. Although the *Workshop* led the way, even commercial shows from *The Chase & Sanborne Hour* to *Cavalcade of America* adapted literature (Twain, Hawthorne, Shaw, Swift, Wilde, Poe, and others), brought middlebrow authors onto the air in original scripts (Robert Sherwood, Carl Sandburg, Thomas Wolfe, Stephen Vincent Benét, William Saroyan, John Steinbeck), and offered young writers opportunities, from fledgling playwrights Arthur Miller and Irwin Shaw to new voices such as Milton Geiger, Leopold Proser, Lucille Fletcher, and others who built enduring reputations on air in the 1940s. MacLeish himself, having evolved from his high modernist works like *Einstein* and *Conquistador*, was increasingly devoting his craft to the problems of the world crisis around him, a project that made his writing focus on public life in mass democracy, something that fit middlebrow radio perfectly. Indeed, radio was one of the media in which the very notion of middlebrow culture developed, not only through drama but also through quiz programs and book review shows, as Joan Shelley Rubin has explained.[19] Consider the authors Orson Welles adapted on his 1930s *Mercury Theater, Campbell Soup*, and *Lady Esther* programs: Daphne du Maurier, Sinclair Lewis, Booth Tarkington, Thornton Wilder, Ernest Hemingway, Victor Hugo, Agatha Christie, John Galsworthy, Dashiell Hammett, Eugene O'Neill, Charles Dickens, Robert Louis Stevenson, Bram Stoker, and Shakespeare. The politics and taste evinced by programmers in these choices aside, the larger point is that at this juncture the framework for "artistic seriousness" came to be framed by standards and sensibilities associated with the literary arts.

The historical role of the *Workshop* will also be forever tied to the masterpiece of this literary moment, MacLeish's "The Fall of the City," an allegory about a conqueror awaited by the citizens of a "City of Masterless Men," as related by a correspondent on the scene. MacLeish intended it as a commentary on fascism and the surrender of liberty; he made it allegorical with a setting inspired by the sixteenth-century conquering of Mexico by Cortés at Tenochtitlàn.[20] With the help of the correspondent in the vast city square, we hear a large crowd listen to the prophecy of a dead woman foretelling that the city will take a master, and hear the attitudes of the citizens being swayed by ministers and priests who argue to embrace pacifism in the face of the threat, as a series of messengers arrive to tell us of the approach of the enemy. We spend most of the play waiting, expecting disaster. Finally, just as a grizzled general convinces the crowd to act in defense of their own liberty, the monster arrives, and the people spontaneously surrender their liberty without resistance of any kind. We hear the conqueror's armor move into the square and climb the high pyramid (the sharpest, clearest sounds in the piece, but also lifeless in movement and sepulchral in tone), only to learn – alone with the correspondent – that it is empty.

Insiders considered the show a new high for the medium, something akin to what D. G. Bridson and Louis MacNeice were doing at the BBC. Director Irving Reis's prediction that "future historians of radio will see it as a most significant occasion" has been borne out, as the innovations begun in "The Fall of the City" were the source of techniques used for decades on network air.[21] At Smith College, "Fall" had such an impact among students that they presented a version of the play in the form of dance. It popularized verse drama as a medium; according to critic Milton Allan Kaplan, in the twelve years after "The Fall of the City," some 200 scripts written in verse had been presented across the Anglo-American broadcast world.[22] It was surely an inspiration for Orson Welles' "War of the Worlds" a year later, and even today it speaks to many historical writers and critics – Michael Denning lists it alongside Picasso's *Guernica*, Langston Hughes's "Air Raid: Barcelona," and the films of Eisenstein and Pudovkin as a paramount example of antifascist international solidarity among Popular Front authors.[23]

It felt, briefly, as if MacLeish and his group had finally brought literary sensibility to the airwaves, or, more precisely, successfully brought the idiom of literary art to the aesthetic framework by which future dramatic radio would be understood. But how welcoming was the audience now that it had an "art?" While the *Times*'s Orrin Dunlap gave "Fall" a favorable review at year's end, *Radio Daily* concluded the program too highbrow for many listeners, a claim that dogged many instances of what critics derisively called "radio culture" in this period.[24] That same year, Orson Welles's "Les Misérables" as well as MacLeish's own adaptation of "King Lear" earned similar responses, while two versions of "Hamlet" were described as shady and hard to follow. The rhetoric was unrestrained. In 1936, *Variety* called the WPA Theater's "Chalk Dust" on WNEW "a tragedy of errors in a lady's washroom," while a program starring Peter Lorre on *Royal Gelatin* using Eugene O'Neill-style interior monologues was not only unconvincing but "had the additional fault of being unwholesome, psychopathic, and occasionally unintelligible."[25] A valiant attempt at Ibsen's "Peer Gynt" on KECA Los Angeles failed – "it ain't for the mob." Compare those contemptuous reviews for high literary content to contemporaneous reactions to Alonzo Deen Cole's campfire tale show *The Witch's Tale* ("about as good as anything on the air . . . dialogue and sound effects through the tale are superb. Likewise the action to the smallest detail") or William Spier's news drama *The March of Time* ("probably the toughest job on the air"), and it becomes clear that the moment of "radio culture" was not proceeding as MacLeish had hoped.[26] Director Earle McGill reserved characteristically mordant sarcasm for the bursting balloon. "Directors touched with the messianic impulse gravitate toward workshop radio," he wrote in 1939. "And workshops have a way of becoming arks of the covenant."[27]

MacLeish himself? He soon learned the messianic path wasn't for him, underestimating how much work went into writing a radio drama – as much as six months, in his case, and all for something lost forever in thirty minutes.[28] His hopes for experimental verse proved too self-certain. He would follow "The Fall of the City" with "Air Raid" the next year, but he wrote little more drama for US audiences until 1944, when he and poet

Muna Lee wrote *The American Story*, a set of ten radio plays for NBC. In his introduction to the published version, it is clear that the poet had grown cynical, confessing that in the end the push for verse literature (at least in the way MacLeish understood it) during the "workshop" era of radio had come to nothing. He wrote that:

> The experimental work in the use of radio as a dramatic medium which centered around the *Columbia Workshop* in the thirties seems to have ended ... Gifted writers and directors have learned how to play the instrument effectively and with feeling. Music has been artfully blended with speech to evoke emotion. Skillful devices have been employed to produce dramatic effects. But the earlier hope for a new stage on which the spoken word, freed of all external paraphernalia, should create by its own power and eloquence the emotions of which it alone is capable, has not been realized. If anything, it is more remote today than it was ten years ago.[29]

By the end of the war, writers from horror scribe Arch Oboler to quizmaster Clifton Fadiman were writing obituaries for radio; critic Gilbert Seldes wrote of radio drama in 1950: "There is a high level of competence and a dead level of sameness."[30] After a decade of attempts, neither had the art found audience nor the audience art. Yet the efforts were not in vain. The drama of "devices" that MacLeish decries was not without merit, and it could not have come about at all without the aspirations that the literary experiment helped bring to the medium.

Sonic Paraphernalia

MacLeish's experience on the air from 1937 to 1939 is but one trajectory among many; the medium was shaped by a number of contradictory impulses, often inside one broadcast. In my work, I've emphasized that rather than bearing a single discernable message about – fascism? liberty? – "The Fall of the City" bears several mutually antagonistic aesthetic mandates at once, and it does so unevenly. For instance, while both script and sound design suggest the importance of what I call audioposition ("where we are" according to "what we hear," where both terms are ascertained using context-specific variables), the play and the production offer different impressions of it. MacLeish firmly positions "us" nearby the elites, while the sound design by director Irving Reis plants us among the crowd, a matter of no small importance in a New Deal-era liberal public culture caught between technocratic progressivism of experts on one hand and populist sentimentality toward the masses on another, something that MacLeish himself struggled with, as Richard Pells has explained.[31]

What Reis and other *Workshop* directors revolutionized about radio – what counted as "serious work" – turned on sonic choices, not literary ones. They created what I've called a "drama of space and time" in which location and movement were far more important than words or characters, in highly kinetic experiments like Pare Lorentz's "Ecco Homo" with its grand assembly lines and migrations, and Leopold Proser's "Broadway Evening," in which we move up Broadway through a soundwalk of effects and rhythms.[32] Sonic marks to indicate space and time are what made "experimental" radio experimental. On these matters, dramas of the 1930s tend to fall into two categories. On the one hand there were "intimate" dramas that follow one character through a deep space, often to explore new worlds and generate intense relationship with the listener, making the lives of those at a distance from us meaningful by way of a being whose life is close to us. On the other hand there were large-canvas pieces I call "kaleidosonic" works that tended to segue from one place to another very quickly across a two-dimensional plane, often to celebrate national occasions or array social "types" before us to celebrate New Deal-era ideas of nationhood.[33] Look at the first major anthology of experimental plays, Douglas Coulter's 1939 *Columbia Workshop*, and you will find both types.[34] Intimate dramas include Dubose Heyward's "Half Pint Flask" in which we follow two white men in the African American community of a South Carolina island, and "The Fall of the City" itself, in which we spend nearly all of the play in intimate audioposition. Kaleidosonic plays are just as numerous, with Irving Reis's Meridian "7–1212," which coordinates nocturnal scenes around a telephone system, and "Nine Prisoners," the story of nine perspectives on a World War I massacre.

Whichever positional strategy a dramatist might select, behind it lay an effort to produce spatial complexity, prompting directors and engineers of the period to busy themselves *adding things* to words (tempo, reverb, sound effects, volume) in order to convey setting, movement, space, and distance. To understand their ramifications for writing, contrast these tendencies with MacLeish's ideas. Where directors wanted to dress utterances in a variety of effects – in one *Washington Post* interview, Reis boasted that his plays had to be structured around sounds, such as heartbeats, the creak of a shoe, the scratch of a dog at the door – MacLeish wanted his words denuded, plain, "free."[35] An aesthetic regime devising inventive and legible sonic residues confronted one devoted to removing them. It is no surprise that the two agendas give one another surprising and energetic counter-pressure, even if they were in constant danger of disarticulating. Perhaps this is what led to the second theme in MacLeish's quote cited earlier, in which writing is problematized as a mere instrument "played," blended, employed as a "device" to produce effects. Writing is less like words and more like music.

"Fall" is about aesthetic struggle, between the verbal and the nonverbal, textual and non-textual, "the word" and "the device," and ultimately between a sense of seriousness in art that is literary and one in which it is sonic. That same struggle also happened in the discourse about the medium. Within months of the *Furioso* letter with which I began this chapter, three publications about creating radio drama appeared by authors directly connected to "The Fall of the City": *Radio Writing* by Max Wylie, a manual by "Fall's" script supervisor that was a touchstone into the war years; *Handbook of Radio Writing* by Erik Barnouw, a book that went on to five printings by an author who would later become a major historian of American radio; and *Radio Directing*, a book by director Earle McGill, who also helped to mount the 1937 broadcast. Each of these texts shares a common thread that reenacts the struggle between Reis and MacLeish. Attempting to dislodge the metaphor of the "stage" from early radio drama and replace it with a more pliable "literary" approach, each text simultaneously fixes the writing around sonic effects.

For Wylie, form was the attribute radio ought to borrow from the stage: "The structure of good radio plays is the structure of good plays," he writes. "I know of no single exception which violates this characteristic."[36] A script supervisor used to sifting through piles of drafts, Wylie understands "structure" to denote targeted features of the writing, emphasizing, for instance, how a radio script can't linger on images before it introduces conflict, a fetishization of the "hook" that aligned radio with short stories rather than films, and proved to have a long life in radio aesthetics.[37] Wylie also advises treating effects as "grace notes" in the script, as he tempts the reader with tales of the 55,000 effects in the studio archives, including thirteen kinds of motors, and twenty models of house doors.[38] For all his efforts to discourage overuse of these devices, his text is bursting with examples of them. For Wylie, one ideal script was Vic Knight's "Cartwheel," in which a silver dollar passes from owner to owner across decades in an epic of transitional coin rolls, fades of footsteps, moans, dead cuts, anvils ringing, horse hooves, organ music, crowds, and traffic. Another great script was Leopold Proser's "Mr. Sycamore," a fantasy about a postman who decides to plant himself in the ground and become a tree, a transformation effected with a harp glissando performed with a fingernail. In the opening of his *Handbook*, Erik Barnouw has a short manifesto of sorts, in which he lays out some lessons that the workshop era had taught his group of writers. The metaphor of radio as a "stage," for one, was discovered to be a mistake; network dramatists realized they spoke not to crowds but to individuals, an important psychological distinction. As a result, the radio writer shared what he called the "bookwriter's problem" in the enlistment of the individuated imagination.[39] This literary frame of reference continues in the chapter: the "variety" of radio arises from its similarity to the printed page; listeners are like "the armchair reader with his book"; Orson Welles's innovations made radio resemble the novel; the theater was at best radio's "foster parent."[40] Soon, however, such references disappear as Barnouw likens radio's components (music, sound effects, words) to singers, and explores how sonic levels are used along with filtering, echo chambers, and choral speech work, precisely the medium-specific sonic representational materials that the novelist lacks. In its focus, Barnouw is much closer to Earle McGill's text *Radio Directing*, which spends more than 200 pages on how to rehearse microphones and use board-fades before any script lines appear on the page. These are either presented without much comment, as in his transcription of *The Columbia Workshop*'s gothic version of Wilbur Daniel Steele's "The Giant's Stair," or to illustrate how amendments to a production script – cuts, choruses, sleigh bells, scene breaks, rewritten lines, timing, continuity, filters, bulletins, fades, bugles – rethink and reinterpret the language long before it escapes the lips of an actor.

In each case, in the course of making an argument designed to take "the word" away from the stage and replace it into narrative structures that resemble literature, these writers get sidetracked, providing models that emphasize the sonic equipment of the medium. This can be heard everywhere in late 1930s radio. Consider the most famous broadcast of that moment, Howard Koch's script for Orson Welles's "The War of the Worlds," a marvelous example of the trends of its period: it uses audio-position deliberately; its first half is kaleidosonic, while its second is intimate. Its blend of drama and news drew on familiar features of 1930s formats. As many have remarked, however, perhaps the most important aesthetic features are its two key silences. The first takes place at the end of the first act, when the feed from a reporter on the scene of the Martian invasion in Grover's Mill, New Jersey, suddenly goes dead. Seconds go by until an announcer takes over to divert us to a piano interlude. The next silence occurs at the end of the second act, as the Martians take over New York, and we hear the microphone of a reporter drop, along with a fading plea on the short wave. The text of the play is everywhere written to emphasize themes of delay, gap, and disjuncture. Here is the opening monologue:

> We know now that in the early years of the twentieth century this world was being watched closely by intelligences greater than man's and yet as mortal as his own. We know now that as human beings busied themselves about their various concerns they were scrutinized and studied, perhaps almost as narrowly as a man with a microscope might scrutinize the transient creatures that swarm and multiply in a drop of water. With infinite complacence people went to and fro over the earth about their little affairs, serene in the assurance of their dominion over this small spinning fragment of solar driftwood which by chance or design man has inherited out of the dark mystery of Time and Space. Yet across an immense ethereal gulf, minds that to our minds as ours are to the beasts in the jungle, intellects vast, cool and unsympathetic, regarded this earth with envious eyes and slowly and surely drew their plans against us.

A play whose sound design will be spattered with makeshift segues, gaps, and abyssal silences is introduced by narration similarly obsessed with scale, interval, and impasse. That is especially true of all the lines that the Welles group added to embellish H. G. Wells's original text: "small spinning fragment of solar drift wood"; "the dark mystery of Time and Space"; "an immense ethereal gulf." In this way, the art of language is "fixed around" the art of sound design.

The same can even be said of "The Fall of the City." Here are some lines that MacLeish himself felt were representative of the piece, at the moment when the conqueror is unmasked:

> There's no one! . . .
> There's no one at all . . . No one!
> The helmet is hollow!
> The metal is empty the armor is empty! I tell you
> There's no one at all there: there's only the metal;
> The barrel of metal: the bundle of armor, it's Empty!
> The push of a stiff pole at the nipple would topple it.[41]

It is a voice reverberating back on itself, as if interacting with the stone of a public square in which it is set; the language is as acoustically live as the environment. Note the echoic repetition of "no one," "empty," and "metal" (itself a kind of distorted echo of "helmet"), as well as the emphasis on the sonic resemblances between the phonemic endings of words (barre*l*, bund*le*, nipp*le*, topp*le*), a sound that propagates over the course of the lines like an outward-moving wave. MacLeish explained the idea for this verse was "using the rhythms of an excited voice, rhythms which are motivated by the excitement and making the excitement the author of the rhythm." In citing the excitation of the actor as the author, MacLeish concedes that "the word" is subordinated to the "external paraphernalia" that bears it on the airwaves. From a historical distance, it is clear that his literary radio had defeated the staginess of radio-as-theater, but in doing so it had become something not quite intended. Intending to make radio sound like literary art, he created literary art that sounds like radio.

Words Stretched to Fit the Sky

I'd like to conclude with a moment from a play that is a harbinger of the radio of the 1940s, a period that would see the marshaling of intimate and kaleidosonic effects for patriotic appeals as well as the parallel rise in denser narratives about interiority as a result of radio's complex aesthetic engagement with the psychic situation of war. "They Fly through the Air with the Greatest of Ease" was one in a cycle of plays that examine the morality of strategic bombing in the wake of Guernica. The play aired in April 1939, almost exactly two years after "The Fall of the City," and was one of the first network plays by Norman Corwin, an author who came to embody the medium in the 1940s – in a light jab at MacLeish and others, Milton Kaplan called Corwin "the first poet brought up with radio, so to speak, in contrast with notable poets who turned to radio," later generations simply knew him as the "Poet Laureate" of radio.[42]

The play is primarily a monologue, written in verse, in which an external narrator calmly tells us of a beautiful morning in an unnamed land, and of Bomber Number Six, a new kind of bird "such birds as God has never dreamed of when He made the skies," with armaments and bombs "as cold and clean as a theorem." The vessel ascends into the skies toward an unnamed town. The poetry focuses on the beauty of the earth, of its timelessness, as the narrator speaks as if addressing each member of the crew ("You, there, Gunner") and brings us to visit the voices of people in the building about to be bombed (a family argument in tenement 3B; a piano player in tenement 5A; a wailing baby in 8F). The reports of explosions come to us above, described in humdrum workaday language ("I'm going to use that church steeple as a marker. Will you steer close so as to pass over it?") and imagery of bodies spreading out like rose petals. The gunner and radio man chat about the chicken tetrazzini on offer at the mess hall while remarking how strafing the civilians reminisces pastoral memories of mowing of wheat, a conceit linking war and agriculture.

The Narrator's ire toward the bomber crew comes through in his response at the uneven odds:

> O Winged Victory!
> The Spartans would have coveted
> The courage of your combat!
> Just think: ten thousand savage roof tops, tarred and tiled,
> Against a single plane!

Yet the voice could be itself accused of a cowardice similar to that of the bomber, assuming a "cold and clean" audioposition close to the bomber for most of the broadcast. The script even specifies how loud the motor should be when we "are" inside the bomber like an invisible compatriot, and when we "are" hovering just outside of it like an accompanying bird.

At a certain point, however, the voice elects to leave the bomber and return to earth to find a silent place in which to compose an ode about the meaning of the bombardment. "What words can compass glories such as we have seen today?" wonders the narrator. "Can phrases tailored to a patch of earth be stretched to fit the sky?"

> Our rhythms jangle at the very start.
> Our similes concede defeat,
> For there is nothing that can be compared to that which lies beyond compare
> You see? We are reduced already to tautologies.
> It's awe does that.
> The wonder of it all has set us stammering.

It is a characteristically modernist gesture about the failure of the literary explicability of war, but it is also a recognition that there are thoughts and experiences that can't be thought in a silent space dominated by the naked power of a literary voice; they require sounds to shape them, to provide room. In the play, the poet stammers through failed classical analogies, then abandons his repose and returns to the bomber, which continues its grim pursuit until it is itself attacked and downed by a defending plane. In order to communicate at all the word cannot do without the motor's sound; the dry critical sarcasm of the speaker needs the wet churn of the machinery to house its critique. The play is a poem that can only take place within the context of a sound effect, which establishes the conditions for articulability.

"They Fly" doesn't just depict the sound of the bomber, I am suggesting; it is a way of thinking about that sound. Consider it a duet for voice and engine. The engines are audible to us for 17:20 of the 26:33 of the play, nearly as long as the narration. When the bomber's motor starts up a few minutes in to the play the sequence lasts more than sixty seconds, unrolling in stages, as a kind of bombastic solo. As the narration continues, both elements undergo a variety of positionings and modulations in relation to one another that are just as significant as the actions and meanings they denote. In a lengthy sequence of fatal descent, the narrator urges the crew to be calm, to behold the beauty around them ("The sun, the air, the earth; they're all the same; It's only you have undergone a change") until they make a final "treaty with the earth." The sequence is memorable for vocal work that matches pace and rhythm with the screech of tumbling fuselage. You can read that conclusion as the duet turning in to a duel, in which a humanist voice conquers and survives a machine. In this way, "They Fly" captures the feel of radio drama as it anticipates war, a force poem inside a force sound, and represents a moment in which the art of broadcasting *as* broadcasting matures. It also rehearses in miniature the evolution of radio drama outlined earlier, leaving action to find a classical, literary quiet, only to discover bare language inadequate to the aesthetic urgency of the moment. But just as Corwin's frustrated ode prompts dramatic commentary on the art of sound design at the heart of the play, the expectation of literary representation in 1930s radio generated crucial self-awareness in the medium. Whether the play actually is a serious work of poetry or literary is beside the point; rather, the poetic seriousness with which it approaches its theme is precisely what makes it a serious work of radio.

Notes

1. From a letter published in *Furioso* 1.1 (1939), 1–2.
2. Archibald MacLeish, "Of Poetic Drama," *New York Times* (April 4, 1937), 171.
3. See Debra Rae Cohen, Michael Coyle, and Jane Lewty, eds., *Broadcasting Modernism* (Gainesville: University Press of Florida, 2009); Tona Hangen, "When Radio Ruled: The Social Life of Sound," *American Quarterly* 66.2 (2014), 465–76; Michele Hilmes and Jason Loviglio, *The Radio Reader* (New York: Routledge, 2002); Kate Lacey, "Ten Years of Radio Studies: The Very Idea," *The Radio Journal* 6.1 (2008), 21–32; Jason Loviglio and Michele Hilmes, eds., *Radio's New Wave: Global Sound in a Digital Era* (New York: Routledge, 2013); Tom McEnaney, "Wireless Materials: Radio Cultures in Ireland, Latin America, and the United States at the Mid-Century" *Sound Studies* 1,.1 (2015), 171–76; and Ian Whittington, "Radio Studies and 20th-Century Literature: Ethics, Aesthetics, and Remediation," *Literature Compass* 11.9 (2014), 634–48.
4. John K Hutchens, "Drama on the Air," *New York Times* (November 2, 1941), X12.

5. Archibald MacLeish,*Reflections* (Amherst: University of Massachusetts Press, 1986), 120.
6. John Drakakis, "Introduction," in *British Radio Drama*, ed. John Drakakis (New York: Cambridge University Press, 1981), 11.
7. Michele Hilmes, "NBC and the Network Idea: Defining the 'American System,'" and Michael J. Socolow, "Always in Friendly Competition: NBC and CBS in the First Decade of National Broadcasting," in *NBC: America's Network*, ed. Michele Hilmes (Berkeley: University of California Press, 2007), 7–24 and 25–43. For a history of radio formats beyond the networks, see Alexander Russo, *Points on the Dial: Golden Age Radio beyond the Networks* (Durham, NC: Duke University Press, 2010).
8. For the definitive study on the episode, see A. Brad Schwartz, *Broadcast Hysteria: Orson Welles's War of the Worlds and the Art of Fake News* (New York: Hill and Wang, 2015).
9. William C Ackerman, "The Dimensions of American Broadcasting," *Public Opinion Quarterly* (Spring 1945).
10. See Richard J. Hand and Mary Traynor, *The Radio Drama Handbook* (New York: Continuum, 2011), 14–21.
11. Shawn VanCour, *Making Radio: Early Radio Production and the Rise of Modern Sound Culture* (New York: Oxford University Press, 2018).
12. Michele Hilmes, *Radio Voices: American Broadcasting, 1922–1952* (Minneapolis: University of Minnesota Press, 1997),97–129. See also Kathleen Battles, *Calling All Cars: Radio Dragnets and the Technology of Policing* (Minneapolis: University of Minnesota Press, 2010).
13. *Advertising Age* (January 5, 1935), 20.
14. Elena Razlogova, *The Listener's Voice: Early Radio and the American Public* (Philadelphia: University of Pennsylvania Press, 2011), 75–97.
15. "Joseph-Koehler-Georgia Bachus, a Brokerage Firm, Largest in Radio Writing," *Variety* (July 28, 1937), 35.
16. Erik Barnouw, *Handbook of Radio Writing: An Outline of Techniques and Markets in Radio Writing in the United States*, 2nd edn. (Boston, MA: Little, Brown and Company, 1947), 1.
17. "Proscription: More Drama" *Printer's Ink* (January 24, 1935), 45. I have more on this development in my book: Neil Verma, *Theater of the Mind: Imagination, Aesthetics and American Radio Drama* (Chicago: University of Chicago Press, 2012), 21–25.
18. Quoted in Milton Allan Kaplan, *Radio and Poetry* (New York: Columbia University Press, 1949), 7.
19. Joan Shelley Rubin, *The Making of Middlebrow Culture* (Chapel Hill: University of North Carolina Press, 1992), 266–329.
20. MacLeish, *Reflections*, 107.
21. "Poetic Drama Wins Hearing," *New York Times* (April 11, 1937), 12x.
22. Kaplan, *Radio and Poetry,* 7.
23. Michael Denning, *The Cultural Front: The Laboring of American Culture in the Twentieth Century* (New York: Verso, 1996), 12–13.

24. Orrin Dunlap, "A Year's Stardust," *New York Times* (January 2, 1938), 124; "The Fall of the City," *Radio Daily* (April 13, 1937), 8.
25. "Chalk Dust," *Variety*, April 15, 1936, 42; "Royal Gelatin," *Variety*, November 11, 1936), 45.
26. "The Witch's Tale," *Variety* (October 8, 1935), 37; "The March of Time," *Variety* (October 2, 1935), 41.
27. Earle McGill, *Radio Directing* (New York: McGraw-Hill, 1940), 270.
28. Scott Donaldson, *Archibald MacLeish: An American Life* (New York: Houghton Mifflin, 1993), 270.
29. Archibald MacLeish, *The American Story: Ten Broadcasts* (New York: Duell, Sloan and Pearce, 1944), xi.
30. Gilbert Seldes, *The Great Audience* (New York: Viking, 1950), 128.
31. Richard Pells, *Radical Visions and American Dreams: Culture and Social Thought in the Depression Years* (Middletown, CT: Wesleyan University Press, 1973), 314–16.
32. Verma, *Theater of the Mind,* 17–88.
33. Ibid., 57–72.
34. Douglas Coulter, ed., *The Columbia Workshop* (New York: Whittlesley House, 1939).
35. Remy Brunel, "Radio Magic Expected to Emerge from Columbia Workshop Experimentation," *Washington Post* (September 6, 1936), AA5.
36. Max Wylie, *Radio Writing* (New York: Farrar, Strauss and Giroux, 1939), 13.
37. See Jessica Abel, *Out on the Wire: The Storytelling Secrets of the New Masters of Radio* (New York: Penguin, 2015), 56–57; Hand and Traynor, *The Radio Drama Handbook,* 113–28; and Nancy Updike "Better Writing through Radio" http://transom.org/2006/nancy-updike/ (accessed April 15, 2016).
38. Wylie, *Radio Writing*, 44–48.
39. Barnouw, *Handbook of Radio Writing,* 12.
40. Ibid., 15, 21, 17.
41. MacLeish, *Reflections*, 111. MacLeish misremembers this: neither the 1937 nor the 1939 airings of the play used the "push of a stiff pole at the nipple" line.
42. Kaplan, *Radio and Poetry,* 9. For more on Corwin, see Jacob Smith and Neil Verma, eds., *Anatomy of Sound: Norman Corwin and Media Authorship* (Berkeley: University of California Press, 2016).

CHAPTER 14

Crime Fiction

Charles J. Rzepka

The most important event affecting American crime fiction during the 1930s was the Great Depression that followed the stock market crash of October 1929 and persisted until the eve of the Second World War. The repeal of Prohibition in 1933, the Dust Bowl drought of 1934–40, Franklin D. Roosevelt's New Deal, and the rise of fascism all take a back seat to this unprecedented economic disaster.

With its devastating impact on blue-collar wages and employment, the Depression shifted the focus of American fiction generally in a proletarian direction. Working-class novels like John Steinbeck's *Tortilla Flat* (1935) and *The Grapes of Wrath* (1939) became commercial successes, and modernists like William Faulkner and Ernest Hemingway turned their attention to the down-and-outs of society. Faulkner's *Sanctuary* (1931) and Hemingway's *To Have and Have Not* (1937) also revealed a growing interest in crime among established writers. Hemingway had dipped his toe in the water in 1927 with "The Killers," a story first published in *Scribner's Magazine*, while Faulkner would go on to feature small-town district attorney Gavin Stevens, from *Sanctuary*, as detective protagonist in stories appearing in *Harper's*, *Scribner's*, and *The Saturday Evening Post*. In 1925, F. Scott Fitzgerald, whose milieu was almost exclusively upscale, had already made a Prohibition gangster his tragic hero in *The Great Gatsby*, a harbinger of W. R. Burnett's Al Capone-inspired *Little Caesar* four years later.

Little Caesar was published by Dial Press and marketed to middle-class households by the Literary Guild of America as "a work of art."[1] It reflected a growing trend toward the *déclassé* in fiction aimed at middlebrow readers. Major publishing houses like Knopf began to feature protagonists drawn from pulp magazines like *Black Mask*, which had originally targeted white working-class males.[2] Soon, this so-called "hard-boiled" genre – violent, action-oriented, and antiestablishment – was challenging the formerly dominant Classical or Golden Age "whodunit" – genteel, puzzle-oriented, and socially complacent – for the middle-income market share, setting the stage for a victory of the proletarian detective during the paperback revolution of the following two decades. By then, Hard-boiled's near cousin, *noir*, had emerged to cast a garish, flickering light on lives of quiet desperation marking time in the abyss of a global economic catastrophe.

In addition to changes in the class orientation of American crime and detective fiction, significant developments were occurring in the genre's representation of race and gender. Prompted by the success of Earl Derr Biggers's Honolulu police detective Charlie Chan, who had made his debut in 1925, white-authored crime fiction began to include Asian American protagonists, while the Harlem Renaissance incited new experiments in the genre among African American writers. The representation of women in American crime fiction, however, regressed from previous decades, with a few exceptions.

British Colonization and Tory Loyalties: Classical Detective Fiction in America

The terms "Classical" and "hard-boiled" are useful starting points for discussion, but it's best to think of them as designating two opposite poles of a spectrum in the genre of detective fiction, which is, in turn, a subgenre of crime fiction in general. Crime fiction is about crime, regardless of the author's choice of protagonist: victim, criminal, detective, witness, or innocent bystander. Gangster or mob fiction like *Little Caesar* features a criminal protagonist. Detective fiction conspicuously features a detective, whether amateur, private professional, or police. Classical or "Golden Age" detective fiction (aka, the "whodunit") focuses the reader's attention on the physical clues and verbal testimony that the detective must piece together to solve the crime, and challenges the reader to find the solution along with or, preferably, in advance of the detective: in short, to assume the detective's investigative role. Hard-boiled (also known as "action adventure" or "tough guy") detective fiction focuses attention on the dangers that the detective must face, and invites the reader to experience them vicariously.[3]

Because there are often dangers threatening the detective at the classical end of the spectrum, and nearly always a puzzle challenge of some sort posed at the hard-boiled end, formal differences between the two types of detective fiction amount to matters of degree rather than kind. However, important contrasts in milieu and attitudes toward society underline these differences. Classical detective fiction generally takes place among the middle-to-upper classes and treats crime as an aberration among a law-abiding, close-knit community. Hard-boiled detective fiction, while fascinated by wealth, likes to muck around in the lower depths from which (in its view) all money originates. Foregrounding the anxieties of deracination and anomie fostered by advanced industrial capitalism, it sees crime among the wealthy as symptomatic of rot at the very foundations of society. The Great Depression, which revealed the factitious basis of the American Dream, helped to popularize this kind of detective fiction among American readers of the 1930s, but the decade began and ended with the classical detective writer in the driver's seat, as hard-boiled author Raymond Chandler acknowledged even as late as 1946: "the English formula still dominates the trade."[4]

Classical detection is often represented as a post–Great War British import to America derived originally from the puzzle-plotting of Arthur Conan Doyle's *fin de siècle* Sherlock Holmes stories and invigorated by the best-selling mysteries of Agatha Christie, beginning with *The Mysterious Affair at Styles* in 1920. There is some truth to this, but Christie was inspired, in turn, by American writer Anna Katherine Green, who vigorously exploited the puzzle element in her mysteries of the 1890s. Moreover, detective stories by Americans like Melville Davisson Post and Jacques Futrelle were challenging readers to solve fictional crimes by brainpower alone well before the British "whodunit" spread to US shores. Nonetheless, it's safe to say that Brits like G. K. Chesterton, Dorothy Sayers, Anthony Berkeley, and R. Austin Freeman, as well as Christie, began to colonize American crime fiction in the 1920s. Among their earliest Tory converts was S. S. Van Dine, pseudonym of art critic Willard Huntington Wright, whose foppish and erudite Philo Vance achieved aphoristic immortality when Ogden Nash opined of him, "Philo Vance/ Needs a kick in the pance."

Already coming up the rear to deliver that kick was a high school dropout and former professional detective named Samuel Dashiell Hammett. Until the Philo Vances could be shown the door, however, they continued to make themselves at home throughout the ensuing decade. Wright, for one, remained prolific until his death in 1939. He was joined at the apex of American "whodunit" fiction by John Dickson Carr, master of the locked room mystery, who had been born in the United States but began his writing career after moving to the United Kingdom in the early 1930s. His detective protagonist, Dr. Gideon Fell, whose corpulence, sartorial affectations, and personality aped G. K. Chesterton's, even had the metafictional temerity to deliver a formal lecture on "The Locked Room Mystery" while investigating the case of *The Three Coffins* (1935).

Two other American masters of the whodunit were Rex Stout and "Ellery Queen." In 1934, Stout introduced the world to the misogynistic, grossly obese beer connoisseur Nero Wolfe. Along with his "Watson," a dapper young private secretary named Archie Goodwin, Wolfe inhabited a posh brownstone on Manhattan's West 34th Street where he met with wealthy clients in the few minutes he could spare from tending to his rare orchid collection. "Ellery Queen" was the corporate pseudonym of cousins Daniel Nathan and Emanuel Benjamin Lepofsky, who began their authorial collaboration as "Frederic Dannay" and "Manfred Bennington Lee" in 1929. Modeling their detective hero on Philo Vance, Dannay and Lee brought the puzzle element to such a degree of machine-like finesse that, just before wrapping up each case, Queen would state that all the necessary clues had now been provided and issue a "Challenge to the Reader" to come up with the solution.

These were the best-known authors in a crowded field that also included women like the prolific Phoebe Atwood Taylor and Leslie Ford. All displayed the telltale symptoms of Golden Age detective fever, including a fondness for eccentric investigators with well-above-average IQs, intricate criminal plots, and implausible murder weapons (e.g., a golf club repurposed to shoot poisoned darts), along with a benign view of modern society (despite a few bad apples) and law enforcement (often incompetent but seldom corrupt).

By the time the Nazis invaded Poland on September 1, 1939, the stable, rational world in which brilliant oddballs like Fell and Wolfe solved their crimes was already a nostalgic memory, supposing it wasn't entirely mythical to begin with. And yet the myth persisted, as it does in the "cozy" of today, perhaps because its fundamental orderliness appealed to readers who'd suddenly found themselves living in a world gone mad. In Agatha Christie's *The Body in the Library*, written in 1941, the only indication that a war is raging outside the prim precincts of St. Mary Mead is the acronym "ARP," which stands for "Air Raid Precautions."[5]

You can't ignore reality indefinitely, however. Like London's civilian population, the classical detective novel was getting blitzed.

The Hard-Boiled Revolution: Founding Fathers

Dashiell Hammett and Raymond Chandler bracketed the hard-boiled revolution of the 1930s. Hammett, its Sam Adams, incited American resistance to the Mother Country by, in effect, throwing her tea into the harbor. Chandler, its George Washington, eventually became first president of a new Tough Guy Nation whose ethos would inform and shape mainstream crime fiction throughout the world and to the present day. There were no Founding Mothers, a topic to which we will return.

Born in 1894 to a philandering justice of the peace and a socially ambitious mother, Samuel Dashiell Hammett spent his early years on a farm on Maryland's western shore until politics forced his father out of office. The family moved to Philadelphia and then Baltimore as the senior Hammett went through a succession of jobs, until young Sam had to drop out of high school to help support his family. Unable to stick with one employer for long, Hammett at last found one he liked, the Pinkerton Detective Agency, and became an "operative," a paid private investigator. When the United States declared war on Germany in 1917, Hammett enlisted in the army's Motor Ambulance Corp, where he promptly contracted the Spanish flu and then tuberculosis, leaving him *hors de combat*. After his discharge, he briefly rejoined the Pinkertons before moving to San Francisco, where he set out to become a writer.

Nothing in Hammett's resume indicated that this was a good choice. But he had devoured books from early childhood – science and philosophy as well as fiction – and had been following developments in the novel, both at home and abroad. In addition, he'd always been a quick study. Looking about him and taking into account his firsthand experience in detection, Hammett decided that crime writing was his fastest route to recognition, and the new action-adventure pulp magazine, *Black Mask*, the nearest doorway. Dropping "Samuel" was the first step he took toward making a name for himself.

"Hammett gave murder back to the kind of people that commit it for reasons, not just to provide a corpse," wrote Raymond Chandler in "The Simple Art of Murder."[6] Much the same could be said for what Hammett did for fictional detectives: he gave murder back to the kind of people who *solve* it for reasons – mainly, it's their job – and not just to provide a "Challenge to the Reader." He began with the Continental Op. Featured in some three dozen stories in *Black Mask* from 1923 to 1930, the anonymous Op (short for "Operative") narrates his adventures tracking down mobsters, grifters, missing heirs, dope smugglers, and ordinary murderers while in the employ of the San Francisco branch of the Continental Detective Agency. In sharp contrast to his *Black Mask* competition, Carroll John Daly's dashing Race Williams, the Op is short, fat, and often out of breath. But while he can't always dish it out, he certainly can take it, as the violent free-for-alls that appear in nearly every Op tale clearly demonstrate. And he knows the professional ropes. Despite his physical shortcomings, it wasn't long before the Op left Race Williams in the dust and the editor of *Black Mask*, Joseph Shaw, made Hammett's prose the gold standard for his stable of contributors.

With his reputation growing, Hammett made the jump to novel writing in 1928 by sending Alfred A. Knopf an Op adventure called *Red Harvest*, originally serialized in *Black Mask*. The manuscript impressed Knopf's influential wife and collaborator, Blanche, who recommended it to her husband after suggesting Hammett cut down on the violence because the excess was implausible.[7] *Red Harvest* – still living up to its sanguinary title – appeared early in 1929, soon followed by another Op tale, *The Dain Curse*, also a *Black Mask* serialization. Having established himself as an author entitled to space on middle-class bookshelves, Hammett turned his attention to the book that would be his masterpiece.

While all five of Hammett's novels except for the last, *The Thin Man* (1934), received trial runs in *Black Mask*, none of these serializations was better timed than that of *The Maltese Falcon*, which began with the September 1929 issue. Penned by a budding socialist (Hammett would join the Communist Party in 1937), here was a contemporary parable of greed, violence, and treachery featuring characters driven by one irresistible desire: to possess an object whose fabulous value would turn out to be just that, a fable. As a comment on commodity fetishism, false credit, and the mirage of exchange value peddled by the fat cats of capitalism (Casper Gutman, the rotund criminal mastermind of the book, dresses like a cartoon version of a Wall Street banker), *The Maltese Falcon* was looking prophetic in the months following October 29, "Black Tuesday," which ended with the worst crash in the history of the US Stock Exchange. By the time Knopf published the novel in February 1930, the world found itself poised on the brink of an unprecedented economic disaster apparently brought about by the same intricate web of con games and self-deception driving the plot of Hammett's book.

Despite the author's leftist sympathies, however, *The Maltese Falcon* wears its allegory lightly and survives for reasons other than its oblique indictment of capitalism. Its hero, Sam Spade, shares none of the Op's antitypical physical features. Tall, powerfully built, with a face made out of *v*'s, Spade, we're told, resembles "a blond Satan."[8] The underworld he inhabits – the mean streets of San Francisco – is one thing he did inherit from the Op, along with his predecessor's most marketable personality traits: toughness, authenticity, cynicism, and a solitary existence. Spade can smell "bunk" from a mile away, he's impatient with "lollipops" (incompetents), and he won't "play the sap" for anybody.[9] Above all, he's a professional. When he refuses to help the *femme fatale*, Brigid O'Shaughnessey, escape punishment despite his attraction to her, it's not because he feels any closer to Miles Archer, the man she killed. In fact, Spade despised Miles. But he was Spade's partner, after all, and letting Brigid go would be "bad for every detective everywhere."[10]

Under the impetus of Humphrey Bogart's unforgettable performance in the 1941 film version of the book, Spade was immortalized as the great progenitor of the hard-boiled PI. What helped him get there, however, was a radical change in Hammett's style that essentially turned the experience of reading the book into the equivalent of watching a film.

After six years of narrating the Op's adventures in the first person, Hammett did a 180-degree about-face and told Spade's from the outside, describing everything – including Spade himself – from a rigidly objective, third-person point of view. Every emotion and intention in *The Maltese Falcon* is registered by speech, gesture, or an almost clinical description of facial features. The effect is to make every character into an emotional enigma and to render every promise of gratified desire, overt or implicit, as dubious as the "black bird" itself. The Falcon is thus not only an icon of capitalist self-delusion, but also a symbol of Hammett's radical experiment in objective narration, one he repeated in his next book, *The Glass Key* (1931), where he pushed it about as far as it could go without making his plot impossible to follow.

Featuring Ned Beaumont, a smart, tough political operative with underworld connections who sets about trying to unravel a murder that threatens to destroy his boss, Mayor Paul Madvig, *The Glass Key* represents for many readers the apex of Hammett's art before he settled for the droll social comedy of *The Thin Man*, in which Nick Charles, a retired detective, and his New York socialite wife, Nora, get pulled into a murder mystery involving one of Nick's former clients and his eccentric family. The Charleses' wit is lubricated throughout by alcohol – lots of it – a reminder that by the time *Redbook* magazine began its prepublication serialization of the book, Prohibition was over and happy days were here again. If we take Nick and Nora to be portraits of Hammett and his late-life companion, Lillian Hellman, their alcoholism is also a portent of the end of Hammett's career. Comfortably well off, he soon left for Hollywood to write and edit screenplays, spend down his fortune, and drink. Hammett would eventually die of lung cancer in 1961 having never published another book.

Other hard-boiled writers were standing in line, however: Hammett admirers like Frederic Nebel, whose Tough Dick Donohue had already replaced the Op in the pages of *Black Mask*, and Raoul Whitfield, another *Black Mask* regular and author of *Green Ice* (1930), which pivots on a frame-up involving stolen emeralds. They were soon joined by a British-educated, former oil company middle manager who made his literary debut in *Black Mask* in December 1933, the same month *The Thin Man* first appeared in *Redbook*.

Raymond Chandler was forty-five by the time he published "Blackmailers Don't Shoot." He'd tried his hand at poetry and *belles lettres* not long after graduating in 1905 from Dulwich College, an English boarding school. Born in Chicago in 1888, Chandler had spent his early childhood in Nebraska until his parents divorced. At the age of seven he accompanied his Irish mother to London, where a wealthy uncle offered to pay for the boy's education at Dulwich. There Chandler earned prizes in both modern and ancient literatures, devoured the medieval and renaissance classics – Malory's *Morte d' Arthur*, the poetry of Christopher Marlowe – and conceived literary ambitions of his own. After graduation he perfected his French and German on the Continent before sitting for the British civil service exams, placing third out of 600. But he soon found himself unhappy with a career in His Majesty's service. Sputtering along as a writer, he eventually returned to the land of his birth to seek his fortune and landed a job as an accountant after taking a correspondence course in bookkeeping. Just months before turning his hand to detective fiction, he had been fired from his job at the Dabney Oil Company in Los Angeles, where he'd worked for ten years. Drunkenness, absenteeism, and womanizing at the office were the ostensible reasons. Chandler liked to think it was for insubordination.

Chandler never hid his admiration for Hammett's accomplishments, and he shared his predecessor's ambition to make hard-boiled writing respectable in the eyes of people who took writing seriously. Lauding Hammett's plain style and realistic attitude, Chandler devised a unique first-person narrative voice reminiscent of the Op's in its laconic self-awareness but unapologetically drawn to eye-catching simile and belonging to a more sentimental and empathetic, if no less tough, detective hero: Philip Marlowe.

Chandler lit upon Marlowe's voice after a six-year process of experimentation in the pages of *Black Mask*, *Dime Detective*, and *Detective Fiction Weekly*, exploring the virtues and limitations of third- vs. first-person narration. Philip Marlowe's name mingles those of two Renaissance poets, the courtier Sir Philip Sidney, who died in military service to the queen who banished him from court, and Christopher Marlowe, who was murdered in a tavern brawl. It reflects Chandler's interest in tough men who are equally good at fighting and writing, as well as his attachment to a chivalric ideal that by the end of the Elizabethan era, as he well knew, had become notional. Marlowe represents a lonely, decent, and mostly honest knight-errant in a violent world lacking any object worth his fealty. In *The Big Sleep*, he goes to work for a venal and decrepit patriarch, General Sternwood, rescuing Sternwood's two spoiled daughters from the clutches of pornographers, blackmailers, and, eventually, the hangman while letting his client "sleep the big sleep" of blissful ignorance – or at least, denial. In the process, Marlowe becomes, despite his intentions, "part of the nastiness" himself,[11] a "shop-soiled Gallahad," as he later calls himself in *The High Window* (1942).[12]

Marlowe is sentimental enough to believe that a cold-blooded killer and adulterer would commit suicide to spare her elderly husband the embarrassment of her murder trial. He's also cynical enough to ply a recalcitrant, elderly dipsomaniac with whiskey in order to pump her for information. He drinks a lot himself, apparently because it helps make the "nastiness" bearable. In *Farewell, My Lovely* (1940), the cheap color reproduction of a Rembrandt self-portrait on the calendar in his office seems indicative of a yearning for higher things. But in Marlowe's eyes the Flemish painter is just another working stiff looking for his next "down payment," with a face "aging, saggy, full of the disgust of life and the thickening effects of liquor."[13]

In "The Simple Art of Murder," Chandler unabashedly describes his ideal detective hero as an embodiment of knightly values: "But down these mean streets a man must go who is not himself mean . . . He is the hero, he is everything . . . a complete man and a common man . . . a man of honor . . . the best man in his world and a good enough man in any world."[14] This is a far cry from the Op or Sam Spade or Ned Beaumont, none of whom pretends to be a good man, just good at what he does and expecting to be paid for it. Marlowe is typically drawn to cases he's not paid to solve and even actively discouraged from pursuing. Hired by Sternwood to take care of a blackmailer, he finds himself investigating, against his employer's wishes, the disappearance of Sternwood's former bodyguard. In *Farewell, My Lovely*, he gets dragged, literally, into a maze of betrayal, fraud, and murder by a gargantuan gangster named Moose Malloy, who's looking for a former girlfriend: "He lifted me up two more steps . . .

I wasn't wearing a gun ... I doubted if it would do me any good. The big man would probably take it away from me and eat it."[15]

This passage is as good an example as any of the straight-faced, often self-deprecatory humor of which Marlowe's voice is capable. It's a voice blazoned by infrequent but startling similes and comparisons fetched from afar but always delivered to the right address. Moose Malloy, for example, is "a big man but not more than six feet tall and not wider than a beer truck." Standing in the middle of Central Avenue, huge and menacing, he's "about as inconspicuous as a tarantula on a slice of angel food."[16] We're meant to take Marlowe's word play as consistent with his education and temperament. He's had a year or two of college, recognizes the subjunctive mood, smokes a pipe, and plays chess – mostly with himself. But he's no show-off, and can tell when he's crossed the line from the acute to the cute. When he says that Mona Mars's voice, in *The Big Sleep*, tinkled "like bells in a doll's house," he adds that he considered the comparison "silly as soon as I thought of it."[17] Marlowe's glaring similes convey the swagger of the American idiom, but the poetics that informs them is as finely balanced as a monogrammed silver butter knife.

While he took a poet's interest in the American language, Chandler was not an ardent admirer of American society, especially its California edition. His cynicism increased after VJ Day, as the nation's renewed prosperity spilled over into the commercial sprawl of postwar Southern California, "the department-store state," as Marlowe calls it in *The Little Sister* (1949): "The most of everything and the best of nothing."[18] America's big business also included big criminals. Gangsters with violent tendencies and catchy epithets – "Little Caesar," "Moose Malloy" – were being elbowed aside by "top-flight racketeers" like Eddie Mars in *The Big Sleep* and Laird Brunette in *Farewell, My Lovely*: quiet, self-effacing men who wore tuxedos and met regularly with their accountants. They "have business brains," says Captain Gregory in *The Big Sleep*. "They learn to do things that are good policy and let their personal feelings take care of themselves."[19]

By 1935, just two years after the end of Prohibition, the most flamboyant of America's so-called Public Enemies – John Dillinger, "Pretty Boy" Floyd, "Baby Face" Nelson, "Ma" Barker, and Bonnie and Clyde – had been hunted down and killed by law enforcement, which included J. Edgar Hoover's new generation of FBI "G-Men." Their imaginary counterparts had loomed larger on the movie screen than in the pages of crime fiction, but more vigorous enforcement of the motion picture industry's Production Code in 1933 led to their virtual disappearance from theaters by the middle of the decade, and from public awareness by the end of it. Organized crime figures soon became about as glamorous as bankers. Except for ostentatious walk-ons like Moose, they blended into the woodwork of endemic municipal and corporate corruption "like rats behind the wainscoting," as Marlowe put it in *The Big Sleep*.[20] Meanwhile, the common threat of the Great Depression had begun to shift readers' attention to criminals more like themselves.

Darkness Visible

The term *noir* was devised by French critics after the Second World War to describe the "dark" look of 1940s American crime films, including those based on hard-boiled detective novels like *The Maltese Falcon* and *The Big Sleep*.[21] It remains a vague descriptor, especially when applied to literature, but for a history of American crime fiction in the 1930s it serves the purpose of separating out an emerging popular subgenre that, unlike the work of Hammett and Chandler, foregrounds the criminal protagonist rather than the detective and dispenses with the puzzle element almost entirely in order to focus on suspense. The animating question of *noir* is not "Whodunit?" but "Can they get away with it?"

Noir fiction of the 1930s provided the tinder for the B-movie bonfire of the 1940s and 1950s. In fact, some of film *noir*'s best known classics, such as *Double Indemnity* (1944), were, like the cinema versions of *The Maltese Falcon* and *The Big Sleep*, adaptations of stories published during the interwar years. Though fictional *noir*'s tarnished heroes (or heroines) may occasionally cross the line between recognizably human and morally insane, they remain in most other respects somewhat ordinary versions of ourselves, never quite sociopathic enough to dispel a reader's sense of emotional complicity. The success of *noir* depends on the author's ability to generate a perverse sympathy with its criminal protagonists that is often based on the reader's shared cynicism toward America's wealthier classes, the millionaires and their minions, including bankers, lawyers, the police, and the media, who really run the show and tilt the table in their favor. While this leads, at times, to casting an innocent man or woman in the role of criminal fugitive, in general the dark star of *noir* is guilty as charged.

The genre's implicit cynicism is starkly conveyed by the title of Edward Anderson's novel, *Thieves Like Us* (1937), which resounds like a musical motif as it is applied by its trio of prison escapees to the police, under-the-counter druggists, politicians, crooked doctors, gamblers, and, above all, capitalists.[22] What distinguishes bank robbers like Bowie, T-Dub, and

Chickamaw from these other thieves is that, along with their support network of near relations, they are "Real People,"[23] which means they share the animus of the have-nots against the haves and an unquestioning mutual trust that makes them especially vulnerable to betrayal: in Bowie's case, being gunned down along with his pregnant girlfriend, Keechie, in an ambush by dozens of police. Anderson, who rode the rails as a hobo and interviewed his cousin, a convicted bank robber, for authentic details, offers in Bowie Bowers a portrait of a basically fair-minded if morally unreflective young man drawn into crime by circumstances he can't control. Anderson's hardscrabble life experiences also gave him a faultless ear for the dirt-kicking *patois* of the American Dust Bowl, an ear that is to Depression-era *noir* what the eye of photographer Walker Evans was to James Agee's contemporaneous portrait of dispossessed Southern share-croppers, *Let Us Now Praise Famous Men* (1941). Many of the people Bowie and his sidekicks meet along the trail of their headline-grabbing bank heists – poor farmers with wives and infants, filling station hands, migrant workers – could have posed for Evans's photos.

This sense of grievance against the system and those it serves appears repeatedly in the *noir* fiction of the 1930s. In Horace McCoy's *They Shoot Horses, Don't They?* (1935), a marathon dancer murders his partner at her request after the two of them reach the end of a contest lasting 879 hours with only $50 each to show for it. In this grueling competition, McCoy creates an allegory of American society as a ruthless struggle to the death that serves none but the monied interests who manipulate it for their advantage and entertainment. His title suggests that injured racehorses put out of their misery with a shot to the head receive more mercy than the fallen victims of American capitalism.

James M. Cain was not unaware of the injuries suffered by the common criminal at the hands of society's puppet-masters, folks like Katz and Sackett, the cynical defense lawyer and DA of *The Postman Always Rings Twice* (1934). But much of the staying power of his two best-known novels arises from his refusal to offer circumstance as an excuse for bad behavior. This refusal is what makes *Postman* and *Double Indemnity* more than just Depression-era indictments of the nation's class system. They are case studies in the perverse consequences of America's relentless pursuit of happiness in general. There is nothing exculpatory about the behavior of Frank Chambers and Cora Papadakis, or Walter Huff and Phyllis Nirdlinger: both pairs of lovers commit homicide out of sheer lust and greed. Frank and Cora in particular are brutally violent, all but carnivorous, in their lovemaking, which reaches a level of intoxication so intense with the murder of Cora's Greek immigrant husband, Nick, that the two are hard to recognize as members of the human race, let alone proletarian victims of The System.

Unlike Anderson and McCoy, Cain was born in 1892 into the cultured, intellectual middle class: his father was a college president, his mother an opera singer. Nothing in his background inclined him to sympathize with society's down and outs. After graduating from Washington College at the precocious age of eighteen, he became a journalist and, eventually, a protégé of H. L. Mencken, editor of the *Baltimore Mercury* and one of the great students of the American vernacular. Almost from the beginning of his writing career, Cain eschewed the "correct" English of his parents, opting for a more authentic American sound. In the first-person narrative voice of Frank Chambers – drifter, hustler, killer – he found the right key.

The enigmatic title of Cain's book may refer (as the author once suggested) to the postal routines of 1930s America, where the letter carrier rang twice if he had a package requiring a signature. But its formal significance is more salient. Everything in the book seems to happen twice: two murder attempts, two trials, two trips to the beach, two failed attempts to hit the road, the second ending in Cora's death in a car accident and, eventually, to Frank's on death row. It's as though Fate itself were "ringing" twice, carrying a parcel marked "postage due." The same goes for speech: nearly everything said in the book seems to "ring" twice. Here are its second and third lines of dialogue, spoken by Frank and Nick when they first meet in Nick's diner: "What you do, what kind of work, hey?" "Oh, one thing and another, one thing and another."[24] This pattern is repeated throughout, like a skipping phonograph needle, as conversations sprawl in search of a direction only to land on pulp clichés – "you look more like a hell cat," "killed her deader than hell," "Rip me! Rip me!" – cheap religiosity – "I looked up at the sky. It was all you could see. I thought about God" – and the verbal channeling of mass entertainment, here, radio comedian Jimmy Durante – "I got a million of them. Am I mortified?"[25]

Cain's ear was devastatingly more accurate than either Chandler's or McCoy's in recording the truly authentic *inauthenticity* of interwar American speech. By the time he wrote *Postman* the movies were talking, radio was a perennial after-dinner guest in American homes, and screen magazines, tabloids, and pulp fiction had become ubiquitous. The nation was on the doorstep of our current postmodern era of yammering simulacra. Joan Didion once wrote that Cain taught ordinary housewives in postwar America how to dream.[26] The dawn of mass entertainment taught the characters in Cain's *Postman* how to talk.

There's little of this discursive self-reflexiveness in Cain's second book, *Double Indemnity*, which was serialized in *Liberty* magazine in 1936 before its publication in book form in 1943. Walter Huff's occasionally faulty grammar shows that he may be a rung or two lower on the social scale than Phyllis Nirdlinger, but he's no drifter, like Frank Chambers, and he has no criminal record. He's got a regular job selling insurance and he's pretty good at it. Also unlike Frank, Walter has dreams of bettering himself. He's been scheming for ways to crook the insurance system well before he stopped by Phyllis's home to renew her husband's auto policy. All he's needed was a "plant out there to put down [his] bet,"[27] and Phyllis, with her half-baked scheme to insure her husband's life and then knock him off, looks like the perfect candidate. All she's needed for her half-baked scheme was the perfect chef.

Walter may be a bit more respectable than Frank Chambers, but Phyllis is a true *femme fatale*, certainly more so than spouse-killer Cora Papadakis, who for all her "hell cat" tough talk seems to be improvising from moment to moment. Phyllis, we learn, murdered Mr. Nirdlinger's former wife to get her out of the way and, after using Walter Huff to help kill Nirdlinger and collect double indemnity, she begins sleeping with her stepdaughter's boyfriend. The stepdaughter is next on her hit list. Phyllis honed her homicidal skills on eight other victims, some of them children, benefiting financially from three of their deaths. She also secretly enjoys dressing up like the "Nightmare Life-in-Death" from Coleridge's *Rime of the Ancient Mariner*.

Although he kept publishing until his death in 1977 and became a competent screenwriter, Cain never again matched the success of his first two novels. Other writers who are closely identified with *noir*, such as Erle Stanley Gardner, Cornell Woolrich, and David Goodis, did not hit their stride until after the war, when film and then TV versions of their stories made them better known, and newcomers like William Lindsay Gresham, Jim Thomson, and Patricia Highsmith extended the genre's sympathy for the devil into bleak, new regions of America's postwar psyche.

No Longer Just White, but Still Mostly Male

It was during the interwar years that American crime fiction first began to feature nonwhite detectives, specifically Asian American and African American. Broadly speaking, this development was initially made possible by China's emergence as a potential democratic ally in America's resistance to Japanese expansion in the Pacific and by the cross-racial marketing of books connected with the Harlem Renaissance. However, it was more proximately initiated by the popularity of Earl Derr Biggers's Charlie Chan, especially the movies based on Biggers's creation. All six of Charlie Chan's adventures were serialized from 1925 to 1932 in *The Saturday Evening Post* before their publication as books. By the time the last, *Keeper of the Keys*, appeared, seven Chan films had reached the screen and another twenty-five would be released by the end of 1940. Whatever we may think nowadays of Chan's stereotypical features, deferential demeanor, and fractured English, his almost yearly serialization in a "slick" (lithographed) family weekly opened the doors of white middle-class households, for the first time, to a nonwhite detective protagonist, prompting Hollywood to sit up and take notice.[28]

In the course of the decade Chan was joined by sophisticated epigones like Hugh Wiley's James Lee Wong, a Yale-educated staple of the *Post*'s direct competitor *Collier's* from 1934 to 1938, and by pulp counterparts like Raoul Whitfield's Filipino police detective Jo Gar, in *Black Mask*, as well as Frederick Lee's Richard Wong, in *G-Men*. John P. Marquand's suave and fluent Japanese special agent Mr. Moto, specifically created to take the place of Chan in the pages of the *Post* after Biggers's death, made his debut in 1935 in *No Hero*.

Meanwhile, the Harlem Renaissance had begun to create bridges between white readers and black writers, some of whom became interested in trying their hand at detective fiction. These included Jamaican American journalist W. Adolphe Roberts and satirist George Schuyler, but the most important by far was Dr. Rudolph Fisher. While the black detective figure has been traced to turn-of-the-century precursors Pauline Hopkins and John E. Bruce, who serialized their work in so-called race publications directed at a black readership,[29] Fisher, like his contemporaries Jean Toomer and Claude McKay, published in venues, including *Atlantic Monthly* and Knopf, mainly targeting white readers. In his books, Fisher surveyed the ghetto from its dives to its "dickty" (well-to-do) private clubs, making his black readers aware of their own class and color prejudices while appealing to white readers drawn to the exoticism of the city's new black colony. *The Conjure-Man Dies* (1932), featuring detective Perry Dart of the NYC police and Dr. John Archer, his friend and sidekick, helped to overturn primitivist stereotypes by placing educated black professionals resembling Fisher himself in roles generically invested by white readers with authority.

While no Native American detectives appeared on the crime-writing scene during the thirties, the decade saw the debut of America's first Native American detective writer, Todd Downing. As a member of the Choctaw nation, Downing worked hard to promote the dignity of the Indian and mestizo cultures of Mexico, where he set most of the nine detective novels he wrote from 1933 to 1941.[30] From what we know of his life and work, Downing was also a closeted gay man whose sexual preference is subtly, but insistently, manifested in his two white detective protagonists, border agent Hugh Rennert and sheriff Peter Bounty. Downing thus belongs to a handful of writers in the '30s who were beginning to "queer" crime fiction without resorting to negative stereotypes like Joel Cairo, indelibly portrayed by Peter Lorre in the 1941 film version of *The Maltese Falcon*.[31]

Although minority detectives were making inroads on white reader-ships, female detectives were faring poorly. The classical, puzzle-oriented detective novel continued to welcome female sleuths, as well as writers, but the new, masculinized hard-boiled and *noir* genres tended to reduce all women, with notable exceptions like Clive F. Adams's coarse, overweight, but effective Violet McDade, to two subservient types: the good-girl assistant and the bad-girl *femme fatale*. Effie Perrine, Sam Spade's secretary, and Brigid O'Shaughnessey, his seductive but deadly nemesis, epitomized the two. While female detectives did appear occasionally in the pulps, they were all created by men and, mostly, for men. The location of Carrie Cashyn's automatic pistol – in a garter holster under her tight skirt – was apparently of more interest to the target audience of *Crime Busters* than the gun's caliber, which went unspecified.[32] The outstanding exception to these sexist tendencies was the appearance of the teenaged Nancy Drew in 1930. Bold, independent, and clever, Nancy thrived under the benevolent care of the Stratemeyer pulp publishing syndicate, juvenile division, until 2004. Since she never grew up, Nancy never became eye candy, or had to choose between playing second fiddle to men and plugging them full of holes.

Before chalking up the misogyny of hard-boiled and *noir* crime fiction to masculinist prejudices, however, it's important to keep in mind that houses like Dial, Knopf, Frederick A. Stokes, and Simon and Schuster (publishers, respectively, of Burnett, Cain, Anderson, and McCoy) depended for their survival on women readers, stalwarts of the Delphian Society reading groups founded to promote female education, as well as the new Book of the Month Club. Blanche Knopf herself had been instrumental in her husband's acceptance not only of *Red Harvest*, but also of *The Postman Always Rings Twice*,[33] which was banned as obscene in Boston and Canada. It's difficult to believe that hard-boiled and *noir* fiction could have managed to enhance the profits of mainstream publishers without attracting the interest of women readers as well as men.

Whatever the explanation for the retrogression in American crime fiction's representation of women, hard-boiled and *noir* literature of the 1930s did manage to break down the class barriers that, until then, had prevented tough, action-oriented protagonists with working-class appeal from occupying the role of detective hero traditionally assigned to erudite eccentrics. As for nonwhite detectives, despite achieving token respectability, most would have to delay their entry through American crime literature's "Whites Only" front door until the civil rights and black power movements of the postwar era had begun to kick out the jambs. First to make it through, in 1957, was Chester Himes's black Harlem police detectives Grave Digger Jones and Coffin Ed Johnson, in *A Rage in Harlem*.

Then came everybody.

Notes

1. Carl Van Doren, "Why the Editorial Board Selected 'Little Caesar,'" *Wings* 3.6 (1929), 4–5, 4. *Wings* was a pamphlet-sized advertising periodical that accompanied each new Dial Press publication in its Library of America imprint.
2. For details of these origins, see Erin Smith, *Hard-Boiled: Working Class Readers and Pulp Fiction* (Philadelphia, PA: Temple University Press, 2000).
3. For a complete genre typology, see Charles J. Rzepka, *Detective Fiction* (Cambridge: Polity, 2005), 9–12.
4. Raymond Chandler, "The Simple Art of Murder," in *Raymond Chandler: Later Novels and Other Writings* (New York: Library of America, 1995), 977–92, 978.
5. Agatha Christie, *The Body in the Library* (New York: HarperCollins, 1992 [1941]), 196.
6. Chandler, "Simple Art of Murder," 989.
7. Letter to Hammett of March 12, 1928. In Diane Johnson, *Dashiell Hammett: A Life* (New York: Random House, 1983), 70.
8. Dashiell Hammett, *The Maltese Falcon*, in *Dashiell Hammett: Complete Novels* (New York: Library of America, 1999), 391–585, 391.
9. Hammett, *Maltese Falcon*, 507, 558, 580.
10. Hammett, *Maltese Falcon*, 582.
11. Raymond Chandler, *The Big Sleep*, in *Raymond Chandler: Stories and Early Novels* (New York: Library of America, 1999), 587–764, 764.

12. Raymond Chandler, *The High Window,* in *Raymond Chandler: Stories and Early Novels* (New York: Library of America, 1999), 985–1177, 1136.

13. Raymond Chandler, *Farewell, My Lovely,* in *Raymond Chandler: Stories and Early Novels* (New York: Library of America, 1999), 765–984, 795.

14. Chandler, "Simple Art of Murder," 991–92.

15. Chandler, *Farewell, My Lovely,* 769.

16. Chandler, *Farewell, My Lovely,* 767.

17. Chandler, *Big Sleep,* 733.

18. Raymond Chandler, *The Little Sister,* in *Raymond Chandler: Later Novels and Other Writings* (New York: Library of America, 1995), 201–416, 268.

19. Chandler, *Big Sleep,* 683.

20. Chandler, *Big Sleep,* 637.

21. For a more nuanced etymological analysis, see Lee Horsley, *The Noir Thriller* (New York: Palgrave Macmillan, 2001), 1–6.

22. Edward Anderson, *Thieves Like Us,* in *Crime Novels: American Noir of the 1930s and 40s* (New York: Library of America, 1997), 217–377. 232, 232, 237, 280, 294, 342.

23. Anderson, *Thieves Like Us,* 285.

24. James M. Cain, *The Postman Always Rings Twice,* in *Crime Novels: American Noir of the 1930s and 40s* (New York: Library of America, 1997), 1–95, 3.

25. Cain, *Postman Always Rings Twice,* 11, 19, 36, 22, 85.

26. Joan Didion, "Some Dreamers of the Golden Dream," in *Slouching towards Bethlehem* (New York: Farrar, Straus and Giroux, 1968), 3–25, 15.

27. James M. Cain, *Double Indemnity* (New York: Vintage Books, 1992), 24.

28. For a more detailed analysis of Chan's impact on interwar detective fiction, see Charles J. Rzepka, "Race, Region, Rule: Genre and the Case of Charlie Chan," *PMLA* 122.5, 1463–81.

29. For a more thorough account of these developments, see Stephen F. Soitos, *The Blues Detective: A Study of African American Detective Fiction* (Amherst: University of Massachusetts Press, 1996).

30. For more details, see Charles J. Rzepka, "Red and White and Pink All Over: Vacilada, Indian Identity, and Todd Downing's Queer Response to Modernity," *Texas Studies in Literature and Language,* 59.3, 353–84.

31. Curtis Evans, "Introduction," in *Murder in the Closet: Essays on Queer Clues in Crime Fiction before Stonewall* (Jefferson, NC: McFarland, 2016), 1–17.

32. Theodore Tinsley, "Riddle in Silk," in *Hard-Boiled Dames,* ed. Bernard A. Drew (New York: St. Martin's Press, 1986), 3–20.

33. Robert Polito, "Note on the Texts," in *Crime Novels: American Noir of the 1930s and 40s* (New York: Library of America, 1997), 983–85, 983.

CHAPTER 15

Documentary Work

Jeff Allred

The Depression years were a period, like our own, in which artists employed new media forms and technologies to capture the everyday lives of the ordinary subjects who suffered most from its social and economic dislocations. These "forgotten" (in Roosevelt's famous figure) were remembered, above all, through documentary, an aesthetic mode that, despite its roots in the late nineteenth century, first emerged as a discursive category in the late 1920s and quickly found wide currency as a cultural keyword of the following decade.[1] Documentary work – a capacious term that encompasses a wide range of artifacts and practices, from films to photo-texts to ethnographies to oral histories – was the central mode by which Americans oriented themselves in the Depression, knitting together fragments of text, image, and recorded voice in a vicarious analog of knitting together a manifestly unraveling body politic into recognizable, sustainable form.[2]

The documentary work that commanded so much attention in Depression-era culture is oddly positioned in literary and cultural histories, wedged between the realism and naturalism of the late nineteenth century and the modernism that consolidated its status in the immediate postwar period as a term for interwar experimental writing. Until recently, Depression-era documentary work appeared as a survival, in the anthropological sense, of naturalist writing kept alive in the hothouse of interwar leftist radicalism but ill suited to a postwar ecosystem dominated by Cold War liberalism and its aesthetic ideology of high modernism. Nor was the dismissal of Depression documentary limited to mandarin modernists: in his influential literary history, *On Native Grounds* (1942), Alfred Kazin describes the recent outpouring of documentary work as a "vast granary of facts on life in America" that constitutes "only a sub-literature ... a preparation for literature."[3] Thus documentary work appeared, even to a left-liberal critic of the era invested in the political dimension of literature, as something relatively inert and ephemeral, more a sheaf of documents in the historian's sense, than a fully realized aesthetic.

In the past several decades, however, post-Habermasian work on publics and counter-publics as well as work in the "new modernisms" tradition have enabled a very different understanding of the place of documentary in literary history. As theories of the "public sphere" have grappled with the coevolution of mass media and mass politics in the early twentieth century, documentary features prominently as a "form of democratic and social pedagogy" that enables a late public sphere in which audiences of documentary texts become aware of themselves as potential members of publics in a process that is much more contingent and fluid than that derived from eighteenth-century cultures of print by Habermas.[4] Jonathan Kahana uses the documentary work of the Depression era as a springboard for thinking about the long arc of an American documentary tradition fundamentally oriented toward the construction of publics and counter-publics. From this perspective, the hallmark of documentary is its self-reflexive positing of a public whose necessary condition of existence and effective political articulation is the documentary text itself. Rather than focusing on the representational problem of the real violence and disorder of the period, documentary addresses the "problem of the public" as articulated by Dewey, Lippmann, and others in the interwar period: how to make the complexity of modernity comprehensible to ordinary citizens and how to hail these citizens as subjects of agency empowered to act upon that modernity rather than being its passive objects.[5]

One can also trace the reemergence of interest in 1930s documentary through the rise of the "new modernisms," and more specifically the articulation of a "late modernist" aesthetic. Late modernism, as most fully theorized in the work of Tyrus Miller, grows out of the wrenching sociopolitical strife of the global depression, capturing in its fragmentary forms the violence and absurdity that characterized everyday life amid the economic collapse and ascendency of extreme political modes in the 1930s and 1940s. Late modernists, Miller argues, "sought to bind the restless, disturbing collective energies of recorded music, fashion, advertising, radio, and film" and "expose(d) to critical view the stigmata where mass politics and urban life left their forceful signatures," a description that maps onto the more experimental examples of documentary work in the Depression.[6] One might expect the documentary mode to be too square and mimetic, too closely aligned with the normative speech of the public sphere to draw from the unruly energy of "late modernism." A close examination of the work of the period, however, reveals that, just as the

Depression era was the "golden age of distortion in the arts," its documentarians deployed their cameras not as mimetic agents but as elements in media assemblages devoted to the expression of grotesque, suffering bodies and the "sensational" affects that orbited around them.[7]

This chapter collates a range of representative examples of Depression-era documentary work, from films to photo-textual essays in books and magazines to novels to poems, and explains how they embody, in different ways and to different degrees, these two major tendencies. On the one hand, I show how works like Pare Lorentz's films and the photo-magazines *Fortune* and *Life* manifest an emergent centripetal mode of documentary that mirrored the broader New Deal's official discourse, calling attention to the "forgotten" at the "bottom of the economic pyramid" and integrating them into the body politic via a disembodied, authoritative state or corporate voice. On the other hand, I examine works that moved against this grain, using recognizably "late modernist" techniques in a centrifugal mode to call attention to fissures in and exclusions from the New Deal order and to summon forth counter-publics bent on imagining new ways of speaking and acting in the first-person plural that exceed the New Deal's discursive norms and imaginative limits. I end with a look forward, considering the legacy of this work in light of more recent experiments in documentary.

Explaining America to Itself: Documentary Continuities

As Cara Finnegan has noted, Roosevelt's classic address to the nation at his second inaugural veils executive power in metaphors of seeing, metaphors enhanced by the abundant circulation of documentary images produced under the auspices of the New Deal's cultural wing:

> I see a great nation, upon a great continent, blessed with a great wealth of natural resources . . .
>   I see millions of families trying to live on incomes so meager that the pall of family disaster hangs over them day by day.
>   I see millions whose daily lives in city and on farm continue under conditions labeled indecent by a so-called polite society half a century ago
>   I see one-third of a nation ill-housed, ill-clad, ill-nourished.[8] . . .

If the central socioeconomic problematic of the New Deal was uneven development – the maldistribution of technology and capital that left the hinterlands in an arrested stage compared to metropolitan zones – Roosevelt's way of seeing allowed Americans to imagine "forgotten" spaces and people as part of an emergent modernity. Seeing here is explicitly an act of benevolent exercise of power, a power available to any of the proper citizens in the audience and, more broadly, to anyone who has "seen" what Roosevelt performatively sees through the diffusion of millions of images of poor people across the continent through the agency of the Farm Security Administration photographic archive, the US Film Service, and other New Deal cultural projects. This rhetorical mode is central to documentary work in the period, though of course it does not originate with Roosevelt or even with the broader act of mechanical "seeing" his administration enabled on such a vast scale.

An important precursor to Roosevelt's rhetoric is the muckraking jour-nalism that emerged several decades prior in the work of Jacob Riis, Ida Tarbell, Lincoln Steffens, and others. One also finds the division between middle-class writers and readers on one hand and abject victims of obscure social forces on the other. Riis's work is especially relevant: *How the Other Half Lives* (1890) arguably invented the genre of the "documentary book" that developed into one of the Depression era's most conspicuous cultural forms. Throughout the text, Riis toggles between a masterful voice that provides a broad survey of social structure and urban policy and a more intimate, homiletic voice that invites readers to partake in a ground-level view of the lives of the "other half." Like a guide of one of the popular "slum tours" of late nineteenth-century cities, Riis binds readers to the narrator in a shared ambience of curiosity, irony, and thrill. Having contextualized the project with several chapters that sketch out a map of the social structures that constrict the lives of the "other half," Riis invites readers to step onto the map, as it were, taking a stroll through the Lower East Side as he plays Virgil to the reader's Dante. "There is nothing to be afraid of," Riis assures readers before guiding them around the Dark Continent of America's urban immigrant poor: the comment allows read-ers to have their cake and eat it, experiencing the immediacy of Riis's documentary mode, especially in light of its shocking photographs, yet remembering that they do so from the safe space of bourgeois domesticity.[9]

Riis's work anticipates Depression-era documentary not merely through similar subject matter and rhetorical mode. Like the photographers, cine-matographers, and radio producers of the New Deal era, he was an relentless tinkerer with the new media of his day, less the author of a book than the architect of a media platform that included "magic lantern" lectures, photographs, books, and journalistic pieces advocating housing reform.[10] Moreover, he aligns his documentary work squarely with the State and its disciplinary project: Riis had reported on law enforcement prior to working on *Other Half*, and in researching the book, he often traveled the beat with police officers. He dramatizes this fact vividly throughout his autobiography, referring to his crew as a "raiding party" that "brought terror wherever it went," a terror rooted in flash powder explosions and the anxiety of public exposure as much as billy clubs and harassment from cops.[11]

The New Deal variant of documentary also rhetorically aligns itself with the State, if in a cooler and more abstract register. The films of Pare Lorentz (e.g., *The Plow That Broke the Plains* [1936] and *The River* [1938]) best represent this strain of documentary. Like Riis's text, Lorentz's best-known films address their audience as part of a "we" aligned with State power and charged with moral urgency to reform dysfunctional policies and disorganized spaces. Lorentz's films, however, radicalize elements of this discourse, replacing Riis's intimate homiletic voice with a transcendent and impersonal voice that speaks to the public in an emergent narrative form conventionally known as the "voice of God."

As recent critics have argued, this voice might be more precisely called a "voice of the State" in Lorentz's work,[12] an act of "ventriloquizing" that "gained its authority by an uncanny ability to produce and fill empty spaces," projecting a unified public of "Americans" out of a scattered, heterogeneous, unevenly developed social field.[13] This expansive voice covers a much broader narrative scope than in the work of Riis and other muckrakers, as both films survey the territory of the United States over its entire history, in the process reducing individual faces and bodies to tiny pieces in a vast mosaic: as Lorentz's voiceover puts it in *Plow*, "This is a record of land ... rather than people."[14] In fact, the films are less records of land than testimonies to the biopolitical aspirations of the State in the New Deal. Following a common trope of the era, Lorentz's films conceive of the nation as a technologically enhanced body with its "nerve center" in Washington, an executive organ that gradually restores/repairs/replaces the body's far-flung, ailing members in the South and West. The rather mundane details of soil conservation and hydroelectric power, then, take on a nobler and more dynamic cast through this allegory of embodiment, especially in light of the lofty iambs of Lorentz's voiceovers set to Virgil Thompson's stirring score.[15]

The most influential source of affirmative representations of America in a "continuity" style of documentary undoubtedly came from Time Inc., and especially from its pioneering photographic magazines *Fortune* and *Life*. By the late 1930s, Time Inc. publications reached, by some estimates, 30 million Americans each month through a stable of publications that spanned media (the photo magazine *Life*, the newsreel and radio segments *The March of Time*, the newsmagazine *Time*) and class positions (the working-class newsreels and *Life*, the professional-managerial *Time*, and the executive class *Fortune*).[16] Like Lorentz's films, Time publications were national in scope and hailed a vast, democratic audience with its distinctive "Timestyle": not the voice of the State, but a corporate voice that dissolved the small army of the company's researchers, photographers, layout artists, writers, and editors into a single, impersonal narrator. What distinguishes Time publications, and especially *Life*, from Lorentz's work and the muckraking tradition it derives from, is its affirmative tone. In the words of founder and board chairman Henry Luce, the "most exciting discovery" of *Life*'s producers "is the extraordinary power of the photograph to dramatize and lend fresh interest ... to the good [to] the normal and calm as distinct from that which is disruptive or fantastic."[17] If the aim of left-wing traditions of social documentary is to agitate and propagandize, to transform disinterested spectators into subjects invested with passion and agency, the aim of *Life* is nearly opposite: to engender the pleasure of what Terry Smith calls "the submission to the spectacle."[18] The prospectus for *Life*, circulated to potential investors in the new enterprise in 1936, captures something of this distinctive pleasure in ways that both draw from Roosevelt's way of looking and revise it in a more conservative direction.

To see through Roosevelt's eyes, or Lorentz's, is to see a dismembered body that awaits reassembly by the Promethean labor of experts and technocrats enabled by the democratic participation of the public that is coalescing among members of the audience of the film itself. To see through the eyes of *Life* is to endure neither agitation nor propaganda: one experiences a teeming world that invites the endless seriality of flipping-through in ways that anticipate the aesthetics of televisual "total flow" and the endless, decentered navigation of Web culture. The very different valence of this mode of continuity becomes clear in an early internal memo from Luce: "To LIFE, the sit-down strike is not Labor Problems or Big Words between a dozen men you really don't give a damn about. In LIFE, the hot news of the sit-down strike is that the people sit down! Or don't. So relaxing. And so true."[19]

One of Luce's employees at *Fortune*, poet, editor, and New Dealer Archibald MacLeish, published a documentary project that, while recognizably part of this centripetal, unitary mode of social documentary in the period, diverges from it in interesting ways. MacLeish's *Land of the Free* (1938) is one of a raft of "documentary books" published between 1937 and 1942 that combined photographs and text to capture some aspect of the Depression's disarray.[20] *Land of the Free* was deeply influenced by Lorentz's films, most obviously in the book's design, which features a printed "soundtrack" that gives the photographs a voiceover of sorts and claims for the book the kind of immediacy and immersiveness associated with film. Like many examples of the genre, MacLeish's text features dramatic layouts with his first-person plural, poetic "soundtrack" on the verso side and full-page photos on the recto. Like *Life* (and many competing documentary books from the period), *Land of the Free* filled the reader's visual field with dramatic two-page spreads that approximate the wide aspect ratio of cinema, bringing the aesthetics of Hollywood into the home a decade before the wide adoption of television.[21] What distinguishes MacLeish's books from both Lorentz's and Time Inc.'s products, however, is his perspectival shift. MacLeish's narrating "we" is neither the voice of the State nor a corporate voice charming readers into submission. MacLeish's narrator is squarely situated among the "folk," the *plebs* rather than the *populus*.[22] This "we" is a paradoxical entity: confronted by the erosion of the economy, social norms, and the earth itself, its primary response is a *lack* of knowledge, in near-perfect opposition to the way Lorentz hails readers as part of an immanent, masterful State. The text's opening line is "We don't know," and what follows recurs constantly to variations on this theme, which resonates with the ubiquitous theme of ordinary Americans as "puzzled" by the Depression (Figure 15.1).[23] Kahana argues that the documentary mode does not issue from an a priori public nor does it index a knowable reality; rather, it is a performance that constructs that which it represents.[24] MacLeish's text is a crystalline example, positing an impossible subject: the subaltern who speaks, but who can only express its refusal to talk and its inability to know, and who is stuck in the subjunctive mood, a "wondering" tone that is remote from the masterful graphs, maps, and blueprints of New Deal-sponsored work. *Land of the Free* thus occupies a kind of fault line in the documentary work of the period, between those projects that assume a unified national culture capable of narrating itself in a continuous form and those that express deep skepticism about such unities. Alfred Kazin claimed that the intent of Depression-era documentarians was "to explain America to itself": MacLeish's text hints at ways in which this attempt at mirroring proved problematic (if productively so) for many writers.[25] The next section considers writers who reflected an "America" back to readers that was not "relaxing" or united but riddled with fissures, opacities, and distortions.

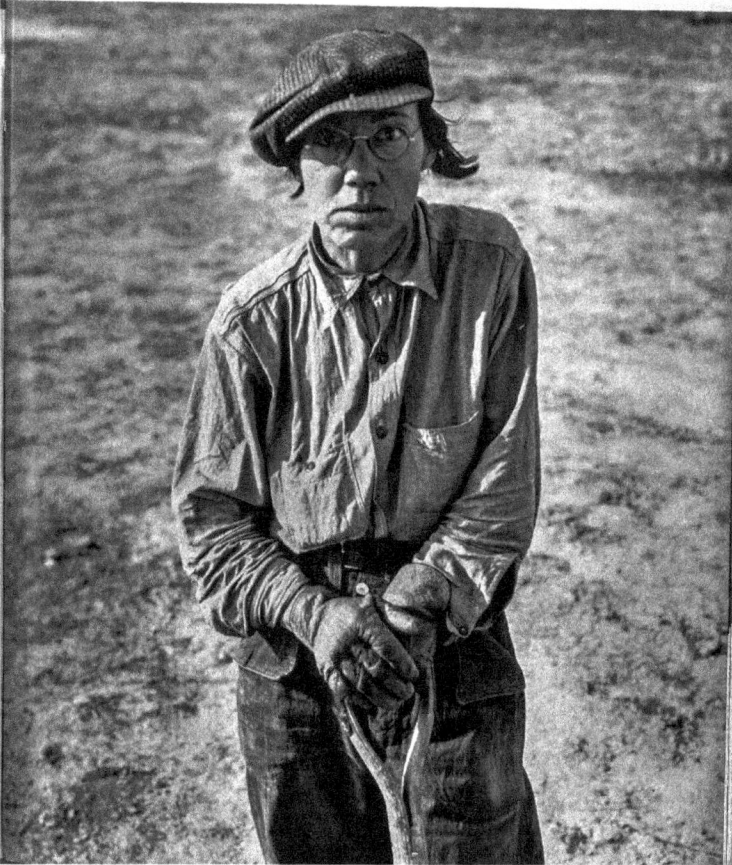

Figure 15.1 Dorothea Lange, "Indian Woman in a Migratory Labor Contractor's Camp in California"

Documentary and/as "Late Modernism"

The mainstream of Depression-era documentary work is clearly oriented toward the production of "official images" that articulate "the people" to themselves in a centripetal, consensus manner via a "voice of the State."[26] Alongside this mainstream, with its clear antecedents in Progressive-era cultural forms, one also finds a very different strain of documentary art, one bound more closely to the modernist aesthetic that transformed multiple areas of culture on both sides of the Atlantic in the early twentieth century. There has been remarkable resistance to linking documentary with modernism until quite recently. Whereas modernism has grown ever-more forceful as a literary critical center of gravity since its consolidation as a critical term in the postwar period, documentary quickly faded from view in literary criticism and history after World War II amid the Red Scare and the predominance of exceptionalist, "vital center" constructions of American culture. To the extent that critics attended to American documentary work in the mid- and late twentieth century, they overwhelmingly insisted on documentary as an enterprise rooted in the ethos of the documentarian as advocate and source of passionate "concern" or "witness" vis-à-vis subaltern subjects and thereby downplayed issues of formal experimentation or narrative subtlety.[27] Thus "modernism" and "documentary" have been kept relatively separate in critical and historical work, a fact that is especially striking given the near simultaneity of their appearance as discursive terms in the late 1920s and the many convergences between in artistic practice.[28]

Moving against the grain of this critical habit of segregating the terms – on the one hand, documentary's mimetic form, its broad public address, and its use of the normative language of the public sphere; on the other, modernism's problematization of representation, its coterie audiences, and its fragmentary play with language – critics have recently begun to examine work that occurs at the intersection of documentary and modernist aesthetics, finding instances of "convergence" and "complementarity" rather than simple opposition in ways that enliven our understanding of how the more experimental face of Depression-era documentary constitutes an important, if neglected, legacy.[29]

Viewed from this perspective, the more experimental documentary work of the Depression era participates in what Tyrus Miller calls "late modernism," a bearer of "recessive traits" within modernism's DNA that used experimental form to engage interwar mass culture and the dislocations of societies on both sides of the Atlantic torn apart by economic catastrophe and war.[30] For Miller, the grotesque is central to late modernism as a figural strategy that reveals how modernity left its "stigmata" on the social body. The modernist strain of Depression documentary makes constant reference to the interruptive force of the "documents" that are inserted into its textual forms, jarring readers out of passive modes of consuming visual spectacles in ways that resonate with Brecht's roughly simultaneous disruption of the conventions of theater. Rather than interpellate readers as part of a social dominant or foundational *plebs*, modernist documentaries produce what Jacques Ranciere calls "dis-identification," convening reader/viewers in ways that enable "new modes of political construction of common objects and new possibilities of collective enunciation."[31] Art becomes political, for Ranciere, insofar as it disrupts habitual dispositions and itineraries and creates a "multiplicity of folds and gaps in the fabric of common experience that change the cartography of the perceptible, the thinkable, and the feasible." The central political/aesthetic problem for documentary modernism, then, is not the technocratic problem of how to bring the unmodern "folk" online, so to speak, through electrification, education, and industry, but the thornier problem of confronting uneven development in ways that privilege disidentification and refuse to assume the stable foundation of collectivities like "America" or the "middle class" to anchor proper political programs.

James Agee vividly exemplifies this practice in his instructions to readers from within the pages of *Let Us Now Praise Famous Men* (1940), his photo-textual collaboration with Walker Evans:

> If I could do it; I'd do no writing at all here. It would be photographs; the rest would be fragments of cloth, bits of cotton, lumps of earth, records of speech, pieces of wood and iron, phials of odors, plates of food and excrement. Booksellers would consider it quite a novelty; critics would murmur, yes, but is it art; and I could trust a majority of you to use it as you would a parlor game.
>
> A piece of the body torn out by the roots might be more to the point.[32]

If the central project of centripetal documentary work like that of Lorentz is to reassemble and quicken a damaged social body in a technocratic mode, modernist documentary sought to interrupt this process, working centrifugally by exploring marginal spaces and broken people and objects on their own terms. Agee implores readers here to linger on the melancholy and suffering of the era, acknowledging ruptures in the social body without seeking to master them. Rather than incorporating the various documents – from photographs to food to odors and clods of dirt – into a continuous fabric by means of a soundtrack or voiceover, Agee wishes to abandon language altogether and force readers to eschew any hope for mastery or unity in a direct confrontation with the quiddities of the lives of his subjects. This emphasis on discontinuity and supplementarity, in the deconstructionist sense, is underscored by the book design of *Famous Men*, which begins with Walker Evans's photographs, presented with no text whatsoever, and continues with Agee's unillustrated text. Thus readers must continually shuffle between pages and, more importantly, shift between sensibilities (Evans's photographs are iconic and stark; Agee's text is torrential and self-reflexive) in order to make sense of the text. Readers of Agee's text are hailed strangely, and in sharp contrast to readers of *Fortune* or viewers of State documentaries: in one of the many moments Agee buttonholes readers, advocating for the most strenuous, serious reading practice imaginable, he argues that Evans's portrait of Annie Mae Gudger should conjure both "a single, holy, unrepeatable individual," and, more abstractly, a unit of humanity "to be multiplied ... by the two billion human creatures that are alive upon the planet today."[33] Facing the union of particular and universal embodied within this photograph, Agee instructs readers to "contemplate, try to encompass, the one annihilating chord" made up of "all these individuals."[34] The vague gesture toward universality and humanism is overwhelmed here by the investment in an "annihilation" that shatters habitual page-flipping consumption of photographs, sentimental appropriation of abject others, and the use of documentaries as instruments of projecting unified publics.

The beginning of Richard Wright's documentary book *12 Million Black Voices* (1941) offers a further case in point. In sharp (and, one imagines, conscious) contrast to Roosevelt's famous performance of *seeing* the "one-third" of poor Americans with such acuity, Wright addresses readers from a very different narrative location than is customary in Depression-era documentary:

> Each day when you see us black folk upon the dusty land of the farms or upon the hard pavement of the city streets, you usually take us for granted and think you know us, but our history is far stranger than you suspect, and we are not what we seem.
>
> Our outward guise still carries the old familiar aspect which three hundred years of oppression in America have given us, but beneath the garb of the black laborer, the black cook, and the black elevator operator lies an uneasily tied knot of pain and hope whose snarled strands converge from many points of time and space.[35]

As in Lorentz's films (and many other texts from the period), Wright's narrator is a first-person plural, but it is a "we" that addresses readers from the far side of a racial and cultural divide, a narrator who confronts readers with their *failure* to see and thus to know the subaltern "black folk" of the title.[36] The photograph of an elderly, blind sharecropper that accompanies this text doubles down on this idea dramatically: whereas an initial glance moves with the grain of long-standing traditions aligning looking with mastery and power, with a majority white audience looking in on a minority subject who is "caught unawares" and thus incapable of dissimulating, a closer look reveals the image as an uncanny mirror for the readers themselves, who are unable to see clearly enough to solve the "knot" of blackness (Figure 15.2). Unable for the present, that is, for the text leads

Figure 15.2 Jack Delano, "Sharecropper, Georgia."

readers through a complex, dramatic history of the "black folk" from the Middle Passage to the present, culminating in a return to the self-reflexive, pedagogical tone of the text's opening: "Look at us and know us, for we are you, looking back at you from the dark mirror of our lives!" (146).

If this closure seemingly resembles that of consensus narratives like Roosevelt's, note the deep differences: Wright's text carefully constructs, rather than assumes, a public, and that public is explicitly a counter-public, a nascent entity that is beginning to know itself as such and demand recognition from peripheral spaces of a broader social sphere. Moreover, through the agency of the dark mirror the documentary text becomes, not a space to express a State-aligned spirit voiced by an immanent "we" but a traumatized, opaque space in which one sees a self that is always already contaminated by others and by a violent history.

The value of linking Depression documentary with "late modernism" is especially apparent when considering Erskine Caldwell and Margaret Bourke-White's *You Have Seen Their Faces* (1937), the most commercially and critically successful documentary book of the period that was vilified, first by Agee in *Famous Men* and later by waves of postwar critics, for its perceived insensitivity to its rural subjects and its fictional overwriting of their voices. Like most examples of the genre, *Faces* combines large, dramatic photographs chronicling Bourke-White and Caldwell's trip through the Deep South in 1936 with a third-person prose analysis contextualizing the photos more broadly in a familiar agit-prop mode. *Faces*, however, features captions composed *post facto* by Caldwell in a blatant breach of the social scientific scrupulousness of Dorothea Lange and Paul Taylor's *American Exodus* or the searing self-reflexive agony of Agee's text. This seeming violation of mimetic and ethical norms has the advantage of denaturing the text, calling attention to its constructedness and allowing the authors to play with readers' expectations in ways that produce powerful moments of disidentification in Ranciere's sense.

Faces includes a range of images that are "sensational" in the double sense employed by Joseph Entin's work on the Depression era: they are shocking and excessive, even to the point of crude stereotype at times, but they also work on an affective register to summon mingled feelings of sympathy and disgust, the terrain of the grotesque. The last section of the text, where Caldwell's narrative shifts from a diagnostic to a prescriptive mode, laying out specific proposals to ameliorate Southern poverty, features images of scarred, damaged bodies and terrain that belie this technocratic confidence. One of the most arresting depicts a family framed by the front doorway of a shotgun house: of the many things out of joint in this picture – the boy's lack of pants, the family's lack of a middle generation, the atmosphere of poverty and inertia – most prominent is the enormous goiter that juts out from the woman's neck (figure 3.15). Goiters are caused by malnutrition, and the image thus simultaneously points unsubtly to the maldistribution of resources that leaves "backward" areas undeveloped, but it also has a subtler register enabled by the caption, "Poor people get passed by."[37] The caption gestures to the setting in which readers consume images of the poor, casually thumbing through particular cases to grasp a general phenomenon, often in a state of pleasurable distraction. Here, however, the authors present an image that is hard to consume, impossible to "pass by," an image that creates an uncanny space of identification in the way it sticks in the reader's craw and refuses to be abstracted as part of a disembodied "half" or "one-third" as mere example. Both coauthors were intimately familiar with mass culture, and both were already wealthy from their work for industry and mass-circulation magazines (Bourke-White) and production of best-sellers (Caldwell). Their recognizably late modernist attempt in *Faces* to problematize such consumption and short-circuit the habitual structure that make it work smoothly, speaks to the rich interplay between mass cultural modes and modernist documentary in this period.

Figure 15.3 Margaret Bourke-White. Sweetfern, Arkansas, "Poor People Get
Passed By."

Conclusion: Extending the Document

In a postscript following *Book of the Dead*, her 1938 long poem documenting the deaths due to silicosis of hundreds (or perhaps thousands) of Union
Carbide employees in West Virginia, Muriel Rukeyser sums up her aesthetic aims thus: "Poetry can extend the document."[38] The statement

resonates with a number of theories from the 1930s linking poetry to the strangeness and evanescence of everyday life in a late modernist manner: Williams's "no ideas but in things"; Moore's definition of poetry as "imaginary gardens with real toads in them"; and Pound's claim that poetry is "news that STAYS news," for example. After a long period of dormancy, the twenty-first century has seen a remarkable resurgence of documentary work of all kinds, but especially work that draws inspiration from late modernists' attempts to "extend the document" by weaving undigested fragments of social reality into dynamic, interpretively unstable texts.

The most direct line of descent of this invocation of the spirit of Depression documentary is the recent rise of "docupoetics" (or simply "DocPo") as a self-aware poetics in the past decade or so. Of the many poets working in this tradition today, from Claudia Rankine to Nikki Finney to C. D. Wright to Adrian C. Louis, Mark Nowak's *Coal Mountain Elementary* (2009) best illustrates contemporary revisions of the Depression-era legacy of documentary work.[39] Like Rukeyser, Nowak surveys a terrain littered with dead and damaged bodies; like Rukeyser, he also works synoptically to compile multiple perspectives, ranging from workers' testimonies to unedited news reports to, most chillingly, excepts from the coal industry's curriculum distributed gratis to K-12 schools to shill the benefits of coal. Nowak extends Rukeyser's project in two ways that point to the ways in which twenty-first century DocPo appropriates late modernist form and theme critically, with an eye to its limitations. First, Novak's text is resolutely global in scope: coal country extends from West Virginia to China, a central locus in the text, especially through the photographs of Nowak's collaborator, Ian Teh, in an attempt to aid readers in sketching for themselves richer cognitive maps of the flows of bodies, technology, and capital that are activated when they casually throw light switches. Second, *Coal Mountain Elementary* signals the roots of documentary in pedagogy (the term derives from the Latin *docere*, "to teach"), mounting a counter-pedagogy that urges pupils to weave together their own interpretations from the resolutely paratactic strands of the text. Nowak writes with the full awareness that such an effort is locked in an asymmetrical war against corporate media and PR apparatuses that enjoy a much greater reach, one that extends even into ostensibly democratic public school systems. Nevertheless, in ways that hearken back to Riis's media platform *avant la lettre*, Nowak maintains a moving blog that simply chronicles the mining disasters that continue to occur after the publication of his poem with appalling regularity. If *Coal Mining Education*, like *Book of the Dead* before it, extends the document through poetry, Novak reverses the poles post-publication, letting reality spill out of the text and calling attention to the ways in which the document might extend poetry.

Notes

Thanks to Sophie Bell, Sarah Chinn, Anna Mae Duane, Joseph Entin, and Hildegard Hoeller for their helpful suggestions on a draft of this chapter.

1. "Documentary," in its current sense to describe aesthetic practice, was coined in 1926 by filmmaker and critic John Grierson to describe the work of filmmaker Robert Flaherty. See J. Grierson (as "The Moviegoer"), "Flaherty's Poetic *Moana*," *New York Sun*, February 8, 1926. Reprinted in Lewis Jacobs, ed., *The Documentary Tradition* (New York: W. W. Norton & Company, Inc., 1979), 25–26.
2. William Stott's book remains the fullest survey of the range of what he calls "documentary expression" in the period. See W. Stott, *Documentary Expression and Thirties America* (Chicago: University of Chicago Press, 1986).
3. A. Kazin, *On Native Grounds: An Interpretation of Modern American Prose Literature* (New York: Reynal & Hitchcock, 1942), 489.
4. J. Kahana, *Intelligence Work: The Politics of American Documentary* (New York: Columbia University Press, 2008), 1.
5. Kahana, *Intelligence Work*, 9–26.
6. T. Miller, *Late Modernism: Politics, Fiction, and the Arts between the World Wars* (Berkeley: University of California Press, 1999), 6.
7. J. Entin, *Sensational Modernism: Experimental Fiction and Photography in Thirties America* (Chapel Hill: University of North Carolina Press, 2007), 11.
8. F. D. Roosevelt, "The Second Inaugural Address. 'I See One-Third of a Nation Ill-Housed, Ill-Clad, Ill-Nourished,' January 20, 1937," in *The Public Papers and Addresses of Franklin D. Roosevelt*, ed. S. I. Rosenman (New York: Macmillan, 1941), 4–5; C. A. Finnegan, *Picturing Poverty: Print Culture and FSA Photographs* (Washington, DC: Smithsonian Books, 2003), xi.
9. J. A. Riis, *How the Other Half Lives: Studies among the Tenements of New York* (New York: Penguin Books, 1997), 26.
10. B. Yochelson and D. Czitrom, *Rediscovering Jacob Riis: Exposure Journalism and Photography in Turn-of-the-Century New York* (Chicago: University of Chicago Press, 2014), 49–53.
11. J. Riis, *The Making of an American* (New York: Macmillan, 1901), 268.
12. Kahana, *Intelligence Work*, 105; C. Wolfe, "Historicising the 'Voice of God': The Place of Vocal Narration in Classical Documentary," *Film History* 9, no. 2 (1997): 149–67.
13. Kahana, *Intelligence Work*, 94.
14. P. Lorentz, *The Plow That Broke the Plains, Documentary, Short, Drama* (US Films, 1936).

15. For examples of the allegory of the national body with the New Deal as its nervous system, see E. Rosskam, *Washington: Nerve Center*, ed. R. Black (New York: Alliance Book Corporation, Longmans, Green and Company, 1939), and H. G. Wells, *Experiment in Autobiography* (New York: Macmillan, 1934), 681–82.

16. D. Macdonald, "'Time' and Henry Luce," *Nation*, 1937, 501.

17. H. R. Luce, "The Photograph and Good News," in *The Ideas of Henry Luce*, ed. J. K. Jessup (New York: Atheneum, 1969), 44.

18. T. Smith, *Making the Modern: Industry, Art, and Design in America* (Chicago: University of Chicago Press, 1993), 343–44.

19. Qtd. in L. Wainwright, *The Great American Magazine: An Insider History of Life*, vol. 1 (New York: Knopf, 1986), 92.

20. For a thorough exploration of this archive, see Stott, *Documentary Expression*, 237.

21. Some of these texts' initial producers and readers made this connection. Photographer and layout editor Edwin Rosskam, for example, wrote that "the two-page spread is the new unit of composition" in books and magazines (Rosskam, *Washington*, 7), and artist James Montgomery Flagg found the first issue of *Life* "fascinating ... all the newsreels on your knee (qtd. in Wainwright, *Magazine*, 82).

22. Both terms translate to "the people," but *populus* is the more subsuming term, whereas *plebs* refers to the "plain people" with no special titles or privileges. I follow Ernesto Laclau in viewing the construction of a *plebs* as the central project of a populist mode of politics. See E. Laclau, *On Populist Reason* (London; New York: Verso, 2005), 81.

23. See, for example, S. Anderson, *Puzzled America* (New York: Charles Scribner's Sons, 1935); E. Wilson, *The American Jitters: A Year of the Slump* (New York: Charles Scribner's Sons, 1932).

24. Kahana, *Intelligence Work*, 103.

25. Kazin, *Native Grounds*, 489.

26. For a collection of FSA and WPA photographs organized around this theme, see P. Daniel, ed., *Official Images: New Deal Photography* (Washington, DC: Smithsonian Institution Press, 1987).

27. For examples of this tendency, see Stott, *Documentary Expression*; G. Garner, *Disappearing Witness: Change in Twentieth-Century American Photography* (Baltimore, MD: Johns Hopkins University Press, 2003); W. A. Bischof, *The Concerned Photographer: The Photographs of Werner Bischof, Robert Capa, David Seymour ("Chim"), Andrè Kertesz, Leonard Freed, Dan Weiner* (New York: Grossman Publishers, 1968).

28. At the risk of reducing a complex phenomenon to mere data, a July 2016 search for refereed journal articles in the MLA International Database published prior to 2006 yields 1,867 hits for subjects containing "modernism," 808 for "documentary," and four containing both. An identical search for work published after 2006 reveals an astonishing increase in work on

documentary – 1,581 hits compared to 1,252 for "modernism" – nonetheless, only four more articles appear that contain both subjects.

29. See, for example, T. Miller, "Documentary/Modernism: Convergence and Complementarity in the 1930s," *Modernism/Modernity* 9.2 (2002), 225–42; T. S. Davis, *The Extinct Scene: Late Modernism and Everyday Life* (New York: Columbia University Press, 2015).

30. Miller, *Late Modernism*, 19.

31. J. Ranciere, *The Emancipated Spectator*, trans. G. Elliott (London: Verso, 2009), 72.

32. J. Agee and W. Evans, *Let Us Now Praise Famous Men* (Boston, MA: Houghton Mifflin, 1941), 12.

33. Agee and Evans, *Praise*, 321.

34. Agee and Evans, *Praise*, 321.

35. R. Wright, *12 Million Black Voices* (New York: Thunder's Mouth Press, 2000), 11.

36. Wright's use of a collective African American narrator is an implicit rebuke to New Deal-sponsored fetishization of poor whites and relative exclusion of people of color, especially from the FSA archive. For a comprehensive treatment of this exclusion (albeit one strangely unsympathetic to Wright's text), see N. Natanson, *The Black Image in the New Deal: The Politics of FSA Photography*, vol. 1st (Knoxville: University of Tennessee Press, 1992). For a reading of Wright's text and its relationship to the broader context of Depression documentary, see J. Allred, "From Eye to We: Richard Wright's 12 Million Black Voices, Documentary, and Pedagogy," *American Literature* 78.3 (2006), 549–83.

37. E. Caldwell and M. B. White, *You Have Seen Their Faces* (New York: Viking, 1937), 49.

38. M. Rukeyser, *U.S. 1.* (New York: Covici, Friede, 1938), 146.

39. For a reading of Rukeyser's poem in light of its influence on recent examples of documentary poetry, see S. Briante, "Defacing the Monument," *Jacket2*, April 21, 2014. http://jacket2.org/article/defacing-monument. And I am indebted to my friend and colleague Michael Dowdy for orienting me to the state of the field.

CHAPTER 16

Modernism

Milton A. Cohen

Introduction

A theme often repeated by leftist literary critics of the 1930s was that the literary modernism of the twenties and teens was thoroughly passé. Its "verbal acrobatics," elitist scorn for the common reader, psychological musings, and pessimist themes no longer resonated in an era of breadlines and Hoovervilles, an era in which politically engaged younger writers strove to win over a new readership of the proletariat.[1] Horace Gregory's 1937 review of new writing, for example, describes younger poets as "no longer concerned with 'mere verbal experiment'" of Joyce, Eliot and Pound, experimenters who now seemed "'arty,' pretentious or distracted."[2]

But if younger writers had indeed turned their backs on modernism – a shaky proposition if one considers the surrealism in Kenneth Fearing's poetry and Nathanael West's fiction – the corollary assumption that older modernists had abandoned the style certainly did not follow. With a few exceptions noted in what follows, modernist poets and writers of the teens and twenties continued to produce novels, stories, and volumes of verse in the challenging styles they had developed earlier, and some pushed their "experiments" even further. Pound's *Cantos* of the thirties were no less abstruse than previous ones (adding Chinese to the foreign language quotations), even as he addressed new topics and saluted Mussolini. Many of Cummings's thirties poems were even more disjunctive than previous ones, as they exploded particles of punctuation, capitals, and words all over the page. The title poem of Marianne Moore's mid-thirties book, *The Pangolin*, also reflects a new expansiveness of her typical style. Faulkner's novels, beginning with *The Sound and the Fury* in 1929, embarked on a continuous series of innovative and challenging narrative structures and prose styles. Dos Passos brilliantly yoked modernist devices to political themes in his *U.S.A.* trilogy (1930–36), and Hemingway experimented with new narrative techniques in *To Have and Have Not* (1937) and loosened his taut sentences in *For Whom the Bell Tolls* (1940).

As modernism carried into the 1930s, however, wobbles in its various trajectories are discernible, as its practitioners responded directly and indirectly to the newly charged political climate. They could scarcely do otherwise. The ravages of the Depression; the new political involvement of writers and critics; the stinging attacks by newly politicized reviewers on the modernists' 1930s publications (what worse fate for this avant-garde than now to be deemed rear-guard?); the menacing rise and expansion of political "isms" playing out on the world stage; the inexorable movement toward another war – amid such buffeting winds, few writers indeed could maintain indifference and equilibrium. Modernist styles may seem intrinsically unrelated to contemporary politics, but styles are created by writers, who, as Wallace Stevens observed in "Mozart, 1935," must "play the present" and live in the modern world, whether they like it or not. Hence, following a few collectivizing generalizations, this study focuses on modernist practitioners, as well as their styles, in the thirties.

That iconoclastic modernists responded diversely to these political and economic pressures, as Stevens called them,[3] is hardly surprising. Some writers, to be sure, did not respond. Marianne Moore and, to a lesser extent, William Faulkner, seemed relatively indifferent to the social and political upheavals of the decade.[4] A few modernists, by contrast, were ahead of the curve, anticipating in their late 1920s work political themes that would soon be widespread. Both John Dos Passos and William Carlos Williams were deeply affected by the Sacco and Vanzetti executions of 1927, and both express an unprogrammatic leftism in the years following. Dos Passos conveyed his liberal-leftist sympathies for underdogs in the grand historical canvas he fashioned in his *U.S.A.* trilogy, which he began writing in 1928 and completed in 1936. By the mid-1930s, Williams turned his long-standing empathy for ordinary people into explicitly political poems, which reflected his own idiosyncratic movement to the left. More belatedly, Ernest Hemingway, smarting from leftist criticism of his social indifference in the early thirties and now deeply involved in covering the Spanish Civil War, recognized economic inequality and the struggles of the working man in *To Have and Have Not* (1937).

If these writers moved left, several modernists shifted to the right or moved further in that direction. As noted, Pound celebrated Mussolini in his 1930s cantos and tracts. Eliot devoted the first half of the decade to works emanating from his religious conversion and espoused a cultural conservatism grounded in his Anglo-Catholicism. By the mid-1930s, both

Cummings and Frost asserted defiance of leftism in their poems and prose. Stevens, by contrast, attempted a thoughtful engagement with the Left in his mid-thirties books: *Ideas of Order*, *Owl's Clover*, and *The Man with the Blue Guitar*.

Modernist styles softened in some cases, as poets like Stevens and Eliot pulled back somewhat from their more abstract styles of the 1920s to more meditative, philosophical verse in the mid-1930s and thereafter. Marianne Moore shows this same movement toward discursive rumination a few years later in her celebrated World War II poem, "In Distrust of Merits." Even the tireless innovator Dos Passos ended the thirties by abandoning the modernist devices – and, not coincidentally, the leftist themes – of *U. S.A.* for the linear narrative of *Adventures of a Young Man*.

POETRY

Eliot

In his survey *Three on the Tower: The Lives and Works of Ezra Pound, T. S. Eliot, and Williams Carlos Williams*, poet and critic Louis Simpson characterized each of his three modernist poets with a single word. For T. S. Eliot, that word was "religion."[5] Eliot scholars may rightly object to the word's inadequacy to represent Eliot before "The Hollow Men" (1925). But it applies quite well to the poetry, drama, and cultural criticism Eliot wrote in the 1930s – with the major exception of "Burnt Norton." Eliot was baptized into the Church of England in 1927 and the following year became a British citizen, declaring himself "classicist in literature, royalist in politics, and anglo-catholic in religion."[6] His first major poem of the 1930s, "Ash Wednesday" (1930), follows close on the heels of his conversion and builds on the shorter religious poems of the late 1920s, such as "Journey of the Magi" (1927).

"Ash Wednesday" symbolically records the speaker's difficult spiritual and penitential journey – "struggle" might be more accurate – to atone for his sinfulness and become worthy of redemption.[7] Though the autobiographical first-person voice marks a partial change from the more impersonal "we" of "The Hollow Men" and the "different voices" of *The Waste Land*, "Ash Wednesday" continues the former poem's extensive use of recondite symbolism, only now the symbols suggest a difficult spiritual journey (climbing flights of stairs, turnings at landings); physical dissolution (the three leopards devouring the speaker), which must precede spiritual rebirth; and, as in *The Divine Comedy*, the beseeching of a divine "Lady of silences" for intercession. Interspersed with these motifs are lines from the Anglican Ash Wednesday service and other liturgical works. Although the journey's difficulty is what the poem most emphasizes, the speaker discernibly progresses from his initial state of self-doubt and despair ("*Because* I do not hope to turn again ... ") to overcoming these spiritually crippling conditions ("*Although* I do not hope to turn again ... " [emphasis added]). And echoing the important *Waste Land* theme of yielding to "controlling hands," Eliot again emphasizes that spiritual submission is essential to achieving inner peace: "Our peace in His will."

Eliot's 1935 essay "Religion and Literature" applies his religious beliefs to literary criticism;[8] but its ex-cathedra tone of certainty is closer to "Tradition and the Individual Talent" (1919) than to the confessional struggle of "Ash Wednesday." Now, secularization replaces romantic egotism as the critical culprit, and the solution Eliot advocates is not to shift our critical attention from author to literary work, but to supplement literary standards with a "definite ethical and theological standpoint" in judging literature. Eliot also wrote two plays in the 1930s, *Murder in the Cathedral* (1935), a verse drama about the murder of Archbishop Thomas à Beckett at Canterbury Cathedral, and *The Family Reunion* (1939). Interestingly, *Murder* was performed by the Federal Theatre Project in the United States in 1937 to rave reviews.

Had Eliot written nothing further, his poetic career in the 1930s might have been seen (by the secular world he disparaged) as contracting to a personal religiosity that most readers could not share. But in 1936, he published a long poem, "Burnt Norton,"[9] in an entirely different style and tone, which subsequently became the first of his much-lauded *Four Quartets* (1943). What immediately stands out in "Burnt Norton" is the poem's directness of speech, free of both the pietistic humility of the religious poems and the magisterial voice of the criticism. Equally important, "Burnt Norton" supplants the earlier symbolist style with a meditative discourse that considers questions of time – past, present, future – and choice. Particularly poignant in this interplay is the past we might have chosen:

> Footfalls echo in the memory
> Down the passage which we did not take
> Toward the door we never opened
> Into the rose garden. My words echo
> Thus in your mind.

Eliot's 1935 trip to the "Burnt Norton" manor house with Emily Hale – who figured as the great "might have been" of Eliot's love life in his middle years – inspired these reveries. But they are carefully structured as analog to a five-movement string quartet (Beethoven's Op. 132 Quartet was the immediate source) with contrasting themes and movements. Unlike the religious symbolism of "Ash Wednesday," the symbols here – the rose garden, children's laughter, music and the dance, for example – are more archetypal, hence more accessible. For many of his readers and critics, *Four Quartets* marks the pinnacle of Eliot's achievement, or at the very least, a major resurgence of his poetic art comparable to Williams's *Paterson*, Hemingway's *For Whom the Bell Tolls*, and Faulkner's *Go Down, Moses*.

Pound

No such renaissance is evident in Ezra Pound's *Cantos* of the 1930s. He wrote forty-one during this decade, published in three books: *Eleven New Cantos* (XXXI–XLI) in 1934, *The Fifth Decad of Cantos* (XLII–LI) in 1937, and *Cantos LII to LXXI* in 1940.[10] In his global and transhistorical examination of banking systems and interest, of moguls and leaders of various states, classical and modern, and of the artistic and political consequences of these systems, he now focused (in *Eleven New Cantos* and in Cantos LXII–LXXI) on those American presidents and others he considered seminal in determining American banking and economics: John Adams (his particular hero), Jefferson, Jackson, Hamilton, and Martin Van Buren (whom he appears to have plucked single-handedly from obscurity). Canto 38 also gives a brief, somewhat garbled account of Major C. H. Douglas's theory of credit and the blockage of exchange created by interest and usury – the theory that, along with World War I, had inspired Pound in 1918 to expand his investigation of modern cultural decline into economics. Cantos LII to LXI shift to a different exemplar of wise ethical leadership and statecraft, Confucius, contrasting his activist philosophy to the passivity of Taoism and Buddhism. Significantly, Pound considered Confucius's activism and wisdom akin to Mussolini's, whom he extravagantly admired and called "Boss" in Canto 41.[11] The prose tract with the startling title, *Jefferson and/or Mussolini* (1933) makes the same kind of questionable analogy to an American president. A concomitant of Pound's fascism was his anti-Semitism (for example, in Cantos 35 and 52). In accordance with medieval church doctrine, if usury was a sin, then its supposed chief practitioners, Jews, were the chief sinners, controlling (in Pound's view) the high finance that fueled World War I. Thus, as most writers and critics in the thirties moved left in politics, Pound moved further right. Though their political destinations seem diametrically opposed, they were really at opposite ends of a political horseshoe not so far apart. Both Pound and Marxist writers were obsessed with economics (Pound's interest more long-standing); expressed their politics directly through their writing; and gravitated toward totalitarian systems – all quite characteristic of the 1930s.

Stylistically, the thirties *Cantos* continued Pound's ideogrammic method of juxtaposing compressed fragments, jumping from one to the next, guided by the assumption that, as in Imagism, meaning would evolve from the juxtaposition itself. That these fragments included allusions to historical personages, some well known, many obscure; parts of quotations (in numerous languages, including Chinese) that Pound came across in his research of letters, diaries, public records, or other documents; "facts" likewise drawn from his research; personal memories and impressions obscure to anyone unfamiliar with the details of Pound's biography; discourse on all manner of subjects, chiefly historical and economic, that interested the poet; and finally that these strings of diverse and arcane allusions lack any apparatus of notes or explanations – all this helps explain the formidable textual difficulty posed by the *Cantos*.

One 1930s canto that partially eludes this obscurity – and for that reason is frequently anthologized – is "Canto 45: 'With *Usura*.'" A relatively straightforward polemic[12] against Pound's *bête noir*, usury, the poem piles example on top of example to show how usury comes between the craftsman and his craft, the bridegroom and his bride (substituting a rich old bedmate instead), hence is unnatural: "CONTRA NATURUM." Nor does usury account for the artistic triumphs (churches and paintings) that the poem lists.

Though he refused to provide glosses, Pound was aware of the problem of clarity and hoped that the whole enterprise would eventually cohere. As early as 1922, he writes a friend: "Perhaps as the poem goes on I shall be able to make various things clearer ... I *have to* get down the colours or elements I want for the poem. Some perhaps too enigmatically and abbreviatedly. I hope, heaven help me, to bring them into some sort of design and architecture later." Five years later, he admits to his father: "Afraid the whole damn poem is rather obscure, especially in fragments."[13] Unwittingly, what Pound did provide was employment for a tribe of scholars to track down and present the exegeses he neglected and for professors to unravel the poems to confused students. For all but those learned exegetes, understanding the *Cantos* themselves cumbersomely requires two books: text and companion glossary.

Stevens

Stevens's style in the 1930s – in *Ideas of Order* (1935, 1936), *Owl's Clover* (1936), and *The Man with the Blue Guitar* (1937) – pulled back from the modernist playfulness and dandyism of *Harmonium* (1923, 1931) into a more reflective and sometimes philosophical rhetoric. No longer do we see the self-satisfied, playful solipsism of "Tea at the Palaz of Hoon," the irreverent teasing of "A High-Toned Old Christian Woman," and the sound play for its own sake in numerous poems (e.g., "flakes of flames" in "Nomad Exquisite"). Stevens reluctantly moved away from what he called "pure art,"[14] for he was painfully aware that "reality" (the pressure of contemporary events) was imposing itself, making it increasingly difficult for the poet to lose himself in the pleasure of art.[15] The poem "Mozart, 1935" (*CP&P* 107–08) perfectly exemplifies the poet's dilemma in the Depression era, as Stevens later told a correspondent (*Letters* 292). The speaker somberly advises the poet-pianist to "play the present," a present of starvation, angry protest, and "besieging pain." Mozart, representing the pure aesthetic delight of the "unclouded concerto," will have to wait for better times. Other poems in Stevens's mid-thirties book, *Ideas of Order*, express moody variants and shadings of this theme. In "Farewell to Florida" (*CP&P* 97–98), the angry speaker, like a rejected suitor, turns his back on the hot, sensual tropics and grimly anticipates returning to the cold North and "a slime of men in crowds." "Sad Strains of a Gay Waltz" (*CP&P* 100–01) declares that the old art, symbolized by the waltz, has grown flat and casts no shadows; that this "epic of disbelief" requires a new kind of poet, a "harmonious skeptic" to unite the anguished "figures of men and their shapes." In some poems, Stevens's unadorned voice shows through like a patch of unpainted canvas: "Marx has ruined Nature, / For the moment. // For myself, I live by leaves" (*CP&P* 109).

Stevens's new sensibility was neither a conversion nor even a transformation, as it still contained remnants of his older one, to which he reverted at times. In the Alfred Knopf edition of *Ideas of Order* (1936), he states in a dust jacket note: "While it is inevitable that a poet should be concerned with such questions [of political and social order] . . . [t]he book is essentially a book of pure poetry" (*CP&P* 997). The central poem, "The Idea of Order at Key West," does indeed ignore the political times to consider the aesthetic relations between cryptic nature, "the ever-hooded sea," and humankind's "rage for order": the order to contain and control the sea in "emblazoned zones" and the poet-maker's order, transforming mindless sea rhythms into "ghostlier demarcations, keener sounds."

If the political themes in *Ideas of Order* express Stevens's grudging acknowledgment of "reality," his next book, *Owl's Clover* (1936), marks a more direct confrontation with the Left, spurred by a negative review of *Ideas* by a Marxist critic Stanley Burnshaw in *New Masses*, the Communist Party USA's literary magazine. Stevens described his intent in a letter: "You will remember that Mr. Burnshaw applied the point of view of the practical Communist to *Ideas of Order*. I have tried to reverse the process: that is to say, apply the point of view of a poet to Communism" (October 31, 1935, *Letters* 289). This poetic response has nothing of the hostility to the Left found in Frost's and Cummings's poems of the period – Stevens even described himself as "headed left" at the time (but not the left of *New Masses*)[16] and that *Owl's Clover* was to be "a justification of leftism" (*Letters* 294–95). Neither statement proved true. The book-length set of four long poems was more a thoughtful description of and rebuttal to the kind of art that Marxism (in Stevens's view) would establish.

The poem that best expresses this rebuttal is "Mr. Burnshaw and the Statue." It envisions a disturbing world of constant change, "A time in which poets' politics / Will rule . . . Yet that will be / A world impossible for poets, who . . . are never of the world in which they live" (*CP&P* 572). In this Marxian world, older symbols of art – a statue of horses – must give way to newer ones that reflect "the Mass." If these newer images are hideous – a "gigantic solitary urn / A trashcan at the end of the world" where "buzzards . . . eat the bellies of the rich" – they may eventually transform into something ideologically attractive when "rose-breasted birds / Sing rose beliefs" (573). Whether or not one subscribes to these depredations, one must accept, Stevens explained, that change is constant and make the best of it (*Letters* 367). The poem shows Stevens at his most conflicted. Not surprisingly, he (and many of his critics) judged *Owl's Clover* a failure, and Stevens excluded it from his *Collected Poems*.

It seems that Stevens had to work through this lengthy exercise in order to arrive at what he really believed in, expressed in the much lighter, more fluent verse of "The Man with the Blue Guitar" (1937). More focused than *Owl's Clover*, "Blue Guitar" opposes the individual imagination of the poet-performer to "they," an amorphous collectivist voice, who demand that he play "things as they are," analytically, for "a million people on one string" (IV, *CP&P* 136). The guitarist questions and ultimately resists this ruthless objectivity, urging "them" to "Throw away the lights, the definitions . . . the rotted names" (XXXII). In so resisting, he preserves a world "washed in his imagination" so that "Things as they are / Are *changed* upon the blue guitar" (XXVI, I, emphasis added). The poem thus repudiates Stevens's efforts to accommodate the "realist" aesthetics of the Left and triumphantly asserts his devotion to imaginative transformation. By 1941, his repudiation of the Left was absolute. He told an audience at Princeton: "I might be expected to speak of the social, that is to say sociological or political obligations of the poet. He has none" ("Noble Rider," *CP&P* 659).

Yet Stevens's brief encounter with leftist politics left a residuum as it forced him to think about the artist's role in society. As early as 1936, he declares that "the poet should be the exponent of the imagination of that society . . . The more realistic life may be, the more it needs the stimulus of the imagination" (*CP&P* 997). His Princeton lecture of 1941, "The Noble Rider and the Sound of Words," develops this idea in memorable prose that remained the bedrock of Stevens's social view of poetry:

> What is [the poet's] function? Certainly it is not to lead people out of the confusion in which they find themselves. Nor is it, I think to comfort them while they follow their leaders to and fro. I think that his function is to make his imagination theirs and that he fulfills himself only as he sees his imagination become the light in the minds of others. His role, in short, is to help people to live their lives. (*CP&P* 660–61)

Cummings

Taken together, Cummings's poems of the 1930s, collected in *ViVa* (1931), *no thanks* (1935), the new poems of *Collected Poems* (1938), and *50 Poems* (1940),[17] describe a kind of parabolic expansion and compression of form. A quick scan of *ViVa* and *no thanks* shows several poems – "SNOW," (*CP* 448), "ondumonde" (*CP* 458) for example – styled with a baroque exuberance, exploding their lines, words, and punctuation over the entire page. "n(o)w" from *ViVa* (*CP* 371) is perhaps the best single example of this expansiveness as it captures a darkening thunderstorm ripping open "n, o; w :" then evolving into the cleansed air of a reborn world: the "N,ew green earth)."

This challenging dispersion accompanied and perhaps reflected another kind of defiance Cummings projected in the 1930s, against the literary intelligentsia's turn to the political left. Following a trip to Russia – an experience the poet likened to a descent into Dante's hell in his 1933 stream-of-consciousness journal *Eimi* ("I am") – he became not only anticommunist, but anti-leftist (including the New Deal), an isolated and increasingly shrill champion of the individual in the 1930s. Like several of Frost's poems in *A Further Range*, many of Cummings's 1930s poems challenge the Left – "kumrads die because they're told" (440) for example – as well as assert his own individualistic philosophy. "if i" (*CP* 506) and "my specialty is living" (*CP* 504) are good examples. And, like Frost, he elicited the Left's ire in negative reviews of his 1930s books. But like Williams's *Complete Collected Poems* of 1938, Cummings's *Collected Poems* of that same year helped solidify his standing in the larger critical community.

In one sense, Cummings's anti-leftism was consistent with his lifelong hatred of conformity in an increasingly collectivistic age. It was just his targets that changed: in the 1920s, they had been mindless warmongering, puritanism, and consumerism. Less heroically, his anti-leftism of the 1930s reflected the bitterness of a poet who was no longer accorded his special status as the bad boy of modernist poetry. Babette Deutsch's wicked parody "e e cummingsesq," suggested that by 1940 his playful devices were growing stale:

> ;printersink s
>   print
> ingdownand sp   (o)
>   ill
>   ing (
>   ver)
>   the
>   page doesn't
>   excite or delight us
>   the same way anymore...[18]

By the end of the 1930s, Cummings's satirical targets returned to consumer culture and middle-class conformity, compressed into the portmanteau "mostpeople" and "mrsandmr collective foetus" (Introduction to *Collected Poems*, 1938). Intensifying the smugness of this cultural repudiation was the other side of Cummings's poetry: the love poems in which "you and i" exclude a benighted world of "them":

> all history's a winter sport or three:
> but were it five, i'd still insist that all
> history is too small for even me;
> for me and you, exceedingly too small.
> . . . . . .

—tomorrow is our permanent address

and there they'll scarcely find us (if they do,
we'll move away still further:into now (*CP* 616)

These oppositions found numerous imaginative expressions in his later poems but never changed their thematic configuration.

What did gradually change by the end of the decade was his poetic style. The baroque exuberance of the early and mid-thirties yielded to a disciplined, more vertical and self-contained style – for example, in "! blac" (*CP* 519) and "air," (*CP* 567). In this sparer style, which became increasingly dominant in Cummings's later poems, classical virtues of balance, order, restraint, and especially symmetry signal not a flagging of stylistic power, but rather an implosion of its energy. In the incomparable masterpiece "l(a)" (*CP* 713), for example, note how the poem balances two contrasting meanings of the falling leaf:

l(a

le
af
fa

ll

s)
one
l

iness

If the first letter is read as lowercase "l," it combines with "one/l//iness" to form "loneliness"; if it is the number "1," the final word becomes "oneliness," which develops "1" and "one" to celebrate individuality. (On Cummings's typewriter, one key represented both letter and number.) While the poem's symmetry – sections of one and three alternating in a 1:3:1:3:1 pattern – is self-evident, other progressions are more subtle: the numerical progression from one ("l") to two ("ll") and back to ("l") compresses a life story of love and loss – the falling leaf representing death as well as separation. And the alternation of tall and short letters in the second section suggests the swinging arcs of the falling leaf. Such poems demonstrate that, although Cummings's political and social themes may have atrophied in tireless (and tiresome) repetitions, his style and lyricism continued to grow.[19]

Williams

In 1935, one could leaf through William Carlos Williams's new book of poems, *An Early Martyr*, and find vertical poems with one-word lines, like the second version of "The Locust Tree in Flower," near a poem entitled "Proletarian Portrait."[20] The former is an extreme example of the stripped-down modernist style Williams had developed beginning in the late teens. The latter poem simply describes a servant girl pulling off her shoe in public to find a painful nail in it. Though anything "proletarian" was a hot topic in 1935, Williams had written "people" poems all his life. And the empathy he now expressed for working-class victims of the Depression was preceded by his stinging critiques of how America exploited its underclass in "To Elsie" (1923) or railroaded Sacco and Vanzetti in "The Suckers" (1927; published 1941).

Still, the sizable number of poems in *An Early Martyr* about Depression victims or quixotic fighters against capitalism was something new, a fusion of Williams's rapport with working-class people and his political activism. More than any of the other modernists in the 1930s, he involved himself in leftist literary politics and causes. He coedited little magazines of proletarian fiction; sent poems and essays to liberal and leftist magazines; forthrightly responded to their survey-inquiries about Marxism and American literature; joined (and subsequently left) several leftist political groups; and actively supported the Loyalists in the Spanish Civil War with poems and translations of Spanish poets, even organizing and chairing the Bergen County Medical Board to Aid Spanish Democracy. But his thinking was too independent merely to parrot a party line or mindlessly follow causes.[21] He was not a communist, he declared often, though much later described his politics as "pink" (*CPWCW* 2, 477). Indeed, his candid declaration that communism would not work in America earned him ridicule in the leftist magazine *Partisan Review.*[22]

Like his political views, Williams's 1930s poems about people caught up in the Depression were idiosyncratic rather than programmatically leftist. The most famous of these poems, "The Yachts" (*CPWCW* 1, 388–89) expresses the division in his aesthetics between the older "art for art's sake" philosophy of modernism and the engaged politics of the present. The poem is weirdly – surrealistically – split between a deep admiration for racing yachts as superbly crafted and skillfully performing objects – the maker's love of things well-made – and condemnation of their class status as toys of the rich, which indifferently run over the drowning poor. A nearby poem, however, "Late for Summer Weather" (384), shows an unemployed couple "ambling / nowhere" but having a good time as they "kick // their way through / heaps of / fallen maple leaves // still green— and / crisp as dollar bills."

These disparate responses to the poor continued through the decade. A poem from 1938, "The Poor" (452–53), delights in "the anarchy of poverty," especially its unpredictable non-conformity: "the dress of the children // reflecting every stage and / custom of necessity." And it admires an old man's pride in sweeping "his own ten feet of" sidewalk. The very next poem, however – "Between Walls" (453) – is virtually a replica of the radically compressed style of "The Red Wheel Barrow" of 1923, even borrowing "Wheel Barrow's" two-line stanzas, in which longer lines top shorter ones. Again, modernist and political poems exist side by side.

Like other poets in the 1930s, Cummings for example, Williams had trouble finding a publisher, at least until his dream publisher, James Laughlin's New Directions Press, came along in 1937. This difficulty turned him to writing more salable fiction. By 1940, he had produced two volumes of stories (*The Knife of the Times*, 1932, and *Life along the Passaic*, 1938) and two novels, *White Mule* (1937) and *In the Money* (1940). Reviewers generally praised his incisive descriptions – dissecting like a surgeon, one critic called them – and his unsentimental matter-of-fact tone. Typical of Williams's idiosyncratic political themes, *White Mule* depicts a working-class printer who runs an open shop – an anathema to unions at the time – yet leftist critics rather liked the novel. Indeed, by the end of the 1930s, with the publication of his *Complete Collected Poems* in 1938, Williams had finally established his critical reputation as a major poet, and his importance would continue to grow for the next generation of poets. And unlike *any* of the other modernists discussed in this chapter, he was about to embark on his most experimental masterwork, the five-book poem blending collage, myth, history, and present-day realism: *Paterson*.

Fiction

The three major modernist novelists of the late 1920s – Dos Passos, Hemingway, and Faulkner – all extended or advanced their styles well into the 1930s. Curiously, Dos Passos's and Hemingway's styles – and their respective political standings with the Left – mark a kind of inverse relationship: Dos Passos moving from modernist experiment to conventional and anti-leftist narrative by the end of the decade, Hemingway the reverse, introducing new narrative techniques and a qualified leftist sympathy in his late thirties fiction.

Dos Passos

For Dos Passos, the 1930s witnessed the full realization of experimental techniques he had begun in the 1920s with *Manhattan Transfer* (1925) and had formalized in the first volume of his *U.S.A.* trilogy: *The Forty-Second Parallel* (1930). The dizzying array of mini-plots in *Manhattan Transfer* now clarified into identified narratives of fewer but still diverse characters in the trilogy, including a vagabond and an entrepreneur, a secretary and a sailor, a dress designer and a socialite, political radicals and Harvard ambulance drivers, and a powerful public relations specialist. Interchanging with and juxtaposed to these plot narratives were several innovative devices for which *U.S.A.* is justly famous. "Newsreels" comprised newspaper headlines of the moment and snippets of popular songs, all carefully culled to form ironic juxtapositions and a meta-commentary on the plot narratives. "The Camera Eye" provided subjective, largely autobiographical, and stream-of-consciousness sequences to complement the "objective" newsreels and the detached tone of the plot narratives. Finally, mini-biographies of famous figures (politicians, moguls, inventors), again highly selective in their facts to convey particular political themes, round out these devices.

Each volume of *U.S.A.* follows the characters' lives within a particular slice of American history: *The Forty Second Parallel* from about 1900 to 1917, when America enters World War I; *1919* (published in 1932) from 1917 to 1920; and *The Big Money* (1936) from 1920 to the Wall Street Crash in 1929. What Dos Passos was after was not conventional historical fiction, but, as he stated, to set his characters "in the snarl of the human currents of [their] time," "to keep up a contemporary commentary on history's changes, always as seen by some individual's eyes, heard by some individual's ears, felt thru some individual's nerves and tissues."[23] His leftist political views colored this commentary, of course, empathizing with the vagabonds and idealists, despising those like public relations wizard J. Ward Moorehouse, who specialized in twisting words and manipulating images to put a noble front on greed. But those leftist sympathies did not overcome a sense of naturalistic futility that governed nearly all of the characters' destinies.

Over the eight-year span of writing this trilogy, Dos Passos's politics gradually shifted toward the center. He recalls his alienation from America in the "Camera Eye" passage (50) about the execution of Sacco and Vanzetti in 1927, but by the time he published *1919* in 1932, he felt he had rejoined America. And in *The Big Money* (1936), the professional communist, Don Stevens, is just as coldly self-seeking and exploitive as any business mogul.

Dos Passos's movement away from the left accelerated with his disillusionment about the Soviets' role in the Spanish Civil War, particularly, the Soviet NKVD's murder of his close friend and translator, José Robles.[24] His final novel of the decade, *Adventures of a Young Man* (1939), a critical failure, abandoned not only the modernist innovations of *U.S.A.*, returning to a conventional, linear narrative, but also the trilogy's leftism. This shift to rightist individualism, paralleling Cummings's, would mark the remainder of Dos Passos's fiction. His many subsequent novels, however, would never come close to the achievement of *U.S.A.*

Hemingway

As Dos Passos's modernist credentials (and political standing with the Left) sparkled in the first half of the decade with the novels of *U.S.A.*, Hemingway's reputation in both regards tarnished following the highly acclaimed *A Farewell to Arms* (1929). His next two books – *Death in the Afternoon* (1932) and *Green Hills of Africa* (1935) – were nonfiction; and although *Green Hills* employed dialog and narrative to convey what the author boasted was "an absolutely true" story, it was essentially a journal and a collection of the author's literary opinions. Virtually all critics complained of the author's self-indulgence in these books, and leftist critics objected to their serene indifference to the Depression and to Hemingway's pot-shots at leftist criticism. The collection of short stories, *Winner Take Nothing* (1933), likewise, was not well received, though it contained such superb stories as "A Clean, Well-Lighted Place."

Hemingway's anti-leftist broadsides in these books (and in some articles for *Esquire* magazine), however, did not prevent him making overtures to the Left, beginning in 1935 with the antigovernment diatribe he published in *New Masses*, "Who Murdered the Vets?"[25] The outbreak of the Spanish Civil War in 1936 accelerated his movement leftward, as he became a strong Loyalist supporter in covering the war as a journalist. His leftism extended even to supporting the Soviet Union's sinister role in Spain because, he argued, it forcibly unified the various leftist factions and provided the best chance of a Loyalist victory. This shift toward the left informs his next novel, *To Have and Have Not* (1937), and of course his Spanish Civil War stories and play *The Fifth Column* (1938). In *THHN*, however, Hemingway carefully distinguishes his protagonist – a typically tough individualist, only now a hard-working "have not" who learns he cannot go it alone –

from programmatic leftists: murderous revolutionaries and a shallow proletarian novelist (read John Dos Passos). The novel also attempts, with
limited success, a number of stylistic innovations, including multiple
narrators, shifting points of view and stream-of-consciousness monologues. Obviously derived from Faulkner and Joyce, these techniques contributed to the novel's disjointed structure, for which it was roundly
criticized.

Hemingway's final novel of the period, *For Whom the Bell Tolls* (1940),
returned to a conventional, though far better developed, narrative. Except
in a few chapters, it stays focused on protagonist Robert Jordan, another
skillful individualist, who fights on the right – that is to say, the left – side.
Unlike the play and short stories about the war, however, *FWBT* assumes
a far more complex stance toward the war, recognizing through its protagonist moral quandaries and contradictions about his own actions and the
Loyalist cause. The novel also marks a loosening of Hemingway's famous
style in notably longer, more complex sentences. Its resounding success
with critics and public alike put Hemingway back on top among American
novelists – at least until Malcolm Cowley published *The Portable Faulkner*
in 1946.

Faulkner

If the 1930s fiction had a champion of modernism, it would have to be
William Faulkner. From *The Sound and the Fury* (1929) to *If I Forget Thee,
Jerusalem*[26] (1939), Faulkner continuously expanded the range of his experiments in narrative techniques, plot sequence, and style in his novels and
stories. Indeed, his fiction was so prolific in this decade that, regrettably,
only a few of the most notable achievements can be considered here.

One of Faulkner's most impressive innovations in these novels is to tell
the story through multiple narrators, voices, and prose styles. In *The Sound
and the Fury*, three brothers and an external narrator present parts of the
story in four radically different styles, ranging from the jumbled memory-
sensations of Benjy, a thirty-three-year-old idiot, to the interior stream of
consciousness of the morbidly subjective Quentin, to the horribly comic
deadpan of Jason, to the refreshingly objective prose of an external narrator. All of these narratives and characters spiral around the mysterious
black hole at the novel's center, Caddy Compson. In *As I Lay Dying* (1930),
Faulkner pushes the technique of multiple narrators to an extreme, interchanging fifteen speakers in fifty-nine brief interior monologues, including
(and most prominently) the corpse's at the center of this comic-absurdist

novel. *Absalom, Absalom!* (1936) presents differing versions of the Sutpen story, told by five different narrators, all rendered in complex, elongated sentences and often a stream-of-consciousness style of narration.

As the multiple narrators in these novels circle *around* the core story, each revealing, but also sometimes withholding, pieces of it, sometimes contradicting each other, often filling in unknown parts with speculation, and nearly always thoroughly subjective and hence unreliable as narrators – and as their narratives consequently ignore conventional linearity – Faulkner's plots (especially in *Absalom, Absalom!*) assume the character of a detective story, which is not complete until the last piece falls into place. "A Rose for Emily" (1931), for example, cleverly employs an unreliable narrator representing the town; from a distance, he guesses at motivations and thoroughly shuffles the plot sequence to enable a shocking ending. These techniques also raise epistemological questions about the validity of a single truth regarding character and history and the impossibility of ever determining it, versus partial, provisional truths. Even in the two conventionally linear and separate narratives of *If I Forget Thee, Jerusalem* (1939), Faulkner interchanges their chapters, enabling an intertextual commentary and ironic comparison on such topics as mythic and realistic levels of the journey motif, the loss of monastic (Edenic?) simplicity, the fearsome pregnant female (versus the subservient male), and, surprisingly, love.[27]

Younger Modernists

This survey has focused on the first generation of American modernists, whose work first appeared in the 1910s and 1920s. Some younger poets and novelists, emerging in the late twenties and thirties, however, also experimented with modernist techniques. Surrealism, still vigorous in the 1930s, influenced both poet Kenneth Fearing and novelist Nathanael West. In the poem "No Credit," for example, Fearing blends bourgeois blandness and political upheaval in describing a "pleasant" dinner "with the windows lit by gunfire" and "a touch of vomit gas in the evening air." West's surrealism ranges from comical nihilism in *The Dream Life of Balso Snell* (1931) to the apocalyptic in *The Day of the Locust* (1939), still one of the best depictions of Hollywood vacuity. Poet Louis Zukofsky may have outdone his friend and mentor Ezra Pound in pushing poetry toward abstraction in his epic-length poem "A." Like Pound's *Cantos*, it is a protean life work, begun when the poet was twenty-three (1927) and continuing, with interruptions, until shortly before his death in 1978. And like the *Cantos*, it is its own universe of diverse styles (including musical), reactions to contemporaneous events, social and political views, and autobiography.

Conclusion

Modernism continued into the 1940s and beyond, as the old warhorses trudged on, writing in styles they had developed decades earlier. A few writers, indeed, had innovative masterworks still to come: Faulkner's *Go Down, Moses* (1942), Eliot's *Four Quartets* (1943), and Williams's *Paterson* (1946–58). But the heyday of modernism had clearly passed if only because newer styles continued to capture the imagination of writers, critics, and reviewers. And, as Apollinaire remarked years earlier, one can't keep lugging around the corpse of one's father. Hence, the efforts to bury modernism – or at least supersede it – continued beyond the Social Realists' shrill attacks in the 1930s. Confessional poets like Robert Lowell and Denise Levertov challenged Eliot's impersonality theory in the fifties. A young Saul Bellow in his first novel, *Dangling Man*, explicitly rejected Hemingway's laconic anti-intellectualism and aimed to discuss ideas freely. The Beats captured both literary and popular attention in the fifties. Even then, however, modernism refused to go quietly, as Pound and especially Williams became mentors for younger poets like Alan Ginsberg and Charles Olson.

Notes

1. As early as September 1930, Mike Gold declared in *New Masses* that the new "Proletarian-Realism" must avoid the "verbal acrobatics" of modernism. The masthead of the *Little Review* perfectly expressed the modernist elitism that leftist critics like Gold also despised: "The common reader be damned!"
2. Horace Gregory, "Some Firsts: New Authors and Their First Books," *Story* 10.54 (January 1937), 103.
3. "The Irrational Element in Poetry" (1936), in *Wallace Stevens: Collected Poetry and Prose* (New York: Library of America, 1997), 788; hereafter cited as *CP&P*.
4. The hardscrabble, nomadic lives of Harry Wilbourne and Charlotte Rittenmeyer in Faulkner's *If I Forget Thee, Jerusalem* (1939) owe something to the Depression, and in *The Mansion* (1959), Linda Snopes is s a communist who fought in Spain alongside her radical husband.
5. Louis Simpson, *Three on the Tower: The Lives and Works of Ezra Pound, T. S. Eliot and William Carlos Williams* (New York: William Morrow &

Company), 90. Simpson's one-word depictions for Pound was "art," for Williams "experience."

6. Preface, *For Lancelot Andrewes: Essays on Style and Order* (London: Fabre and Gwyer, 1928).

7. *T. S. Eliot: Complete Poems and Plays* (New York: Harcourt, 1980), 60–67.

8. *Selected Prose of T. S. Eliot*, ed. with introduction Frank Kermode (New York: HBJ Harvest Books, 1975), 97–106.

9. First published in *Collected Poems: 1909–1935* (London: Faber, 1936).

10. *The Cantos* (New York: New Directions, 1996); subsequent page citations refer to this edition.

11. The admiration was partly mutual, for Canto 41 begins by quoting Mussolini's mild praise for Pound's poetry: "This is diverting" (202).

12. Carroll F. Terrell, Pound's chief exegete, glosses a mere twenty allusions in this poem (*A Companion to "The Cantos" of Ezra Pound* [Berkeley: University of California Press, 1993], 178–79).

13. *The Selected Letters of Ezra Pound: 1907–1941*, ed. D. D. Paige (New York: New Directions, 1971), 180, 210. Cf., Pound's later contradictory views in his last Canto (CXVI) on whether "the whole thing coheres."

14. Letter to Ronald Lane Latimer, October 31, 1935, *Letters of Wallace Stevens* (Berkeley: University of California Press, 1996), 288; hereafter cited as *Letters*.

15. Stevens discusses these pressures – and the poet's need to resist them – in two seminal lectures: "The Irrational Element in Poetry" (1936) and "The Noble Rider and the Sound of Words" (1941), in *CP&P* 781–92, 643–65.

16. *Letters* 286. In another letter (292), Stevens clarified "left" as a belief in "up-to-date capitalism," citing Edward Filene, the liberal owner of a Boston department store, who espoused redistribution of wealth to temper the abuses of capitalism (Alan Marsh, *Money and Modernity: Pound, Williams and the Spirit of Jefferson* [Tuscaloosa: University of Alabama Press, 1998], 157).

17. In *E. E. Cummings: Complete Poems 1904–1962*, revised, corrected, and expanded edition, ed. George James Firmage (New York: Liveright, 2016); hereafter cited as *CP*.

18. *The Nation*, May 17, 1941, 591; rpt. in *E. E. Cummings: A Miscellany Revised*, ed. S. V. Baum (New York: October House, 1965), 112.

19. In his last two volumes of poetry–*95 Poems* (1958) and *73 Poems* (1963)– Cummings's themes also grew beyond the "you and i vs. them" oppositions to recognize the transcendent mystery of ever-approaching death.

20. *The Collected Poems of William Carlos Williams*, Vol. I (1909–39), ed. A. Walton Litz and Christopher MacGowan (New York: New Directions, 1991), 379–80, 384–85; hereafter, cited as *CPWCW* 1; subsequent page citations refer to this text or to Vol. II (*CPWCW* 2).

21. See, for example, his letter to Marianne Moore, May 2, 1934, in *Selected Letters of William Carlos Williams* (New York: New Directions, 1957), 147.

22. "Sanctions against Williams: Correspondence," *Partisan Review*, III.4 (May 1936), 32.

23. "The Business of a Novelist," *The New Republic*, April 4, 1934, 220; "What Makes a Novelist," *National Review*, January 20, 1968, 31.

24. Dos Passos's public denunciation of the Soviets in Spain ("Farewell to Europe," *Common Sense* [1937]; rpt. in *John Dos Passos; Travel Books and Other Writings 1916–1941* [New York: Library of America, 2003], 618–22) led to a bitter falling out with his former friend, Hemingway, and to virtual expulsion from the Left.

25. *New Masses*, September 17, 1935, 9–10; rpt. in *New Masses: An Anthology of the Rebel Thirties*, ed. with a prologue, Joseph North (New York: International Publishers, 1969), 181–87.

26. Originally titled *The Wild Palms*.

27. If in *To Have and Have Not*, Hemingway emulated Faulkner's device of multiple narrators and points of view, Faulkner returned the compliment in *If I Forget Thee, Jerusalem*, in attempting to outdo *A Farewell to Arms* in the Harry Wilbourne/Charlotte Rittenmeyer love-pregnancy-death odyssey.

CHAPTER 17

The American Stage

Mark Fearnow

Sociologists Robert and Helen Lynd returned to Muncie, Indiana, in 1935. Their 1925 analysis of the "typical American town" had become a surprise bestseller when published in 1929 as *Middletown: A Study in Contemporary American Culture.*[1] Now they returned to see how the city had changed after ten years of economic catastrophe coinciding with rapid technological innovation in transportation, communication, and manufacturing. Their new book, published in 1937 as *Middletown in Transition: A Study in Cultural Conflicts*, culminated in the chapter "Middletown Faces Both Ways" (487–510). The Lynds describe a culture that is dwelling in an "unresolved duality," a culture that "wants to be adventurous and embrace new ideas and practices" but that also "desperately needs security . . . clinging largely to tried sources of security rather than venturing out into the untried" (491–92).

The Lynds' description of the 1930s United States as living in an "unresolved duality" is a memorable one. A nation that had powered through the 1920s on a fuel of economic expansion mixed with belief in never-ending "progress" found itself in a struggle for survival. The dream of progress and a future of marvels endured but vied with the daily reality of massive unemployment and the descent of many into poverty. "People want to continue to live hopefully and adventurously into the future," wrote the Lynds, "but if the future becomes too hazardous, they look steadily toward the known past" (493).

American theatre, like the culture itself, underwent radical expansion in the later 1910s and 1920s. The middle class, freed by technology from hours of labor and transportation, spent part of its new leisure time in the burgeoning "Little Theatre" movement. The Provincetown Players, emerging in 1916 from its status as a casual summer retreat for writers and political radicals on Cape Cod, helped to initiate the "Downtown" arts scene in lower Manhattan. Here it hosted Expressionist works by Eugene O'Neill, most notably *The Emperor Jones* (1920) and *The Hairy Ape* (1922).

341

Uptown, at the Bandbox Theatre on East 57th Street, the Washington Square Players was founded in 1915 and produced a mixture of new American plays alongside European and Russian works by writers such as Chekhov, Maeterlinck, and Wedekind. By the mid-1920s, these two theatres had "grown up." The Provincetown Players became a fully professional theatre in 1922, and in 1919 the Washington Square Players transformed into the Theatre Guild, a Broadway producer of innovative theatre.

Emboldened by the audience appeal of these theatres and their experimental plays, commercial producers joined in, and the New York theatre scene of the 1920s became an exciting artistic environment. New York saw lavish productions and long runs for Elmer Rice's *The Adding Machine* (1923) and Sophie Treadwell's *Machinal* (1928), landmarks in American Expressionist drama. Eugene O'Neill was a questing artist in the 1920s, working in one style, setting it aside, and trying another. O'Neill's twin influences were Greek tragedy and the plays of August Strindberg, a volatile mixture most evident in *Desire under the Elms* (1924) and the monumental, four-hour psychoanalytic experiment, *Strange Interlude* (written 1923), a sensation when produced by the Theatre Guild in 1928.

The risks of periodization of history are well known, but the break between the United States of the 1920s to that of the 1930s is an unusually clear one. US stocks reached unprecedented heights in September 1929, but between October 24 and 28, values fell more than a third and panic led the economy into a downward spiral. Corporations cut investment in an attempt to preserve cash, and as a result consumption fell, prices fell, wages were cut, and unemployment exploded.[2] By the time Franklin Delano Roosevelt took office in March 1933, the nation was in a dire condition. Compared to the economy's peak in September 1929, the Gross National Product had fallen by 29 percent, consumption by 18 percent, construction by 78 percent, and investment an astonishing 98 percent.[3] Meanwhile, unemployment had risen from 3.2 percent in 1929 to 24.9 percent.[4]

With the drastic change in the economy, culture changed rapidly. A cultural product based on aestheticism could be seen as frivolous and even immoral in a context of widespread poverty. Artistic experiment was by no means extinct in the Depression years. The Gertrude Stein–Virgil Thomson *4 Saints in 3 Acts*, a surreal "opera to be sung," was the high-art phenomenon of 1934. Orson Welles emerged as a brilliant stage director with his radical reinterpretations of classic texts, and the Federal Theatre Project's "Living Newspapers" brought techniques from Irwin Piscator's Epic Theatre to their elaborate staging of raging issues of the day.[5] Nevertheless, a general tendency of this decade of emergency was the creation of Realistic social dramas, Realistic comedies, escapist farce, nostalgic dramas and comedies, socially conscious musicals, and escapist musicals.

In the face of this complexity, what is most distinctive about 1930s drama is the rise of Realism as the dominant style of American theatre. The advance of Realism was rapid. During these ten years, a new standard was achieved, a new playing field outlined. Writers including Lillian Hellman, Clifford Odets, Robert E. Sherwood, and William Saroyan explored the possibilities of this flexible and accessible style, as did comic writers such as George S. Kaufman, Moss Hart, Philip Barry, and Clare Boothe Luce, who infused Realistic comedies with notable social purpose. Thornton Wilder, a peculiar and unavoidably brilliant playwright, more in tune with the aesthetic of Gertrude Stein than that of Ibsen, is better understood when held up in contrast to the main artistic project of his generation of serious American playwrights. At the same time, Eugene O'Neill, for so many a cultural hero of the previous decade, drove on in the 1930s to expand Realistic techniques to encompass his obsession with Greek tragedy, and at last to embody his most personal and devastatingly honest plays.

The student of American culture should keep in mind that most of the Broadway "smash hits" of the 1930s were – perhaps unsurprisingly – sex farces, musicals, and musical revues. Of the many impressive Realistic plays of the decade, only one made the list of the ten longest-running Broadway productions – *The Children's Hour* by Lillian Hellman, which ran for 691 performances in 1934–35.[6] This play, with its Ibsenesque structure carrying a clear if complex message, is a meaningful entry point to the socially conscious Realistic drama of the 1930s, in that its commercial success proves the accessibility and audience appeal of what came to be seen as a distinctly American style of serious play.

The Children's Hour was Hellman's first produced play and the most commercially successful of her career. Hellman (1905–84) had worked as a script-reader for MGM, written short stories, and coauthored (with Louis Kronenberger) an unproduced comedy when she happened upon an 1810 Scottish legal case concerning two women who ran a boarding school for girls. The women's reputations were ruined by an accusation of lesbianism from one of the students.[7] Hellman saw potential for a "drama of morality," a play not about lesbianism but on the theme of the insidious power of lies.[8] Though by no means the first American playwright to use Ibsen as a model – James Herne, Clyde Fitch, and Rachel Crothers had explored that method effectively – Hellman brought extraordinary talent for truth-ful characterization to the fateful machinery of life and circumstance.[9]

Hellman's later plays were more personal in their origins, but in *The Children's Hour*, she followed the advice of her mentor and romantic partner, novelist Dashiell Hammett, in choosing a subject about which she could feel detached.[10] Hellman reset the story in New England and created a powerful representative of bourgeois ruthlessness in the grandmother of one of the schoolgirls. The two young women who run the school bring suit but lose their case. The play's twist is that one of the women admits, in the last act, that she does feel sexual attraction for her friend, and then promptly commits suicide. In the final scene, the grandmother who had raised the public alarm arrives to say that her granddaughter has confessed that she made up the story of seeing the women together. Everyone is very sorry.[11]

The play has faced criticism – in the 1930s because it dared to discuss homosexuality, and in more recent decades because it propelled a decades-long artistic cliché – that if any character comes out as gay or lesbian, he or she must die by the final scene.[12] Despite these detractions, *The Children's Hour* has continued to hold a place in the repertory. Writing about the political theatre of the 1930s from the position of 1964, Gerald Rabkin called Hellman "the hardiest dramatic survivor of the thirties," her plays staged more frequently than work by Lawson, Odets, or Sherwood.[13]

Hellman is a writer who "faces both ways." She looks to the past for her dramatic technique and finds a working model in Ibsen, and to the future, with an ideological urge for a better, more just and humane civilization. Ibsen's plays tend toward an acceptance of human weakness and corrup-tion that could be called Realistic but might be called cynical. Hellman uses Realism to draw a corrupt world, but with a measure of hope left in it. Her next play, *Days to Come* (1936), was her most overtly political play, about a labor strike in Ohio. Though intelligently conceived and artfully constructed, the play was unsuccessful, closing after only seven perfor-mances. The script is oddly cool, the playwright trying to depict the union leader and the capitalist owner in a moral balance.

Hellman seemed to find the ideal mixture of realistic technique, moral determination, and political implication in *The Little Foxes* (1939). Set in an Alabama town in 1900, the play depicts the competition for wealth within the middle-class Hubbard family, members of whom resort to theft and homicide in pursuit of money. The protagonist, Regina, succeeds in her quest for wealth, but she alienates the one person she loves – her teenaged daughter – who vows in the final scene to spend her life fighting against uncaring, avaricious people like her mother and uncles.

Critics have sometimes offered the play faint praise, emphasizing its mechanical perfection and calling it a melodrama, while denying its social meaning or lingering significance as literature. Brooks Atkinson set the pattern upon the play's premiere in 1939:

> Miss Hellman writes with melodramatic abandon, plotting torture, death, and thievery like the author of an old-time thriller. She has made her drama air-tight; it is a knowing job of construction, deliberate and self-contained. In the end she tosses in a speech of social significance, which is no doubt sincere.[14]

The Little Foxes is more than a thriller. If it is a melodrama, so are *Macbeth* and most of Ibsen. The most relevant comparison is to *A Doll's House* (1879). Psychologically complex characters move through an action that – unfolding with seeming inevitability – exposes an underlying social condition that surfaces in the final scene as the subject of dialogue. A difference between the plays is that Hellman does all of this rather more subtly than Ibsen had done sixty years earlier. The machinery of her storytelling is nearly invisible and when the "message" emerges in the final scene – Alexandra's rejection of her mother's barbarian capitalism – the dialogue grows plausibly from the arc we have seen the daughter travel. Ibsen's Nora, in that pioneering work of Realism, enters her last scene, wherein she presents her decision to leave her husband and children, a completely different person – logical, analytical, self-possessed in a way we have never seen her.

Hellman's play is clear without being expository. The playwright looked to the past for setting and a dramatic tradition, but the "thought" of her play was of its moment. Hellman's theme of the power of capitalism to convert people to obsessed money-grubbers is remarkably similar to Bertolt Brecht's *The Good Person of Szechwan* (1943). The Brecht work is told in a mode of anti-realistic theatre, but the moral and economic analysis is consistent with Hellman's.

As an American Realistic social drama of the 1930s, *The Little Foxes* has few rivals in terms of its artistic quality. A leading contender is *Awake and Sing!* (1935), a vibrant, energetic, ideologically committed play of modern urban life by Clifford Odets, distilled in the pressurized vessel of the legendary Group Theatre. Odets joined the Group – a communitarian, idealistic set of young people who split off from the Theatre Guild in 1930 – as an actor and dishwasher in their summer workshops. Odets was only twenty-nine in 1935 when the Group presented *Waiting for Lefty* and *Awake and Sing!*, his first two plays, and those with which he is most identified.

Waiting for Lefty (1935) is a Realistic one-act play with five scenes inside a framing story about a union meeting. The roles were written for Group members, who relished the passionate material and rehearsed it in their spare time. When the union members learn that Lefty – a charismatic labor leader – has been murdered, actors scattered around the theatre stood up one by one to join the cry, "STRIKE, STRIKE, STRIKE!!!" and the audience joined them. In his engrossing book, *The Fervent Years*, Harold Clurman called this electrifying moment in January 1935 "the birth cry of the Thirties."[15]

> Our youth had found its voice. It was the call to join the good fight for a greater measure of life in a world free of economic fear, falsehood, and craven servitude to stupidity and greed. "Strike!" was Lefty's lyric message, not alone for a few extra pennies of wages or for shorter hours of work, strike for greater dignity, strike for a bolder humanity, strike for the full stature of man. (148)

While *Waiting for Lefty* was being presented on Sunday evenings at labor events, the Group was preparing its Broadway production of Odets's first full-length play, *Awake and Sing!* This play, its title drawn from the book of Isaiah – "Awake and sing, ye that dwell in the dust" – looks back to Realistic or Naturalistic dramas that depict characters trapped in misery by economic circumstances. Like the characters in Maxim Gorky's *The Lower Depths* (1902) and Gerhardt Hauptmann's *Rose Bernd* (1903), Odets's struggling New Yorkers dream of happiness and fulfillment, but find exploitation and disappointment. The Berger family "share a fundamental activity," Odets wrote – "a struggle for life amidst petty conditions."[16] The misery of the characters is tempered by what is, in a sense, a hopeful ending. The most humane of the characters, the old grandfather, commits suicide by jumping from the roof, making it appear as an accident, so that his grandson, the frustrated Ralph, can claim his life insurance and find a better life. (This plot idea anticipates one used by Arthur Miller, much influenced by Odets, in *Death of a Salesman* in 1949.) In the final scene, Ralph eschews the money, vowing to make his grandfather's sacrifice mean something by organizing his coworkers. Ralph vows to work for a better future, where "life won't be printed on dollar bills."[17]

The play was a critical and financial success, propelling Odets and the Group Theatre to new prominence. Odets would write three more dramas in the Thirties – *Paradise Lost* (1935), *Golden Boy* (1937), and *Rocket to the*

Moon (1938), but none achieved the stature of *Lefty* or *Awake and Sing!* *Golden Boy* was a commercial success, but its overwrought story of a violin virtuoso who wastes his talent pursuing fast money as a boxer feels implausible and its conclusion – the boxer and his girlfriend dying in a car crash – unnecessarily dire. Odets famously moved to Hollywood in 1936 and married a film star. His defection from the Group was seen by Group members as Odets's own version of chasing easy money.[18]

John Howard Lawson, who shone in the 1920s with his Expressionist work, turned in the 1930s to Realism, in parallel to his commitment to Communist ideology. After joining the party in 1934, Lawson wrote his influential *Theory and Technique of Playwriting* (1936), synthesizing his reading of Marx with a study of Aristotle. Lawson's playwriting text was widely read and a major influence on the era. His emphasis on the necessity of conflict in the dramatic action fuses with the Marxist principle of the progressive clash of forces in dialectical materialism. Lawson's *Marching Song* (1937) was his attempt to write, in Gerald Rabkin's phrase, "the model of the revolutionary drama."[19] *Marching Song* follows the pattern for proletarian literature advanced by Soviet authorities in the mid-thirties, but Lawson's attempts at Socialist Realism never found an audience. In Clurman's view, the play lacked a sense of real life, causing the Group to reject it. Angry at their decision, Lawson demanded of Clurman, "Don't you think proletarian plays should be written at this time?" leading Clurman to reply, "Perhaps, but not by you."[20]

Rivaling O'Neill in literary reputation, Robert E. Sherwood was a serious, hard-working intellectual and political liberal who created his most important work in the 1930s, winning Pulitzer Prizes for *Idiot's Delight* in 1936 and *Abe Lincoln in Illinois* in 1939.[21] John Mason Brown emphasized Sherwood's attentiveness to his social milieu in the title of his biography, *The Worlds of Robert E. Sherwood: Mirror to His Times.*[22] Sherwood's plays *The Petrified Forest* (1935) and *Idiot's Delight* (1936) reveal a cultural subtext of the 1930s animated by the grotesque.[23] The grotesque, a condition in which the irreconcilable are held in uncomfortable and unresolved relationship, is an effective critical term for conflicts of the 1930s, as Americans found themselves caught between an agrarian past and the promise of a technological future. Sherwood's plays, artful and entertaining, reward the reader with insights into the 1930s American "mind," in a sense derived from Siegfried Kracauer's method of cultural history.[24] Sherwood's plays seem at times to be uncanny predictors of the future. In *Idiot's Delight*, the playwright brings together a collection of oddly assorted Americans, a German arms dealer, and a variety of Europeans, stranded in an alpine hotel in an unnamed country just as war breaks out. Though written four years before the onset of World War II, Sherwood anticipates the moves of the major powers in a play uncomfortably balanced between sex comedy and political drama.

The Petrified Forest, staged the previous year, used a similar device of strangers stranded in a remote outpost to sculpt an enduring metaphor for America's and the developed world's teetering position, competed for by idealists, cynics, and fascists. Enjoyable on the level of gangster melodrama, the play is enriched with Sherwood's characteristic analogic situation and philosophical dialogue. Here, the wandering poet, Alan Squier, articulates the theme. A spiritually exhausted intellectual, Squier welcomes the arrival of the murderous gangster. He volunteers to be shot, convinced that he is taking part in nature's handing over the world from the intellectuals to the brutes.

Sherwood's 1938 Lincoln play was part of a larger American obsession with that president in the decade.[25] Of the many 1930s plays on Lincoln, Sherwood's is the most substantial and effective. He depicts Lincoln as a suffering savior who battles doubt and depression and overcomes them. The play ran for more than a year and was seen by most critics as Sherwood's finest. Lincoln's reluctant acceptance of the need for war to preserve liberty was emphasized by many commentators. Brooks Atkinson captured the attitude in a memorable review:

> Full of admiration for his chief character, [Sherwood] is also overflowing with love for the principles that Lincoln reluctantly accepted from destiny and made his own. They are Mr. Sherwood's now, and also ours; and "Abe Lincoln in Illinois" is a noble testament of our spiritual faith.[26]

President Roosevelt's assistant, Harry Hopkins, attended the opening night party for the play. A short time later, Sherwood went to work as a writer for the administration.[27]

Some of the socially relevant plays of the decade were comedies. Realistic comedies by S. N. Behrman, especially *Rain from Heaven* (1934) and *End of Summer* (1936), applied the style Behrman developed in the 1920s to the new cultural paradigm. Like his contemporary Philip Barry (*The Philadelphia Story*, 1939), Behrman wrote about the world of the upper classes. These tense, self-conscious comedies show the quaking of that world as the problems of the Depression and global conflict – unemployment, Communist organizing, and political refugees – burst into what had in the 1920s been placid drawing rooms, garden parties, and amusing country weekends.

George S. Kaufman turned away from the satires and farces of his earlier career to join with Moss Hart in crafting a series of highly successful Realistic comedies. Most effective was their 1936 collaboration, *You Can't Take It with You*. This enduring play has many thematic similarities to Odets's *Awake and Sing!*. The theme of the stories of Odets's Berger family and Kaufman and Hart's Vanderhof household is the same – the determination to build a life that is not based on acquiring money. Ralph's search for a life that is not "printed on dollar bills" could be found if he ventured a mile downtown to the Vanderhofs', where Grandpa and his household of eccentrics persuade a titan of business and even the Internal Revenue Service that life is about enjoyment, not the struggle to get ahead.

Kaufman directed another comic hit of 1936, *The Women* by Clare Boothe Luce. A pitiless, witty play of language and character, Luce's comedy ridiculed wealthy women she observed through her editorial work at *Vogue* and *Vanity Fair*, and with whom she later associated as a peer through her marriage to *Time* and *Life* publisher Henry Luce.[28] The play is not an indictment of all women but of a trendy set who are wasting their opportunities and resources in idleness and consumption. The protagonist's conversion over the course of the play from a nice but ineffective time-waster to a fighter who goes after what she wants is consistent with Luce's life-long attitude, one that she continued in her later career as a member of Congress and foreign policy advisor to Republican administrations.[29]

William Saroyan's fanciful, dreamy, delicate comedies of the 1930s were like no others. A writer of immense linguistic skills, Saroyan was reluctant to include any "bad" characters in his whimsical and optimistic worlds, leaving them as plays without adequate conflict to drive the action. The exception is his best play and a beautiful document of the decade, *The Time of Your Life* (1939). Set in a San Francisco waterfront dive, the play is presided over by Joe, a benevolent young man with money but no observable profession. The barroom is peopled by a colorful variety of types – an old-timer of the Old West who tells tall tales, a tap dancer who wants to become a comedian but is not funny, an elderly Arab man given to philosophy, a young man in love, and another who cannot stop playing the pinball machine.

Joe facilitates his right-hand man's courtship of a young prostitute who wants to change her way of life. The love story is nearly blocked and all happiness ruined by a malicious vice cop with the unforgettable name of Blick, who is determined to jail the young woman. All works out in the end. The Old West braggart assassinates Blick, the young couple is united, and even the pinball player is victorious, winning the highest score, prompting the machine to celebratory sounds and waving of American flags.

Though written in Saroyan's distinctive "I am in love with America" style, the play has much in common with Kaufman and Hart's *You Can't Take It with You*. Both plays avoid the unpleasant realities of poverty by centering on protagonists with unusual sources of cash to shield the beloved characters from harm. Grandpa Vanderhof owns undefined real estate that provides him a substantial annual income (upon which, through a ruse, he avoids paying income tax), and Saroyan's fantasy is lifted by Joe's mysterious funds, allowing him to live the life of barroom loafer and benevolent God. These plays offer wish fulfillment that Depression audiences were eager to receive. Grandpa and Joe face opposition to their benevolence, but the threats are defeated in ways more than reassuring, approaching the miraculous.

No consideration of American drama of the 1930s should omit the strange and lasting contributions of Thornton Wilder, whose plays emerge from no obvious tradition, fit no recognized category, and have preserved their strangeness and audience appeal across many decades. An abstract thinker and highly intellectual writer, Wilder came to public attention as winner of the Pulitzer Prize for Fiction for his short, subtly philosophical novel, *The Bridge of San Luis Rey*, written while Wilder was teaching French at a school in New Jersey. In 1931, Wilder published a collection of short plays unlike any other. *The Long Christmas Dinner and Other Plays in One Act* compress, through a variety of simple dramatic and theatrical techniques, huge universal stories into stage actions of thirty to forty-five minutes. The title play depicts multiple generations of a family at a continuous Christmas dinner; a doorway on one side of the room allows for births and an arch on the other supplies an exit for the characters who have – adding white wigs as they age and moving along the table – lived their lives and then escape our view. "Pullman Car Hiawatha" compresses life, love, death, madness, and even the motions of the stars and planets into the overnight journey of one sleeper car. Simplest and perhaps most effective of all is "The Happy Journey to Trenton and Camden," in which a family of four makes a short drive in New Jersey to visit the oldest daughter and in so doing suggests a universal story of familial love, birth, and death. This play, like others in Wilder's collection, calls for no scenery save a few chairs.

Though the influence is subtle, Wilder's aesthetic was inspired by his study of James Joyce and, later in the thirties, his friendship with Gertrude Stein. Wilder objected to Realism in the theatre as not being "Real" at all.

When you emphasize place in the theater, you drag down and limit and harness time to it. You thrust the action back into past time, whereas it is precisely the glory of the stage that it is always "now" there. Under such production methods the characters are all dead before the action starts. You don't have to pay deeply for your heart's participation. No great age in the theater ever attempted to capture the audience's belief through this kind of specification and localization.[30]

What Wilder wanted was a Theater of Unique Occasion. As he explained in a lecture to the James Joyce Society in 1954, he wanted to capture what Joyce captured in *Ulysses* (1922) – the avoidance of "generalization," and the recreation of the truly "real," the uniqueness of a moment of experience. "Every human being lives only unique occasions, just as we all die one death," Wilder told the audience. People have said "I love you" millions of times and millions are saying it each day. But "each time it is really said just once . . . The participation in essential love or essential death is, as they are now saying, 'existential' – totally individual."[31]

Wilder's masterwork of the 1930s is *Our Town* (1938), for which he won the Pulitzer Prize, becoming the first person to win Pulitzers for different categories. This deceptively simple play, constantly in print and – according to Wilder's estate – in perpetual stage production, was influenced by Wilder's friendship with Gertrude Stein, whom he met on her US lecture tour in November 1934.[32] The two became frequent correspondents and Wilder made a close study of Stein's work. He wrote to her in 1937 that he was well along in writing a play called "Our Town" that was "a little play with all the big subjects in it; and it's a big play with all the little things of life lovingly impressed into it."[33] He was at that time working on the play's third act. It was, he wrote Stein, "based on your ideas, as on great pillars."[34]

As with Wilder's one-act plays, *Our Town* eschews scenery and most stage properties. Plain wooden chairs, a table, two ladders, and some black umbrellas (carried by mourners at a funeral) create the Unique Occasions that comprise the action. Wilder's use of the Stage Manager as intermediary between audience and dramatic world allows for the isolation of particular moments. The Stage Manager introduces short scenes, brings on a "professor" to provide historical information, skips over months and years, and focuses the audience's attention on the moments he determines they will see.

These techniques bear some resemblance to the Epic Theatre of Erwin Piscator and Bertolt Brecht. Wilder was familiar with Epic plays and staging from his visits to Berlin in 1928 and 1931.[35] Max Frisch called Wilder's technique a "glorious imitation" of Brecht, and Friedrich

Dürrenmatt referred to *Our Town* as "Episches Theater."[36] The comparisons are sensible, but Wilder uses the techniques in *Our Town* for purposes completely opposite from those of Piscator and Brecht, who wished to prevent emotional identification with the characters and belief in their actions such that the audience maintained a critical intellectual position. Most spectators, in their guided witness to a few small scenes of daily life in a New Hampshire village, find *Our Town* to be an intensely moving play. Wilder's real source is more distant in time – Shakespeare, Lope de Vega, and Molière – a theatre of pure conventions, wherein the "bareness of the stage releases the events from the particular and the experience of Juliet partakes of that of all girls in love, in every time, place, and language."[37]

Eugene O'Neill entered the 1930s as the most prestigious American playwright and one of the few American writers – along with Hemingway, Faulkner, Upton Sinclair, and Sinclair Lewis – to have achieved an international reputation. His impressive body of work from the 1920s included some of the best Realistic plays yet written by an American – *Beyond the Horizon* (1920), *Anna Christie* (1921), and *Desire under the Elms* (1924) – as well as successful experiments in Expressionism – *The Emperor Jones* (1920) and *The Hairy Ape* (1922). O'Neill had prominent work in more genres, including historical drama and masked tragedy. His boldest creation thus far, the four-hour *Strange Interlude* (1928), was produced to great acclaim by the Theatre Guild, now O'Neill's "home" theatre, won the writer his third Pulitzer Prize and – extremely rare for a play – became an international bestseller in book form. So esteemed was O'Neill that when Sinclair Lewis won the Nobel Prize for Literature in 1930, he turned in his acceptance speech to praise for O'Neill. Lewis told the Swedish Academy that O'Neill,

> has done nothing much in the American drama save to transform it utterly in ten or twelve years from a false world of neat and competent trickery to a world of splendor, fear, and greatness. [O'Neill has] seen life as something not to be neatly arranged in a study, but as terrifying, magnificent and often quite horrible, a thing akin to a tornado, an earthquake or a devastating fire.[38]

O'Neill, at age forty-two in 1930, was at the height of his powers. Success had brought him substantial wealth as well as fame, and he and his third wife, former actress Carlotta Monterey, began what would be a life-long search for privacy, building a series of large and secluded homes. O'Neill launched into the decade with a work of major scope and ambition.

Mourning Becomes Electra (1931) is a trilogy, each play having either four or five acts, its action based on Aeschylus's *The Oresteia*. The playwright transforms the world of Greek tragedy according to a Realistic vision, setting the plays in a New England village in the nineteenth century.

The Theatre Guild presented the trilogy in one long evening, the first play beginning at five in the afternoon, and the second commencing after a dinner break from seven to eight. A short intermission was allowed between the second and third plays, and the drama concluded at nearly midnight.[39] The play had the appearance of Realism, with characters acting in a recognizable setting upon motivations with plausible, if extreme, psychological motivations; but the characters and dialogue were also abstracted. O'Neill conceived the trilogy as a masked drama, but later chose to instruct the actors to wear mask-like makeup. In the words of Alice Brady, who played the central role of Lavinia (based on Electra), "I feel that Mr. O'Neill meant Lavinia to be a symbol rather than a living, breathing human being who buys hats and gloves and eats lamb chops."[40]

The critical success of *Mourning Becomes Electra* was followed by a popular success – O'Neill's only full-length comedy, the nostalgic coming-of-age play, *Ah, Wilderness!* (1933), and then by one of his greatest failures, *Days without End* (1934), a drama that uses two actors to portray dueling aspects of the central character (a technique used successfully three decades later by Brian Friel in *Philadelphia, Here I Come!*) After the launch of *Ah, Wilderness!*, O'Neill and Carlotta Monterey retreated to their newly built ocean-front home on Sea Island, Georgia. O'Neill had a closely held plan to write his largest work ever – a cycle of five plays, later expanded to eight, then nine, then to eleven plays – tracing the fate of an Irish-American family in New England from 1754 to the present. This ambitious project took an enormous toll on the writer as he toiled over the plays in an isolation deplored by his friends but effectively enforced by Carlotta.[41] The cycle – to have been titled *A Tale of Possessors Self-Dispossessed* – and O'Neill's painstaking work on it from 1934 to 1939, ultimately proved a failure. O'Neill accumulated cartons of outlines, notes, and drafts, but completed only one play, *A Touch of the Poet*, and all but this play and a wayward typescript of another – *More Stately Mansions* – were destroyed by O'Neill and Carlotta in 1953 when, extremely ill, he accepted that he would never finish the plays and did not want them to be completed by anyone else.[42]

O'Neill's health declined drastically during the 1930s. What began as a tremor in his hands progressed to a general loss of motor control, making it difficult for him to walk, write, or even swallow. The illness was diagnosed in the 1930s as Parkinson's disease, but an autopsy in 1953 showed it to have been a rare form of cerebral cortical atrophy.[43] O'Neill's mind was unaffected by the illness, yet he was so physically debilitated by 1936 that he could not attend the ceremonies when he became the second American, and the first American playwright, to be awarded the Nobel Prize for Literature. O'Neill tried writing via dictation, but found the method impossible, telling friends, "my pencil has become part of my brain."[44]

Believing that his life was nearing an end, O'Neill abandoned work on his cycle in June 1939 to write three plays that had been on his mind for years and held personal urgency. This decision was an important one in the history of American drama, because it led to O'Neill's composition of three of the most critically admired American plays – *The Iceman Cometh* (written 1939, staged 1946), *Long Day's Journey into Night* (written 1939–41, staged 1956), and *A Moon for the Misbegotten* (written 1943, staged 1947). These long Realistic dramas were closely drawn from O'Neill's personal history. In them, the writer confronted the dark stories of his past – the years spent in an alcoholic haze in New York dives; his painful relations with his parents – his father a famous Romantic actor privately driven by an obsessive parsimony, his mother a sensitive dreamer addicted to morphine, and his brother, Jamie, who blamed himself for introducing Eugene to the demimonde of Bowery bums and prostitutes. O'Neill's dedication of *Long Day's Journey into Night* to Carlotta on their anniversary captured his idea of the play's importance:

> Dearest: I give you the original script of this play of old sorrow, written in tears and blood. A sadly inappropriate gift, it would seem, for a day celebrating happiness. But you will understand. I mean it as a tribute to your love and tenderness which gave me the faith in love that enabled me to face my dead at last and write this play – write it with deep pity and understanding and forgiveness for all the four haunted Tyrones. These twelve years, Beloved One, have been a Journey into Light – into love. You know my gratitude. And my love![45]

The play deals unsentimentally with his family but the unpleasant reality is offset by countervailing gentleness and generosity. Its pages are filled with a miasmic sadness. The characters wander the gloomy Connecticut house like elegiac ghosts, searching out the means of their own remembrance. In his last work, *A Moon for the Misbegotten*, nearing a time when he himself would long for death as a release from physical suffering, O'Neill offered a benediction upon his brother's memory. Josie Hogan – a kind of giantess-virgin farmer who represented for O'Neill the source of all goodness – speaks O'Neill's final dramatic line. Josie has provided Jamie a night of peaceful sleep on her breast, beneath a benevolent moon. As Jamie takes his leave from her and walks down the road, O'Neill writes:

> JOSIE: (*Her face sad, tender and pitying – gently*) May you have your wish and die in your sleep soon, Jim, darling. May you rest forever in forgiveness and peace. (*She turns slowly and goes into the house.*) (*Curtain*).[46]

O'Neill, who began his career writing Realism in his early one-act plays (1913–17) and then experimented widely in the 1920s, returned to that style in his maturity with unmeasured artistic skill and wisdom. His last three plays set a new standard for what could be achieved in serious American drama in a Realistic style. Both Arthur Miller and Tennessee Williams wrote to O'Neill after the publication of *The Iceman Cometh*, praising its quality and importance.[47] (*Long Day's Journey into Night* was, at the playwright's insistence, withheld from publication or production until after O'Neill's death).[48] Miller and Williams, along with dramatists such as William Inge and Lorraine Hansberry, carried the tradition of American Realism into the 1940s and 1950s, which – with the assistance of Hollywood adaptations of their plays – propelled American drama to an esteemed position in world theatre. The foundation for that achievement was the work of O'Neill, declared by Sinclair Lewis as early as 1930 as the inventor of American drama as a serious art form. Decades later, Tennessee Williams, with characteristic drama, spoke of the suffering O'Neill had endured in creating his later works. "O'Neill gave birth to the American theatre," Williams told a biographer, "and died for it."[49]

Notes

1. Robert S. Lynd and Helen Merrell Lynd, *Middletown: A Study in Contemporary American Culture* (New York: Harcourt Brace and World, 1929).
2. Robert S. McElvaine, *The Great Depression: America, 1929–1941* (New York: Three Rivers Press, 1984), 73–74.
3. McElvaine, *The Great Depression*, 75.
4. McElvaine, *The Great Depression*, 75.
5. Pierre de Rohan, ed., *Federal Theatre Plays: Triple-A Plowed Under, Power, Spirochete* (New York: Random House, 1938).
6. Samuel L. Leiter, *The Encyclopedia of the New York Stage, 1930–1940* (Westport, CT: Greenwood Press, 1989), 1083.
7. Jackson R. Bryer, *Conversations with Lillian Hellman* (Jackson: University of Mississippi Press, 1986), 25.

8. Bryer, *Conversations with Lillian Hellman*, 7.

9. See Mark Fearnow, "A New Realism," in *The Oxford Handbook of American Drama*, ed. Jeffrey H. Richards and Heather S. Nathans (Oxford: Oxford University Press, 2014), 173–88.

10. Bryer, *Conversations with Lillian Hellman*, 25, 96.

11. Lillian Hellman, *The Children's Hour* (New York: Random House, 1934).

12. See Mary Titus, "Murdering the Lesbian," *Tulsa Studies in Women's Literature* 10 (1991), 215–32.

13. Gerald Rabkin, *Drama and Commitment: Politics in the American Theatre of the Thirties* (Bloomington: Indiana University Press, 1964), 40.

14. Brooks Atkinson, "Tallulah Bankhead in Lillian Hellman's Drama of the South, 'The Little Foxes,'" *New York Times*, February 16, 1939.

15. Harold Clurman, *The Fervent Years: The Group Theatre and the Thirties* (New York: Knopf, 1975), 148.

16. Clifford Odets, *Awake and Sing!* in *Waiting for Lefty and Other Plays* (New York: Grove Press, 1993), 37.

17. Odets, *Awake and Sing!* 97.

18. Odets's struggle between idealism and pleasure was captured provocatively in *Barton Fink*, a 1991 film by Ethan and Joel Coen, with a title character based on Odets.

19. Rabkin, *Drama and Commitment*, 157.

20. Clurman, *The Fervent Years*, 187.

21. Sherwood won a third Pulitzer in 1941 for *There Shall Be No Night*.

22. John Mason Brown, *The Worlds of Robert E. Sherwood: Mirror to His Times* (New York: Harper and Row, 1962).

23. Mark Fearnow, *The American Stage and the Great Depression: A Cultural History of the Grotesque* (New York: Cambridge University Press, 1995), 56.

24. Siegfried Kracauer, *From Caligari to Hitler: A Psychological History of the German Cinema* (Princeton, NJ: Princeton University Press, 1947).

25. Mark Fearnow, "The Meaning of Pictures: Myth and American History Plays of the Great Depression, or, Lincoln Died (So You and I Might Live)," *Journal of American Drama and Theatre* (Fall 1993), 1–15.

26. Brooks Atkinson, "Raymond Massey Appearing in Robert E. Sherwood's 'Abe Lincoln in Illinois,'" *New York Times*, October 17, 1938.

27. Brown, *The Worlds of Robert E. Sherwood*, 386.

28. Mark Fearnow, *Clare Boothe Luce: A Research and Production Sourcebook* (Westport, CT: Greenwood, 1995), 8.

29. See Fearnow, *American Stage*, 76–79.

30. Thornton Wilder, "Preface to Three Plays: Our Town, The Skin of Our Teeth, The Matchmaker," (1957), in *American Characteristics and Other Essays* (New York: Harper and Row, 1979), 108.

31. Thornton Wilder, "Joyce and the Modern Novel," (1954), in *American Characteristics and Other Essays* (New York: Harper and Row, 1979), 174.

32. Edward M. Burns and Ulla E. Dydo with William Rice, eds., *The Letters of Gertrude Stein and Thornton Wilder* (New Haven, CT: Yale University Press, 1996), xv.
33. Burns et al., *The Letters of Gertrude Stein and Thornton Wilder,* 175.
34. Burns et al., *The Letters of Gertrude Stein and Thornton Wilder,* 175.
35. Charles H. Helmeteg, "Mother Courage and Her American Cousins in The Skin of Our Teeth," *Modern Language Studies* (Autumn 1978), 65.
36. Helmeteg, "Mother Courage and Her American Cousins," p. 65.
37. Thornton Wilder, "Some Thoughts on Playwrighting" (1941), in *American Characteristics and Other Essays* (New York: Harper and Row, 1979), 124.
38. Sinclair Lewis, Nobel Prize Lecture, "The Fear of American Literature," delivered December 12, 1930, Stockholm. www.nobelprize.org/nobel_prizes/literature/laureates/1930/lewis-lecture.html.
39. Arthur Gelb and Barbara Gelb, *O'Neill* (New York: Harper and Row, 1962), 751.
40. Gelb and Gelb, *O'Neill,* 748.
41. Gelb and Gelb, *O'Neill,* 797–98.
42. Gelb and Gelb, *O'Neill,* 938.
43. Recent evaluations of O'Neill's autopsy materials differ as to whether the nervous system deterioration was related to heavy alcohol use in the playwright's youth. See Denise Grady, "Medical Researchers Revise O'Neill's Death Tale," *New York Times,* April 13, 2000.
44. Gelb and Gelb, *O'Neill,* 887.
45. Eugene O'Neill, Dedication to *Long Day's Journey into Night* (New Haven, CT: Yale University Press, 1956).
46. Eugene O'Neill, *A Moon for the Misbegotten* (New York: Random House, 1952), 177.
47. Dan Isaac, "Founding Father: O'Neill's Correspondence with Arthur Miller and Tennessee Williams," *Eugene O'Neill Review* (Spring/Fall 1993), 124–133.
48. The story of the publication and production rights of *Long Day's Journey into Night* is a complicated one. See Gelb and Gelb, *O'Neill,* 862.
49. Gelb and Gelb, *O'Neill,* 877.

PART III

Institutions

CHAPTER 18

Federal Writers' Project

Jerrold Hirsch

It seems simple. Had there been no Great Depression there would have been no New Deal Federal Writers' Project (FWP). But it isn't. The Congress that approved the FWP in 1935 did so largely because it was part of the work relief program that became the Works Progress Administration (WPA). Eventually that program employed more than 6,000 people. But the members of the House and Senate who voted for all those jobs showed little interest in creating a FWP, a Federal Art Project, a Federal Music Project, and a Federal Theatre Project. They just wanted to put people to work.

However, the New Deal administrators who directed these projects sought more. They wanted to address unemployment, but they wanted also to make significant contributions to American culture and to create national cultural institutions that would sustain a new vision of American life and character. They saw the American Guide Series (AGS) they promoted and the American folklore and oral history interviews they conducted as being as much a part of American literature as any authored poem or novel.[1] They sought to argue a politics of culture, what national folklore editor B. A. Botkin called a "cultural strategy,"[2] that linked their work to romantic nationalist literary theory[3] at home and abroad, to the New Deal ethos, and to the Popular Front politics of the late 1930s.

Unfortunately, early students of the FWP did not treat the project as part of American cultural history. Rather those historians treated the FWP as another New Deal bureaucracy, some of whose work needed to be praised with a few brief laudatory comments. In recent years, however, FWP studies have begun to examine the cultural vision underlying the project's work, leading not only to the study of the FWP's AGS, but also to examination of its experimental, genre-blurring, academically challenging work in ethnic and racial studies, folklore, literature, and oral history. We certainly have not "assimilated" those experiments into American life and culture as B. A. Botkin, the national FWP folklore editor, had hoped American scholars, critics, and citizens eventually would.[4]

True, we have gone beyond listing the names of prominent FWP writers and begun to consider how project work may have affected their own and American writing. We have begun to recognize that although the FWP employed more out-of-work teachers, librarians, newspaper reporters, secretaries, recent college graduates, and other literate Americans than it ever did writers, the project was still a literary endeavor that had an impact on all the writers it employed. Nevertheless, much more work is required. National FWP officials worked under many limitations. They had to take from the relief rolls unemployed literate individuals who needed to be on white collar projects, rather than construction jobs, but who were often inadequate to the research and writing assignments they were given. A small exemption for needy writers, who did not qualify for work relief, played a crucial role in the FWP officials' intention of "introducing America to Americans," their catchphrase for a nation of citizens whom they thought knew far too little about each other.[5] But their dreams were much grander. National FWP officials sought nothing less than to create new genres of art, literature, criticism, and history. They tried to shape the FWP into a permanent government agency that could continue to study American life and culture. Although they failed in that goal, their legacy deserves more study, if we are ever to learn from it.

***

National FWP officials were an ethnically and racially diverse group of cosmopolitan intellectuals who sought to reconcile a romantic nationalist outlook with cultural pluralism, to reconcile diversity with unity, and to contribute to creating a society that was inclusive, egalitarian, and democratic. Almost all of them had been influenced by anthropologist Franz Boas's cultural relativism, which had turned the hierarchical cultural ladder of evolutionary anthropology on its side. Henry Alsberg, who directed the FWP, organized the project so that the study of American folklore, African American life, common laborers, the nation's various regions, and social ethnic groups – the last term is one of the earliest formulations of the term "ethnicity" – would be seen as central to understanding American identity. Alsberg hired John Lomax as the first folklore editor, and later hired as Lomax's successor folklorist, poet, and social historian B. A. Botkin. He chose African American poet Sterling A. Brown as Negro Affairs Editor and Morton Royse as Social Ethnic Studies Editor, with the goal of using the terms "folk" and "lore" to answer questions raised by the history of romantic nationalism in Europe and the United States as well as by the impact of the Great Depression on American cultural and social identity. Brown, for example, wanted to focus not just on the contributions of prominent African Americans, important as they were, but on the participation of blacks in all facets of American life and culture; while Royse argued that if there is a Massachusetts town with a mostly Polish population, then that cultural experience is not peripheral to "American culture" but the American culture in that town.[6]

It needs to be remembered, as national FWP officials knew well, that the 1920s era of Republican ascendency saw an intense rise in WASP nativism bounded not by class but by race and religion. The 1920s witnessed, for example, the nationwide rebirth of the KKK as a middle-class organization and the passage of immigration restriction laws designed to discriminate against southern and eastern Europeans and Asians. FWP officials knew as well that fascist racial ideologues were rising to power in Europe at the very moment Roosevelt's New Deal coalition of recent immigrants and their American-born children, the working class, the rural poor, African Americans, was beginning to exercise political and cultural power. Finally, they acknowledged their own leanings toward the Popular Front, a wide cultural and political movement aimed at uniting all liberals and leftists in the support of industrial unionism, anti-racism and antifascism, and toward the working-class immigrant and minority writers and artists who played a central role in shaping its ethos. Many of these artists were their friends, and their ability to survive and create because of the federal arts projects only strengthened the FWP's ability to affirm a pluralistic nationalism and cosmopolitan appreciation of American diversity.[7]

The AGS was the FWP's major and most public undertaking. Book reviewers in the popular press and magazines followed the release of each volume. The books in the AGS series were divided into three sections: essays on topics such as history, literature, music, and folklore, descriptions of major cities, and then the automobile tours that crossed the state. Prominent critics, such as Bernard DeVoto, writing in the *Saturday Review of Literature*, saw the tours as the guide's great literary triumph and cultural contribution to American self-understanding. He called them "a rich, various, and rewarding spectacle . . . a heartening reminder of how complex the current scene is and on what a variegated and fascinating base it rests."[8] Lewis Mumford, reviewing some of the guides, argued that by grounding American art in the details of American life and experience, by studying the "American Scene," optimistic romantic nationalists like himself could agree with national FWP officials that "the Federal Writers

Project together with the other creative projects will gradually tend to make literature and art an integral part of the national life."[9]

The roots of these arguments lay in the belief that awareness of the cultural creativity of the "people" would provide the basis for great national achievements in the high arts. The Tennessee guide essay on "Writers of Tennessee" provides an example typical of this AGS boldness: "the literature of the early settlers is found in the written forms in which they transacted the business of their everyday lives."[10] The fundamental assumption here and in the many other guide essays on literature was that by poring over the documents of daily life in the past, by examining indigenous forms of expression, and by studying local traditions, new literary achievement would automatically issue, since the artist would then be ready to realize his own creativity. And since he was working with a shared American tradition he would have an audience for his work.

The same romantic nationalist theme appeared in the essays on the arts in every FWP guide. Again, the Tennessee guide provides a good example of this sometimes naïve faith. Tennessee's guide writers are not at all embarrassed by the lack of high art among the pioneers, for "the pioneer folk of Tennessee produced ... an exceedingly rich assortment of handicrafts and domestic patterns. Spinning, hand-weaving, furniture-, broom-, and basket- making ... constituted Tennessee's earliest and most native participating in American art."[11] More recently literary theorist Hans Georg Jauss, as did Botkin earlier, argued that forms of folk expression lie, "in advance of historically realized manifestations of a literary culture."[12] Botkin would have differed with Jauss in thinking of folklore and creative writing as two forms of literature, each deserving respect and analysis as under modern conditions they influenced each other.

Virtually all the book reviews noted how the guides celebrated American pluralism and especially how the tours captured that diversity by exploring the extraordinary in the ordinary, and the ordinary in the extraordinary – the Sales Mondays that took place in South Carolina, the singing schools in Missouri, the church suppers in Iowa, the Czechs of Cedar Rapids, many of whom worked in the town's packing plants, the German dairy farmers in Wisconsin. Traditional "historical" sights were noted, but so were the diverse enclaves of various eastern and southern Europeans in the Midwest and the romantic sublime of Gary, Indiana's steel mills.

By 1938, Alsberg had concluded that with many of the state guides completed it was time for the FWP to pursue deeper cultural studies. As he put it, "the building up of our country knows no parallel in historical times – in the influx of peoples from all ends of the earth, and in the freedom and opportunities which beckoned to the impoverished and oppressed of all lands. How a social and cultural unity was achieved by these people, without stamping cultural differences into one mold, producing the unique American civilization and how the fabric was enlarged is the crux of our story."[13] Alsberg saw Botkin as the key figure who would tie together these new studies, some already begun by Sterling Brown and Morton Royse, and in spring 1938 he hired him to succeed John Lomax as national folklore editor.

Alsberg talked about books on "Composite America," a "National Negro Book," a volume of ex-slave narratives, and an "American Folklore Caravan."[14] The latter title echoes the annual *American Caravan* anthologies of new American experimental and modernist writing, poetry and fiction that Van Wyck Brooks, Lewis Mumford, and Paul Rosenfeld had edited in the 1920s, and the very naming of the proposed American folklore book encapsulated Botkin's view of contemporary folklore as a form of modern literature. Although none of these books was ever completed, the published and unpublished materials continue to demand analysis, which they are now receiving, but not to the degree that they deserve.[15]

The different approaches of Lomax and Botkin to American folklore illustrate how the FWP moved from a romantic nationalism that viewed American folklore as a closed and finished part of American literature to one that viewed it as unfinished and compatible with diversity and modernity.[16] Both Lomax and Botkin thought that there was a made-in-America American folklore, not just folklore survivals brought here from other places. But they differed greatly on the crucial matter of whether folklore was *still* being created in the industrialized, urbanized, and increasingly diverse United States of the thirties. Because of these developments Lomax thought the conditions for creating folklore in American were vanishing. Botkin totally disagreed.[17] Lomax's romantic "closing account" view of American folklore was clearly stated in the folklore manual FWP workers were given. While it dismissed folklorists who valued "only what could be traced back to a past for which they have a nostalgia; a ballad to interest them must have an Elizabethan origin," it did not assert that contemporary American life was likely to produce new examples and genres of folklore. Lomax was interested in "America, not in Europe," and his manual argued Federal Writers should value "a recital of Clementine and her forty-niner parent above those of Lady Claire," but it also assumed that "machine civilization" was gradually destroying the widespread conditions for an American folklore. For Lomax, American folklore and folksong were still being performed, still had a function in some communities, and still could be collected before it passed away, but it was unlikely to continue to be made.[18]

In sharp contrast, Botkin rejected the view that modern life destroyed folklore. For him, folklore both survived and was newly made. He also had moved beyond the pastoralism that dominated American folklore studies. Instead he argued that there was also an urban and labor lore, a folk and lore of the present as well as of the past. Sure that folk creativity persisted, Botkin sought to reconcile romantic creativity with cultural pluralism by maintaining that there existed a multiregional and multiethnic American folklore that was more than mere survivals from the past. Focusing on intercultural contact and hybridity, instead of on isolation and purity, he saw new lore being created continuously in the modern technological, industrial, and urban world.[19]

Botkin's idea of "folklore in the making" – the continual creative response of various American subcultures to their world – was attractive to national FWP officials who saw in it a basis for revitalizing American culture. Unlike most folklorists of that time, Botkin talked about the lore of the present as well as of the past; he saw that for every form of folklore in decay, there was a new living, contemporary folklore in the making. For Botkin, this emerging lore was created in the factory as well as on the farm, in the cities as well as in the countryside, among the educated and the unlettered. Some was a product of interactions between cultural groups, some a product of class conflict, and some a form of resistance that grew in the interstitial places bureaucracy could not eliminate in its desire for seamless control, but all was alive, new, and vital.

Botkin thought that this new American lore could be understood through collecting what he called "own stories."[20] He saw an interview not only as a way of recording folklore but also as a way of capturing the experiences of individuals and their communities. Beyond that he saw opportunity for creative writers on the FWP to gather material for their poems and novels by collaborating with their interviewees as coworkers in doing oral history interviews. The documentary impulse was a sign of the times, and there had been earlier twentieth-century works along these lines in England and the United States. However, the crucial new factor was that now many Depression-era writers wanted to write about "the people" – a key popular front term – and thus go beyond the middle-class realistic novel, beyond much of the formulaic proletarian literature of the time, and beyond formal descriptions of traditional elites. In the southeast, W. T. Couch had begun a Southern life histories project, focused largely on sharecroppers and cotton mill workers, which led to the publication of the powerful and moving *These Are Our Lives* (1939).[21] Botkin respected Couch's focus on the impact of poverty on many Southerners, but he intended to add a focus on lore as a symbol of artistic self and group expression.

The FWP's ex-slave interviews eventually became the project's most famous oral history project. Unlike Lomax, Alsberg and Botkin realized "the ex-slave stories were a source of information about contemporary life as well as the past, since in many instances we have been able in these stories to carry the picture of slavery in the United States back to the beginning of the nineteenth century and on the other side through the reconstruction era and later period in the South."[22] George Cronyn, assistant national FWP editor, articulated a sentiment widely shared among project officials: "Such documentary records by the survivors of a historic period in America are invaluable, both to the student of history and to creative writers."[23] But then Congress in June stripped the national FWP office of its ability to supervise the state projects and renamed it the Writers' Program. In a few bits and pieces published in *Direction*, a left literary magazine, the FWP had only begun to introduce this work as a part of thirties literature, but the full cultural import of the FWP's work both in its era and beyond is only now beginning to be appreciated.

***

Scholars have just begun to address the impact the FWP had on the creative output of some of the writers who worked on it. Superficial assumptions regarding the FWP and ignorance of and hostility to forms of American left-leaning romantic nationalist argument, especially after the rise and defeat of fascism, led literary scholars to ignore the FWP as part of the "story" of American literature. If romantic nationalism had any resonance for most post–World War II students of American literature, it suggested only chauvinism and fascism, not something compatible with inclusiveness, diversity, and egalitarianism. With little investigation too many literary scholars have assumed the FWP's experiments in creative writing were "merely" exhausted forms of naturalism, or superficial social realism, or formulaic proletarian fiction, or lacking any political thrust at all. They have also assumed mistakenly that these FWP undertakings had no connection to interwar modernist literature or the emphasis in post–World War II American writing on self-examination, confession, and subjectivity.

From the beginning, Alsberg had thought about what the project could do for writers, beyond the obvious life support it provided, and certainly there is evidence that some FWP writers pursued the same thoughts. Botkin clearly believed that his theories on living lore were designed to promote a distinctive and different kind of post–WWII American literature and it is equally clear that writers such as Nelson Algren, Jack Conroy, and Ralph Ellison welcomed the larger opportunities Botkin gave them. But it is also clear that many FWP writers working exclusively on the guidebooks embraced his dream with enthusiasm. FWP writer Jack Balch described in his novel *Lamps at High Noon* (1941) the conflicts on the Missouri project over political patronage, time servers, and incompetent employees desperate to hold on to their jobs. With a keen eye, he presented knife-sharp conflicts over political allegiance, the experiences of a failed strike. Despite these back steps, one of his characters still holds on to the idealism of the National Office and the New Deal: "America will have, for always, things now that it never could afford; hospitals, schools, roads, books, theater; most of all, a research, a consciousness and a possession of a culture."[24]

Alsberg repeatedly insisted that the very act of working on the AGS would make FWP workers better writers. Indeed, he believed, guidebook writing required aesthetic skill and discipline. "The tour form," he argued, "can contain as excellent material and skillful writing as any sonnet or ballad."[25] Cultural critics Lewis Mumford and Charles Glicksberg added their support. Mumford argued, "in the long run, this apprenticeship, this seeing of the American scene, this listening to the American voice, may mean more for literature than any sudden forcing of stories and poems." Glicksberg thought that the FWP "together with the other creative projects will gradually tend to make literature and art an integral part of the national life." As much as Alsberg agreed with Mumford and Glicksberg, he knew their "faith" did not itself meet the FWP's creative writers' need for self-expression, if for no other reason than that they told him so.[26] But he believed he should try to support their desires as much as he could. To that end, in 1937 Alsberg went to the meeting of the American Writers' Congress in an attempt to establish friendly ties between Popular Front writers and the FWP. He was also unhappy that all he could offer "his" creative writers was the opportunity to work on the guide series. He explained he wished he could subsidize creative writers to work full time on their own writing, but he knew that political realities demanded "production in order to justify the project at all." He pointed out that *American Stuff: An Anthology of Prose and Verse by Members of the Federal Writers' Project* (1937) would appear in a couple of months and that he hoped this would lead to a regular magazine of creative writing – it didn't, but he was unable to mollify the writers at the congress or get them to do more than support continued appropriations for the project.[27]

In his introduction to *American Stuff*, Alsberg elaborated on the problems of trying to find a way to give Project workers a chance to write novels, short stories, and poems. He stressed that he saw the work of FWP authors as establishing a new literary tradition favoring a new social realism best suited to depression realities. No one picking up the volume, he wrote, should expect anything that would remind "him of the classics" or that would be an "echo of the higher aestheticism or the delicate attenuation of emotion." True, he noted, much of the writing reflects "a solid passionate feeling for the less prosperous millions."[28] Ironically, Alsberg never mentions the pages of folklore sayings included in the volume. Despite an emerging cultural nationalist rhetoric, neither Alsberg nor most project workers had yet made a connection between the theory and practice of folklore, their creative writing, and their folklore collecting, despite the fact that many of them were fascinated by oral literature. That literary self-literary awareness would develop only after Botkin joined the project.

For many years before joining the FWP, Botkin had been exploring ways to integrate oral and written literature. *Folk-Say: A Regional Miscellany*, which he created and edited between 1929 and 1932, had been one effort in this direction.[29] Despite the financial and political problems that had brought the venture to an end, he had learned much, including his firm conclusion that to counter the domination of eastern sensibilities and publishers, writers needed to form compact groups to support each other and to develop ties to regional publishing houses. When Alsberg asked Botkin to join the FWP, it must have seemed to Botkin that one of his dreams now had a chance of becoming reality.[30]

Building on his ideas about the relationship between folklore, literature, and history, Botkin established "Living Lore units," special projects in places such as New York City, Chicago, and New England designed to give FWP writers an opportunity to explore the relationship between the folklore collection and creative writing processes functioning much like modern university-based writers' programs. Botkin directed special meetings with the Living Lore writers at which they workshopped each other's work.[31] Ralph Ellison remembered collecting folklore in Harlem while engaged in work-based discussions about the relationships between romantic theory, pluralism, cosmopolitanism, and race, class, and the folk. And while these Living Lore units lasted only a year, they influenced alumni such as Ellison, Studs Terkel, Margaret Walker, Nelson Algren, Jack Conroy, and Chester Himes.[32]

Botkin asserted that living lore should have a special appeal for the creative writer. For one thing, he insisted, "it supplies imaginative color and flavor, human interest; and human fantasy." Beyond that it "gave the writer a social and cultural consciousness too often lacking in ivory tower writing." In living lore, Botkin thought, writers would find an answer to their search for "a new subject matter and a new technique." He maintained living lore had a "direct relationship to contemporary or recent social structure and is an expression of social change and cultural conflict."[33] He placed the personal interview at the heart of the work of the Living Lore units because he believed it best captured a subject's individuality while also representing her or him as a part of a group. He thought the interviewers needed to encourage a personal voice to emerge that would render the interview as literature. He believed that an interviewee's subjectivity and narrative had to be allowed to develop into a performance monologue complete with characters. From his point of view, the interviewee's speaking of his own story turned his subjectivity into the subject of his narrative. The speaker became his own character in his own story until at a certain point he no longer differentiated his invented self from his "real" self.

Botkin had been thinking through these issues for quite some time. In imagining a role for the interviewer/writer who becomes an interpreter of and a voice for the folk, Botkin shared the modernist impulse seen in T. S. Eliot's wish to heal the "dissociation" between thought and sensibility without resorting to a confessional discourse. For Botkin, there was no need to become an expatriate or alienate oneself from one's culture to achieve this end. Instead, like the American modernists who stayed home – think especially of Carl Sandburg – he believed that "[w]hen one has assimilated folk consciousness ... one becomes, like the folk, symbol-minded." For Botkin, folk consciousness had no need to separate the moment of creation from the thing created. He held that the distinction between symbol minded in the folk, anthropological, and aesthetic senses was small if one defined symbol-minded thinking "as identification of the subject with the object."[34]

Many of the Living Lore unit authors shared the working-class experience of their subjects or were not far removed from it. They were open to Botkin's argument that the terms "folk" and "proletariat" were not mutually exclusive. Nor did such Living Lore writers as Herman Spector, Joseph Vogel, and Nicholas Wirth see modernist and proletarian literature as antagonistic. They had ties to poets Ezra Pound and Louis Zukofsy and had contributed their own efforts to the "revolution of the word." Spector had published a prose piece in Ezra Pound's *Exile* in 1928. Vogel had corresponded with Pound about literary issues. In 1934, Spector, Vogel, and Wirth founded *Dynamo, a Journal of Revolutionary Poetry.* Their experiments, however, moved in the direction of adapting and transforming such sources as oral tradition, popular culture, folk expression, and personal experience narrative into new written forms.[35]

"The streets are full of people, some of them talking. You walk into a park and sit down on a bench. What do you listen for among the afternoon voices?" New York City Federal Writer Hyde Partnow asked his audience at the Third American Writers' Conference. "Next to you sits a kid ... You perceive him picking you out by secret signs, but you say nothing. Nor does he. Then you hear: 'Can you spare a cigarette?' In a few minutes he's spilling his heart." Partnow claimed he could tell when he was really listening creatively: "After a while you get so sharp even your mother begins sounding like folk-say. Then you're all right, you're beginning to hear things." He thought that each time he listened creatively he was "watching a more or less submerged person come to the top." It was an approach that emphasized a dynamic view of individuals and folk groups in a state of transition; nothing was static: "he's enduring change and violence and conflict, and he's got notions and ways of looking at these things that are his own and yet not wholly his own, because they are also his folks."[36]

Partnow's "I'm a Might Have Been" was published in *Direction* in the spring of 1939. In such lines as the following, one hears a series of vernacular expressions used to convey an individual and group perspective, a personal lyric and a group experience: "I'm among the world of missing men. I'm so insignificant if they sent out a radio call for me in a hundred years nobody would find me. Economically, I'm collapsed, I could write my whole will on a postage stamp, not a single coin of the realm you'll find in my pocket, I ain't got enough real estate to put in a flower pot. Tell me, then, why should I sing my country tis of thee or welcome sweet springtime I greet you in song."[37]

Partnow talked about the importance of Walt Whitman to his work, but NYC Living Lore writer David Silver stressed instead the importance of Carl Sandburg to FWP writers like him who were interested in the language of work. "In *Good Morning America*, Sandburg had announced the arrival of a code-language, lingo, slang ... the proverbs of a people."[38] Federal Writers, Silver noted, wanted to record that code, and "provide a key to its significance." They had, according to Botkin, amassed evidence "that urban industrial life creates its own types of 'isolation' and 'homogeneity' and consequently evolves its own types of 'folkways' and its own fantasy patterns."[39]

Botkin also encouraged Living Lore writers to think in terms of story-telling as entirely monologue or dialogue in which action, drama, and lore emerged out of a voice or voices. Grace Outlaw's reconstruction of con-versations overheard in policy stations situated the folklore of playing the numbers in a living conversation:

CLERK IN POLICY STATION: "Where've you been Miss Simmons? . . . haven't had any luck . . . or have you been ill?"

POLICY PLAYER: (old woman) "Both . . . chile, my rheumatics has had me down . . . guess' I'll play my same gig . . . 16–29–39 . . . bout good as any; play it in the North and South, then put it in the one leg book . . . ten cents on the first two and a nickel on the other one . . . that's a quarter," and Miss Simmons counted out fifteen pennies and two nickels."

CLERK: "Hope you're lucky this time . . . be careful about your rheumatism . . . didja ever try rubbing with coal-oil and salt? My mother used to use it . . . see you this afternoon . . . goodbye."[40]

Few folklorists in that period would have looked for urban lore, but if they had they most likely would have extracted the folklore items from the foregoing conversation – gig, one-leg book, cures for rheumatism – and ignored the rest. Such an item-centered approach would be lifeless and tell the reader nothing about folklore as it is lived. Not until the 1960s would scholars begin to focus on folklore as performance. My point is not simply that Botkin was ahead of his time; rather it is that he saw such a shift in scholarly attention as a contribution to an emerging American literature.

Botkin also encouraged Living Lore writers such as Jack Conroy and Nelson Algren to develop occupational stories they had heard into what were in effect the tall tales of the "industrial-urban frontier." For example, Conroy's "The Boomer Fireman's Fast Sooner Hound," a story of a dog who can outrun a railroad, uses the persistent structural elements of the tall tale to frame a populist resentment toward the railroads. And his "Slappy Hooper, World's Biggest, Fastest, and Bestest Sign Painter" announces in its very title its debt to tall-tale stories.[41]

Given their modernist sensibilities and their personal experiences, Living Lore unit writers were open to a view of folklore as a mix of the traditional, the contemporary, and the popular. To hear this mix in the unofficial poetry of the workplace, they thought writers needed to put dogma aside and listen. In this way, they concluded writers could serve the cause of leftist politics by capturing on paper the intellectual complexity of folk knowledge, folk speech. and folk fantasy and ensure that the language and oral literature of industrial workers and the like did not go unwritten. Like Botkin, their form of modernism located creativity in the community of ordinary folk. For them, proletarian literature did not mean formulaic propaganda. It meant giving voice to the real fears, desires, and needs of those who spoke but were never heard. Indeed, the split between the techniques of high modernism and the left literature of the 1930s was never as great as later New Critics thought and the depth and nature of proletarian writing was never as narrow and shallow as claimed by those who later recommended this literature be dismissed out of hand.

Harold Rosenberg, an FWP art editor who worked closely with Botkin, directed the *Men at Work* (*MAW*) project, one of the program's more significant literary experiments (unfortunately not published until recently). Ironically, Rosenberg insisted later that the Writers' Project had done nothing for writers as writers.[42] (Rosenberg became famous after World War II as an advocate, explicator, and defender of abstract expressionism, a form of art that whatever its other virtues, erased all signs of ethnic, class, or regional differences.) Still while in the FWP, Rosenberg treated *MAW* as a serious project, whose goals were a response to the literary trends of the 1930s. *MAW* was intended to provide readers with narrative accounts depicting the physical labor Americans did across the nation. Proletarian fiction, Rosenberg claimed, had focused on either the social life of workers or their struggles as an exploited class, but not on the actual labor central to "the productive, and hence powerful and dynamic core of [the worker's] existence." FWP writers who worked on *MAW* paid attention to class and racial issues as they emerged in actual labor.[43]

Middle-class condescension toward those who earned their livelihood through factory labor, Rosenberg claimed, explained why descriptions of "the operations performed in the factory" are missing from most literature.[44] Actual factory work, Rosenberg suggested, struck most modern writers as deadly monotony. He thought writers who had no sense of the relationship between a laborer's work and his imaginative life lost a sense of the human, social, and political possibilities in the situation. He thought an FWP project could offer thirties writers another way of capturing worker-class consciousness. Since *MAW* was not published at the time, one could argue it had no effect on thirties literature and was thus irrelevant to understanding the writing of the era. That would be a mistake. Rosenberg's goals remain critical evidence of the left literary thinking of his time.

Nevertheless, as Rosenberg acknowledged, FWP authors often turned to what he called "'transitional' industries, those not yet modernized like mining, fishing, lumbering, or they picked jobs which still linger on in smaller plants." Rosenberg also conceded that although the FWP writers focused on work still more central to modern production methods than the "work of the artisan or handicraftsman," they usually ignored the new mass production industries that "baffle the writer with their lack of human content." So even in *MAW* there were limits to how writable FWP workers thought factory work could be. Surprisingly, Rosenberg's conclusion sounded a preservationist tone regarding *MAW*: the volume "had the added value of being a preserver of work memories and fast-disappearing folkways."[45]

The FWP writers who focused on the actual laborer of workers described in *MAW* constructed their work narratives in a variety of ways. Whether telling the story in the first person or in an omniscient third-person voice, *MAW* authors kept the focus on the worker and the work. For example, in a story about a worker at the Anaconda copper mines, one finds not a word about the role of George Hearst, William Randolph Hearst's father, nor about the role of the mine in the global economy. Instead, Edward Reynolds tells the story of the Anaconda through the eyes of a worker who walks us through the operation of the mine. Only the most literary of readers will notice the third-person narrator, so closely entwined does the reader become with the main character from the opening line: "he shoved the white card into the timekeeper's window and growled a greeting" until the last line when he leaves the mine. There is no one between the reader and the actions, the thoughts, and the conversations of the central character.[46]

Right from the beginning one hears the terminology of the miners and their folk speech with its group dimensions and individual variations, with its possibilities for performance and shared lore. After being given a card for the Stack, "rappin' treaters or dumping flue dust," the main character reveals his sense of social hierarchy, when he insists this is a job really for "Okies" and "Arkies," and "not a job for a guy that had been born and raised here on the ground, here in Anaconda, whose residents, we are told, do not look at the morning sky to see how the weather is, but whose first glance is at the Big Stack to see how the smoke's coming out. They don't ask one another's health, they ask, 'What shift you on?' 'How she's going' is hello; 'Tap her light' is good-by."[47]

Because this individual has to walk to the Stack, the omniscient narrator can guide us through this complex, as if we were walking with this worker and being introduced to his view of the regimen and techniques of each department. We become listeners to conversations about work. As one worker describes "the how to's" of a job, we are privy to a work tradition being passed on orally from one worker to another: "'We're dumping flu dust,' he said. 'I'll show you how to wrap up.'"[48] And we feel as if we were being wrapped up: "fur tripped goggles went over the cheesecloth on his face." The mixture of danger and fear the workers experience becomes palpable. Any feeling of pride in work performed well is outweighed by alienation: "When they got out in the sunlight again it was like coming into a new world."[49] Rosenberg had built on ideas he had discussed with Botkin. And he had included in *MAW* tall tales of folk work done by members of the Living Lore units.

Botkin had found in the FWP a way of continuing the experimental literary work he had begun in *Folk-Say*. In retrospect, as literary historian Douglas Wixson observes, Botkin's *Folk-Say* was one of the reasons in the early thirties that "there was hope that the experience of migratory workers, the dispossessed, the assembly line stiffs, mill workers, and farmhands might serve to reintegrate culture into everyday life." "In the beginning," Wixson argues, "the possibilities seemed very fresh that a new strain of literature might evolve," a literature "deriving from orality, certain types of speech acts, folk tradition, and ordinary experience, reflecting the hetero-geneity of American common life." The irony, Wixson writes, was that "the United States government filled a vacuum created when the left largely abandoned its sponsorship of worker-writing." Irony aside, that vacuum was not filled for long.[50]

And the story since? Bits and pieces of the work of the Living Lore units have been published but most of the work still lies unseen and unstudied in archival folders. Consider again Ralph Ellison. Although *Invisible Man* was not published until 1951, it still has strong ties to the FWP's literary experiments he witnessed and participated in. The point is not that in Ellison we have found an FWP writer who later became famous, but that his later work reflected the ethos of the FWP and its Living Lore units. In *Invisible Man* Ellison found a way to write that in its very structure wrestled with all the lessons that Botkin had hoped Federal Writers in the Living Lore units would learn: how to craft the relationship between the individual and the folk group, how to balance provincialism and cosmo-politanism, tradition and modernity, the fact of diversity and the need for unity. To be sure Ellison was both unique and special among FWP writers. Still, as American literature's best example of the creative reciprocity between the individual in a folk community and his group, Ellison's *Invisible Man* can be read as an epic of black migration and a description of the impact of changing and diverse social contexts on the performance of folklore.

Folk cultures, Botkin had told Living Lore writers, were not merely a part of the American past, not something behind us, but beside us and among us. They were "not static but dynamic and transitional, on their way up." It is easy to conjure Ellison's Invisible Man in these claims residing not behind us, but below the surface of our consciousness, caught only in the sideways glance, affirming that his experience is a part of the American experience, that it is a possibility of rising up. In the last chapter of *Invisible Man*, Ellison uses the same image Franklin Roosevelt employed: "America," he tells us, "is woven of many strands; I would recognize them and let it so remain." He reminds us that a cosmopolitan view of the world only works when linked to one's background and past, and only succeeds when it celebrates its ties to the experiences of other Americans and asks them to do the same.[51]

***

Legacies are constructed as much by those who inherit them as they are by those who create them. Regarding that of the FWP, it is easy to say that since there was no longer a Writers' Project (1935–39) or a Writers' Program (1939–43), that the FWP simply came and died. From that perspective, we can note the efforts that FWP officials made to keep their agency alive and that their political opponents made to kill it. That approach by itself can give us an informative obituary, but it does not tell us if there is anything to learn from those who saw the FWP as a prelude to a new future for American literature or their political opponents who saw it as a political weapon to use against the New Deal. The arts projects' friends and enemies both struggled to imagine whether and how government should play a role in American art and culture.

None of this is surprising. Alsberg himself knew that the future of the FWP hung in the balance every time Congress had to provide a new appropriation for the arts projects. Nevertheless, he tried to plan programs as if the FWP would become a permanent government agency. He promoted the project with all those individuals and groups he knew could help secure its future. He and other FWP officials promoted the AGS in every mainstream way they could without, they thought, abandoning their grand cultural ambitions. They touted what the guides might do for tourism to the railroads, chambers of commerce, and state congressional delegations, while trying not to betray their commitment to travel as a search for America's pluralist identity. They cooperated with mainstream publishing houses and universities, hoping to tie the FWP to institutions that had cultural authority and prestige. They knew that they needed the practical skills of academics, but they clearly also wanted the prestige and legitimacy that could come with such cooperation.

Both Alsberg and Botkin also reached out repeatedly to the left literary world by appearing at the Second American Writers' Congress. After assuming full-time responsibility for the FWP folklore studies, Botkin set to work to create a Joint WPA Folklore Committee. In June 1938, Donald Daugherty of the American Council of Learned Societies suggested that the various New Deal agencies gathering material on American culture consider how the results of their research could be preserved and made available to scholars.[52] Botkin also gave major theoretical and research papers at meetings of the Modern Language Association and the American Historical Association.[53] He and other members of the Joint Committee saw themselves as developing scholarship that would be addressed to a public audience.

None of these efforts at institutionalization protected the FWP when the Martin Dies-led House Un-American Activities Committee began hearings in 1938 at about the same time Botkin was creating the WPA Joint Committee on Folklore and the Living Lore units. Historians have thoroughly documented the falseness of HUAC's charges of Communist subversion, the slanderous attacks, and the lack of logic in many of its false allegations. But what is most important about the hearings was the effort to delegitimize the FWP as a federal agency. The Dies Committee rejected the national FWP's vision of a pluralistic and egalitarian America in flux, a nation still, indeed always, in the process of becoming. For Dies and his cohorts, American identity was fixed, white, Anglo-Saxon, Protestant, and under attack by a New Deal, Popular Front culture that sought to mongrelize America. When World War II provided the opportunity, they provided the coup de grâce.[54]

A renewed interest in the FWP emerged in the late 1960s when questions of national identity and pluralism again became unavoidable. However, the FWP's vision only came close again to an institutional center of American government when folklorist William Ferris, who served as head of the National Endowment for the Humanities (1997–2001) and was himself influenced by colleagues of Botkin, tried to create regional humanities centers with limited success.[55] Since 2011, The Writing Democracy Project has self-consciously tried to build on the legacy of the FWP and create a new institutional nexus for a similar project. Project directors concluded that colleges and universities seeking to serve their communities could become an important vehicle for their efforts by using college students to do the work Federal Writers' Project had done.[56]

The Writers' Project ended, but it may not be dead. The answer to that implicit question lies in the hands of Americans who will decide if they want to pick up the FWP's legacy. It remains to be seen if such a task might yet begin.

Notes

1. For a sociological approach that stresses the impact of the federal/state structure in shaping the FWP and the work it did over ideas, see Wendy Griswold, *American Guides: The Federal Writers' Project and the Casting of American Culture* (Chicago: University of Chicago Press, 2016). Note that Paul Fusell, *Abroad: British Literary Traveling between the Wars* (Oxford: University Press, 1980), 212–15, argues "that the status of [poetry and prose] is largely an unearned and unexamined snob increment from late romantic notions of art."

2. The term "cultural strategy" is used repeatedly in the official correspondence between Botkin and Charles Seeger of the Federal Music Project. For an example of how they used this term, see Seeger to Walter Spivacke (Head of the Music Division, Library of Congress), April 4, 1940, Box 212, Federal Writers' Project, Works Progress Administration Records Group 69, National Archives, Washington, DC (hereinafter FWNA). Botkin also used the phrase in later writings. See Benjamin Botkin, "Folklore and World Understanding," *New York Folklore Quarterly* 8 (1952), 157; Botkin, "Applied Folklore: Creative Understanding through Folklore," *Southern Folklore Quarterly* 17 (1953), 205–06; Botkin, "L. Zemlajonva on Folklore and Democracy," *New York Folklore Quarterly* 2 (1965), 226.

3. William Wilson, "Herder, Folklore, and Nationalism," *Journal of Popular Culture* 6 (1973), 819–35.

4. For a solid administrative history, see Monty Penkower, *The Federal Writers' Project: A Study in Government Patronage and the Arts* (Chicago: University of Illinois Press, 1977). Recent approaches to the cultural history of the FWP can be seen in Jerrold Hirsch, *Portrait of America: A Cultural History of the Federal Writers' Project* (Chapel Hill: University of North Carolina Press, 2003); Christine Bold, *The WPA Guides: Mapping America* (Jackson: University Press of Mississippi, 1999); Christine Bold, *Plumbers and Anarchists: The WPA Writers' Project in Massachusetts* (Amherst: University of Massachusetts Press, 2006); Sharon Ann Musher, *Democratic Art: The New Deal's Influence on American Culture* (Chicago: University of Chicago Press, 2015); and Sara Rendene Rutkowski, "The Literary Legacy of the Federal Writers' Project," unpublished PhD thesis, City University of New York (2015); B. A. Botkin, "WPA and Folklore Research: 'Bread and Song,'" *Southern Folklore Quarterly* 3 (1939), 11.

5. *The American Guide and the American Guide Series: Their Task: To Introduce America to Americans*, n. d., Box 74, FWPNA.

6. Hirsch, *Portrait of America*, 5, 9, 26–32, 107–26, 138–39; Susan Rubenstein DeMasi, *Henry Alsberg: The Driving Force of the New Deal Federal Writers' Project* (Jefferson, NC: McFarland 2016), 5–10, 156–61.

7. The central work on the Popular Front as a social and cultural movement is Michael Denning, *The Cultural Front: The Laboring of American Culture in the Twentieth Century* (London: Verso, 1997). See also Hirsch, *Portrait of America*, 2–3.

8. Bernard DeVoto, "New England via the WPA," *Saturday Review of Literature* 18 (May 14, 1938), 4.

9. Lewis Mumford, "Writers' Project," *New Republic*, October 20, 1937, 306–07.

10. Federal Writers' Project, *Tennessee: A Guide to the State* (New York: Viking Press, 1939), 145.

11. Federal Writers' Project, *Tennessee*, 167.

12. Hans-George Jauss as quoted in Douglas Wixson, *Worker-Writer in America: Jack Conroy and the Tradition of Midwestern Literary Radicalism, 1898–1990* (Chicago: University of Illinois Press, 1994), 346.

13. Alsberg to All State Directors, no date, description of studies for a composite America, Box 191, FWPNA.

14. Alsberg to Ellen Woodward, WPA Director of Professional and Service Projects, July 22, 1938, Box 195, FWPNA.

15. Van Wyck Brooks, Lewis Mumford, Paul Rosenfeld, and Alfred Kreymborg, eds., *American Caravan: A Yearbook of American Literature* (The Macaulay Company, 1927–29, 1931). Brooks was only involved in editing the 1927 volume.

16. The "closed account" idea is presented in Francis Gummere, *The Popular Ballad* (Boston, MA: Houghton Mifflin, 1907), 16, 337.

17. For an overview of Botkin and Lomax's thinking about American folklore, see Jerrold Hirsch, "Folklore in the Making: B. A. Botkin," *Journal of American Folklore* 100 (1987), 1–38; the essays in Lawrence Rogers and Jerrold Hirsch, eds., *America's Folklorist: B. A. Botkin and American Culture* (Norman: University of Oklahoma Press, 2010); and Jerrold Hirsch, "Modernity, Nostalgia, and Southern Folklore Studies: The Case of John Lomax," *Journal of American Folklore* 105 (1992), 183–207.

18. John Lomax, Supplementary Instructions No. 9 to the American Guide Manual, "Folklore and Customs," March 12, 1936, and No. 9C; "Folklore and Folk Customs," August 4, 1936, Box 69, FWPNA; John Lomax and Alan Lomax, eds., *American Ballads and Folk Songs* (Basingstoke: Macmillan Company, 1934), xxvi.

19. For an overview of B. A. Botkin's thinking on folklore, see Hirsch, "Folklore in the Making," 3–38.

20. Botkin, "Regionalism and Culture," in *The Writer in a Changing World*, ed. Henry Hart (New York: Equinox Cooperative Press, 1937), 157; "Old and

New in New England. Background of Social-Ethnic Studies," September 18, 1940, Box 210, FWPNA.

21. See Couch's preface to Federal Writers' Project, *These Are Our Lives: As Told to Us by the People and Written by Members of the Federal Writers' Project of the Works Progress Administration in North Carolina, Tennessee, and Georgia* (Chapel Hill: University of North Carolina Press, 1939), ix–xx.

22. Alsberg to Woodward, July 22, 1938, Box 195, FWPNA. For an analysis of conflicting visions of the purpose of the FWP ex-slave narratives, see the excellent study *Long Past Slavery: Representing Race in the Federal Writers' Project* (Chapel Hill: University of North Carolina Press, 2016).

23. Cronyn, undated document, Box 134, Benjamin A. Botkin Papers, Benjamin Botkin Collection of Applied Folklore, University of Nebraska-Lincoln.

24. Jack S. Balch, *Lamps at High Noon* (Chicago: University of Illinois Press, 2000 [1941]), 229.

25. Supplementary Instructions No. 11E, Box 69, FWPNA; Mumford, "Writers' Project," *New Republic* 92 (1937), 67; Charles I. Glicksberg, "The Federal Writers' Project," *South Atlantic Quarterly* 37 (1938), 159.

26. Alsberg to Anzia Yezierska, February 1937, Box 34, FWPNA.

27. Federal Writers' Project, *American Stuff: An Anthology of Prose and Verse by Members of the Federal Writers' Project* (New York: Viking Press, 1937.), V.

28. Federal Writers' Project, *American Stuff*, V.

29. B. A. Botkin, ed., *Folk-Say: A Regional Miscellany* (Norman: University of Oklahoma Press, 1929–32).

30. Botkin, "Folk-Say and Space: Their Genesis and Exodus,"*Southwest Review* 20 (1935), 329–34.

31. Botkin, "'Living Lore' on the New York City Writers' Project," *New York Folklore Quarterly* 2 (1946), 254, 255.

32. Rutkowski, "Literary Legacy of the Federal Writers' Project," 9–10, 28–29, 87–162.

33. Botkin, "Folklore as a Neglected Source of Social History," in *The Cultural Approach to History*, ed. Caroline F. Ware (New York: Columbia University Press, 1940), 311–12. The papers in this volume were all first delivered at the annual meeting of the American Historical Association in 1939).

34. Botkin, "The Folk and the Individual: Their Creative Reciprocity," *English Journal* 27 (1938), 132–33.

35. On the careers of these writers, see Douglas Wixson, *Worker-Writer in America: Jack Conroy and the Tradition of Midwestern Literary Radicalism, 1898–1990* (Chicago: University of Illinois Press, 1994), 144, 146, 179–80, 208, 232, 276, 301, 350–51, 396–97, 465–66, 476, 516, 586.

36. Donald Ogden Stewart, ed., *Fighting Words* (New York: Harcourt Brace, 1940), 6–7, 9.

37. Hyde Partnow, "I'm a Might Have Been," *Direction* 2 (May–June 1939), 14.

38. David Silver, *Direction* 2 (May–June 1939), 14.

39. Botkin, "Living Lore on the New York Writers' Project," *New York Folklore Quarterly* 2 (1946), 257–58.

40. Grace Outlaw interview, name of informant not given, April 17, 1939, Chicago Folkstuff, FWP files, Library of Congress, Washington, DC.
41. Jack Conroy, "The Boomer Fireman's Fast Sooner Hound," and "Slappy Hooper, World's Biggest, Fastest, and Bestest Sign Painter," in *Men at Work: Depression Era Stories from the Federal Writers' Project*, ed., Matthew L. Basso (Salt Lake City: University of Utah Press), 39–42, 232–36.
42. Rosenberg, "Anyone Who Could Write English," *New Yorker* 49 (January 20, 1973), 102.
43. Harold Rosenberg, "Original Preface," in Basso, *Men at Work*, 3.
44. Rosenberg, *MAW*, p. 3.
45. Rosenberg, *MAW*, 6, 7.
46. Edward B. Reynolds, "Anaconda," in *MAW*, 137–44.
47. Reynolds, "Anaconda," 137.
48. Reynolds, "Anaconda," 141.
49. Reynolds, "Anaconda," 143.
50. Wixson, *Worker-Writer in America*, 169, 418, 421.
51. Botkin, "The Folk and the Individual," 126; Roosevelt to Green, March 2, 1934, as quoted in "Folk Music in the Roosevelt White House: A Commemorative Program Presented by the Office of Folklife Programs at the National Museum of American History, Smithsonian Institution, Washington, DC, January 31, 1982," 10–11, n.p.
52. "Minutes – First Meeting Joint Committee on Folk Arts, W.P.A.," December 7, 1938, Box 195, FWPNA. Herbert Halpert to B. A. Botkin, October 4, 1939; "Draft: Coordinating Committee on Living Folklore, Folk Music and Folk Art, Federal Project Number One, Works Progress Administration," November 23, 1938, Box 195, FWPNA outlines the aims, functions, and program of the committee and lists members and consultants.
53. Botkin, "WPA and Folklore Research," 7–14, paper first presented at the annual meeting of the Modern Literature Association, Botkin, "Folklore as a Neglected Source of Social History," 308–15.
54. Hirsch, *Portrait of America*, 197–212.
55. Hirsch, *Portrait of America*, 230–31, 236–37.
56. Shannon Carter and Deborah Mutnick, "Writing Democracy: Notes on a Federal Writers' Project for the 21st Century," *Community Literacy Journal* 7 (2012), 1–14; Jerrold Hirsch, "Rediscovering America: The FWP Legacy and Challenge," *Community Literacy Journal* 7 (2012), 15–32.

CHAPTER 19

Hollywood

William Solomon

Hollywood may be full of phonies, mediocrities, dictators and good men who have lost their way, but there is something that draws you there that you should not be ashamed of.

Budd Schulberg, *What Makes Sammy Run?* (1941)

That's why for each and every person Hollywood is a touchstone. You either love it or it fills you with horror from . . . your first step onto its streets.

Blaise Cendrars, *Hollywood* (1936)

When Edmund Wilson railed in *The Boys in the Back Room* (1941) against the manifestation in James M. Cain's *Serenade* (1937) of "something we know all too well: the damned old conventions of Hollywood," he was voicing a critical opinion that would be echoed over and over again in the years to come.[1] Although this novel was "a definite improvement on" the cliché-ridden *The Postman Always Rings Twice* (1934), *Serenade* also lacked the formal inventiveness that would have marked it as a significant literary achievement; it too had "its trashy aspect, its movie foreshortenings and its too-well oiled action" that kept it in constant "danger of becoming unintentionally funny" (14). While "there is enough of the real poet in Cain" that one might expect something better from him in the future, it is equally plausible that his immersion in the film industry will prevent him from realizing his creative potential, that in the end he will prove to have been one more promising artist added to the "already appalling record of talent depraved and wasted" in Hollywood (72). Throughout the postwar era, the cultural commentary of Cold War intellectuals frequently expressed in similar fashion their aversion for the motion-picture business due to its debasing effect on writers caught up in its economic machinations. For instance, Arthur Schlesinger Jr. complained in *The Vital Center: The Politics of Freedom* (1949) that "the Hollywood writer . . . has abandoned his serious work in exchange for large weekly paychecks."[2] Correlatively, in "Masscult and Midcult" (1960), Dwight Macdonald lamented the current state of affairs such that "before a proper Hollywood film can be made," the book as "work of art has to be defeated."[3] For him, whereas in the past literature had admirably aimed to "satisfy popular tastes," Hollywood now reprehensibly seeks "to exploit them" (14).[4]

Some of the most severe denunciations of the film industry can be found in the recollections of those who had been commercially successful screenplay writers during the 1930s. For instance, admitting in his autobiography, *A Child of the Century* (1954), that he fell victim to the "double lure" Hollywood perpetually held for him ("tremendous sums of money for work that required no more effort than a game of pinochle"), Ben Hecht nevertheless condemned the movies as being "one of the bad habits that corrupted" the nation, the "eruption of trash" for which it was responsible having "lamed the American mind and retarded Americans from becoming a cultured people."[5] His complicity in the industry notwithstanding, Hecht accused moviemakers of having manufactured a duplicitous, morally banal form of entertainment strictly for profit; in so doing, they stand guilty of having fed the American populace "naivete and buncombe in doses never before administered to any people. They have slapped into the American mind more human misinformation in one evening than the Dark Ages could muster in a decade. One basic plot only has appeared daily in their fifteen thousand theatres – the triumph of virtue and the overthrow of wickedness" (259). Moreover, so politically retrograde are the stereotyped productions of the industry, that "all fifteen thousand" movie theatres in "the U.S.A." amount to "a single backward front" (260). Even more amusingly vitriolic and humorously hyperbolic are the reminiscences his interviewers at the *Paris Review* managed to squeeze out of S. J. Perelman in 1963. Replying (with perhaps feigned weariness) that he looks back on his activities in Hollywood (including his work with the Marx Brothers) with regret and revulsion, Perelman proceeds to compare the place to "the Sargasso Sea an immense, turgidly revolving whirlpool in which literary hulks encrusted with verdigris moldered until they sank."[6] Indeed, a few "made a great deal of loot out there," but it remains the case that Hollywood was "a dreary industrial town controlled by hoodlums of enormous wealth, the ethical sense of a pack of jackals, and taste so degraded that it befouled everything it touched" (20). So disgustingly sordid did he find the locale, that when he drove along "the Sunset Strip and looked at those buildings, or when" he "watched the fashionable film colony arriving at some premiere at Grauman's Egyptian," he "fully expected [as if channeling the prophetic vision of Tod Hackett in Perelman's brother-in-law Nathanael West's *Day of the Locust* (1939)] God in his wrath to obliterate the whole shebang" (20).[7]

All such emotionally intense reactions to Hollywood (whether contemporaneous or retrospective) are best comprehended as symptoms of a historically determined vocational crisis. From the 1930s forward, the aggression American writers and literary critics have frequently exhibited toward the film industry (an aggression occasionally tempered by recognition of certain impressive achievements in the newer medium) has functioned as the mode of expression of the feeling that one's position in a shifting field of cultural practice has been destabilized. This has not been simply a case of authors worrying that literature was under siege, for the novel had been long before the rise of the movies as much a popular commodity as an artistic phenomenon. Sensing (correctly) that the publishing industry was being displaced from the center to the periphery of the cultural marketplace, novelists and short story writers in the United States in the Depression era logically felt compelled to reflect on their dilemma. Even as many of them came into close contact with their primary other by securing employment as screenwriters, they continued to struggle in their narrative fictions to establish their identities in opposition to mass-produced culture.[8] Since the borderline separating literature and Hollywood film was at the time the site where a series of affectively charged encounters took place, it is not surprising that the Hollywood novel flourished in the period. And while the number of stories dealing with the situation of literature vis-à-vis its highly commercialized opponent cannot be limited to the thematically explicit approach of this subgenre, the Hollywood novel remains a solid point of access to the myriad ways in which American writers under economic pressure both registered the psychic distress the film industry was causing them and sought to meet the professional challenge it constituted.

As Hollywood established its dominance in the realm of mass entertainment, the gravitational pull it exerted became strong enough to draw a vast number of talented American writers into its orbit. The list of Depression-era figures who moved, temporarily or permanently, to Southern California and participated in the studio system in order to supplement their incomes is a lengthy one and includes (to name just some of the canonical examples) Cain, West, F. Scott Fitzgerald, William Faulkner, William Saroyan, John Dos Passos, Dorothy Parker, John Fante, John O'Hara, Horace McCoy, Daniel Fuchs, Lillian Hellman, Dashiell Hammett, and Budd Schulberg – and in subsequent decades, Raymond

Chandler and James Agee. It is also worth mentioning in this context a few of the Hollywood Ten – left-wing playwright John Howard Lawson and proletarian novelist Albert Maltz, as well as Dalton Trumbo and Alvah Bessie – all of whose careers were damaged when they were blacklisted during the postwar Red Scare. And Mike Davis's account in *City of Quartz* of Langston Hughes's disillusionment with Hollywood upon discovering that the only job he could get was as the composer of degrading dialogue in dialect for black characters (followed shortly thereafter by Chester Himes's humiliating treatment at Warner Brothers in the 1940s) alerts us to the role race played at this time in the possibility (or lack thereof) of turning to the film industry as a means of financial survival (42–44).[9]

Although the determining effects of Hollywood on American literature in the 1930s extended beyond those writers to whom it either offered or denied employment, it was an especially important point of reference for those whose career paths led to Los Angeles. For Budd Schulberg, the son of a studio mogul, the industry epitomized all that was wrong with capitalism in the country in that it rewarded the ruthlessly competitive at the expense of those seeking to maintain their moral integrity. Thus Sammy Glick, the despicably self-promoting enigma at the center of *What Makes Sammy Run?* (1941) is entirely comfortable thinking of "pictures as a commodity like any other." More than willing to "forget this prestige business," he is happy to accept as his primary task "making sure that every shipment will make a profit." "'After all,' he says to his Wall Street backer, 'pictures are shipped out in cans. We're in the canning business'" (249). Correlatively, Sammy adheres to an assembly-line-like approach to story construction, plundering as much as he can get away with from older films: "he could lift ready-made situations from the shelves in the back of his mind, dust them off and insert them into our yarn like standard automobile parts" (240). Any investment in creative originality is to him a waste of time and energy since the merchandise sells just as well when it is the formulaic result of repetition and reshuffling. The cognitive burden of the novel in turn is to comprehend the motivations of such an unscrupulous person, to discover what has driven the malignant character as he has rapidly ascended to the top of his profession, to the point where he can look out his office window at the "processional of laborers, extras, waitresses, cutters, writers, glamour girls, all the big cogs and the little ones that must turn together to keep a film factory alive," and declare happily "it's mine. Everything's mine" (258).

Conversely, Al Manheim, the unambitious yet intrigued first-person narrator, is the rhetorical device that enables Schulberg to pursue an answer to the question as to why a certain kind of individual (a new economic type in the nation) so mean-spiritedly runs over anybody standing in his way. Having "collected ... evidence" that "the only love" "a swift little rodent like Sammy Glick" is "capable of was a violent passion for his own future" (84), Al does not manage to grasp the causal forces determining the viciously predatory character's twisted egotism until he researches his brutal upbringing as an ethnic minority on Manhattan's Lower East Side. The conclusions Al reaches have a bit more nuance than the Darwinian paradigm of survival of the fittest that Sammy himself uses to justify his own behavior, but environmental circumstances are eventually disclosed as factors contributing to the historical molding of this unrepentant "heel" (109). The narrator's sustained commitment to solving "the mystery" of Sammy – a seemingly conscienceless manifestation of unredeemable evil – helps ground the epistemological and ethical specificity of literary undertakings in relation to the motion pictures. "[B]y drilling into" its ignoble subject "deeper and deeper" (61), the novelist resists Hollywood's tendency toward psychological superficiality. If most "of our characters on the screen are sandwich men for different moral attitudes" (60), the book counters such satisfying images with the more honest and honorable account of someone for whom spiritual renewal is an impossibility. Unwilling to perpetuate the industry's insistence that good inevitably triumphs in the end, the narrator, who here is close to Schulberg (whose father, B. P., was the recently deposed head of Paramount), willingly runs the risk of "heresy" in scrutinizing in detail the trajectory of a truly unpleasant creature who will never be "Regenerated" ("one of Hollywood's favorite words" [60]).

Al's self-consciously decent behavior toward others functions on another semantic level, allegorizing the ethical superiority of the (realist) novelist over his cultural foil (Hollywood). *I Should Have Stayed Home* (1938), Horace McCoy's distinctively *noir* variant of the literary subgenre – the Hollywood novel – under discussion, is similarly structured. Taking direct aim at the devastatingly systematic way in which the entertainment industry exploits (economically and sexually) those desperate to break into it, the novel in so doing indirectly affirms the integrity of the socially conscious writer.

Narrated in retrospect (and in a manner that corresponds to the cinematic deployment of voice-over technique) by a severely disillusioned and regretful would-be actor (Ralph Carston), the story he has to tell is one of ideological manipulation and material degradation. Convinced by a talent scout to leave Georgia and come to Hollywood for a screen test, the naïve youth has not seen this initial opportunity pan out, and he has been reduced to sitting by the phone all day waiting for a call that never comes. He eventually allows himself to be seduced by a wealthy and well-connected widow, who has assured him she will smooth his way toward becoming a celebrity if he serves as her escort. What Ralph has grasped at this stage of his education is that prostitution is a virtually institutionalized prerequisite for securing a break. "Now she had bought me ... Now I realized that nobody can beat the movie game without help – and the quicker you play ball, the quicker you succeed."[10] Unfortunately, unavoidable obstacles remain: his heavy Southern accent makes it unlikely that he will be cast in a speaking role.

While he continues his quest, he is supported and housed by Mona, an aspiring actress who has already lived through the series of defeats he is currently enduring. Having resigned herself to working as an extra to keep going, she directs her fury at fan magazines, blaming the falsehoods they perpetuate for the ruinous path she is on and that many others will take after her. Marketing deceit verbally and visually ("Printing all those goddam lies, all those goddam pictures of Crawford and Gaynor and Loy and Lombard ... beside their pools" [38]), the magazine's fairy tale accounts of easily obtained luxury, of how such performers "started at the bottom and rose to fame and fortune," mislead "millions of waitresses and small-town girls" in the country" (38) into believing they can do it too. But what inevitably happens, she blurts out before breaking down into sobs, is "they come to this goddam town and starve to death" (38). The immediate source of her rage is the imprisonment of her friend Dorothy for stealing groceries; after the latter hangs herself in her cell, Mona places "three or four movie magazines" in the corpse's hands at the morgue and then taunts a group of photographers, challenging them to shoot these "instruments" of death insofar as they are (as opposed to Dorothy's stocking) "what really killed her." "Isn't it glamorous enough? Go ahead – show the world an authentic picture of Hollywood" (101). If disseminated, morbid images might negate the persuasive force of a contemporaneous film like *A Star Is Born* (1937), the partial validity of which Johnny, a minor character, has previously qualified as "not *the* true story" since it leaves out all "the tragedy and heartbreak ... all the viciousness and cruelty" (61).[11] To counteract the effect of such motion pictures he plans "to write a novel about extras in the movies. How they live, what they think ... there's a big field there" (61). Although in the fiction the character eventually abandons this project, McCoy managed to complete it in reality, titling it *I Should Have Stayed Home*. From this perspective, the story the text ultimately tells is that the

novel may be distinguished from mainstream films on ethical grounds, on
the basis of the author's seriousness of social purpose.

In partial contrast, in his unfinished final novel, *The Last Tycoon* (1941),
Fitzgerald evoked the possibility that commercial and aesthetic demands
might be reconciled in a morally satisfying fashion within the confines of
the film industry. While one might have anticipated a hostile diatribe
against the system of mass production along the lines Henry Miller
articulated in his 1938 essay, "The Golden Age," Fitzgerald in fact extolls
the achievement of Monroe Stahr, praising him (and by extension his
deceased real-life counterpart, Irving Thalberg) as a visionary leader whose
efforts took the new medium "way up past the range and power of the
theatre, reaching a sort of golden age before the censorship in 1933."[12]
In sharp contrast to Miller's castigation of Hollywood (the "herculean
efforts" of its inventive directors notwithstanding) as the supplier of "a
drug" designed to "counteract the insomnia of the mob,"[13] Fitzgerald
characterizes his protagonist as a pioneering figure who "in a 'long
shot' ... saw a new way of measuring our jerky hopes and graceful
rogueries and awkward sorrows" (21). What sincerely mattered to him
was the discovery of a way to utilize the medium to express emotion
precisely and to depict actions with meaningful accuracy. Rather than
blame the commercially successful producer for having helped prevent
a genuinely avant-garde cinema from realizing its artistic potential,
Fitzgerald endorses his doomed hero's accomplishments. By seizing control over and rationalizing the process of manufacturing popular entertainment, he had "almost single-handed[ly] ... moved pictures sharply
forward through a decade, to a point where the content of the
'A productions' was wider and richer than that of the stage" (107).
Though Stahr admittedly dealt with writers and directors as if they were
replaceable parts, reassigning them from one project to another as he saw
fit, his authoritarian manner of exercising his supervisory prerogative was
mitigated by his aspiration to legitimate the movies as a quality product.
Instead of convicting the character of pandering to "the public's lack of
taste" (Miller, 50), Fitzgerald defends Stahr's desire to convince the skeptical that mainstream films are worth patronizing.

The opening scene of the novel boldly stakes out an attitude beyond the
quintessentially (high) modernist loathing for Hollywood. The narrator,
Cecilia Brady (a former Bennington coed whose father is "in the picture
business as another might be in cotton or steel" [3]), recalls that her English
teachers "pretended an indifference to Hollywood or its products" but that
in truth they "really *hated* it ... way down deep as a threat to their

existence" (3). In contrast, Cecilia (clearly speaking for the author here) declares that the film industry is a phenomenon one might comprehend by focusing on one of the few men who has "been able to keep the whole equation of pictures" in his head instead of dismissing "it with the contempt we reserve for what we don't understand" (3). And what we learn from Stahr is that organizing the filmmaking process efficiently is a crucial step toward the overall goal of reconciling commercial and artistic priorities. The requirement of appealing broadly does make it mandatory that the movies function ideologically and reflect received wisdom back to its consumers. "Our condition is that we have to take people's own favorite folklore and dress it up and give it back to them" (107). But there is more to cinematic storytelling than this; as the frustrated novelist turned screenwriter Boxley eventually realizes, there are creative ideas proper to the medium and it is worth one's while to pursue these. Presented in the quasi-allegorical fiction as more than a mere "merchant," the impression *Last Tycoon* gives of Thalberg is that he was an ethically admirable individual, was an icon of sincerity worth emulating insofar as he pushed himself to his physical and emotional breaking point in the hope of establishing the movies as an authentically popular art.

West's *The Day of the Locust* (1939) adopts an equally unexpected attitude toward Hollywood. A grotesquely stylized examination of those living on the fringes of the motion-picture business in the 1930s, the novel surprisingly attributes to the film industry a creative energy one customarily associates with artistic undertakings. An important scene featuring two of the book's main characters – Tod Hackett, a painter whose day job is as a studio set and costume designer, and Faye Greener, an impoverished yet aspiring young starlet who has thus far in her career only secured bit parts as an extra – will help illustrate this point (the significance of which has eluded many of the book's best commentators).

At the start of the scene, as the two characters converse, a theatrical analogy articulates Faye's effect on Tod. "Being with her was like being backstage during an amateurish ridiculous play. From in front the stupid lines and grotesque situations would have made him squirm with annoyance. But because he saw the perspiring stagehands and the wires that held up the tawdry summerhouse with its tangle of paper flowers, he accepted everything and was anxious for it to succeed."[14] Although her verbal mannerisms and physical gestures are blatantly artificial, the performance when viewed from the proper angle excites him erotically because of all the effort she puts into it. It is the labor she expends as she acts (in everyday life) that impresses him and that he envies. What the sweating bodies of the stagehands indicate figuratively is the quantity of work required to produce the spectacle of beauty, and it is this same potency that his own artistic endeavors demand but that he is not sure he possesses. In other words, Tod observes here the same discrepancy that the starers are said at the beginning of the novel to discern in the masqueraders: the latter inhabitants of Los Angeles tend to dress not as who they are but as who they would like to be; and the starers are jealous of and enraged by those who fabricate their appearance because the exhibitionism of the latter shows that they have what the voyeuristic émigrés to the region really want: the capacity to desire (60–61). Gazed at from the side, Faye as the quintessential masquerader displays the subjective lack or nothingness that is constitutive of artistic creativity. Tod doesn't want to possess her as the object of desire; he wants to be like her, to be the subject of desire.

It therefore makes sense that in the scene in question Faye is also associated with the kind of imaginative power that keeps the commercial cinema going. Hoping to make loads and loads of money collaborating with Tod, Faye describes how she comes up with plot lines. Once in the mood, she goes "over them in her mind, as though they were a pack of cards" until she finds the suitable story and selects it. She admits her method is "too mechanical for the best results," that it would be preferable "to slip into a dream naturally (104)"; nevertheless her strategy will do for their purposes since "beggars couldn't be choosers." Faye later adds that she plans to continue acting as well because of her existential devotion to her craft ("acting was her life"), and at this point Tod realizes that ironically the financial proposition in its entirety is another one of her fantasies, that "she was manufacturing another dream to add to her already very thick pack" (105). However, rather than interpret the passage as one more cynical account of the film business as a debased form of entertainment that recycles preexisting materials to turn a profit, West's intended meaning is that we take it as a clue as to why Hollywood has managed to secure a position of cultural hegemony in the world. (Tod's expressionist painting is to be taken, then, not as a displaced figuration of the novel itself but as a symptom of cultural envy. The canvas of "The Burning of Los Angeles" reveals the aggressive attitude of the visual *artist* toward his rival. Jealous because he can't match the collective force of desire animating the dream factory, he envisions its destruction).

Tod's oft-praised comparison during his stroll through the studio lots of the surrealistic remnants of past movie sets with Janvier's "Sargasso Sea" supports this thesis. If this "final dumping ground" is analogous to the "imaginary body of water [that] was a history of civilization in the form of a marine junkyard," it is because both sites consist of the material traces of previous desires. The dump will continue to grow in size because "there is not a dream afloat somewhere which wouldn't sooner or later turn up on it, having been made photographic by plaster, canvas, lath and paint" (132). In other words, the unconscious wishes of troubled subjects function as the generative source of mass culture. From this critical perspective, artists should be wary of laughing at the decaying evidence of a "monstrous" yearning "for beauty and romance, no matter how tasteless, even horrible, the results of that" may be, lest they exclude themselves from the impassioned origin of aesthetic production: the dissatisfied populace (61).

As we have seen, one of the recurrent features of Depression-era fictions focused on Hollywood is their self-reflexive attentiveness to the specificity of literature in relation to its mass cultural other. An allegorical articulation of the differences or similarities between the author's enterprise and those of his or her cinematic adversary tends to supplement the main narrative. Matters pertaining to the social aspects of the dominant mode of cultural *production* customarily come to the forefront in this context: the collaborative nature of story composition; the mechanical devices and persons required to shoot scenes properly; the importance of securing adequate funding and of marketing strategies; the interplay between directors, stars, screenwriters, and producers, as well as technically skilled and unskilled workers, etc.[15] A complementary area of critical interest often explored outside the subgenre were processes occurring at the level of motion picture *consumption*. During the 1930s, the emotional solace and ideological drawbacks associated with movie going emerged as a particularly pressing issue for writers from relatively disenfranchised communities. With limited access to the forces of cinematic production as a means of engaging in acts of collective representation, but well aware of the psychic impact of Hollywood on ethnic and racial minorities in the United States, writers from these groups on occasion registered film spectatorship as an important topic. An experimental chapter in Richard Wright's *Lawd Today!* and a short story by William Saroyan are exemplary in this regard.

Though published posthumously in 1963, Wright's novel was circulated in manuscript form (under the title "Cesspool") to presses in the late 1930s. Influenced by Dos Passos (as well as by James Joyce and Gertrude Stein), it records a day in the life of Jake Jackson, an emotionally volatile black postal worker in Chicago whose subjectivity is shaped (for the worse) by his media-saturated environment. Newspaper coverage of contemporary events misleads him; the sales pitch of advertising leaflets fools him; while propagandistic radio broadcasts (it is Lincoln's birthday) annoy

him. Wasting time in the city streets before heading to work, he is attracted
by a luridly colorful billboard with several placards in the front of a movie
house. Wright then describes at great length the protagonist's response to
the posters, which display scenes from an action film called *The Death
Hawk*. That the villainous characters resemble "foreigners" (they are
"gangsters who looked like mexicans or japs or reds or huns"[16]) reinforces
Jake's repellent nativist xenophobia about which we have been informed
earlier. Equally problematic is the poster's solicitation of identification
with a Caucasian hero who gazes "with love into the eyes of the gold-
enhaired blueeyed girl who lay on the ground gagged tied bound trussed"
(53). For when Jake thinks to himself that "*Being an aviator must be fun*"
(54), he is simultaneously embracing white femininity as an object of desire
and absorbing the notion that it is acceptable to derive perverse pleasure
from the suffering of women ("his eye lingered on the poster where the girl
was tied so that her thigh was exposed" (54). The irony, which escapes him,
is not simply that mainstream films fail to offer him either admirable or
empowering role models to imitate but that in addition the images of black
men projected on the screen convey an impression of vulnerability comparable to the one evoked by the heroine's predicament in *Death Hawk*.
This becomes evident after he is reprimanded later in the day for performing badly at work. His resentment at this point encompasses the frustrating
fact that all Hollywood offers him are scenes that recall a traumatic past,
that in effect enact a return of repressed experiences. "When he went to the
movies he always wanted to see Negroes . . . shown against the background
of urban conditions, not rural ones. Anything which smacked of farms,
chaingangs, lynchings, hunger, or the South in general was repugnant to
him. These things had so hurt him once that he wanted to forget them
forever; to see them again merely served to bring back the deep pain for
which he knew no salve" (138).[17]

Saroyan's "Love, Death, Sacrifice and So Forth" articulates from the
perspective of the film viewer the discrepancy between Hollywood's classical narrative strategies and contemporary reality. Addressing the reader in
the second person as part of the audience ("You are sitting in the theatre
waiting for what you know is going to happen"[18]), the speaker in the
literary text summarizes the predictable movie plot to the point where
the male hero of the film, a railroad magnate, is on the threshold of killing
himself after learning about his son's incestuous relationship with his
stepmother. As the grand finale approaches, the speaker comments sarcas-
tically on the two leads' gestural exaggerations on screen as their beginning
"to act." He also disparages the sentimental reaction the abandoned first

wife's destruction of herself produces: it is "so touching . . . that tears came to the eyes" (69). Mocking the tendency of the entranced spectator to admire the wife for her dedication to her husband, a "great man," the literary work seeks to alienate its reader from the tragic paradigm on which too many films rely. Hollywood's perpetuation of glib theological explanations of transgressive behavior as fated is bad enough ("It simply had to happen. Man is flesh, and all that" [70]); but what is even worse is the emotional compensations such hackneyed spectacles furnish those who adore them, inducing in filmgoers who lose themselves in the illusion an otherwise unobtainable state of ecstasy. Those "who have spent the better parts of their lives in the movies, loving, dying, sacrificing themselves to noble ideals, etc." experience "a moment of great living" at the climax of the picture (71).

To ensure the detachment of the reader from the moral simplicities of Hollywood melodrama, the speaker doubles the stakes of the main character's obligation to do himself in. His existential crisis is simultaneously an ideological and economic one for the form of mass entertainment: "For his honor's sake, for the sake of Hollywood ethics, for the sake of the industry (the third largest in America, I understand) . . . Tom has got to commit suicide. If he doesn't, it will . . . mean we have been deceiving ourselves all these years" (71). What is in suspense is whether the theatrical conventions to which we adhere and the heroic tradition they enforce will remain valid. "A long while back we made the rules, and now, after all these years, we wonder if they are genuine ones, or if, maybe, we didn't make a mistake at the outset" (71). Fortunately, the character goes through with it, to the feigned relief of the speaker. "He remains a great man. Once again the industry triumphs . . . Everything is hotsytotsy. It will be possible for Hollywood to go on making pictures for the public for another century" (72). The naïve spectator is left weeping joyfully "in the pious darkness" yet the critical discourse continues. The speaker now references an actual or "regular" suicide he once overheard. His next door neighbor nearly botched the job, attempting to shoot himself in the heart and then hollering in agony when he missed. The ensuing chaos as the suddenly sincere speaker recollects it stands in stark contrast to the reassuringly coherent cinematic death he has just finished describing ironically. The only viable solution to this gross disparity is to cease representing the desperate acts of troubled individuals in a vacuously standardized manner: "we've got to stop committing suicide in the movies" (74).[19]

If, like Wright, one of Saroyan's primary motivations was to depict sympathetically the hardships of everyday life for ethnic and racial minorities in the 1930s, a supplementary goal of both writers was to maintain the status of reading literature as an activity with more referential reliability than the watching of movies. "Pat Hobby, Putative Father," one of the seventeen short pieces Fitzgerald composed featuring this character – an aging reprobate whose moment of glory during the silent era is long gone – also embraced this critical task, if only in passing.[20] At one point the narrator interrupts the comic action to disclose a trade secret, to explain the way trick photography is used for "process" shots:

> [A] projecting machine threw a moving background upon a transparent screen. On the other side of the screen, a scene was played and recorded against this moving background. The projector on one side of the screen and the camera on the other were so synchronized that the result could show a star standing on his head before an indifferent crowd on 42nd street – a *real* crowd and a *real* star – and the poor eye could only conclude that it was being deluded and never guess how.[21]

The insight Fitzgerald had acquired as a participant-observer in mass culture enabled him to demystify a bit of the magic of the movies, to reveal the tactics filmmakers employed to manipulate spectators at the level of their sensory organs into accepting a distorted view of the world.

Dos Passos's *U.S.A.* trilogy took this epistemological imperative as its *raison d'etre*. By naming two of the formal devices he utilized in his experimental enterprise after aspects of the cinema, Dos Passos recognized the medium as a force with which the politically committed novelist must reckon. His designation of the lyrical or subjective portion of the three volumes "the Camera Eye" and the more historical or objective dimension "the Newsreel" does reveal Dos Passos's desire to incorporate formal traits (such as montage[22]) associated with his photographic rival into his own print or typographical undertaking. However, the goal of this late modernist project was not to assimilate into literature the expressive thrust and perceptual acuity of technologically mediated modes of seeing; nor was it to tap into the documentary genre's capacity to record the momentous events and trivial affairs that constituted everyday life in the early decades of the twentieth century. Rather his main priority was to cancel out the representational claims of more naïve uses of language, whether image-based autobiographical poetry or journalistic description. The experimental writer's anti-illusionism and correlative deployment of an aesthetic of painful shocks mark the stance he adopted toward the film industry and its pleasurable spectacles as a hostile one.[23]

This is not to say, however, that Depression-era authors in this country regarded Hollywood from an exclusively skeptical or negative point of view. On the contrary, the work of several writers who may be categorized as "ghetto pastoralists" conveyed the affinity they felt for a nearly obsolete brand of motion picture fun: American slapstick.[24] Though out of synch with his Objectivist poetics, Louis Zukofsky's "A Keystone Comedy" (1941) is a telling indication of this sensibility. A modest achievement, the short story details the amusing adventures of a (Jewish) family operating a cocaine business out of their home in a neighborhood in the Bronx. Conversational topics in the dwelling range from complaints about nosy neighbors to arguments over the proper amount of sugar to use to cut the drug, the denouement coming when the dealers are forced to flush "ten thousand dollars worth" of the narcotic down the drain to avoid arrest.[25] Edward Dahlberg's regrettably forgotten *From Flushing to Calvary* (1932) is a more significant manifestation of this literary tendency. The most revealing moment for my purposes in this remarkably innovative novel takes place when its autobiographical protagonist (Lorry Lewis) gazes into a plate glass window and sees reflecting back at him a "silly helpless Harry Langdonesque image."[26] The pathetic character's comparison of himself to the least well-remembered of the four great silent screen comedians – though James Agee would subsequently praise Langdon as being "as remarkable a master as Chaplin of subtle emotional and mental processes"[27] – indicates that Dahlberg was seeking to answer in his creative prose the critical call he had made a few years before to American writers to take advantage of the expressive possibilities of the puppet-like performer. For in "Ariel in Caliban" (1929), Dahlberg had proposed that the screen performer's "inelastic jerks and movements ... bodied forth Bergson's theory of the comic," albeit in a tragic vein.[28] (Though she cannot be classified as a ghetto pastoralist, Eudora Welty shared this penchant for using the cinematic genre for practical inspiration. Looking back over her career, she pointed to "the antic pantomime of the silent screen," naming Chaplin, Keaton, and the Keystone Kops as decisive influences on her understanding of how to "make fictional comedy."[29] "Lily Daw and the Three Ladies" and "Why I Live at the P.O.," collected in *A Curtain of Green* (1941), would be two Depression-era cases in point.)

Daniel Fuchs's first two novels – *Summer in Williamsburg* (1934) and *Homage to Blenholt* (1936) – epitomize the ghetto pastoralist's response to the film industry. Though geographically set far from Hollywood, both novels survey in a nonjudgmental fashion the myriad ways in which the motion pictures, one of "two positive institutions in Williamsburg," remain close to the hearts of the neighborhood's predominantly Jewish residents.³⁰ In *Summer*, for example, sexual awakening is shown to take place customarily under the sign of the movies. Although "characters in moving picture romances are men and women, and grown-ups claim love as an adult privilege," young Davey disagrees, consequently taking his seduction cues, albeit ineptly, from stars like Adolph Menjou (67–68). His friend Natie, who is "actually in love" with Marion Davies, the discrepancy between their ages and her unattainability notwithstanding (30), prefers to mimic the behavior of either George Raft or John Gilbert (331–32). Similarly, Julie is said to live "on the tabloids and movie fan magazines," and the "surest access to her favors" is therefore "to take her to a show" (37). The circular entanglement of erotic intimacy in the real with cinematic fantasy culminates in a lengthy account of two adolescents attending a "love picture" together. While fascinated by the affairs imaged on screen, they eventually begin to explore the pleasures of physical contact with each other:

> Natie followed the story with furious interest. Yetta was absorbed by the picture. Natie said, what the hell, this will tell. He pressed his knee against hers. Yetta did not flinch. Knees too could be soft and warm. She really liked him, Natie thought, else she would have taken her leg away ... Natie en rapport with this lovely girl beside him, elbows and knees touching, felt as though he were sitting next to Marion Davies and the picture couldn't be too long. (337).

Film's formative effect on the love life of slightly older persons is apparent in the relationship between Philip and Tessie. The latter, we are told, has been struggling "with her eternal soul in an effort to discover truth," i.e. to figure out whether she cares about Philip, but her introspective quest for knowledge is "clouded by the shadowy influence of the movies" (56). Philip, well aware of her predilection for copying the famous ("Ah, Tessie, Tessie, who studies the amorous postures of movie stars and tries them out on me" [56]), eventually accuses her of playing the part of Gloria Swanson in a formulaic tragedy (91).³¹

Homage to Blenholt extends this moderately sympathetic scrutiny of the movies' capacity at the point of reception to shape relationships in the world, but this sequel also incorporates elements of slapstick film at the stylistic level. While one character (Max Balkan) remains fixated on the figure of Tamburlaine from Marlowe's Elizabethan drama, his girl-friend, when not poring over photographs and gossip columns in *Screenplay*, keeps trying to drag him away from his literary obsession and go with her to the Miramar to see her idol Joan Crawford. Though Max resists, he too is plagued by the disparity between his comic clumsiness in reality and "the ease and smoothness with which the petty events of life were accomplished" at the movies. Whereas the gestures of actors tend to be effortless and faultless, when preparing for a journey he inevitably breaks his trunk, loses the key, and will then "fall in a pool of mud" on the way to the station.[32] Correlatively, the novel's most inspired scenes function as literary extensions of the Keystone studio's legacy of comic lunacy. For instance, the bursts of anarchic fury Max's alcoholic friend Coblenz periodically indulges in derive directly from this film tradition. Similarly when Max himself is trampled at a funeral, the painful brutality of the incident is tempered by its hilarity, as is the violent conflict between two grammar school kids. When one traps the other in a dumbwaiter and viciously assaults his victim with rotting fruit and vegetables, we are amused rather than horrified. It is in this light telling that Max's father, a former tragedian on the Yiddish stage reduced to wearing a sandwich board while bizarrely made up as a clown to advertise a local beauty parlor, is referred to as a "real Charlie Chaplin" (47). Part of an ensemble cast, as was Chaplin at the beginning of his career when working for Sennett, the elder Balkan is endlessly harassed by his voluble wife, who is in a constant state of hysteria. "[T]aking it out on Pop just as though it was a silent moving picture" (94), she makes fun of any attempt on his part to reestablish his dignity as "a sketch. If you saw it in the movies, people would laugh their insides out" (43), as the reader here is encouraged to do. Max's father may be "the kind of man who was bothered intensely when he saw furniture or pies or automobiles destroyed in the moving pictures, the heedless destruction of material causing him real anguish," but he is himself a character in a literary version of such cinematic recklessness (172).

In light of his predilection for examining the role of the movies in everyday life, it is not surprising that after his Williamsburg novels sold poorly Fuchs departed for Hollywood. The move across the country and into a different medium ultimately turned out to be both permanent and rewarding. Looking back a quarter century later on his career to date, he defended the cultural product he had helped turn out "as indigenous as our cars or skyscrapers or highways, and as irrefutable. Generations to come, looking back over the years, are bound to find that the best, most solid creative effort of our decades was spent in the movies."[33] Notably, one of his first assignments in the industry was to collaborate with Faulkner on a rewrite of the script for a Raoul Walsh-directed spy-thriller (*Background to Danger*) — a task Fuchs found daunting ("I was paralyzed by awe.

It happened that I had a deep, longtime admiration for this man and his achievement" [5]). Faulkner himself rarely had anything good to say about the time he spent in the industry and tended (like Hecht and Perelman) to get out of town as soon as he got what he came for: money. Nevertheless, one of the most vital topics in Faulkner studies recently has been the reciprocity between his literary and cinematic endeavors. Critical scholarship on the author has started to explore the repercussions of his sustained involvement in screenwriting on his subsequent novels, and has also continued to pursue an elusive understanding of the connection between his Depression-era output and motion-picture entertainment.[34]

The interplay between Faulkner and Hollywood opens out onto the dizzying series of transactions from the 30s to the present between crime or hardboiled fiction and film noir. *Sanctuary* (1932) merits attention in this respect, as does *The Wild Palms* (the original title of which–*If I Forget Thee, Jerusalem* (1939)—has been restored). The latter is of particular interest here due to the oft-noted allusion to it in Jean-Luc Godard's feature-length debut, *Breathless* (1960). In this groundbreaking film, Patricia, a young American reporter asks her love interest, the ill-fated anti-hero, Michel, if he has read Faulkner's novel (given to her in a previous scene by a rival for her affections) and then quotes an existentially resonant passage from the text.[35] In the same year, Francois Truffaut rechristened the main character in his second picture–*Shoot the Piano Player* (1960)–Edouard *Saroyan* in apparent homage to William Saroyan.[36] If the obvious implication of these two references is that the postwar French directors recognized an affinity between themselves and certain Depression-era American prose stylists, my accompanying claim is this affinity was grounded in a comparable cultural predicament. Like their late modernist predecessors, the New Wave auteurs felt compelled to negotiate the specificity of their interventions in critical dialogue with Hollywood traditions. The enduring appeal to the directors of the latter is evident in the structural derivation of *Breathless* and *Shoot the Piano Player* from B-movie paradigms. In contrast, the hostility Godard and Truffaut felt toward the products of the American film industry is evident in their shared commitment to mutilating the narrative codes of the generically standardized fare to which they remained indebted.[37] It would seem, then, that one of the legacies of Depression-era American writers to innovative artists elsewhere in the world was a contradictory blend of sincere admiration for and ironic rejection of the dictates of the commercial cinema.

The present inquiry has proposed, however, that mapping Depression-era responses to Hollywood in accordance with the degrees of disgust expressed and desire articulated is only the starting point for an interpretation that seeks to do justice to a complex historical predicament: the need of American novelists to negotiate their (declining) status in relation to an institution that had decisively altered the nature of artistic production for the foreseeable future. Only after this experience would authors in this country find themselves prepared to ride "into a new destiny, purified in the crucible that men call Hollywood" (Perelman, "Strictly from Hunger," 91).

Notes

1. Edmund Wilson, *The Boys in the Backroom: Notes on California Novelists* (San Francisco, CA: Colt Press, 1941), 13.
2. Quoted in Saverio Giovacchini, *Hollywood Modernism: Film and Politics in the Age of the New Deal* (Philadelphia, PA: Temple University Press, 2001), 217.
3. Dwight Macdonald, "Masscult and Midcult," *Partisan Review* 27.2 (Spring 1960), 208.
4. "They try this and that and if something clicks at the box office, they try to cash in with similar products, like consumer-researchers with a new cereal, or like a Pavlovian biologist who has hit on a reflex he thinks can be conditioned" (14). The anti-Communist aspects of Macdonald's critique of "masscult" are patent throughout the essay.
5. Ben Hecht, "Enter the Movies," in *Film: An Anthology*, ed. Daniel Talbot (Berkeley, CA: University of California Press, 1966), 257–58.
6. Tom Teicholz, ed., *Conversations with S. J. Perelman* (Jackson: University of Mississippi Press, 1995), 19.
7. Perelman also composed numerous satiric attacks on Hollywood. See especially "Scenario" and "Kitchenware, Notions, Lights, Action, Camera!" as well as "Strictly from Hunger." The latter is a Depression-era piece that wittily details the absurd misadventures of a screenwriter as he migrates to California to work for a major studio ("Plushnick Productions").
8. Because poetry has rarely been as financially a remunerative activity as literary prose, poets have not tended to react to the presence of Hollywood with the same urgency, much less animosity. For a critical survey of this topic, see Laurence Goldstein, *The American Poet at the Movies* (Ann Arbor: University of Michigan Press, 1995).
9. Jack Warner apparently fired Himes on the basis of skin color alone; see *City of Quartz; Excavating the Future in Los Angeles* (New York: Verso, 2006), 43.
10. Horace McCoy, *I Should Have Stayed at Home* (New York: Signet, 1951), 35.
11. Dorothy Parker was nominated for an academy award for her contribution to this film's screenplay. One of her best-known stories, however, "Big Blonde" (1929), is much closer in spirit to McCoy's novel. Though it does not deal with the film industry, it does address the misery of women positioned as

disempowered objects of exchange between men. Though it falls outside the
historical scope of the present inquiry, Joan Didion's *Play It as It Lays* (1970) is
pertinent in this context as well. On the motif of the "extra" in Depression-era
motion pictures, see David E. James, *The Most Typical Avant-Garde: History
and Geography of Minor Cinemas in Los Angeles* (Berkeley: University of
California Press, 2005), 39–66.

12. F. Scott Fitzgerald, *The Love of the Last Tycoon: A Western* (New York:
    Scribner, 1993), 28. Miller's title is a reference to Luis Bunuel's *l'age d'or*.
    Coincidentally, late in the novel Stahr screens at his home the surrealist classic
    Un Chien Andalou (directed by Bunuel in collaboration with Salvador Dali).

13. Henry Miller, *The Cosmological Eye* (New York: New Directions, 1961), 50.
    Because Miller had access to an alternative mode of literary production in the
    form of a Paris-based independent press (Obelisk), he did not feel the need (as
    most of his contemporaries did) to make any concessions to commercial as
    opposed to avant-garde film ventures. Before seeking a rapprochement with
    moving pictures, Fitzgerald expressed his reservations about them in "The Crack-
    Up" (1936), worrying that "the novel," formerly "the strongest and supplest
    medium for conveying thought and emotion from one human being to another,
    was becoming subordinated to a mechanical and communal art ... capable of
    reflecting only the tritest thought." In the new art, the power of words was
    succumbing to "a more glittering, a grosser power" – images. *The Jazz Age*
    (New York: New Directions, 1996), 66.

14. Nathanael West, *The Day of the Locust* (New York: New Directions,
    1962), 104.

15. The impact of left-wing politics on the industry is also something Fitzgerald,
    McCoy, and Schulberg all deal with in their respective Hollywood novels.
    The latter's treatment of the effort to gain recognition for the Screen Writers'
    Guild is the most sustained of these, though McCoy weaves into his text
    a subplot involving union organizing in the region. Doing justice to the
    genealogical link of the proletarian to the Hollywood novel in the 1930s is
    beyond the scope of the present discussion, yet the fact that West, in letters to
    Malcom Cowley and Jack Conroy, apologetically acknowledges he had
    excised material from *Day of the Locust* dealing with "the strong progressive
    movement" is in this context highly suggestive. See Jay Martin, *Nathanael
    West: The Art of His Life* (New York: Carroll and Graf, 1970), 334–36.

16. Richard Wright, *Lawd Today!* (Boston, MA: Northeastern University Press,
    1991), 53.

17. James Baldwin echoes and critically elaborates this assessment in his
    autobiographical essay, *The Devil Finds Work* (1976), though he makes
    an exception for Sylvia Sidney and Henry Fonda, who appeared together
    in Fritz Lang's *You Only Live Once* – released in 1937 when Baldwin was
    twelve. He credits the former with being the "only American film actress
    who reminded me of a colored girl, or woman – which is to say that she
    was the only American film actress who reminded me of reality"
    [New York: Vintage], 2011: 21); whereas the latter was to him "the only

actor of the era with whom I identified ... I was not alone. A black friend of mine, after seeing Henry Fonda in *The Grapes of Wrath*, swore that Fonda had colored blood" (21–22).

18. William Saroyan, *The Daring Young Man on the Flying Trapeze* (New York: New Directions, 1997), 67.

19. Also relevant in *Daring* is "Dear Greta Garbo," a faux letter from a young Italian to the movie star. He hopes to impress her and get her to help him break into the business by drawing her attention to his appearance in a newsreel of a strike that turned into a riot outside a local Ford factory. Though he was knocked unconscious, he feels he looked good on screen.

20. Suggestive parallels notwithstanding, the lazy character in truth bears only a faint autobiographical resemblance to his author. Matthew J. Bruccoli's research has shown that Fitzgerald took his script assignments seriously in the hopes of salvaging his career as a writer. See *Some Sort of Epic Grandeur: The Life of F. Scott Fitzgerald* (New York: Harcourt Brace Jovanovich, 1981), esp. 424–60.

21. F. Scott Fitzgerald, "Pat Hobby's Secret," in *The Pat Hobby Stories* (New York: Scribner, 2004), 66.

22. Many commentators have taken note of Sergei Eisenstein's probable influence on Dos Passos in this respect. For a fictive account of the Russian director and his crew's labors on *Que Viva Mexico?* (1931), a project he had initially planned to complete under the auspices of Hollywood, see Katherine Anne Porter's "Hacienda" (1934).

23. I unfold this admittedly counterintuitive argument in *Literature, Amusement, and Technology in the Great Depression* (Cambridge: Cambridge University Press, 2002). Notably, in the interim between the composition of *1919* (1932) and *The Big Money* (1936), the second and third installments of the trilogy, Dos Passos participated as a screenwriter in the making of Joseph Von Sternberg's *The Devil Is a Woman* (1935), which starred Marlene Dietrich, for Paramount Studios. As he explained it in a letter to Ernest Hemingway: "I've just signed up to serve a term of five weeks in Hollywood teaching Spanish or something like that to Von Sternberg – I was in a sort of a gap in my work and thought I might as well take a stab at it, restoring my finances and taking a look at the world's great bullshit center." *The Fourteenth Chronicle: Letters and Diaries of John Dos Passos* (Boston, MA: Gambit Incorporated, 1976), 437. Though exasperating, his "enormously instructive" (446) stay in Hollywood did furnish the basis for the unflattering portrait he drew of Margo Dowling in the last installment of *U.S.A.*

24. The term is Michael Denning's; see *The Cultural Front: The Laboring of American Culture in the Twentieth Century* (New York: Verso, 1996), 230–58.

25. Louis Zukofsky, *Collected Fiction* (New York: New Directions, 1990), s14.23.

26. Edward Dahlberg, *From Flushing to Calvary* (New York: Harcourt, Brace and Company, 1932), 244.

27. James Agee, "Comedy's Greatest Era" (1949), in *Agee on Film* (Boston, MA: Beacon Press, 1958), 13.

28. Edward Dahlberg, *Samuel Beckett's Wake and Other Collected Prose* (Elmwood, IL: Dalkey Archive Press, 1989), 4.

29. Eudora Welty, *One Writer's Beginnings* (Cambridge, MA: Harvard University Press, 1984), 36. In "The Golden Age," Miller too suggests the compositional value to him of the "thousands of slap-stick, pie-throwing Mack Sennett films" (54) he had viewed as a child.

30. Daniel Fuchs, *Summer in Williamsburg* (New York: Carroll and Graf, 1983), 165. Venues to watch films are ubiquitous in the area: "within a radius of seven blocks of Ripple Street there were no fewer than eight movie houses, three of them pretentious movie palaces, the rest of the dump variety" (166).

31. For a more panicky contemporaneous critique of such mimetic behavior, see Henry James Forman, *Our Movie-Made Children* (1935). Of the numerous tracts of this sort commissioned by the Payne Foundation, Laurence Goldstein singles this one out for explication (91–92). Goldstein's interpretation of the mind/cinematic machine metaphor in Delmore Schwartz's "In Dreams Begin Responsibilities" (1935) and reading of the latter's poem "Metro Goldwyn Mayer" and short story "Screeno" are also pertinent to the present discussion (96–106).

32. Daniel Fuchs, *Homage to Blenholt* (New York: Basic, 1961), 106.

33. Daniel Fuchs, "Writing for the Movies: A Letter from Hollywood, 1962," *The Golden West: Hollywood Stories* (Boston, MA: Black Sparrow, 2005), 20.

34. For an overview, see Robert W. Hamblin, "Faulkner and Hollywood: A Call for Reassessment," in *Faulkner and Film*, ed. Peter Lurie and Anne J. Abadie (Jackson: University of Mississippi Press, 2014), 3–24. Hamblin interprets Faulkner's "Golden Land" (1935) as a precursor of West's *Day of the Locust*, 15–16.

35. For a thorough discussion of this topic, see "C'est vraiment Dégueulasse": Meaning and Ending in *A bout de souffle* and *If I Forget Thee Jerusalem*," in *A Companion to William Faulkner*, ed. Richard Moreland (Malden, MA: Blackwell, 2007), 65–83.

36. The actor who played "Eddie" – Charles Aznavour – was, like William Saroyan, of Armenian descent. The film is an adaptation of David Goodis's *Down There* (1956). Also pertinent in this context are the references in Louis Malle's *The Fire Within* (1963) to Fitzgerald. As Alain, a suicidal alcoholic, paces around his room in a rehabilitation clinic, several shots suggest he has been reading *Babylon Revisited* (1931), thus prompting the viewer to draw a parallel between the world-weary Charlie in the short story and the protagonist of the film. The camera also shows that Alain's book collection includes *This Side of Paradise* and *Tender Is the Night*.

37. Truffaut called his film "a *respectful pastiche* of the Hollywood B-films from which I learned so much," explaining that his goal was "*the explosion of a genre* (the detective film) *by mixing genres* (comedy, drama, melodrama, the psychological film, the thriller, the love film, etc." (emphasis in the original). Quoted in James Monaco, *The New Wave: Truffaut, Godard, Chabrol, Rohmer, Rivette* (New York: Oxford University Press, 1976), 41.

CHAPTER 20

Time Inc.

Donal Harris

After spending the bulk of the 1920s in Paris as an expatriate poet, Archibald MacLeish returned to the United States in 1928 and shortly thereafter received a job offer that would indelibly mark his occupational identity. Henry Luce, the cofounder of Time Inc., said that for a half-year's salary, MacLeish could work six months out of twelve at his magazines and devote the rest of his time to whatever he wanted. Having spent time in the modernist institutions of Gertrude Stein's salon and Pound's "Ezraversity," and having penned so recently the closing lines of "Ars Poetica" (1926) – "A poem should not mean / but be" – one could imagine the poet balking at such a brazenly commercial agreement. Yet it is a deal that MacLeish called "one of the luckiest things that happened to me in a fairly lucky life." As he recalled, "[i]n 1929, when the offer was made, jobs were not easily available, particularly jobs for writers of verse with wives and children, and, more particularly still, jobs such as Luce was willing to provide . . . I had begun by saying that I needed a job desperately, so desperately that there was only one thing I needed more – time enough to finish a long poem I had started in Paris two years before."[1] That poem was *Conquistador*, which won the Pulitzer Prize for Poetry in 1933, and the job was an editor at *Fortune*, the newest title in Time Inc.'s stable of periodicals.

MacLeish's sharp ascent in the editorial ranks at Time Inc. was only a prelude to the mark he left on a number of governmental and cultural institutions. Roosevelt nominated him as the librarian of Congress in 1939, and he served as the director of the Office of Fact and Figures and the assistant director of the Office of War Information during World War II. This bureaucratic acumen, along with his continued success as a writer of verse, made him an administrative-poet extraordinaire, both because his corporate journalism underwrote so much of his poetry, and because the questions about writing that arose because of his administrative positions seeped into his ostensibly personal work. The tension between the artist and the patron is a central component of *Frescoes for Mr. Rockefeller's City*

(1933), most obviously, but it is also on view in *Conquistador*, which at heart
addresses how two different administrators aestheticize the legacy of their
employer. The poem documents Cortez's conquest of the Aztec Empire in
the name of Spanish colonialism from the point of view of an amateur poet
and professional soldier, Bernardo Diaz del Castillo. Diaz repeatedly
contrasts his own underappreciated and anti-literary verse, "Cold on the
page with the spilt ink and the shunt of the / Stubborn thumb," with the
smooth style of Cortez's officially sanctioned historian, "with the school-
taught skip of his writing."[2] Diaz's poetry is better than the administrative
poet's, in *Conquistador*'s logic, because it arises out of his own *aficion* rather
than professional obligation. Diaz's valorization of writing that is not
sanctioned as work, then, might offer a glimpse of MacLeish's earlier,
unencumbered poetic identity lashing out against the polished sheen of
his current, managing-editor self. It certainly amplifies the tension between
definitions of writing already present in the conditional closing of "Ars
Poetica": poems "should" be free from the obligation to mean, and poets
from thinking of their task as another kind of work, but for MacLeish they
cannot. *Conquistador*, then, could be said to dramatize two complementary
poetic styles of the same system of patronage; after all, the same person
signs both of the soldier's and poet's checks, so to speak.

It is more than coincidence that *Conquistador*'s imagined battle between
inter-organizational professional styles was produced during MacLeish's
tenure at Time Inc. The media company, founded in 1923, actively sought
to realign the professional procedures of journalistic and literary writing.
Though this goal was present from the outset, it intensified in the 1930s,
and the company had a pronounced influence on both the field of commercial magazines and literary culture in the period. Certainly, Time Inc.
did not invent the tension between journalism and literature; Stephen
Crane's lament about the "double literary life" of a serious writer, who
imagines her efforts outside of economics, but who must also write to pay
the bills, was well known by the 1920s.[3] MacLeish claimed that writers of
his generation were taught to "avoid the practice of journalism like wet sox
and gin before breakfast," yet his own poetic success depended on Luce's
corporate largesse for both economic and creative reasons.[4] "I got more of
my own work done in my years at *Fortune* than in any other comparable
period in my life," he gushed, making him one of the few Time Inc.
employees who went on record in support of the organization's influence
on his literary efforts.[5] In fact, he refers to journalism and literature as "the
two ends of the typewriter keyboard," suggesting their similar methods of
production creates a broader likeness in their output.[6] For a period in the

1930s it can begin to feel like everyone at Time Inc. thought the same, even if they did not share MacLeish's enthusiasm for Time Inc.'s influence. This chapter surveys how and why so many novelists and poets ended up in Luceland, and then considers how this institutional affiliation shaped the media company's print publications as well as the employees' literary endeavors. Certainly MacLeish is more salutary than most when discussing the effects of corporate journalism on literary production, but his experience is representative of the way that Time Inc. offered a space of tenuous mutual benefit for mass media companies and writers in the 1930s.

The proof of mutual benefit can be found in the sheer number and range of Time Inc.-sponsored literary feats from the period. Although Time Inc. editors shared an overwhelming homogeneity in terms of demographics – white, male, Protestant, and Ivy League-educated, like the company's founders, and reflecting larger trends in journalism and publishing – their outside writing was anything but. Along with MacLeish's poetry, James Agee's and Walker Evans's *Let Us Now Praise Famous Men* (1941) began as an assignment for *Fortune* in 1936; John Hersey's Pulitzer Prize–winning first novel *A Bell for Adano* (1944), as well as his ground-breaking *Hiroshima* (1946), emerged out of his war reporting at *Time*; Kenneth Fearing began his now classic crime novel *The Big Clock* (1946) while an editor at *Time*, and it takes place in a fictionalized Time Inc. editorial office; Robert Cantwell's social novels from the 1930s were produced while he worked at Time Inc.; much of Dwight MacDonald's most scathing cultural criticism responds directly to his career there; nearly all of Margaret Bourke-White's and many of Gordon Parks's most iconic photographs were taken while they were staff photographers at *Fortune* and *Life*. Time Inc.'s patronage supported many other intellectual endeavors, as well: Daniel Bell's *The End of Ideology* (1960) grew out of his labor reporting for *Time*, and William Whyte's *The Organization Man* (1956), which eulogized the death of young American business people's desire to strike out on their own, was assigned to him as a *Fortune* story.

As this impressive canon of Time Inc. texts suggests, Luce's company was adept in the 1930s in its willingness to help artists and intellectuals square the two needs of a steady income and free time to pursue one's own "serious" work. "It is easier to turn poets into business journalists than to turn bookkeepers into writers," Luce was fond of saying, and Time Inc. perfected a method of bringing authors and artists into the fold of mass media production that would be replicated by other media corporations for decades.[7] Alfred Kazin, who sporadically wrote for both *Time* and *Fortune*, recounts with awe visiting the *Time* offices in the 1930s: "Part of the fascination of going up to see Harriet [his friend] in the new *Time* offices in Rockefeller Center was running into James Agee, Walker Evans, Robert Fitzgerald, John Hersey." At *Fortune*, he met and befriended MacDonald, MacLeish, Cantwell, Ralph Ingersoll, Louis Kronenberger, and James Gould Cozzens.[8] Partially this concentration of novelists and poets at a media corporation had to do with the economics of authorship in the 1930s: as MacLeish alludes, the Great Depression made it extraordinarily difficult for artistically minded authors to scrounge a living by publishing their work in noncommercial arts journals. As the patronage systems of modernist little magazines dried up, working at a mass-market periodical sat alongside finding a job in one of the New Deal arts programs or moving to Hollywood as the obvious career options for those trying to sell their most valuable skill set: the ability to write well.[9] Time Inc. was especially attractive because of its active recruitment of what Kazin called "poet-reporters," individuals interested in literary craft but willing to write copy for a news outlet. Time Inc. provided these poet-reporters with a healthy salary to weather economic downturns, but also with a legitimate path to literary prestige. "Never as in the Thirties," Kazin wrote, "when history proclaimed itself every day in the significances of daily struggle, could a story in *Time* have seemed so significant to a writer." A story for *Time* amounted to "a literary feat because of the harsh stylistic frame to which a story had to be fitted," one for which "you got paid well, praised as only great writers are ever praised, and felt like you were an artist, of sorts."[10]

The "harsh stylistic frame" that Kazin refers to was *Time* style, the magazine's idiosyncratic editorial voice: inverted sentence structures, a chatty tone, and the aggressive compression of content and words. Unlike the upside-down triangle model of reportorial writing in the newspapers, which emphasized objectivity and in-depth coverage, *Time* style consisted of highly compressed stories (at the beginning, no more than 400 words apiece) that relied on a chatty, "smart" tone. The compressed coverage went so far as to combine words: *Time* made a point of employing portmanteaus such as "cinemactor," "socialite," "filmen," "Hindenburglary," and "detectifiction."[11] One might claim the transition in 1927 from self-identifying as "News-Magazine" to "Newsmagazine" marks the full internalization of this tendency. The goal of *Time* style, according to its advertising material, boiled down to three alliterative words: "Curt. Clear. Complete."

Time's compression of journalistic style responded to the success of general interest magazines and newspapers, both of which, according to Luce and Hadden, produced far too much information for the average reader. The late nineteenth and early twentieth centuries witnessed exponential increases in the amount of printed material available: between 1890 and 1905, newspaper circulations in the United States rose from 36 million to 57 million, and during the same period, magazine circulations tripled. Periodical historian Matthew Schnierov claims that magazines, at the turn of the century, became America's "first national mass media."[12] As the circulation of specific magazines increased, so did the variety of available titles and genres. Edward Munsey of *Munsey's*, Edward Bok of *Ladies Home Journal*, and George Horace Lorimer of the *Saturday Evening Post* were only the most prominent pioneers of a hybrid magazine genre alternately titled the general interest or "family home" magazine that brought together the high tone of older "quality" magazines such as the *Atlantic Monthly* and *Harper's* and the economic model of the penny press. Spurred on by advertising revenues – which were tied to circulation numbers – and new marketing strategies, these magazines understood the path to more readers as more content of greater variety. This content-based approach is embedded in the etymology of "magazine," which comes from *magasin*, the French for "storehouse," an architectural metaphor Edward Bok reimagined as analogous first to a general store and then to the middle-class home. The different "departments" within the table of contents were like a house's functionally divided living and work spaces, and Bok attempted to generically replicate each in his magazine. Fiction for the easy chair, recipes for the kitchen, gossip for the parlor, advice columns, sporting news, celebrity profiles, travel articles, political stories, advertisements, questionnaires: all between two covers, all under one roof.

As circulation numbers and magazine genres both exploded, the page counts of each issue also grew in number. For example, a typical issue of the *Saturday Evening Post* – one of the most popular magazines in the United States – in 1926 exceeded 200 pages. A 1926 *Ladies Home Journal* issue was 270 pages, and it was common for *Cosmopolitan* or *McClure's* to close in on 150 pages. The result, according to Time Inc., was an early instance of information anxiety. "As it is now," wrote Luce in the early 1920s, "people have to think too hard as they read."[13] A *Time* advertising circular from 1925 dramatizes this: two distraught characters, "Busy Man" and "Busy Woman," sit sadly in a living room surrounded by newspapers. The man laments, "I bought this mass of printed matter to find out what is going on in the world, but it's no use! I am not abreast of the news in anything outside of my business." Lo and behold, "TIME" knocks on the door and saves the day, representing "a new idea of journalism. In my twenty-six pages is every fact of significance in all those newspapers and periodicals on your floor."[14] In the Prospectus, the publishers call their solution to the debilitating mass of printed matter "a complete ORGANIZATION of the news," and in the first issue, they write that the goal is to "compartmentaliz[e] the news into 22 departments, written to be read from the first page to the last at one sitting in the span of the hour" – an edict that recalls Edgar Allan Poe's single-sitting time limit for fiction.[15] By front-loading the work of aggregating and stylizing the news, the magazine reduces the effort that goes into reading while expanding the benefits of that activity; one need only consume *Time* and replicate its language to remain current and culturally viable. *Time* decides that a news organ matters, to quote the Prospectus one last time, "not in how much it includes between its covers – but in HOW MUCH IT GETS OFF ITS PAGES INTO THE MINDS OF ITS READERS."[16]

To accomplish this narrative compression, Luce and Hadden heavily emphasized the creative task of writing, rather than the more journalistic activity of reporting. In fact, until the late 1930s, Time Inc. did not employ reporters at all; instead it hired editors who would read the dailies and, like a Dadaist collage, remake the content of newspapers into an aesthetic object. As longtime Time Inc. editor T. S. Matthews put it, "the trouble with journalism was that you didn't have enough poets in it,"[17] and one appeal of the rigorous compression of *Time* style was that some imagined it to be akin to poetic craft. As Luce explained, "It takes *brains and work* to master all the facts dug up by the world's 10,000 journalists and to put them together in a little magazine."[18] The magazine did not found itself on informational originality but on the way that it translated other people's research into its own voice. And because of this emphasis on a uniform voice, all of the Time Inc. publications excised bylines in favor of a staff list in the frontmatter of each issue. The end products of different writers, after passing through the sieve of *Time* style, were supposed to be indistinguishable, so attaching names to the stories became counterproductive for establishing a single periodical persona.

Because of its emphasis on a recognizable editorial voice, it is both ironic and telling that the most famous single instance of *Time* style comes from outside of the magazine's own pages: Walcott Gibbs's acerbic 1936 *New Yorker* profile of Henry Luce, in which he parodies how, in *Time*, "backwards ran sentences until reeled the mind!"[19] In fact, the *Time* style parody became something of a micro-genre in the 1930s, turning up everywhere from a 1931 University of Washington alumni magazine, to a 1934 truck manufacturer's promotional pamphlet, to a letter to Luce from his mother.[20] It was famous enough by the 1930s that both James Agee and Whittaker Chambers lampooned *Time* style in their job applications. After defecting from his position as a Communist spy in 1939, Chambers sought out a position at Time Inc. because he wanted the most public job he could find. He spent almost a decade working for Luce in some capacity, a tenure that ended only when his central role in the Alger Hiss trial made him too much of a liability for the company. Though he resigned with a bang, he auditioned with a sample review of a war history that began, "One bomby Sunday afternoon . . .," mimicking the pun-filled copy of *Time*'s editorial style.[21] Agee accomplished a similar but far more elaborate feat. While president of the *Harvard Advocate*, he compiled a parody issue of *Time*, imagining it reporting on major historical events of the Western world: for instance, he wrote about "J. G. Caesar," who "scribbles a good deal; not for publication, just for the pure fun of the thing," and reviewed the first performance of Aeschylus's *Electra*, his "latest nerve-shatterer," a play "well worth a trip to the new State Theater."[22] That is, Agee imagined *Time* style compressing not just the events of a week but entire centuries between the covers of a single, slim volume. Agee's and Chambers's job applications make clear how easily *Time* style hops off the page of its own magazine and into many other formats.

Though *Time* style originated with Britton Hadden, the style slowly matriculated from his personal editorial taste into a work ethic distributed across the corporation. T. S. Matthews remembers, "All neophytes were expected to memorize Hadden's invented words and phrases and to use them at every opportunity." The task had lasting effects, according to Matthews; when he and his colleagues tried to stop writing in *Time* style, "the iron had so far entered our souls that the attempt at reform was never successful."[23] William Gottfried, another Time Inc. lifer, describes how the magazine's compression and stylistic tics quickly transformed into a form of self-censure: "The original Prospectus said that no story would occupy more than about seven inches of type. We tried to write this way, but gradually we found our medium changing under our hands . . . *Time*-style became not a formula of words, but a kind of mental discipline."[24] Gottfried describes the mutation of formal or spatial constraints into an approach to thinking about writing and then into an automatic way of writing that no longer requires thinking.

Time Inc.'s expansion into business news with *Fortune* in 1930, radio and newsreels with its *The March of Time* series in 1931, photojournalism with *Life* in 1936, and many other print-based and multimedia endeavors, created one of the most expansive and wealthiest media corporations of the twentieth century. As the range of publications grew, the "mental discipline" of *Time*-style was applied to a specific method for each new endeavor – the "corporation story" of *Fortune* and the "photo-magazine" format of *Life*, for example – but the ethos of "group journalism" continued to guide Time Inc.'s overarching editorial system. Each magazine developed its own focus, but the organizational model that makes editorial work transferable between writers also makes the administration of that work transferable between titles. Perhaps the best evidence of this is the promiscuous reappropriation of writers between periodicals within the organization. MacLeish wrote the Education column for *Time* and edited *Life*, alongside his role at *Fortune*. James Agee spent four years at *Fortune*, began writing book and later film reviews for *Time* in 1939, wrote special pieces for *Life*, and after 1945 served as a "rover," writing in any capacity and for any magazine that Luce required of him. For *Time*, Whittaker Chambers repeatedly moved between Foreign News and Books and wrote a cover story on Joyce's *Finnegan's Wake*, but then moved over to *Life* where, in 1947, he began a serialized history of Western civilization from the Middle Ages until the present.

For some, the flexible, anonymous form of group journalism signaled something positive. John Updike reflected on the reams of unsigned work James Agee published for Time Inc. by concluding, "surely a culture is enhanced, rather than disgraced, when men of talent and passion undertake anonymous and secondary tasks."[25] Following Updike's lead, it is only a slight stretch to place the Time Inc. employee's work alongside that of T. S. Eliot's ideal poet. Rather than emphasizing individual genius, Eliot claims "poetic originality is largely an original way of assembling the most disparate and unlikely material to make a new whole."[26] Both Luce and Eliot imagine the writer's project as organizing the sum total of one's reading into a new form that ideally cannot be tied to a single author. *Time* style's sublimation of individual writers into a corporate voice can look like a bowdlerized version of modernist "impersonality," especially the one laid out in "Tradition and the Individual Talent," where Eliot claims that an artist does not have a "personality" to express but rather "a particular medium which is only a medium and not a personality." "The poet cannot reach this impersonality without surrendering himself wholly to the work to be done," Eliot argues.[27] Ironically, this theory of impersonal authorship, in which "the work to be done" overrides the writer doing the work, also guides the editorial model at Time Inc. The difference is that no one questions who wrote either *The Waste Land* or *Ulysses*. Eliot's ideal author still gets to sign the finished product – and, in the case of *Ulysses*'s closing "Trieste-Zurich-Paris, 1914–1921," a date and location stamp of authorial composition. At Time Inc., the lofty hand that guides Eliot's individual poet, what he calls "the historical sense," materializes in the suspect form of a corporate "house style," a purely textual identity that supersedes the agents that work in its name.

Time Inc., as to be expected, had a different idea about its relationship to modernist experimentation. In its first issue, between a positive review of Gertrude Atherton's novel *Black Oxen* (1922) and a quotation about cubism from Clive Bell, "English critic and pontiff of modernism," *Time* gave an astonished takedown of *The Waste Land* and *Ulysses*. "Has the Reader Any Rights before the Bar of Literature?" asked the reviewer. In response to Joyce's and Eliot's perceived abuse of readerly rights, the reviewer claimed, "[t]here is a new kind of literature abroad in the land, whose only obvious fault is that no one can understand it."[28] Unlike *Time* style, Eliot's and Joyce's mode seemed to experiment for its own sake, rather than for the reader's benefit. Even worse, though, is that this intentionally meaningless writing found supporters in the periodical world: the article mentions that Eliot recently won *The Dial*'s prize for Outstanding Service to Letters. In addition, it outlines how Burton Rascoe at *The New York Tribune*, Edmund Wilson at *Vanity Fair*, and John Middleton Murry at *The Athenaeum* (referred to only as "a British critic") all positively review, and hence legitimize, Eliot's and Joyce's experiments.[29] All of this amounts to a "literary dictatorship," according to another article. A "semisecret cabal of radical young critics," a

> "youthful intelligentsia, occupying strategic positions in the publicity section of the literary world as editors and contributors to the "highbrow" weeklies, critics of books and drama, colyumnists [*sic*] and readers for publishing houses, have combined to form not alone a mutual admiration society; but also an exclusive literary coterie, admission to which is denied candidates who have not the personal friendship of the charter members. Only thoroughgoing social radicals are welcome. Clearness and cleanness, coupled with a sound belief in American institutions, is a fatal bar.[30]

Note *Time*'s singling out of the radicals' renunciation of "clearness and cleanness," two adjectives that closely echo Time Inc.'s self-designation as "Curt. Clear. Complete." And in juxtaposing two approaches to narrative experimentation, these early articles show what modernism's aesthetic and institutional "counterspace" looked like from the outside – a tentative and skeptical picture of the literary coterie from the position of those who can only access modernist prestige through the cloudy window of what the reviewers feel to be inscrutable texts.[31] *Time*, itself only two months old, does not say that an older generation refuses to let it in. Instead, it portrays a literary market quietly overrun by a minority of young "highbrow[s]" who are cutting out their forebears and "traditional" younger writers.[32]

Time Inc., then, saw itself in competition for market share with other commercial periodicals, but it also imagined a contest of legitimacy concerning various models of linguistic innovation.

The combination of organizational and artistic experimentation, and yet clear interest in commercial competition, led Time Inc. to be extremely possessive of its stable of writers, many of whom claimed that the organization made an indelible impression on their craft. Chambers claimed that his nine years at Time Inc. "was time enough in which to accumulate a body of work faithfully and carefully done, and to develop habits of working and thinking, a way of life and of the mind, very difficult to dismiss when it was abruptly broken off."[33] After only a few months at *Fortune*, Agee wrote more ambivalently about Time Inc.'s effect on his own writing: "For the past two weeks, particularly, writing has been very much on my mind. I've been steadily trying to do it, and haven't written a single good thing. The only writing I do which approaches decency is on this job – and on other stuff I seem to be pretty well congealed."[34] For Dwight MacDonald, whose most trenchant cultural criticism was often directed at his former employer, the eventual imbalance of personal writing and work writing was part of Time Inc.'s organizational model. While writing for *Fortune*, MacDonald also wrote for a little magazine, *The Miscellany*, in his "spare time." When he sent a copy to Luce, he received an irate letter in return, arguing that to write for anyone else constitutes a "betrayal of Time Inc." This "was not just a job, it was a vocation worthy of a man's whole effort, and pay was thought up by so-and-so [one of my fellow editors] late one night on the West Side subway between the Seventy-second and the Seventy-ninth street stations . . . This is a twenty-four hour profession, you never know when you may get an idea for us, and if you're all the time thinking about some damn little magazine," then MacDonald is not fulfilling his writerly obligations to Luce.[35] John Hersey's *Hiroshima* (1946) is another example of this. Hersey, who served as one of *Time*'s first correspondents during World War II (rather than an editor, who rewrote reports from other agencies), published his account of the bombing in the *New Yorker* rather than a Time Inc. title, which earned him Luce's eternal disdain. MacDonald's, Agee's, and Hersey's experiences register the company style becoming a discipline so pervasive, and something applied to all aspects of an employee's authorial career, that to write for someone else, even if that person is oneself, is considered theft.

Along with Agee's and Evans's *Let Us Now Praise Famous Men*, Kenneth Fearing's novel *The Big Clock* (1946) offers one of the most sustained fictional accounts of Time Inc.'s effect on a writer's outside activities.

Throughout the twenties and thirties, Fearing was a fairly well-known leftist poet. Associated with the Dynamo school and supported by two Guggenheim fellowships, he published several books of poetry that received high marks from reviewers. Despite this success he still faced financial trouble when not on a stipend, so to make ends meet he worked for *Time*, *Newsweek*, and several other news publications, while also writing pornographic crime stories for pulp magazines.[36] Unlike MacLeish's seamless integration into Time Inc.'s institutional life, Fearing took pains to keep his worlds separate. "I always begin to get suspicious," he told his son, "when I hear a poet talking about his *work*," implying that even using the same word for art and occupation is to allow the logic of labor into one's vocation.[37] In his 1956 essay "Reading, Writing, and the Rackets," Fearing reflected on how the collective composition model developed at Time Inc. presents a "curious reversal of custom that once prevailed in print." "The writer is paid (and very well paid) by the sponsoring corporation," he explained, "while he himself has become a corporate writer, one member of a large team . . . The writer has a private name, probably, and he probably has a distinct personality. But his divorce from the transmitted material is complete."[38] What Fearing laments here is a corporate publishing entity, or what he calls the "theaters of communication," that transforms from intermediary between writer and public into the primary agent.

   With this in mind, *The Big Clock* might be seen as a limit case for the total integration of work and writing, because the logic of the editorial office draws a thick outline around each character's existence. The main character, George Stroud, is an editor at *Crimeways* newsmagazine, one title in a vast media company called Janoth Enterprises clearly modeled on Time Inc. Echoing Kazin's litany of literary types that fill *Time*'s office, Stroud registers the strange scene of an office building filled with "frustrated ex-artists, scientists, farmers, writers, explorers, poets, lawyers, doctors, [and] musicians."[39] Stroud refers to the cumulative effect of this group as an "empire of intelligence" that shares the boundless perspective of Agee's parody: "Whatever the subject, it scarcely mattered," says Stroud. "What did matter was our private and collective virtuosity," which can turn any topic into a Janoth story. "What we decided in this room," he thinks, "more than a million of our fellow-citizens would read three months from now, and what they read they would accept as final . . . they would follow the reasoning we presented, remember the phrases, the tone of authority, and in the end their crystallized judgments would be ours" (23–24). What Luce and Hadden intimated, Fearing makes explicit:

it is the memorable phrases and "tone of authority" that are the wellspring of the company's appeal.

The problem for Stroud, as for Fearing, resides in the collective pronoun repeated earlier: the "we" of a depersonalized corporate voice, and the blanket "tone of authority" that erases the author. The novel captures this uneasy transformation of individual perspectives into a plural voice in its narrative structure, which offers successive, chapter-length first-person accounts from Stroud, Janoth, and the characters that come into contact with the company. In this way, Fearing borrows the experiments in fragmented narrative perspective associated with modernist novels such as Gertrude Stein's *Three Lives* (1909) and William Faulkner's *The Sound and the Fury* (1929) and turns them toward describing corporate life.[40] When George Stroud asks himself who or what, exactly, provides he and his fellow writers with the words they disseminate to the millions of readers, he cannot quite explain: "The moving impulse simply arrived, as we, on the face that the giant clock turned to the public, merely registered the correct hour of the standard time" (24). Uncovering the source of that "moving impulse," and how one connects to it, generates the fairly standard detective-murder plot of the novel. Earl Janoth's girlfriend, Pauline Delos, is found dead in her apartment, and George Stroud is handpicked to lead the investigation into who killed the woman. The novel builds its dramatic irony on the fact that Stroud's higher-ups do not know that he was having an affair with Pauline Delos, and hence that they put him in charge of finding himself. To take the informational imbalance between the employee and the employer one step further, Stroud also knows that Earl Janoth is the real killer. The plot that actually provides the novel's thrust, then, is not a whodunit – the reader and main character know that from the beginning – but instead a kind of shadow story in which we see Stroud redirecting the path of the investigation away from clues that lead to him, and toward clues that lead to Janoth.

To cover up his affair and expose his boss's guilt requires Stroud to see "the face of the giant clock" everywhere, which results in the all-encompassing visions of the clock:

> [T]he big clock was running as usual . . . Sometimes the hands of the clock actually raced, and at other times they hardly moved at all. But that made no difference to the big clock. The hands could move backward, and the time it told would be right just the same. It would still be running as usual, because all the other watches have to be set by the big one, which is even more powerful than the calendar, and to which one automatically adjusts his entire life. (6–7)

Though the novel clearly has no love for the automatic adjustments that one makes inside the clock, it does suggest the impulses that it imparts are not necessarily malevolent. Stroud describes the organization's perfect bureaucratic movement as "smooth and infinitely powered" (91), running on the energy of "five hundred sightless eyes" (138), "all of whom spent their lives conforming ... to a sort of overgrown, aimless, haphazard stenciling apparatus" (107). Yet to Stroud's surprise, the machinery of "the big clock" is extremely easy to manipulate. Part of its efficiency comes from being "blind, clumsy, [and] unreasoning" (91). When Stroud describes his goal to turn this unreasoning Clock against itself, he says, "If I picked the right kind of staff, twisted the investigation where I could, jammed it where I had to, pushed it hard where it was safe, it might be a very, very long time before they find George Stroud." All of this pushing, jamming, and twisting of the investigative machine is just, as Stroud repeatedly says, "the big clock running as usual." And rather than getting squashed, or crushed, or defiantly stripping the gears, he discovers the pliancy of its systematized work – really, its total indifference to the content that the machinery produces. From the outside, "the big clock" may seem monolithic, cold, and inhuman. But Stroud, with his jamming and pushing, discovers the opposite: he finds out how easily, even if unintentionally, someone aware of the way that the administration functions can take advantage of it. As an outsider on the inside, so to speak, Stroud can make the system work for him.

So "the big clock" describes the media corporation, Janoth Enterprises, and its role as a "haphazard stenciling apparatus" that standardizes the lives of its workers and readers by way of highly organized editorial work and the "tone of authority" housed in the periodical's content. However, when it is described as "haphazard," "blind," "sightless," and "clumsy," one begins to suspect the effectiveness of the clock's rational organization of employees and their work. The ease with which Stroud uses the clock-like media corporation for his own purposes makes it hard to read Janoth Enterprises as the embodiment of machine-like conformity, or, in turn, to read the novel as an outright excoriation of Fearing's corporate work. Part of the allegorical ambiguity of the clock comes from the difficulty of pinning down exactly where the technological center of that clock resides, or how it functions. Unlike the 1948 film adaptation, which places a clock tower in the center of the corporate offices, and features a fight scene inside of it, there aren't any actual clocks in the novel. Early on, Stroud philosophizes, "[f]or of course the clock that measures out the seasons, all gain and loss, the air Georgia [his wife] breathes, Georgette's [his daughter] strength, the figures shivering on the dials of my own inner instrument board, this gigantic watch that fixes order and establishes the pattern for chaos itself, it has never changed, it will never change, or be changed" (13). The big clock is so big that one can only glimpse its movements in the changing of the seasons; and at the same time it is so particularized one can breathe it in. More than this, Stroud's "own inner instrument board" makes him clock-like too, so that company, employee, and environment are seamlessly integrated. "The big clock," then, transforms from agent to background, from evil mover of things to a more banal medium through which things move. Or, put another way, Fearing evidences the way that *Time* style turns everything into company work, but he does so without Macdonald's outrage. The representations of Stroud's work as an editor in *The Big Clock* look increasingly like what one usually does outside of work: he eats with his family, goes to restaurants and bars, buys antiques and paintings, talks with friends. For Stroud, each of these actions now constitutes work, as his "work" at Janoth Enterprises is to investigate himself. Or, as Mark Seltzer might phrase it, when the media system that is the novel turns its attention to the daily work of media systems, in this case Janoth Enterprises, then the text models its own doubling of the world.[41] And, ultimately, this reflexive self-modeling is just how the world of modernity works – it is simply "the big clock running as usual," with no judgment attached.

If one can read reception history back into the novel, then *The Big Clock*'s grand statement about the effect of writing on company time is at best a tortured one. Despite the disapproval of Fearing's former avant-garde literary circle, who interpreted his trade of poetry for the detective novel as giving in to economic demands, *The Big Clock* became a runaway bestseller. A laudatory review in none other than *Time* magazine was followed by brisk sales and popular approval. All told, he made more than $60,000 from royalties, republications – including a condensation for *The American Magazine* – and film rights. *The Big Clock* even spawned its own subgenre of anti-Time Inc. crime procedurals: Ralph Ingersoll's *The Great Ones* (1948), John Brooks's *The Big Wheel* (1949), and William Brinkley's *The Fun House* (1961) are only a small sampling of fictional responses to Time Inc. employee-dom. In a strange way, though, this genre reinforces, rather than rejects, the magnetic pull of Time Inc.'s patronage. Certainly, *The Big Clock* and its followers start as ripostes to Luce's and Time Inc.'s roles in the lives of their authors, but then they end up carrying over their corporate jobs into the mental space of "serious" writing they hoped to cordon off. A similar feature shows up in James Agee's and Walker Evans's *Let Us Now Praise Famous Men*, which offers itself as an antidote to Time Inc.'s coverage of American poverty, but retains the basic organizational structure of its original setting – a three-part story for *Fortune* – as well as that magazine's skepticism toward governmental interventions in addressing economic inequality.

The contamination of authors' extracurricular work by their commercial day job can look like the dark mirror of the Popular Front's ideal of the writer as "total propagandist," someone who "take[s] an interest in as many imaginative, aesthetic and speculative fields as he can handle" and applies the same leftist politics to all.[42] Yet to place such a judgment on Time Inc.'s role in the organization and aesthetics of mass media and literature is to miss the variety of political positions of its staff and the eclectic artifacts it produced. While one can fault the company for the lack of gender and racial diversity on its masthead, the office culture was capacious enough in terms of politics and literary style for both Whittaker Chambers and Dwight MacDonald, for both *Let Us Now Praise Famous Men* and *Conquistador*. *The Big Clock*, for all its bluster, ends on an ambivalent note concerning what corporate patronage can do for an underfunded art culture. Stroud collects the abstract paintings of an unfashionable artist, Louise Patterson, and one particular painting he buys at an antique story on the night that he spent with Pauline becomes a key plot piece. The location of this painting, rather than that of the killer, becomes the subject of a media frenzy: articles are written about its centrality to the case, the magazine sends a team of investigators in search of it and the person who painted it, and, as one *Crimeways* reporter puts it, "we'd automatically find the picture when we found the man," a phrase that both semantically and syntactically prioritizes the aesthetic object over the nondescript suspect (153). In the course of all this publicity for the painting, its price tag skyrockets, as does the reputation of its artist. By the end of the novel, Patterson paintings are the new trend in art, and Stroud's painting is the most valuable piece. In another book, produced under different organizational circumstances, this might be characterized as a degradation of artistic value by bringing it into contact with a financially motivated media company. But Fearing has something else in mind. The painting depicts two hands exchanging a gold coin: one character names it "The Temptation of St. Judas," another names it "Toil," but Patterson, the artist who produced it, corrects them, calling it "Study in Fundamentals." The popular, multimedia success of a novel that was born in a media company and thematizes an all-encompassing idea of work suggests that, by 1946, a writer was much more likely to find success by aestheticizing corporate media than by rejecting it.

Notes

1. Archibald MacLeish, "The First Nine Years," in *Writing for Fortune* (New York: Time Inc., 1980), 10.

2. Archibald MacLeish, *Conquistador*, in *Collected Poems: 1917–1982* (Boston, MA: Houghton Mifflin, 1985), 180, 175.

3. See Willa Cather, "When I Knew Stephen Crane," in *Willa Cather: Stories, Poems, and Other Writings* (New York: Library of America, 1992), 932–38.

4. Archibald MacLeish, *Poetry and Journalism: A Lecture Delivered at Northrop Memorial Auditorium* (Minneapolis: University of Minneapolis Press, 1958), 3.

5. MacLeish, "The First Nine Years," 10.

6. MacLeish, *Poetry and Journalism*, 3.

7. Qtd. in Robert T. Elson, *Time Inc.: The Intimate History of a Publishing Enterprise, 1923–1941* (New York: Atheneum, 1968), 129.

8. Alfred Kazin, *Starting out in the Thirties* (Boston, MA: Little, Brown, 1962), 105.

9. For the impact of federal programs on literature, see Michael Szalay, *New Deal Modernism: American Literature and the Invention of the Welfare State* (Durham, NC: Duke University Press, 2000); for the Hollywood studios, see Jerome Christensen, *America's Corporate Art: The Studio Authorship of Hollywood Pictures* (Stanford, CA: Stanford University Press, 2012).

10. Kazin, *Starting out*, 104.

11. For a more complete treatment of *Time*'s portmanteaus and neologisms, see Joseph J. Firebraugh, "The Vocabulary of 'Time,'" *American Speech* 15.3 (1940), 232–42; Norris Yates, "The Vocabulary of *Time* Magazine Revisited," *American Speech* 56.1 (1981), 53–63.

12. Matthew Schnierov, *The Dream of a New Social Order: Popular Magazines in America 1893–1914* (New York: Columbia University Press, 1994), 6.

13. Qtd. in Elson, *Time Inc.*, 6.

14. Alan Brinkley, *The Publisher: Henry Luce and His American Century* (New York: Knopf, 2010), 136.

15. Qtd. in Frank Luther Mott, *A History of American Magazines, Vol. 5: 1905–1930* (Cambridge, MA: Harvard University Press, 1968), 295; *Time*, March 3, 1923, 2.

16. Qtd in Mott, *History*, 295.

17. Qtd. in Robert Vanderlan, *Intellectuals Incorporated: Politics, Art, and Ideas inside Henry Luce's Media Empire* (Philadelphia: University of Pennsylvania Press, 2012), 17.

18. Qtd. in Elson, *Time Inc.*, 197.

19. Walcott Gibbs, "*Time* ... *Fortune* ... Life ... Luce," *New Yorker* 12.41 (1936), 21.

20. For a longer list of *Time* parodies, see Brinkley, *The Publisher*, 129.

21. Chambers recounts his early days at Time Inc. in *Witness*, 85–90. The review he mentions is "The Menacing Sun," *Time* (May 1, 1939), reprinted in Whittaker Chambers, *Ghosts on the Roof: Selected Journalism of Whittaker Chambers, 1931–1959*, ed. Terry Teachout (Washington, DC: Regnery Gateway, 1989), 49.
22. Qtd. in Laurence Bergreen, *James Agee: A Life* (New York: Penguin, 1985), 105–06.
23. Qtd. in Brinkley, *The Publisher*, 128.
24. Qtd. in Elson, *Time Inc.*, 84.
25. Qtd. in James Agee, *Selected Journalism*, ed. Paul Ashdown (Knoxville: University of Tennessee Press, 1985), xv.
26. T. S. Eliot, *The Frontiers of Criticism* (Minneapolis: University of Minnesota Press, 1956), 9.
27. T. S. Eliot, "Tradition and the Individual Talent," in *The Sacred Wood* (1920; repr. London: Methuen, 1960), 57, 59.
28. "Shantih Shantih Shantih," *Time* (March 2, 1923), 12.
29. In 1939, Burton Rascoe emended his praise of Eliot and wrote a relatively well-known reappraisal in *Newsweek*. See Rascoe, "Shreds and Tatters," *Newsweek*, April 3, 1939, 40.
30. "Free for All?" *Time*, April 28, 1923, 11.
31. See Lawrence Rainey, *Institutions of Modernism: Literary Elites and Public Culture* (New Haven, CT: Yale University Press, 1998).
32. For a reading of how writers appropriate or distance themselves from experiments in news coverage, rather than vice versa, see David Rando, *Modernist Fiction and the News: Representing Experience in the Early Twentieth Century* (London: Palgrave, 2011).
33. Chambers, *Witness*, 87.
34. James Agee, *Letters of James Agee to Father Flye* (New York: George Braziller, 1962), 56.
35. Dwight Macdonald, *Against the American Grain* (New York: Random House, 1952), 33; interpolation in original.
36. Funding highbrow endeavors with popular projects certainly is not unique to Fearing. In fact, during this period it is fairly close to the norm. One might read it as analogous to H. L. Mencken subsidizing *The Smart Set* with the *Black Mask*.
37. Qtd. in Robert M. Ryley, "Introduction," in *Complete Poems of Kenneth Fearing* (Orono, ME: National Poetry Foundation, 1994), xiii.
38. Kenneth Fearing, "Reading, Writing, the Rackets," in *New and Selected Poems* (Bloomington: Indiana University Press, 1956), ix–xxiv.
39. Kenneth Fearing, *The Big Clock* (1946; repr. London: Orion, 2001), 107. Hereafter cited parenthetically in the text.
40. Socially minded fiction in the 1930s and 1940s often appropriated the techniques of modernism for overtly political ends, especially the genre that Barbara Foley calls "the collective novel." See *Radical Representations:*

Politics and Form in U.S. Proletarian Fiction, 1929–1941 (Durham, NC: Duke University Press, 1993), 398–442.

41. See Mark Seltzer, *The Official World* (Durham, NC: Duke University Press, 2016).

42. Kenneth Burke, Address to the 1935 American Writer's Conference, qtd. in Michael Denning, *The Cultural Front: The Laboring of American Culture in the Twentieth Century* (London: Verso, 1997), 103.

CHAPTER 21

The Communist Party

Christopher Phelps

"The night the bank failed, Frank's baby died." Given its succinct association of capitalism with darkness, dolorousness, and death, this austere line from a short story published in the *New Masses* in 1931 might serve as a one-sentence distillation of the proletarian fiction championed by the Communist Party of the United States of America (CPUSA) in its Depression heyday. The story in which it appeared, "Can You Make Out Their Voices," tells of a rural region facing drought, economic severity, and starvation. The impoverished farmers take matters into their own hands by shouldering rifles and marching on the Red Cross to seize milk and bread for their children and community. The story may be classed within the preferred genres of left-wing literature in the Depression decade – social realism and proletarian literature – but it fit a more select category as well: dramatic representation of the American Communist experience.

At its height in the early thirties, "proletarian literature" was pervaded by ambiguity. Was it to be written by proletarians? To take proletarians as its subject? Or simply to inspire a revolutionary view of the world – and if the latter, could it be written by anyone and could its protagonists be drawn from the middle class or even the rich?[1] "Can You Make Out Their Voices" somehow managed to satisfy the stricter side of all these criteria at once. It was authored by a young, impecunious, déclassé writer; it placed hardscrabble dirt farmers at the center of its drama; and it exemplified the potential for an avowedly Communist fiction focused upon the revolutionary organizer as its subject. Here was a Bolshevism of the backcountry, Lenin's *What Is to Be Done?* set in a fictive American landscape. The story's protagonist, a militant Communist, is thought "queer" by his community because of his politics, but that very iconoclasm enables him to fan the flames of discontent and inspire mass action. Although the story is bleak, foreboding, and ominous, it conveys a desperate heroism, implying that class uprisings will not arise spontaneously from hard times or injustice –

that they require a tiny dedicated core, stoked with a proper analysis of social forces, ready with appropriate strategies and tactics, willing to transgress law and convention, and courageous enough to lead the way as a revolutionary vanguard.

In the year "Can You Make Out Their Voices" was published, 1931, its thirty-year-old author published three more stories – a total of four – in the *New Masses*. One, set in China, depicts revolutionaries who skirmish with soldiers and face capture and death, concluding, "The march to victory is up the sharp side of mountains." The October *New Masses* cover story was "Our Comrade Munn," a portrayal of a Communist in a New England factory town who challenges a complacent Party branch leadership before he is shot and killed by police on a picket line. "Death of the Communists" portrays men before a prison firing squad who go to their deaths singing "The Internationale." Each of the four tales, then, puts Communist activity at its crux. Each is told omnisciently, suggesting how others might view Communists, rather than in a first-person mode getting at the interiority of Communist experience. Most of the stories end in ruination, with historical necessity supplying ultimate justification for revolutionary commitment, and with death as motif. The stories, in short, are philosophical existentialism *avant la lettre*, with Communist commitment cast as a desperate way of imbuing life with purpose. Their ambience, a Spenglerian Stalinism, borders on despondence.[2]

Yet the first of the stories, especially, resonated in its time and place. International Publishers, the Party imprint, released it as a pamphlet under the modified title *Can You Hear Their Voices?* A Soviet literary critic in *International Literature* praised the author as one of the *New Masses*' "best contributors" and said the story "for the first time in American literature gives a revolutionary exposition of the problem of the agricultural crisis and correctly raises the question of the leading role of the Communist Party in the revolutionary farmers' movement."[3] The story was made into a play by Hallie Flanagan of the Vassar Experimental Theatre and subsequently staged around the nation, a breakthrough that set Flanagan on course to direct the Federal Theatre Project under the New Deal. *The New Masses* bestowed recognition on the story's author by drafting him onto its editorial board and, in 1932, elevating him to managing editor. In the following year, Lincoln Steffens – the muckraking journalist whose autobiography, published in 1931, sparked interest in the Soviet Union among intellectuals – wrote to the author, saying, "My hat came off while I was reading today a story of yours. How you can write! ... Whenever I hear people talking about 'proletarian art and literature,' I'm going to ask them to shut their mouths and look at you."[4]

By the time Steffens wrote that, however, the intended recipient had vanished from view. He was living under assumed names, having become a secret operative for Soviet intelligence in the United States. It was a furtive, underground form of Communist commitment, one that his fiction – focused on the agitator – did not anticipate. Despite a note in the *New Masses* saying he was "at work on a novel" and had "just completed a one-act play on a miners' strike," the author never again published any creative fiction.[5] The demands of his new life, followed some six years later by his rupture with Communism out of disillusionment over the Moscow Trials, brought an end to his left-wing literary output. His failure to ever publish a novel may explain why his four *New Masses* stories are mentioned only in passing, if at all, in histories of proletarian literature and American Communist fiction, but another reason lies in his name: Whittaker Chambers.

Chambers would become famous when, as an editor at *Time* magazine, he testified before the House Committee on Un-American Activities (HUAC) in 1948 at the dawn of the Cold War, accusing high-ranking State Department official Alger Hiss of having passed classified government information to him in the thirties. In *Witness* (1952), his bestselling autobiography, he would marshal the same mood he once brought to the *New Masses* – dark, portentous, with a tragic sense of history – but against Communism. Hiss went to prison, convicted for perjury for denying Chambers's charges under oath, but in years to come a number of commentators would portray that verdict and Chambers's *National Review* conservatism as inseparable from McCarthyism's unjust crescendo. Their doubts about Chambers's veracity seemed vindicated as Richard M. Nixon, the Republican HUAC member who first gained prominence by championing Chambers, became President, prolonged the Vietnam War, and then resigned from office after the Watergate cover-up, suggesting he might have been mendacious in the Hiss–Chambers affair too. However, compelling evidence – especially the Venona archival releases referring to a Soviet source high in the State Department code-named "ALES" – now indicates that Chambers testified far more accurately than Hiss.[6]

Chambers's forgotten left-wing literary career, followed by his pathway from Soviet agent to conservative renegade, is emblematic of the dual quality of the American Communist cultural experience. On the one hand those published in the *New Masses*, whether Party members or close to the Party (a group far larger in number), generated a body of work that amalgamated radical political consciousness with creative literature, fostering a culture of labor and class resistance combined with opposition to empire, racial oppression, and war. Varied in quality, sometimes stulti-fying, it was also at times quite original and finely tuned in its craft and art. Although American, these works of fiction, poetry, and reportage may not have come into being at all if not for the inspiration provided by the Russian Revolution and the promise it seemed to hold of a society better than capitalism, as well as the resources and cultural institutions the Communist movement supplied, such as the *New Masses*. Chambers's life equally demonstrates, however, that the Communist movement, by subordinating the fortunes of American radicalism to the leadership of a foreign state, left itself vulnerable to the twists and turns, at times jolting, of a political line set abroad. As the reality of the Soviet party-state headed by Joseph Stalin became plain, the trickle of defections became a flood. In Chambers, this double-sidedness is embodied within one life.

Communism, this is to say, *structured* intellectual commitment and literary production. It did so by means of internalized discipline, institu-tional control, resource deployment, and a resolutely applied political line. Consequently, the Party structured a swathe of intellectual life well beyond its membership. It accomplished that both by formal front groups and the influence of members in such influential professions as publishing, the arts, music, theatre, and journalism. Chambers's *New Masses* fictional represen-tations were imbued with the value and meaning of this structuring – his heroes were Communist Party militants – and he manifested such rever-ence for it in his own life that he was willing to set aside his artistic ambition and literary work to take up an underground existence.

Recent literary histories have tended to portray Communist writers and intellectuals in largely favorable terms as American radicals first and fore-most, admirable for their social and political commitments. Some of these studies adopt a biographical method, whether in focusing on individual lives or weaving composite tapestries. Others are framed by themes or ideas such as the "laboring" of culture. Both approaches, biographical and thematic, abound with insights and archival findings that have expanded and enriched our understanding of the Communist literary experience of the 1930s generation.[7] Out of desire to locate a usable past and exonerate past radicalisms, however, some contemporary scholars have obscured or downplayed the nature of the Communist Party's organizational discipline and congruence with Stalin's Soviet Union – or even romanticized, cele-brated, or justified that dependency in some manner.[8] While McCarthyist caricatures of American Communists as regimented or robotic are properly discredited, a corrective or supplementation is in order that gives greater consideration to the core *structuring* of Communist life. The CPUSA was significant not only for the doctrines and ideas it promoted, such as Marxist philosophy, but for structuring the everyday experience of those in and near it. Communists and their fellow-traveling allies adhered willingly to a politics and organizational flowchart that tied them to Joseph Stalin's Soviet Union, with disastrous moral and political consequences.

The political line functioned less often as a set of explicit directives (though sometimes that was its exact nature) than as a tether granting latitude within a prescribed circumference, with room for variance in local application. Liberal critics of Communism, particularly during the Cold War, often compared Communism to a religion with its own dogmas, scriptures, rituals, and saints. The analogy is plausible but it is better to comprehend the CPUSA as an outpost in a bureaucratic mode of production. In the Soviet Union, the promised workers' control of the early revolutionary years had given way to single-party administrative rule in replacement of private property. That state provided a foundation for the American Communist Party, a base upon which forms of culture arose. This structuring of political and intellectual life explains why Communist policy, ideology, and even aesthetic criteria could shift quite dramatically, for all were linked to the foreign policy of the Soviet Union.

How structure illuminates the individual American Communists' lived experience may be seen, up close, in one forgotten New York writer's life, that of Hank Fuller. Shortly after the New Year in 1934, Fuller wrote to his girlfriend Muriel Rukeyser, whose *Theory of Flight*, published the following year, would help make her a major American poet, to inform her that "a new branch, Ernst Torgler, has been formed on the lower East Side." The branch's name, he felt no need to say, signified antifascist ardor by alluding to the name of the leader of the German Communist Party's Reichstag delegation prior to the Nazi seizure of power. "It now has about 25 members, the vast majority unemployed. They are such fine people. We do business in three languages . . . I am tactless, tend to be dictatorial at times, other times giving in too easily. There is friction, most of it healthy and work goes on." In the prior year, Fuller and Rukeyser had journeyed to Alabama, where nine young African-American men were on trial for rape of two white women at Scottsboro in what Communists believed a frame-up. He and she shared a commitment to writing, although Fuller's orientation was more down-market. Once he had written for the *New Republic* and a leading African-American newspaper, the *Chicago Defender*; now his output was for pulps. "The sex story sold without difficulty at the place which was interested in things miscegenated," one of his letters reported. "The new editor likes me," he wrote in another. "I left some rank pornography and hope the hell they pay a little something ... I once wrote a lot of things for him which sold to the sidewalk sex-starved and all the hunters of perverts."[9]

Fuller needed the money. Having lived in New York six years since migrating from Florida, he was making only $15 a week at a Civil Works Administration job as a clerk, plus his haphazard pay as a Communist organizer. "The Section owes me about $7 to $10. It may pay sometime." Fuller's political organizing did not always go smoothly. "Things, even the Party line," he wrote, "do not travel directly from point of inception to point of culmination." The police broke up demonstrations at Union Square. Fear abounded, with one comrade believing "there will be a massacre and the Party will be driven underground." Still, the pulse of action was quickening. By August, Fuller was pleased to relate that the *Daily Worker* would go into three editions at the beginning of October: "There will be a morning and an evening one here in the city also an enlarged national."[10]

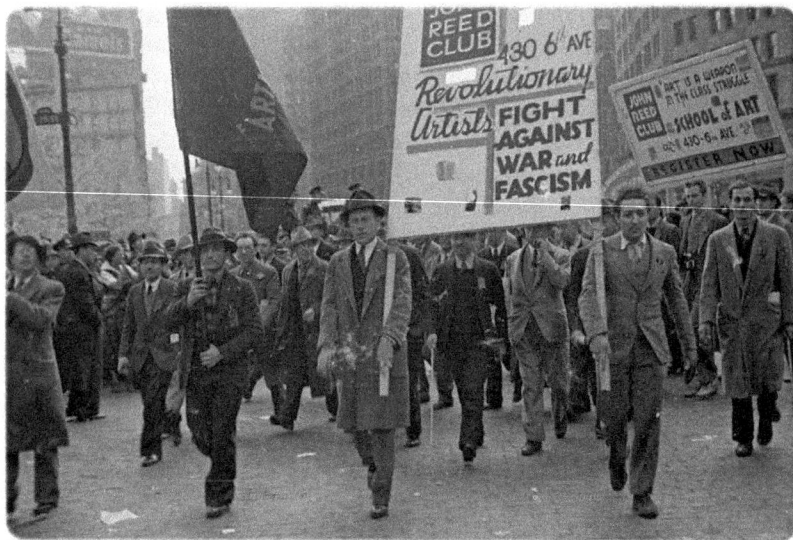

Figure 21.1 Ben Shahn. A John Reed Club demonstration in Manhattan, May Day 1935.

As a Party organizer, Fuller's life was highly structured every day of the week. "During the week it was class on Monday and later a political meeting on a street corner," he wrote to Rukeyser.

> Then Tuesday it was a long street corner meeting at which I spoke over an hour. Wednesday I again spoke on the Lower East Side and Thursday I spoke in the Square ... Tonight it is a Slovak branch meeting and god knows I speak no Russian, Ukrainian, or whatever it may be that the members of the Slovak branch speak. Sunday, as yet, is not scheduled for activity beyond an executive meeting at 1. In between I have worked two days for the city, run around for the District, and chased halls, individuals, etc.

Even within a single day, the Party supplied structure. "Am tired out and wanting you so much tonight," he wrote one evening.

> First Buro, then Section Committee and it was nearly 4PM. Then at the District in search of a definition, 5:45. Ate. Downtown to a boys' club, nearly all Jewish and the kids are afraid to protest against Hitler terror. The bosses' America. "Only the Communists kick and they get nowhere." Then two churches, Negro, and so much God they have no time for lynchings. Then a strike, food workers and there was an arrest, and now home. Made contact with one nice Negro family. Found one preacher a rat and no kidding. Have made one friend among the boys and have arranged to speak at a boys' club and at the strike tomorrow night. In between times, so lonesome. A Jewish comrade, member CP, USSR, moves in here tomorrow. He is older.[11]

Meetings, demonstrations, speeches, fund-raising, leaflet-writing: every day and night in the life of the dedicated Communist in the 1930s was shaped by structure. Orrick Johns, who joined in San Francisco and went on to edit the *New Masses* in New York, said that during his four years in the CPUSA, "I no longer had a personal life, in the sense of being my own master. I was the servant of a cause, and a semi-legal cause, under the control of my superiors at all times." Quotidian life in the Party was "dry, dull, and repetitious," he wrote, a phrase echoed in Granville Hicks's description of Party life as "dull as dishwater," akin to a volunteer fire association. A workhorse culture meant that Communists were often credited for being the ones in unions and other social movements who, in the words of Elizabeth Hawes, "do all the work, distribute the leaflets, sweep the hall, make the sandwiches" – "the only ones who always turn up and can be depended upon."[12]

By this structuring of activity, the Party superseded the subjective intentions of those who comprised it. Contrary to psychoanalytic claims that all Communists were disturbed, individual Communists were of every personality type. "Of the admirable persons I have known in my life, a considerable proportion belonged – and some still belong – to the Communist Party," wrote Hicks after breaking with it. "There is more self-seeking in the average church, more hypocrisy on the average college faculty, more opportunism in the average charitable society than there is in the Communist Party."[13] According to Hawes, there were two kinds of Party members. One was the Catechismic Communist who "knew everything out of books and if life did not accord with the book, then life was wrong." This sort "couldn't live unless under strict orders" and "believed themselves very disciplined but in reality . . . were either afraid to use their heads or couldn't." The other was the Common Comrade or "average CP member one met in union work," who had an "unusual staunchness" derived from a "deep belief in socialism" that "made him an unusually hard worker along whatever line he chose to go." This divided assessment was impressively honest to an extent, but Hawes's portrait of a Communist picking up "whatever line he chose" was fanciful, for as she well knew, Party commitment mitigated against pure individualism.[14]

Just as the prism of structure clarifies the nature of individual Communist experience and helps explain how the Party melded varied personalities into a common purpose, structure illuminates the broader left-wing political and cultural landscape of the 1930s. Across the decade, the CPUSA sponsored key cultural institutions and initiatives corresponding to strategic phases set by the Communist International. With the ultra-left "revolutionary" phase between 1928 and 1933 came a "proletarian" emphasis on art as a weapon in the class struggle. After the shock of the 1933 Nazi triumph came a less determinate phase that in 1935 crystallized as the People's Front, with opposition to fascism elevated to the foreground. Last came a brief ultra-leftism brought on by the Nazi–Stalin "non-aggression" pact that ended with the 1941 Nazi invasion of the Soviet Union. Political-diplomatic history, given its focus on espionage, has come to consensus about Soviet oversight of the American Communist apparatus. A good deal of social-historical and literary scholarship on American Communism, however, continues to emphasize Party members' organizing among the unemployed and labor, opposition to racism, resistance to fascism, and contributions to arts and letters while downplaying the hierarchical nature of Party structure, dependency on Soviet direction, and reversals of line. Earlier treatments in the secondary literature minced no words over these realities and their consequences. "Stalin converted the literary practitioners into a public information army of the Soviet state," wrote Daniel Aaron in *Writers on the Left* (1961) – still the best single-volume history of the American literary left between the wars, one careful to resist crudities regarding Communist writers and their work.[15]

In the 1930s, the CPUSA openly boasted that its "democratic centralism" required members' structural subordination to a Central Committee and loyalty to the Communist International and Soviet Union.[16] Granville Hicks, a Harvard instructor who was among the most prominent of Communist literary intellectuals, came to regret that he "refused to see that the Communist Party of the United States was completely subservient to the Soviet Union," but he may not have been so unaware since at the American Writers Congress in 1937 he declared himself "confident that sooner or later Communism will be established throughout the world, and that its establishment will begin – that, indeed, the founding of the Soviet Union has already begun – a new era in human history."[17] Devotion to the Soviet Union was the sine qua non of Communist politics. It is precisely what the Communists' critics on the radical left most objected to, as when Dwight Macdonald faulted the American Writers Congress for requiring "an a priori agreement on Stalinist policies," or when Socialist leader Norman Thomas, in a 1935 Madison Square Garden debate with Earl Browder, said, "I trust the democracy of a party more than I trust a rule from on top, a centralization so great that orders are handed down from Moscow ... so that some of you have been made rather dizzy changing your minds to keep up with the correct line."[18]

On one level, of course, the Soviet Union functioned purely as inspiration. The October Revolution, in the words of Joshua Kunitz, was a "cultural revolution."[19] Its example gave American writers and artists permission to explore themes of class struggle between exploiters and exploited. Strikes abounded in the plays of Clifford Odets, the fiction of Michael Gold and Agnes Smedley, and the art of William Gropper and Hugo Gellert, among others. Out of the mines, mills, logging camps, and factories, it was hoped, a new drama, art, poetry, and literature would originate. Gold, an advocate of American emulation of Soviet "Prolet-Kult," wrote, "When there is singing and music rising in every American street, when in every American factory there is a drama-group of workers, when mechanics paint in their leisure, and farmers write sonnets, the greater art will grow and only then."[20] This "proletarian realism" had its left-wing critics from the beginning, such as Edmund Wilson, who argued that proletarian literature made no more sense as a concept than proletarian chemistry, or the Harlem writer Claude McKay, who, worrying over the likely diminution of literary standards, mocked Gold for wanting to print "doggerel from lumberjacks and stevedores and true revelations from chambermaids."[21]

Nevertheless, the worker-writer impulse allowed the Party to sponsor the John Reed Clubs of the early thirties, which promoted raw, untutored writers in the Communist orbit. Meanwhile, the economic crisis was radicalizing new swathes of traditional intellectuals. Soviet Russia, with its Five-Year Plan and claim of full employment, provided a stark contrast with the wasteful, anarchic, capitalist economies. "I have been over into the future, and it works," declared Lincoln Steffens upon returning from Moscow.[22] Theodore Dreiser, author of *Sister Carrie* (1900), took a trip to Kentucky to report on the bitter Harlan County coal mining strike and returned to say, "My solution for the difficulties of the world, and particularly those in America, is Communism."[23] By 1932, fifty-three writers and intellectuals, from John Dos Passos to Langston Hughes, were prepared to endorse the Communist ticket, declaring in *Culture and the Crisis*: "As responsible intellectual workers we have aligned ourselves with the frankly revolutionary Communist Party, the party of the workers."[24]

That rhetorical fusion of party and class was telling, for it made "proletarian" synonymous with Communist. Rather than being open to all radical working-class currents, however, the Communist Party was monolithic, having expelled two key factions at Moscow's insistence.[25] Despite having only 10,000–15,000 members, the Party projected itself as the vanguard of millions. "The leader of the revolution in all its stages is the Communist Party," presidential candidate William Z. Foster wrote in *Toward Soviet America* (1932), promising a "proletarian dictatorship" of single-party rule through suppression of all political rivals. "Under the dictatorship all the capitalist parties – Republican, Democratic, Progressive, Socialist, etc. – will be liquidated, the Communist Party functioning alone as the Party of the toiling masses."[26]

The quest for a proletarian art superior to bourgeois culture was embedded within the mindset of the Third Period (1928–33), a phase of Comintern policy in which vitriol was directed against all rivals on the left as "social-fascists." This policy led to physical attacks on Socialists, most famously at Madison Square Garden in 1934. Such attitudes, and the regime originating them, had begun to produce revulsion. In his "Ballad of an Intellectual" (1932), poet e. e. cummings, whose trip to the Soviet Union persuaded him that Communism was authoritarian, wrote:

Now all you morons of sundry classes
(who read the Times and who buy the Masses)
... I mightn't think (and you mightn't too)
that a Five Year Plan's worth a Gay Pay Oo
and both of us might irretrievably pause
ere believing that Stalin is Santa Clause.[27]

Lewis Mumford, similarly, wrote to Edmund Wilson and Malcolm Cowley in 1932 that he saw no value in "being tied up even temporarily with a party whose official ideology – dialectical materialism – seems to me as unsound as it is cocky and self-confident, and whose political tactics are so transparently opportunist."[28]

Viewed from another angle, however, the Communists could seem impressively bold compared to the weak tea of social democracy. The perception that Communists "really meant it" carried through after 1933 as the menace of Hitler began to propel artists, teachers, writers, journalists, and professionals leftward. In the context of the New Deal, with a revived labor movement in the offing, there was immense appeal in the People's Front against fascism announced by the Seventh World Congress of the Communist International in August 1935. "Every anti-fascist is needed in this united front," Gold pronounced. "There must be no base factional quarrels."[29] With right-wing authoritarianism and militarism ascendant in Italy, Germany, and Japan, even the flagship American liberal periodicals, *The Nation* and *The New Republic*, supported a "democratic front" that included the Soviet Union. As Party membership soared to some 80,000 members, the Spanish Civil War of 1936–39 seemed the frontline battle in halting the advance of fascism. Some Americans, including Hank Fuller, journeyed there to fight in the Abraham Lincoln Brigade, while far more attended fund-raising cocktail parties for Loyalist Spain, from Hollywood to Park Avenue. More people from upper-class origins than ever before were attracted to what one called "the fashionable pose of being a Communist."[30]

In this context the worker was displaced by "the people" in the left-wing literary imagination. The John Reed Clubs, with their untrained proletarian writers, were shunted aside for new Popular Front efforts drawing on illustrious literary names such as those of Ernest Hemingway, John Steinbeck, and Dorothy Parker. This disbanding of the John Reed Clubs – opposed by Richard Wright, for one, who became a writer through them – was a decision made by Earl Browder on the Ninth Floor of Party headquarters on East Thirteenth Street in New York City, and passed down by Alexander Trachtenberg, informally considered the Party's "cultural commissar."[31] The result was the American Writers Congress, which gave birth to the League of American Writers. In *The Nation*, Kenneth Burke declared that "this congress was unquestionably made possible only by the vitality and organizational ability of the Communist Party."[32] In the exuberance of the moment, American Communists were given to writing articles with titles such as "USSR – Land of Real Democracy," but democracy, as all of this indicates, was never the organizing principle of the Communist movement.[33] Interventions by midlevel Party functionaries, particularly if heavy-handed, could rankle writers and intellectuals. Budd Schulberg, the Hollywood screenwriter and author of the satirical novel *What Makes Sammy Run?* (1941), broke with the Party after his brush with one such authority, V. J. Jerome: "I came away with the conviction that the Communists I had known before, with two possible exceptions, were innocent amateurs, and that I had seen at last the true face of the Party, the face of the political commissar, rigid, narrow, dictatorial, defending each devious twist and turn of the Party Line as if it were eternal truth."[34]

The antifascism of the Popular Front was itself structured. Despite ritual appeals to unity, it would admit no radical, no matter how resolutely opposed to fascism, who was fundamentally critical of Stalin's Soviet Union – an exclusion that transpired at the very moment when Stalin's Great Purges were extinguishing millions of lives. When Waldo Frank, first chair of the League of American Writers, came to doubt the Moscow Trials, he was immediately removed from his honorary position in 1937. Browder, speaking to the American Writers Congress, spoke of "a broad unity of all democratic and progressive forces against the rising menace of fascist barbarism" – and then, in the same breath, condemned anarchists and Trotskyists in Spain as "agents of the fascists."[35] From exile in Mexico, Leon Trotsky denounced the Soviet "Thermidor," arguing that Popular Front conciliation of bourgeois liberalism and the purges were conjoint manifestations of the Stalinist bureaucracy's conservative retreat from proletarian revolution. A number of talented intellectuals – including James T. Farrell, Edmund Wilson, John Dos Passos, V. F. Calverton, Sidney Hook, C. L. R. James, and the editors of *Partisan Review*, originally an organ of the John Reed Clubs of New York – criticized the Communist Party from the left.[36] The Communist press branded them all "Trotskyite," a term of abuse meant to place them beyond the pale and inhibit others from considering their perspectives seriously.

A coda to the decade came with the Nazi–Soviet pact of August 1939. It and the ensuing invasion of Poland appalled Popular Front liberals who had imagined the Soviet Union to be an implacable bulwark against fascism and war. The Party's reputation would never recover as the consequences of structure became painfully apparent. "Even if our efforts had done no harm," wrote Hicks, remembering various Popular Front initiatives, "they did almost no good, for the Party liquidated the whole antifascist front, which we had worked so hard to create."[37] Although two years later the United States would enter a Grand Alliance with the Soviet Union, never again did many intellectuals trust the CPUSA. Fidelity to Stalin's foreign policy left Communists vulnerable in the McCarthy era, by which time Common Comrades were difficult to discern from Catechismics. "When an individual has accepted three or four changes of line, reversing his stated opinions each time," wrote Hicks, "he does not have much left with which he can resist."[38] Though some Communists may still have had the best of intentions, their minds were, in a word, structured.

Notes

1. These questions are posed in Irving Howe and Lewis Coser, *The American Communist Party* (1957; New York: Da Capo, 1974): 302–03; and Walter B. Rideout, *The Radical Novel in the United States, 1900–1954: Some Interrelations of Literature and Society* (Cambridge, MA: Harvard University Press, 1965): 166–70.
2. These four stories of 1931 were "Can You Make Out Their Voices," *New Masses* 6.10 (March 1931), 7–16; "You Have Seen the Heads," *New Masses* 6.11 (April 1931), 14–16; "Our Comrade Munn," *New Masses* 7.5 (October 1931), 13–17; and "Death of the Communists," *New Masses* 7.7 (December 1931), 10–12.
3. A. Elistratova, "New Masses," *International Literature* 1.1 (1932), 110. One American Communist who traveled to Moscow found that Elistratova, a regular and stern Soviet judge of American literary production, was "a twenty-year-old apple-cheeked girl who knew English imperfectly and absolutely nothing about the United States," according to Daniel Aaron, *Writers on the Left: Episodes in Literary Communism* (New York: Harcourt, Brace, 1961), 437.
4. *The Letters of Lincoln Steffens, Vol. II: 1920–1936* (New York: Harcourt, Brace, 1938), 961.
5. *New Masses* 7.5 (October 1931), 31.
6. This turning of consensus began with Allen Weinstein, *Perjury: The Hiss–Chambers Case* (New York: Knopf, 1978). See also National Security Agency and Central Intelligence Agency, *Venona: Soviet Espionage*

and the American Response, 1939–1957 (Washington, DC: Center for the Study of Intelligence, 1996).

7. For landmark works, consider Michael Denning, *The Cultural Front* (London: Verso, 1997), and the trilogy by Alan M. Wald: *Exiles from a Future Time: The Forging of the Mid-Twentieth-Century Literary Left* (Chapel Hill: University of North Carolina Press, 2002); *Trinity of Passion: The Literary Left and the Antifascist Crusade* (Chapel Hill: University of North Carolina Press, 2007); *American Night: The Literary Left in the Era of the Cold War* (Chapel Hill: University of North Carolina Press, 2012).

8. A prolific and emphatic historian of this school is Gerald Horne; softer forms exist in others, including some with great talent and influence, such as Robin D. G. Kelley.

9. Hank Fuller to Muriel Rukeyser, January 3, 1934 and n.d. (Muriel Rukeyser Papers, The Henry W. and Albert A. Berg Collection of English and American Literature, The New York Public Library, Astor, Lenox and Tilden Foundations).

10. Hank Fuller to Muriel Rukeyser, January 3, February 7, and August 28, 1934, August 28, n.y. (Rukeyser Papers).

11. Hank Fuller to Muriel Rukeyser, "Saturday" [n.d., n.y.] and 12:40A.M. [n.d., n.y.] (Rukeyser Papers).

12. Orrick Johns, *Time of Our Lives* (New York: Stackpole Sons, 1937), 322, 351; Granville Hicks, *Where We Came Out* (New York: Viking, 1954), 43; Elizabeth Hawes, *Hurry Up Please It's Time* (n. p.: Cornwall Press, 1946), 84.

13. Granville Hicks, "Communism and the American Intellectuals," in *Whose Revolution? A Study of the Future Course of Liberalism in the United States*, ed. Irving DeWitt Talmadge (New York: Howell, Soskin, 1941): 99, 102.

14. Hawes positioned herself merely as a "non-Red-Baiter" despite a long history of writing for the *Daily Worker*. The book appeared in the postwar period when the Party was expunging "Browderism" and taking a Stalinist "revolutionary" turn under William Z. Foster. In elevating the Commoner over the Catechismic, Hawes faulted the latter for hewing to the moderate wartime line of Earl Browder. She therefore managed to both signify loyalty to the Party's new "proletarian" line by celebrating the simple working-class members and simultaneously object to Party dogmatism. Hawes, *Hurry Up Please It's Time*, 84–85.

15. Aaron, *Writers on the Left*, 145.

16. See, for example, J. Peters, *The Communist Party: A Manual on Organization* (New York: Workers Library, 1935), and M. J. Olgin, *Why Communism?* (New York: Workers Library, 1935).

17. Hicks, *Where We Came Out*, 7; Hicks, "The Writer Faces the Future," in *The Writer in a Changing World*, ed. Henry Hart (n.p.: Equinox Cooperative Press, 1937), 182.

18. Dwight Macdonald, "The American Writers' Congress," *The Nation*, June 19, 1937, 714; *Debate: Which Road for American Workers, Socialist or Communist? Norman Thomas vs. Earl Browder* (New York: Socialist Call, 1936), 8.

19. Joshua Kunitz, "Introduction," *Azure Cities* (New York: International, 1929), 10.
20. Aaron, *Writers on the Left*, 89.
21. Aaron, *Writers on the Left*, 93.
22. Justin Kaplan, *Lincoln Steffens* (1974; New York: Simon and Schuster, 2013), 250.
23. Aaron, *Writers on the Left*, 178.
24. League of Professional Groups for Foster and Ford, *Culture and the Crisis* (New York: Workers Library, 1932), 3.
25. The former leadership bloc of the Party, headed by Jay Lovestone, was disgorged in 1929, shortly after the Trotskyists in 1928. These expulsions were crucial in sealing the American Communist leadership's strict fidelity to Soviet direction thereafter.
26. William Z. Foster, *Toward Soviet America* (New York: Coward-McCann, 1932), 275.
27. The GPU (pronounced "Gay Pay Oo") was the Soviet secret police, forerunner of the KGB. e. e. cummings, *Complete Poems, 1904–1962*, ed. George James Firmage (New York: Liveright, 1991), 279.
28. Aaron, *Writers on the Left*, 258.
29. Aaron, *Writers on the Left*, 156.
30. Burton Rascoe, *We Were Interrupted* (Garden City, NY: Doubleday, 1947), 163.
31. Richard Wright, *American Hunger* (1944; New York: Harper & Row, 1977), 98; Aaron, *Writers on the Left*, 282; Rideout, *Radical Novel*, 148.
32. Kenneth Burke, "The Writers' Congress," *The Nation*, May 15, 1935, 571.
33. *Educational Vanguard* (July 23, 1936), published by the Teachers College and Columbia Units of the Communist Party.
34. Budd Schulberg, "Collision with the Party Line," *Saturday Review of Literature*, August 30, 1952, 32.
35. Earl Browder, "The Writer and Politics," in *The Writer in a Changing World*, 50, 52.
36. The anti-Stalinist radical left is detailed in Alan Wald, *The New York Intellectuals* (Chapel Hill: University of North Carolina, 1987); and Christopher Phelps, *Young Sidney Hook* (Ithaca, NY: Cornell University Press, 1997).
37. Hicks, *Where We Came Out*, 44.
38. Hicks, *Where We Came Out*, 47.

Epilogue
Echoes of the 1930s

Morris Dickstein

The chapters in this volume are telling, not only for their range of subjects but for the fresh approach they represent. Thinking about the 1930s, we have long since gone beyond the stereotype of the Red Decade popularized by the 1941 book of that name by Eugene Lyons. In fact we have gone so far afield that more recent scholars, including Alan Wald, Michael Denning, Barbara Foley, and others, have made a strong case for the often criticized left-wing culture of the Depression decade. Postwar artists and critics ranging from Abstract Expressionist painters and formalist critics to New York intellectuals had defined themselves against the cultural manifestations of the Popular Front, just as mainstream liberals and centrists rejected the populist politics of the Communist Party. This, in turn, led the generation of scholars that came of age in the 1960s and later to recover some of the buried work inspired by the historical left.

The war, along with the economic lift-off and unexpected prosperity that followed, marked a sharp break in American culture. From the perspective of the 1950s, the arts of the thirties were either forgotten or seen at best as a cautionary example – too radical, too propagandistic, above all too journalistic, caught up in the topical demands of the economic and social crisis. In the fifties, the major arts were seen as a bastion of high culture, an intransigent minority culture sharply distinguished from middlebrow and popular taste. Postwar critics were still in the process of assimilating the challenging work of twenties modernists from Proust to Kafka. They erected a canon that emphasized cultural hierarchies and separated this often difficult work from more traditional, more easily consumed fiction and poetry, especially the domain of bestsellers and book clubs, the Broadway theatre, popular music, and representational painting. The democratizing features of thirties art, ranging from interview books to public murals, were seen by critics as outright betrayals of the higher, more challenging goals of art.

No one would look to the 1930s as a period of art for art's sake. Those of us drawn to the period were precisely interested in the intersections between art and politics, in the burning immediacy of the arts as they confronted the social and economic crisis. The contributors to this volume dexterously bridge the barriers between art and journalism, between high art and popular art, between aesthetic conscience and social purpose. On this expanded terrain their subjects include radio drama, bestsellers, and government-sponsored arts programs, in short a capacious, inclusive notion of literature itself, something typical postwar critics would hardly have recognized. This also reflects a shift from a purely literary history to one that embraces cultural and social history, a turn from text to context, form to function.

It's hard to imagine an earlier literary history of the thirties that would have included essays on hard-boiled crime fiction, on Hollywood, and especially on Time, Inc., though all of them attracted serious writers, not always happy with what they were doing. From the point of view of the postwar little magazines, Hollywood and *Time* magazine were scarcely more than ways of selling out, or at best simply of putting food on the table (and Impressionist paintings on the wall). But neither would they have expected a separate chapter on modernism, a subject rarely associated with the arts of the 1930s, which were invariably accused of reverting to an unsophisticated realism or a crude naturalism under the pressure of the times. This is yet another boundary that has grown blurry in recent years. It's revealing that the work most frequently mentioned in these essays is *Let Us Now Praise Famous Men*, its text by James Agee preceded by photographs by Walker Evans, a failure when it appeared belatedly in 1941 but a greatly admired classic after it was republished (with a larger selection of pictures) in 1960, five years after Agee's early death.

Their book is at once an epitome of the art of the thirties and an angry exception to it. In the most artful manner possible, in prose greatly influenced by Joyce and Faulkner, Agee expresses his hostility toward the "emasculation of acceptance" he identifies with art, any aesthetic framing that would distance his sharecropper families from the urgency of their actual condition. He sees his subjects as innocent and vulnerable, "an undefended and appallingly damaged group of human beings," helpless even before the camera itself. In an oft-quoted passage, he wishes he could substitute some material fragments of their lives for any mere writing about them. As real people, he insists, they demand more from us – empathy, recognition, respect – than any imagined characters. Walker Evans's understated photographs underline this reality. Quietly posed, free of all captions or identification, separated from the body of the text, avoiding the least hint of social protest, they make a general statement about human dignity in the most unlikely of settings. Seemingly artless, altogether direct, they make for a striking contrast with Agee's involuted, self-reflexive text, though it pursues exactly the same goal of providing them and their ramshackle homes with a solemn and immediate presence.

Agee's book bridges the divide between modernism and naturalism, between the avant-garde currents of the 1920s and the social reportage of the following decade. This is also a feature of other books that were little appreciated then, neglected or soon forgotten only to be rediscovered decades later, as if they had appeared before their times. Such a list would include Henry Roth's ghetto novel *Call It Sleep*, Nathanael West's four novels, particularly *Miss Lonelyhearts* and *The Day of the Locust*, Zora Neale Hurston's feminist and erotic *Their Eyes Were Watching God*, and even the novels of Fitzgerald and Faulkner, out of fashion (and partly out of print) by the late thirties but acclaimed and canonized after the war. Roth's, Hurston's, and Faulkner's novels are at once documents of their time and place and florid enactments of individual consciousness, some-thing often attacked by politically engaged thirties critics, who saw individuality as an indulgence and preferred the collective subject, the plain style, the illusion of transparency. At once complex and palpably immediate, they are among the thirties books best loved and most widely read today.

The specter of modernism haunts many of the essays in this volume. It may be something of a reach to see the proletarian novel as experimental work – few would deny its formal conservatism – but this experimental thrust, indentured to the ordinary and the real, is surely a feature of the whole documentary movement. Here, as Jeff Allred suggests, "mundane details" take on "a nobler and more dynamic cast." Even more strikingly, Donal Harris sees the anonymity and "rigorous compression" of *Time* journalism as analogous to modernist collage, though, from the very first number in 1923, the magazine mocked modernist texts for their obscurity. Harris portrays even the much-satirized deformations of *Time* style as part of "a contest of legitimacy of linguistic innovation."

These enduring novels and other writings are but a sampling of the legacy of twenties modernism in the Depression years, but they also point to powerful echoes of the 1930s in the following decades. No doubt the most far-reaching effect of the Depression decade was the welfare state created by the New Deal, involving the new role of the federal government in everything from labor relations and retirement income to codes and standards enforced by regulatory agencies. This New Deal order would long remain the basic glue of the Democratic constituency, attacked but never seriously undermined by Republican presidents and intermittently hostile majorities in Congress. With the coming of the war, some New Deal programs, long under fire, were finally scrapped, especially in the cultural sector. Among them were WPA initiatives like the Federal arts projects, repeatedly accused of Communist sympathies or of spreading New Deal propaganda. Here the echoes of the 1930s were notable in the writers they spawned, the indigent young painters they supported, as well as in the work they produced, from the American Guide series to the murals decorating public buildings. The creation of the National Endowments of Art and Humanities in the 1960s could be seen as a revival of New Deal funding of culture, though not as relief or public works programs.

The crisis of the thirties caused artists to turn inward, looking for sources of strength and national identity in American history, folklore, or simply the American heartland. Lincoln and Whitman became ubiquitous icons of the common man. Once-difficult composers like Aaron Copland, trained in Paris in the 1920s, would look to the resources of the American tradition to write more accessible music, music that had a singular American sound. The road trip, the interviews with ordinary people, the text-and-picture book would all become vehicles of national self-examination. Both the Popular Front and the WPA helped create a progressive vision of American values that would later contribute to wartime unity and morale.

The alliance with the Soviet Union provided a temporary respite for the American left. The focus on the ordinary American family in plays like Clifford Odets's *Awake and Sing!* would echo through the late forties in plays like Arthur Miller's *Death of a Salesman* and films like Elia Kazan's *A Tree Grows in Brooklyn*, as Judith E. Smith showed in *Visions of Belonging*, a book that also explores the spate of socially conscious films and novels of the late forties focused on prejudice and discrimination – against Jews, blacks, homosexuals – including *Gentleman's Agreement*, *Crossfire*, *Home of the Brave*, *Pinky*, and *No Way Out*.[1]

By 1950, when Senator McCarthy made his debut on the national stage, such films could no longer be made, though gritty crime films that channeled the dark mood of thirties hard-boiled fiction could still fly below the radar, exposing a scene of social corruption and personal betrayal. The American self-celebration and national unity promoted in the 1930s and the war years took a nativist turn with blacklists, loyalty oaths, and congressional witch hunts targeting not only putative spies but virtually any past left-wing activity, from the New Deal to the Popular Front. Nothing did more to curb the impact of thirties programs, of liberalism itself, than the onset of the Cold War. As leftist screenwriters went to jail, other survivors of thirties radicalism, such as Paul Robeson or Woody Guthrie and the Weavers, were kept from performing and lost much of their audience. Writers like Langston Hughes and Malcolm Cowley put out sanitized versions of their earlier work, books from which all traces of previous Communist leanings were expunged. This began to change in the late fifties and early 1960s with the stirrings of the New Left, though its impact on the arts was at first limited.

The most explicit and widely influential throwback to thirties culture came with the Beats starting in the mid-1950s. Jack Kerouac revived the road novel but peopled it with his own friends rather than ordinary Americans. Photographer Robert Frank, a friend of the Beats, took to the road as well, and the resulting book, *The Americans* (1959), with an introduction by Kerouac, harked back to the probing and democratic cast of Walker Evans's work, his intrinsic respect for his subjects. Meanwhile Allen Ginsberg turned the tables on postwar formalist poetry with impassioned Whitmanesque free verse, a form of vernacular modernism, at once popular and surreal, that had some of its roots in his own Communist youth. In "America," written in 1956 in a vein of comic exasperation, he evoked the sacred causes of the left in the thirties, from the Scottsboro boys to the Spanish loyalists.

The stifling atmosphere of the Cold War gave rise to a nostalgia for an earlier era in which radicalism thrived while culture and politics crossed paths explosively, a time of crisis that seemed more appealing, even glamorous, and certainly more morally demanding than the complacent Eisenhower years. Despite its tony Camelot veneer, the Kennedy presidency, with its youthful energy and its trumpet call to a revived idealism, gave unlikely impetus to this critical spirit. The New Left was very different from the old, prizing spontaneity over organization and moral witness over a dogmatic appeal to historical necessity. It preferred the egalitarian ideals enshrined in American sources, however unfulfilled, to the theoretical framework and Party discipline of European Marxism. The music of this early New Left could be found in the renascent folk culture, grounded in the ethnomusicology of the 1930s, which set out to record and preserve America's oral heritage. Three decades later, folksingers in Greenwich Village and Berkeley turned this into mellifluous social complaint. When the young Bob Dylan sat at the feet of the grievously ill Woody Guthrie, the two decades met and joined hands. Something vibrantly embedded in the arts in the 1930s had been transmitted to a new generation, the heritage of an embracing popular culture and an authentic social conscience.

Note

1. Judith E. Smith, *Visions of Belonging: Family Stories, Popular Culture, and Postwar Democracy, 1940–1960* (New York: Columbia University Press, 2004).

Index